Mauritius

Rodrigues • Réunion

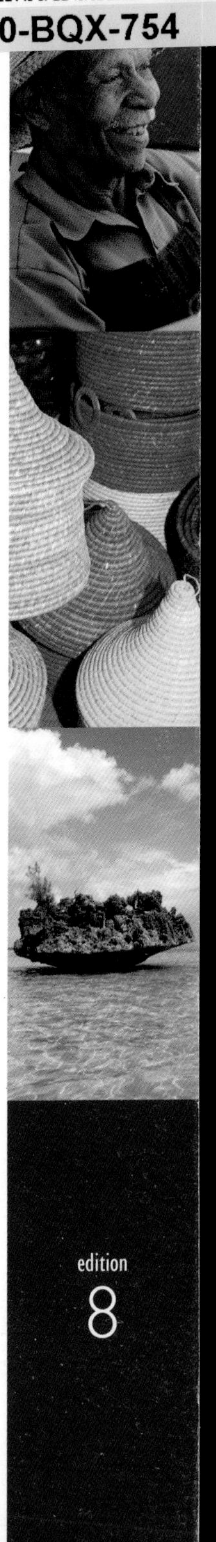

the Bradt Travel Guide

Alexandra Richards

edition 8

www.bradtguides.com

Bradt Travel Guides Ltd, UK
The Globe Pequot Press Inc, USA

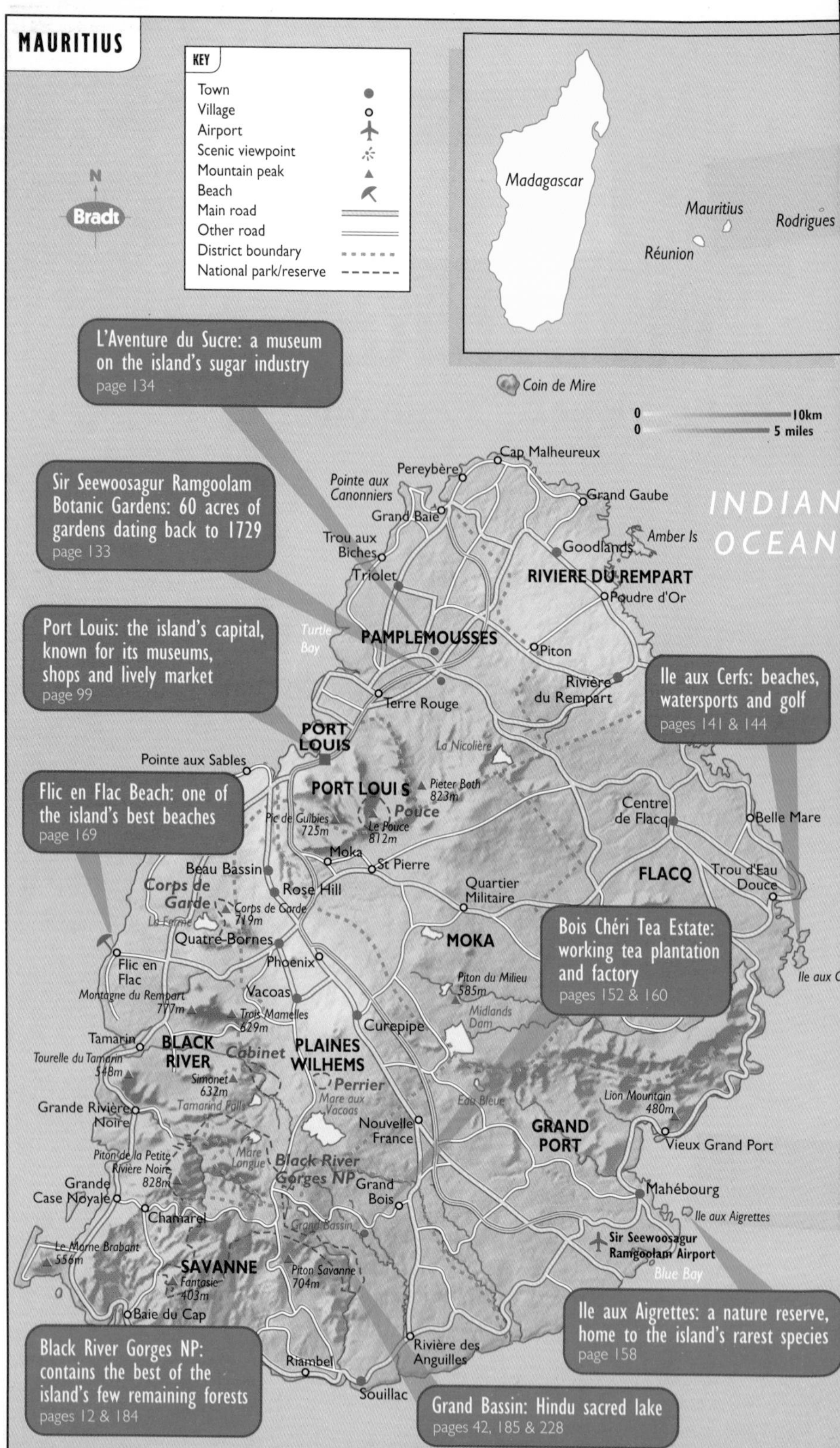
MAURITIUS
KEY
Town
Village
Airport
Scenic viewpoint
Mountain peak
Beach
Main road
Other road
District boundary
National park/reserve
N
Bradt
Madagascar
Mauritius
Rodrigues
Réunion
L'Aventure du Sucre: a museum on the island's sugar industry
page 134
Coin de Mire
0 10km
0 5 miles
Sir Seewoosagur Ramgoolam Botanic Gardens: 60 acres of gardens dating back to 1729
page 133
Port Louis: the island's capital, known for its museums, shops and lively market
page 99
Flic en Flac Beach: one of the island's best beaches
page 169
Ile aux Cerfs: beaches, watersports and golf
pages 141 & 144
Bois Chéri Tea Estate: working tea plantation and factory
pages 152 & 160
Ile aux Aigrettes: a nature reserve, home to the island's rarest species
page 158
Black River Gorges NP: contains the best of the island's few remaining forests
pages 12 & 184
Grand Bassin: Hindu sacred lake
pages 42, 185 & 228
INDIAN OCEAN
Cap Malheureux
Pereybère
Pointe aux Canonniers
Grand Gaube
Grand Baie
Trou aux Biches
Amber Is
Goodlands
Triolet
RIVIERE DU REMPART
Poudre d'Or
Turtle Bay
PAMPLEMOUSSES
Piton
Rivière du Rempart
Terre Rouge
PORT LOUIS
La Nicolière
Pointe aux Sables
PORT LOUIS
Pieter Both 823m
Pouce
Pic de Gulbies 725m
Le Pouce 812m
Centre de Flacq
Belle Mare
Moka
St Pierre
Beau Bassin
Rose Hill
FLACQ
Trou d'Eau Douce
Quartier Militaire
Corps de Garde
Corps de Garde 719m
La Ferme
Quatre Bornes
MOKA
Phoenix
Flic en Flac
Ile aux Cer
Piton du Milieu 585m
Montagne du Rempart 777m
Vacoas
Trois Mamelles 629m
Midlands Dam
Curepipe
Tamarin
BLACK RIVER
PLAINES WILHEMS
Tourelle du Tamarin 548m
Cabinet
Simonet 632m
Perrier
Mare aux Vacoas
Eau Bleue
Lion Mountain 480m
Grande Rivière Noire
Tamarind Falls
Nouvelle France
GRAND PORT
Vieux Grand Port
Piton de la Petite Rivière Noire 828m
Mare Longue
Black River Gorges NP
Grand Bois
Mahébourg
Grande Case Noyale
Chamarel
Grand Bassin
Ile aux Aigrettes
Sir Seewoosagur Ramgoolam Airport
Le Morne Brabant 556m
SAVANNE
Piton Savanne 704m
Blue Bay
Fantasie 403m
Baie du Cap
Rivière des Anguilles
Riambel
Souillac

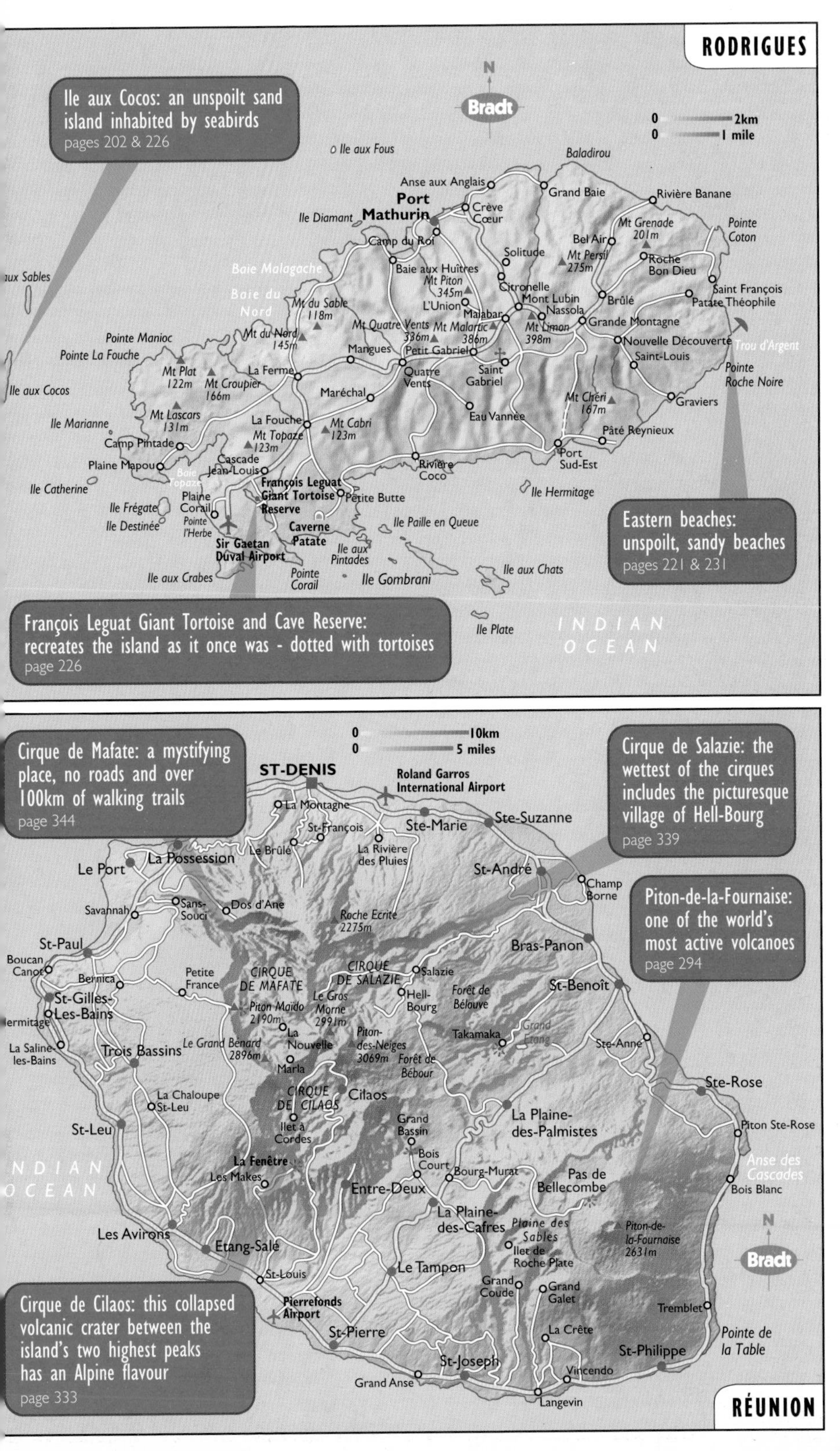

RODRIGUES
Ile aux Cocos: an unspoilt sand island inhabited by seabirds
pages 202 & 226
Eastern beaches: unspoilt, sandy beaches
pages 221 & 231
François Leguat Giant Tortoise and Cave Reserve: recreates the island as it once was - dotted with tortoises
page 226
Port Mathurin
Bradt
0 2km
0 1 mile
Ile aux Fous
Baladirou
Anse aux Anglais
Grand Baie
Rivière Banane
Crève Cœur
Ile Diamant
Camp du Roi
Mt Grenade 201m
Pointe Coton
Bel Air
Solitude
Mt Persil 275m
Roche Bon Dieu
Baie Malagache
Baie aux Huîtres
Mt Piton 345m
Citronelle
Baie du Nord
Mt du Sable 118m
L'Union
Mont Lubin
Brûlé
Saint François
Patate Théophile
Malabar
Nassola
Grande Montagne
Mt Quatre Vents 336m
Mt Malartic 386m
Mt Limon 398m
Mt du Nord 145m
Nouvelle Découverte
Trou d'Argent
Pointe Manioc
Mangues
Petit Gabriel
Saint-Louis
Pointe La Fouche
Mt Plat 122m
Mt Croupier 166m
La Ferme
Quatre Vents
Saint Gabriel
Pointe Roche Noire
Ile aux Cocos
Maréchal
Graviers
Mt Lascars 131m
Eau Vannée
Mt Cheri 167m
Ile Marianne
La Fouche
Mt Cabri 123m
Camp Pintade
Mt Topaze 123m
Pâté Reynieux
Plaine Mapou
Cascade Jean-Louis
Rivière Coco
Port Sud-Est
Baie Topaze
Ile Catherine
François Leguat Giant Tortoise Reserve
Petite Butte
Ile Hermitage
Plaine Corail
Ile Frégate
Ile Destinée
Pointe l'Herbe
Caverne Patate
Ile Paille en Queue
Sir Gaetan Duval Airport
Ile aux Pintades
Ile aux Chats
Ile aux Crabes
Pointe Corail
Ile Gombrani
Ile Plate
INDIAN OCEAN
Ile aux Sables
Cirque de Mafate: a mystifying place, no roads and over 100km of walking trails
page 344
Cirque de Salazie: the wettest of the cirques includes the picturesque village of Hell-Bourg
page 339
Piton-de-la-Fournaise: one of the world's most active volcanoes
page 294
Cirque de Cilaos: this collapsed volcanic crater between the island's two highest peaks has an Alpine flavour
page 333
0 10km
0 5 miles
ST-DENIS
Roland Garros International Airport
La Montagne
St-François
Ste-Marie
Ste-Suzanne
Le Brûlé
La Rivière des Pluies
La Possession
Le Port
St-André
Champ Borne
Savannah
Sans-Souci
Dos d'Ane
Roche Ecrite 2275m
St-Paul
Bras-Panon
Boucan Canot
Bernica
Petite France
CIRQUE DE MAFATE
CIRQUE DE SALAZIE
Salazie
Hell-Bourg
Forêt de Bélouve
St-Benoît
St-Gilles-Les-Bains
Piton Maïdo 2190m
Le Gros Morne 2991m
Hermitage
La Nouvelle
Piton-des-Neiges 3069m
Takamaka
Grand Etang
La Saline-les-Bains
Trois Bassins
Le Grand Bénard 2896m
Marla
Forêt de Bébour
Ste-Anne
Ste-Rose
La Chaloupe St-Leu
CIRQUE DE CILAOS
Cilaos
St-Leu
Ilet à Cordes
Grand Bassin
La Plaine-des-Palmistes
Piton Ste-Rose
INDIAN OCEAN
La Fenêtre
Les Makes
Bois Court
Bourg-Murat
Pas de Bellecombe
Anse des Cascades
Bois Blanc
Entre-Deux
La Plaine-des-Cafres
Plaine des Sables
Piton-de-la-Fournaise 2631m
Les Avirons
Etang-Salé
Ilet de Roche Plate
St-Louis
Le Tampon
Grand Coude
Grand Galet
Pierrefonds Airport
Tremblet
St-Pierre
La Crête
Pointe de la Table
St-Joseph
St-Philippe
Vincendo
Grand Anse
Langevin
RÉUNION

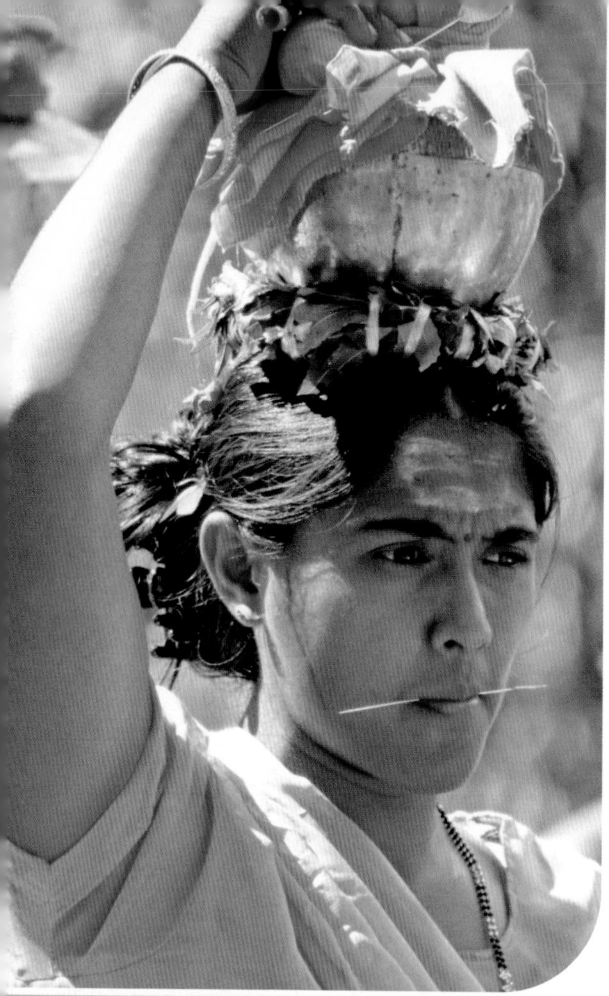

Mascarene Islands Don't miss...

Local traditions and culture
Thaipoosam Cavadee is an awe-inspiring procession made by Tamil pilgrims every year
(AR) page 71

Stunning beaches and bays
Rodrigues's unspoilt eastern beaches are typically deserted
(AR) page 197

Rugged landscapes
The stunning Piton-de-la-Fournaise is one of the world's most active volcanoes
(AR) page 294

Colourful markets
The hustle and bustle among the displays of fruit, vegetables and spices at Port Louis market provides a snapshot of everyday life
(AR) page 110

Colonial Creole architecture
Carefully restored, Château de Labourdonnais in the north of Mauritius is a fine colonial sugar planter's mansion
(AR) page 134

above **Subsistence farmers in Rodrigues take pride in their livestock and crops** (AR) page 203

left **Particular efforts have been made to restore and maintain Réunion's many delightful '*ti cases*, the humble dwellings of ordinary families** (AR) page 246

below **A typical Rodriguan smallholding provides food for the family as well as produce to sell at the Port Mathurin weekly market** (AR) page 203

above left **A child musician on Belle Mare Beach during the Ganesh Chaturthi festival** (AR) page 72

above right & below **Vital to *séga* music is the drum beat provided by the *ravane*, a goatskin tambourine** (below; AR). ***Séga* dancers traditionally wear colourful, billowing skirts** (above right; AR) page 39

above left Horseriding along Flic en Flac Beach, Western Mauritius (AR) page 169

above right Many Mauritian fishermen still employ traditional methods (AR) page 33

below Rodrigues is blessed with unblemished natural beauty. Here, St François Beach (AR) page 231

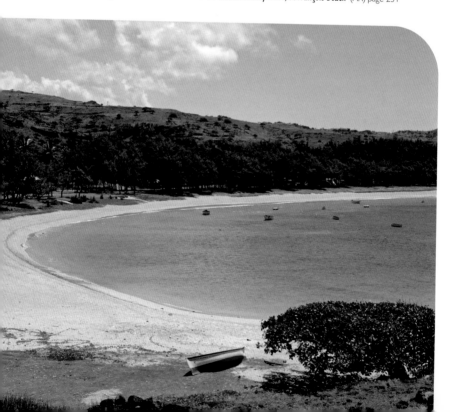

AUTHORS

EDITIONS 5 TO 8

Alexandra Richards (*www.alexandra-richards.com*) grew up in Dorset, where she developed a love of rural life, the natural world and outdoor pursuits. She graduated from Durham University in 2000, where she read modern European languages. During her studies she spent a year teaching English in Réunion and took the opportunity to travel in the Mascarenes. She has kept in touch with many of the friends that she made on the islands and returns as often as possible. Having worked in the travel industry, she is now a freelance travel writer with a passion for photography, natural history and adventure. In 2004, she undertook a writing/photography assignment travelling to Australia on a cargo ship via the Suez Canal, and has divided her time between Dorset and Australia ever since.

EDITIONS 1 TO 4

Royston Ellis (*www.roystonellis.com*) is a travel writer, novelist and biographer who first visited Mauritius in 1983 to research a bestselling series of historical novels, *The Fleshtraders*, set in Black River. He conceived and wrote as sole author the first edition of *Mauritius* published by Bradt in 1988, and two further editions, as well as contributing updates to subsequent editions on which this eighth edition is based. He is the author of over 60 books, many set in Indian Ocean countries and written under pseudonyms, as well as of Bradt guides to the Maldives and to Sri Lanka, the latest editions of which were published in 2008 and 2011 respectively. He lives in Sri Lanka.

Derek Schuurman is a freelance travel writer, author and keen naturalist. He first visited Mauritius in 1986. Subsequently he has returned to all the Mascarene Islands as a specialist tour operator and on press assignments. He now works in London for the specialist tour operator, Rainbow Tours. His other books include *Madagascar Wildlife: A Visitor's Guide* with Nick Garbutt and Hilary Bradt.

UPDATES WEBSITE AND FEEDBACK REQUEST

At Bradt Travel Guides we're aware that guidebooks start to go out of date on the day they're published – and that you, our readers, are out there in the field doing research of your own. You'll find out before us when a fine new family-run hotel opens or a favourite restaurant changes hands and goes downhill. So why not write to us and tell us about your experiences? Contact us on ☎ 01753 893444 or e info@bradtguides.com. Alternatively you can add a review of the book to www.bradtguides.com or Amazon.

If you send an email to info@bradtguides.com about changes to information in this book we will forward it to the author who may include it in a 'one-off update' on the Bradt website at www.bradtguides.com/guidebook-updates. You can also visit this website for updates to information in this guide.

PUBLISHER'S FOREWORD

Hilary Bradt

My association with Royston Ellis goes back to the mid 1980s when he approached me as a possible publisher for a guide to Mauritius, an island he knew intimately since many of his novels were set there. I saw the book as a partner for my own Madagascar guide which was in the pipeline, so we agreed to go ahead. And anyway, how could I resist a writer who had, in 1960, performed his beat poetry with a group he dubbed The Beatles? This group went on to greater things, keeping Royston's spelling of their name. Now the book is under the equally expert and knowledgeable authorship of Alexandra Richards, a former resident of Réunion, who has restructured, updated and expanded the guide through four editions, and added her own personal stamp on the contents.

Eighth edition October 2012 First published 1988

Bradt Travel Guides Ltd, IDC House, The Vale, Chalfont St Peter, Bucks SL9 9RZ, England
www.bradtguides.com

Print edition published in the USA by The Globe Pequot Press Inc, PO Box 480, Guilford, Connecticut 06437-0480

Book packager: Jonathan Gilbert, Azalay Media

British Library Cataloguing in Publication Data
A catalogue record for this book is available from the British Library

ISBN 978 1 84162 410 5
e-ISBN: 978 1 84162 743 4 (e-pub)
e-ISBN: 978 1 84162 644 4 (mobi)

Photographs Alamy: F1 online digitale Bildagentur GmbH (F1DB/G/A), Guichaoua (G/A), Hemis (H/A), Thierry GRUN (TG/A); FLPA: Biosphoto/Gregory Guida (B/GG/FLPA), Imagebroker (I/FLPA); Alexandra Richards (AR); Shutterstock: marvellousworld (MW/S); Neal Sullivan (NS); SuperStock (SS)
Front cover Taxi-boat, Mauritius (H/A)
Back cover Tamil temple (AR), Horserider on beach (AR)
Title page Hand-woven bags (AR), Stall-holder, Port Mathurin (AR), Crystal Rock, Mauritius (MW/S)

Maps David McCutcheon FBCart.S; colour map relief base by Nick Rowland FGRS

Typeset from the author's disc by Wakewing, High Wycombe
Production managed by Jellyfish Print Solutions and manufactured in India
Digital conversion by the Firsty Group

Acknowledgements

For the time and effort they devoted to this eighth edition, I am very grateful to Air Mauritius, in particular Nicole Hansen, and to the following for their help with the maps: B&T Directories, Kartaplus and Option Service Ltd.

I am also grateful to Lone Raffray of the Mauritius Wildlife Foundation for her contributions to the sections on natural history and conservation.

The Rodrigues Tourist Office provided invaluable help and support. A special thank you to Jean-Paul André, our wonderful, entertaining guide in Rodrigues. For his assistance with the chapters on Rodrigues, I would like to thank Paul Draper. My thanks and best wishes go to everyone at CARE-Co – a truly inspirational team.

For their assistance with the section on Réunion, I would like to thank the Comité du Tourisme de la Réunion. My thanks go to my dear Réunionnais friends, Dominique Vendôme and Richard Thesée, for their help and companionship, and for making living in Réunion such fun.

For their help, guidance and inspiration I must thank Alf and June Wallis, and Chris and Cleo Campbell. My heartfelt thanks to the Rt Hon Baroness Sharples for many years of unstinting support.

A special thank you to my parents. To my late father, himself a writer who wrote wonderfully entertaining books and articles about his travels. And to my mother, for her companionship on previous research trips and for her endless hours of proofreading.

My sincere thanks to my Australian friends, in particular Teena, Dave and Anne.

My thanks to Neal Sullivan for accompanying me on my last research trip, and for his assistance with the maps and photography.

Finally, I must thank Zouk and Kaya, my two dogs who take their names from the Mascarenes, and who kept me company while I wrote this edition.

Alexandra Richards

Contents

PART FOUR REUNION 233

LIST OF MAPS

Introduction

Whenever my mother is struggling for an answer (usually prompted by a particularly tricky question on a television game show), she turns to one of her enormous collection of ancient books and invariably comes up with the goods. I had always dismissed this practice as pure eccentricity. However, after fumbling for some time for inspiration for this introduction, I gave in and reluctantly asked if she had any old books that may help. It didn't surprise me in the least that she happened to have handy a copy of the 1879 edition of *The Illustrated Globe Encyclopaedia of Universal Information*.

I searched for a little-known gem of information on the Mascarene Isles, as Mauritius, Rodrigues and Réunion are known, and came up with this authoritative pronouncement on Réunion: 'The climate of late has greatly deteriorated, and is now very deadly to Europeans.'

I have been travelling to the Mascarenes since 1998 and can assure you that the encyclopaedia got it wrong. And just in case you think mine was a fluke escape, official statistics show that hundreds of thousands of Europeans visit the Mascarenes each year and survive to bore friends and relatives with their holiday photos.

Mauritius, in particular, has become a 'dream holiday' destination, especially popular with honeymooners and couples wishing to tie the knot on a classic white-sand beach. It is easy to see why: luxurious hotels, a tropical climate, a glorious coastline, excellent diving and fascinating flora and fauna combine to make this island idyllic. In fact, sooner or later someone in Mauritius will tell you that when God made the island he liked it so much that he fashioned paradise in its image. Mark Twain is responsible for perpetuating that idea: 'You gather the idea that Mauritius was made first and then heaven, and that heaven was copied after Mauritius.'

Like heaven, Mauritius exudes an air of exclusivity, partly because the government does not allow charter flights and pursues a tourism policy of quality not quantity. However, holidays to Mauritius needn't be expensive, as I hope to show in this guide.

By contrast, the island of Rodrigues, although part of Mauritius, is a place of simple charm. Whenever I visit, I am struck by the tremendous sense of community, and the laid-back way of life is certainly a lesson to us all. I am told that it resembles the Mauritius of 30 years ago and a visit to the island is a welcome escape from our fast-paced world, where high-tech time-saving devices, multi-tasking and real-time connectivity seem key to survival. Tourism in Rodrigues isn't only in its infancy – it has barely left the maternity ward. Although development of the island's tourism potential has begun, with the expansion of the airport and creation of the island's first mid-range hotels, tourists are still a novelty here and receive an incredibly warm welcome. My advice is to get to Rodrigues as soon as possible, before it all changes.

Réunion is an island of contrasts. Officially part of France, and therefore part of the European Union, it is inhabited by a cocktail of people of African, Indian, European and Chinese origin. The Creole culture is strong here and *séga* (a traditional dance with African roots), sorcery and occasional cockfights contrast with the ubiquitous croissants, Citroëns and boules tournaments.

Réunion was my home for almost a year. It is a kind of user-friendly, flat-packed paradise, where life is exotic yet easy and familiar. The atmosphere is tropical, yet the roads, doctors' surgeries and hospitals are of a reassuringly European quality.

Whilst Réunion's beaches may not rival those of Mauritius, its natural beauty is world class. The rugged, mountainous interior attracts hikers, naturalists and adventure sports enthusiasts from around the globe.

Each of the Mascarenes has its own trump card, as I am sure you will discover. However, in combination they are unrivalled. If you visit just one you'll love it, but if you can take in all three you'll be smitten.

I leave you with the thought that you shouldn't believe everything you read in an encyclopaedia and wish you a very enjoyable trip to the Mascarenes.

Alexandra Richards

Part One

MAURITIUS: GENERAL INFORMATION

MAURITIUS AT A GLANCE

Country Mauritius is an independent state, consisting of the islands of Mauritius, Rodrigues and dependencies; it is known as Ile Maurice in French
Location In the Indian Ocean, south of the Equator and just north of the Tropic of Capricorn
Size Mauritius 1,864km^2; total area with dependencies 2,045km^2
History Discovered by Arabs, then the Portuguese, Mauritius was first settled by the Dutch in 1598. It was claimed by the French in 1715 as Ile de France and captured by the British in 1810. It was a British colony until 1968 when it became an independent member of the Commonwealth. It became a republic in 1992.
Climate Hot summers (November to April) with average coastal temperatures of 30°C; warm winters (May to October), averaging 24°C. Interior temperatures are 3–5°C lower. Rainy season January to May; possibility of cyclones from January to March.
Nature Mountainous with plateaux; flowers, forests and crops; rare wildlife and nothing dangerous; fine beaches within coral reefs
Visitors Tourists come all the year around; November to January and August most popular months; May and October most pleasant
Capital Port Louis
Government Parliamentary democracy based on the Westminster model of government. The president is the head of state but the prime minister and cabinet have constitutional power.
Population 1,286,340 (July 2011) of Indian, African, European and Chinese origin
Economy Based on industrial and agricultural exports, tourism and financial services
Language Official language English, but Creole most widely used. Most people speak (and read) French, with Hindi, Tamil and Chinese as the main alternatives.
Religion Hindusim, Islam, Christianity, and also Confucianism and Buddhism
Currency Mauritian rupee (Rs), which is divided into 100 cents (cs). The international exchange rate fluctuates daily, linked to a basketful of currencies.
Rate of exchange £1=Rs47; US$1=Rs30; €1=Rs37 (August 2012)
International telephone code +230
Time GMT+4
Electricity 220 volts
Weights and measures The metric system was officially introduced in 1985.

Background Information

GEOGRAPHY

Its isolated location kept Mauritius from being settled until 1598 and even today, many people don't know where it is. On a world map, it is an insignificant dot in that vast expanse of ocean between southern Africa and Australia, at longitude 57°E, latitude 20°S, overshadowed by its much larger neighbour, Madagascar, 855km to the west.

Africa is the nearest continent, with Mombasa some 1,800km away. Perth is 6,000km from Mauritius and London is 9,755km away.

Mauritius is part of the Mascarene Archipelago, together with its closest neighbour, the French island of Réunion (161km away), and its own territory, Rodrigues, which lies 560km to the east. The Cargados Garayos Archipelago, also known as the St Brandon Islands, 395km northeast of Mauritius, and the two Agalega Islands, 1,200km to the north, are Mauritian dependencies.

Mauritius also claims Tromelin Island, a French possession, and would like to reclaim the Six Islands, Peros Banhos, Salomon, Trois Frères and Diego Garcia, which have, since 1965, been the British Indian Ocean Territory (BIOT).

The island of Mauritius is 65km at its longest, and 45km across at its widest. There are 160km of coastline, almost entirely surrounded by coral reefs, while the centre is a great plateau punctuated by impressive mountains. The whole state, including its dependencies, has a land area of only 2,045km^2, although, because the islands are so spread out, its sea area is vast.

Around Mauritius itself there are more than 15 islets lying in their own lagoons. North of the island, uninhabited except for wildlife, are six small islands: Serpent, Round, Flat, Gabriel, Amber and Coin de Mire.

The origins of the island of Mauritius date back some 13 million years, when masses of molten lava bubbled up beneath the ocean floor. It took five million years to surface through the activity of two volcanic craters. The weathered crater rims of these once enormous peaks still remain as the mountain ranges of Black River, Grand Port and Moka.

Further volcanic activity followed four million years later, opening up the craters of Trou aux Cerfs, Bassin Blanc and Kanaka. The island's volcanoes have now been extinct for 200,000 years, although odd lava flows may have occurred up to 10,000 years ago.

The island's rugged profile is a constant reminder of these cataclysms. The jagged volcanic peaks tower over coastal plains smothered in sugarcane, leaves waving like long green ribbons in the wind. The broad plain of the north rises to an extensive, fertile plateau, itself broken by more volcanic steeples and gorges. This tableland (600m/1,970ft high) is bordered by mountains which roll down to the crags of the southern coastline. In some areas there are deep, and seldom explored, lava caves.

It is not the height of the mountains that is impressive, but the sheer oddity of their shape. The highest is Piton de la Petite Rivière Noire at 828m (2,717ft). Pieter Both is next at 823m (2,699ft) with Pouce – the thumb-shaped mountain looming behind Port Louis – at 812m (2,664ft).

Despite the mountains and a rainfall on the windward slopes of the central plateau that can amount to 5m (197in) a year, Mauritius is not an island of great rivers. There are some 60 small rivers and streams, many degenerating as they reach the coast into rubbish-clogged trickles through cement ditches and culverts. The Grande Rivière Sud-est is the largest at 39.4km long.

The main harbour is at Port Louis, the capital, on the west coast. The airport is at the opposite side of the island, at Plaisance, not far from the old east coast harbour of Grand Port.

The island is divided into the same nine districts as it was when the British captured it in 1810. In a clockwise direction from the capital, these districts are Port Louis, Pamplemousses, Rivière du Rempart, Flacq, Grand Port, Savanne and Black River, with Plaines Wilhems and Moka in the centre. Rodrigues is a district in its own right.

The eccentric terrain of Mauritius means that the island is blessed with a diversity of scenery not usually found in such a small area, and since there are good roads, travel is not time-consuming. When the brashness of the northwest coast is too much, sanctuary is easily found in the tranquillity of the southwest or the dramatic coastline of the south.

CLIMATE

Basically, there are two seasons: summer is hot and wet (November to April), whilst winter is warm and dry (May to October).

Its proximity to the Tropic of Capricorn assures Mauritius of a subtropical climate that is typically warm and humid. Temperatures during summer range from 24°C at dawn to 30°C at noon on the coast, and during winter from about 18°C at dawn to 24°C at noon. On the central plateau it is normally about three to five degrees cooler. The western and northern regions are slightly drier and warmer than the east and the south.

Winter brings the trade winds, which are predominantly southeasterly and are at their strongest in July and August. The south and east coasts can be unpleasantly windy at this time of year, while in summer the sea breezes offer welcome relief from the humidity. The rainy season is roughly January to May, although rain is spasmodic, not a constant downpour for the entire five months. On the west coast the rainfall is about 1m or less a year, whilst the central plateau and windward slopes can have up to 5m in a year.

Mauritius, Réunion and Madagascar are prone to cyclones between January and March. A cyclone is a violent tropical storm that can have a devastating effect on vegetation, insecure buildings and roads. It is a tropical zone low-pressure system with winds circulating in a clockwise direction, spiralling with force towards a centre, or eye, around 4km wide. They usually form in the southwest Indian Ocean, north of Mauritius, embracing the island as they move southwards. Gusts can reach over 250km/h.

Around the centre of a cyclone, where most uplift occurs, there are torrential rains (up to 50cm per day). The cyclone season starts in November with the onset of summer. An average of ten storms is tracked in each summer period but few represent a real threat to Mauritius. Each is given a name, beginning at 'A' then working through the alphabet.

The lifecycle of a cyclone is around nine days but its effect on the island lasts only a day or two, according to its velocity. It moves at a speed of 8–15km/h. Damage is caused by continuous winds and gusts, and flooding.

Mauritius has a well-structured system of cyclone warnings and procedures. The warnings range from Class I, preliminary precautions (usually 36–48 hours before the cyclone strikes), to Class IV, striking moment, when people are confined indoors.

The Mauritius Meteorological Service has a website giving up-to-date weather information, which is particularly useful when a cyclone is approaching (*http://ncb.intnet.mu/meteo.htm*).

NATURAL HISTORY

VOLCANIC ORIGINS OF FRAGILE ECOSYSTEMS Around 7½ million years ago, the lava that created Mauritius rose above sea level, throwing up the mountain ranges of Grand Port, Moka and Black River. Later, light grey rock, also of volcanic origin, was scattered across the island on a northeast–southwest axis, giving rise to Bassin Blanc, Trou aux Cerfs and the Kanaka Crater. Fragile ecosystems evolved gently in a predator-free haven.

First to appear on the lava formations were pioneer plants, like lichens, mosses and ferns. These were followed by other plants, seeds of which were brought by birds or washed on to the shores by the sea. In time, most of the island was swathed in lush rainforest. Where rainfall was lower, palm savanna replaced forest.

Some invertebrates, birds and bats found their way to Mauritius deliberately; others came accidentally due to gale-force winds. Reptiles (and more invertebrates) arrived by means of floating vegetation or driftwood. In time these evolved into a myriad species unique to Mauritius. When examining Mauritian fauna in terms of its links elsewhere, connections with the other Indian Ocean islands, Africa, Australasia and Asia are apparent.

Man's arrival in the Mascarenes signalled a wave of extinctions paralleled only by that which occurred in the Hawaiian Archipelago. Magnificent tropical hardwood forests were felled for construction, export and agriculture. It is not clear exactly how many endemic plant species were lost. Today, only token remnants of the original forests remain, mostly in the Black River Gorges National Park. But even there, fast-growing introduced plants have swamped the indigenous species.

With the original forests went a remarkable ensemble of animals, the most famed of which is the dodo (*dronte*). Also wiped out quickly – as in the other Mascarenes – were herds of giant tortoises and, offshore, the gentle, vulnerable dugong. Apart from the dodo, at least 20 species of endemic birds were exterminated.

The situation was worsened considerably by the introduction of man's ghastly, invasive animal entourage: dogs, cats, rats, monkeys, rabbits, wild pigs, goats and deer all wreaked havoc on the island ecosystem, just as they have done on other islands around the globe. Further introductions were tenrecs (similar to hedgehogs) from Madagascar, mongooses and musk shrews, all of which have affected native fauna adversely. Snakes were also introduced, along with a host of birds, most of which now far outnumber the few remaining indigenous species.

By 1970, the situation for the remaining endemic Mauritian plants and animals looked horribly bleak. Some conservation organisations abroad wrote the Mascarenes off as 'paradise lost'. In the mid 1970s, the Durrell Wildlife Conservation Trust (then the Jersey Wildlife Preservation Trust) and the Mauritian Government stepped in.

ENDEMIC AND INDIGENOUS FLORA *with the Mauritian Wildlife Foundation*

There are 671 species of indigenous flowering plant recorded in Mauritius, of which 311 are endemic (Mauritius has eight endemic plant genera), and 150 are endemic to the Mascarene Islands. Of the indigenous plant species, 77 are classified as extinct and 235 as threatened.

Widespread habitat destruction has rendered many endemic plants extremely rare: some species are now down to just one or two specimens. Indigenous species, which are shared with Réunion and/or Rodrigues, have stood a better chance of survival. However, as on Réunion and Rodrigues, most of the flora you'll see on Mauritius is of introduced species.

ISLAND COMMUNITIES *Jonathan Hughes*

Remote islands throughout the world house rather special communities of animals and plants. In order to colonise an isolated island a species must pass three great challenges. The first challenge is to arrange transportation, the second to establish a stable population upon arrival, and the third to adapt to the island's habitats. At each stage the chance of failure is high, but with luck, and a certain degree of 'evolutionary skill', some inevitably succeed.

Species arrive on remote islands either by 'active' means, such as swimming or flying, or by 'passive' means, such as floating with ocean and air currents or hitching a ride on or in another individual. This degree of mobility is not available to all animal and plant groups, hence on isolated archipelagos there is often a characteristic assemblage of flying animals such as birds, bats and insects, light animals such as spiders and micro-organisms, buoyant animals such as tortoises and snakes, and plants employing edible seeds such as fruit trees, airborne seeds such as grasses, or floating seeds such as the coconut palm. Large land mammals, amphibians and freshwater fish have obvious difficulties in colonising remote islands and are therefore often absent, unless introduced by humans.

Assuming the problem of transport is overcome, there is then the task of establishing a permanent population on the island. Pioneers with the highest chance of success are single pregnant females, or in the case of plants, individuals able to self-fertilise. Flying species may arrive en masse, while species carried by currents must chance successive landings on the same island.

As populations establish, the animal and plant community begins to exploit the island's resources, and some animals take on very unusual roles in the community, but one role that is left vacant is that of the large, fierce predator at the top of the food chain. Large predators need a lot of space and a lot of resources. Without an extensive range there simply isn't enough food to support a population of such animals. Hence, on all but the largest of islands, large predators are absent, leaving meat-eating to smaller, less demanding species.

The absence of large predators has a profound effect on species that are normally on their menu – their worries are over. Ground-foraging birds, with no need for a quick escape, tend to lose the ability to fly, marooning themselves in the process. The downfall of Mauritius's most famous former resident, the dodo, was a lack of fear, evidence of its worry-free lifestyle. Even where flightless birds are absent today, most remote islands have had them in the past. Island giants, such as the giant tortoises which used to wander through the Mauritius scrub, are also indications of a short food chain. Free from predators, but in stiff competition

To find examples of the impressive tropical hardwood trees that once covered much of Mauritius, go to the Black River Gorges National Park, where many are still represented. Only approximately 1.3% of Mauritius's virgin forest remains, and most of it is found in this national park.

Undoubtedly the island's best-known hardwood, the Mauritius ebony (*Diospyros tesselaria*) was in particularly high demand because it has the darkest wood of any tree. Its congener on Réunion (*D. borbonica*) is still quite plentiful but the Mauritian species was almost wiped out. Other impressive protected hardwoods found in Black River Gorges include various species of the genera *Mimusops* and *Sideroxylon*, as well as *Labourdonnaisia*. Quite a few of the rare, slow-growing hardwoods are

with each other, the bigger, stronger individuals tend to survive and the smaller, meeker ones don't, so that, over time, the population attains giant proportions.

Although a remote island offers unusual opportunities, it cannot carry an infinite number of animals and plants. As each new population arrives, the competition for food and space increases, and the community has to adjust. The pressure to adapt is intense and species change their characteristics dramatically in a short time. Less mobile species such as inland birds and plants, isolated from their mainland ancestors, soon spread throughout the various habitats found on the island and gradually adapt to each one; after a period of time the original founding species evolves into a string of new species. This explains why many of the animals and plants found on remote islands are endemics – types found nowhere else in the world.

Inevitably, at some point, after repeated immigrations, an island 'fills up' – the diversity of species reaches a maximum and there is literally 'no room at the inn'. Biologists have found that the number of species that any one island can support depends on several factors. The size of the island is the most influential of these. Larger islands, not surprisingly, can cater for more species, but the number of different habitats is also important. Islands that have forests, lagoons, lakes, scrub and cliffs, simply offer more opportunities than those covered in one type of vegetation, and consequently sustain more species. Nevertheless, at some point the island will be full, and from this moment on any new arrival will either perish from lack of food or be forced to usurp one of the residents – an act that leads to extinction. The rate at which species immigrate and cause such disruption is determined by the remoteness of the island. Islands distant from other lands experience few new arrivals and hence suffer extinctions less frequently. Islands near to a mainland have far more disruption, receiving new species and losing old ones at a daunting rate.

The remoteness of the Mascarenes protected the islands from excessive immigrations for millions of years, while the size of Mauritius and Réunion nurtured a diverse community. Then we arrived, in a wave similar to any other immigration. Like large predators, we needed space and resources too, but unlike the predators, we made sure that we got what we needed. We chopped down forests and introduced our favourite species, animals and plants that would never have been able to overcome the three challenges of island colonisation. Exposed to the new, advanced species from the mainland, the island community quickly lost many of its older residents in an event more profoundly disruptive than any witnessed by these islands since their abrupt beginnings.

shared with Réunion, such as the takamaka (*Calophyllum tacamahaca*), the 'rat' tree (*Tarenna borbonica*) and the *bois blanc* (*Hernandia mascarenensis*).

There are 89 species of orchid found in Mauritius. Of those, 94% are endemic to the Mascarenes/Madagascar region. Nine species are endemic to Mauritius only. Certain orchids, like *Oeniella polystachys* and *Angraecum eburneum*, have become rare, so attempts are being made to conserve them on Ile aux Aigrettes, where they can be seen in the wild. (For details of visits to Ile aux Aigrettes, see page 158).

Seven species of palm are endemic to Mauritius. Most of these are in cultivation because in the wild they are all gravely threatened. Two palms – *Hyophorbe amaricaulis* and *Dyctosperma album* var. *conjugatum* – are down to a single wild individual each. The latter, which is sought-after for heart-of-palm salad, has been cultivated successfully by the Mauritian Wildlife Foundation (MWF) as part of a project to rescue all endangered flora. However, the species *Hyophorbe amaricaulis* appears to be doomed.

A problem facing botanists and conservationists currently is lack of information about the indigenous flora. For instance, very little is known about pollinator agents. However, the MWF, in conjunction with several foreign universities, has been engaged in studies of Mauritian plant pollinators: bats, invertebrates like hawk moths, butterflies and beetles, passerine birds and reptiles like *Phelsuma* geckos. Where plants have been decimated, their pollinators suffer likewise, particularly those that are specifically associated with one or two plant species.

In terms of flowering plants, one of the most impressive endemics is the *bois bouquet banané* (*Ochna mauritania*). In summer (November to January), this small deciduous shrub can be seen covered in a display of white flowers, at Pétrin and in Black River Gorges National Park.

Of the various plants with medicinal properties, the best known is the *bois de ronde* (*Erythroxylon laurifolium*), the bark of which is used to treat kidney stones.

Finally, the national flower of Mauritius is the rare and beautiful *Trochetia boutoniana* (or *boucle d'oreille*, which means 'earring') of the Serculiaceae family. Forget about seeing this stunner in the wild, though – it is confined to a single mountaintop. But being the national flower, it is cultivated in various sites, for example at the Special Mobile Force Museum in Vacoas and in the grounds of the Forestry Service. The closely related (and just as beautiful) *Trochetia blackburniana* is a little more plentiful and can be seen along the road at Plaine Champagne. It also has lovely pinkish-crimson flowers.

FAUNA *with the Mauritian Wildlife Foundation*

The sole surviving endemic mammal is the striking Mauritius fruit bat (*Pteropus niger*), which still exists in fair numbers. Like its endangered cousin, the Rodrigues fruit bat (*P. rodericensis*), the much darker Mauritius fruit bat roosts in large trees by day and forages for fruit and flowers at night. These fruit bats belong to a predominantly Asian genus also present in Madagascar and the Comoros, where they reach their westernmost limit. A third Mascarene fruit bat, *Pteropus subniger*, is sadly extinct. To see fruit bats, go to Black River Gorges, the Moka Mountains, Savannah or the Grand Port Mountains.

Birds Birdwatchers visiting Mauritius are in for a treat. Although only nine endemic species still remain, they include some of the world's rarest birds.

By 1974, the fabulous pink pigeon (*Nesoenas mayeri*) was down to some 24 individuals. Following intensive captive-breeding efforts by the DWCT and MWF, this gorgeous pigeon (yes, it really is pink!) is now more plentiful, numbering some

NARCOTIC INDULGENCES OF THE PINK PIGEON

The pink pigeon's continued existence has left some naturalists puzzled. It has been questioned why this bird survived the colonisers' presence on the island, when the similarly sized Mauritius blue pigeon, with which it shared its habitat, was exterminated.

The answer seems to lie in the pink pigeon's dietary preferences. Apparently, its favoured food was the fruit of a shrub known as *fangame* (*Stillingis lineata*), which has an intoxicating effect. It is said that when *fangame* berries were in season, the pink pigeons would gorge themselves and flop to the ground in a drug-induced daze. As such, they were an even easier target for hunters. However, the Dutch soon realised that every time they ate a pink pigeon pie, they felt quite dreadful. So the pink pigeons were left alone and are still around today, whilst the last Mauritius blue pigeon (*Alectroenas nitidissima*) was shot as long ago as 1826.

400 birds. A substantial population is held in various captive-breeding centres and large numbers of captive-bred birds have been reintroduced into the wild. Successful predator-control programmes, carried out in woodland where wild pink pigeons nest, help tremendously. What was once the world's rarest pigeon can now be seen in its natural habitat at Black River Gorges National Park and Ile aux Aigrettes.

Another rarity which the DWCT and MWF have saved from certain extinction is the sole-surviving Mauritian raptor, the Mauritius kestrel (*Falco punctatus*). In 1973, when only four individuals could be found, it was declared the world's rarest bird. Causes for its dramatic decline included the extensive use of DDT, which was sprayed everywhere except for the Black River Gorges.

Captive breeding of the Mauritius kestrel started in very basic and primitive conditions in 1974 but was hampered by lack of knowledge about the bird. By 1978, the situation had become desperate and so little progress had been made that Carl Jones of the MWF was sent to close down the project. Fortunately his keen interest in hawks and his enthusiasm saw him revive the project and restart the captive breeding, which has led to such spectacular results. Hundreds of kestrels have been bred in captivity and released into the wild; today between 400 and 500 kestrels are estimated to be flying around Mauritius

The phenomenal success which conservationists had with the pink pigeon and Mauritius kestrel meant they could turn their attention to yet another Mauritian endemic in dire straits – the echo parakeet (*Psittacula eques*). By the 1990s, about 15 birds remained, all in the upland forest of Macchabée ridge. It was regarded as the world's rarest wild breeding bird. In 2001/02, 21 hand-reared birds were released into the wild and management of wild nests allowed a further 21 birds to fledge naturally. The population now stands at around 600 birds.

For four of the five remaining endemic birds, all passerines (perching birds), things do not look too rosy at present. The Mauritius cuckoo-shrike (*Coracina typica*), Mauritius bulbul (*Hypsipetes olivaceous*), Mauritius olive white-eye (*Zosterops chloronothus*) and Mauritius fody (*Foudia rubra*) have all suffered heavy losses, caused by introduced predators (rats, mongooses, cats and monkeys) raiding their nests. All are classified as 'uncommon' in the definitive field guide *Birds of the Indian Ocean Islands* (Olivier Langrand and Ian Sinclair, 1998) and are on the International Union for Conservation of Nature red list. At present there is particular concern for the striking Mauritius fody and olive white-eye, both of which have declined to fewer than 150 breeding pairs. In breeding plumage, the male fody is a living jewel, with a ruby-red head and upper breast and dark green underparts. The olive white-eye is equally spectacular, with its olive green back and spectacled eye ring. All of these threatened birds can be seen in the Black River Gorges National Park, their last stronghold. The MWF has released the Mauritius fody and olive white-eye on Ile aux Aigrettes and they have taken to their new home, with nearly 170 and 30 birds respectively now on the island.

Strangely enough, one endemic, the Mauritius grey white-eye (*Zosterops mauritanus*, locally known as *zozo maniok* or *pic pic*), has adapted very successfully to man's encroachment of its habitat. It is very common all over the island, entering hotel gardens freely, as its near relative on Réunion does there.

The Mascarene swiftlet (*Collocalia francica*) and Mascarene paradise flycatcher (*Terpsiphone bourbonnensis*) are shared with Réunion, where both are more plentiful than on Mauritius. Also shared with Réunion (and with Madagascar) is the larger Mascarene martin (*Phedina borbonica*).

Finally, of great interest to visiting birders is the Round Island petrel (*Pterodroma arminjoniana*). Amazingly, it is found only around Round Island (where it nests) and on the other side of the globe, around Trindade Island, Brazil. Some authorities previously considered it a full species (separate from the birds of Trindade). However, recent work has shown it is a hybrid of several gadfly petrels; research by the MWF is ongoing. It is endangered but, thanks to all the rehabilitation work that has been conducted on Round Island, its chances for survival have been improved significantly.

Reptiles The endemic birds – and to a lesser extent, plants – of Mauritius have received much international press coverage, but few people know that a fascinating ensemble of endangered reptiles exists there also, most significantly on a small chunk of volcanic rock called Round Island, 22km north of Mauritius.

Other offshore islets and the mainland itself support four endemic day geckos (genus *Phelsuma*), two more night geckos (genus *Nactus*) and two small skink species (genus *Gongylomorphus*).

Round Island is a tilted volcanic cone rising 278m above the sea. Its surface area covers 219ha. Surrounded by rough seas and often buffeted by strong winds, the island has remained uninhabited by man and rats, allowing reptiles, seabirds and plants that have perished elsewhere to survive. Five of Round Island's eight reptile species are now endemic to the island and endangered: the large Telfair's skink (*Leiolopisma telfairi*); the strangely nocturnal Round Island 'day' gecko (*Phelsuma guentheri*); the tiny nocturnal Durrell's night gecko (*Nactus durrelli*); and the remarkable keel-scaled boa (*Casarea dussumieri*). The fifth, the Round Island burrowing boa (*Bolyeria multocarinata*), was last seen in 1975 and is sadly presumed extinct. (For more information on Round Island, see pages 15–19 and 130).

In recent years, a number of initiatives have been implemented to improve the long-term outlook for these species. As part of the Darwin Initiative Reptile Conservation Project, Telfair's skink was reintroduced to Ile aux Aigrettes and Coin de Mire. In January 2008, the MWF announced that the first of a new generation of Telfair's skinks had been discovered on Ile aux Aigrettes. This was the first time for 150 years that the skink had been known to reproduce naturally in the wild, outside of Round Island. Since 2008, the MWF has translocated 382 orange-tail skinks (*Gongylomorphus fontenayi* spp.) from Flat Island to Coin de Mire. Initial observations show that they are doing well and starting to produce offspring.

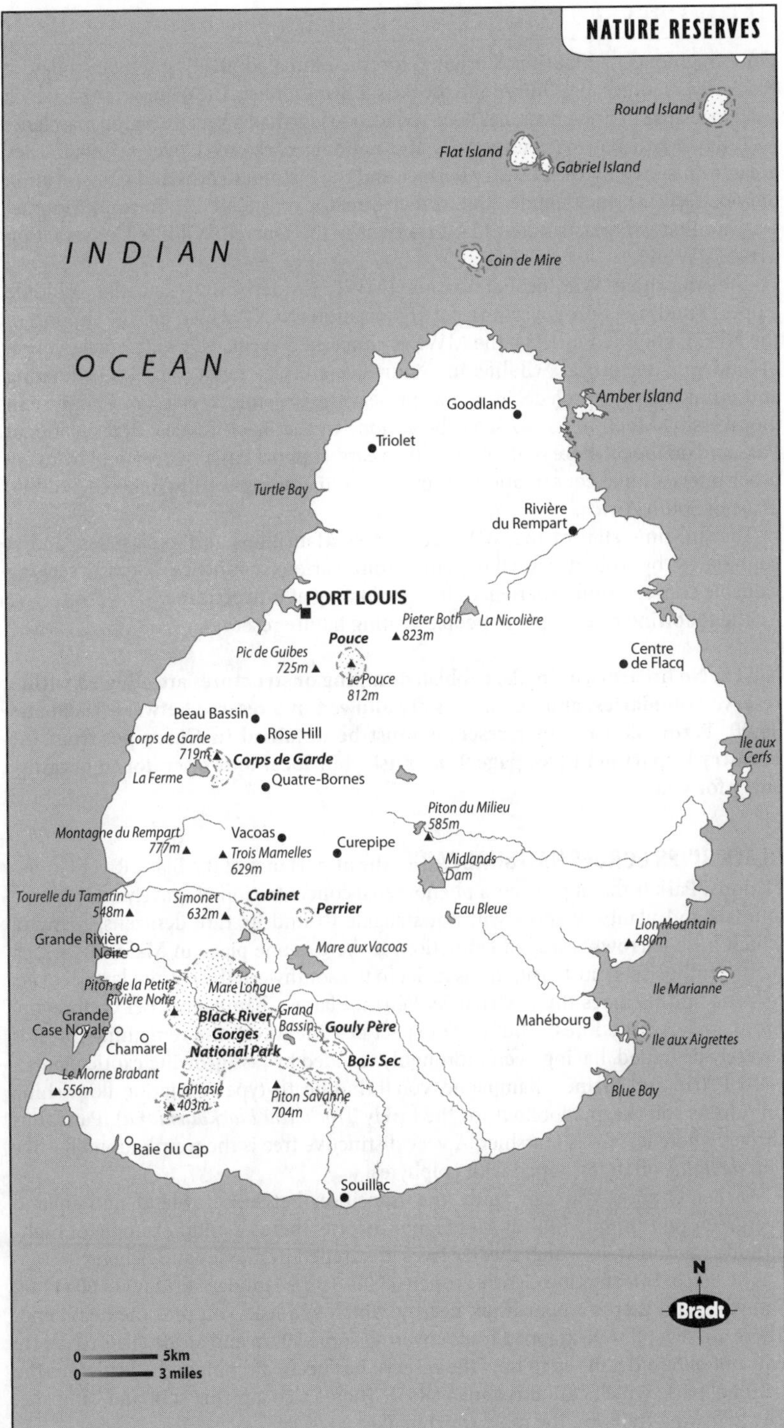
NATURE RESERVES
Round Island
Flat Island
Gabriel Island
INDIAN
OCEAN
Coin de Mire
Amber Island
Goodlands
Triolet
Turtle Bay
Rivière du Rempart
PORT LOUIS
Pieter Both 823m
La Nicolière
Pouce
Pic de Guibes 725m
Le Pouce 812m
Centre de Flacq
Beau Bassin
Rose Hill
Corps de Garde 719m
Corps de Garde
La Ferme
Quatre-Bornes
Ile aux Cerfs
Piton du Milieu 585m
Montagne du Rempart 777m
Vacoas
Trois Mamelles 629m
Curepipe
Midlands Dam
Tourelle du Tamarin 548m
Simonet 632m
Cabinet
Perrier
Eau Bleue
Lion Mountain 480m
Grande Rivière Noire
Mare aux Vacoas
Piton de la Petite Rivière Noire
Mare Longue
Ile Marianne
Grande Case Noyale
Black River Gorges National Park
Grand Bassin
Gouly Père
Mahébourg
Ile aux Aigrettes
Chamarel
Bois Sec
Le Morne Brabant 556m
Fantasie 403m
Piton Savanne 704m
Blue Bay
Baie du Cap
Souillac
N
Bradt
0 5km
0 3 miles

NATURE RESERVES AND CONSERVATION

Only fragments of Mauritius's original forests, estimated at 1.3%, remain today, at Black River Gorges, Bel Ombre and the Bassin Blanc Crater. The palm savanna, which used to feature in drier areas, has been reduced to less than a hectare on the mainland.

Today, Mauritian nature reserves and national park cover over 6,700ha. They are administered by the Forestry Service and the National Parks and Conservation Service (NPCS). Incidentally, the former director of the NPCS, Yousoof Mugroo, was the first overseas student to be trained by the Durrell Wildlife Conservation Trust (DWCT).

The Mauritian Wildlife Foundation (MWF, formerly the Mauritian Wildlife Appeal Fund) is a non-governmental organisation (NGO) which has the support of the NPCS. Founded in 1984, the MWF is concerned exclusively with conservation of endemic terrestrial wildlife in Mauritius and its territories, co-ordinating and administering projects aimed at preserving endemic species and ecosystem biodiversity. Much of its work has been done in the Black River Gorges National Park and on the offshore islands. Over the years, support has also been lent by many other international conservation organisations, including the Endangered Wildlife Trust of South Africa.

The full-time staff of the MWF comprises Mauritians and expatriates, and is augmented by volunteers who come from various countries abroad, seeking valuable conservation experience after graduating at universities.

The following rules apply to people visiting nature reserves:

NOTE: No firearms, animals, rubbish dumping or structures are allowed within reserve boundaries, and no visitors are allowed in a reserve between 18.00 and 06.00. Permission to enter reserves must be obtained in Curepipe, from the Forestry Department (see page 95), or ask your local tour operator to organise entry for you.

BLACK RIVER GORGES NATIONAL PARK The importance of the Black River Gorges National Park is that it protects a phenomenal concentration of gravely endangered animals and plants. Visitors will not struggle to find its rare denizens, many of which have narrowly escaped extinction. If there is one place in Mauritius which nature enthusiasts must visit, this is it. Set in the southwest, the national park covers 6,754ha and includes the Macchabée, Pétrin, Plaine Champagne, Bel Ombre and Montagne Cocotte forests. But don't expect pristine forest: the remaining forest is severely degraded, having been thoroughly invaded by fast-growing exotic plants.

At Pétrin and Plaine Champagne, you'll find heath-type vegetation flourishing on porous soil (keep a lookout for the lovely *Trochettia blackburniana*). Pandanus thrives where terrain is marshier. A very distinctive tree is the weird, umbrella-like *bois de natte*, often festooned with epiphytes.

At Bel Ombre, you can study the transition between lowland and upland evergreen rainforest, whilst at Montagne Cocotte, there's a good example of high-altitude rainforest, in which shorter trees are draped in mosses and lichens.

The Pétrin Information Centre is open 08.00–15.15 Monday–Friday, 08.00–11.00 Saturday, and there's a boardwalk nearby, which will lead you into the heathland. There are several well-mapped trails covering some 50km and at the visitors' centre you can obtain details as to how the reserve has been laid out, and a leaflet on the national park, which contains a map (Rs5). There's also a picnic spot and campsite. The following trails are the most worthwhile:

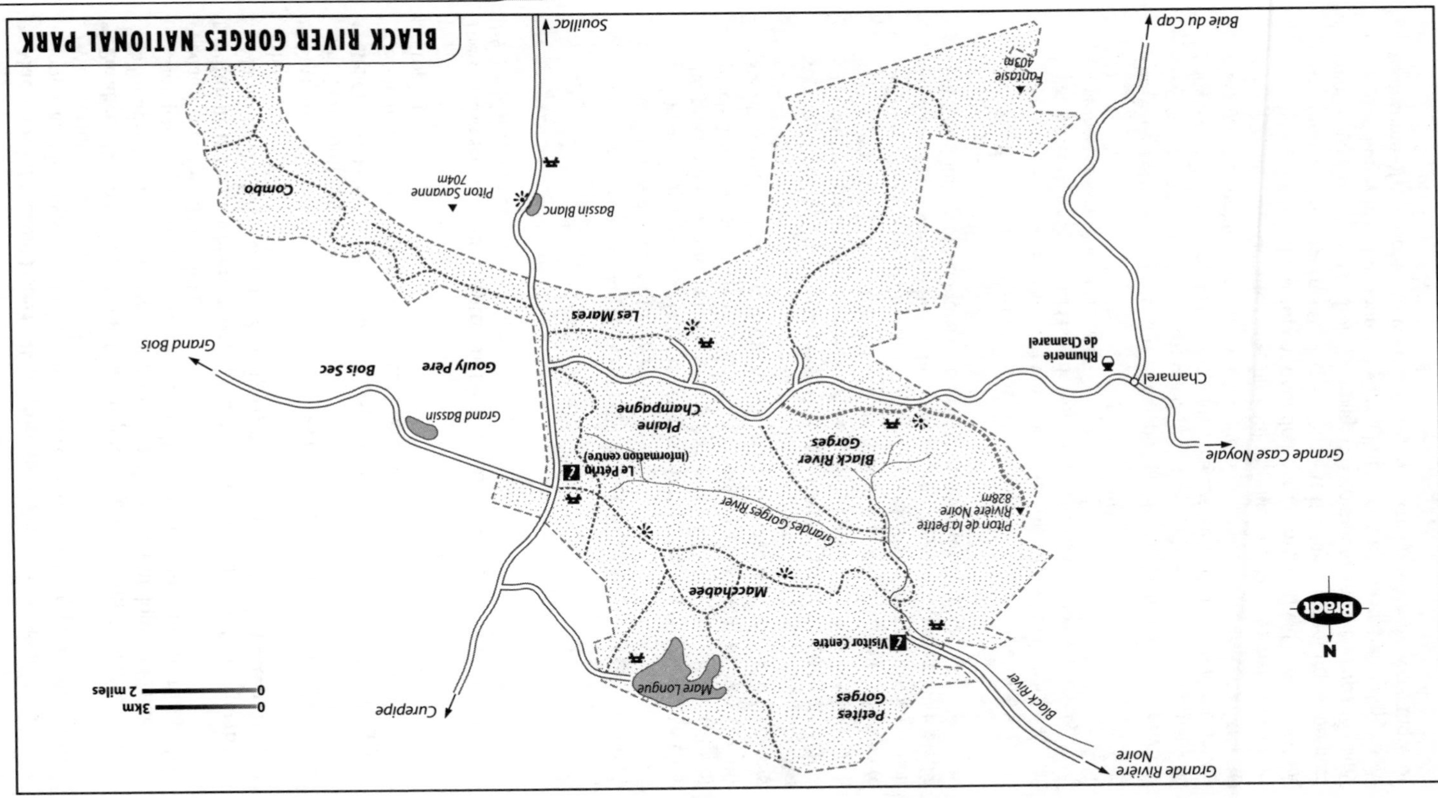
BLACK RIVER GORGES NATIONAL PARK
Souillac
Baie du Cap
Fantasie
403m
Combo
Piton Savanne
704m
Bassin Blanc
Les Mares
Grand Bois
Bois Sec
Gouly Père
Rhumerie
de Chamarel
Chamarel
Grand Bassin
Plaine
Champagne
Black River
Gorges
Le Pétrin
(Information centre)
Grande Case Noyale
Grandes Gorges River
Piton de la Petite
Rivière Noire
828m
Macchabée
Visitor Centre
Bradt
N
Mare Longue
Petites
Gorges
Black River
0 3km
0 2 miles
Curepipe
Grande Rivière
Noire

- **Macchabée (Macabe) Forest** 14km return from Pétrin (moderate). This loop trail allows visitors the best experience of Mauritian tropical rainforest. Wonderful views, good birding.
- **Parakeet** 8km one-way: Plaine Champagne to visitors' centre (tough). This is for adventurous, fit hikers, who will enjoy the steep trail joining Plaine Champagne with the gorges area. The really energetic can combine this with Macchabée for a 15km hike.
- **Piton de la Petite Rivière Noire** 6km return (moderate). This takes you to Mauritius's highest peak, at 828m. Fairly easy except for the last, steep stretch to the top.
- **Savanne** 6km return, from the end of Les Mares road (easy). Offers scenic views of southern Mauritius.
- **Bel Ombre** 18km return, Plaine Champagne to the reserve boundary (tough). Good birding in the tropical forest at lower elevations. Also, fruit bats and tropic birds.

There is also second visitor centre on the other side of the park inland from Grande Rivière Noire, on Les Gorges Road.

DEAD AS A DODO

Neal Sullivan

Most people have heard of the world's most famous extinct creature but few are aware that it was endemic to Mauritius.

The dodo (*Raphus cucullatus)* is believed to have been a flightless relative of the pigeon and a close relative of the Rodrigues solitaire (*Pezophaps solitaria*), which is also extinct. It would seem that the dodo lost its ability to fly due to the abundance of food close to the ground and the absence of mammalian predators.

With the arrival of Europeans in the late 16th century, the dodos' numbers started to decline and it is believed they were extinct by 1681. Dodos laid their eggs on the ground, making them easy targets for introduced predators, such as rats and pigs. The destruction of their habitat and these new predators were the principal causes of their demise, although the early settlers certainly ate their way through a good number of the hapless birds. Heyndrick Dircksz Jolinck led a Dutch exploration of Mauritius around 1598 and wrote:

> we also found large birds, with wings as large as of a pigeon, so that they could not fly and were named penguins by the Portuguese. These particular birds have a stomach so large that it could provide two men with a tasty meal and was actually the most delicious part of the bird.

The early settlers sketched the rather peculiar-looking birds but no physical evidence of their existence was found until the 19th century, leaving many to conclude in the interim that it was a mythical creature. This led to a fascination among the scientific community with finding dodo remains. In 1865, after 30 years of searching, George Clark, an English primary schoolteacher working in Mahébourg, found an assortment of dodo bones in marshy land known as Mare aux Songes, in the southeast of the island. At the time, indentured labourers were digging a railway line from Curepipe to Mahébourg and piling up the many assorted bones that they found. A young British civil engineer, Harry Higginson, took some of the bones to George Clark, who confirmed they were those of

For more information about the reserve, contact the National Parks and Conservation Service of the Ministry of Agriculture and Natural Resources at Le Réduit (☎ *464 4016*; **f** *465 1184*; **e** *npcs@mail.gov.mu*) or pop into either of the visitor centres.

ROUND ISLAND *with the Mauritian Wildlife Foundation*

Round Island's troubles began in the 19th century, when goats and rabbits were introduced as a food source for fishermen, seabird-egg hunters and shipwreck victims. True to their form, these animals multiplied like flies, relentlessly munching away the hardwood forest on the upper slopes and the palm savanna on the lower slopes, which resembled that present in the drier areas of Mauritius, circa 1500.

Conservationists realised that urgent action had to be taken if Round Island's remaining plants and animals were to be saved. In 1976, the late Gerald Durrell and John Hartley made their first visit there. They were aghast at what they found: only two hurricane palms and eight Round Island bottle palms remained. The three species of skink and three species of gecko fed on a dwindling insect supply, and the two species of primitive boa on the diminishing lizard supply. Immediately, captive-breeding programmes were started at Jersey Zoo for the endemic reptiles. The

the dodo. Clark returned to the site to supervise further excavations he sent hundreds of bones to the British Museum, for which he was paid a pound a piece, and those bones ended up in museums around the world.

In 1904, Louis Etienne Thirioux, a Port Louis hairdresser and amateur naturalist, found a complete dodo skeleton, which at the time was the only one in the world. The skeleton is now in the Natural History Museum in Port Louis.

In 2005, an international team of researchers excavated part of the Mare aux Songes and found fossilised dodo remains that had accumulated over centuries. Subsequent excavations suggested that dodos, along with other animals, became mired in Mare aux Songes trying to reach water during a long period of severe drought about 4,200 years ago.

In 2007, the discovery of 'Dodo Fred' added further to our knowledge of these birds. Fred and Debbie Stone were looking for cave cockroaches near Bois Chéri when they discovered bones that were later confirmed to be those of a dodo. These were the first dodo remains found in the highlands and proved that dodos inhabited that area. It is thought that Dodo Fred entered the cave to seek shelter from a violent cyclone, fell down a deep hole and could not climb out. Interestingly, during the excavation of the remains, the remains of another extinct bird, the Mauritian owl, were found. This discovery provided important DNA for determining the dodo's closest relatives. DNA testing of other dodo remains had been inconclusive but the cave conditions were ideal for DNA preservation. Results of these tests are yet to be determined.

The dodo has to be one of the world's most famous birds and has become the reigning symbol of extinction. Its rather ridiculous appearance has contributed to its fame, and it is always depicted as a friendly and harmless creature as it was in Lewis Carroll's *Alice's Adventures in Wonderland*. In 2009, a previously unpublished 17th-century Dutch illustration of a dodo was sold at Christie's in London for £44,450, evidence that 300 years after its demise the dodo still fascinates us.

Mauritius Government, under the Conservator of Forests and Wildlife Director A Wahab Owadally, rid the island of its goats by 1979. But the 3,000 undernourished rabbits still presented a major problem. So, the DWCT finally enlisted the assistance of the equally renowned New Zealand Department of Conservation. In 1986, the rabbits were completely eradicated.

The results have been spectacular, to say the least. Almost immediately, most of the island's endemic and indigenous plants began sprouting scores of seedlings. The subsequent increase of fruit and insects has resulted in substantial increases in the reptile populations. The Forestry Department and a MWF botanist carried out an extensive programme to weed exotic plants and replant indigenous species. Today, the keel-scaled boa, Round Island day gecko and Telfair's skink are present in healthy, flourishing populations and new projects to fully restore the vegetation of the island and study the reptiles have been initiated by the MWF and its partners. Round Island represents one of the most spectacular examples of a DWCT-led conservation triumph and there are now plans to apply for

INVADERS

The poor Mascarene ecosystems! Not only have they been hammered by man and his animal followers, but they're riddled with invasive alien plants. Most of the animals and plants are species that have been introduced, and have subsequently run rampant to the detriment of indigenous flora and fauna.

Very prominent introductions include the *filao* (casuarina) tree (*Casuarina equisetifolia*), which often lines beaches and is useful as a windbreak. It originates in Malaysia. Great banyan trees (*Ficus benghalensis*) were brought from India, recognisable by their weird root systems dangling from their branches to the ground. Two distinctive Malagasy introductions are the flamboyant tree (*Delonix regia*) and the fan-shaped ravenala palm (*Ravenala madagascariensis*).

Privet and Chinese guava (*goyavier*) have spread at an alarming rate in the montane rainforests, often choking seedlings of slow-growing indigenous hardwoods. A horribly invasive bush is *Lantana camara*, the worst nightmare of conservationists. It is native to tropical America and has spread like wildfire in the Mascarenes.

Other tropical American invaders include sisal (*Furcraea foetida*), the morning glory creeper (*Ipomoea purpurea*), the prickly-pear cactus (*Opuntia vulgaris*) and the unmistakable poinsettia (*Euphorbia pulcherrima*).

In marshy areas, pampas grass (*Cortaderia selloana*), introduced from southeast Asia, is common. The originally Asian elephant ear (*Colocasea esculenta*) also frequents damp places. The staghorn fern (*Platycerium bifurcatum*), which one sees on so many rainforest trees, is actually Australian. Two of the most commonly used ornamentals, the bougainvillea (*Bougainvillea glabra*) and the frangipani (*Plumeria alba*), are tropical American species.

When the earlier settlers arrived in Mauritius, they introduced a selection of destructive animals, intentionally and by accident. A truly senseless introduction was the southeast Asian long-tailed macaque monkey (*Macaca fasicularis*), courtesy of the Dutch back in 1606. These primates are now abundant in Mauritius, where eradicating them is very difficult because Indo-Mauritians consider them sacred. They pose a very real threat to the endemic birds, reptiles, invertebrates and flora.

Wild pigs (*Sus scrofra*), of Asian origin, abound too, but are very secretive and wary. No doubt they don't do terrestrial fauna much good, being the highly adaptable omnivores that they are, and are very destructive in native forests.

World Heritage status for Round Island. British zoologist/author Nick Garbutt, who visited Round Island several times while working in Mauritius, provides a fascinating report:

> I was surprised at the density of vegetation, for despite the rugged nature of the slopes and the apparent lack of soil, latan palms (*Latania loddigesii*) and pandanus or screwpines (*Pandanus vandermeerschi*) covered the majority of the western slopes. I recalled photographs of these same slopes looking barren and lifeless, taken in previous years, when the goats and rabbits were still present. The difference was absolutely remarkable and it was clear that the palm savanna was beginning to recover. The helicopter swung in over the south coast and landed on the one flat piece of rock on the island. It was not long before I spotted our first visitor, a Telfair's skink, scurrying over a hot rock surface towards the camp. It was followed by three more, then a further four from various directions. This large skink often reaches a length of 1ft. It is very bold, showing no fear of man, and congregates around visitors. Because

Brown rats and black rats arrived by means of ships and thoroughly invaded all the Mascarenes. Other introductions include the musk shrew, the black-naped hare (*Lepus nigricollis*) and the wild rabbit (*Oryctolagus cuniculus*), which was eradicated on Round Island after severely damaging the ecosystem there. The lesser Indian mongoose (*Herpestes javanicus*) is fairly often seen bolting across rural roads and was introduced in 1900 to reduce rats. It also munched its way through native bird populations.

Of the reptile introductions, the aggressive Indian wolf snake (*Lycodon aulicus*) is most often seen. We can only imagine what species this reptile wiped out while establishing itself in Mauritius, where it is now quite common.

Many birds have been introduced and those that established themselves are generally common and highly successful species. They are the birds you'll see in hotel gardens, parks and towns. Sadly, where they have an endemic relative, they far outnumber that species; like the red-whiskered bulbul, an Asian introduction, which is numerous, while the endemic Mauritius bulbul is uncommon.

The aggressive Indian mynah is to be seen in any urban centre, as are the house sparrow and house crow. Also regularly seen and heard is the zebra dove. The ring-neck parakeet (*Psittacula krameri*) can be confused with its endangered, endemic relative, the echo parakeet. However, their calls differ and both sexes of the ring-neck have red beaks, whilst only female echoes have black beaks.

Three small passerines (an order of birds characterised by the perching habit) from Africa are the spotted-backed weaver, the common waxbill and the yellow-eyed canary, all of which are now abundant. The bright red Madagascar fody has colonised all the Mascarenes. Seeing this little bird is guaranteed, but to stand the best chance of seeing its rare native congener, the Mauritius fody, you will need to go to Ile aux Aigrettes.

Some of the introduced birds have been far less invasive and are actually quite interesting. The Meller's duck (*Anas melleri*) is uncommon in its native Madagascar and is known to breed in Mauritius, where there are no other wild ducks or geese left. The common Indian francolin is present in grasslands and in sugarcane fields. More often seen is the Madagascar turtle dove.

they are highly adept at locating any food, all supplies had to be stored in 'skink-proof' boxes well above the ground. The skinks also prey on smaller lizards present, namely Bojer's skinks, night geckos and ornate day geckos.

Bojer's skink (*Gongylomorphus bojeri*) is the island's most common reptile, also being present on several of the outlying islands, including Coin de Mire, Flat and Gabriel islands, and was probably exterminated on Mauritius by introduced rats, mongooses and Indian wolf snakes (*Lycodon aulica*).

MARINE ENVIRONMENTAL AWARENESS *with Tom Hooper*

By following a few simple guidelines you can enjoy the wonderful marine environment of the Mascarenes without damaging it.

BE CAREFUL WHERE YOU WALK There are many delicate organisms on the reef edge and shoreline which will break or be crushed if you walk on them. Corals are particularly vulnerable and are likely to die from being touched or smothered by silt. When you are diving and snorkelling be especially careful with your fins to make sure you don't break corals.

DON'T BUY SHELLS There are good reasons for not buying shells. The most beautiful and pristine shells are very rarely collected dead. They are taken live from the seabed and the animal inside is killed. While looking for and collecting shells there is also damage to the surrounding marine life. Lastly, even empty shells serve a useful purpose as homes for hermit crabs or a hard substrate for new growths of coral.

DON'T BUY CORALS, TURTLE SHELLS OR OTHER MARINE CURIOS Creating a market in these organisms leads to them being targeted for capture and the destruction of their surroundings during collection.

DISPOSE OF YOUR LITTER CAREFULLY A single piece of litter can destroy the illusion of wild remoteness and ruin a beach walk. With the introduction of cans and plastic bottles, wrappers and bags, even the coastlines of Rodrigues are beginning to suffer from the eyesore of scattered litter. Some of these items will take tens or hundreds of years to biodegrade.

SEAFOOD The demand for particular types of seafood can set a marine ecosystem off balance. In addition, some harvesting techniques are particularly damaging to the environment. Octopus populations are currently vulnerable in Rodrigues and the collection method damages the marine environment. Good fish to eat are the herbivorous fish which are caught in basket traps such as unicorn and rabbit fish. These have a delicate taste and are excellent grilled.

AVOID EATING SHARK World populations of shark are in serious decline and as the top predators this has led to an imbalance in marine food chains. Areas of the Caribbean and Far East still use the lamentable practice of finning, which involves cutting fins from sharks for use in shark-fin soup, and then throwing them back alive.

Another skink found on Round Island is the pan-tropical Bouton's skink (*Cryptoblepharus boutonii*). Because of its long legs and claws, it is capable of staying on a rock while raging whitewater crashes over it. The ornate day gecko (*Phelsuma ornata*) remains common on Mauritius and Round Island. It forages by day for insects and nectar. The endemic Round Island day gecko (*P. guentheri*) is unusual among day geckos in that it is most active at night and is not brightly coloured like its relatives. Reaching a total length of nearly 300mm (1ft), it is the largest day gecko which still exists. They are often to be seen foraging in latan palms, for which they are important pollinators. Another gecko to be found on Round Island is the diminutive Durrell's night gecko (*Nactus durrelli*).

Round Island is best known among zoological circles for its two endemic snakes, which are so distinctive taxonomically that they have been accorded a family of their own, the Bolyeridae. Intriguingly, the only other animal family unique to the Mascarenes is the Raphidae – the remarkable dodo and solitaires – all of which are extinct. The considerable regeneration of native vegetation on Round Island following the rabbit eradication means that the keel-scaled boa is now thriving and there may just be a faint glimmer of hope for the Round Island burrowing boa. The keel-scaled boa is largely nocturnal, preying wholly on lizards. During the day, the boas tend to curl up in rock crevices or between fallen latan palm fronds. Sadly, no-one knows what the burrowing boa ate or how it lived.

The importance of Round Island as a refuge for a unique group of reptiles and plants cannot be overstated.

ILE AUX AIGRETTES Ile aux Aigrettes is a 25ha reef-ringed coral islet about 1km off the southeast coast. It contains the last remaining traces of the lowland ebony forest that once dominated much of coastal Mauritius, as well as numerous other endemic animal and plant species threatened with extinction.

Since the MWF obtained the long-term lease of the islet in 1986, they've been engaged in extensive rehabilitation of the ecosystem there, which had been severely damaged over 400 years. The aim is that Ile aux Aigrettes should one day resemble its original state as closely as possible. To this end, the MWF has been weeding the islet and replanting with native plants, restoring the forest and reintroducing endemic birds and reptiles known to have once lived there. In recent years, the olive white-eye, Telfair's skink, Guenther's gecko and seabirds have been reintroduced. As the threat from highly invasive plants, such as giant acacia, is very real, general maintenance weeding will continue for years to come. Reintroductions of fauna will also continue.

Visitors can enjoy fascinating guided tours of the islet, see some very rare flora and fauna and witness conservation work in process. It is one of the best places to see the rare pink pigeon and the Mauritius fody, and the only place in the Mascarenes where giant Aldabra tortoises roam completely freely. Two tortoise species are known to have existed in Mauritius; both are now extinct, having been used as a source of protein by passing sailors. The giant Aldabra tortoises, which can weigh as much as 200kg, are native to the Seychelles but have been introduced to the island as the closest surviving relative of the lost species. Visitors are also likely to see colourful day geckos basking in the sun. Tours last around two hours and the guide will take the time to explain the geology and history of the island (for details see page 158).

OTHER PROTECTED AREAS North of Black River are two small mountain forest reserves, **Corps de Garde** and **Le Pouce**. The island's smallest reserve, **Perrier**, is only 1.5ha and is between Curepipe and the Mare aux Vacoas reservoir. It protects a small remnant parcel of transition forest between lowland and montane rainforest and harbours a large number of endemic plants.

Other nature reserves include Bois Sec, Cabinet, Combo, Flat Island, Gabriel Island, Coin de Mire, Gouly Père, Les Mares, Marianne Islet and Serpent Island.

MARINE LIFE The marine life of Mauritius has also suffered since man's arrival, although it is still an important attraction for visitors.

It is easy to visit coral gardens in depths of 7–20m through hotel diving centres (see *Chapter 3, Scuba diving*, pages 89–92). The range of fish to be seen, especially those engaging in antics like the boxfish with their curious sculling action and the trumpet fish with their darting movements, is fascinating.

The appeal of the reef is enhanced by the variety of the coral that is among the most beautiful in the world. Because of the sunlight that filters through sea of the right salinity and temperature, the coral thrives better in the waters of Mauritius than elsewhere. There are notable coral gardens at the southern corners of Mauritius, off La Morne Brabant and Blue Bay.

Shell collecting has been rapacious since the 1960s and the Mauritius Scuba Diving Association now considers collecting unacceptable. To meet demand for souvenirs, shells are imported from the Philippines to be sold to tourists who want something pretty.

The rarest and most valuable shells in the world, such as the several varieties of conus, *Lambis violacea* and *Cypraea onyx-nymphal*, have been found off Mauritius. There is an extensive collection of shells at the Mauritius Museum Council in Port Louis (see page 112). A model of the rare cone (*Conus milneedwardsi*) can be seen among the exhibits. This was brought up in a fisherman's basket net from a depth of 40 fathoms, off the coast of Black River. Also exhibited is a giant clam (*Tridacna gigas*), the largest clam ever evolved.

Cone and cowrie shells, while delightful, can be deadly if of the *Conus aulieus*, *geographicus*, *marmoreus*, *rattus*, *textile* or *tulipa* species. Poison injected from their sharp ends can bring death within 150 minutes, with no known antidote. There have been 105 species recorded. Harp shells, four species with ribs resembling the strings of a harp, are attractive to collectors, especially the double harp (*Harpa costata*), which is not found outside Mauritian waters. There are 135 species of mitre shells (*Mitridae*), which are spindle- to oval-shaped and notched in front. Murex shells, such as *Murex tenuispina* with its elongated, jagged stem, are popular. The purple fluid secreted by them was used in ancient times as a dye.

Starfish are common and the presence of the crown of thorns (*Achantaster plancei*) is destructive to coral. An excellent specimen of the very rare *Acanthocidaris curvatispinis*, which is known only in Mauritius, is on display at the Natural History Museum in Port Louis. The collection of echinoderms there also contains a remarkable specimen of *Chondrocidaris gigantea*, exhibited in a special showcase as it is considered to be the most beautiful sea urchin in the world.

HISTORY

The delightful mélange that is Mauritius has its origins in a mixed-up history. It was Dutch … French … and finally British until the country's independence in 1968.

DISCOVERY The first recorded discovery of Mauritius was by Islamic colonisers, when, in AD975, Hasan ibn Ali, a mercurial leader from Shiraz, Iran, left his homeland with a fleet of seven ships and a band of followers.

Most of them eventually settled in Mombasa and Pemba, although one of their ships went as far as the Comoros. From there they reached Madagascar and the islands to the east of it. On 15th-century maps, these were shown as Dina Arobi (Mauritius), Dina Margabim (Réunion) and Dina Moraze (Rodrigues).

It is unlikely that the colonisers actually settled in Dina Arobi. The island was uninhabited then and no evidence of Arab settlements has ever been found. Its neighbour, Madagascar, was inhabited but according to a 12th-century observer, Idrisi, its inhabitants had no boats capable of crossing the sea.

THE ARRIVAL OF THE EUROPEANS In the wake of Vasco da Gama's penetration of the Indian Ocean via the Cape of Good Hope, came the Portuguese *conquistadores*. While they progressed along the African and Indian coasts, they never tried to establish themselves properly in Madagascar and neighbouring islands. Pedro Mascarenhas (after whom the Mascarenes were named) is credited with the European discovery of Réunion in 1512 and Mauritius is said to have been discovered by navigator Domingo Fernandez in about 1511, although there is some doubt that he ever saw the island. No Portuguese settlement was started despite the island's ideal situation on the route from the Cape to India.

Mauritius became known on Portuguese maps as Ilha do Cirne, Island of the Swan, possibly after the 'land swan' which then inhabited the island: the dodo. A more prosaic theory is that the name was derived from that of a Portuguese vessel.

In 1528, Diego Rodriguez gave his name to the island still known as Rodrigues. Portuguese names have also survived on other neighbouring islands including Diego Garcia in the Chagos Archipelago, which was named after another Portuguese navigator.

If the Portuguese did visit Mauritius, it was infrequently. On their way to and from India they preferred to use the Mozambique Channel, staying close to the African coast rather than risking the open sea. Mauritius remained uninhabited except by bats and tropical birds, many of which, like the dodo, are now extinct.

The great bay on the southeast corner of the island, now known as Grand Port, was a natural haven for ships. During the latter part of the 16th century, Swan Island was probably used by pirates who preyed on the pilgrim route between India and Jeddah. Vessels from a Dutch fleet on its way from Amsterdam to Java sailed in during a violent storm in September 1598. Many of the crew were suffering from scurvy and the landfall was seen as a godsend.

Admiral Wybrandt van Warwyck was in command of the fleet and he arrogantly named the bay Warwyck Haven, a name immediately forgotten. His choice of a name for the island, however, had a catchier ring to it – he claimed possession for the Stadtholder of the Netherlands, Prince Mauritius van Nassau.

The Dutch were fascinated by the island, especially by the trusting curiosity of the birds which had yet to learn fear and allowed themselves to be knocked down with a club. In Grant's *History of Mauritius*, published in London in 1801, the dodo is described as 'a feathered tortoise' whose sluggish movements made it an easy target for the laziest hunter. Although the Dutch called occasionally for shelter, food and fresh water they took little interest in developing the island.

The French and British, too, began to see possibilities for both trade and strategy in the Mascarenes and sent out expeditions in 1638. Their ships arrived too late. In May 1638, Cornelius Simonsz Gooyer had set up the first permanent Dutch settlement in Mauritius. He was sent by the Dutch East India Company and became the first governor, over a population of 25 colonists who planned to exploit the island's resources of ebony and ambergris, as well as rearing cattle and growing tobacco.

Over the next few years, 100 slaves were imported from Madagascar and convicts sent over from Batavia (now Jakarta). The convicts were Europeans, Indonesians and Indians and were employed in cutting ebony. The free colonists came from Baltic and North Sea ports, hardened men who were settlers out of desperation and coercion rather than through brave ideals. From its very first settlement, Mauritius had a mix of races that was to set a pattern for its future.

The settlers supported themselves by raising vegetables and livestock, which they sold to the company or, for more profit, to the crews of visiting French, English and pirate ships. Yet although the settlement grew to 500, it did not prosper.

The slaves from Madagascar escaped to the forest and began to exact revenge for Dutch cruelties by destroying their crops and slaughtering their cattle. Invasions by hungry rats added to the problems of the settlement. The lack of interest shown by the Dutch East India Company finally demoralised the colonists.

A few years after the Dutch founded a colony at the Cape of Good Hope in 1652, the island was abandoned completely, the European market for ebony being glutted. Only the sugarcane that had been introduced from Batavia and the runaway Malagasy slaves in the forests remained.

The Dutch tried again in 1664, starting a settlement under the aegis of the Cape colony. They were more ambitious this time with attempts at agriculture on a commercial scale, including tobacco, sugarcane, indigo and maize. Deer, introduced from Java, thrived in the forests and were hunted for food and pelts. Forts were built on the eastern coast, forests cleared and domestic animals raised.

Legend has it that the Dutch were driven off for a second time in 1710 by the rats they had themselves accidentally introduced. Resentment at colonial bureaucracy also played its part, since the colony at the Cape received preferential treatment from the Dutch authorities. The settlers were ill-suited to be colonists – they suffered from the heat, were undisciplined, lazy and prone to drunkenness.

Meanwhile, a new state was forming in Madagascar. Called Libertalia, it was a pirate republic founded by a French adventurer and a defrocked Italian monk. There was no shortage of tough men, mostly pirates from every nation, who made Libertalia their home. From there they successfully plundered shipping throughout the Indian Ocean and their community thrived. These men were to contribute to the new colonisation of Mauritius.

FRENCH RULE The French East India Company had already occupied Bourbon (now Réunion) as a trading centre, but although the island had fertile soil and attracted as settlers a great number of pirates and their offspring by Malagasy women, it lacked harbours. The attraction of a vacant Mauritius with its well-protected bays was irresistible.

A preliminary expedition led by Guillaume Dufresne d'Arsel took possession of Mauritius in the name of King Louis XV of France in September 1715, naming it Ile de France so its ownership would be in no doubt. D'Arsel placed the French flag near what is now Port Louis, drew up a document witnessed by his officers declaring the island French and, after three days, sailed away.

Nearly seven years passed before the French East India Company actually occupied the island. In 1721, a motley crew of company officials, settlers and slaves from Madagascar, Mozambique and west Africa landed. Swiss mercenaries made up the garrison; pirates and their women accompanied them. More women were rounded up on the waterfronts of St Malo and Bordeaux and shipped out to swell the island's population. It was hoped that a grant of land, a sum of money and the prospect of an imported wife would be enough to tempt men to settle.

For the first 14 years, the French colony followed the dismal experience of the Dutch. Only the most desperate and toughest of settlers survived, eking out a living from the pittance they earned from the company. Their appallingly treated slaves escaped to become *marrons* (runaway slaves), living in the forest and sabotaging the plantations.

A forlorn settlement of palm-thatched cabins sprang up near the west coast harbour of Port Louis, where the French East India Company decided to build the capital. The company, however, maintained its headquarters in Bourbon, despairing of ever controlling their reluctant settlers or making a profit on their investment in Ile de France.

The solution was an inspired one. As the new Governor of Ile de France and Ile Bourbon, the French East India Company appointed an aristocratic sea captain, Bertrand François Mahé de Labourdonnais. He was 38 and full of ambition when he sailed into Port Louis harbour in 1735.

The wretched conditions of the settlers dismayed Labourdonnais. There were 190 whites on the island and 648 blacks, most of them African or Malagasy slaves, together with a few Indians.

Labourdonnais transformed the island from a colony of malcontents into 'the star and key of the Indian Ocean'. He was a born leader and as a naval man understood the lusty spirit of men with pirate blood flowing in their veins. Despite – or was it because of? – his own blue blood, he had an affinity with the struggling colonisers. He began by giving them self-respect and ambition.

He ordered that the seat of government of the two colonies be transferred from Bourbon, which was better established, to Ile de France and set up a council to administer the islands. He channelled the seafaring abilities of his settlers back to the sea, deliberately creating a navy of buccaneers.

The thatched hovels were demolished and in their place rose forts, barracks, warehouses, hospitals and houses, many of which survive in part of Port Louis today. Government House was built of coral blocks, roads were opened throughout the island and a shipbuilding industry commenced.

Although he had to import slaves, Labourdonnais made their lot easier by also importing ox-carts so slaves could be utilised for more skilled tasks. He turned many of them into artisans to make up for the lack of skilled men among the settlers. He also pushed through an agriculture programme that concentrated on feeding the islanders and on marketable produce. On his own estates he grew sugarcane, encouraging new settlers to start plantations of cotton, indigo, coffee and manioc. The first sugar factory was opened at Villebague in 1744, a salt pan was started and he even tried to rear silkworms.

Gradually a civilised life evolved in Port Louis, attracting colonisers from Bourbon, and even from good French families. Labourdonnais is known as the father of the colony.

In 1746, with England and France at war, Labourdonnais led an expedition of nine ships from Ile de France to India. There they defeated a British squadron and captured Madras, the most important British outpost.

Labourdonnais's actions resulted in a conflict with Dupleix, his superior in India and caused his downfall. Dupleix wanted Madras razed to the ground but Labourdonnais refused because he knew the British would pay a ransom to get Madras back. He was accused of accepting a bribe to preserve Madras and was replaced as Governor of Ile de France. On his return to France he was thrown into the Bastille. Although in 1751 he was found innocent, he died a broken man two years later, aged 54. His statue stands in Port Louis facing out across the harbour.

The town of Mahébourg (started in 1805) is named after him. So, too, is Mahé, capital of the Seychelles.

In 1764, the French East India Company, brought to bankruptcy by the Seven Years War, made over its assets, including the Ile de France, to the French king. In 1767, the Royal Government was established on the island. At that time there was a population of 18,773 that included 3,163 Europeans and 587 free blacks, mostly Hindus. The rest were slaves.

The appositely named Pierre Poivre (Peter Pepper) was picked as administrator. He introduced varieties of plants from South America, including pepper, and even offered tax incentives to planters to grow them. Under his influence, the colony developed as an agricultural and trading centre.

A French nobleman, Vicomte de Souillac, was made governor (1779–87), bringing an era of extravagance to the colony. Port Louis became renowned for its bright social life, duelling, gambling and hunting. Public affairs were neglected; fraud, corruption and dishonesty were commonplace and land speculation and scandals were rife.

In January 1790, a packet-boat arrived in Port Louis harbour from France, flying a new flag, the Tricolour. It brought news of the revolution. An elected assembly and municipal councils were set up and tribunals replaced courts of justice. A National Guard was formed, streets were renamed and revolutionary clubs started. Church property was confiscated and white, red and blue cockades were sported with delight. A guillotine was even erected in the Champ de Mars but its only victim was a dog (some historians say a goat), decapitated to try it out.

The colonists' enthusiasm for the revolutionary principles of liberty, equality and fraternity faltered when in 1796 two agents of the Directoire, wearing splendid orange cloaks, arrived from France and informed the startled colonists that slavery was abolished. The news was received with anger and the agents had to flee for their lives.

The last French governor of Ile de France was appointed by Napoleon Bonaparte in 1803 to bring the colony back to order after 13 years of autonomy. With such a task, it was inevitable that the governor, General Charles Decaen, would be unpopular. He dissolved all the elected councils and adopted a dictatorial attitude to administration.

BRITISH RULE Meanwhile, the British were expanding their influence in the Indian Ocean and in 1809, British forces from both the Cape and India occupied Rodrigues from where they prepared their attack on all the Mascarenes. Bourbon, which had been renamed Réunion during the revolutionary years, was taken. A major battle was fought between the French and British fleets off Grand Port in August 1810, and after prolonged fighting, the French won a victory that no-one expected.

In December 1810, 70 British vessels and 11,500 soldiers set sail from Rodrigues for the north of Ile de France. Their aim was not colonisation, but to neutralise the island so that it wouldn't be used as a base for French attacks on British vessels bound for India. British spies and reconnaissance had found a passage near Coin de Mire. Decaen was taken by surprise as he awaited the invasion in Port Louis. The British forces under General Abercrombie marched on the capital, meeting only token resistance.

Faced with the might of the British forces and the indifference of the settlers to remaining French, Decaen surrendered.

Soldiers were allowed to leave the island and settlers who did not want to stay under a British administrator were permitted to return to France with all their possessions. These generous capitulation terms also included British pledges to preserve the island's laws, customs, language, religion and property.

The majority of settlers remained. Perhaps some expected the colony to be restored to France in peace time. The Treaty of Paris did restore Réunion in 1814 but Mauritius was confirmed as a British possession.

A dashing, unorthodox personality in the Labourdonnais mould, Robert Farquhar became the first British governor in 1810. He soon revealed himself as remarkably independent of the British Government in London, taking advantage of the long time it took for despatches from London to reach Mauritius to act as he thought best.

Farquhar quickly won over the French settlers, particularly through his scrupulous interpretation of the capitulation terms. Since the settlers were allowed their customs, he permitted them to continue with the slave trade despite the British law of 1807, which prohibited trading in slaves in the British Empire.

Farquhar had to contend with many calamities during his administration, including an outbreak of smallpox in 1811 and of rabies in 1813. There was a disastrous fire in Port Louis in 1816 when 700 houses, mostly wooden, were destroyed, which resulted in new ones being built of stone. A cholera epidemic broke out in 1819, and there were fierce cyclones in 1818 and 1819.

Farquhar campaigned for reliance on sugarcane because it was the only money-making crop able to withstand cyclones, encouraging the planters to abandon coffee, cotton and their other crops. He also established Port Louis as a free port, open to ships of all nations, and stimulated food production and road building. He proved to the inhabitants that there were distinct economic advantages in being British rather than French.

He mixed with everyone and opened dialogue with non-white leaders. Although his stance on slavery seemed ambivalent, he believed in attacking the slave trade at its source (in this case Madagascar) and worked for its elimination there as a way of ending the trade to Mauritius. He set up an office for the registration of slaves and tried to improve their conditions in the face of hostility from their owners.

Yet like Labourdonnais before him, Farquhar ran foul of his home government and was recalled to England in 1817. He returned to Mauritius, though, in 1820 as Sir Robert and governed for a further three years.

The attempts by the British Government to abolish slavery in Mauritius met with resistance from the planters who, having been persuaded to concentrate on sugar as an income-earning export crop, relied on slave labour to produce it. The arrival of Attorney General John Jeremy in 1832 to force through emancipation led to clashes and Jeremy was obliged to flee the island.

This time the planters' triumph was short-lived and slavery was abolished on 1 February 1835. The planters were paid over £2 million compensation, which they considered to be half the total value of their 68,613 registered slaves.

For the slaves the pleasure of emancipation was dulled by the imposition of a four-year period of apprenticeship during which they were supposed to work for their former masters in return for meagre wages. Not surprisingly, the scheme failed and slaves took up residence in unpopulated coastal areas where they suffered years of neglect. The wily planters turned to an alternative source of compliant labour: Indian migrants, known in Mauritius as 'the coolie trade'.

INDIAN MIGRATION Indian migrants had been in Mauritius since 1736 when Labourdonnais brought in 40 artisans from Pondicherry. In 1834, just prior to the abolition of slavery, Mauritius's sugarcane planters began to recruit workers from India to meet the demands of the rapidly expanding sugar industry. Following the abolition of slavery, the need for labour increased further. The indentured, or contracted, labour system was institutionalised in 1842 and, although most of the immigrants came from India, some also arrived from China, Madagascar and east Africa. Each of them was bound by a contract for a stipulated period but many settled permanently in Mauritius.

An immigration depot, Aapravasi Ghat, was built in Port Louis in 1849 to process the indentured labourers as they arrived. Today it is recognised as a UNESCO World Heritage Site and is open to the public (see pages 111–12).

By 1923, when indentured immigration ceased, almost half a million people had arrived in Mauritius under the system. The impact of Indian immigration changed the course of the island's history and shaped its population. Now the majority, the Indians came to wield influence in all spheres, not only by their contribution of an efficient workforce that sustained the economy, but also by a vigorous intellectual force in politics.

The political reforms of 1886, however, excluded the Indian population, although they launched the beginning of a parliamentary democracy. Universal franchise was finally granted in 1959.

In 1901, Mohandas Gandhi (later Mahatma Gandhi) visited Mauritius and as a result sent Manillal Doctor, an Indian lawyer, to Port Louis in 1907 to organise the indentured labourers who had no say in politics and no civil rights. A Royal Commission from Britain visited in 1907 and made wide-ranging recommendations for the reorganisation of agriculture, the civil service, education and the constitution, under which only 2% of the population were then qualified to register as electors.

THE 20TH CENTURY AND POLITICAL CHANGE Party politics followed the constitutional reforms of 1886 with the 'oligarques' of the conservative Parti de l'Ordre dominant over the 'democrats' of Action Libérale until the early 1920s. The socialist Mauritius Labour Party (MLP) founded in 1936 represented one side of the traditional two-party system with the Railliement Mauricien on the right. A multi-party system based on ethnic as well as political appeal evolved after 1950.

World War I brought suffering to the island with drastic cuts in shipping causing food shortages and price rises. There was a local campaign after the war for Mauritius to be returned to France but the so-called 'retrocessionist' candidates were heavily defeated in the 1921 general election.

World War II brought infrastructural development. The British based a fleet at Port Louis and Grand Port, as well as building an airport at Plaisance and a seaplane base at Baie du Tombeau. A large telecommunications station was built at Vacoas, although the first underwater telephone cable, linking South Africa to Australia, had been laid to Mauritius in 1901.

In the election held after the war, the MLP won the majority of seats in the Legislative Council set up under the 1948 constitution. This success was repeated in 1953. After the 1959 election (the first held following the introduction of universal adult franchise), Hindu doctor (later Sir) Seewoosagur Ramgoolam, leader of the MLP, became chief minister, then premier in 1965, holding the post until 1982. In 1968, Mauritius became an independent country within the Commonwealth of Nations, with Queen Elizabeth II as head of state represented by a governor general.

In 1971, social and industrial unrest led by the Mouvement Militant Mauricien (MMM) resulted in a state of emergency. The party's leaders, including Paul Berenger, a Franco-Mauritian born in 1945, were jailed for a year.

In the election of 1982, the MMM, with Paul Berenger as general secretary and a Hindu, British-trained lawyer, Anerood Jugnauth, as president, captured all 62 directly elected seats. Anerood Jugnauth became prime minister with Berenger as his finance minister.

Tensions among the ministers resulted in a break when Berenger resigned with ten of his cabinet colleagues. Jugnauth formed a new party, the Mouvement Socialiste Militant (MSM), drawing on defectors from other parties and allying himself with Sir Seewoosagur's MLP and the Parti Mauricien Social Démocrate (PMSD).

The new alliance scored a victory that gave them 41 of the directly elected seats and five of the eight 'best loser' seats. (The 'best loser' system was devised by the British to ensure that every ethnic group has adequate representation.) Sir Seewoosagur became governor general.

Following the defection of some party members and the resignation of six parliamentarians because of a drug-smuggling scandal, the next general election was held a year early, on 30 August 1987. This resulted in a win for the alliance of parties led by Prime Minister Anerood Jugnauth. Knighted in 1988, Sir Anerood Jugnauth became prime minister again after a general election in 1991, when he led an alliance of the MSM and MMM. In March 1992, Mauritius became a republic within the Commonwealth and the then governor, Sir Veerasamy Ringadoo, became the first president. In June 1992, Cassam Uteem, a former minister, was nominated as president, an office he held until February 2002.

At the general election held in December 1995, there was a curious repeat of history when, as in 1982, the opposition captured all the 60 seats on Mauritius and allies took the two seats on Rodrigues. The victors were an opposition coalition and their leader, Dr Navin Chandra Ramgoolam, son of the much-revered Sir Seewoosagur Ramgoolam, became prime minister.

Born in 1947, Dr Navin Ramgoolam is a Dublin-qualified medical practitioner and a barrister called to the Bar in London in 1993. In 1994, he formed an alliance with the MMM of Paul Berenger and it was this alliance that captured all the elected seats. However, on 18 June 1997, the Labour Party and MMM split from one another. The Labour Party ruled the country while the MMM headed the opposition.

By the September 2000 elections, Navin Ramgoolam's popularity had fallen considerably. Many Mauritians felt he was out of touch with the island, having spent much of his life abroad, and allegations of corruption plagued his time in government. The elections saw Ramgoolam defeated by an alliance of the MSM and MMM, who won 50 seats in the parliament. In an unusual step, it was agreed that Sir Anerood Jugnauth would be prime minister for the first three years of the parliamentary term, followed by Paul Berenger for the second three.

February 2002 saw another unexpected shake-up for Mauritian politics. President Cassam Uteem, a Mauritian Muslim, was forced to resign after refusing to give his assent to the proposed prevention of terrorism legislation in the wake of the 11 September 2001 terrorist attacks in New York. His vice president also resigned and on 25 February 2002, Karl Auguste Offman was sworn in as the third president of the Republic of Mauritius. Offman's term as president lasted just over a year, with Sir Anerood Jugnauth assuming the role when Berenger became prime minister.

When he became prime minister in 2003, Paul Berenger was not only the first white but also the first non-Hindu prime minister since independence in 1968. His time as prime minister came to an end in July 2005, when his party was defeated by the newly formed Socialist Alliance and Dr Navin Ramgoolam once more became prime minister. The result was not unexpected with rising unemployment in the sugar and textile industries, high-profile figures resigning from the government to join the opposition alliance and allegations of corruption all conspiring against the governing MSM–MMM coalition.

In 2010, a coalition comprising the MLP, MSM and PMSD was elected, with the MMM in opposition. Power was again in the hands of two men who have dominated Mauritian politics for decades: President Air Anerood Jugnauth and Prime Minister Dr Navin Ramgoolam. In August 2011, the president's son, Pravind Jugnauth, pulled his party, the MSM, out of the alliance following allegations of corruption against some of his colleagues. He then joined forces with the opposition MMM.

Sir Anerood Jugnauth resigned as president on 20 March 2012 at the age of 82, saying he could not support current government policies. At the time of writing, the acting president was Monique Ohsan Bellepeau, who had served as vice president since 2010.

GOVERNMENT AND POLITICS

Mauritius is a parliamentary democracy on the Westminster model, with 62 members of parliament elected every five years by universal suffrage. Mauritius is divided into 20 constituencies, each returning three members. Rodrigues is a single constituency, returning two members.

The 'best loser' system allows for ethnic representation of MPs in the legislative assembly. Currently, more than 45 of the 70 members of parliament are Hindu. The ministries are also allocated on a communal basis. Hindus hold 16 ministries out of 22, three ministries are allocated to Muslims and three to Christians.

The role of the president, although important, is limited in powers to official and ceremonial procedures. Authority is delegated by him to the Council of Ministers, a body of ministers headed by the prime minister.

Government by coalition is a common feature of Mauritian politics and reflects the way of life of the people. The class divisions and communal differences of the post-war period are gradually crumbling as the economic situation improves. Education, industrialisation and improving prosperity have also helped people attain better status and heightened their aspirations.

One of the main challenges facing any government of Mauritius is the constant effort that must be made to maintain harmony between the island's various ethnic groups. The growth of tourism has made this an even greater priority. It is no secret that many Mauritians of African descent feel disadvantaged and under-represented in politics. You only to have to visit the southwest of the island, the most Creole area, to see that this is one of the poorest parts of Mauritius. The social unrest that occurred following the death of the popular Creole singer, Kaya, in February 1999, is a reminder of how dangerous underlying discontent can be (see box *Kaya*, page 167).

MILITARY Mauritius has no military forces as such. A paramilitary unit called the Special Mobile Force (SMF) numbers about 1,000 and has its headquarters at Vacoas. The upper ranks have usually been trained in Europe and India; French military advisers offer supervision and further training and there is also a lingering British connection. The National Coast Guard is a branch of the Mauritius Police Force.

NATIONAL FLAG The flag of Mauritius consists of four equal-width horizontal stripes. In descending order these are red, blue, yellow and green, so when the flag is flying, red is at the top. The colours have been interpreted as red for freedom and independence; blue for the Indian Ocean; yellow representing the light of independence shining over the nation; and green standing for the agriculture of Mauritius and showing the country's colour throughout the 12 months of the year.

A second interpretation maintains that the colours stand for the island's different religious and ethnic groups. Red represents the Hindus, blue the Catholic population, yellow the Tamils and green the Muslims.

Crest The crest of Mauritius reflects its past more than its present, flanked by a dodo and a stag, both clutching shoots of sugarcane. The shield portrays a medieval ship, presumably representing the island's discoverers, and three stylistic trees.

There is also a key and a shining star, depicting the country's motto that appears below it: STELLA CLAVISQUE MARIS INDICI (Star and key of the Indian Ocean).

ECONOMY

The influence on the economy of Sir Robert Farquhar, the first British governor, only waned 168 years after his departure from Mauritius. Farquhar realised the value of an export-oriented economy but encouraged a reliance on one export only: sugar. It was not until 1985 that sugar was displaced as the country's main foreign-exchange earner by the manufacturing sector.

The reliance on a one-crop economy meant that the prosperity of Mauritius depended on the world demand for sugar and on home climatic conditions. When both were favourable, Mauritius benefited.

This is what happened in the early 1970s when economic growth averaged 9% per year. The standard of living improved visibly; new houses were built of concrete blocks and electricity served 90% of the island's dwellings. However, the pace of economic advance slowed as the sugar boom fizzled out.

The salvation was the Export Processing Zone (EPZ) set up in 1970 to attract foreign, as well as to encourage local, investment. According to the 1995 report of the Chamber of Commerce, 'The EPZ which has been the main engine of growth for a decade is giving way to an economic growth supported more and more by local demand.' The report noted that, from a macro-economic point of view, there was an urgent need to reduce consumption and increase savings and investment. This was based on the observation that 'new shopping centres with modern concepts have been well received by the population. Their immediate success is evidence of the aspirations of the population for better services and greater choice.'

Inflation, which was 14.5% in 1981, dropped to 6.7% in 1985 and was running at 3.5% in March 2012. Unemployment, which reached 19% of the registered workforce in 1983, was at 7.5% in 2011. Unemployment hardship relief of just Rs220 per month is available to the registered unemployed, who are actively seeking work. Since the 1990s Mauritius has had to import labour from abroad, mainly from Taiwan and Sri Lanka, for the construction and textile industries.

The challenge for the Mauritian economy is to look for new areas which can drive economic growth. Although sugar, textiles and tourism are likely to remain important, new avenues are opening up which take advantage of Mauritius's greatest natural asset: its skilled and multi-lingual workforce.

Offshore banking (see pages 81–2), pharmaceuticals, communications and information technology have already started to gain a foothold and it is perhaps these new industries that will direct Mauritius's economic development over the coming decades. It is already in a strong position: Mauritius is considered a relatively stable, peaceful democracy, has attracted considerable foreign income and has one of the highest per capita incomes in the African region.

INDUSTRY When industrialisation began in the 1960s the objective was to produce locally the goods that were being imported, creating jobs and saving on foreign exchange. Small industries were set up by local entrepreneurs, encouraged by fiscal incentives. Scope for profitable expansion was limited, however, by the size and buying power of the local market.

The Yaoundé Convention, allowing African countries associated with the European Economic Community (EEC) to have access to European markets for their goods, provided the fillip Mauritius needed. An Export Processing Zone (the EPZ) was set up in 1970 and policy switched to the labour-intensive production of goods for export.

A package of fiscal incentives, including exemption from certain taxes and duties, freedom to repatriate capital and profits, and a guarantee against state takeovers was offered. The scheme attracted investors from around the world, including the UK, France, Germany, Holland, India, South Africa, Hong Kong, Singapore, Taiwan and Australia.

The EPZ produces 95% of all Mauritius's industrial exports. Nearly 540 enterprises have been established under its banner and about 70,000 new jobs have been created. Nearly half the workforce are engaged in the knitwear industry.

The manufacturing sector is the largest employer in the country, with some 128,000 employees, and contributes 21% of the GDP. Although a variety of goods are produced, the textile industry dominates the manufacturing sector, accounting for 80% of its total earnings. In fact, Mauritius is amongst the world's largest exporters of woollen knitwear and produces clothing for numerous famous brands, such as BHS and Littlewoods in the UK. However, this sector is coming under pressure from cheaper producers such as China and Bangladesh. This is forcing textile companies like Floréal Knitwear to shift from producing basic products to more upmarket, niche products, as well as moving some of its production to countries with lower labour costs, such as Madagascar.

After the success of the EPZ, concern was expressed that the concentration on textiles could be as risky as the reliance on sugar had been. The industrial development strategy now aims for diversification and new target areas include electronics, information technology, jewellery and printing and publishing.

Meanwhile Mauritius has become world famous as a reliable supplier of manufactured goods. The 'made in Mauritius' label is familiar and much sought after as the country gains a reputation for high standards of quality.

The Mauritius Export Development and Investment Authority (MEDIA) was opened in 1985 by government and private sector officials to promote the industrialisation process of the country, help industries find new markets for their products and attract the right type of entrepreneur to the EPZ. This has now been replaced by the Mauritius Investment and Development Authority (MIDA), which promotes the export of goods and services from Mauritius. (For further information see *Chapter 3, Business*, pages 80–2.) The success in displacing sugar's importance to the economic base of Mauritius was crucial. The industrialisation of sugar itself is also taking place with such by-products as molasses, rum, ethyl alcohol and acetic acid.

AGRICULTURE AND FISHING

Sugar When the sugarcane is fully grown, the roads of the flat lands in the north of Mauritius are like tunnels through the cane fields. With nothing to be seen except the blue sky above and the green ribbons of cane waving in the wind, it is easy to imagine that the whole of the island is one vast sugar plantation.

While the overall economy may be less reliant on sugar than it once was, it still dominates the agricultural sector with nearly 90% of agricultural land being used for sugarcane. On average 600,000 tonnes of sugar is produced annually with most of it being exported to Europe. However, the proportion of land devoted to sugarcane is in decline. Recently, some of the large sugar estates have begun to diversify, establishing so-called Integrated Resource Schemes (IRS) consisting of hotels, luxury villas and golf courses (see page 48). Bel Ombre in the south and Médine in the west are two such examples.

Although sugar's importance in the economy may be dwindling, it still plays a vital role, representing about 18% of exports and about 3% of GDP. Thanks to an increasingly competitive international environment, the industry is now facing one of its most challenging periods. There is, however, a market for the island's delicious raw, unrefined sugar.

The number of sugar factories has also been in steady decline for some years. In the 19th century there were 250 sugar factories. Now tall, crumbling chimney stacks are all that remain of many of them – monuments to the early days of the industry that made Mauritius.

Sugarcane was introduced from Batavia (Jakarta) by the Dutch in 1639. A plaque recording the date can be seen set into a portion of stone wall standing in a palm grove on the Ferney Sugar Estate near Vieux Grand Port.

It was the French governor, Labourdonnais, who began sugar production in earnest. He set up the first sugar factory at Villebague in the centre of the island in 1744, using slave labour. By the time the British arrived in 1810 there were 10,000 acres under cultivation. The British governor, Farquhar, persuaded the settlers to expand their cane cultivation because of the crop's ability to withstand cyclones.

It was not until the abolition of duties on Mauritius-grown sugar in 1825, which allowed it to be imported into Britain on the same terms as sugar from the Caribbean, that the industry really began to thrive.

The early sugar mills relied on slaves and oxen to turn the rollers to crush the cane. The juice was extracted and collected in cauldrons where foreign matter was skimmed off. Then it was boiled, using the *bagasse* (crushed cane) as fuel, and the syrup was cooled until it crystallised into sugar. A copy of an early sugar mill showing how sugar was produced in 1770 can be seen in action at Domaine les Pailles (see page 188).

Animal-driven mills were gradually replaced by machinery, with the last one closing in 1853. From 1864, railway lines opened to transport sugarcane. The main railway system operated until 1964, when it was closed down as being uneconomic, since its use for profitable freight was confined to the crop season. One of the few remaining locomotives used to haul the sugarcane trolleys rests in splendour on public display in the unusual setting of La Vanille Réserve des Mascareignes (see page 160).

Owing to the island's volcanic beginnings, which caused the soil to be strewn with boulders and stones, every inch of the land used for cane growing has had to be cleared by hand. The gaunt piles of rock in the midst of the cane fields are a forceful reminder of the toil of the men and women who worked in the blisteringly hot sun to clean these patches in the volcanic blanket.

The stony nature of the soil still restricts mechanical harvesting, although tractors and forklifts are used to transport the cut cane for processing.

New cane is planted in cycles to be harvested after 14 to 18 months. The ratoons (shoots) appear from the second year onward. They are harvested every 12 months during the June to December cropping period.

When cane is cut, it is transported as soon as possible to the nearest factory where it is bulk fed into mechanical crushers. A constant supply of cane is needed to maintain production, so the pace is frenetic. The factories are self-powered, as they were in the 19th century, only now it is more scientific. The *bagasse* is used to produce electricity, not only for the factories but to augment the national supply.

The factories that remain have become ultra-efficient in sugar production and highly adaptable. They are also required to cultivate other crops, such as potatoes and tomatoes, which are planted between the rows of cane. Some estates have branched out into growing flowers, particularly the red, wax-like anthuriums (*Anthurium andraeanum*) for export, and into pineapple and watercress cultivation, hotel development and other projects.

The history of the sugar industry and the processes of sugar production are brilliantly explained at L'Aventure du Sucre, a museum housed in the former Beau Plan sugar factory near Pamplemousses (see page 134).

Tea The tea you drink in Mauritius is produced on the island and comes in a variety of locally inspired flavours, such as vanilla and coconut.

Teas with the best flavour are grown at heights greater than the altitude of the tea plantations in Mauritius. However, the Mauritius tea is popular for blending and it is the island's second major crop. Much of Mauritius's tea is exported, while the balance is sold on the local market.

The central highlands around Curepipe are the main plantation area. The cooler temperatures and the greater rainfall of the highland plateau suit tea. Being a plant that grows as a sturdy bush with deep roots and a long life, it can withstand winds of cyclonic force.

Tea's roots in Mauritius actually go back to the 18th century, when it was grown by settlers for their own use. From the early 1960s, extensive planting was pursued until, 25 years later, there were 40km^2 of land under tea.

The crew-cut tops of the bushes have a uniform appearance, thanks to the nimble fingers of tea pickers and to an electric shearer. The picking is done with incredible dexterity early in the morning, mainly by women. Only the top two or three young leaves are removed from the branches. The green leaf is then bagged and transported to a factory where it dries, ferments and is sorted and prepared for packing.

In recent years the fortunes of the tea industry have fluctuated, with its demise seeming likely in the late 1970s. Then the Tea Development Authority was reconstructed, factories expanded with new processing equipment, tea plantation land was rehabilitated and inducements offered for improved cultivation methods. By the mid 1990s, with tea prices dropping and sugar prices rising, some tea bushes were being torn up to be replaced by sugar. Tea, being labour intensive, used to be regarded as a good crop when there was an abundance of labour. With labour in short supply and with Mauritian tea having to compete with that produced by traditional tea-growing countries like Sri Lanka, its value to the economy of Mauritius is doubtful.

It is worth taking the time to visit the working tea factory of Bois Chéri, near Curepipe, and see the production in progress (see pages 160–1).

Tobacco Tobacco has been grown in Mauritius since 1639, when it was introduced by the Dutch. In 1926, the British American Tobacco Company opened a cigarette factory on the outskirts of Port Louis.

Although it is a major crop, tobacco is not exported and often falls short of local demand. Most of the tobacco is Virginia flue-cured, although Amarello air-cured is also produced. It is grown on small plantations by private planters under the supervision of the state-controlled Tobacco Board.

In recent years, tobacco production has declined and the volume of imported tobacco has increased. At the same time, smoking in Mauritius has been in decline.

Other produce The staple diet of Mauritians is rice, which has to be imported. However, enough potatoes for local demand are now grown, in excess of 20,000 tons a year. Maize production is increasing, although a substantial proportion has to be imported.

Groundnuts, onions, garlic, manioc, various leaf vegetables and spices are grown locally, as well as the tiny, round Mauritian tomato known quaintly as *pomme d'amour* (love apple). The growing of pulses such as peas and beans is being encouraged.

Fruits abound, especially pineapples, which are offered, already peeled in spirals, for sale at every major street corner and bus station. Bananas, papayas and traditional tropical fruit such as mangoes, lychees, watermelons, coconuts and citrus thrive and are of commercial importance.

Coffee is grown only on a small scale because it is in flower during the risky cyclone season. It can be found in the Chamarel area of the south, growing in sheltered places by the ridges of the hillsides.

Enough poultry and eggs are produced for domestic needs. Cattle-rearing has been developed on some sugar estates as part of the diversification policy but meat is still imported. Goat meat is popular and is produced commercially. Pigs and sheep are also raised, but in smaller numbers than cattle or goats. Venison, too, is farm-reared.

Fishing The romantic sight of a small rowing boat, bobbing peacefully in a sun-drenched lagoon while its crew pull up a net full of fish, is a glimpse of the tradition behind an expanding fishing industry. Mauritius has 1.7 million km^2 of marine surface area, known as its Exclusive Economic Zone (EEZ), which it is intent on developing.

Since the first settlers came to Mauritius, fishing has been confined to the lagoon and offshore lagoon areas. Most fishermen, being Creoles of small means, do not have the equipment or the inclination for fishing far beyond the reefs. They use traditional methods, with wooden (or sometimes fibreglass) boats of 6–7m in length. The crew fish with handlines, basket traps, seines, gill nets and harpoons. These artisanal fishing grounds, the only source of fresh fish supply, spread over an area of 1,020km^2 for Mauritius and 1,380km^2 for Rodrigues.

Banks fishery is conducted by motherships using small dories with outboard motors, operated by a crew of three. The mother vessel remains at sea for 35 to 55 days with the dories bringing in their catch for gutting and freezing twice a day.

The mothership's load is landed at the fishing port of Trou Fanfaron in Port Louis as frozen fish, more than 90% of it *Lethrinus mahsena* (or *Sanguineus*), known locally as Dame Berri.

The areas fished are the St Brandon, Nazareth and Saya de Malha banks on the Mauritius/Seychelles ridge, and the Chagos Bank around the Chagos Archipelago submarine plateaux, which lie 20–25m below the surface.

Tuna fishing for mainly skipjack (*Katsuwonus pelamis*) and yellow-fin tuna (*Thunnus albacares*) is a major industrial activity. Tuna canning started in 1972 when most of the fish had to be imported from the Maldives.

International big-game fishing competitions are held frequently and are popular with tourists who pay high fees to participate. The catch is mainly marlin (*makaira*) and swordfish (*Xiphias gladius*). Smoked marlin is a delicious delicacy served in most upmarket hotels and restaurants.

If you like eating fish, look out for Mama Rouge (orange rock cod: *Cephalopholis aurantius*), a grouper. It is much in demand, with a flesh that tastes like crab. Mauritian cooks complain that it is priced beyond their pockets or exported to Réunion where people pay more for it. A fish frequently to be found on menus is capitaine (*Lethrinus nebulosos*), a snapper sold frozen as *poisson la Perle*.

Fish farming is an old tradition, using *barachois*, or artificial sea ponds, to breed finfish, crabs and oysters. The local oyster (*Crassostrea cuculata*) lives in brackish water on rocks and mangrove roots. Efforts to introduce faster-growing species from the USA were tried without success.

A few species of seaweed with commercial importance for the food, cosmetic and medical industries have been identified, as have four marine shrimp species with potential for commercial aquaculture.

The growing of freshwater fish is another possibility. Mauritius, being an oceanic island remote from continental land masses, is limited in endemic freshwater fauna and does not have any freshwater fish or crustaceans suitable for culture, but researchers are experimenting with introducing a wide variety of species for commercial cultivation.

Sea salt, incidentally, is produced in Mauritius, with salt pans along the coast in the Black River district, in the area known as Les Salines. The salt is used for local consumption only.

Development of the EEZ is at present confined to the expansion of all sections of the fishing industry. For the future, however, studies have revealed a wealth of minerals on the ocean floor and there is also the possibility of ocean thermal energy conversion. It all seems a long way from the tranquil sight, beloved by tourists, of a fisherman casting his net in a picturesque lagoon.

TOURISM The first tourists to arrive in Mauritius by air were 50 passengers and crew on a Qantas flight from Australia to South Africa, who landed in 1952. The airline agents were asked in advance to find overnight accommodation for them and, seeing the possibilities, bought a colonial mansion in Curepipe. This became the Park Hotel and is now the administrative offices of the island's Beachcomber group of hotels.

Today, tourism is the island's third-largest foreign-exchange earner after the EPZ and sugar. The industry provides employment for nearly 30,000 people. Since earnings from tourism circulate very quickly into the economy, the impact is considerable. However, tourism has also been a factor in the increase in imports, especially foodstuffs.

In 2011, Mauritius attracted around 965,000 tourists. Of these, 12% came from Réunion, 9% came from the UK, around 6% from Germany, 9% from South Africa, 5% from India and 2% from Australia. France (excluding Réunion) topped the charts with 31% of tourist arrivals. Russia and China are becoming increasingly important markets for the Mauritian tourism industry and in 2011 arrivals from those countries rose 85% and 99% respectively against the previous year's figures.

The popularity of Mauritius with French tourists is not only because of the common language; with cheap flights from France to Réunion and a separate ticket on to Mauritius, the French can reach Mauritius at much less expense than their European neighbours flying direct. For them, too, the cost of living in Mauritius is remarkably low compared with that of France and Réunion. Many – whether affluent middle-aged or youthful backpackers – visit as independent travellers and keep the non-package hotels and guesthouses and self-catering units in business.

Studies have been made on the careful development of tourism in the future and the prospects are, with careful management, that tourism will continue to be an asset and not a blight on the island.

At present the government policy of preserving Mauritius as an upmarket destination continues. Charter flights are not allowed and the emphasis throughout the industry is on quality rather than quantity.

In recent years, the global economic slowdown has taken its toll on the tourism industry. However, the island retains the numerous assets that set it apart from its competitors, including beautiful beaches, luxurious hotels, exceptional service and a fascinating blend of cultures. These assets, if well managed, will stand it in good stead for the future.

The Mauritius Tourism Promotion Authority is responsible for marketing the country as a tourist destination. As well as offices in Port Louis, the MTPA has representatives in many counties worldwide (see *Chapter 2, Tourist information*, page 44).

INFORMATION TECHNOLOGY In an attempt to reduce its dependence on sugar and textiles, in 2001 the government launched an ambitious project to make Mauritius a 'cyber island'. A few kilometres south of Port Louis, the Ebène Cyber City, the island's information technology hub, stands on land formerly used for sugar production. It provides an internet data backup centre and servers for web-hosting, e-commerce and financial transactions. It is also being promoted as a bridge between Africa and Asia, acting as a landing point for a high-speed submarine communications cable linking Malaysia with South Africa.

It is early days for this industry in Mauritius and there has been considerable investment in IT education to ensure the population can benefit from the jobs that are created. Mauritius is seen as relatively secure and stable, which encourages companies to take advantage of the cyber city's facilities.

PEOPLE

With a population of almost 1.29 million, you would expect Mauritius to feel crowded, but it doesn't. Although the main towns are frequently teeming with pedestrians and the roads jammed with cars, deserted areas of beach and forest are easy to find.

The population is overwhelmingly young with about 22% being under 15 years of age and only 7.5% over 65. In 2012, life expectancy at birth was 71.25 years for a man and 78.35 years for a woman.

INTOXICATING MIXTURE In the enthusiastic prose of the MTPA, 'the people are unique for their sheer diversity – Indians, Africans, Europeans, Chinese and an intoxicating range of mixtures'.

It is potentially an explosive mixture, although few tensions are apparent to the visitor. Instead there is an admirable respect for the beliefs and lifestyles of others.

Mauritians are usually delighted to speak to visitors, although the stranger may have to start up the conversation. The ethnic diversity means that, unless dressed like a typical tourist, you won't stand out and can wander around without being the object of curiosity outside the tourist areas. If people approach to talk to you, it will probably be a genuine offer of help or hospitality, rather than a sales ploy.

Since all Mauritians are descended from immigrants (many have grandparents who were born in another country), the ethnic groups are distinctive in appearance, religion and language, although the distinctions are getting blurred and the many ethnic labels have now been whittled down to the General Population, the Indo-Mauritians and the Sino-Mauritians.

General Population The General Population (those who can't be tagged as being of Indian or Chinese descent) make up about 30% of the islanders. They are the whites and the Creoles (people of mixed European and African origin), with European influences of culture and religion.

Mauritian Creoles are a diverse group, the result of intermarriage that cuts across class and ethnic considerations. They constitute just over a quarter of the total population and form a large working class. Their influence is a unifying one and their language, Creole, is the lingua franca of the entire population, spoken by all races.

The whites are descended from European, mostly French, settlers. Curiously, despite 158 years of British presence, only a handful of families think of themselves as Anglo-Mauritian. Franco-Mauritians make up only around 2% of the population but hold much of the island's private wealth and dominate the business world.

Indo-Mauritians Indian immigrants arrived in numbers under the indentured labour system, although some came later from the Indian subcontinent. By 1861, the Indian population outnumbered the whites and Creoles by 192,634 to 117,416, forming the ethnic and cultural majority. They now make up 68% of the population.

There are two major groups by religious definition: Hindus (some of whom are actually Tamils) and Muslims. Many of the Muslims migrated independently from India and Pakistan as traders.

To confuse the situation, intermarriage has resulted in an Indo-Mauritian element being introduced into the (Christian) General Population as well.

As well as forming the backbone of the labouring and agricultural communities, the Indo-Mauritians have developed through a history of industrial and political agitation to take vital roles in the economic and political life of the island.

Sino-Mauritians Mauritians of Chinese origin are a small but ubiquitous ethnic community forming about 3% of the population. The first Chinese migrants came from Canton in the 19th century but the largest group is the Hakkas, from the province of Honan in northeast China.

There is a large Chinese quarter in Port Louis but Sino-Mauritians are to be found throughout the island, mostly as retailers or traders.

Their noticeable contribution to the development and unification of Mauritius is Chinese cuisine, which is found in private homes, as well as in restaurants and food stalls.

In spite of this wide variety of peoples, one of the attractions of Mauritius is its ethnic mix, not its ethnic division. Former prime minister of Mauritius, Sir Anerood Jugnauth, summed up his people aptly when he said: 'The single great wealth of this island nation is its people, a multi-national group with an amazing blend of cultures, a political maturity admired by friend and foe alike and a jealously guarded freedom … The hospitality of Mauritians is legendary and spontaneous.'

Young Mauritians tell me that in the past decade marriages between ethnicities have increased, further blurring the lines between the various ethnic groups.

LANGUAGE

The official language of Mauritius is English, although most Mauritians are more comfortable speaking French. The language of the people, however, is Creole.

Although the Mauritians working in the tourism industry speak good English, the English-speaking visitor should not count on being understood everywhere on the island. English is the medium of teaching in schools and the working language of government and business, but beyond school and work it is rarely used. Fewer than 3,000 Mauritians speak English at home.

French, however, is spoken at home by about 35,000 Mauritians. It is used in polite and formal circumstances, although not at government level. The daily newspapers are predominantly in French with occasional articles in English.

Creole is the lingua franca of Mauritius, understood and spoken by all Mauritians. It is the mother tongue of about 80% of the population but, incredibly, is not officially recognised as a language, and has no popular written form. It was not until 2011, after much debate, that Creole was added as an optional subject to the primary school curriculum. It is a patois, structurally distinct from French but borrowing most of its vocabulary from that tongue, although pronunciation is different. It evolved from the pidgin used by the French masters of the 18th century to communicate with their slaves, also incorporating words from African and Malagasy dialects.

Its popularity stems from the ease with which it can be learnt. Since the African population was disinclined to learn Indian or Chinese languages, the new immigrants of the 19th century took to Creole as a simple means of communicating. It requires little intellectual effort to speak, and English, French and Indian words can be adapted by 'Creolising' them. There are no grammatical rules and foreigners settling in Mauritius soon speak it without embarrassment at making errors.

Creole's lowly origins have caused the language to be treated with contempt in the past but its unifying value as the one language that all Mauritians speak and understand is clear. While it shares characteristics with the Creole spoken in the Caribbean and the bayous of Louisiana, a Mauritian would not immediately understand, for example, the Creole of Dominica. Even the Creole of neighbouring Réunion is not identical.

For the visitor wanting to speak Creole, there are several locally printed Creole phrase books on sale in Mauritius. The language is written phonetically and the hardest part seems to be to understand the odd spelling used, such as *ahn-kohr* (meaning 'more'). Although it sounds an aggressive language it is very colourful, rich in clichés and ribaldry. (For useful phrases, see *Appendix 1, Language*, pages 347–8.)

The main mother tongue of the country's largest ethnic group is Hindi and is spoken at home by over 100,000 people. While Hindi is the medium for religious ceremonies and is looked on as a sign of education and prestige, the Indian equivalent of Creole is Bhojpuri, spoken by around 12% of the population. Tamil was actually the first Indian language spoken in Mauritius and today is spoken at home by about 35,000 people. Other Indian languages spoken as mother tongues are Urdu, Telegu, Marathi and Gujarati.

Arabic is also spoken, although most of the preaching in the mosques is in Creole. Less than a third of the Chinese community speak Chinese languages, including Hakka, Mandarin and Cantonese.

RELIGION

There are nearly 90 different religious denominations represented in Mauritius. Since there is complete freedom of religion, new sects or groupings have emerged within the main religions of Hinduism, Christianity and Islam. Throughout Mauritius there are Gothic-style churches, high-domed temples, minareted mosques and ornate pagodas in the most unlikely places – the middle of a sugarcane field, by the racecourse – testifying to the strong Mauritian belief in religion. It is not fanaticism but an enduring way of life, which Mauritians relish.

HINDUISM About 48% of Mauritians are followers of one of the many Hindu sects, the majority being Sanatanists, or orthodox Hindus.

Devout Hindus proclaim their faith with small shrines and red or white pennants fluttering outside their homes. Several villages have Hindu temples, the largest being at Triolet. Saints of other religions, especially the Roman Catholic Père Laval, whose shrine is at Sainte Croix, are also worshipped by Hindus.

Local Tamils have their own religion which has evolved since 1771, when the French granted permission for a Tamil temple in Port Louis. The reformist movement of Arya Samaj, in which worship is of the spirit Brahma and not of statues or idols, took hold from 1910, when the first 'Samaj' was opened in Port Louis. Tamils sometimes indulge in spectacular forms of worship in honour of different deities, such as fire walking and piercing their flesh with enormous needles (see *Chapter 3, Working hours, public holidays and festivals*, pages 70–3). As with Christianity, there is a variety of sects including Kabir Panthis, a reformist group, Rabidass, and the Hare Rama Krishna sect.

CHRISTIANITY Christianity was the first religion in Mauritius and is now the religion both of the general population and of more than 80% of the Sino-Mauritians. Roman Catholicism became the official religion of the Ile de France in 1721, spreading with the French conversion of their slaves and still permitted to flourish after the British arrived. There is a Roman Catholic cathedral, St Louis, in Port Louis.

Anglicans, Presbyterians and the evangelical Christian religions such as the Assembly of God and Adventists all play a part in society, as do at least a dozen other denominations including Jehovah's Witnesses, Methodists and Swedenborgians.

With its various sects, Christianity is the second-largest faith in the country, and over 30% of the population are Christians of some kind. In Rodrigues, 97% of the population is Roman Catholic.

ISLAM The Muslims of Mauritius form about 16% of the total population. The majority consists of Sunni Muslims and is divided into three subgroups: Sunni Hanfites, Sunni Surtis and Meimons. The Meimons are a small aristocracy with responsibility for the best-known mosque in Mauritius, the Jummah (Friday) Mosque in Port Louis.

The Shi'ite Muslims are very few and are subdivided into groups. One is the Cocknies from Cochin in the southwest of India, who came as boatbuilders to Mauritius. Since intermarrying with Creoles they have created a people known as Creole Lascars.

CHINESE RELIGIONS The Chinese religions are almost dying out since the majority of Sino-Mauritians have embraced Roman Catholicism. However, Buddhism and Confucianism are still practised by around 2% of the population.

The first Chinese temple was opened in Port Louis in 1846. Other temples have since been opened by the Cantonese Nam Shun Fooye Koon society and the Hakka Heeh Foh society.

EDUCATION

The education system in Mauritius is based on the British model and is free up to university level. Education is compulsory up to the age of 16. The country's literacy rate is respectable, around 85%, and over 95% of all children attend school.

The education boom began in the 1960s, with the opening of scores of private colleges. Free education at secondary level was introduced in 1977 with an immediate doubling of the number of students enrolled, and with new schools being opened by the government.

The majority of schools are state run, but a significant number are controlled by the Roman Catholic Education Authority and the Hindu Education Authority.

Lessons are conducted mostly in English, whilst French is taught. The majority of papers for public examinations are marked in the UK.

The University of Mauritius at Le Réduit was opened in 1965, originally to train civil servants in preparation for independence. It now runs schools of administration, agriculture and technology. The Mauritius Institute of Education trains the country's schoolteachers and is responsible for the national certificate of primary education. The Mahatma Gandhi Institute at Moka concentrates on African and Asian studies.

Many Mauritians strive to study at universities overseas, particularly in the UK, France and Australia.

CULTURE

Each of Mauritius's ethnic groups and religions brings its own unique qualities to the island's rich and varied culture. An exciting variety of cuisine, musical styles and languages are a part of everyday life.

MUSIC Mauritians grow up with music and dancing playing an important role in their lives: at family gatherings, festivals and celebrations.

Ubiquitous is the *séga* (pronounced 'say-ga'), which evolved from the spontaneous dances of African and Malagasy slaves. At night, after a day's toiling in the cane fields, slaves used improvised instruments to create a primitive music to which they could dance and forget their woes. At times, this meant defying their masters' prohibition of music and dancing, which aimed to sever the slaves from their African and Malagasy roots.

Songs were often about the slaves' plight and were highly critical of their masters. Girls danced to songs composed and sung by their admirers while the spectators encouraged them with hand clapping, foot stomping and chanting. The more impassioned the lyrics, the more heated the music and the more tempestuous the dancing.

On Mauritius's accession to independence, *séga* was adopted as the national dance and it has been flourishing and evolving ever since. Traditional *séga* is a courtship drama, beginning slowly with couples dancing apart from each other. As the beat intensifies, they shuffle closer together, hips swinging in time, but they never quite touch. The girl will sink to her knees at the cry of *en bas*, leaning back in the manner of a limbo dancer passing under a pole. Her partner leans over her, still not touching, as they both shimmer and shake, while the music races to a crescendo. The music slows and the partners retreat. What makes *séga* unique is the combination of musical influences it has absorbed over the centuries, until it has assumed its own immediately recognisable beat. Like the *ka-danse* or *zouk* music of the French West Indies, also sung in Creole patois, it has a similarity to Latin American music in its jaunty rhythms. *Séga* is as prolific on Rodrigues and Réunion as it is in Mauritius, but each of the islands has developed its own distinctive version.

Descendants of the primitive instruments used by the slaves can still be seen in *séga* bands today. Vital to *séga* is the distinctive drumbeat provided by the *ravane*, a goatskin tambourine. The *maravane* is a container (either wooden or fashioned from a gourd) filled with seeds or pebbles, which is shaken like the maracas. A triangle beaten with vigour adds a carillon voice echo, just as a cowbell does in *ka-danse*.

Séga is a fantastic dance with a wonderful, joyful music that seizes spectators with an urge to join in, which they are encouraged to do at hotel performances. At hotel shows, the men will usually wear the traditional pedal pushers and a colourful shirt, while the women are sensational in a billowing skirt.

Kaya, the popular Creole singer who was found dead in a police cell in February 1999, pioneered a new musical style in the late 1980s: *séggae*, a blend of reggae and *séga*. Kaya's work has been continued by his fellow Creole musicians and the mellow *séggae* is now popular throughout the western Indian Ocean islands (see box *Kaya*, page 167).

ARCHITECTURE Creole architecture can be appreciated both in small, simple dwellings and in grand colonial mansions, such as Eureka (see pages 188–9) and Château de Labourdonnais (see pages 134–5). A charming characteristic feature of such buildings is the carved wooden or metal fringes that decorate the roof, the *lambrequin*. Sadly, examples of colonial architecture, such as Government House in Port Louis, are sometimes overwhelmed by the modern monstrosities erected next to them.

Contemporary architecture in Mauritius mostly finds expression in new hotels since new houses tend to be standard, cyclone-proof concrete boxes. The best known of the island's architects is Maurice Giraud, who has had a hand in designing many of the hotels.

2

Practical Information

WHEN TO VISIT

Mauritius is a place to visit at any time of the year for someone from northern climes who craves tropical beauty and warmth. The one time when it is not ideal to visit is January–March, when cyclones are most likely to occur. They don't happen every year but the cyclonic rains, which can last for several days, are an annual event. Humidity is high then and it can be a depressing, unsettling time. (See *Climate* on pages 4–5 for more information.)

The high season for tourism, when holiday packages cost more, is November to early January. Hefty peak-season supplements are charged over Christmas and Easter. Flights should be less crowded outside European school holiday periods and hotels are noticeably so.

December is the time when local fruits are in abundance: it's summer and the temperature on the coast is about 30°C. The weather is cooler from June to September with the temperature at sea level being about 24°C, and it can be windy at this time. Package holiday prices are lower and hotels tend to host conference and incentive groups. September to October is perhaps one of the best times to travel as the weather is good but peak-season prices and crowds have not yet set in.

If climate is not the governing factor, choose when to visit according to your interests. For instance, the horse-racing season is from May to late November and the best deep-sea fishing is from November to May. You may like to time your visit to coincide with one or more of the island's many colourful festivals (see *Festivals*, pages 70–3).

There are many websites which offer useful tips and information to help you prepare for your visit. For details see *Appendix 2, Further information*, pages 349–52.

HIGHLIGHTS

Mauritius is small enough for you to base yourself in one place and explore the island's highlights.

NATURAL HISTORY Natural history enthusiasts and hikers should head to the **Black River Gorges National Park**. There are **hiking trails** of varying difficulty, where glimpses of the rare **pink pigeon** and **Mauritius kestrel** are possible. Also worth a visit is **Ile aux Aigrettes**, a coral island off the south coast, which the Mauritian Wildlife Foundation is working hard to restore to its natural state.

SHOPPING A visit to one of the island's lively **markets** is fascinating – Port Louis's daily market is by far the largest but Mahébourg's Monday market also has plenty of variety. The hustle and bustle amidst the colourful displays of fruit, vegetables, spices and souvenirs represents an unforgettable snapshot of everyday life in the island's towns. For a shopping experience of a different kind, visit one of the upmarket **shopping centres** where tourists are tempted at every turn by diamonds, clothing and model ships. These include Caudan Waterfront in Port Louis and Ruisseau Creole in the island's west. You may as well make the most of Mauritius being a **duty-free island**. In recent years a series of new, large, modern shopping malls has sprung up across the island, such as Les Halles in Phoenix, Bagatelle in Moka and Cascavelle in Flic en Flac. Thanks to the unstable economic climate, they are struggling to fill the shops in some of these malls and it remains to be seen how they will fare in the future.

HERITAGE One of the island's most impressive attractions is **L'Aventure du Sucre** (Sugar World), a former sugar factory which has been transformed into a well-organised, modern museum telling the story of the industry on which the island was built. Its display on the island's history is one of the best in Mauritius. Equally fascinating are guided tours of the **Bois Chéri Tea Factory**, which are followed by a tasting. The tour can also be done as part of **La Route du Thé** (The Tea Route), which takes in three sites linked to the Bois Chéri Tea Estate.

Mauritius is home to two UNESCO World Heritage Sites: **Aapravasi Ghat**, the immigration depot built in 1849 to receive indentured labourers in Port Louis, and **Le Morne**, the distinctive mountain in the southwest of the island that is regarded as a symbol of resistance to slavery.

CULTURE Mauritius's 'melting pot' of ethnicities provides a wealth of opportunities to experience local **culture**. Most organised tours will include a stop at **Grand Bassin**, where visitors can learn about this sacred Hindu lake and watch the worshippers who flock to its shores. The Tamil festivals are colourful and fascinating – if you have a chance to watch **fire walking** or the **Thaipoosam Cavadee** pilgrimage, don't miss it.

BEACHES I couldn't write about the highlights of Mauritius without mentioning the beaches – and, yes they really are as good as they look in the holiday brochures. Belle Mare, Trou aux Biches and Flic en Flac are considered by locals to be among the island's finest.

Beyond the beaches all manner of **watersports** are on offer, from kayaking to kitesurfing. Non-motorised watersports may well be included in your accommodation package. Under the waves there are colourful coral reefs and a wealth of **diving and snorkelling sites**. For those who wish to explore the underwater world without getting wet, there are **submersible vessels** (classic submarines and ingenious underwater scooters) – a great option for children and non-divers.

Sailing, **deep-sea fishing** and **dolphin-watching** cruises are all popular with visitors.

RODRIGUES A trip to the island of Rodrigues is an ideal add-on to a stay in Mauritius. It is not a beach-lovers' paradise but an opportunity to stray well off the beaten track and retreat into a world where simplicity rules.

SUGGESTED ITINERARIES

Most people who visit Mauritius are seeking relaxation rather than adventure. However, there is plenty to see and around two weeks will allow you enough time to wind down and relax, as well as to explore some of the elements that make Mauritius distinctive. Mauritius is small enough that you can base yourself in one place and explore by taking day trips. For a memorable contrast, consider adding a few days in Rodrigues.

PORT LOUIS AND NORTHERN MAURITIUS A day will give you ample time to visit the island's invariably hectic capital, Port Louis, which is best explored on foot, making sure that you stop in at the bustling market, the waterfront, Aapravasi Ghat (where indentured labourers were processed) and your pick of the various museums.

You can combine a trip to Port Louis with contrastingly peaceful visits to the nearby Pamplemousses Botanic Gardens and the historic Château de Labourdonnais, a renovated Creole mansion. Also in the area is L'Aventure du Sucre, a fascinating museum that tells the story of the sugar industry. The north (at Mont Choisy) is where you can take a submarine or underwater scooter to view the coral reef at the edge of the lagoon (see page 93). Mont Choisy also has a good beach, as does nearby Trou aux Biches, and while in the area, you can stop in at the tourist resort of Grand Baie. As you potter along the coast, stop in at Cap Malheureux to see the distinctive red church featured in so many postcards.

A catamaran cruise out to the islands off the north will take the best part of a day and provides some excellent snorkelling opportunities.

EASTERN MAURITIUS Less developed than the north, the east has some fabulous beaches, such as Belle Mare, and some of the island's finest golf courses. This coast is popular for sailing excursions, which typically take in the tourist trap of Ile aux Cerfs.

SOUTHERN MAURITIUS Wherever you are staying on the island, the south is worth a visit. It cleverly combines unspoilt scenery and diverse manmade attractions. Starting in the southeast, drop in to the historic town of Mahébourg, which hosts a lively Monday market. Nearby is the beautifully simple Rault Biscuit Factory, where manioc biscuits are made the old-fashioned way.

Just south of Mahébourg you can snorkel in the impossibly turquoise waters within the protected marine reserve of Blue Bay and take a trip to Ile aux Aigrettes, a Mauritian Wildlife Foundation nature reserve. Back on the mainland is Vallée de Ferney, another nature reserve, which you can explore on foot or by 4x4.

Continuing along the south coast, **La Vanille Réserve des Mascareignes** is primarily a crocodile farm but is home to giant Aldabra tortoises, Rodrigues fruit bats and other wildlife from the region.

Nearby St Aubin, a colonial house built in 1819 is a good spot for lunch and you can take fascinating tours explaining the production of vanilla, sugar and rum.

Inland lies tea plantations and the unmissable Bois Chéri Tea Factory, which offers guided tours and tea tastings. From there it is a short drive to the sacred lake at Grand Bassin, a cultural highlight of the south.

WESTERN MAURITIUS The west has excellent beaches, notably the ever-popular Flic en Flac, and is the best part of the island for deep-sea fishing. Casela Nature and Leisure Park has all manner of attractions, the best of which is Safari Adventures with its interactive big cat experiences.

Heading inland towards Chamarel takes you through agricultural land, where sugarcane and pineapples cover the hillsides. The Rhumerie de Chamarel provides an insight into the rum-making process or, if you prefer something a little more active, La Vielle Cheminée provides some of the island's best horseriding.'

CENTRAL MAURITIUS The island's largest nature reserve, the Black River Gorges National Park, is popular for hiking and is easily accessed from the south and the west of the island. Although the centre of the island is where most of the population lives, it holds the least interest for visitors. For most tourists, the only reason to venture to the traffic-heavy centre is to pick up a bargain at the market in Quatre Bornes.

TOURIST INFORMATION

The **Mauritius Tourism Promotion Authority (MTPA)** is the best source of information both prior to your trip and during it. They publish information booklets on the island and have a website that is packed with useful information and links. **MTPA Head Office** 4th Fl, Victoria Hse, Saint Louis St, Port Louis; ☎ 210 1545; **e** mtpa@intnet.mu; www.tourism-mauritius.mu. The MTPA has an information desk at the airport in Plaisance (☎ *637 3635*) and a kiosk in Trou d'Eau Douce (*Coastal Rd, La Pelouse;* ☎ *480 0925*).

For tourist information during your stay in Mauritius, you can call the tourism 24-hour information line (☎ *152*), which provides details of exchange rates, night-duty pharmacies, events, restaurants etc in English and French.

The MTPA has the following representation overseas:

China Lavender Media, B1601, GUO JI GANG, No Wu 2, Dongsanhuan-beilu, Chaoyang District, Beijing 100027; ☎ +86 10 8447 1364; **f** +86 10 8447 1034; **e** hzhou@lavender-media.com

France Interface Tourism, 11 bis Rue Blanche, 75009, Paris; ☎ +33 1 53 25 11 11; **f** +33 1 53 25 11 12; **e** ilemaurice@interfacetourism.com

Germany Aviareps Tourism GmbH, Josephspitalstr. 15, 80331, Munich; ☎ +49 89 5525 33825; **f** +49 89 5525 33489; **e** Mauritius@aviareps.com

India TRAC Representation Pvt Ltd, A-61, 6th Fl, Himalaya Hse K G Marg, New Delhi 110001; ☎ +91 11 2335 2550; **f** +91 11 2335 0270; **e** mtpaindia@tracrep.com

Italy AIGO Comunicazione, Piazza Caiazzo 3, 20124 Milan; ☎ +39 2 669 9271; **f** +39 2 669 2648; **e** mtpa@gigacomunicazione.com

Russia Aviareps Tourism, Olimpic Plaza, 39 Prospect Mira, Bldg 2, 129110 Moscow; ☎ + 74 959 375950; **f** + 74 959 375951; **e** robolgogiani@aviareps.com

South Africa Baird's Renaissance, PO Box 3674, Ranburg 2125; ☎ +27 11 504 4000; **f** +27 11 8882474; **e** yvette@bairds.co.za

Spain Aviareps AG, Airline Centre España SL, Avda de Concha Espina 65 – 2a planta, 28016 Madrid; ☎ +34 91 458 5560; **f** +34 91 344 1726; **e** gvaca@aviareps.com

Switzerland PRW Public Relations & Werbe AG, Kirchenweg 5, PO Box 1323, 8032 Zurich; ☎ +41 44 388 4100; **f** +41 44 388 4103; **e** info@prw.ch

UK Hills Balfour, Colechurch Hse, 1 London Bridge Walk, London SE1 2SX; ☎ +44 20 7367 9023; **f** +44 20 7407 3810; **e** carolinel@hillsbalfour.com

TOUR OPERATORS

Below is a non-exhaustive list of tour operators that feature Mauritius:

UK

Aardvark Safaris RBL Hse, Ordnance Rd, Tidworth, Hampshire SP9 7QD; ☎ +44 1980 849160; **e** mail@aardvarksafaris.com; www.aardvarksafaris.co.uk

Beachcomber Tours Direction Hse, 186 High St, Guildford, Surrey GU1 3HW; ☎ +44 1483 445621; www.beachcombertours.co.uk

Onyx Travel 26 Woodford Cl, Caversham, Reading RG4 7HN; ☎ +44 118 947 2830; **f** +44 118 946 3104; **e** information@onyxtravel.co.uk; www.onyxtravel.co.uk

Partnership Travel White Lion Hse, 64a Highgate High St, London N6 5HX; ☎ +44 20 8347 4020; **e** info@partnershiptravel.co.uk; www.partnershiptravel.co.uk

Rainbow Tours 305 Upper St, London N1 2TU; ☎ +44 20 7666 1250; e info@rainbowtours.co.uk; www.rainbowtours.co.uk

Sunset Faraway Holiday Sunset House, 6 Bedford Pk, Croydon, Surrey CR0 2AP; ☎ +44 20 8774 7100; e info@sunset.co.uk; www.sunset.co.uk

AUSTRALIA

Abercrombie & Kent Level 3, 290 Coventry St, South Melbourne, VIC 3205; ☎ +61 1300 851 800; e contact@abercrombiekent.com.au; www.abercrombiekent.com.au

Beachcomber Tours 10/5 Canopus St, Bridgeman Downs, QLD 4034; ☎ +61 7 3353 6204; e info@beachcomber.com.au; www.beachcomber.com.au

Mauritius Holidays 439 North Rd, Ormond, VIC 3204; ☎ +61 3 9597 9877; e travel@mauritiusholidays.com.au; www.mauritiusholidays.com.au

FRANCE

Kuoni various offices; www.kuoni.fr

Nouvelles Frontières various offices; www.nouvelles-frontieres.fr

GERMANY

Escape Tours Hohenzollernstrasse 112, D-80796 Munich; ☎ +49 89 8299 480; e info@escape-tours.de; www.escapetours.de

Trauminsel Reisen Summerstrasse 8, D-82211, Herrsching; ☎ +49 81 529 3190; e info@trauminselreisen.de; www.trauminselreisen.de

ITALY

Best Tour Via Tito Speri 8, 20154 Milan; ☎ +39 2 336 33310; e mho@besttours.it; www.besttours.it

Idee Per Viaggiare Via Leonetto Capiello, 14 – 00125 Rome; ☎ +39 6 520 981; e info@ideeperviaggiare.it; www.ideeperviaggiare.it

SOUTH AFRICA

True Blue Travel Adventures 188 Bree St, Cnr Buitensingel, Cape Town 8000; ☎ +27 21 426 0881; e info@truebluetravel.co.za; www.truebluetravel.co.za

Origin Tours & Safaris 3 Sir Lowry St, Gordons Bay, Western Cape; ☎ +27 21 856 5851; www.origintours.co.za

US

Aardvark Safaris 312 South Cedros Av, Suite 315, Solana Beach, CA 92075; ☎ +1 888 776 0888; e info@aardvarksafaris.com; www.aardvarksafaris.com

RED TAPE

ENTRY REQUIREMENTS To enter Mauritius, you will need a passport valid for at least six months beyond the end of your stay, proof of a return or onward ticket and the address of confirmed accommodation on the island.

Tourists and business visitors travelling on passports from the following countries are among those who do not require a visa: the UK, other European Union countries, the US, Canada, Australia, New Zealand, Israel, Botswana, South Africa, Zambia, Zimbabwe, Norway and Sweden. Holders of passports from certain other countries are granted stays of a limited duration on arrival; for instance, visitors from Albania, Comoros and Madagascar are granted two weeks, while visitors from Russia, India, China and Fiji are granted 60 days. For those travelling on passports from some other countries, a visa is required prior to travel; for instance, Democratic Republic of Congo, Pakistan, Philippines, Rwanda, Sri Lanka, Thailand and most Latin American countries; visitors are usually granted a stay of up to 90 days, or for the duration of their visit if less. For further information on business visits see page 82. Entry requirements change so, please check with your nearest Mauritius representative or the MTPA website.

VISA ISSUE Visas can be obtained from Mauritian embassies and high commissions (see pages 48–9). Visa application forms are available online from the Passport and

Immigration Office (*http://passport.gov.mu*). In addition to the form, you will need to send two recent passport-sized photographs and a photocopy of the data pages of your passport.

IMMIGRATION During your flight to Mauritius you should be given an international embarkation/disembarkation card and a health-related form. These need to be filled in before you join the immigration queue. Have them ready, together with your return air ticket and passport. The process may require some patience on your part.

You will be required to provide the address where you intend to stay or at least the name of your hotel. If you don't know where you're going to stay, expect questions, since immigration needs an address for you. If you are hoping to camp bear in mind that there are no official campsites and camping is discouraged.

You must have a return air ticket otherwise you may be asked to purchase one on the spot. You may also be asked to provide proof that you have sufficient funds to cover your stay. The amount of money that you have in your possession is not the sole criterion: your access to funds in an emergency is important too. According to the MTPA, you will be expected to have at least US$100 (around £63) per night.

The visitor who comes on a package holiday does not raise the same doubts that independent travellers do because the package tourist has prepaid accommodation and is under the auspices of the tour company. However, providing the independent traveller is a genuine tourist who will not engage in 'profit-making activities', which is forbidden, entry is granted after a short interview at the desk.

There is a list of undesirable types who will not be admitted to Mauritius. Anyone who is likely to be a charge on public funds will be refused entry, as will chronic alcoholics, so don't overdo the drinks on the plane.

The second desk you come to is manned by a Ministry of Health official. You will need to hand over the health form you filled in on the aircraft and you may be asked whether you are carrying any plant or animal material and whether you have visited a farm recently. This is part of the continual campaign to prevent malaria returning to Mauritius. If you have come from a malaria-infected country you could be asked to give a blood sample for precautionary analysis within a few days of your arrival.

CUSTOMS The red and green channel system operates in Mauritius but even if you opt for the green channel, you may be questioned before being allowed through.

Incoming visitors aged 16 and over are allowed to import free of duty:

Tobacco	up to 250g
Spirits	1 litre
Wine/beer	2 litres of wine, ale or beer
Perfume	10cl of perfume & 25cl of eau de toilette

Goods for personal use up to the value of Rs15,000 (Mauritian passport holder), Rs7,500 (Mauritian passport holder under 12 years of age), Rs7,500 (foreign passport holder)

Restricted and prohibited goods The following goods are either restricted or prohibited: arms and ammunition, fishing guns, drugs, publications, films or videos of an obscene nature, sugarcane cuttings, plant material, animals and animal products. It is illegal to import or possess cigarette papers.

Prescription drugs If you are carrying prescription drugs, they may be illegal for import into Mauritius. It is advisable to keep them in the manufacturer's box with your prescription. Be prepared to present them for inspection to the customs officials.

Plants and animals All plants and plant material must be declared to customs and will be subject to inspection. A plant-import permit must be obtained in advance from the Ministry of Agriculture, including for cuttings, bulbs, fresh fruit, vegetables and seeds. It is illegal to import sugarcane, soil or micro-organisms.

The same procedure of import permits must also be followed for animals and animal material, which must be accompanied by a health certificate issued by the veterinary authorities of the exporting country. Animals must be declared on arrival. The importation of invertebrates is prohibited. Dogs and cats undergo a six-month quarantine period, birds and other animals two months. The cost is met by the importer.

Animal- and plant-import permits are available from Agricultural Services (*Head Office, Port Louis;* ☎ *454 1091*).

Money There is no restriction on the importation or exportation of foreign or Mauritian currency.

Drugs The penalties for trafficking drugs of any kind are severe. Don't risk it.

STAYING ON

Visa extensions Each application to stay longer than the period written by the immigration officer in a visitor's passport is treated according to the individual visitor's circumstances, not by standard published guidelines.

Applications are dealt with by the Passport and Immigration Office (*Sterling Hse, 9–11 Lislet Geoffrey St, Port Louis;* ☎ *210 9312;* **f** *210 9322;* **e** *piomain@mail.gov.mu; http://passport.gov.mu;* ⏱ *09.00–14.30 Mon–Fri, 09.00–11.00 Sat*).

You will need to take with you a letter addressed to the Officer In Charge, Passport and Immigration Office, in which you explain your reason for wanting to stay longer, and until what date you want to stay. You should state also that you have a ticket out of Mauritius and give details of your confirmed reservation to leave. Include details of where you are staying and of the amount of funds you have available to cover your costs, including lodging and personal expenses. Be prepared to furnish proof of everything you say in the letter.

If your case is genuine and you satisfy the examining officer that you do not intend to work and will not become a charge on public funds, an extension may be granted for up to three months as a tourist.

Work permits Because Mauritius is developing with the aid of considerable private foreign investment, the authorities accept the need of those foreign investors to employ foreign personnel (usually as directors or financial controllers) to represent their interests. Expatriates with technical or professional ability are also likely to be granted work permits if they have been offered employment by a Mauritian company and qualified nationals are not available. Applications for work permits are made through the Board of Investment and further information is available on its website (*www.boimauritius.com*).

Your potential employer will apply for the work permit and pay the fee, which rises for each year of employment. It is likely to take several weeks before it comes through. Forms are available from the Employment Division of the Passport and Immigration Office (*10th Fl, Sterling Hse, 9–11 Lislet Geoffrey St, Port Louis;* ☎ *213 2370; http://labour.gov.mu/empment/download/wpermit.pdf;* ⏱ *09.00–16.00 Mon–Fri*).

Residence permits Applications for permanent residence permits are made to the Prime Minister's Office (*4th Fl, New Government Centre, Port Louis*). Each application is investigated thoroughly and if it is from a foreigner wishing to invest in Mauritius, it is considered in conjunction with the proposed investment project. If applying for a work permit (investor, professional or self-employed), you apply for a residence permit at the same time and receive what is called an 'occupation permit' to allow you to live and work on the island. Information on living, working and retiring in Mauritius is available from the Board of Investment (*www.boimauritius.com*).

Integrated Resort Schemes/Real Estate Scheme Since 2002, non-Mauritian individuals and companies have been allowed to purchase properties that are part of an Integrated Resort Scheme (IRS). An IRS must have certain characteristics, but broadly speaking, in return for purchasing a luxury villa, which is part of an IRS and costs a minimum of US$500,000, the individual is entitled to acquire Mauritian residence for the duration of the villa ownership. There is no restriction on the length of time that the villa can be rented out.

IRS are not usually built on the beachfront but they are finished to a high standard and have extensive facilities. As well as luxury villas, they typically have restaurants, shops, swimming pools and a golf course. Maintenance, gardening and security are usually included. In 2007, the Government of Mauritius announced that the IRS concept would be extended to small landowners under a new scheme called the Real Estate Scheme (RES). This is essentially a slimmed-down version of the IRS with smaller land sizes (up to 10ha) and no minimum investment amount.

EMBASSIES AND CONSULATES

High commissions, embassies and consulates can provide information on Mauritius and deal with visa or work permit enquiries. (See also *Red tape*, pages 45–8.) Embassies, high commissions and their consular offices do not exist as 'minders' or information bureaux.

ABROAD

Australia (High Commission) 2 Beale Cres, Deakin, ACT 2600, Canberra; +61 2 6281 1203; e mhccan@cybeone.com.au

Belgium (Embassy) 68 Rue des Bollandistes, Etterbeek, 1040 Brussels; +32 2 733 9988; e ambmaur@skynet.be

China 202 Dong Wai Diplomatic Office Bldg, Dongzhi Men Wai Da Jie No 23, Beijing 100600; +86 10 653 25695; e mebj@mail.gov.mu

Egypt (Embassy) 1st Fl, 33 Ismail Mohamed St, Zamalek, Cairo; +20 22736 5208; e embmaur@thewayout.net

France (Embassy) 127 Rue de Tocqueville, 75017 Paris; +33 1 42 27 30 19; e paris@amb-maurice.fr

India (High Commission) EP-41 Jesus & Mary Marg, Chanakyapuri, New Delhi 110021; +91 11 2410 2161; emhcnd@bol.net.in. Mauritius Consulate, Office 1105, 11th Fl, Regent Chambers, Jamnalal Bajaj Marg, 208 Nariman Point, Mumbai 400021; +91 22 2284 1410; e mumbcon1@yahoo.com

Italy (Consulate) Via G B Morgagni 6/A, 00161 Rome; +39 6 4424 5652; e consmaur@libero.it

Madagascar (Embassy) Villa David IV, Manakambahiny, Antananarivo 101; +261 20 223 2157; e memad@moov.mg

Malaysia (High Commission) 17th Fl, West Block, Wisma Selangor Dredging, Jalan Ampang, 50450 Kuala Lumpur; +60 3 2163 6306; e maurhckl@streamyx.com

Pakistan (Embassy) Hse No 13, St No 26, Sector F-6/2, Islamabad; +92 51 2828 985; emauripak@dsl.net.pk

Russia (Embassy) Nikoloyamskaya 8, 109240 Moscow; +74 95 915 7617; e moscow_emb@mail.gov.mu

South Africa (High Commission) 1163 Pretorius St, Hatfield 0083, Pretoria; +27 12 342 1283; e mhcpta@mweb.co.za

UK (High Commission) 32–33 Elvaston Pl, London SW7 5NW; +44 20 7581 0294; e londonmhc@btinternet.com

US (Embassy) 1079 N St, NW, Washington, DC 20036; +1 202 244 1491; e Mauritius.embassy@verizon.net

IN MAURITIUS

Australia (High Commission) 2nd Fl, Rogers Hse, 5 President John F Kennedy St, Port Louis; 202 0160; e ahc.portlouis@dfat.gov.au; www.mauritius.embassy.gov.au

China Royal Rd, Belle Rose; 454 9111; e chinaemb_mu@mfa.gov.cn

France (Embassy) 14 St Georges St, Port Louis; 202 0100; e ambafr@intnet.mu; www.ambafrance-mu.org

Germany (Honorary consulate) Royal Rd, St Antoine Industrial Zone, Goodlands; 283 7500; e germanconsul@intnet.mu

India (High Commission) 6th Fl, LIC Bldg, President John F Kennedy St, Port Louis; 208 3775; e hicompol@intnet.mu;

Italy (Honorary consulate) Nicholson Rd, Vacoas; 686 4233; e consolatoitalia@myt.mu

Madagascar (Embassy) Rue Guiot Pasceau, Floreal; 686 5015; e madmail@intnet.mu

Pakistan (High Commission) 9-A Queen Mary Av, Floréal; 698 8501 e pareportlouis@hotmail.com

Russia (Embassy) Queen Mary Av, Floréal; 696 1545; e rusemb.mu@intnet.mu

South Africa (High Commission) 4th Fl, British American Insurance Bldg, 25 Pope Hennessy St, Port Louis; 212 6925; e sahc@intnet.mu

Sweden (Embassy) 2 Jules Koeing St, Port Louis; 208 8763

US (Embassy) 4th Fl, Rogers Hse, 5 John Kennedy St, Port Louis; 202 4400; e usembass@intnet.mu

UK (High Commission) 7th Fl, Les Cascades Bldg, Edith Cavell St, Port Louis; 202 9400; e bhc@intnet.mu

GETTING THERE AND AWAY

A package including flights and hotel accommodation is one of the most cost-efficient ways of visiting Mauritius as tour operators are able to negotiate special fares with airlines and hotels. Many offer visits to Mauritius in combination with another destination; particularly popular is a stay in Mauritius after a safari in Africa. Going on a package holiday need not restrict your freedom to explore the island.

BY AIR

From Europe It takes around 12 hours to fly to Mauritius direct from Europe. The fact that it is a long way and that there are no cheap charter flights has helped Mauritius preserve the qualities that make it attractive. It also makes getting there the biggest expense of a visit.

UK Air Mauritius and British Airways each offer several non-stop flights per week from London. It is also possible to fly via Paris with Air France, via Dubai with Emirates and via the Seychelles with Air Seychelles.

France Air Mauritius and Air France operate frequent codeshare flights from Paris Charles de Gaulle. Alternatively, you can fly via Réunion with Air France or Air Austral.

Germany Both Condor and Air Mauritius operate direct flights from Frankfurt and Munich.

Air Mauritius also offers direct flights from **Milan** and **Geneva**.

From Africa The closest mainland gateways are those in Africa. It takes around four hours to fly from Nairobi, Durban or Johannesburg to Mauritius and around five hours from Cape Town. From **Johannesburg**, **Durban** and **Cape Town** there are flights by Air Mauritius and South African Airways. British Airways also flies from Cape Town to Mauritius via Johannesburg. Air Mauritius operates flights from **Nairobi**. Regular Air Mauritius and Air Madagascar flights link **Madagascar** and Mauritius; flight time to Antananarivo is just under two hours.

From other Indian Ocean islands Air Mauritius offers several flights a day between **Réunion** (Roland Garros and Pierrefonds) and Mauritius; flight time is around 45 minutes from Roland Garros and 55 minutes from Pierrefonds. Air Austral also operates regular flights on the Mauritius–Réunion route. Air Mauritius flies several times a day between Mauritius and **Rodrigues** (flight time around 1 hour 30 minutes).

From the US/Canada There are no direct flights between North America and Mauritius. The best option is usually to fly via London or Paris.

From Australia Air Mauritius operates flights from **Perth** and from **Sydney** via **Melbourne**. Approximate flight times to Mauritius are Perth 8 hours 30 minutes, Sydney 12 hours 50 minutes and Melbourne 11 hours 25 minutes.

From the Middle East Air Mauritius operates direct flights in a codeshare arrangement from **Dubai** with Emirates Airlines. Flight time is around 6 hours 30 minutes.

From Asia Air Mauritius operates flights from **Mumbai**, **Delhi**, **Bangalore** and **Chennai**. Flight times from Mumbai, Bangalore and Chennai are around 6 hours, and from Delhi around 7 hours 30 minutes. Air Mauritius flies between Mauritius and **Hong Kong** (9 hours 45 minutes), and **Shanghai** via Kuala Lumpur (11 hours 20 minutes). Air Mauritius flights to/from **Kuala Lumpur** (7 hours) and **Singapore** (7 hours 10 minutes) are in a codeshare arrangement with Malaysian Airlines.

Whichever way you fly to Mauritius, it is absolutely essential that you have a confirmed return, or onward, ticket in your possession when you arrive. Passengers without a valid ticket to leave Mauritius aren't welcome and won't be allowed in until they buy one. There is more on the immigration requirements in *Red tape*, pages 45–8.

Air Mauritius: the nation's airline When Air Mauritius began in 1967, it was an airline without an aircraft. It has remained small ever since although it is known in international aviation circles for doing big things. In 1987, it became the first airline in the world to order higher gross weight 767/200 Extended Range jetliners from Boeing which entered service in 1988. This philosophy continued with the introduction in 1994 of Airbus A340-300 aircraft to replace the airline's ageing Boeing 747SPs. This aircraft carries around 300 passengers in two classes (economy and business).

In 2012, the fleet consisted of four Airbus A340-300s, two Airbus A340-300Es, two Airbus A319-100s, two Airbus A330-200s, two ATR 72-500s (used on the Réunion and Rodrigues routes) and three Bell 206 Jet Ranger helicopters (available for charter).

By 2012, Air Mauritius was serving 25 destinations on four continents. The airline also acts as the ground handling agent for all other airlines at the international airport.

I have heard few negative reports from passengers flying with Air Mauritius. As a rule, the cabin crew are professional and friendly. As airline food goes, the quality is good in all classes, but don't forget to make the airline aware of any special dietary requirements at the time of booking. The Airbuses have a satisfactory seat pitch of 81cm (32in) in economy class, personal video screens and in-seat telephones in all classes, whilst business-class passengers enjoy 'lie-flat seats' with a 180cm (60in) pitch. Air Mauritius no longer offers a first-class category. All flights are non-smoking.

You are allowed 23kg (50.6lb) of checked baggage in economy class, but only 15kg (33lb) on flights to/from Rodrigues. The business-class allowance is 30kg (66lb). A small extra allowance is provided for sports equipment. If you are carrying a wedding dress, you can ask that it be stored in the business-class coat compartments, otherwise it can be stowed in the overhead lockers or boxed and checked in as hold baggage.

The airline's head office is located in President John F Kennedy Street in Port Louis and has an efficient ticketing office on the ground floor. Tickets can also be purchased via the company's website (*www.airmauritius.com*) and call centre (see below).

If you do choose to fly Air Mauritius, the in-flight magazine, *Islander*, is worth a read as it frequently contains worthwhile articles on culture, activities, tourist attractions, shopping, etc.

Air Mauritius offices

Mauritius Air Mauritius Centre, President John F Kennedy St, Port Louis; 207 7070; reservations & reconfirmation of tickets, 207 7575; e reservations_mru@airmauritius.com: Air Mauritius, SSR International Airport, Plaisance; 603 3030: Air Mauritius Cargo, Plaine Magnien; 603 3698; e cargo@airmauritius.com

Australia Level 18, Suite 1805, 264 George St, NSW 2000; +61 2 9394 1401; e mksydney@airmauritius.com: Level 7, 246 Bourke St, Melbourne, VIC 3000; +61 3 9251 5047; e mkmelbourne@ airmauritius.com; Level 3, 189 Georges Terrace, Perth, WA 6000; +61 89442 6070; e mkperth@airmauritius.com

China Suite 1008, Bldg A, COSCO Happiness Mansion, 3 Dongsanhuan North Rd, Chaoyang District, Beijing 100027; +86 10 8446 7002; e bjsmk@jpkexpress.com.cn

France 4th Flr, 23 Rue de la Paix, 75002, Paris; +33 1 49 240 425; e mkparis@airmauritius.com

Germany Poststrasse 2–4, 60329 Frankfurt; +49 69 2400 1999; e info-fra@airmauritius.com

Hong Kong Room 701A, Admiralty Centre Tower 1, 18 Harcourt Rd; +852 2523 1114; e hkgmk@jpkexpress.com.hk

India 403/408 Arcadia Bldg, 195 Nariman Point, Mumbai 400021; +91 2202 6430; ebominfo@airmauritius.com

Italy Via Paolo da Cannobio 10, 20122 Milan; +39 2 804 661; e info@airmauritius.it

Kenya 3rd Fl, Sasini House, Loita St, Nairobi; +254 20 2229 166; e airmauritius@imaanair.com

Madagascar Làlana, Solombavambahoaka, Frantsay, 77, BP3673 Antsahalova, Antananarivo 101; +261 20 2235 990; e airmauritius@ariomad.com

Malaysia CP 05, Suite 2201, 2nd Fl, Central Plaza, 34 Jalan Sultan Ismail, 50250 Kuala Lumpur; 2142 9161; e sales@airmauritius.com.my

Réunion 113 Rue Charles Gounod, 97400 St-Denis; +262 948383; e airmauritius@wanadoo.fr: 7 Rue François de Mahy, 97410 St-Pierre; +262 960600; e ariofrance@wanadoo.fr

Rodrigues ADS Bldg, Max Lucchesi St, Port Mathurin; +230 831 1558; e mkrodrigues@airmauritius.com

Seychelles Kings Gate Travel Centre, Independence Av, PO Box 356, Mahé; +248 297 000; e 5ticket@seychelles.net

Singapore 80 Robinson Rd, 22–30, Singapore 068898; +65 6 222 3033; e mk@aviationservices.com.sg

South Africa Upper Ground Fl, Lakeside Pl, 1 Ernest Oppenheimer Dr, Bruma Lake Office Pk, 2198 Johannesburg; 0800 983 537; e jnbmk@airmauritius.com:

Switzerland 1–3 Rue de Chantepoulet, Case Postale 1060, 1211 Geneva; +41 22 732 0560; e gvamk@airmauritius.ch

✈ **United Arab Emirates** PO Box 1520, Al Maktoum St, Dubai; ☎ +971 4 221 4455; e nasatour@emirates.net.ae

✈ **UK** Ground Fl Suite, Chiswick Pl, 272 Gunnersbury Pl, London W4 5QB; ☎ +44 20 7434 4375; e information@airmauritiusuk.com; at London Heathrow: Room 2502A, Terminal 4, Middlesex TW6 3YG; ☎ +44 20 8897 3545; e mklhr@airmauritius.com

✈ **US** Los Angeles: 16250 Ventura Bd, Suite 310, Encino, CA 91436; ☎ +1 800 537 1182; e samk@airmauritiusna.com; New York: 450 Seventh Av, Suite 705, NY 10123; ☎ +1 800 537 1182; e kirtis@sitanet.com; Houston: 3050 Post Oak Bd, Suite 1320, TX 77056; ☎ +1 800 537 1182; e ravinm@airmauritiusna.com; Chicago: 101 North Wacker Dr, Suite 350, IL 60606; ☎ +1 800 537 1182; e kazimg@airmauritiusna.com

The Air Mauritius website (*www.airmauritius.com*) is excellent and very informative, and includes timetables, descriptions of the packages they offer and the hotels used.

Airline offices in Mauritius

✈ **Air Austral** Ground Fl, IBL Hse, Caudan, Port Louis; ☎ 202 8050; e Maurice@air-austral.com

✈ **Air France** c/o Rogers Aviation & Travel Services, 5 President John F Kennedy St, Port Louis; ☎ 212 2666

✈ **Air Madagascar** c/o Rogers Aviation & Travel Services, 5 President John F Kennedy St, Port Louis; ☎ 208 6801

✈ **Air Seychelles** c/o Rogers Aviation & Travel Services, 5 President John F Kennedy St, Port Louis; ☎ 202 6671

✈ **British Airways** c/o IBL, Duke of Edinburgh Av, Port Louis; ☎ 208 1039

✈ **Condor** c/o Harel Mallac & Co, 18 Edith Cavell St, Port Louis; ☎ 204 4802

✈ **Emirates** Ground Fl, Harbour Front Bldg, Place d'Armes, Port Louis; ☎ 213 9106

✈ **Malaysian Airlines** c/o Airworld Ltd, Blendax Hse, Dumas St, Port Louis; ☎ 208 4935

✈ **Singapore Airlines** c/o Currimjee Jeewanjee & Co, 5 Duke of Edinburgh Av, Port Louis; ☎ 208 0791

✈ **South African Airways** c/o Rogers Aviation & Travel Services, 5 President John F Kennedy St, Port Louis; ☎ 208 6801

Sir Seewoosagur Ramgoolam International Airport The airport at Plaisance, in the southeast of the island, is small but modern with good facilities. At the time of writing, the construction of a new terminal building was under way adjacent to the current one.

There are a few duty-free shops both on arrival and on departure. In the departure area are a café and shops selling local goods, from handicrafts to smoked marlin, although these are more expensive than in many other outlets on the island. Money can be changed at the bank counters in the main hall, which are open during all international arrivals.

The public are not allowed to enter the check-in departure area and baggage security screening is done at the entrance to the building.

For more information about the airport, visit http://aml.mru.aero.

Luggage Delivery of luggage is usually prompt unless there are several aircraft arriving at the same time and there are usually plenty of trolleys available. If you use the services of the porters, who wait outside the arrivals lobby, you may want to give a small tip, say about Rs100.

Getting to your hotel If you have booked your holiday as part of a package, transfers to your hotel will probably be included. Even budget hotels booked independently can usually arrange transfers for a fee.

All the major car-hire companies have desks at the airport. If a friend is meeting you, they will have to wait outside since the general public are not allowed into the arrivals lobby and have to congregate with the taxi drivers, beyond the doors. Tour operators and hotel representatives wait inside the lobby.

If you need a taxi it helps to know the current fare to your destination and the tourist information counter at the airport should be able to tell you. At night you could well be charged double. It is best to agree the price before starting your journey.

During the day there are public bus services from the airport to Mahébourg and Curepipe, from where buses serve other parts of the island. The information counter can provide details on bus services from the airport.

See *Getting around*, pages 62–5, for further information on car hire, bus services and driving.

BY SEA Cruise liners occasionally call at Mauritius, either on round-the-world voyages or on cruises from southern and eastern Africa. A Costa Croisières (*www.costacroisieres.fr*) ship is based in Port Louis from December to March and operates cruises in the region, taking in Réunion, Madagascar, the Seychelles and east Africa.

Cargo ships come frequently but few of them carry paying passengers and those that do only carry about a dozen.

There are regular passenger sailings between Mauritius and Réunion and between Mauritius and Rodrigues. For detailed information contact the Mauritius Shipping Corporation (*Suite 412, St James Court, Saint Denis St, Port Louis;* ☎ *208 5900;* e *info@mscl.mu; www.mauritiusshipping.intnet.mu*).

Réunion *Mauritius Pride*, operated by Mauritius Shipping Corporation (*see above*), sails around seven times a month between Mauritius and Réunion. There are 248 aircraft-style seats and nine double-berth cabins. The crossing takes 12 hours. For non-residents of Mauritius, seats cost from Rs3,250 per person return and cabins are Rs4,500 per person return. *Mauritius Trochetia* is a new, well-equipped ship with first- and second-class cabins and suites. Facilities include a gym, shop and restaurant. It sails around five times a month between Mauritius and Réunion, and once a fortnight continues on to Toamasina in **Madagascar**. Cabins cost from Rs3,450 per person return.

Rodrigues See page 211.

HEALTH

The only proof of vaccination required is against yellow fever for those over one year of age arriving from areas at risk of yellow fever transmission. This includes most of sub-Saharan Africa and parts of South America. The decision whether to take the vaccination will depend on which country you are coming from and whether the vaccine suits you. If you are arriving into Mauritius from an endemic zone then seek specialist advice as to whether you need the vaccine or can take an exemption certificate.

The traveller to any tropical country will benefit from the following vaccinations: tetanus, diphtheria and polio and hepatitis A. For longer trips, ie: four weeks or more, typhoid and hepatitis B vaccine should also be considered. You are advised to visit your doctor well in advance of your trip to plan the vaccine schedule.

According to the Mauritian authorities, there is no malaria risk in Mauritius or Rodrigues. Visitors generally do not take anti-malaria medication.

To combat the annoyance of mosquitoes during the night, most hotels supply an electric mosquito repellent vaporiser. You should use a DEET-containing repellent

(50–55%) for the body, particularly in the evenings. Remember though that there may also be day-biting mosquitoes that can carry dengue fever (see below) or chikungunya (see box, page 58) so keep your repellent to hand at all times.

Although the water in Mauritius is officially safe to drink in most places, water, and ice, can be the cause of minor upsets. A sensible precaution is to drink only bottled water (obtainable everywhere), to clean your teeth with bottled water and to do without ice in your drinks. Bottled soft drinks, mixers and soda water are usually served cold. Do not drink tap water during or after a cyclone or heavy rains as bacteria and viruses can be washed into the water supply and treatment problems may occur.

Mauritius is considered to have no rabies in terrestrial animals but does potentially have rabies in bats. Exposure to bat saliva or brain tissue should be considered a potential risk and medical help should be sought as soon as possible. On the whole the risk for travellers is very low.

For those who are looking for it, romance is easy to find in Mauritius. However, AIDS is present on the island and visitors should be aware of the dangers.

DENGUE FEVER This acute febrile illness is caused by the dengue virus and is transmitted by day-biting mosquitoes. The incubation period of the disease is from 3–14 days and classically starts with pain behind the eyes, followed by fever, rash and joint pain, among other symptoms. The illness is often self-limiting though unpleasant and treatment is supportive and symptomatic. There are no vaccines or tablets to prevent dengue fever. There are four serotypes; second infections with a different serotype can lead to more serious and potentially fatal disease. It is wise to use insect repellents on exposed skin during daylight hours.

TRAVEL CLINICS AND HEALTH INFORMATION A full list of current travel clinic websites worldwide is available on www.istm.org. For other journey preparation information, consult www.nathnac.org/ds/map_world.aspx. Information about various medications may be found on www.netdoctor.co.uk/travel.

UK

✚ **Berkeley Travel Clinic** 32 Berkeley St, London W1J 8EL (near Green Park tube station); ☎ 020 7629 6233; ⏲ 10.00–18.00 Mon–Fri, 10.00–15.00 Sat

✚ **Cambridge Travel Clinic** 41 Hills Rd, Cambridge CB2 1NT; ☎ 01223 367362; f 01223 368021; e enquiries@travelcliniccambridge.co.uk; www.travelcliniccambridge.co.uk; ⏲ 10.00–16.00 Mon, Tue & Sat, 12.00–19.00 Wed/Thu, 11.00–18.00 Fri

✚ **Edinburgh Travel Health Clinic** 14 East Preston St, Newington, Edinburgh EH8 9QA; ☎ 0131 667 1030; www.edinburghtravelhealthclinic.co.uk; ⏲ 09.00–19.00 Mon–Wed, 09.00–18.00 Thu/Fri. Travel vaccinations & advice on all aspects of malaria prevention. All current UK prescribed anti-malaria tablets in stock.

✚ **Fleet Street Travel Clinic** 29 Fleet St, London EC4Y 1AA; ☎ 020 7353 5678; www.fleetstreetclinic.com; ⏲ 08.45–17.30 Mon–Fri. Injections, travel products & latest advice.

✚ **Hospital for Tropical Diseases Travel Clinic** Mortimer Market Centre, 2nd Fl, Capper St (off Tottenham Ct Rd), London WC1E 6AU; ☎ 020 7388 9600; www.thehtd.org; ⏲ 09.00–16.00. Offers consultations & advice to certain higher-risk travellers & pre-existing patients – see the website for relevant information & booking details. Runs a healthline (☎ 020 7950 7799) for country-specific information & health hazards. Also stocks nets, water purification equipment & personal protection measures. Travellers who have returned from the tropics & are unwell, with fever or bloody diarrhoea, can attend the walk-in emergency clinic at the hospital without an appointment.

✚ **MASTA** (Medical Advisory Service for Travellers Abroad), at the London School of Hygiene & Tropical Medicine, Keppel St, London WC1 7HT; ☎ 09068 224100; e enquiries@masta.org; www.

masta-travel-health.com. This is a premium-line number, charged at 60p per min. For a fee, they will provide an individually tailored health brief, with up-to-date information on how to stay healthy, inoculations & what to take.

✚ **MASTA pre-travel clinics** ☎ 01276 685040. Call or check www.masta-travel-health.com/travel-clinic.aspx for the nearest; there are currently 30 in Britain. They also sell malaria prophylaxis, memory cards, treatment kits, bednets, net treatment kits, etc.

✚ **NHS travel website** www.fitfortravel.nhs.uk. Provides country-by-country advice on immunisation & malaria prevention, plus details of recent developments, & a list of relevant health organisations.

✚ **Nomad Travel Stores** 3–4 Wellington Terrace, Turnpike Lane, London N8 0PX; ☎ 020 8889 7014; f 020 8889 9528; e turnpike@nomadtravel.co.uk; www.nomadtravel.co.uk; walk in or appointments ⏱ 09.15–17.00 daily, with late night Thu. 6 stores in total countrywide: 3 in London, also in Bristol, Southampton & Manchester. As well as dispensing health advice, Nomad stocks mosquito nets & other anti-bug devices, & an excellent range of adventure travel gear.

✚ **InterHealth Travel Clinic** 111 Westminster Bridge Rd, London, SE1 7HR; ☎ 020 7902 9000; e info@interhealth.org.uk; www.interhealth.org.uk; ⏱ 08.30–17.30 Mon–Fri. Competitively priced, one-stop travel health service by appointment only.

✚ **Trailfinders Immunisation Centre** 194 Kensington High St, London W8 7RG; ☎ 020 7938 3999; www.trailfinders.com/travelessentials/travelclinic.htm; ⏱ 09.00–17.00 Mon–Wed & Fri, 09.00–18.00 Thu, 10.00–17.15 Sat. No appointment necessary.

✚ **Travelpharm** The Travelpharm website (*www.travelpharm.com*) offers up-to-date guidance on travel-related health & has a range of medications available through their online mini-pharmacy.

Irish Republic

✚ **Tropical Medical Bureau** Grafton St Medical Centre, Grafton Bldgs, 34 Grafton St, Dublin 2; ☎ 1 671 9200. Has a useful website specific to tropical destinations (*www.tmb.ie*).

USA

✚ **Centers for Disease Control** 1600 Clifton Rd, Atlanta, GA 30333; ☎ 800 232 4636 or 800 232 6348; e cdcinfo@cdc.gov; www.cdc.gov/travel. The central source of travel information in the USA. Each summer they publish the invaluable *Health Information for International Travel*.

✚ **IAMAT** (International Association for Medical Assistance to Travelers) 1623 Military Rd, #279 Niagara Falls, NY 14304-1745; ☎ 716 754 4883; e info@iamat.org; www.iamat.org. A non-profit organisation with free membership that provides lists of English-speaking doctors abroad.

Canada

✚ **IAMAT** (International Association for Medical Assistance to Travelers) Suite 1, 1287 St Clair Av W, Toronto, Ontario M6E 1B8; ☎ 416 652 0137; www.iamat.org

✚ **TMVC** Suite 314, 1030 W Georgia St, Vancouver, BC V6E 2Y3; ☎ 905 648 1112; e info@tmvc.com; www.tmvc.com. One-stop medical clinic for all your international travel medicine & vaccination needs.

Australia, New Zealand, Thailand

✚ **TMVC** (Travel Doctors Group) ☎ 1300 65 88 44; www.tmvc.com.au. 22 clinics in Australia, New Zealand & Thailand, including: *Auckland* Canterbury Arcade, 170 Queen St, Auckland; ☎ 09 373 3531; *Brisbane* 75a Astor Terrace, Spring Hill, Brisbane QLD 4000; ☎ 07 3815 6900; e brisbane@traveldoctor.com.au; *Melbourne* Dr Sonny Lau, 393 Little Bourke St, 2nd Fl, Melbourne VIC 3000; ☎ 03 9935 8100; e melbourne@traveldoctor.com.au; *Sydney* Dr Mandy Hu, Dymocks Bldg, 7th Fl, 428 George St, Sydney NSW 2000; ☎ 02 9221 7133; f 02 9221 8401

✚ **IAMAT** PO Box 5049, Christchurch 5, New Zealand; www.iamat.org

South Africa

✚ **SAA-Netcare Travel Clinics** e travelinfo@netcare.co.za; www.travelclinic.co.za. 12 clinics throughout South Africa.

✚ **TMVC** NHC Health Centre, cnr Beyers Naude & Waugh Northcliff; ☎ 011 214 9030; e traveldoctor@wtmconline.com; www.traveldoctor.co.za. Consult the website for details of clinics.

Switzerland

✚ **IAMAT** 57 Chemin des Voirets, 1212 Grand-Lancy, Geneva; e info@iamat.org; www.iamat.org

Medical services in Mauritius Wherever you are staying, the management will recommend the nearest doctor or dentist for an emergency. The larger hotels have a nurse and small dispensary on their premises, and a roster of doctors on call.

Medical facilities in Mauritius are reasonable, with private clinics and public hospitals available if a doctor advises hospitalisation. The standard is the equivalent of developed countries and the cost of treatment will be a lot less than private treatment in Europe. The island's most modern hospital is Apollo Bramwell (see below). However, medical services in Rodrigues are limited and many patients are sent to Mauritius for treatment (*see Chapter 12, Health and safety*, page 211).

Main hospitals

✚ **Dr Jeetoo Hospital** Volcy Pougnet St, Port Louis; ☎ 212 3201
✚ **ENT Hospital** Vacoas; ☎ 286 2061
✚ **J Nehru Hospital** Rose-Belle; ☎ 603 7000
✚ **Mahebourg Hospital** Cent Gaulettes St, Mahebourg; ☎ 631 9556
✚ **Moka Eye Hospital** Moka; ☎ 433 4218
✚ **Princess Margaret Orthopaedic Hospital** Candos; ☎ 425 3031
✚ **Sir Seewoosagur Ramgoolam National Hospital** Pamplemousses; ☎ 243 3661
✚ **Souillac Hospital** Souillac; ☎ 625 4218

Private clinics

✚ **Apollo Bramwell** Royal Rd, Moka; ☎ 605 1000; www.apollobramwell.com
✚ **City Clinic** Sir Edgar Laurent St, Port Louis; ☎ 241 2951
✚ **Clinique Darné** Georges Guibert St, Floréal; ☎ 601 2300
✚ **Clinique de Greffe de Cheveux** 15 Chemin de la Coline, Pointe aux Canonniers; ☎ 269 0566
✚ **Clinique de Lorette** Higginson St, Curepipe; ☎ 670 2911
✚ **Clinique de Quatre Bornes** Stevenson Av, Quatre Bornes; ☎ 425 0429
✚ **Clinique du Bon Pasteur** Thomy Pitot St, Rose Hill; ☎ 464 2640
✚ **Clinique du Nord** Coast Rd, Baie du Tombeau; ☎ 247 2532; e ndnord@intnet.mu
✚ **Clinique Ferrière** College Lane, Curepipe; ☎ 676 3332
✚ **Clinique Mauricienne** Le Réduit; ☎ 454 3061

Vaccination centres & pharmacies

✚ **International Vaccination Centre** Mutual Aid Bldg, Victoria Sq, Port Louis; ☎ 212 4464

Pharmacies Pharmacies are well stocked with European/US proprietary medicines, are open in the evenings in most towns, and there are dispensaries and health centres in most villages.

MEDICAL TOURISM

Medical tourism, particularly cosmetic surgery and dentistry, is on the rise with a growing number of clinics offering treatment and recovery in Mauritius for procedures such as hair transplants, breast augmentation and cosmetic dentistry. Special packages are available, including flights, accommodation and treatment. Facilities are generally modern and treatment in Mauritius may be cheaper than in your home country but, as with all medical tourism, it pays to do your research. Many of the doctors seem to be trained in France, so it is worth checking whether English is spoken at your preferred clinic.

One of the larger clinics is Centre de Chirurgie Esthétique de l'Océan Indien in Trou aux Biches (☎ *265 5050;* e *info@esthetiqueoceanindien.com; www.esthetiqueoceanindien.com*), which offers hair transplants and cosmetic surgery, including breast augmentation, lipo-sculpture, rhinoplasty and face lifts. It also incorporates a cosmetic dentistry clinic, Challenge 32 (☎ *265 5498;* e *infos@challenge32.net; www.challenge32.info*), which has a team of French-trained dentists.

SAFETY

As with all travel, it is worth checking your own government's advice for Mauritius before deciding whether to travel and what precautions to take while travelling. The UK Foreign and Commonwealth Office provides useful advice for travellers (*www.fco.gov.uk*), as do the US Department of State (*www.travel.state.gov*) and the Australian Department of Foreign Affairs and Trade (*www.smartraveller.co.uk*).

Although Mauritius enjoys a relatively low crime rate, petty crime is on the increase. Many attribute this to an increase in drug taking. Pickpockets are reported to target tourists in busy areas such as Port Louis market and Grand Baie, whilst self-caterers should be aware of the increase in reports of housebreaking. Visitors should take sensible precautions, including avoiding walking alone at night, not leaving valuables visible in cars and taking care of bags and valuables when walking in towns and tourist areas.

Mid-range, upmarket and luxury hotels typically have robust security arrangements but, as in any country, you should secure any valuables in your hotel safe and always make sure your room is locked. In January 2011, an Irish tourist was murdered in her room on a resort in the north of the island. This was an extremely unusual occurrence and a huge shock to the tourism industry in Mauritius; as such it received a good deal of publicity around the world but is not indicative of an increased threat to tourists from crime.

In 2003, the Police du Tourisme (Tourism Police) was set up to patrol tourist areas and assist local police in the investigation of crimes against tourists. The Tourism Police can often be seen patrolling the beaches in specially marked 4x4 vehicles and they have a hotline number – 213 2818 – for the reporting of incidents.

The Tourism Police publishes a leaflet entitled 'Spend a safe holiday in Mauritius'. Its advice includes: secure your valuables in the hotel safe, avoid carrying your passport unless needed, do not leave valuables in your car, park your car in well-lit areas, avoid showing large sums of cash in public, do not walk alone at night and ensure service providers hold a valid licence. The leaflet specifies that tourists should check that any provider of boating excursions or watersports holds a pleasure craft licence. The craft should display a registration number preceded by PC for commercial activities, and not PPC (private pleasure craft). A small coastguard service operates in Mauritius and hotel watersports centres are generally well run.

Hawkers operate on many of the island's beaches and in some towns. You will have no recourse if any items you buy from them are faulty, and please do not buy items made from shells as this contributes to the destruction of the marine environment.

A vast army of dogs wanders the streets and beaches of Mauritius: some are strays but others simply have careless owners. There is always the possibility of confrontation, particularly as they often go around in packs. I was told by a friend living locally that the best defence while walking alone is an umbrella. If a dog with dubious intentions approaches, simply erect the umbrella in its direction and its shield-like appearance should be enough to deter the beast. Take care whilst driving as the roads are not well lit and dogs tend to appear from nowhere.

An increasingly common menace, which my mother and I experienced first hand on our last trip to Mauritius, is the terrifying 'mugger monkey'. Over the years, the island's monkeys have come to associate people with food, and in some areas bold monkeys try to intimidate passers-by into handing over an edible bounty by rushing at them, teeth and gums bared. You don't need to be carrying food to be subjected to this kind of attack. I almost lost my camera bag to a monkey who

CHIKUNGUNYA VIRUS INFECTION

Chikungunya is a viral disease that is transmitted by mosquitoes. It is endemic to large parts of Africa, the Middle East, India and southeast Asia, and has some similarities to dengue fever, which is widespread in most tropical regions.

During 2006 there were increased numbers of cases of chikungunya reported in Réunion, Mauritius and the Seychelles, with over 1,100 cases reported in Mauritius by March 2006. The main preventive measure taken by the authorities is to spray against mosquitoes and to reduce their breeding grounds. Cases continue to occur though in smaller numbers in more recent years but it is still wise to take precautions as described below.

Symptoms appear between four and seven days after a bite by the infected mosquito. A high fever and headache occur, with significant pains in the joints (eg: ankles and wrists). Most patients recover fully over a period of a few weeks, although 5–10% of patients will experience joint symptoms that can persist for a year or more. The virus is rarely fatal.

There is no vaccine available to protect against chikungunya. Travellers are advised to take precautions against insect bites (ie: use insect repellent on areas of exposed skin), particularly during daylight hours when these mosquitoes are active. Pregnant women and those with chronic illnesses should seek specific expert advice before travelling.

assumed the bag contained a hidden stash of bananas. Areas where you need to be particularly vigilant to 'mugger monkeys' include the Alexandra Falls lookout and Grand Bassin sacred lake.

On one of my visits to Mauritius I met a charming British couple who specifically asked me to write about the dangers of slippery tiles in bathrooms. I met them in a Mauritian hospital – the husband had fallen on wet tiles in the bathroom of an upmarket hotel and broken his leg. As a result, they discovered that there are no regulations requiring non-slip tiles in bathrooms in Mauritius, and, in fact, there are almost no non-slip bathrooms on the island. While many of the hotel bathrooms look spectacular, they are pretty slippery. So, tread carefully.

A relatively new danger is that presented by speedboats and jet skis, which roar along the coasts in front of hotels. There have been reports of swimmers being seriously injured, so be vigilant or stick to marked bathing areas.

Don't let all this spoil your holiday; simply use common sense and don't take unnecessary risks.

WOMEN TRAVELLERS

Lone women travellers receive a fair amount of attention from males. It is usually well-meaning curiosity but don't take chances that you would not take in your home country. For instance, don't accept a lift from a lone male or group of men. Don't walk alone at night and try to avoid dimly lit areas, such as beaches. Even during the day, make sure that you are not too isolated on a beach.

Dress standards in Mauritius are conservative. While swimwear is perfectly appropriate on the beach and around the pool, it is not appropriate elsewhere.

Women who are expecting to visit a temple or sacred site should dress appropriately or carry a shawl to cover their shoulders and/or head, if required.

DISABLED TRAVELLERS

While most modern buildings in Mauritius conform to international standards for disabled access, there is no requirement for hotels to construct rooms equipped for the disabled. Even large modern hotels built in the last few years lack specially designed rooms.

However, most hotels claim that they can accommodate disabled guests by giving them a room on the ground floor. This is all very well but many hotels have numerous steps linking their facilities and lifts are not always on hand. Contact the hotel direct in order to gather as much information as possible.

Hotels which have rooms equipped for the disabled include Hilton Mauritius Resort and Spa, Le Preskil, Le Touessrok, One&Only Le St Géran, Sugar Beach Resort and the Indian Resort. Domaine les Pailles is one tourist attraction that has full wheelchair access and even holds conferences for the disabled.

Although pavements are present in large towns, such as Port Louis and Curepipe, they are often poorly maintained. The coastal resorts tend to be quite spread out and frequently lack pavements, making wheelchair access difficult. Public transport does not offer wheelchair access but local ground handlers, such as White Sand Tours (see page 62), can assist by providing wheelchair-friendly transport.

TRAVELLING WITH KIDS

Mauritius is a very child-friendly destination. While a few of the island's hotels are geared towards couples rather than families, most cater very well for children. You can expect mid-range, upmarket and luxury hotels to have well-equipped kids' clubs; some also have teenagers' clubs and a baby-sitting service. The programme of activities at these clubs is impressive and means parents can have plenty of child-free time should they need it. For those who fear their holiday may be ruined by other people's screaming children, many hotels (such as Sugar Beach Resort) endeavour to keep one end of the hotel child-free.

GAY/LESBIAN TRAVELLERS

Mauritians are generally friendly and welcoming to all travellers. However, traditional values are tightly held and homosexuality is not accepted by everyone. There are no gay clubs or bars on the island but gay parties are sometimes organised at one of the clubs or privately. The Mauritian gay community has a strong online presence and websites such as www.gaystaymauritius.com can provide further information on travelling to the island. Travellers should avoid public displays of affection and note that, while the law does not criminalise homosexuality in itself, the act of sodomy is illegal regardless of sexual orientation.

WHAT TO TAKE

The glib answer is plenty of money as there are endless opportunities to spend it in Mauritius. Credit cards are widely accepted and all the main towns have ATMs.

Apart from specific personal items like prescription medicines, you should be able to get everything you need but some items may be more expensive than in your home country. Suncream, insect repellent, camera equipment and other such essentials are very expensive locally.

For clothes, casual elegance is a good watchword. On the coast at any time of the year, you will need lightweight, preferably cotton clothing. Something warmer will be necessary in the evenings, particularly in the highlands. Most hotels require men to wear trousers and shirts in the restaurant in the evenings. If you plan to do some hiking, sturdy trainers are sufficient for the trails in Mauritius. Hotel boutiques and shops in Port Louis and Curepipe have a range of clothing appropriate for the climate.

Three-pin and continental two-pin sockets are both used, so take the appropriate adaptors if you need to. Modern buildings and hotels tend to have three-pin UK-style plugs, whilst budget hotels and self-catering accommodation often have two-pin plugs. Occasional power failures do occur so it is prudent to carry a pocket torch.

Finally, don't forget adequate travel insurance.

MAPS There are several small maps of Mauritius and Rodrigues available as part of the tourist office literature, which will be sufficient for most visitors. Ground handlers can also provide good maps of the island. The Globetrotter travel map has useful detail and includes maps of Port Louis Curepipe, Grand Baie. For hikers, a map of the Black River Gorges National Park is available from the Forestry Department.

MONEY

The legal unit of currency is the Mauritian rupee (Rs), which is divided into 100 cents. There are banks with automatic teller machines (ATMs) in most towns around the island, including several in Grand Baie and Flic en Flac. Banking hours are generally 09.00–15.00 Monday–Friday; some are open on Saturday mornings. Banks are closed on Sundays and public holidays. Foreign-exchange counters in tourist areas often have longer opening hours.

The Bank of Mauritius, the Central Bank (*www.bom.mu*), oversees the proper functioning of the banking system and implements the financial and monetary policies of the government. It used to administer exchange control but since 1983 the rupee has been linked to a basket of currencies relevant to foreign trade. The exchange rate fluctuates daily and is determined by the Central Bank.

You can change foreign currency at banks and exchange bureaux; you will usually need to have your passport with you. Some mid-range and all upmarket and luxury hotels offer foreign-exchange services, where guests can change travellers' cheques and cash, although the commission may be higher than at banks.

Credit cards, such as Visa and MasterCard, are widely accepted in Mauritius. Most upmarket and luxury hotels will also accept American Express.

Currency exchange rates in April 2012 were as follows: £1=Rs46; US$1=Rs29; €1=Rs38.

BUDGETING

The thrifty, independent traveller staying in cheap, basic accommodation and eating in budget restaurants, travelling by bus, and enjoying free outdoor pursuits could live on £40 per day. Since there is bound to be a time during your stay when you will want to do or buy something you haven't anticipated, allow extra.

If you are on a half-board (dinner, bed and breakfast) package holiday at an upmarket beach resort, you will have to buy lunch, which can be expensive in hotels. However, there is always the opportunity to eat outside the resorts and you can get a decent lunch in a reasonable local restaurant for Rs400. Alternatively, you can pick up ten *samoussas* or similar snacks from roadside stalls for around Rs20. Drinks are expensive in hotels; even bottled water with your dinner can cost over Rs200. A number of resorts offer all-inclusive packages, which may be an economical option if you plan to spend a lot of time in your hotel.

If you're staying in self-catering accommodation you should find the cost of household items and food averaging out at less than at home, particularly if you buy your food at local markets. For beer drinkers, you can keep the cost of drinks down by buying local Phoenix beer, rather than imported beers (see page 69).

Taxis have meters but drivers will only use them if you insist. It is often better to negotiate the fare before the journey. Taxi drivers know their value, especially as resort hotels are isolated and a taxi is usually the only way to reach or leave them, so allow extra cash for unexpected taxi journeys, particularly since the island-wide bus service stops running early in the evening.

There is a 15% government tax on hotel accommodation but this is usually included in the room rate. There is also a tax of 15% on meals in restaurants and this may or may not be included in the prices on the menu. A footnote will explain if it is.

TIPPING Tipping in restaurants is usually left to your discretion, although you should check that a service charge is not going to be added to the bill before you dish out tips. In restaurants where no service charge is added, you could leave 5–10% of the bill, according to your satisfaction with the service. In basic eateries tipping is not expected.

Many hotels ask that you do not tip individual staff, but instead place any tips in the tipping box at reception to be divided among all staff. For airport porters Rs100 is usually sufficient. Taxi drivers don't expect tips but they are gratefully received.

GETTING MARRIED

In keeping with the romantic ambience of Mauritius, the island has become a popular place for visitors to get married – not to Mauritians, but to each other. Wedding packages feature in the brochures of most overseas tour operators, whose local representatives handle the arrangements.

Most wedding packages mean that many of the administrative formalities are carried out for you. The tour operator will usually arrange a special licence to allow you to be married from three working days after your arrival in Mauritius. You will need to visit the Civil Status Office in Port Louis before your wedding day to obtain special dispensation under Mauritian law. Divorced ladies must allow a minimum 300-day gap between the divorce and new wedding date, or a pregnancy test taken locally must be negative.

It is possible to arrange a wedding independently but allow plenty of time to gather the required paperwork. If your hotel is not organising your wedding, local ground handlers can assist. You will need to take to Mauritius originals of all documents plus copies certified by a solicitor. For any documents not in English, you will need a certified translation. Vital is a certificate issued under the authority of the prime minister to the effect that the couple are not citizens or residents of Mauritius. This is obtainable on application (at least ten days before the date of the proposed wedding) to the Registrar of Civil Status (*7th Level, Emmanuel Anquetil Bldg, Port Louis;* **t** *201 1727;* **f** *211 2420;* **e** *civstat@mail.gov.au*). The documents needed for the application are two photocopies of each birth certificate and two photocopies of the pages showing the issuing authority and personal details of each passport, and any other documents in case of proving divorce, or demise of former spouse. This certificate has to be produced to the Civil Status Officer at the time of publication, and the marriage can take place the following day.

A couple can choose to be married at the Civil Status Office, on a beach or in their hotel, in which case the ceremony is performed by the Civil Status Officer of the locality where the couple are staying. There are more unusual options too, like Ile des Deux Cocos, a small island off the coast, or on board a catamaran or even the Blue Safari submarine off the north coast.

Religious weddings are also possible but you will need to be on the island at least 15 days before the wedding takes place. For Roman Catholic weddings, you need to contact the Episcopate of Port Louis (*208 3068*). Information should also be obtained from the diocese in which you normally reside.

If you are carrying a wedding dress, you can ask the airline to store it in the business-class coat compartments, otherwise it can be stowed in the overhead lockers or boxed and marked as fragile and checked in as hold baggage.

Information on getting married abroad is available at www.weddings.co.uk.

GETTING AROUND

INBOUND TOUR OPERATORS If you are happy to forego your independence for a while, the easiest way to get around and see the sights of Mauritius is by taking one of the conducted tours run by a tour operator. They provide an instant introduction to the island, enabling the visitor to discover places that they can return to later and explore independently. Inbound tour operators (ground handlers) meet arrivals at the airport on behalf of the hotels and overseas tour operators. They provide leaflets about their services to incoming guests and many have desks at hotels.

The larger tour operators, listed below, can organise almost anything, including car hire, private driver/guide and all manner of activities and excursions. They can also provide guides fluent in a range of languages. Group excursions last either a half or full day and most include lunch and entrance fees to the attractions visited.

White Sand Tours was established in 1974 and is one of the most successful and innovative destination management companies in Mauritius. The company employs 200 highly competent staff and has its own fleet of well-maintained vehicles. In 1996, it was the first destination management company in the Indian Ocean to obtain the ISO9002 certificate, an internationally recognised quality assurance standard. In 2008, it was the first to launch a Sustainable Development Charter, which encompasses employee welfare, environmental awareness, socially responsible tourism, corporate responsibility for the wider community and a collective movement for sustainable development. As well as the usual tours, either chauffeur-driven or in groups, the company can arrange activities such as deep-sea fishing, sailing, helicopter flights, horseriding, mountain climbing and trekking.

Smaller tour operators usually specialise in a few organised group tours and most are to be found around Grand Baie and Trou d'Eau Douce. Their prices may not include entrance fees.

GBTT (Grand Baie Travel & Tours) Royal Rd, Grand Baie; 263 8771; e resa.gbtt@intnet.mu; www.gbtt.com

Mauritours S Venkatesananda St, Rose Hill; 467 9700; e mauritours@mauritours.net; www.mauritours.net

Mautourco 84 Gustave Colin St, Forest Side; 670 4301; e info@mautourco.com; www.mautourco.com

SummerTimes 5 Av Bernardin de St Pierre, Quatre Bornes; 427 1111; e summer@summertimes.intnet.mu; www.summer-times.com

White Sand Tours M1 Motorway, Port Louis; 212 3712; e wst@whitesandtours.com; www.whitesandtours.com

DRIVING There are around 2,000km of good, tarred roads throughout Mauritius. A well-maintained motorway crosses the island diagonally from the airport in the southeast corner, travelling through Port Louis and north to Grand Baie.

Little-used country roads are not in such good condition.

Driving is on the left. Although the standard of driving is generally fairly good (higher than in neighbouring Réunion), drivers are not courteous. Do not expect other drivers to give way or to stop at pedestrian crossings, or to wait for a safe moment to overtake. Outside the towns, there are stretches of open road without traffic, which make driving pleasant. However, roads are not well lit at night so watch out for pedestrians and stray dogs. Take care to observe the speed limit of 80km/h on the motorway and 50km/h in built-up areas; police operate on-the-spot fines. As of December 2008, it is compulsory for cars registered in Mauritius to be fitted with rear seatbelts and the driver is held responsible if they are not worn.

Negotiating Port Louis by car requires patience as traffic builds up to horrendous proportions during the day. Most of the streets are one-way, which adds to the confusion for the uninitiated. If you only want to hire a taxi for one day, let it be the day you go to Port Louis.

Parking zones, applicable if you are parking on the street, exist in Port Louis, Rose Hill, Quatre Bornes and Curepipe between 09.00 and 16.30. Parking tickets must be purchased in advance from a filling station and displayed inside the windscreen. In Port Louis, there are car parks near the Caudan Waterfront, such as the Granary, where you can simply buy a ticket on arrival.

Both petrol and diesel are readily available at filling stations throughout the country, but it is worth keeping your tank full, especially for distance driving at night.

Private cars have black number plates, taxis white, hire cars yellow and diplomatic cars blue. However, I have heard that this system is likely to change.

Car hire The minimum age for hiring a self-drive car varies from 20 to 25 years, according to the hire company. All companies require that the driver has been in possession of a valid driver's licence for at least one year. The car-hire company will need to view your licence.

The rental must be paid in advance. Payment of a daily premium reduces the insurance excess and a daily driver and passenger personal accident insurance is available.

Cars can usually be delivered and recovered anywhere on the island and there are car-hire desks at the airport.

Europcar operates one of the largest fleets of rental cars in Mauritius, with cars ranging from Hyundai Atos to BMW X3s or convertible Mini Coopers. They have desks at many hotels around the island and their staff are efficient and helpful. As an example of daily rates, Europcar charges around Rs2,500 per day (one to six days) for a small, three-door car with unlimited mileage (fuel is not included).

If you don't want to drive yourself, the car-hire companies will provide a driver. Not only does this save you having to cope with local driving conditions but there is also the bonus of having a private guide too. A chauffeur-driven service provided by the main companies will add around Rs750 per eight-hour day to your bill. Overtime, Sundays and public holidays may be extra.

Car-hire companies

ABC Car Rental Albion Docks Bldg, Trou Fanfaron, Port Louis; 216 8889; e abccar@intnet.mu; www.abc-carrental.com

Avis DML Bldg, M1 Motorway, Port Louis; 208 6031; e avis@avismauritius.com; www.avismauritius.com

Budget Rent a Car S Venkatesananda St, Rose Hill; 697 2014; e budget@mauritours.net; www.budget.com.mu
Dodo Touring & Co Ltd St Jean Rd, Quatre Bornes; 425 6810; e dtc@intnet.mu
Europcar Av Michael Leal, Les Pailles; 286 0143; e europcar@intnet.mu; www.europcar.com
GBTT (Grand Baie Travel & Tours) Royal Rd, Grand Baie; 263 8771; e resa.gbtt@intnet.mu; www.gbtt.com
Hertz Gustave Colin St, Forest Side; 670 4301; e hertz@mautourco.com; www.hertz.com
Mango Beach Tours Royal Rd, Triolet; 767 1411; e mbt@intnet.mu; www.drive-mauritius.com
Sixt Rent a Car 5 Av Bernardin de St Pierre, Quatre Bornes; 250 9999; e sixt@intnet.mu; www.sixt.mu
Wind Surf Tours Royal Rd, La Preneuse; 255 7779; e resa@carhiremauritius.com; www.carhiremauritius.com

Motorbike hire There are few places offering mopeds and fewer still offering motorbikes, and it is risky to hire from an unofficial provider. Mopeds are available from around Rs800 a day, including helmet. Crash helmets are compulsory when driving or riding a motorbike or moped.

Motorbike- and moped-hire companies

AKD Holidays Cap Malheureux; 765 3281; e adeegamber@yahoo.com; www.akdholidays-mauritius.com
Imarco Royal Rd, Triolet; 255 8059; e imarco@intnet.mu; www.mauritius-rental.com
Wind Surf Tours Royal Rd, La Preneuse; 255 7779; e resa@carhiremauritius.com; www.carhiremauritius.com

Bicycle hire In 2009, the MTPA began a campaign promoting Mauritius as a cycling-friendly destination (*www.cyclotourism.com*). Suggested cycle routes are available on the website, along with a list of races held on the island. While short rides along the coast can be very pleasant, the towns are not generally cyclist-friendly and in areas of heavy traffic there are no cycle lanes into which one can escape. All bikes used on the road need to be registered at a police station for a small fee but if you hire a bike, this will already have been done.

Bicycles can be hired from the major hotels by the hour, half day and day. The cost is usually from Rs350 per day and several hotels organise group bicycle tours. Some agencies in Grand Baie and most inbound tour operators can arrange bicycle hire.

TAXIS One thing Mauritius is not short of is taxi drivers. Wherever you go, taxi drivers will shout out to you and do their best to persuade you that you need their services. Although most taxis now sport nifty modern meters, they are rarely used. It is as well to negotiate a fare before you start your journey but be prepared to bargain. A taxi ride from Port Louis to Flic en Flac should cost around Rs350.

Most taxi drivers will be only too happy for you to rent their taxi for several hours or a whole day and will act as a de facto tour guide. You can expect a day tour of the island in a taxi to cost around Rs2,000. Bear in mind that taxi drivers are paid a commission by certain shops and attractions to take tourists there, so if you have a fair idea where you want to go you may have to be fairly insistent to ensure you don't spend too much time deviating to the taxi driver's preferred haunts.

Most hotels have a taxi stand and display the fares agreed with the drivers at reception. However, if you take a taxi from a stand not linked to a hotel and negotiate a price, you will often find it is even cheaper than hotel taxi prices.

In most towns taxis are to be found close to the bus station but tend to be available only at conventional times (06.00–20.00). They can also be telephoned (there are two dozen companies listed in the phone directory) and there are 24-hour and night services. Many drivers have mobile phones with numbers also listed in the directory. There are a number of private cars operating as illegal taxis (*taxi marron*).

Taxi trains tout for custom among passengers queuing for buses or follow regular routes, picking up passengers on the way and charging little more than the bus fare for a seat in a shared car. These taxis are usually old boneshakers but they do offer a cheap alternative and will operate late into the night on popular routes.

HELICOPTER HIRE The Air Mauritius Bell Jet Ranger helicopter, with seats for four passengers, is available for hire with pilot for sightseeing and for transfers from/to the airport.

In 2012, the cost of transfer from the airport to a hotel was Rs20,000 for two people plus Rs5,000 for each additional passenger. Sightseeing helicopter flights start at Rs12,000 for two people for 15 minutes, rising to Rs32,000 for one hour.

Bookings should be possible through your hotel or tour operator. Alternatively, contact Air Mauritius directly (*603 3754*; e *helicopter@airmauritius.com*; *www.air-mauritius.com*).

BUSES Mauritius is blessed with a decent bus service, a boon to the independent traveller. It is run on a co-operative basis by different operators: the National Transport Corporation (NTC) (*427 5000*; *http://ntc.intnet.mu*); Rose Hill Transport (RHT) (*464 1221*); United Bus Service (UBS) (*212 2026*); Triolet Bus Service (TBS) (*261 6516*); Mauritius Bus Transport (MTB) (*245 2539*); and individual operators. Since so many people live outside the towns where they work, they depend on the bus service for transportation and their patronage keeps it flourishing.

Compared with the bus services of Africa and Asia it is a disciplined, well-run operation, although the buses can be pretty ancient and many of the bus drivers seem to think the size of their vehicle is enough to intimidate other road users to get out of their way. Catching the bus can be a fun experience – for a start, the buses usually proudly sport amusing names painted on their sides.

Express buses are not non-stop but take a shorter route between points and stop less frequently, although they charge the same fare as the slower buses. The fares are low, with a trip across the island from Port Louis to Mahébourg (which involves a change) costing Rs120 or so, and from Port Louis to Flic en Flac around Rs20. It is important when getting on a bus to ask the conductor where it is going since the town on the front is not necessarily its destination. You can buy your ticket from a conductor on the bus. As the usual flow of passenger traffic is to Port Louis in the morning and out of Port Louis in the evening, making a connection in country districts sometimes takes ages.

Buses operate from 05.30 to 20.00 in urban areas and from 06.30 to 18.30 in rural areas. There is a late-night service until 23.00 between Port Louis and Curepipe via Rose Hill, Quatre Bornes and Vacoas. During the day, services tend to operate as the bus fills up, rather than to a strict timetable.

There are no published timetables so your best source of information is the National Transport Authority (*202 2800*) or the bus companies themselves.

HITCHHIKING Hitchhiking is seldom practised by Mauritians. With the bus service reaching the depths of nearly every village, Mauritians are knowledgeable about how to get around their island easily and inexpensively. Foreigners do hitchhike though and cars will stop. As with hitchhiking in any country, you should be wary, particularly at night, and women should definitely not hitchhike alone.

ACCOMMODATION

Mauritius provides a vast range of accommodation, from budget guesthouses to some of the world's most luxurious hotels; camping, however, is not encouraged and there are no official campsites.

Service throughout Mauritius is superb, a fact which owes much to the Hotel School of Mauritius. The school offers courses for all hospitality and tourism personnel, from chefs to airline cabin staff.

Until recently there was no official rating or classification system for hotels in Mauritius, rather hotels which used a star rating would award it themselves. In April 2012, the MTPA launched an official hotel classification system based on international standards. For the purposes of this guide, we have divided accommodation into five categories, determined principally by the hotel's public rates. The categories, which are defined below, are luxury, upmarket, mid range, budget and shoestring.

Almost all hotels in Mauritius publish their rates in euros only as most of their guests are Europeans and the euro is considered more stable than the Mauritian rupee. Therefore, we have provided rates in euros below.

LUXURY These hotels and resorts regard themselves as six-star properties. Rooms will be spacious and superbly finished with all the facilities that you would expect – a large en-suite bathroom, air conditioning, satellite television, DVD, international direct-dial (IDD) telephone, minibar and safe. Many will include 24-hour private butler service. Luxury villas and presidential suites with rooms for staff are often a feature of these resorts. There will be a choice of restaurants and bars offering world-class cuisine and at least one of the restaurants is likely to be endorsed by a renowned chef. Facilities will be extensive, usually including numerous free watersports, a dive centre, several pools, tennis, a gym and a kids' club. Many of these resorts will have their own golf course or offer access to one nearby. No luxury hotel would be complete without a spa, offering a variety of massages and treatments, as well as saunas, steam rooms, jacuzzis and relaxation areas.

UPMARKET Equates roughly to four- and five-star international standards. Rooms will be en suite and equipped with air conditioning, television (including some satellite channels), IDD telephone, minibar and safe. There will be excellent resort-style facilities, usually including free, non-motorised watersports, such as snorkelling, glass-bottom boat trips, pedaloes and kayaks. Many hotels also offer free water skiing but this is sometimes limited to a certain number of hours. These hotels typically feature a spa, several pools, a dive centre, a gym, tennis courts and a kids' club. Some of these resorts will have their own golf course or offer access to one nearby. There will be regular evening entertainment and activities are often organised during the day. At such hotels there is typically a choice of restaurants and bars, and the standard of cuisine is high.

MID RANGE A wide selection of acceptable hotels offering comfortable accommodation. Many of the large hotels in this category, particularly those owned by the main hotel groups, such as Beachcomber and Naiade, have extensive facilities. Rooms will be en suite and typically have air conditioning, television, IDD telephone and safe. Hotels by the coast will usually offer some free non-motorised watersports, such as pedaloes, kayaks and snorkelling. Other watersports may be payable.

ACCOMMODATION PRICE CODES

Double room per night on HB:

Luxury	**$$$$$**	£450+; US$711+; €549+; Rs2,957+
Upmarket	**$$$$**	£200–450; US$316–711; €244–549; Rs1,314–2,957
Mid range	**$$$**	£100–200; US$158–316; €122–244; Rs657–1,314
Budget	**$$**	£50–100; US$80–158; €62–122; Rs333–657
Shoestring	**$**	up to £50; US$80; €62; Rs333

AI means all-inclusive: breakfast, lunch, dinner, snacks and drinks are included in the room rate. Usually available only as part of a package at a resort hotel.
FB means full board: breakfast, lunch and dinner (meals are often buffets or *table d'hôte* menus) are included in the room rate.
HB means half board: breakfast and dinner are included in the room rate. Few hotels allow you to change to breakfast and lunch.
BB means bed and breakfast is included in the room rate.
RO means room only: no meals are included in the room rate.

BUDGET No frills but usually fun, ranging from boarding houses to self-catering accommodation to medium-sized hotels offering basic facilities.

SHOESTRING Basic accommodation aimed at those on a very limited budget, likely to be self-catering.

PRICES AND TERMS Price brackets have been supplied as a guide only – rates do change regularly, according to season and demand. It is therefore better to judge a hotel by its description than by the price. In any case, if the hotel is booked as part of a package holiday including flights, the public rate is never what you, the guest, actually pay. Even for those who make their own hotel bookings direct, there could be significant discounts on the public rates at luxury, upmarket and mid-range properties. The vast majority of hotels offer considerable discounts for children and infants are often accommodated free of charge. It is worth visiting the websites of hotels as many, particularly the larger ones, publish special offers on the internet.

The price brackets are based on the hotels' public rates for a standard double room, per room per night during high season on half board (dinner, bed and breakfast), two people sharing. However, budget and shoestring properties are likely to be sold on a bed and breakfast or self-catering (room only) basis, rather than half board.

EATING AND DRINKING

FOOD Just thinking about the food I've eaten in Mauritius makes my mouth water, from the delicious French-style crêpes served with local coffee for breakfast to the delight of *salade de palmiste* (heart of palm salad) and the beguiling taste of *fish vindaye* (fish curry) for lunch, then a dinner of *samoussas* and Chinese soup from a street stall.

If you have your meals only in your hotel, you may wonder what I mean. However exceptional its standards, by definition a hotel catering for tourists has to serve international dishes that are familiar to guests and with a taste that is tolerable to nervous palates. Most hotels make an effort to showcase local cuisine and will have Creole and Indian nights at least once a week. The true adventure of eating in Mauritius is for the streetwise since so many delicious – and cheap – dishes are available from pavement hawkers or in noisy dives. Of course, there are also many restaurants that specialise in Creole food or European dishes with a local zest.

The influences of Creole cuisine are African and Indian, with a dash of French. The recipes of slaves and indentured labourers have been blended with French ingenuity to produce an array of irresistible dishes, most of which are mildly spiced. The Chinese influence has been confined to particular areas, such as *mine* (noodles) and the ever-popular fried rice.

A favourite local dish, available from street vendors, is *dholl purées*: thin pancakes, made from wheat flour dough and ground split peas and cooked on a griddle. They are served plain, or rolled around a spoonful of *rougaille* or *brèdes*, and wrapped in paper. The Indian-originating *purée*, with its African/French filling, is an example of the successful blend of culinary traditions. *Rougaille* is a spicy condiment often made with *pommes d'amour*, the tiny cherry tomatoes that are grown and eaten all over the island. *Brèdes* are part of the daily diet of Mauritian country dwellers, cooked either plain or with meat or fish. They are green leaves – such as watercress, spinach, the leaves of tuber plants and Chinese cabbage – tossed with onions, garlic and red chillies in hot oil until the water has evaporated.

More substantial meals are also available from street sellers, such as *poisson vindaye*, seasoned fried fish coated with a *masala* of mustard seeds, green chillies, garlic and turmeric, often eaten cold with bread. *Achards légumes*, pickled vegetables mixed with spicy paste and vinegar, are also sometimes eaten with bread.

The sweet tooth is catered for with many Tamil specialities, such as *gâteau patate*, a wafer-like pastry of sweet potato and coconut. There is an abundance of tropical fruit too, especially the small pineapples dextrously peeled into spirals, with the stem remaining as a handle.

All street eating costs little since office and shop workers on small salaries are the main customers. Some workers carry their lunch with them in plaited reed baskets, dainty square boxes suspended from a string handle with a cover concealing the contents. These containers, called *tentes*, are made from vacoas leaves. They are sold in the markets and make good souvenirs.

Mauritians do not only eat in the street. There are inexpensive eateries in all the towns, where the typical dishes will be meat, chicken or fish served either as *carri* (curry), *daube* (stewed with potatoes and peas) or *kalya* (cooked with saffron and ginger/garlic). Snacks, called *gadjacks*, are served in bars on small saucers, like Spanish *tapas*, to accompany drinks. The range is generous, from *rougaille ourite* (octopus in tomato) to *croquettes volaille* (chicken bites).

RESTAURANT PRICE CODES

To assist you in choosing a restaurant, we have provided a rough indication of the price using codes to represent the average price of a main course:

Expensive	$$$$$	£30+; US$48+; €36+; Rs1,380+
Above average	$$$$	£20–30; US$32–48; €24–36; Rs920–1,380
Mid range	$$$	£10–20; US$16–32; €12–24; Rs460–920
Cheap and cheerful	$$	£5–10; US$8–16; €6–12; Rs230–460
Rock bottom	$	£0–5; US$0–8; €0–6; Rs0–230

Snoeck rougaille (salted fish in tomato) is a frequent standby if fresh fish is not available, and shrimps or lobster are also sometimes served in *rougaille. Camarons* (prawns) served with watercress salad are a favourite with Franco-Mauritians. Wild boar, hare and venison are widely available in restaurants, even out of the hunting season. Goat (*cabri*) is sold in the meat markets in the way that mutton is sold in Europe and is served in curry. The exotic *palmiste* (for which miniature palm trees are especially cultivated to yield their hearts) is sometimes served boiled instead of in a salad, with a Creole sauce.

Most restaurant menus do not contain many options for vegetarians. However, the majority of establishments will proudly create a dish especially for you, usually *carri de légumes* (vegetable curry). If you eat fish you'll be spoilt for choice, with delicious red snapper, dorado (mahi mahi), tuna and swordfish on offer. One of the highlights is, of course, *marlin fumé* (smoked marlin), served as an expensive but superb starter.

Restaurant prices may not include 15% tax, so be prepared for it to be added to your final bill.

DRINKS A popular Mauritian drink is *alooda*, sold on the streets and in markets by energetic salesmen praising their own product. It consists of dissolved, boiled china grass (*agar agar*) and sugar, which has been strained and allowed to set and then grated, to which is added water, milk, rose syrup and soaked *tookmaria* (falooda) seeds.

As you would expect, beer, wine and spirits are far more expensive in hotels than they are in local shops.

Beer At the beginning of the 1960s, Pierre Hugnin listened to the suggestion of a friend from Tahiti that he should start a brewery. At the time, 18,000 hectolitres of beer were imported into Mauritius annually. While going into the figures for the project, Hugnin had the well water at his proposed site in Phoenix analysed and found it ideal.

The first Mauritian beer, Phoenix, was brewed by Mauritius Breweries Limited in August 1963. With beer seen as an acceptable drink in multi-religious Mauritius, MBL launched a second beer, Stella, two years later and began to distribute Guinness, which has been brewed under licence since 1975. Phoenix (5% vol) has become synonymous with beer for Mauritians and is the company's bestseller. In 2003, MBL merged with another beverage firm to form the Phoenix Beverages Group (*Phoenix Hse, Pont Fer, Phoenix;* ☎ *601 2000;* **e** *pbl@pbg.mu; www.phoenixbeveragesgroup.com*). The company now produces non-alcoholic beverages as well as an expanded range of alcoholic drinks, including Blue Marlin, a stronger beer (6% vol), Phoenix Special Brew (6.5% vol), Stella Pils (a lager) and Phoenix cider.

Mauritius beer has won many international awards for its quality, including Monde Selection gold medals for Blue Marlin (2007) and Stella Pils (2009). Mauritius sugar is used in the production of beer (where other breweries might use maize or rice) since it produces a beer that is more digestible. Top-quality hops come from Australia and Europe. The beer has a clean and refreshing taste with lots of flavour.

Spirits Almost 200 years ago, a commentator on Mauritius complained: 'The facility with which spirits, especially arrack of inferior quality, are to be procured is more fatal to the soldiers than exposure to the sun, or any other effect of the climate.'

Rum-making on the island dates back to 1639, following the introduction of sugarcane by the Dutch, when it was made from cane juice even before people knew how to extract the crystals. Alcohol is now the most successful by-product of sugar, obtained by turning molasses into fine spirit.

There are many rums produced in Mauritius, including the romantic-sounding Green Island Rum. Most households and bars keep a variety of *rhum arrangé*, made by adding their own choice of fruit and/or spices to a large bottle of rum and leaving it to mature for a few months. The story of rum-making on the island is told at the Rhumerie de Chamarel (see page 176).

Wine In a tasting of rosé wines from South Africa, France and Portugal conducted by a wine writer in South Africa a few years ago, a bottle of Château Bel Ombre featured well. It was determined by half the tasters as being South African in origin and by others as being from southern France or Portugal. Everyone was flabbergasted when they learned it came from Mauritius, produced by E C Oxenham & Co Ltd (*St Jean Rd, Phoenix; ↘696 7950; e eureka@intnet.mu; www.oxenham.bz*).

The absence of vineyards in Mauritius has led sceptics to dismiss Oxenham's wines as being obtained through the fermentation of Mauritian fruits. Not so. The wine is made from grape must, concentrated for travel, and imported into Mauritius in plastic blowpacks.

Edward Clark Oxenham, a descendant of British colonials, was a pioneer who tried to grow grapes on his farm in Rodrigues. He failed, but with help from the Pasteur Institute of Paris started to produce wine from dried grapes and local fruits in 1931. He moved to Mauritius and in 1932 founded the company that now bears his name.

Mauritian white and rosé wines can be drunk young, but the red is stored in oak vats to mature. The Oxenham range begins with Eureka, the everyday wine of Mauritians, through the pleasant and inexpensive Rosé Chaptalin, to finer wines with the St Nicholas label, as well as the full-bodied Mon Hussard red.

Wines produced in Mauritius have the added attraction for the drinker of their low retail price, although hotel or restaurant mark-up can increase the price by as much as five times.

PUBLIC HOLIDAYS AND FESTIVALS

PUBLIC HOLIDAYS Public holidays for religious and state occasions threatened to overwhelm working life in Mauritius, multiplying until there were 28 official days off work a year, in addition to weekends. Now the number of statutory public holidays has been reduced to 15. These are as follows:

New Year's Day	1 January
New Year	2 January
Chinese Spring Festival	variable (January/February)
Thaipoosam Cavadee	variable (January/February)
Abolition of Slavery	1 February
Maha Shivaratree	variable (February/March)
National Day	12 March
Ougadi	variable (March/April)
Labour Day	1 May
Assumption	15 August
Ganesh Chaturthi	variable (August/September)
Divali	variable (October/November)

Arrival of Indentured Labourers	2 November
Id El Fitr	variable (November/December)
Christmas Day	25 December

Employees are also permitted to have two additional days' leave a year to celebrate religious festivals that are no longer official public holidays. Leave is granted at the employee's request even if the employee doesn't belong to the religion celebrating the festival. Some of these festivals are so popular with everyone, regardless of their religion, that they become like public holidays, with shops and businesses closed.

Since many of these festivals depend on different religious calendars, the days on which they are held vary each year and will not always be in the months shown below.

FESTIVALS

Sankranti	January
Holi	March
Mehraj Shariff (Muslim)	March
Varusha Pirappu (Tamil New Year)	April
Shabbe Baraat (Muslim)	April
Good Friday	March/April
Easter Monday	March/April
Seemadree Appana Parsa (Telegu)	May
Sittarai Cavadee (Tamil)	May
Corpus Christi	May/June
Id El Adha (Muslim)	August
Raksha Bandhan (Hindu)	August
Anniversary of Père Laval's Death	9 September
Mid-Autumn Festival (Chinese)	October
All Saints' Day	1 November
Yaum Un Nabi	November
Ganga Asnan	November
Boxing Day	26 December

Sankranti The first of the year's religious festivals, it is celebrated in the beginning of the Tamil month Thai, and is also known as Thai Pongal. It is an occasion of thanksgiving for the harvest which is represented by the ceremonial boiling of rice. It is customary to wear new clothes at this time.

Chinese Spring Festival This is New Year's Day and spring-cleaning combined. The festival begins on the eve of the Chinese New Year with an explosion of firecrackers to chase away evil spirits. It takes place in January or February and does not fall on the same day every year because of the irregularity of the lunar month.

During the week before New Year's Day there is a thorough spring-cleaning of the home. Traditionalists visit pagodas on New Year's Eve with offerings and prayers of thanksgiving. Neither scissors nor knives are used on the day and the colour red, symbolic of happiness, is favoured. Food is displayed in an honoured place in the home in the hope of abundance in the coming year. Cakes made of rice flour and honey, called wax cakes because of their texture, are shared with relatives and friends.

Thaipoosam Cavadee This Tamil ritual is named after the wooden yoke – the *cavadee* – decorated with flowers and palm leaves and with a pot of milk suspended from each end, which a devotee fulfilling a vow carries across his/her shoulders in procession to their temple. There it is placed before the deity when, despite the long, hot ordeal, the milk should not be curdled.

The *cavadee* procession, while colourful and spectacular, is awe-inspiring because of the penance undergone by the participants who walk with their bodies pierced with needles, hooks hanging from their flesh and skewers threaded through their tongues and cheeks.

Maha Shivaratree The Great Night of Shiva is a solemn occasion for Hindus which begins with a night-long vigil in worship of the god Shiva. The following day, devotees dressed in pure white carry the *kanwar*, a wooden arch decorated with flowers, paper and tiny mirrors, in procession to the sacred lake, Grand Bassin.

The Hindus carry water from the lake home to their temple. *Poojas* (worship with food) are celebrated that night in the temples dotting the banks of the lake, the air heavy with the sweet smell of burning incense sticks and reverberating with prayers broadcast from loudspeakers.

This is reputed to be the largest Hindu festival celebrated outside India and is reminiscent of the great rituals on the banks of the holy Ganges. Worshippers believe the lights they launch on the lake on banana leaves and their offerings of flowers will float somehow to the Ganges.

Holi A happy time for Hindus when greetings are exchanged and revelry erupts with the squirting of coloured water and the spraying of coloured powder on one another, and on everyone else the revellers come across. A noisy and cheerful festival.

Ougadi Telegu New Year.

Id El Fitr The annual month of fasting (Ramadan) by Muslims, during which they neither eat nor drink between sunrise and sunset, comes to an end with this festival. Prayers are offered at mosques during the day.

Ganesh Chaturthi Celebrated on the fourth day of the lunar month of August/September by Hindus of Marathi faith as the birthday of Ganesh, the god of wisdom and remover of all obstacles. Processions are held with devotees escorting pink, elephant-nosed effigies to the sea and dusting onlookers with scarlet powder.

Corpus Christi Devout Roman Catholics join in a procession through the streets of Port Louis in May or June on the occasion of Corpus Christi.

Id El Adha Sheep and goats are sacrificed in ceremonial slaughter for this Muslim festival and the meat is shared with family and friends. The day commemorates Abraham's willingness to sacrifice his son for god, and the events symbolise the Muslim ideal of sacrifice and dedication.

Père Laval Pilgrims of all faiths gather at the tomb of Father Jacques Desiré Laval throughout September, but particularly on 9 September, the anniversary of his death. Many come in hope of a miracle cure. For more information see page 113.

Divali Clay oil lamps and paper lanterns with candles in them are placed in front of every Hindu and Tamil home on this Festival of Lights. Hills and valleys sparkle in the night as lights burn to celebrate the victory of Rama over Ravana, and Krishna's destruction of the demon Narakasuran, the victory of good over evil.

All Saints' Day The day on which cemetery cleaning takes place and flowers are placed by Roman Catholics on the graves of the dead.

Yaum Un Nabi The birth and death anniversaries of the Prophet Muhammad are commemorated on the Prophet's Day, following 12 days during which the faithful gather in mosques throughout the island, devoting themselves to religious study.

Ganga Asnan For Hindus this is the time of ceremonial bathing in the sea for purification, since they believe the holy water of the Ganges will be able to purify them through it. At the beaches special lifeguard units are set up to ensure the safety of bathers.

Muharram An important Muslim festival known in Mauritius as Yamsey, featuring figures and towers called *ghoons*, carried in procession through the streets in commemoration of the death of the grandson of the Prophet.

Firewalking At the Tamil temple in Terre Rouge and at other temples in predominantly Tamil areas, *teemeedee* (firewalking) takes place between October and March. Worshippers walk over beds of red-hot embers which represent the outstretched sari of Draupadee. They prepare for the ordeal by fasting, ritual bathing and a blessing before walking unscathed on the glowing embers to the accompaniment of chants from supporters.

Details of where to see firewalking, and the dates each year of the religious festivals and public holidays, are given in a leaflet about 'Coming Events' available bi-monthly from the tourist office.

CHURCHES

For Christians there are both Roman Catholic and Anglican cathedrals in Port Louis with Presbyterian and Evangelical churches close by and churches of all denominations throughout the island. Hotels display details of religious services held near them on their noticeboards. The following churches regularly conduct services in English: St Joseph's Chapel, Rose Hill (*464 2944*) – Roman Catholic Mass; St Paul's Church, Vacoas (*686 4819*) – Anglican Mass; St Columba's Church, Phoenix (*696 4404*) – Presbyterian Sunday Service.

SHOPPING

Mauritius is billed as a 'shopping paradise' and a lot of money could be spent buying intricately carved model ships, duty-free diamonds and designer clothing. Many tourists find it hard to resist the clothing factory outlets, where the clothes produced in Mauritius for export are sold at discounted prices. Although such shops are found throughout Mauritius, they are concentrated around Port Louis waterfront, Grand Baie, Flic en Flac, Curepipe, Floréal and Quatre Bornes. A shopping trip to these areas can be organised by most tour operators.

The government is doing all it can to promote shopping in Mauritius. In 2005, it announced plans to become one of the world's few duty-free islands by abolishing, over the next four years, its 80% tax on 1,850 different types of goods, including clothing, electronics and jewellery. It offers incentives for investors to build large retail centres and shopping malls, such as Ruisseau Creole in the island's west.

Shops in Port Louis sell everything from the latest electronic goods to coconut husks for polishing wooden floors. Near the harbour, the large and modern **Caudan Waterfront** (☎ *211 9500;* **e** *caudan@intnet.mu; www.caudan.com*) offers something for everyone with duty-free jewellery and carpets, clothing boutiques, bookshops, model ship shops and an excellent craft market, where local artisans can be seen at work. Many of the handicrafts on sale in Mauritius are imported, mostly from Madagascar. However, if you head to one of the National Handicraft Promotion Agency (NHPA) or Small Enterprises & Handicraft Development Authority (SEHDA) shops, you can be sure not only that the handicrafts you are buying are made in Mauritius, but also that a percentage of the proceeds goes to the artisan. (For more information see *Travelling positively*, pages 83–4.)

Shops in Port Louis are open 09.00–17.00 on weekdays. On Saturday they close at midday and only a few shops open on Sunday mornings. Shops in Curepipe and Quatre Bornes are open 10.00–17.30 daily except Thursday and Sunday, when they close at midday.

Discounts on marked prices may be available if you have the courage to ask, although it's usually Mauritians who are successful. Bargaining on unmarked prices, particularly in markets, is acceptable if you have time.

MARKETS Markets are good places to shop, as prices tend to be lower than in shops, and you can pick up vanilla and other spices to take home. Self-caterers will find a good range of fresh fruit and vegetables. They are held in the following towns:

Port Louis	daily
Curepipe	Wednesday and Saturday
Quatre Bornes	Thursday and Sunday
Vacoas	Tuesday and Friday
Mahébourg	Monday
Centre de Flacq	Wednesday and Sunday
Plaine Verte	Tuesday and Saturday

DUTY-FREE GOODS The duty-free shops primarily sell jewellery, watches and electronic goods. Particularly popular are the duty-free diamonds, which can range from 0.1 to 10 carats and from £50—£300,000. For duty-free purchases, buyers need to show a foreign passport and air ticket in the same name, so remember to take both when you go shopping. Payment must be made with foreign currency, travellers' cheques or credit card, and at least 48 hours before the purchaser's intended departure. You can claim back 15% VAT at the airport, provided you have the paperwork for your purchase.

JEWELLERY The production of jewellery for export has become a thriving industry, and some jewellers even have boutiques in the upmarket hotels. For handmade work – even to your own design – try the award-winning **Ravior** (*88 St Jean Rd, Quatre Bornes;* ☎ *454 3229;* **e** *ravior@intnet.mu; www.ravior.com*). Ravior also has shops at Newton Tower in Port Louis (☎ *212 8021*) Ruisseau Creole shopping centre in Rivière Noire (☎ *483 6585*) and at the airport.

Family-run business **Adamas** has been selling diamonds and jewellery in Mauritius since 1987. Adamas has a diamond showroom in Mangalkhan, Floréal (☎ *686 5246;* **e** *adamas@intnet.mu; www.adamasltd.com*), where visitors can learn about diamond cutting and polishing, or even watch their commissions being made.

It also has outlets at the Caudan Waterfront in Port Louis (☎ *210 1462*), Richmond Hill complex in Grand Baie (☎ *269 1609*) and Cascavelle shopping centre in Flic en Flac (☎ *450 9018*).

Another well-known name in the local jewellery industry is **Poncini**, which has its headquarters in one of the handsomest buildings in Port Louis – a wooden, colonial Creole house built in 1850 (*Place du Théâtre, 2 Jules Koenig St;* ☎ *212 0818;* e *contact@poncini.com; www.poncini.com*). It also has shops at the Caudan Waterfront in Port Louis (☎ *211 6921*), on Royal Road in Curepipe (☎ *674 7044*) and Sunset Boulevard in Grand Baie (☎ *263 8607*).

The newly converted Citadel in Port Louis contains a series of shops targeting the tourist market, including **Trésor**, a diamond and jewellery shop (☎ *217 4040;* e *info@tresordiamonds.com*).

MODEL SHIPS The model shipbuilding industry started small in the 1960s but has become so successful that there are now several workshops on the island.

The 150 or so different models available include replicas of famous ships such as the *Golden Hind*, HMS *Victory*, HMS *Bounty*, *Mayflower*, USS *Constitution* and *Cutty Sark*. Each is made by hand exactly to scale, using camphor or teak: camphor for the keel, hard *bois de natte* for the masts, yards and pulley blocks, soft lilac for the helm and capstan. Prices are generally high, ranging from Rs1,000 to over Rs30,000, but it is easy to see why as a large detailed model can take up to 450 hours to make. Model ships can be sent worldwide, or packed for taking in the hold, as checked baggage, on the plane home (a surcharge may apply). Many of the workshops also produce fine furniture.

One of the best-known manufacturers is **Historic Marine** in Goodlands (☎ *283 9304;* e *hismar@intnet.mu; www.historic-marine.com*), which has been producing model ships since 1982. The company now makes around 2,000 models per year. Visitors can visit the model ship workshop and buy the finished articles on site (see page 132).

You will find model ship shops around the island and in some hotels but most are concentrated around Curepipe. **Comajora** at La Brasserie Road, Forest Side (☎ *676 5345*), has a shop just outside Curepipe. **Bobato** has a showroom at 53A Sir John Pope Hennessy Street, Curepipe (☎ *675 2899; www.mauritiusshipmodels.com*). **First Fleet Reproductions** is at 74–76 Royal Road, Phoenix (☎ *698 0161;* e *fstfleet@intnet.mu; www.firstfleetreproductions.com*). On the west coast, there are two model ship shops on the way into Flic en Flac, **Pirate Ship Models** (☎ *453 9028*) and next door, **Superbe Ship Shop**. **Qetsia Boutique** at the Citadel in Port Louis (☎ *233 2800*) also sells model ships.

MAURITIUS GLASS GALLERY The aim of the Mauritius Glass Gallery is to produce handmade glass objects from recycled glass and promote environmental awareness. The workshop at Pont Fer, Phoenix, is open to the public and there are regular glass-blowing demonstrations (for details see page 187). The products can be bought at Pont Fer (☎ *696 3360;* e *mgg@intnet.mu*), in the craft market at the Caudan Waterfront (☎ *210 1181*), at the Super U Commercial Centre in Grand Baie (☎ *269 0376*) and at the airport. A glass dodo costs around Rs115, a paperweight is about Rs200 and lamps are around Rs1,000.

TEXTILES Textiles are now one of the largest industries in Mauritius. While most of the finished goods are exported to Europe, once the manufacturers have completed their quotas, the remainder can be sold at home, at very attractive prices.

The island has made a name for itself in the knitwear field and shops can be found all across Mauritius. In the Floréal Square, there are a number of shops that sell good-quality clothes at factory prices. Floréal Knitwear makes clothes for a number of well-known international brands but you can pick up the garments in Mauritius at a fraction of the price, often before the brand label has been sewn in. Harris Wilson, Maille Street, Café Coton, Equateur and Diesel are all decent brands made in Mauritius. Visitors to Mauritius used to flock to the innumerable 'designer' stores on the island believing that they were getting fabulous discounts on famous brands, Ralph Lauren in particular. It wasn't until 2004 that it was confirmed that these shops stocked fake designer clothing made on the island and the government ordered them to be shut down. Canny shoppers will be quick to spot that fakes (often Dolce and Gabbana, Chanel, Armani, etc) are still sold in some shops.

If you want custom-made clothing, dressmakers and tailors can run up garments in a few days. Short-term visitors should commission the work on arrival to ensure that it is ready in time for departure.

SOUVENIRS Those looking for a reminder of Mauritius to take home with them are spoilt for choice. If your home country allows the importation of plant material, the wax-like anthuriums grown in Mauritius are sold packed in cardboard boxes for travelling. They should keep for a few weeks when you get them home.

Local delicacies such as smoked marlin, tea, sugar, rum and vanilla make lovely gifts and can be bought at the airport just before departure if you have left your shopping until the last minute. Spices are easy to transport and are inexpensive in markets.

The **Small Enterprises & Handicraft Development Authority** sells a range of souvenirs made in Mauritius and Rodrigues. Buying souvenirs from its outlets is a good way of supporting the local economy. For more information see *Travelling positively*, pages 83–4.

ARTS AND ENTERTAINMENT

The arts flourish in Mauritius despite a lack of appreciation and encouragement from the outside world. Local authors and poets who want to be published often have to pay for the printing of their own works unless they can find sponsorship from foreign cultural organisations.

The Ministry of Arts and Culture runs a useful website (*www.creativearts.mu*) with information on Mauritian artists, a list of art galleries and museums, and opportunities to invest in the Mauritian arts scene.

The **Alliance-Française** (*1 Victor Hugo St, Bell Village, Port Louis;* ☎ *212 2949;* **e** *afim@intnet.mu; www.afmaurice.com*) is very active in its encouragement of the arts and the French language, so much so that the **British Council** (*Royal Rd, Rose Hill;* ☎ *403 0200;* **e** *general.enquiries@mu.britishcouncil.org; www.britishcouncil.org/mauritius*), which had slumped into inactivity, was revived at the end of 1987 with the appointment of a new representative.

LITERATURE Several slim volumes of verse, belles-lettres and travelogues by local authors are to be found hidden away in Mauritian bookshops. Robert Edward Hart, who died in 1954, was Mauritius's most renowned poet, and was awarded the OBE and the French *Légion d'honneur*. His house at Souillac is now a museum (see page 160).

Mauritian writer and painter, Malcolm de Chazal (1902–81), is best known for his *Sens Plastique*, a compilation of several thousand aphorisms and pensées. Born in Vacoas of a French family, de Chazal wrote in French. His surrealist work was highly praised by French literary figures.

Much of Mauritian literature is written in French, some in English and very little in Creole. Playwright Dev Virahsawmy, a retired politician, is an advocate of the Creole language and writes works only in that language.

Each June, Le Prince Maurice Hotel hosts Le Prince Maurice Prize for literature with a theme of love. The prize alternates between English and French writers each year and the winner receives a two-week stay at the hotel.

Shelf-loads of books, mostly in French, have been written about Mauritius, many with slavery as their theme. The island has been the setting for novels, too, the most famous being the pastoral French novel, *Paul et Virginie*, by Bernadin de Saint Pierre, which was first published in 1773. Its sentimental tale of love and heartbreak, based on the wrecking of the *St-Géran* in 1744, is remarkable for the accuracy of its nature notes and description of an idyllic Mauritius when it resembled a garden of Eden.

Bookshops For its population and high literacy rate, Mauritius is poorly served for bookshops (*librairies*). While there are a number of them on the island, most of these combine stationery supplies with a stock of books for students and a few general volumes in French and some in English. The best bookshops are in Curepipe and Port Louis.

THEATRE, DANCE AND ART There are some local folklore and dramatic societies that occasionally perform cultural shows and plays. The old opera house in Port Louis (*Municipal Theatre; ☎ 212 1090*), built in 1822, has been lovingly restored and is a fine setting for local drama with performances usually in the evenings. The Plaza Theatre (*Royal Rd, Rose Hill; ☎ 424 1145*) is part of the Beau Bassin/Rose Hill town hall complex, a Baroque 1920s creation by Coultrac Mazérieux which has become a prestigious venue for Mauritian and foreign cultural activities.

For tickets to concerts and plays, contact the island's ticket office, Otayo (*☎ 466 9999; e info@otayo.com; www.otayo.com*).

An art gallery also at the Beau Bassin/Rose Hill town hall complex is named after the Mauritian artist, Max Boullé (*☎ 454 9500*), and often features exhibitions by local artists.

In Port Louis there is the Galérie d'Art de Port Louis in Mallefille Street, just behind the Mauritius Museum Council, which holds occasional exhibitions of local artists' work. Commercial art galleries are found in Quatre Bornes, Grand Baie, Pointe aux Cannoniers, Rivière Noire and Port Louis (see page 111). There is a greater concentration of galleries around the touristy areas. Galerie du Moulin Cassé in Pereybère (*☎ 727 0672; ⏲ Fri 10.00–18.00*) is in a converted 19th-century sugar mill and has permanent exhibitions by Diane Henry, natural world photographer, and Malcolm de Chazal (1902–82), Mauritian artist. Seebaluck Art Gallery in Pointe aux Canonniers (*☎ 263 6470; ⏲ Mon–Sat 09.30–19.00*) has works by local and international artists.

NIGHTLIFE For most tourists, nightlife will centre on their hotel since the hotels themselves are isolated on the coast and far from whatever local action there is. Hotel evening entertainment is of good (but not international) standard, with live bands, floor shows, discotheques and occasional concert parties and fashion shows organised by the hotel's 'animation' staff. Most hotels feature weekly *séga* shows.

In recent years, a few hotels have established upmarket clubs open to the public. Shanti Maurice in the south of the island has the Fish and Rhum Shack, a barefoot restaurant rustic beach bar (see page 155). C Beach Club at Heritage Le Telfair is a similar concept with a beachside bar, restaurant and regular live entertainment (see page 156). Entry for the day will cost around Rs400 and includes use of the pools, watersports facilities and access to the bar and restaurant.

For nightlife outside the hotels, the focal points are the tourist areas of Grand Baie and Flic en Flac. Grand Baie used to be the place to go but Flic en Flac is becoming increasingly popular. Many nightclubs open on Wednesday, as well as Friday and Saturday evenings. Expect an entrance charge (from around Rs300), although entry is sometimes free for women. For additional information, see the chapter on the relevant geographical area.

Casinos Mauritians love to gamble. Most casinos offer fruit machines as well as a variety of tables (roulette, blackjack, etc). Dress standards call for more than beachwear. The casinos are generally open from early evening for playing the slot machines, but only from 21.00 for gambling at the tables. On Sundays, they open at about 15.00, when they are popular with wealthier residents, particularly the Chinese.

The hotels with casinos are One&Only Le St Géran and La Pirogue. Gamblers can also indulge their passion at:

L'Ámicale Casino 6 Chausée St, Port Louis; ☎210 9713
Casino de Maurice Teste de Bush St, Curepipe; ☎675 1535
Flic en Flac Casino Pasadena Village, Flic en Flac; ☎453 8022
Le Casino du Caudan Port Louis Waterfront; ☎210 4203
Le Grand Casino du Domaine Domaine Les Pailles; ☎286 0405
Ti Vegas Royal Rd, Quatre Bornes; ☎454 8800
Ti Vegas Super U, Grand Baie; ☎269 1448

PHOTOGRAPHY

The cost of photography paraphernalia and processing is likely to be higher than in your home country. Processing of colour print film in 24 hours is available at several outlets in Port Louis and Curepipe. Digital photography equipment and printing are available in outlets around the main tourist resorts. Printing and downloading of photos onto disk are available at the main internet cafés.

Most Mauritians are quite happy to have their photos taken but you should ask permission first. Permits are not required for photography but you are not allowed to take photographs of the harbour and the airport.

MEDIA AND COMMUNICATIONS

MEDIA Newspapers in Mauritius enjoy a reputation for lively debate and freedom of expression, with the independent press curbed only by self-censorship. The first newspaper was published in 1773 and there have been more than 600 titles since then, including *Le Cernéen*, started in 1832 as the first newspaper that did not have to be submitted to the government for approval.

The most popular daily papers are *Le Matinal* (*www.lematinal.com*), *Le Mauricien* (*www.lemauricien.com*) and *L'Express* (*www.lexpress.mu*), which are published in French, with occasional articles and advertisements in English. L'Express also publishes a version in Rodrigues. Mauritius now has an English-language daily newspaper, *The Independent* (*www.theindependent.mu*). Larger hotels often sell

English and other foreign newspapers, and provide daily news summaries in several languages.

The *Mauritius News* (*583 Wandsworth Rd, London SW8 3JD;* ☎ *+44 20 7498 3066;* e *editor@mauritiusnews.co.uk; www.mauritiusnews.co.uk*) is published monthly in the UK for Mauritians living overseas and is also available in France, Belgium, Switzerland, Australia and Canada. A copy is also held in La Librairie Allot in Curepipe. Five thousand copies are produced each month and the cover price is 70p or £15 for an annual subscription in the UK.

The Mauritius Broadcasting Corporation (MBC) (*Louis Pasteur St, Forest Side;* ☎ *674 0475; www.mbc.intnet.mu*) operates six radio stations, which broadcast in English, French, Creole and Hindi. Mauritius's first private radio station, Radio 1, was officially opened on 11 April 2002. The BBC World Service can be received on kHz1575.

Television broadcasting began in Mauritius in 1964 but was not introduced to Rodrigues until 1987. MBC has embraced digital television and operates a total of 17 television channels with programmes in French, English, Hindi, Creole and Chinese. Most hotels in the mid-range, upmarket and luxury categories have satellite channels, including BBC World and CNN.

POST In 1815, it took 17 weeks for news of Napoleon's defeat to reach Port Louis. Today the postal service is quick and reliable. Mail to/from Europe takes about a week, and approximately ten days to/from the US.

A useful local service is Express Delivery, which can result in a letter mailed before 09.00 being delivered to an address within a radius of three miles a few hours later the same day. Two forms have to be filled in for this service.

Most towns and villages (and the airport) have a post office. The general post office in Port Louis is a squat Victorian granite-block building in Quay Street on the waterfront. Adjacent to it is the Mauritius Postal Museum (see page 112).

Interactive kiosks have been installed in many of the island's post offices. These offer local and international phone calls, internet access, email and printing. Prepaid cards to use the kiosks can be purchased at the counters or you can use a credit card.

Mauritius Post offers a poste restante facility for visitors who need a temporary mailing address for their incoming mail.

Post offices are open 08.15–16.00 Monday–Friday and 08.15–11.45 Saturday.

TELEPHONE The International Direct Dialling code to telephone or fax Mauritius or Rodrigues from overseas is 230, followed by a seven-digit number. To call Rodrigues from Mauritius, the code 095 should be used in front of the seven digits.

The telephone system is run by Mauritius Telecom, whose corporate office is at Telecom Tower, Edith Cavell Street, Port Louis (☎ *203 7000; www.mauritiustelecom.com*).

IDD phones are nationwide; just dial 020 followed by the country code, area code and local number. An IDD call to the UK, Australia, France, the USA, South Africa, Italy and Germany from Mauritius costs about Rs15 per minute. Hotels, of course, add their own, often considerable, mark-up to the basic cost.

In recent years, a number of companies have launched prepaid phonecards. These offer very attractive call rates to major destinations and can be used from any phone. For example, using Mauritius Telecom's Sezam Global Prepaid to call the UK, USA, France or South Africa costs Rs5.70 for the first minute and Rs0.095 per second thereafter; for Australia it is Rs5 and R0.0833. Cards are available in Rs75, Rs150 and Rs250 denominations.

Payphones using coins or prepaid phonecards are available throughout Mauritius but are not always in working order. Phonecards are sold in the busier places but do not expect them everywhere. If you have a mobile phone, you should be able to use it in Mauritius as coverage is very good in most areas. You will need to inform your service provider prior to travel. However, coverage is not as good in Rodrigues. The principal mobile network providers are Cellplus (code CELLPLUS-MRU or CELL+) and Emtel (code Emtel or MRU10).

Mauritius Telecom customer service centres can send faxes and have payphones. They are to be found in many towns, including Mahébourg, Rivière du Rempart, Rose Hill, Terre Rouge, Triolet, Vacoas and in Port Mathurin, Rodrigues.

Useful telephone numbers are:

Operator assistance 191
National directory enquiries 150
International directory enquiries 190
International call assistance 192
Tourist information 152

FAX Faxes can be sent through the Mauritius Telecom customer service centres at much less mark-up than that charged by hotels. See above for locations.

INTERNET ACCESS/EMAIL Most mid-range, upmarket and luxury hotels offer internet access (sometimes at a fee), either in your room or in the hotel business centre. Many of the hotels now offer wireless internet, available either in your room or in a given area of the hotel. Some offer this as a free service, whereas others charge around Rs250 per hour.

Mauritius Post is progressively installing interactive kiosks in post offices, which include internet access. Post offices in the larger towns and tourist areas, including Flic en Flac, Grand Baie, Grand Gaube, Trou d'Eau Douce and Mahébourg, have these kiosks. You need to purchase a prepaid card from the post office counter or use a credit card. It costs Rs10 for 15 minutes.

Internet cafés are not widespread through the island and are usually limited to the main towns and tourist areas. Tariffs for email vary but you can expect to pay around Rs35 for 15 minutes or Rs200 for one hour. For those with a laptop, some internet cafés, restaurants and bars offer Wi-Fi.

BUSINESS

Over the past four decades Mauritius has successfully followed an economic strategy of diversification and industrialisation. One element of this was to attract direct foreign investment, with the result that Mauritius has developed good facilities for business. There are direct scheduled flights from Europe, Africa, the Far East and Australasia, a reliable infrastructure and sophisticated communication links. The local workforce is an added advantage with Mauritius enjoying the highest adult literacy rate in Africa and most individuals being fluent in English and French. The success which Mauritius has experienced has been recognised by a number of international organisations. In the World Bank's *Doing Business Survey 2012*, Mauritius was ranked 23 out of 183 countries and first in the sub-Saharan African region.

BUSINESS ASSISTANCE There are a number of organisations that exist both to develop and promote Mauritius as a centre for business and investment, and also to provide support to existing companies.

Mauritius Chamber of Commerce (MCCI) 3 Royal St, Port Louis; ☎ 208 3301; e mcci@intnet.mu; www.mcci.org. Founded in 1850, the MCCI now has 400 members representing a wide spectrum of economic sectors from commerce & industry to banking, insurance, transport & tourism. Affiliated to the MCCI are the Chinese Chamber of Commerce, the Indian Traders' Association & the Mauritius Chamber of Merchants. The MCCI's activities include constant dialogue with government, trade fair & mission organisation, providing commercial information & defending the economic interests of Mauritius through contact with the European Union. There is a consultancy service for small businesses & computer & system analysis courses are held. Every year the MCCI issues an annual report, essential reading for anyone interested in doing business in Mauritius.

Board of Investment (BOI) 10th Fl, 1 Cathedral Sq Bldg, 16 Jules Koenig St, Port Louis; ☎ 203 3800; e contact@investmauritius.com; www.boimauritius.com. The BOI was established in March 2001 as the body responsible for promoting Mauritius as an international investment & business centre. It is also charged with considering investment proposals & issuing investment certificates. In recent years, the BOI has opened offices in Paris & Mumbai. Its website contains useful information on working & living in Mauritius, investment opportunities & legislation relevant to doing business.

International Management (Mauritius) Ltd (IMM) Les Cascades Bldg, Edith Cavell St, Port Louis; ☎ 212 9800; e ds@cimglobalbusiness.com; www.cimglobalbusiness.com. IMM is a member of the CIM Financial Group, which is a wholly owned subsidiary of the Rogers Group, one of the largest & best-known companies in Mauritius, with representation in the UK, Australia, South Africa & Singapore. IMM helps clients to set up, manage & administer offshore entities including companies, trusts & funds & to liaise with the FSC (see below). IMM carries a stock of ready-formed shelf companies & can obtain name approval for new companies within 2 working days. IMM also provides consultancy services to clients wishing to be onshore rather than offshore & provides advice on obtaining residency permits.

Financial Services Commission (FSC) FSC Hse, 54, Cybercity, Ebene; ☎ 403 7000; f 467 7172; e fscmauritius@intnet.mu; www.fscmauritius.org. The FSC was established in 2001 under the Financial Services Development Act & is the independent regulator of non-bank financial services. The FSC licences, regulates & supervises the non-banking offshore sector, while co-ordinating government agencies & private organisations dealing with the sector.

OFFSHORE BUSINESS CENTRE As part of its continuing diversification strategy and in order to sustain economic growth, the government initiated offshore business in Mauritius in 1992. Offshore activities include banking, insurance, fund management, trusteeship of offshore trusts, operational headquarters, international consultancy services, shipping and ship management, and aircraft financing and leasing.

Offshore banks operating in Mauritius include Bank of Baroda, Banque Internationale des Mascareignes, Barclays, Deutsche Bank and Investec.

There are considerable incentives for offshore business activities in Mauritius. Personal and corporate tax rates are only 15% and dividends are tax-free. Furthermore, Mauritius has double taxation agreements with 36 countries and several more currently under negotiation. Those already completed include China, France, Germany, India, Italy, Pakistan, South Africa, Sweden, Singapore and the UK. Offshore companies can take advantage of those treaties and may obtain a certificate of fiscal residence from the Mauritian tax authorities stating that a company is resident in Mauritius for the purpose of tax.

Other financial institutions which support the development of Mauritius as a financial centre include the Development Bank of Mauritius, State Investment Corporation, Mauritius Leasing Company and Stock Exchange of Mauritius.

The **Stock Exchange** (*4th Fl, 1 Cathedral Sq Bldg, 16 Jules Koenig St, Port Louis;* ☎ *212 9541;* f *208 8409,* e *stockex@sem.intnet.mu; www.stockexchangeofmauritius.*

com) was launched in 1989 and is playing an important role in mobilising funds on behalf of companies listed on the Stock Exchange. Similarly, the offshore banking sector is authorised to provide loans in foreign exchange to the EPZ sector at competitive rates. The Mauritius Leasing Company provides financial leases up to 100% of the value of production equipment for a period of three to seven years.

Mauritius is also a freeport which was established in 1992 under the control of the Mauritius Freeport Authority (*10th Fl, 1 Cathedral Sq Bldg, 16 Jules Koenig St, Port Louis;* ☎ *203 3800;* e *contact@investmauritius.com; www.efreeport.com*). The freeport is a regional warehousing, distribution and marketing centre and has seen significant infrastructure development in recent years by private developers. Companies import goods mainly from China, India and Thailand and then re-export to Madagascar, Hong Kong, Singapore and African countries. The principal products re-exported are frozen fish, textiles, machinery and electronic equipment, chemicals, foodstuffs and pharmaceuticals.

However, Mauritius should not be thought of as a tax haven manipulated by 'brass plate' operators. A proven presence locally must be established (for which accountants and company formation firms can be hired) to obtain a tax residence certificate. This enables offshore companies to have an optional zero tax rate and exemption from profit tax, stamp duties and capital gains tax.

BUSINESS ACCOMMODATION Most luxury, upmarket and some upper mid-range hotels cater extremely well for business guests. Business and conference centres provide all the facilities you may need, including secretarial services and assistance with local contacts. Such hotels regularly host conferences and incentive groups. For business accommodation in Port Louis, the **Labourdonnais Waterfront Hotel** (see page 107) and **Le Suffren Hotel & Marina** (see page 107), both near the Caudan Waterfront Complex, are popular.

BUSINESS VISA As with tourist visas, business visitors from certain countries do not require a visa (see page 45). For stays longer than 90 days per calendar year, a work permit is required. Applications are made through the Board of Investment – further information is on its website (*www.boimauritius.com*). For more information see *Red tape*, pages 45–8.

WORKING HOURS For the public sector, working hours are 09.00–16.00 Monday–Friday and 09.00–12.00 Saturday. The number of staff is reduced on Saturdays, so for the sake of your sanity it is advisable to carry out administrative formalities on weekdays.

Private enterprises are usually open 08.30–16.15 Monday–Friday and 09.00–12.00 Saturday.

CULTURAL ETIQUETTE

Reproduced here (translated from the French by the MTPA) is the Code of Ethics for Tourists, since it shows how great is the concern of Mauritians for the right approach to visitors to their country:

You are already most welcome in Mauritius. You'll be even more so if you will readily appreciate that our island …

- considers its most important asset is its people. They are well worth meeting and enjoying a friendly chat with;

- possesses a rich capital of cultures, needs and values which it cherishes more than anything else;
- is ready to give you value for money, but is not prepared to sell its soul for it;
- has wealth of its own, which deserves to be preserved;
- treats all its visitors like VIPs, but does not take kindly to those who overact the part;
- is not all lagoon and languor, and boasts a host of many-splendoured sights;
- considers, without being prudish, that nude when flaunted can be provocative and offensive;
- is not a faraway paradise of unlimited licence;
- takes pride in serving you with a smile and would be grateful for a smile in return;
- and will bare its soul willingly if you will handle it with care.

Beachwear is acceptable in tourist resorts but is less so in local towns and villages. Tourists should dress appropriately when visiting religious buildings (no shorts, miniskirts, etc). It is a good idea for women to carry a light cardigan or shirt and sarong for this purpose. Shoes should be removed when entering temples and mosques, and you may also be asked to remove leather items at some Hindu temples. At mosques you may be required to cover your head. Nudism is not allowed anywhere on the island. Although some female tourists sunbathe topless, it is not encouraged.

Mauritians are generally traditional and conservative – public displays of affection are best avoided, particularly away from the resorts. Pointing at people is considered to be impolite – a general wave in the right direction is more appropriate. When Mauritians walk into a shop or restaurant they greet those present and they appreciate it when visitors do likewise. As you explore Mauritius, be prepared for lots of questions. Mauritians are curious and their motivation is usually simply a desire to learn about your country and practise their language skills.

In recent years there has been an increase in the number of people begging, including children, particularly around the main commercial centres, markets and tourist attractions. Beggars are not usually aggressive and a gentle refusal to a demand for money, accompanied by a smile, is normally accepted immediately.

Although it should not affect travellers, many Mauritian women are the victims of sexual abuse and domestic violence. There is a hotline for reporting incidents of domestic violence (☎ *211 0725*).

TRAVELLING POSITIVELY

I am sure that you will thoroughly enjoy visiting Mauritius and Rodrigues. You may feel that you wish to repay the hospitality you experience by helping the local community in some way. Below is a selection of particularly worthwhile projects and details of how you can lend support.

CARE-CO (RODRIGUES) CARE-Co (Rodrigues), formerly known as Craft Aid Rodrigues, is a wonderful project, giving people with disabilities a vastly improved life and a place in society. I am fortunate enough to have visited the CARE-Co workshop in Rodrigues several times and can assure you that donations are put to excellent use, including hearing aids, family support, educational tools, and equipment for the Gonzague Pierre-Louis Special Learning Centre. For further information, see box *CARE-Co*, page 230.

How you can help

- Buy CARE-Co products. You can also buy the jewellery online at www.beaucoco.co.uk. For UK partners, write to: CARE-Co, Camp du Roi, Rodrigues, Mauritius.
- For coconut jewellery (*bijoux coco*), you can order a full-colour catalogue. The catalogue costs £3 to produce so any contributions are very welcome. The cost of the catalogue will be reimbursed on your first order.
- Cheques or donations can be sent in any major currency. Donate to CARE-Co (Rodrigues), Mauritius Commercial Bank, Port Mathurin; account number 360000940.
- Those who donate any amount exceeding £15 receive direct reports from the Gonzague Pierre-Louis Special Learning Centre.

MAURITIAN WILDLIFE FOUNDATION (MWF) The Mauritian Wildlife Foundation conserves Mauritius's remaining plants and animals.

How you can help

- Book an excursion to Ile aux Aigrettes, which contains the last remnants of native coastal forest and is the probable site of the dodo's extinction. Excursions are offered in most Mauritius hotels and a portion of the tour fees supports wildlife conservation. For further details see page 19.
- Donations are vital to the continuation of the MWF's work. You can donate via the MWF website, or contact the MWF directly (*The Fundraising Manager, Mauritian Wildlife Foundation, Grannum Rd, Vacoas;* ☎ *697 6097;* **f** *697 6512;* **e** *lraffray@mauritian-wildlife.org; www.mauritian-wildlife.org*).
- The MWF is staffed by Mauritians and expatriates, as well as overseas volunteers. To apply for a volunteer placement with the MWF, please consult the website and contact the Conservation Manager (**e** *executive@mauritian-wildlife.org*).

SHOALS RODRIGUES Shoals Rodrigues is a non-governmental organisation (NGO) that studies and monitors the marine ecology of Rodrigues and, through various programmes, promotes marine environmental awareness amongst Rodriguans of all ages thus working towards a sustainable development of the lagoon.

The organisation accepts volunteers from around the world on placements. If this interests you, or you would like to make a donation to the organisation, please contact Jovani Raffin at Shoals Rodrigues, Pointe Monier, Rodrigues (☎ *831 1225;* **e** *admin@shoalsrodrigues.intnet.mu; www.shoals-rodrigues.net*).

See box *Shoals Rodrigues*, pages 204–5.

SMALL & MEDIUM ENTERPRISE AUTHORITY (SMEDA) SMEDA (*www.smeda.mu*) supports and facilitates the development of entrepreneurship in Mauritius and Rodrigues. It promotes the manufacture and sale of handicrafts and by buying goods from SMEDA outlets you ensure part of your payment goes to the Mauritian and Rodriguan artisans who made them. Handicrafts sold in other outlets, including the markets, are often imported. SMEDA craft shops can be found at:

Craft Market Caudan Waterfront, Port Louis; ☎ 210 0139
Plaine Corail Airport Rodrigues; ☎ 832 7653
SMEDA Tourist Exhibition Centre Industrial Zone, Coromandel; ☎ 233 0500
SSR International Airport Plaine Magnien; ☎ 637 4828
Village Artisanal Mahébourg Museum Compound, Mahébourg; ☎ 631 3879

3

Activities

For many visitors, turning over to tan the other side will be the extent of their physical exertion whilst in Mauritius. However, there is plenty to keep the more energetic amused. Activities, watersports in particular, are generally run by the large resort hotels.

SPA TREATMENTS

While most of the luxury, upmarket and mid-range hotels on the island have their own spa (some of which are open to non-hotel residents), those who are staying in smaller establishments without such facilities can take advantage of the growing number of spas opening outside the hotels.

The island's spas are typically operated by well-trained staff and offer a range of massages and treatments. Some even offer comprehensive wellness programmes lasting several days. You can expect to pay around Rs1,500 for a 45-minute facial, Rs1,600 for a 45-minute body massage.

The following are spas which operate outside the hotels:

Surya Coastal Rd, Pereybère; ☎/f 263 1637; e info@spasurya.com; www.mauriweb.com/surya; ⌚ 09.00–20.00 daily. This Ayurvedic spa between Grand Baie & Pereybère offers a range of relaxing massages & treatments. As well as one-off treatments, programmes lasting from 3 days to 3 weeks are available. Yoga classes are available.

Grand Baie Gym & Hydrospa X Club Rd, Grand Baie; ☎ 263 4891; f 263 9291; e info@grandbaiegym.com; www.grandbaiegym.com; ⌚ 06.00–21.00 Mon–Fri, 07.30–19.30 Sat, 09.00–13.00 Sun & public holidays (spa closed Sun. Offers a gym, pool, spa, beauty treatments, weight-loss programmes, hairdresser & a range of group classes, such as martial arts, dance & aerobics. There is a café selling healthy treats. Temporary membership of the gym is from Rs1,398 per week, Rs 690 per day.

Trou aux Biches Beach Spa Coastal Rd, Trou aux Biches; ☎ 256 2012

Emeraude Spa Emeraude Beach Attitude Coastal Rd, Belle Mare; ☎ 401 1400; f 415 1109; www.emeraudebeachhotel.com; A small spa with 2 massage rooms, offering a complete range of massages, body care & facials.

Rituals Bois Rouge/Fond du Sac; ☎ 266 9595; f 266 9029; e rituals@spaconcept.mu; www.rituals.mu; ⌚ 09.00–19.00 Mon–Sat including public holidays. Has 5 treatment rooms & a spacious spa suite for couples with outdoor bath. The spa also includes a hamman, vichy shower & a power plate studio for slimming programmes & muscle toning.

Rituals Level 1, Tower C, Nexteracom Bldg, Ebène; ☎ 468 1800; e ritualsebene@spaconcept.mu; www.rituals.mu; ⌚ 09.00–19.00 Mon–Thu, 09.00–20.00 Fri–Sat.

Om Spa Complex Les Flamboyants, Coastal Rd, Flic en Flac; ☎ 769 2676; e omspa–mu@yahoo.com; ⌚ 09.15–17.30 Tue–Sat, 09.15–13.00 Sun & public holidays. Offers traditional & Ayurvedic massage, plus beauty treatments.

Om Spa Hillside Bldg, Royal Rd, Candos, Quatre Bornes; ☎ 750 2880; ⌚ 09.15–17.30 Tue–Sat; 09.15–13.00 Sun–public holidays

Spa Viva 102 St Jean Rd, Quatre Bornes; ☎ 467 8907; e spaviva@intnet.mu

GOLF

For golfers, there are plenty of courses to choose from, with most located at the upmarket hotels. While some are only open to hotel residents, the following are also open to non-residents on payment of a green fee. Expect to pay around Rs4,000–6,000 for 18 holes at the top courses; children pay approximately half price. Clubs, trolleys and other equipment can usually be hired. The price of club hire varies enormously, but expect to pay Rs500–1,600 for a full set, and around Rs275 for a trolley. A golf cart will cost around Rs1,750 for 18 holes, a caddy around Rs350. Lessons with a golf pro will cost in the region of Rs3,000 per hour. It is advisable, and often a requirement, to book tee-off times.

18-HOLE COURSES

The Anahita Golf Course Beau Champ; ☎ 402 3125; e teetime.anahita@fourseasons.com; www.anahita.mu. An 18-hole, par-72 championship course designed by Ernie Els. The course claims one of the most stunning 18th holes in the world, with its fantastic ocean backdrop. Green fees, including buggy, GPS & practice balls are Rs7,500.

Constance Belle Mare Plage Belle Mare; ☎ 402 2600; f 402 2616; e headpro@bellemareplagehotel.com; www.bellemareplagehotel.com. 2 impressive courses designed with both professional & amateur golfers in mind. The Legend is an 18-hole, par-72 course designed by Hugh Baiocchi, with accuracy on the tree-lined fairways the main challenge. The Links is an 18-hole, par-71 championship course designed by Rodney Wright & British player/commentator Peter Alliss, 3-time winner of the PGA Championship. Only the Links course is open to non-residents of the hotel.

Heritage Golf Club Coastal Rd, Bel Ombre; ☎ 623 5600; f 623 5601; e info@heritagegolfclub.mu; www.heritagegolfclub.mu; ⏲ 07.00–16.00 daily. An 18-hole, par-72 championship course designed by South African architect, Peter Matkovich, plus a 9-hole course. In a stunning setting on 100 acres sandwiched between hills covered with sugarcane & the ocean. The course was designed to be accessible to a wide range of golfers yet be able to host a championship; it therefore offers 5 tee options. Residents of Heritage Le Telfair & Heritage Awali Hotels will have green fees included in their package. The green fees (inc buggy) for others are Rs4,400 for 18 holes & Rs2,700 for 9 holes. Residents of Mauritius can expect rates to be cheaper.

Mauritius Gymkhana Club Suffolk Rd, Vacoas; ☎ 696 1404; f 698 1565; e mgymclub@intnet.mu; www.mgc.intnet.mu. An 18-hole, par-68 course, the oldest on the island & the only private club. The charge of Rs1,500 pp per day includes access to the club, green fees & insurance. Tee-off times must be booked in advance.

Paradis Hotel Le Morne Peninsula; ☎ 401 5050; f 450 5140; e paradis@bchot.com; www.paradis-hotel.com. An 18-hole, par-72 championship course set against the stunning backdrop of Le Morne.

Tamarina Golf Estate & Beach Club Médine Sugar Estate ☎ 401 3000; f 483 0300; e info@tamarinagolf.mu; www.tamarinagolf.mu. Another stunning 18-hole par-72 course, with views of Mt Rempart & the waters of Rivière du Rempart featuring on many of the holes. The course was designed by Rodney Wright & undulates over 206ha. There are 5 tee options. Many of the hotels on the west coast can arrange for guests to play at this course.

Le Touessrok Golf Course Le Touessrok; ☎ 402 7720; e info@letouessrokgolf.mu; www.letouessrokgolf.com; ⏲ 06.30–18.30 daily, last tee-off time for 18 holes is 14.00. An 18-hole, par-72 championship course endorsed by Bernhard Langer & voted tenth in the World's Top One Hundred Courses by *Golf World* magazine. An incredible course on the small offshore island of Ile aux Cerfs – all 18 holes have views of the sea. The 9 lakes & the obvious space limitations of playing on an island make this a challenging course. There is a superb clubhouse, which includes an impressive restaurant & bar with views of the course. Green fees are from Rs6,325 for 18 holes.

9-HOLE COURSES

Le Saint Geran Poste De Flacq; ☎ 401 1888; f 401 1888; e reservations@oneandonlylesaintgeran.com; www.lesaintgeran.oneandonlyresorts.com. A 9-hole, par 33-course, complete with clubhouse & the One&Only Golf Academy.

Le Shandrani Blue Bay; ☎ 603 4343; **f** 637 4313; **e** shandrani@bchot.com; www.shandrani-hotel.com. A 9-hole, par-29 'pitch & putt' course. Only open to residents of Le Shandrani Hotel & Mauritian residents.

HORSE RACING

Horse racing takes place at the **Champ de Mars** racecourse in Port Louis every Saturday during the season from May until the end of November/early December. The highlight is the **Maiden Plate**, which is usually run in September. The sport is very popular amongst Mauritians, primarily because they love to gamble, and the centre of the racecourse fills with stalls, snack bars and bookmakers on race days.

Admission to the course is free but entry to the stands costs Rs120–175, depending on the races being held, and entry to the outside terraces is Rs20. For more information contact the **Mauritius Turf Club**, Eugene Laurent St, Port Louis (☎ *211 2147;* **e** *shanip@mauritiusturfclub.com; www.mauritiusturfclub.com*).

HORSERIDING

Most hotels can arrange horseriding, although it is often cheaper to arrange it directly with the stables. The standards of horses and safety vary and, if you are not offered a riding hat, you should ask for one (you may have to insist). Do check that all the equipment is safe before setting off. Jodhpurs and riding boots are not usually available, so suitable clothing (long trousers and sensible, enclosed shoes) must be worn.

Some hotels offer horseriding along the beach, something many people dream of doing, but don't overlook the inland estates which offer riding – it is a great way to explore the island's interior.

One-hour treks typically costs Rs800–1,200, a half-day ride with lunch around Rs1,800.

Domaine les Pailles Les Guibies, Pailles; ☎ 286 4225; **e** domaine.sales@intnet.mu; www.domainelespailles.net. Located in the centre of the island, just off the motorway between Port Louis & Moka. Well-managed stables run by qualified & experienced staff. Safety is taken seriously – riding hats must be worn & can be borrowed. Medical insurance is included in the rates. The countryside is beautiful & on early-morning rides you are likely to see monkeys. Reservations should be made at least 24hrs in advance.

Domaine de l'Etoile Royal Rd, Moka; ☎ 729 1050; **e** cieletnature@drbc-group.com; www.cieletnature.com. Offers guided rides through the 2,000ha estate.

Horse Riding Delights Mont Choisy Sugar Estate, Grand Baie; ☎ 265 6159/421 1166 (after hours); **e** horseriding@montchoisy.com. A highly professional stables offering rides through the estate's private deer park. It is a fantastic, historic setting, featuring a charming traditional home as the centrepiece. The remains of the sugar factory & lime kilns add to the atmosphere & even the horses enjoy stabling in imposing, old, stone buildings. Riding hats must be worn & can be borrowed on site. There are 17 horses & rides are limited to groups of 10.

Maritim Hotel Turtle Bay, Balaclava; ☎ 204 1000; **f** 204 1020; **e** info.mau@maritim.de; www.maritim.com. Offers riding to hotel residents only, along the beach & through the countryside around the hotel.

La Vieille Cheminée Route Principale, Chamarel; ☎ 483 5249; **f** 483 5250; **e** caroline@lavieillecheminee.com; www.lavieillecheminee.com; ⌚ Mon–Sat. Riding is on the 250ha working farm, through sugarcane, pineapple fields & forest. These have to be the best cared-for horses on the island – owner Caroline adores them. There are 5 horses, most of which are Boerpeds, well suited to the terrain. Rides are tailor-made to suit clients' riding ability.

Refreshingly, they will not lump you in with a group of other riders of varying ability but will instead take you out in your own small group. No horseriding experience necessary; 1hr, 2hr (€45, or €55 with a picnic) & full-day rides are available.

HUNTING

Java deer and wild boar were first brought to Mauritius by the Dutch in 1639. They were introduced in order to assure a supply of fresh meat to the new colony. These new inhabitants flourished and hunting is used to keep their numbers under control and to protect vegetation.

Hunting is a status sport in which wealthy or well-connected Mauritians take part. The traditional season for deer hunting is June to September. Visitors can hunt at the following:

Domaine des 7 Vallees Ligne Barrique, Mare Aux Vacoas; ☎ 631 3336; **f** 631 3198; **e** dchasseur@intnet.mu; domainedes7vallees.com. A 4,000ha estate with more than 2,500 deer & wild boar. Rifles & ammunition are provided.

Kestrel Valley Anse Jonchée, Le Vieux Grand Port; ☎ 634 5011; **f** 631 5261; **e** ledomaine@intnet; www.kestrelvalley.com. Stalking is possible throughout the year. Hunters have the option of using either rifle or bow on the 300ha property.

FOOTBALL

Football is Mauritius's national sport and is played by amateur teams throughout the island. All the main towns have a stadium for local league matches, although unofficial games are played with passion wherever there is a space large enough.

Mauritians are devoted fans of English football and the shirts of English clubs are everywhere. The addiction is perpetuated by the fact that there is more English football on television in Mauritius than in England itself!

The Mauritius Football Association is at Football House, Trianon (☎ *465 2200;* **e** *info@mauritiusfootball.com; www.mfa.mu*).

DEEP-SEA FISHING

Mauritius has some of the best deep-sea fishing waters you can find and people come from all over the world just for that reason. World-record catches off Mauritius include the mako shark, blue shark, skipjack tuna and the renowned blue marlin. In 2010, the island had its best fishing year for around 15 years. Although the west coast is regarded as the best area for deep-sea fishing, the northern and eastern coasts can offer rewarding trips.

If the primary purpose of your visit to Mauritius is fishing, you may want to take account of the following seasons:

Wahoo/hammerhead shark	September–December
Blue marlin/sailfish	November–March
Mako shark	November–April
Yellow fin tuna	March–May
Black marlin, skipjack tuna, barracuda	all year

Most of the deep-sea fishing companies operate modern, well-equipped boats that can reach deep waters in no time at all. The boats usually have three 'fighting' chairs in the stern and outriggers so that three baits can be trolled at a time. Any fish that is caught remains the property of the boat owner, although 'tag and release' is starting to be practised in Mauritius, and is used at Beachcomber hotels.

Almost all hotels will be able to arrange deep-sea fishing and some of the more upmarket ones will have their own fishing centres. Tour operators will also be able to organise trips.

In most cases, the crew of deep-sea fishing boats are incredibly poorly paid, particularly when you consider the amount of skill involved. If you feel that they have looked after you well, a tip will make a lot of difference to them.

The price will vary between boats, but a half-day trip (usually six hours) costs from around Rs15,000 per boat (usually six people) and a full day (usually nine hours) Rs20,000. This will include all the equipment, snacks and drinks.

DEEP-SEA FISHING OPERATORS

Northern Mauritius

Organisation de Pêche du Nord (also known as Corsaire Club) Mont Choisy; ☎ 265 5209; f 265 6267

Sportfisher Sunset Bd Complex, Grand Baie; ☎ 263 8358; ☎/f 263 6309; e sportfisher@orange.mu; www.sportfisher.com

Southern Mauritius

Domaine du Pêcheur Vieux Grand Port; ☎ 634 5097; f 634 5261; e dchasseur@intnet.mu

Western Mauritius

JP Henry Charters Ltd Black River; ☎ 729 0901; f 483 5038; e info@blackriver-mauritius.com; www.blackriver-mauritius.com. Widely acknowledged as the island's best deep-sea fishing operator, this long-established, family-run firm has a superb range of modern boats & knowledgeable crew. They can arrange a trip to suit all levels of experience & ability. Also offers jigging.

La Pirogue Big Game Fishing Flic en Flac; ☎ 453 8054; f 395 1445; e info@lapiroguebiggame.com; www.lapiroguebiggame.com

Morne Anglers Club Black River; ☎ 483 5060; e lmaclub@intnet.mu; www.morneanglers.com

While all deep-sea boats are equipped for anglers, the enthusiast who wants to buy equipment can do so from:

Quay Stores 3 President John F Kennedy St, Port Louis; ☎ 212 1043

Rods & Reels La Preneuse; ☎ 483 5060; e jphenry@intnet.mu

SCUBA DIVING AND SNORKELLING

The reefs off Mauritius offer excellent conditions for scuba diving and snorkelling: warm, crystal-clear water, calm seas and varied marine life. Although pollution, overfishing, poaching in protected waters and the stealing of shells have taken their toll in some areas, there are still numerous excellent dive sites around. Many experts rate them as better than those to be found around the main Seychelles islands or off Sri Lanka.

Although diving can be done throughout the year, June–July is considered by experienced divers to be the least suitable time, on account of the weather.

Most hotels offer snorkelling equipment and trips, either free of charge or for a small fee. Masks, snorkels and flippers can be bought quite cheaply in tourist areas. The lagoons of the northeast and west coasts are good snorkelling areas, as are the waters around Trou aux Biches and Blue Bay.

There are plenty of scuba-diving centres on the island. Instructors should have Professional Association of Diving Instructors (PADI) or Confédération des Activités Subaquatiques (CMAS) qualifications, which ensure that they have undergone professional training and rigorous safety tuition. Many of the dive centres belong to the Mauritian Scuba Diving Association, based at Route Royale in Beau Bassin (☎ *454 0011;* e *msda@intnet.mu; www.msda.mu*).

Prices start at around Rs900 for a single dive including all equipment. For a course of five dives, expect to pay about Rs7,000–9,000 with equipment, and about Rs16,500-17,500 for ten dives. For beginners, many dive centres offer a resort course, which consists of a lesson in a pool followed by a sea dive and these cost around Rs1,650–1,800. Rates do not usually include insurance, so if your travel insurance does not cover diving, you would be advised to pay the additional amount, usually about Rs150–250, for medical insurance. Many dive centres also offer PADI courses and will be able to provide more information and prices.

The Mauritius Underwater Group (MUG, for short), has given rise to the Mauritian Marine Conservation Society, a group actively engaged in conservation of the reef environment. MUG is linked to the Professional Diving Association and to the International Diving Confederation. Members meet on Tuesday and Sunday nights over beers, discussing their latest dive experiences. Visitors are welcome; a week's temporary membership costs about Rs150, but you must be a qualified diver to join. Temporary members can hire equipment from MUG, which is considerably cheaper than at many of the big resorts. The clubhouse is open most days. It is near Phoenix, just off the main Port Louis–Curepipe road.

Divers should not touch any seashells underwater and should remember that it is illegal to remove shells from the sea.

DIVING CENTRES The following list is not exhaustive but covers most of the diving operators. All of those listed are members of the Mauritius Scuba Diving Association.

Northern Mauritius

Atlantis Diving Centre Trou aux Biches; ☎ 265 7172; e vb@atlantisdiving.info
Blue Water Diving Le Corsaire, Trou aux Biches; ☎/f 265 7186; e hugues@bluewaterdivingcenter.com; www.bluewaterdivingcenter.com
Cap Divers Paradise Cove Hotel, Anse La Raie; ☎ 204 4000; e bluesdiving@intnet.mu; www.bluesdiving.net
Diving World Le Canonnier, Le Victoria & Le Mauricia hotels; ☎ 263 1225; e divwor@intnet.mu
Easydive Diving Centre Pointe aux Piments & Le Morne; ☎ 204 3481; e easydive@intnet.mu; www.easydivemauritius.com
Merville Diving Centre Merville Beach Hotel, Grand Baie; ☎ 209 2200
Mon Plaisir Diving Centre Villas Mon Plaisir, Pointe aux Piments; ☎ 261 7980; e villasmp@intnet.mu
Nautilus Trou aux Biches Hotel; ☎ 265 5495; e ricana@intnet.mu; www.nautilusdivers.com
Ocean Spirit Pereybère; ☎ 263 4468; e gringospirit@yahoo.com
Turtle Bay Nautics Maritim Hotel, Turtle Bay; ☎ 204 1000; e judexcassadin@hotmail.com

Eastern Mauritius

East Coast Diving One&Only Le St Géran, Poste de Flacq; ☎ 401 1688; e marilyn@intnet.mu
Pierre Sport Diving Le Touessrok Hotel, Trou d'Eau Douce; ☎ 402 7400; e psdltd@intnet.mu
Sea Fan Diving Centre Belle Mare; ☎ 431 1069; e explorer@intnet.mu

Southern Mauritius

Coral Dive Centre Blue Bay; ☎ 631 9603; e contact@coraldiving.com; www.coraldiving.com
Shandrani Diving Le Shandrani Hotel, Blue Bay; ☎ 603 4343; e divwor@intnet.mu
Southern Adventures Le Telfair Hotel, Bel Ombre; ☎ 263 1225; e divwor@intnet.mu

Western Mauritius

Abyss Morcellement Anna, Flic en Flac; ☎ 4538836; f 453 8109; e tof110@yahoo.fr
Diving Style Centre Klondike Hotel, Flic en Flac; ☎ 452 2235; e giosteen007@yahoo.com
Exploration Sous-marine Villas Caroline, Flic en Flac; ☎ 453 8450; e szalay@intnet.mu; www.pierre-szalay.com

Island Diving Hotel Indian Resorts, Le Morne; ☎ 728 9127; e pascalava@yahoo.com
Sofitel Imperial Diving Centre Sofitel Imperial Hotel, Wolmar; ☎ 453 8700; e sofitel@intnet.mu
Sun Divers La Pirogue Hotel, Wolmar; ☎ 453 8441; e sundiver@intnet.mu; www.sundiversmauritius.com

DIVE SITES The Mascarenes are volcanic isles, so much of the terrain you see whilst diving consists of rock formations like overhangs, walls and caverns. Abundant and diverse corals colonise such formations – some 200 species are said to be present.

The best dive spots include Le Morne in the southwest, the west coast off Flic en Flac and north to Trou aux Biches and Grand Baie. In the southeast, diving is good off Vieux Grand Port. Some of the very best diving, however, is around the northern offshore islets, like Coin de Mire.

The southwest coast Most of the sites in this area are about 30 minutes by boat from the shore and they are all on the seaward side of the barrier reef, where marine life is abundant. You can explore sites like **Needle Hole**, **Jim's Place** and **Anthony**, all of which are shallow dives (12–18m). Highlights include magnificent corals and swarms of fish like sergeant-majors, goldies and surgeonfish, and all boast excellent visibility with exceptional conditions for underwater photography. A deeper dive is **Michel's Place**, at 38m, which features flat corals, lots of clownfish, and triggerfish. Apparently green and hawksbill turtles are also common.

Another deep one is the drop-off called **Cliff** (average depth 22m) opposite Le Paradis Hotel. Conditions can be quite badly affected by a strong tidal surge. Moray eels are seen on most dives.

One of the most beautiful and popular sites in the area is known as the **Japanese Gardens**. At 14–28m, they are so named because of the diversity of corals in the coral garden there. There is very little current and visibility is good. Abundant fish include parrotfish, pipefish and ghost morays.

A flat, horseshoe-shaped reef well known to divers is **Casiers** (average depth 26m), where shoals of barracuda, kingfish and surgeonfish are usually encountered. Tidal influence is a little more pronounced and visibility can be adversely affected by suspensions in the water.

The west coast Ideal for beginners is **Aquarium**, a rocky reef area that harbours the likes of angelfish, clownfish and butterflyfish plus lots of wire coral. The dive starts at 7m and descends to 18m. Visibility is usually good but watch out for poisonous stonefish. This is the site where night dives are conducted for experienced folk.

For some cave diving, try the **Cathedral** (18–27m). The dive takes place on the drop-off, enters a chamber and then a huge underwater cave, in which lionfish, squirrelfish, kingfish and crayfish are often seen. Light filters into the cave through a crack in the ceiling creating the impression of being in a cathedral. Experienced divers rate the site highly.

Also for experienced divers is **Manioc**, a deep dive on rock faces, which begins at 32m and descends to 45m. Game fish, including kingfish, tuna and barracuda, often make an appearance. Impressive emperor angelfish abound and white-tipped reef sharks are occasionally seen. Divers are almost guaranteed sharks, rays, tuna and barracuda at **Rempart L'Herbe**, also known as **Shark Place**. The sharks are typically grey reef sharks, although hammerheads occasionally visit the area. It's a deep dive (42–54m) on a pinnacle with steep slopes covered in pink and black coral.

Off the coast opposite the Villas Caroline is the ***Kei Sei 113***, a barge which was deliberately sunk in 1988 to form an artificial reef at a depth of 40m. It is partly covered with corals and residents typically include giant moray eels, red snappers and hawkfish.

The north coast The Trou aux Biches area is some 300m from a large reef. This is great for snorkelling, as there's little in the way of surf. From the northwest, you could visit about ten different sites, of which **Coin de Mire** and **Flat Island** are among the best. It takes about 90 minutes to reach Coin de Mire, where the rock walls drop to about 100m. The sites around the island are suitable only for experienced divers because of the tides and currents. Average depth is 10–20m and the dives are usually drift dives. Barracuda, dogtooth tunny, large parrotfish, wahoo and white-tipped shark are common and there are lots of oyster clams, cowries and hermit crabs. To the north of Coin de Mire is Flat Island, but because of strong currents and rough seas this is dived only during the summer and only by highly experienced divers. On the southwest side of Flat Island, beneath Pigeon Rock, is the famous **Shark Pit**, where divers can watch sharks swirling around the pit for oxygen from the waves crashing above.

There are also a number of sites off Grand Baie. One of the best is **Tortoise** (13m), which lies just 1.5km offshore. The flat reefs are home to a variety of colourful tropical fish, moray eels, octopus, stonefish and lionfish. **Coral Gardens** (average depth 15m), halfway between Grand Baie and Coin de Mire, consists of coral banks between which are sand gullies. The coral and the visibility are generally good, and the site is popular for night dives. Commonly seen are squirrelfish, trumpetfish and goldies. **Night dives** off **Grand Baie** are said to be incredible. At night, colours on the reefs are far brighter than by day and a mass of marine animals emerge from their daytime hideouts.

A good option for novices is the **Pereybère** site, at only 12m, where tropical reef fish abound. Divers may see octopus, moray eels and stonefish.

In 1987, the ***Stella Maru***, a Japanese trawler, was deliberately sunk 1.5km west of Trou aux Biches by the Mauritius Marine Conservation Society. The ship lay on its side until 1992 when a cyclone forced it upright, where it remains. Stonefish, spotted morays and green morays are often seen. This dive, which reaches a depth of 26m, is highly recommended by experienced divers.

The east coast A bit wilder and rather less affected by mass tourism than the other regions, the east coast offers some excellent diving. Drift dives are typical in the area. At **The Pass** (8–25m) you can drift-dive through the 'pass' in the barrier reef, admiring the psychedelic tapestries of coral and reef fishes. Turtles and sharks are often seen.

Lobster Canyon (25m), approximately 1.6km offshore, takes divers through a short cave full of crayfish, along a wall and into a canyon, where sharks and eagle-rays may be seen. At times visibility is limited to 10m owing to high levels of plankton.

OTHER UNDERSEA EXPERIENCES

There are plenty of alternatives to diving and snorkelling for those who want a glimpse of underwater life. Most hotels offer trips in **glass-bottom boats**, which sail over the reef. This is a good way for children to see and learn about marine life.

UNDERSEA WALKS Undersea walks involve plodding along the seabed wearing a lead belt, whilst air is pumped into your helmet from the boat above. It is advertised as being suitable for children over seven years of age. Sadly, this activity is damaging the marine environment and thousands of pairs of feet per year gradually destroy what lies beneath them. If you are still interested, walks usually last 20–25 minutes and cost around Rs1,000 per person. The main operator is **Captain Nemo's Undersea Walk** (*Coastal Rd, Grand Baie; ☎ 263 7819; e captainnemo@intnet.mu*).

SUBMERSIBLES Submersibles are another option suitable for children and adults alike (although not claustrophobics!).

Blue Safari Submarine Coastal Rd, Grand Baie; ☎ 263 3333; **f** 263 3334; **e** bluesaf@intnet.mu; www.blue-safari.com. A 15min boat trip takes you to the holding ship, from where you board the submarine for the 40min dive. The submarine can hold 10 people & reaches a depth of 35m. There you can see the coral reef, a shipwreck & tropical fish. The submarine departs every hour 08.30–16.30 in summer & 08.30–15.30 in winter. You need to allow about 2hrs for the whole experience, including time to complete the paperwork, etc. Adult/child Rs3,900/2,300. Reservation essential. You can book exclusive use of a 5-person submarine for a special meal or even a wedding (Rs25,000). Blue Safari Submarine also offers 30min rides on 2-seater, James Bond-style, submersible scooters. You can pilot the scooter yourself & it is simple to operate. The driver & passenger can talk to each other during the dive. You dive in a group of 5 scooters, accompanied by 2 divers for safety. You must be over 16 years of age to drive a scooter & over 12 years to be a passenger. As with the submarine, the experience takes around 2hrs, departing every hour 09.00–16.00 in summer & 09.00–1500 in winter. Double scooter Rs5,000 (2 people), Rs3,900 (1 person).

Le Nessee Centre Sport Nautique, Sunset Bd, Grand Baie; ☎ 263 8017; **f** 263 5500; **e** info@centrenautique.com. A yellow semi-submersible boat with underwater viewing. Departures at 10.00, 12.30 & 14.30. Trips last 1½hrs & include 30mins of snorkelling. Adult/child Rs800/450.

SAILING

Conditions for sailing are usually excellent. The large beach hotels have small sailing dinghies which guests can use within the waters of the lagoon.

Catamaran cruises are popular and full-day trips usually include snorkelling and lunch. They cost around Rs2,000. Sadly, some crews, particularly in the touristy north of the island, are unaware of the destruction that their actions cause to the marine environment. Many drop their anchors on the coral in the same area each day and it has become such a big business that as many as half a dozen catamarans will be anchored in the same place at the same time for snorkelling. A cruise from the west coast is likely to be more relaxing and less crowded than one from the north and JP Henry Charters are one of the best, most environmentally aware operators on the island. A more expensive but far more pleasurable experience is to charter a yacht.

Grand Baie Yacht Club (☎ *263 8568*), near the Veranda Hotel, has a temporary membership scheme for visitors. **Magic Sails** in Cap Malheureux specialises in catamaran cruises, including overnight cruises, which allow you to sleep on board for one or two nights. For contact details, see below.

YACHT/CATAMARAN CHARTER AND CRUISES

Catsail Ltd Coastal Rd, Pointe aux Piments; ☎/**f** 261 1724; **e** is.advent@intnet.mu

Centre Sport Nautique Sunset Bd, Grand Baie; ☎ 263 8017; **f** 263 7479

Croisières Australes Coastal Rd, Grand Baie; ☎ 263 1669; **e** cruise@c-australes.com

Cruises Océane (Croisières Océanes) Coastal Rd, Trou d'Eau Douce; ☎ 480 2767 **f** 480 1615; **e** oceane@intent.mu

Gamboro Yacht Charters Coastal Rd, Pointe aux Canonniers; ☎ 263 7808; **e** bowenint@intnet.mu

JP Henry Charters Ltd Black River; ☎ 729 0901; e info@blackriver-mauritius.com; www.blackriver-mauritius.com

Magic Sails Cap Malheureux; ☎ 262 7188; e sales@magicsails.mu

Yacht Charters Coastal Rd, Grand Baie; ☎ 263 8395; e yacht@bow.intnet.mu

DOLPHIN-WATCHING CRUISES Dolphin-watching cruises depart early in the morning (around 07.00) and usually last a couple of hours. The west coast is the best for dolphins and most hotels can organise these excursions. Many of the operators encourage you to jump into the water and snorkel near the dolphins once you have found them, allowing you to watch these graceful creatures underwater. It can get a little frantic and crowded if several operators find the same pod of dolphins, and remember the smaller the boat you go on, the fewer people there will be. The dolphins have not been tamed in any way and there is no guarantee you will find them on a particular outing. It is reassuring to know they are free to go if the mood takes them. A dolphin-watching cruise typically costs around Rs1,400.

JP Henry Charters Ltd Black River; ☎ 729 0901; e info@blackriver-mauritius.com; www.blackriver-mauritius.com. Will only take a max of 6 people, which is good for both the dolphins & the people.

WINDSURFING

The popularity of windsurfing and the ideal conditions for it have resulted in many competitions, including World Championships, being held in Mauritius. The majority of hotels in the luxury, upmarket and mid-range categories will have windsurfers available for their guests and many will also offer instruction (usually payable). Sailing or reef shoes should be worn to prevent coral cuts.

KITESURFING

One of the newer sights to be seen in the waters off Mauritius is kitesurfers, who skim along the water on a small board while attached to a large kite and float into the air intermittently, performing a variety of impressive mid-air acrobatics. It is advisable not to attempt kitesurfing unless you are a good swimmer, and have some experience of surfing, windsurfing, paragliding and kiting. The best spots for kitesurfing are Le Morne (not for novices) and La Prairie (good for beginners) in the southwest, Belle Mare and Pointe d'Esny in the east, Cap Malheureux and Grand Gaube in the north. Kitesurfing schools are found at Kuxville at Cap Malheureux (see page 130), Le Shandrani Hotel in Blue Bay (see page 150) and at Indian Resort at Le Morne Peninsula (see page 166).

Kitesurf Paradise Ltd Trou d'Éau Douce ☎ 743 4298; e mauritius.kitesurf@gmail.com; www.mauritius-kitesurf.com. Kitesurfing school with IKO-qualified instructors.

WATER SKIING

With its calm lagoons, Mauritius is an ideal location for water skiing, particularly for beginners. At luxury, upmarket and some of the better mid-range hotels, water skiing is free, although it may be limited. Other mid-range hotels may offer water skiing at a fee. If your hotel does not offer water skiing, it can be arranged through an independent watersports company.

HIKING AND ADVENTURE SPORTS

While you can arrange hiking excursions independently, it is probably better to do so through a reputable local tour operator, such as White Sand Tours or Mauritours, or one of the companies that specialise in hiking. Speak to your operator about places like the Black River Gorges National Park, Combo Forest or Bassin Blanc – all of which have great potential as hiking venues. (For information on hiking in the Black River Gorges National Park, see pages 12–14.)

Many of the island's best hiking spots are found in nature reserves and permission from the Forestry Department (*675 4966*) is required to enter these. Their offices are next to the botanical gardens in Curepipe. They can also provide maps. A growing number of the island's private estates or *domaines* are opening up to the public and typically offer **guided nature walks** and **hiking**, as well as **quad biking** and **4x4 tours** (see page 96).

As you would for hiking anywhere, be sure to take appropriate footwear, water, rain gear, suncream and protective wear for the tropical sun. The Mauritian mountains really don't require any special skills and you need only an average level of fitness to attempt them. However, to avoid the risk of getting lost, it's advisable to contact your tour operator about arranging a local guide for you.

There are some impressive **caves** in Mauritius, many of which were used as shelters by runaway slaves or by pirates in days gone by, but these should never be explored alone. Again, speak to a local tour operator if you wish to visit any of them. They should be able to arrange transport, entry permission and an experienced local guide.

Adventure sports, like **canyoning**, **climbing**, **ziplining (flying-fox)**, **mountain biking** and **off-road driving**, are not as big in Mauritius as they are in Réunion. Nevertheless, there are a number of companies that offer these types of activities:

Incentive Partners Ltd Domaine de Chazal Chamouny; 422 3117; e info@incentivepartnersltd.com; www.incentivepartnersltd.com. Offers a range of land- & water-based activities including ziplining.

Kart Loisir La Joliette, Petite Rivière; 233 2223; f 233 2225; e kartloisir@intnet.mu; from 09.00 daily. Offers go-karting & quad biking. Go-karting from Rs300 pp for 10mins, quad biking from Rs1,380 pp for 1hr.

Otelair 696 6750; e otelair@yahoo.com; www.otelair.com. Offers hiking, canyoning, rock climbing, mountain biking & kayaking. Team-building days can be arranged.

Parc Aventure Chamarel; 234 4533; f 234 5866; e parcaventure@intnet.mu; www.parc-aventure-chamarel.com; 09.00–16.00 Thu–Tue. An elaborate obstacle course through 12ha of forest, with rope bridges, climbing nets, etc. The course takes around 2½hrs to complete. Wear long trousers, trainers, gloves & insect repellent. There is a minimum age requirement of 6 years. Also on offer are mountain biking, hiking, kayaking & canyoning. Reservation necessary.

Trekking Ile Maurice Black River; 785 6177; e yan@trekkingilemaurice.com; www.trekkingilemaurice.com. Offering guided hikes & trail running around the south west of the island.

Vertical World PO Box 289, Curepipe; 251 1107; e vertical@verticalworldltd.com; www.verticalworldltd.com. Specialises in hiking, canyoning & rock climbing.

Yemaya 752 0046/754 4234; e adventure@yemayaadventures.com; www.yemayaadventures.com. Specialises in hiking, mountain biking & sea kayaking. Tickets are sold at HABIT clothing shops across the island.

The following private estates offer activities such as hiking, mountain biking, quad biking and 4x4 tours. For more information see the *What to see* section of the relevant chapter.

EASTERN MAURITIUS

Kestrel Valley Anse Jonchée, Le Vieux Grand Port; ☎ 634 5011; **f** 631 5261; **e** ledomaine@intnet; www.kestrelvalley.com

SOUTHERN MAURITIUS

Frederica Nature Reserve Bel Ombre; ☎ 623 5522; **e** info@domainedebelombre.mu; www.domainedebelombre.mu

Vallée des Couleurs Chemin Grenier; ☎ 251 8666; **e** info@lavalleedescouleurs.com; www.lavalleedescouleurs.com; ⌚ 09.00–16.30 daily; adult/child Rs150/75. About 10km north of Souillac lies this multi-coloured exposed area of earth, similar to the Seven Coloured Earths of Chamarel. It is far less visited than Chamarel & claims to have 23 colours of earth as opposed to 7. It is within a pleasant forested area with good views of the coast. A walking circuit takes you past areas of endemic plants, a few animals (deer, ducks, tortoises, etc) & waterfalls, as well as the coloured earth. Quad biking, ziplining & pedaloes are available for the energetic. There is a café on site.

WESTERN MAURITIUS

Casela Nature & Leisure Park Royal Rd, Cascavelle; ☎/**f** 452 2828; **e** casela@intnet.mu; www.caselayemen.mu. A safari-park-style area, with resident zebra, ostrich, deer, wild pigs & giant tortoises, can be explored in a safari bus (Rs85 for 1hr), on a Segway (Rs1,100 for 1hr) or on a quad bike (Rs2,160 for 1hr). It is the zebra which make this worthwhile. Casela also offers ziplining, consisting of 11 lines which criss-cross the ravines surrounding the sugarcane fields (Rs880 for 1hr, Rs2,420 for a full day) & canyoning (Rs2,810 for a full day). New to Casela is the adventure trail (Via Ferrata circuit). It involves climbing, trekking & ziplining in either a half-day (Rs1,710) or a full-day circuit (Rs2,310).

CENTRAL MAURITIUS

Domaine les Pailles Les Guibies, Pailles; ☎ 286 4225; **f** 286 4226; **e** domaine.sales@intnet.mu; www.domainelespailles.net

Domaine de l'Etoile Royal Rd, Moka; ☎ 729 1050; **e** resa.cieletnature@drbc-group.com; www.cieletnature.com

BEACHCOMBER 'SPORT AND NATURE' Beachcomber's Le Shandrani Hotel runs a daily programme of sports and nature activities which cater for all levels of fitness. It's open to non-residents and bookings can be made via Le Shandrani (☎ *603 4540*).

The programmes, which last either a full day or half day, are an ideal way to see beautiful parts of the island, whilst doing some exercise. Some of the programmes are suitable for children.

SKYDIVING

Skydive Austral Riviere du Rempart; ☎ 499 5551; **e** info@skydivemauritius.com; www.skydivemauritius.com. Offers tandem skydiving from 10,000ft. Prices from Rs11,500.

Part Two

MAURITIUS AND ITS DEPENDENCIES

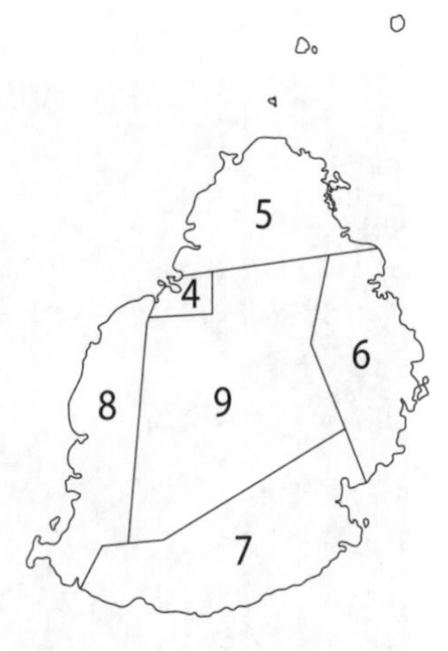

4

Port Louis

Port Louis looks best from the sea. It is a chaotic but charming city that combines new buildings with old, contrasting with the spires and peaks of the threadbare mountain range behind. In the centre is Pouce, poking 812m into the sky like Jack Horner's thumb. On its left is Pieter Both, a peak named after a Dutch notable who drowned in the bay, distinguished by the boulder balanced precariously on its tip. To the right the city's boundary extends along a switchback of daunting crags: Snail Rock, Goat Rock, Spear Grass Peak and Quoin Bluff. The sheer sides of Signal Mountain (323m) dominate the western flank of the town.

Solid Victorian warehouses and modern concrete towers, like sawn-off skyscrapers, crowd the flat expanse of the city. Houses claim the land right up to the foothills of Pouce Valley, leaving open spaces only on the plain of the Champ de Mars and the isolated 86m-high hill in the middle of the city, on which perches the battered vulture of a fort called the Citadel. Tall royal palms have somehow survived the city's growth to form an avenue of greenery leading from the waterfront up the centre of the Place S Bissoondoyal (formerly Place d'Armes) to Government House.

Port Louis is the seat of government and the most populous town in Mauritius, with some 150,000 inhabitants. The French pronunciation is *Por' Louie*, whilst the English is *Port Loo-iss*, while others compromise with *Port Loo-ee*.

HISTORY The city was first settled by the Dutch but was named Port Louis in 1722 by French settlers. The name was chosen either to honour the then young King Louis XV (1715–74) or to link the settlement with Port Louis in Brittany from which, at that time, French seamen sailed for India. When Mahé de Labourdonnais arrived here in 1735, dense vegetation covered the area, except for land cleared between where the theatre now stands and the Chien de Plomb at the bayside, which was the ships' watering point.

There were 60 mud huts thatched with palm leaf in this clearing, the homes of the French East India Company staff. Soldiers lived in makeshift shelters of straw. The stream running down from Pouce Mountain formed a swampy gully dividing the plain in two. The right side, as viewed from the sea, became the residential area while the left was given over to commerce.

A statue of Mahé de Labourdonnais, erected in 1859, stands overlooking the harbour he created. Nearby, a stone set into the patch of lawn at the foot of the palm trees commemorates the 250th anniversary of his founding of Port Louis.

AROUND TOWN

THE CITADEL Viewed from the Citadel hill, the layout of the city is uncomplicated: rectangular street blocks as far as the eye can see. A French post existed here in the

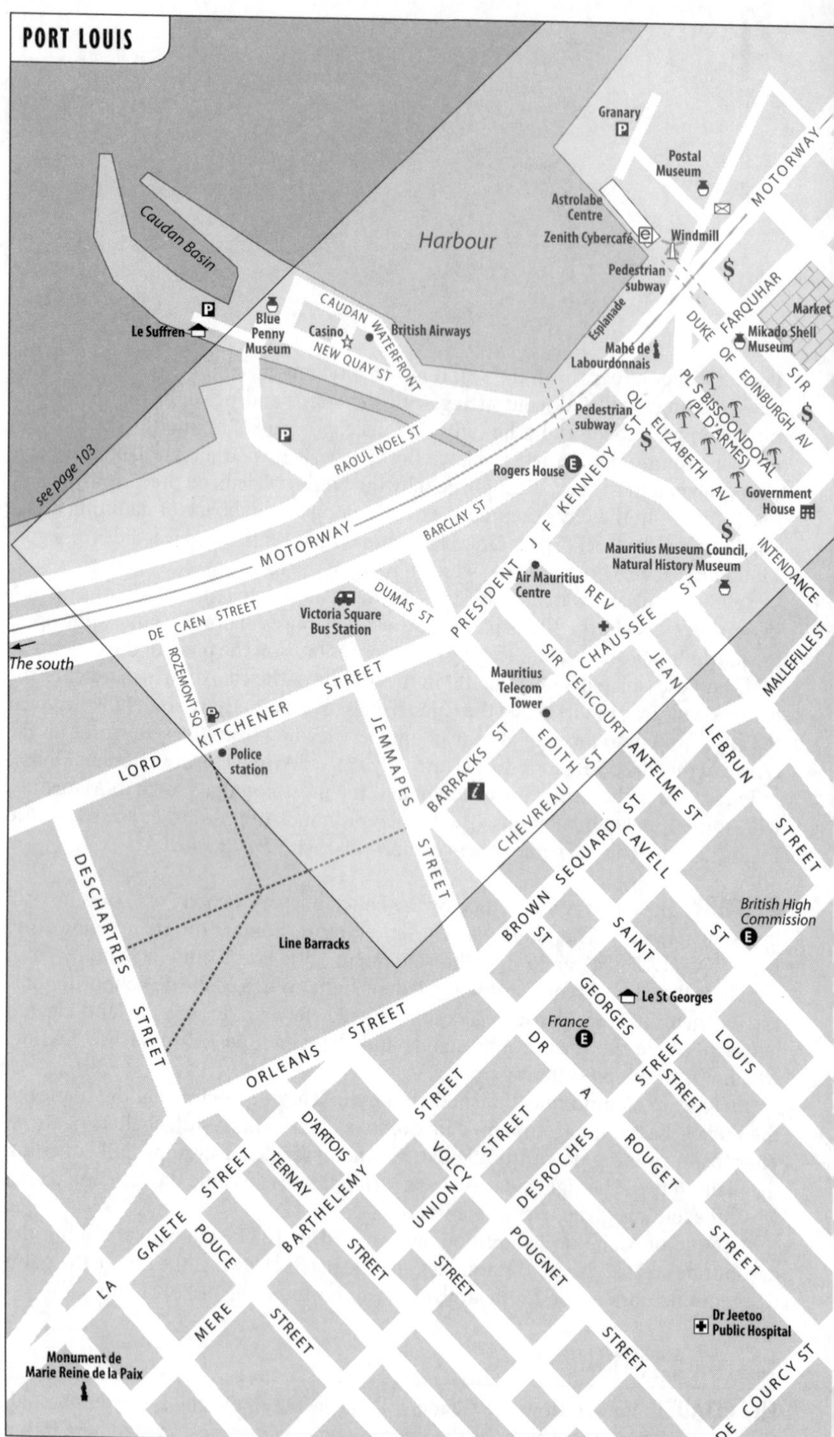
PORT LOUIS
Harbour
Caudan Basin
Granary
Postal Museum
Astrolabe Centre
Zenith Cybercafé
Windmill
Pedestrian subway
Esplanade
Market
Mikado Shell Museum
Mahé de Labourdonnais
Le Suffren
Blue Penny Museum
Casino
British Airways
CAUDAN WATERFRONT
NEW QUAY ST
RAOUL NOEL ST
see page 103
MOTORWAY
DUKE OF EDINBURGH AV
FARQUHAR
SIR
PL S BISSOONDOYAL (PL D'ARMES)
QU ELIZABETH AV
Pedestrian subway
Rogers House
PRESIDENT J F KENNEDY ST
Government House
INTENDANCE
Mauritius Museum Council, Natural History Museum
BARCLAY ST
DUMAS ST
Air Mauritius Centre
REV JEAN
CHAUSSEE ST
MALLEFILLE ST
DE CAEN STREET
Victoria Square Bus Station
The south
ROZEMONT SQ
LORD KITCHENER STREET
SIR CELICOURT ANTELME ST
Mauritius Telecom Tower
Police station
JEMMAPES STREET
BARRACKS ST
EDITH CAVELL ST
LEBRUN STREET
CHEVREAU ST
BROWN SEQUARD ST
DESCHARTRES STREET
Line Barracks
British High Commission
SAINT GEORGES STREET
Le St Georges
France
DR A
LOUIS STREET
ORLEANS STREET
D'ARTOIS STREET
VOLCY STREET
UNION STREET
TERNAY
BARTHELEMY STREET
DESROCHES
ROUGET STREET
LA GAIETE STREET
POUCE
MERE STREET
POUGNET STREET
Dr Jeetoo Public Hospital
DE COURCY ST
Monument de Marie Reine de la Paix

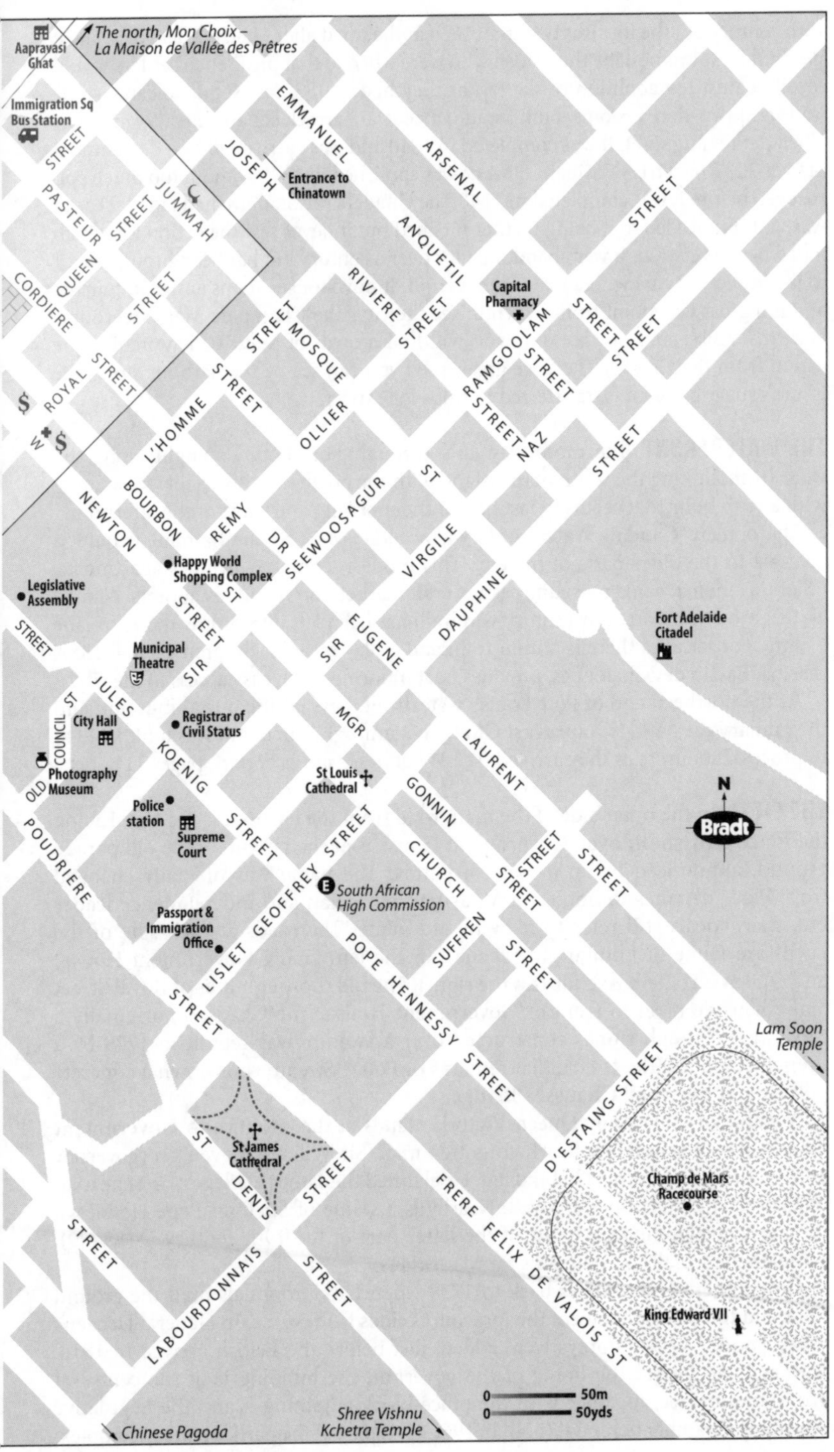
The north, Mon Choix – La Maison de Vallée des Prêtres
Aapravasi Ghat
Immigration Sq Bus Station
Entrance to Chinatown
Capital Pharmacy
Happy World Shopping Complex
Legislative Assembly
Municipal Theatre
City Hall
Registrar of Civil Status
Photography Museum
Police station
Supreme Court
St Louis Cathedral
South African High Commission
Passport & Immigration Office
Fort Adelaide Citadel
St James Cathedral
Champ de Mars Racecourse
King Edward VII
Lam Soon Temple
Chinese Pagoda
Shree Vishnu Kchetra Temple
EMMANUEL
ARSENAL
JOSEPH
ANQUETIL
RIVIERE
MOSQUE
RAMGOOLAM
NAZ
OLLIER
DR SEEWOOSAGUR ST
VIRGILE
DAUPHINE
SIR EUGENE
MGR
LAURENT
GONNIN
CHURCH
POPE HENNESSY STREET
SUFFREN
LISLET GEOFFREY STREET
D'ESTAING STREET
FRERE FELIX DE VALOIS ST
LABOURDONNAIS
ST DENIS
POUDRIERE
SIR JULES KOENIG STREET
OLD COUNCIL ST
NEWTON
BOURBON
REMY
L'HOMME
ROYAL
CORDIERE
QUEEN
PASTEUR
JUMMAH
STREET
N
Bradt
0 50m
0 50yds

18th century but the fort was begun in 1834 and named after Queen Adelaide, wife of William IV. It was built by the British who were worried that the French settlers would revolt against the abolition of slavery, as they had in 1832. Its solid, volcanic stone walls and two-tiered rooms, built around a central barrack square, are a formidable, albeit depressing sight. It was completed in 1840 and was garrisoned by a detachment of over 200 Royal Irish Fusiliers. Slavery was abolished in 1835 without too much ado so, even before it was completed in 1840, the Citadel's raison d'être had faded. Fear of war with France led to it being further fortified but it never saw the action for which it had been prepared. It was abandoned for over a century but has been brought back to life in recent years with a major renovation. It now houses shops aimed at tourists and is a great viewpoint from which to see the city. The Champ de Mars racecourse is clearly visible and on race days you will find crowds of Mauritians watching the action from the Citadel. The large green shed you can see by the harbour stores the island's sugar before it is transferred to ships for export.

THE WATERFRONT The motorway cuts through Port Louis, straight along the waterfront, linking the south of the island with the north. It is invariably slow going with a rush hour that seems to last half of the morning and most of the afternoon.

The opulent **Caudan Waterfront** (*www.caudan.com*) by the harbour is quite a contrast to the older parts of the city. This modern complex includes apartments, offices, a cinema, bank, museum, casino, craft market, shops and restaurants. Amidst all this modernity, an 18th-century windmill has been left intact, near the Astrolabe Centre. For families there is a mini train and a play area for children aged 4–15. A marina, Bassin des Chaloupes, provides boat moorings with easy access to the city.

At the northern end of Port Louis's waterfront, beyond the postal museum and the granary car park, is **Aapravasi Ghat**. This immigration depot was built in 1849 to process labourers as they arrived (see *What to see in Port Louis*, pages 111–12).

THE CITY On the other side of the main road from the harbour is the city. Facing the **Place S Bissoondoyal**, Government House is at the far end of the old parade ground, announced by an avenue of palms. The name was officially changed from Place d'Armes to honour a Mauritian politician and independence leader but many locals still refer to it by its old name. The roads at each side of the lawns are Duke of Edinburgh Avenue (on the left, facing Government House) and Queen Elizabeth Avenue (on the right). The old thoroughfares of Royal Street and Chaussée meet in front of Government House. The Chaussée, originally a causeway of rough stones constructed over a swamp, was rebuilt in 1779 by a French engineer. The trickle that remains of Pouce Stream runs down a concrete gully under the small **Chaussée Bridge**.

A statue of a matronly Queen Victoria stands at the entrance to **Government House**, with a statue of a nearly forgotten man, Sir William Stevenson (governor 1857–63), in the forecourt behind her. He claimed the same privileges for Mauritian officials that British ones enjoyed. Nearby is a statue of Sir John Pope Hennessy, the most outstanding governor of the latter part of the 19th century (1883–89), sympathetic to calls of Mauritius for Mauritians.

Government House dates back to 1738 when Labourdonnais built the ground floor and the wings that form the forecourt's sides from stone. In General Decaen's time, wooden upper storeys were added, just before the British arrived in 1810. Although no longer the home of the governor, the building is at the centre of government since, together with the office block adjoining it and the Legislative Assembly Chamber behind it (built in 1965), it is part of the parliamentary complex.

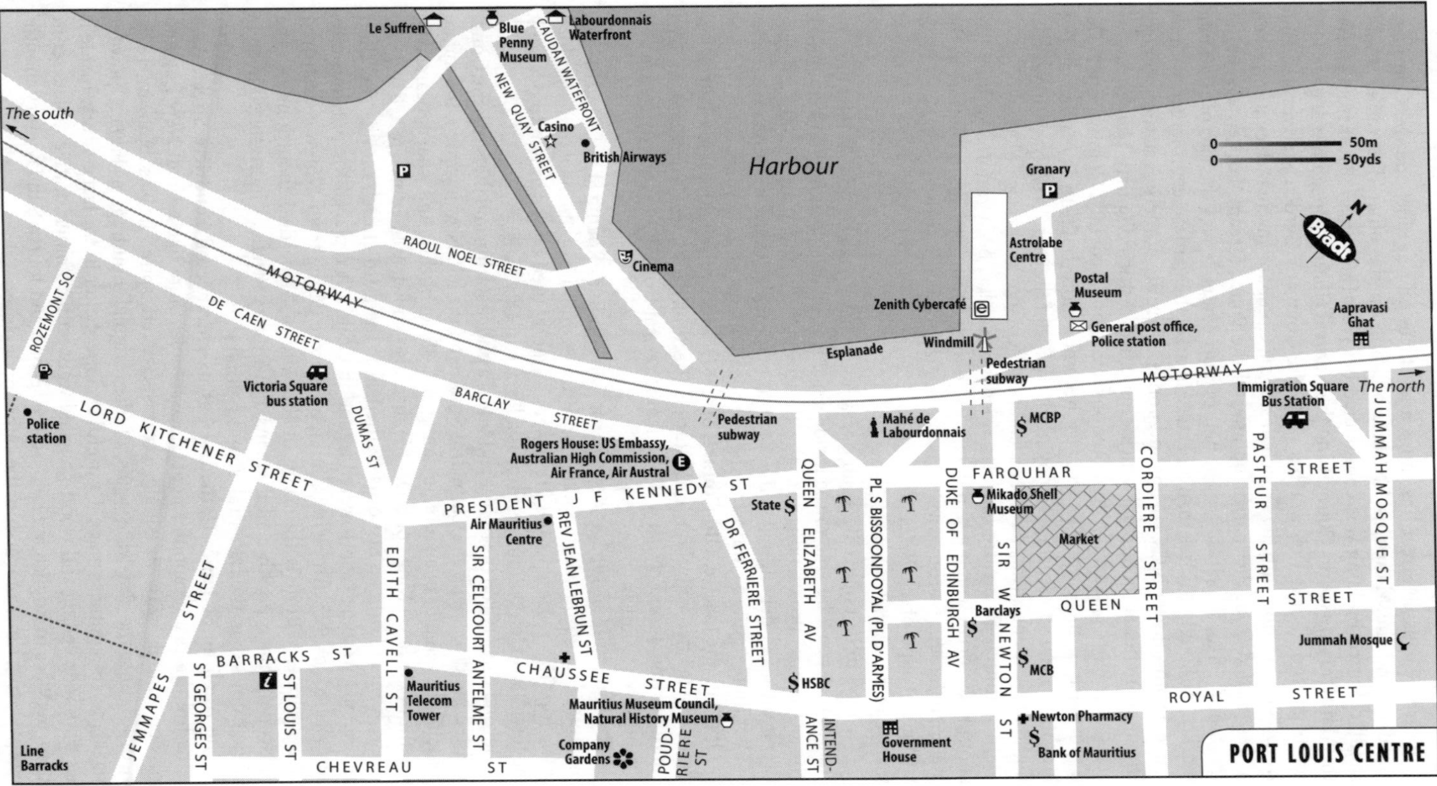
PORT LOUIS CENTRE
Harbour
0 50m
0 50yds
Bradt
N
The south
The north
Le Suffren
Blue Penny Museum
Labourdonnais Waterfront
CAUDAN WATEFRONT
NEW QUAY STREET
Casino
British Airways
P
RAOUL NOEL STREET
Cinema
MOTORWAY
DE CAEN STREET
ROZEMONT SQ
Police station
Victoria Square bus station
LORD KITCHENER STREET
DUMAS ST
BARCLAY STREET
Rogers House: US Embassy, Australian High Commission, Air France, Air Austral
Pedestrian subway
Esplanade
Zenith Cybercafé
Windmill
Astrolabe Centre
Granary
Postal Museum
General post office, Police station
Aapravasi Ghat
Immigration Square Bus Station
PRESIDENT J F KENNEDY ST
Air Mauritius Centre
REV JEAN LEBRUN ST
DR FERRIERE STREET
State
QUEEN ELIZABETH AV
PL S BISSOONDOYAL (PL D'ARMES)
Mahé de Labourdonnais
DUKE OF EDINBURGH AV
SIR W NEWTON ST
FARQUHAR STREET
MCBP
Mikado Shell Museum
Market
CORDIERE STREET
PASTEUR STREET
JUMMAH MOSQUE ST
QUEEN STREET
Jummah Mosque
ROYAL STREET
Barclays
MCB
Newton Pharmacy
Bank of Mauritius
Government House
INTENDANCE ST
HSBC
CHAUSSEE STREET
Mauritius Museum Council, Natural History Museum
POUDRIERE ST
Company Gardens
SIR CELICOURT ANTELME ST
EDITH CAVELL ST
Mauritius Telecom Tower
BARRACKS ST
ST LOUIS ST
ST GEORGES ST
JEMMAPES STREET
CHEVREAU ST
Line Barracks

Nearby Chaussée Street has shops and offices on one side, and the **Company Gardens** and the **Mauritius Institute** building on the other. The rather grand, sandy coloured building was constructed between 1880 and 1884; it now houses the **Mauritius Museums Council** and the **Natural History Museum** (see page 112) on its ground floor is well worth a visit. The Company Gardens derives its name from its connection with the French East India Company in the 18th century, when it was created from the marshland around the Pouce Stream. For ten years after the fire of 1816, which destroyed half of Port Louis, it was the site of the town market. Although it is less than a hectare in area, the garden seems larger, with its narrow paths, flower beds, shrubs and ponds. There are numerous statues, some of which are national monuments, including one of Adrien d'Epinay, planter, lawyer and campaigner against the abolition of slavery, and Léoville l'Homme, poet. The importance of the garden as the city becomes more built-up is evident and at lunchtimes you will see locals enjoying the shade of the impressive banyan trees. At night, the gardens attract a rather seedier element and are best avoided.

The **Municipal Theatre** on Jules Koenig Street has been restored to look like another Victorian warehouse but with its colonnaded front a sharp contrast to the mediocre buildings around it. It was opened in 1822 with a production by a Creole amateur troupe of *La Partie de Chasse de Henri IV* and is said to be the oldest theatre in the southern hemisphere.

The days of its popularity as an opera house have passed and it is now only by chance that you'll be able to see inside since it is invariably closed and shuttered. The occasional productions that the theatre puts on today are mostly amateur Creole musicals, depending on the rhythms of local *séga* music to emphasise stories of liberation – quite a contrast to the European operas of its heyday.

Opposite the theatre, **Old Council Street** (Vieux Conseil Street) is an attractive cobbled lane lined with shops and eateries. The **Souk du Vieux Conseil** has modern boutiques and a food court; it is a welcome retreat from the hectic city centre and a good spot for lunch.

City Hall, built in 1962, is a few yards away on Jules Koenig Street. Outside is a concrete block tower without walls, with steps spiralling up its interior to the clock at the top. This represents the fire towers formerly used by watchmen to overlook the town's wooden buildings. There is a library in City Hall.

Beyond City Hall on the right-hand side is a **police station** and the **Supreme Court** (a listed building), with the **Cathedral Square** on the left. Now a garden, the square contains the remains of a fountain dating to 1788, an obelisk, and what appears to be a statue of medieval King Louis IX of France, also known as St Louis, erected in 1896.

The Roman Catholic **St Louis Cathedral** is the third church on this site. Built in 1932 in awesome twin-towered imitation Gothic, it replaced the previous one, demolished in 1925. An earlier church on the site dating from 1756 was destroyed by a cyclone. Within is the tomb of the wife of Mahé de Labourdonnais. The **Episcopal Palace**, a 19th-century mansion with airy verandas more suited in style to the tropics than the cathedral, stands behind it.

The Anglican **St James Cathedral** has its entrance on Poudrière Street. As a cathedral this is a disappointment, since it looks more like a small New England mission church with its single, cream-plastered spire. It was built in 1828, incorporating the 2m-wide walls of the original building, a French powder magazine. Its stoutness made it a useful cyclone shelter in the last century. Inside it has a wooden ceiling and wood-panelled walls with commemorative tablets set in them. Services in English are held on the second and fourth Sunday every month; except during times of worship, the cathedral is closed.

There are some small wooden mansions from the French period in the block between Poudrière Street and St George Street. There are also a large number of embassies and high commissions in the area. (For details see *Chapter 3, Embassies and consulates*, page 49).

At the end of Pope Hennessy Street is the **Champ de Mars Racecourse**. People still promenade here as they did in the 19th century, although joggers and children have taken the place of crinolined ladies and their beaux. There is a statue of King Edward VII in the centre and the tomb of Malartic (governor 1792–1800) at the far end. This is a striking setting for racing with a backdrop of gaunt mountains like a natural amphitheatre for the drama played out on the plain. (See also pages 87 and 105.)

The Champ de Mars has been a racecourse since the Mauritius Turf Club was founded by an English army officer, Colonel Edward Draper, in 1812, making it the oldest racecourse in the southern hemisphere and one of the oldest in the world. Draper oversaw the building of the track on what was then the army parade ground. At first, only horses belonging to the English garrison were ridden by young army officers, until the French settlers showed interest and entered their own horses. By 1837, horse racing was firmly established. Today the Mauritians' love of gambling ensures that races are always well attended.

On the north side of the Champ de Mars, at the corner of Dr Eugene Laurent and Corneille streets, is the **Lam Soon Temple** (🕘 *06.00–14.00 daily*), which is actually two temples. The newer one, built in the 19th century, is in the foreground, a curious adaptation of British colonial architecture to Buddhist needs, the columns of the veranda painted red and gold and the interior devoted to worship. The centre altar is extravagantly carved while the interior walls are simple.

The ancient custodian makes a point of telling visitors the temple is independently run and depends on offerings for its upkeep, indicating the offertory box. Once you've put something in, you're invited to walk through to the more dilapidated wooden temple beyond. This temple doubles as a commercial enterprise, selling not only incense sticks and flags but also soft drinks and pickles. Business, according to the old custodian, is brisk on race days.

The **Shree Vishnu Kchetra Temple** is in a tranquil location in St Denis Street, parallel to the Champ de Mars, one block away. It serves Hindus and Tamils. The older Hindu temple is simply laid out with bright paintings and statues and places for offerings of coconuts and incense. Worshippers toll the bell to wake the gods.

In the same compound is a new Tamil temple and an ancient, sacred peepul tree (*Ficus religiosa*, known as a 'bo-tree' in Sri Lanka). The temple is closed for five minutes at midnight when it is considered a dangerous time to disturb the gods.

The **Jummah Mosque**, with its 'wedding cake' architecture, is, unsurprisingly, on Jummah Mosque Street. The mosque extends an entire block, its white towers and friezes imposing grace on the clutter of lock-up shops beneath its balconies. Its huge teak doors are priceless, ornately carved and inlaid with ivory. The muezzin's call from the minaret before dawn is the signal not only for prayer but for the cacophony of the city to erupt. This mosque, built in the 1850s and extended over the years, is the island's most impressive and opened when Muslims formed an exclusive merchant group in the neighbourhood. A group of Muslim merchants banded together and bought two properties and built the mosque on the site. Visitors can enter the inner courtyard outside prayer times. In the courtyard is an old badamia tree, older than the mosque itself.

Near the mosque in Royal Street is **Chinatown**, a clutter of stores, warehouses and restaurants, its shops bright with the plastic and chrome knick-knacks much in demand by modern-day Mauritians. The location of Chinatown so near to the mosque has caused some tension between the two communities, which at its height resulted in the burning down of the Chinese-run Amicale Casino.

Between Farquhar and Queen streets is Port Louis **market**, selling fruit and vegetables, meat, fish, clothing and handicrafts. The wrought-iron work above the entrance has the initials VR (Victoria Regina) intertwined in it. In 2004, the market buildings were completely renovated. As a result, the market lost some of its grubby charm and a greater proportion of it (mostly the first floor) was taken over by souvenir stalls. It may not feel as 'authentic' as it once did but it is still an exciting, bustling place, which offers an insight into the everyday lives of Mauritians. (See also, *Shopping*, page 110.)

At the southern end of the city, along Jemmapes Street from the Victoria Square bus station are the **Line Barracks**, whose foundations go back to the early days of the French occupation, when they housed 6,000 men, as well as rebel colonists after the French Revolution. A police station, the police headquarters and the traffic branch are there now.

Signal Mountain between Plaine Lauzon and the city marks the western end of the mountain range around Port Louis. A beacon used to be kept alight on its summit at night, and flags hoisted there during the day as a guide for approaching vessels. At the foot of the mountain is the **Marie Reine de la Paix monument** and its pleasant gardens, where the first Mauritian bishop was consecrated in 1989. The Edward VII Boulevard provides a spectacular view of the city and harbour.

Sainte-Croix, a suburb of Port Louis nestling below Long Mountain, is famous for its church, a modern-style replacement of the original, with its shrine containing the body of **Père Laval** (see page 113).

GETTING THERE AND AWAY

BY BUS The **Immigration Square bus station** is at the end of Pasteur Street, still known by city denizens as Hospital Street, because of the hospital that was in the square. It is difficult to know which bus queue to join since there are limited signs and no enquiry office, but other passengers are helpful. Buses from here serve the north of the island and include an express service to Grand Baie.

The **Victoria Square bus station** is off Dumas Street. Buses leave throughout the day bound for central towns, such as Curepipe, from where you can get buses to the south (including the airport) and west. The long, dilapidated, two-storey building used to be the main railway station and offices.

BY CAR Apart from the traffic jams, it's easy to get to Port Louis by **car** as the motorway goes right through the city. Parking zones exist in Port Louis, for which you have to purchase tickets in advance from a petrol station (see page 63) if you intend to park on the street. The most convenient car park for the centre, market and waterfront is **The Granary**, on the harbour side of the highway. The Granary allows you to buy a ticket on the spot and avoid the hassle of the parking zone system. In 2011, the rates were Rs25 for the first two hours, and Rs25 for every additional hour or part thereof. The Granary is a short walk from the Astrolabe Centre and Port Louis Waterfront (the esplanade), and from there a pedestrian subway leads to the city. You can also park at the Caudan Waterfront, near the Blue Penny Museum.

BY TAXI Taxis are more expensive in Port Louis than elsewhere and the attitude of the drivers is predatory. Be sure to negotiate a reasonable fare. There is a taxi stand at Place S Bissoondoyal (Place d'Armes) and one at the Victoria Square bus station.

TOURIST INFORMATION

There is a **tourist office** (☎ *210 1545;* **e** *info@mtpa.mauritius.net; www.tourism-mauritius.mu;* ⌚ *09.00–16.00 Mon–Fri*) on the fourth floor of Victoria House in St Louis Street. They can't make arrangements for you but they have a healthy supply of leaflets and basic information. The Caudan Waterfront complex has its own small information centre at Barkly Wharf.

For the location of embassies and high commissions, see page 49.

WHERE TO STAY

UPMARKET

Labourdonnais Waterfront Hotel (109 rooms) Caudan Waterfront; ☎ 202 4000; **f** 202 4040; **e** info@labourdonnais.com; www.labourdonnais.com. By far the most elegant accommodation in the city, overlooking the harbour. Caters largely for business guests. En-suite rooms have AC, TV, phone, internet connection, minibar & safe. Wi-Fi is free in the public areas. Facilities include 3 restaurants, a pool, casino, health centre, business centre, elaborate conference facilities & free shuttle bus to Ebène Cyber City. **$$$$**

Le Suffren Hotel & Marina (100 rooms) Caudan Waterfront; ☎ 202 4900; **f** 202 4999; **e** info@lesuffrenhotel.com; www.lesuffrenhotel.com. Sister hotel of the Labourdonnais, this hotel also targets business travellers & overlooks the harbour. It has a nautical theme; the rooms have either harbour or mountain views & are equipped with AC, TV, phone, safe, minibar & tea/coffee facilities. Wi-Fi is free in the public areas. There is a manmade beach area, pool, restaurant & bar, & guests can use the restaurants at the Labourdonnais. Not suitable for disabled guests as there is no lift. **$$$$**

MID RANGE

Le Saint Georges (82 rooms) 19 St Georges St; ☎ 211 2581; **f** 211 0885; **e** reservation@saintgeorgeshotel-mu.com; www.saintgeorgeshotel-mu.com. Centrally located hotel popular with businesspeople. Comfortable en-suite rooms with AC, TV, phone, safe & minibar. There is a restaurant & a pool. **$$$**

Mon Choix – La Maison de Vallée des Prêtres (4 rooms) Senneville; ☎ 217 0505; **e** dodoisland@intnet.mu; www.ecomauritius.com. Friendly guesthouse in a quiet location in the hills above Port Louis. You will need a car to reach this one but there is a lot to be said for its peaceful setting with views of the valley towards the capital. The 4 rooms (2 en suite) are nicely furnished & have minibar & tea/coffee facilities. There is a kitchen, pleasant dining & sitting rooms, a pool & large garden. Breakfast is provided & dinner is available on request. The owners make a real effort to run an eco-friendly guesthouse. Not suitable for children. **$$$**

WHERE TO EAT

Cheap eateries abound: snack bars, *samoussas* sellers and even fast-food outlets. There are restaurants scattered throughout the Port Louis Waterfront area and a food court in the Caudan Waterfront with numerous outlets serving snacks, ice creams and fast food.

Le Courtyard Cnr St Louis & Chevreau sts; ☎ 210 0810; ⌚ for lunch Mon–Sat, for dinner Thu/Fri. Cuisine: European. As the name suggests, tables are arranged in an attractive courtyard, providing a welcome retreat from the city streets. A sophisticated restaurant & very popular. Reservation recommended. **$$$$**

Café du Vieux Conseil Old Council St; ☎ 211 0393; ⌚ for lunch Mon–Fri. Cuisine: French, Creole. In a quiet, restored cobbled lane, opposite the theatre. Al fresco dining & an almost Mediterranean atmosphere. Excellent food & service. The menu lists only a few dishes & is changed frequently, but there is sufficient variety, including vegetarian specialities & Australian beef. **$$$**

✕ **Carri Poulé** Duke of Edinburgh Av; ☎ 212 4883; ⏲ for lunch Mon–Sat, for dinner Fri/Sat. Cuisine: Indian, Creole. A sophisticated restaurant serving well-prepared Indian dishes with a Mauritian touch, not the stereotyped offerings of European 'Indian' restaurants. **$$$**

✕ **Le Capitaine** Caudan Waterfront; ☎ 213 0038; ⏲ for lunch & dinner daily. Cuisine: seafood, Creole, Indian. A good location by Port Louis's standards, overlooking the harbour. Superb seafood & good service. Seafood platter for 2 from Rs3,000. **$$$**

✕ **Namasté** Caudan Waterfront; ☎ 211 6710; ⏲ for lunch & dinner Mon–Sat, for dinner Sun. Cuisine: north Indian. Fine cuisine in the historic setting of the old observatory building. The décor is fascinating, with the original walls of the observatory adding atmosphere. The food is authentic & delicious, carefully prepared with spices imported from India. Live Indian music on Fri, Sat & Sun evenings. Reservation recommended. **$$$**

✕ **Beer & Spice** Astrolabe Centre; ☎ 208 0351; ⏲ 09.00–01.00 daily. Cuisine: Italian, Creole. At the city end of the Astrolabe Centre. Informal dining on a terrace overlooking the harbour. Friendly service & excellent pizzas, plenty of options for vegetarians. The owner is happy to prepare dishes not on the menu for those with special dietary requirements. The large portions make this good value for Port Louis. **$$**

✕ **Black Steer** Grill House, Caudan Waterfront; ☎ 211 9147; ⏲ 12.00–23.30 Mon–Sat, 12.00–14.30 & 18.00–23.00 Sun. Happy hour 17.30–19.00. Cuisine: grills. A large, modern American-style steakhouse. Popular for its Sun lunch buffet. **$$**

✕ **La Bonne Marmite** 18 Sir William Newton St; ☎ 212 2403; ⏲ for lunch Mon–Fri. Cuisine: Creole, French, Indian, Chinese. A café, pub & restaurant in one. The café is on the ground floor behind which is the Rocking Boat Pub (see *Nightlife & entertainment* below). The restaurant is upstairs in a grand room with *table d'hôte* & à la carte menus. Reservation recommended. **$$**

✕ **La Flore Mauricienne** 10 Intendance St; ☎ 212 2200; ⏲ 08.30–17.00 Mon–Fri, 08.30–14.00 Sat. Cuisine: French, Creole. This well-known bar, café & restaurant first opened in 1848. There is a smart open-air terrace, a buffet restaurant & an elegant dining room. The accent is on European cuisine & clientele. French pastries are a speciality.

PHILATELISTS' HEAVEN

Mauritius holds a special place in the affections of stamp collectors since the first stamps issued there are now among the greatest rarities in the philatelic world. In 1993, at an auction in Zurich, a buyer paid the equivalent of US$3.3 million for 'the crown jewel of philately', an envelope – 'the Bordeaux cover' – with two stamps on it, sent from Mauritius to a Bordeaux wine importer in 1847. This is the only cover known with the two values (one penny and twopence) of the Mauritius 'Post Office' series.

Mauritius was the first British colony to use adhesive postage stamps, and was only the fifth country in the world to issue stamps, in 1847. The first 1,000 postage stamps (500 at a penny value and 500 at twopence) were produced by Joseph Barnard, a watchmaker and jeweller of Port Louis, who engraved the dies on a copper plate and laboriously printed the stamps one at a time, direct from the engraving. Despite his skills as a craftsman, the results were very primitive compared with the famous penny blacks of Britain. They also contained an error. Instead of the words POST PAID he engraved POST OFFICE in the left-hand margin.

The stamps were released on 21 September 1847. On the same day, Lady Gomm, the governor's wife, used a considerable number of the orange-red one-penny value on invitations to a ball at Le Réduit. Only 15 one-penny stamps and 12 of the blue twopenny value are believed still to exist.

Barnard was instructed to produce further stamps in 1848. To facilitate printing, he engraved each stamp 12 times on the plate. The result was that no two stamps

Patronised by regulars, so some feel it has a cliquish atmosphere. $$

Le Bistrot du Port Astrolabe Centre, Caudan Waterfront; 210 6586; 08.30–late Mon–Sat. Cuisine: French, Creole. Casual dining on the waterfront; has an extensive menu. $$

First Restaurant Cnr Royal & Corderie sts; 212 0685; for lunch & dinner Tue–Sun. Cuisine: Chinese. Tasty, reasonably priced dishes in pleasant surroundings. Regarded as one of the best Chinese restaurants on the island; Sun lunch yum-cha is popular. Try the roast duck. $

NIGHTLIFE AND ENTERTAINMENT

In 1722, there were 125 drinking shops known to the police in Port Louis. The French governor, Ternay, found this excessive and closed all but 30, eventually reducing that number to four. Since then, they have seen a resurgence and there is now a plentiful supply.

The Caudan Waterfront is the place to go of an evening, with its restaurants, bars, cinema and casino. **Le Patio** (*213 5353*) is a modern café/wine bar at the Dias Pier section of the waterfront complex. Very popular is the **Shooters Sports Pub and Grill** (*210 9737*) on the first floor in the Observatory. A restaurant during the day, it transforms into a bar/nightclub in the evenings with live bands playing on the weekends. **Latitude 20 Cocktail Bar** at the Labourdonnais Waterfront Hotel is a popular watering hole. Its sister hotel, Suffren Hotel and Marina, has two good bars: **Spinnakers**, where sports matches are played on large plasma screens, and **On the Rocks,** a trendy lounge bar. The **Rocking Boat Pub** at La Bonne Marmite Restaurant has been skilfully designed to project the ambience of a European drinking den with low lighting, dark décor and a cocktail bar with stools for the steadier drinkers.

The **Caudan Waterfront Casino** (*210 2191*) is open daily except Monday. The slot machines are open 10.00–02.00 and the tables 20.00–04.00.

were identical, although they had the correct words POST PAID on them. These stamps, which were in use until 1859, are also highly prized among collectors.

Another fascinating rarity turned up in a philatelist's collection in 1994. Two twopenny blue stamps postmarked 9 November 1859 revealed spelling errors. One shows 'Mauritius', the other 'Mauritus'. The issue appears to have been withdrawn from circulation the same day. Being unique, the stamps are priceless.

After 1859, mass-produced stamps, printed in Britain, were issued. However, stocks of frequently used stamps were often exhausted before fresh supplies arrived from London. Consequently, the lower-value stamps were surcharged, creating more stamps of interest to collectors.

The first pillar boxes were erected in Port Louis in the early 1860s. Special date stamps for mail collected from them were used from 1885 to 1926 in Port Louis, Beau Bassin, Curepipe, Mahébourg and Rose Hill. Examples of such cancellations are rare.

Other historical events have also given Mauritius stamps special value. Airmail services were launched to Réunion in 1933 and to Rodrigues in 1972. The first use of aerogrammes in Mauritius was on 27 December 1944.

Today, used postage stamps and first-day covers are sold in shops selling tourist souvenirs in Port Louis and Curepipe, and stamps can be bought in the General Post Office and at the Postal Museum in Port Louis.

CINEMA **Star cinema** (☎ *211 5361*) in the Caudan Waterfront Complex has three screens showing international films.

THEATRE The tourist office can provide information about productions at the theatre on Sir William Newton Street, or try contacting the theatre direct (☎ *212* 1090), or the island's ticket office, Otayo (☎ *466 9999;* e *info@otayo.com; www.otayo.com*).

SHOPPING

Shops in Port Louis are typically open 09.30–17.00 Monday–Friday and 09.00–12.00 Saturday. A few open on Sunday morning.

The **market** between Queen and Farquhar streets is open 06.00–18.00 Monday–Saturday and 06.00–12.00 Sunday. There is a fantastically colourful fruit and vegetable market, which contains two intriguing *tisane* (herbal remedy) stalls. Both have been there for generations and claim to offer a cure for every imaginable ailment, from rheumatism to cellulite, with their unassuming bundles of twigs and leaves. Their cures have become so well known that they now take orders from overseas via email. On the opposite side of Farquhar Street is the meat and fish market.

Above the fruit and vegetable market, on the first floor, is the place for souvenirs, although you may have to look hard to find items made in Mauritius. The colourful bags, wooden objects and spices are largely imported from Madagascar or Africa. Pickpockets are said to operate around the market and, although the atmosphere isn't threatening, the tenacious sales techniques can be rather tiresome. You are expected to barter.

The **Caudan Waterfront** (☎ *211 6560*) contains a vast range of shops: jewellery, fashion, carpets, crafts and souvenirs, some of which are duty free. Opening hours are 09.30–17.30 Monday–Saturday, 09.30–12.30 Sunday, and there is an information kiosk in the Barkly Wharf building. It's relatively hassle-free shopping with no real hard sell, although prices may be a little elevated. On the ground floor of Barkly Wharf, **Bookcourt** (☎ *211 9146*) is a well-stocked bookshop which has English-language titles on the Mascarene Islands, including this one. There is a **craft market** within the Caudan Waterfront, not far from the casino, where you can see artisans at work. The **Mauritius Glass Gallery** has an outlet here (☎ *210 1181*). Spices, sugar products, tea, art and locally produced essential oils are also on sale.

The **Small Enterprise To Help Development For All (SEHDA)** has a shop in the Astrolabe Centre and in the Caudan Waterfront craft market, where you can be sure of buying locally made products (see also *Travelling positively*, pages 83–4).

On weekend evenings there is an open-air market at the Caudan Waterfront, called **Le Souk**.

Air Mauritius has its own building, **Air Mauritius Centre**, in President John F Kennedy Street. The smart arcade of shops on the ground floor is known as **Paille en Queue** shopping centre. Reservations and reconfirmations for Air Mauritius flights can be made in the ground-floor ticket office. (For further details of this and other airline offices, see pages 51–2).

OTHER PRACTICALITIES

MONEY AND BANKING Branches of the major **banks**, including HSBC (*Pl d'Armes;* ☎ *203 8333*) and State Bank of Mauritius (*1 Queen Elizabeth Av;* ☎ *202 1111*). Mauritius Commercial Bank (*9–15 Sir William Newton St;* ☎ *202 5000*) and Barclays (*Sir William Newton St;* ☎ *207 1800*) can be found a short distance from the harbour.

COMMUNICATIONS The **General Post Office** (☎ *208 2851;* ⏲ *08.15–11.15 & 12.00–16.00 Mon–Fri, 08.00–11.45 Sat*) and the Postal Museum are near the harbour at the end of Sir William Newton Street.

Payphones can be found around the Caudan Waterfront.

Internet access

Zenith Cybercafé Astrolabe Bldg, Port Louis Waterfront; ☎ 213 2435; ⏲ 09.00–22.00 Mon–Sat, 10.00–16.00 Sun. Also offers Wi-Fi.

MEDICAL CARE The **Dr Jeetoo Public Hospital** (☎ *212 3201*) is on Volcy Pougnet Street. There are several pharmacies, including the well-stocked **Newton Pharmacy** (*10 Sir William Newton St;* ☎ *208 7048*) and **Capital Pharmacy** (*50 Sir Seewoosagur Ramgoolam St;* ☎ *216 9000*).

WHAT TO DO IN PORT LOUIS

HORSE RACING At the historic Champ de Mars racecourse. The season lasts from May until the end of November/early December, with race days usually every Saturday. A memorable day out but expect lively crowds as Mauritians love their racing. For more information, see *Chapter 3, Horse racing*, page 87.

ART The **Galérie d'Art de Port Louis** in Mallefille Street (☎ *208 0318*) holds occasional exhibitions of local artists' work. There also are several commercial art galleries in Port Louis, including **Didus** (☎ *210 7438*) in the Caudan Waterfront, which has a permanent exhibition, sells works by local artists and can arrange shipment.

HIKING The mountains around Port Louis provide superb views of the city and surrounding countryside. Hiking **Le Pouce** (812m) takes around three hours (return) and the path is well signed. It is relatively easy but steep in parts, particularly towards the summit of the thumb from which it takes its name. You can tackle the walk either from near Moka or from Port Louis. Coming from Port Louis along the M2 take the second exit marked Moka and the first left marked Eureka. Around 100m before Eureka turn right and you will see a track marked 'Le Pouce'. Alternatively buses from Port Louis's Victoria Square bus station to Nouvelle Découverte will drop you off at the start of the track. Local adventure sports companies, such as Otelair (☎ *696 6750; www.otelair.com*) and Yemaya (☎ *752 0046; www.yemayaadventures.com*) offer guided hikes of Le Pouce.

Scaling **Pieter Both** (820m) is rather more strenuous and requires a guide; the summit demands climbing gear. Vertical World (☎ *697 5430;* **e** *vertical@verticalworldltd.com; www.verticalworldltd.com*) offers guided hikes – allow a full day.

WHAT TO SEE IN PORT LOUIS

AAPRAVASI GHAT (*1 Quay St;* ☎ *217 2481; www.aapravasighat.org;* ⏲ *09.00–16.00 Mon–Sat; admission free*). Free guided tours take you around the buildings of the immigration depot built in 1849 to receive indentured labourers, now a UNESCO World Heritage Site. Between 1834 and 1923 almost 500,000 indentured labourers arrived in Mauritius to replace the labour lost following the abolition of slavery in 1835. While many worked in the island's sugar plantations, others were transported from Mauritius to other British colonies. The majority came from India but some also arrived from southeast Asia, Madagascar and east Africa.

The depot originally consisted of a gatekeeper's office, hospital block, kitchens, immigration office, other staff offices, sheds, stables and privies. Today only parts of it remain, including the gatekeeper's office, hospital block, wharf steps and immigrants' sheds. On a guided tour you will walk up the steps, as those early immigrants did when they disembarked their ships, and then wander around the remaining stone buildings.

MAURITIUS MUSEUM COUNCIL (*Mauritius Institute Bldg, Chaussée St;* ☎ *212 0639;* **f** *212 5717; www.mauritiusmuseums.com*) A complex containing a number of museums, including a natural history museum, an historical museum and a cultural centre.

NATURAL HISTORY MUSEUM (*Mauritius Institute Bldg, Chaussée St;* ☎ *212 0639;* **f** *212 5717;* **e** *mimuse@intnet.mu; www.mauritiusmuseums.com;* 🕘 *09.00–16.00 Mon/Tue & Thu/Fri, 09.00–12.00 Sat; admission free*) It is certainly not the most modern or high-tech museum but still worth a visit for its exhibits on the natural history of the Mascarenes. The natural history museum was established in 1826 and moved to its current site 1885. Its most famous display is a goose-down-clad dodo replica; there are also skeletons of a dodo and a Rodrigues solitare. Numerous other displays on animals, birds and marine life, extinct or otherwise, are to be seen.

PHOTOGRAPHY MUSEUM (*Old Council St;* ☎ *211 1705;* **e** *photomuseemaurice@yahoo.com;* 🕘 *10.00–15.00 Mon–Fri; admission adult/child Rs200/100*) In a restored street on the opposite side of Jules Koenig Street to the theatre. An intriguing little private museum containing old cameras and prints of Port Louis in colonial days, many showing horse-drawn taxis. One photograph, dated 1956, shows the last passenger train leaving Curepipe for Port Louis. A highlight is the daguerreotype, the first commercially successful photographic apparatus, developed in 1839 by Jacques Daguerre. It created an image of a silver-surfaced copper plate but the process was superseded by other technologies and had almost completely died out by the 1860s. Mauritius received its first daguerreotype in 1840, just six months after France bought the licence from Daguerre.

BLUE PENNY MUSEUM (*Le Musée, Caudan Waterfront;* ☎ *210 8176;* **f** *210 9243;* **e** *bluepennymuseum@intnet.mu; www.bluepennymuseum.com;* 🕘 *10.00–17.00 Mon–Sat, last entry is at 16.30; admission adult/child Rs225/100*) The stamp collection includes the famous 'Post Office' stamps issued in 1847 (see box *Philatelist's heaven*, pages 108–9). Paintings, photos, documents and nautical charts from the island's colonial days are also on display, and the museum provides a good history of Port Louis. The shop sells books on the Mascarene Islands and souvenirs.

POSTAL MUSEUM (*Quay St;* ☎ *213 4812;* **e** *postalmuseum@mauritiuspost.mu; www.mauritiuspost.mu;* 🕘 *09.00–16.00 Mon–Fri, 10.00–15.30 Sat; admission adult/child Rs150/90*) Within a stern Victorian granite-block building on the waterfront that once served as a public hospital. The neatly laid-out museum displays cancelling machines, letter boxes and vending machines, as well as stamps. Most of the really famous rare stamps that you see here are reproductions, although there is an original penny black. Souvenir packs of stamps, letter openers, paperweights and other objects with a postal theme are on sale.

MIKADO SHELL MUSEUM (*6 Sir William Newton St;* ☎ *208 1900;* e *Mikado@ intnet.mu;* ⌚ *09.00–17.00 Mon–Fri, 09.00–13.00 Sat; admission free*) Above the jewellery shop, this is one of the most significant shell collections in the Indian Ocean – some 3,000 shells from around the world.

SSR MEMORIAL CENTRE FOR CULTURE (*87 Sir Seewoosagur Ramgoolam St, Plaine Verte;* ☎ *242 0053;* ⌚ *09.00–16.00 Mon, Tue, Thu, Fri, 09.00–12.00 Sat; admission free*) This house, where Sir Seewoosagur Ramgoolam lived from 1935 to 1968, contains exhibits on the life of this much-loved former Mauritian leader. The centrepiece is a photographic exhibition showing significant events in his life. At the time of writing, the museum was closed for renovation.

PERE LAVAL'S SHRINE (*Ste-Croix;* ☎ *242 2129*) Father Jacques Desiré Laval (known locally as Père Laval) was born in France in 1803 and brought up in a strict religious atmosphere, qualifying as a medical doctor before becoming a priest. In 1841, he arrived in Mauritius as a missionary and converted thousands of recently freed slaves to Catholicism, becoming known as the Apostle of the Blacks. He died on 9 September 1864. He was beatified in 1979, following Pope John Paul II's visit to Mauritius, and is regarded as the island's 'national saint'. He is venerated by followers of all faiths who attribute miraculous healing powers to his name. Throughout September, and particularly on the anniversary of his death, people from around the world flock to his tomb in Ste-Croix, many in hope of a miracle healing. The tomb can be visited at any time of year. A rather gaudily coloured plaster effigy covers it. Ste-Croix is a suburb of Port Louis and is easily reached by bus from the Immigration Square bus station.

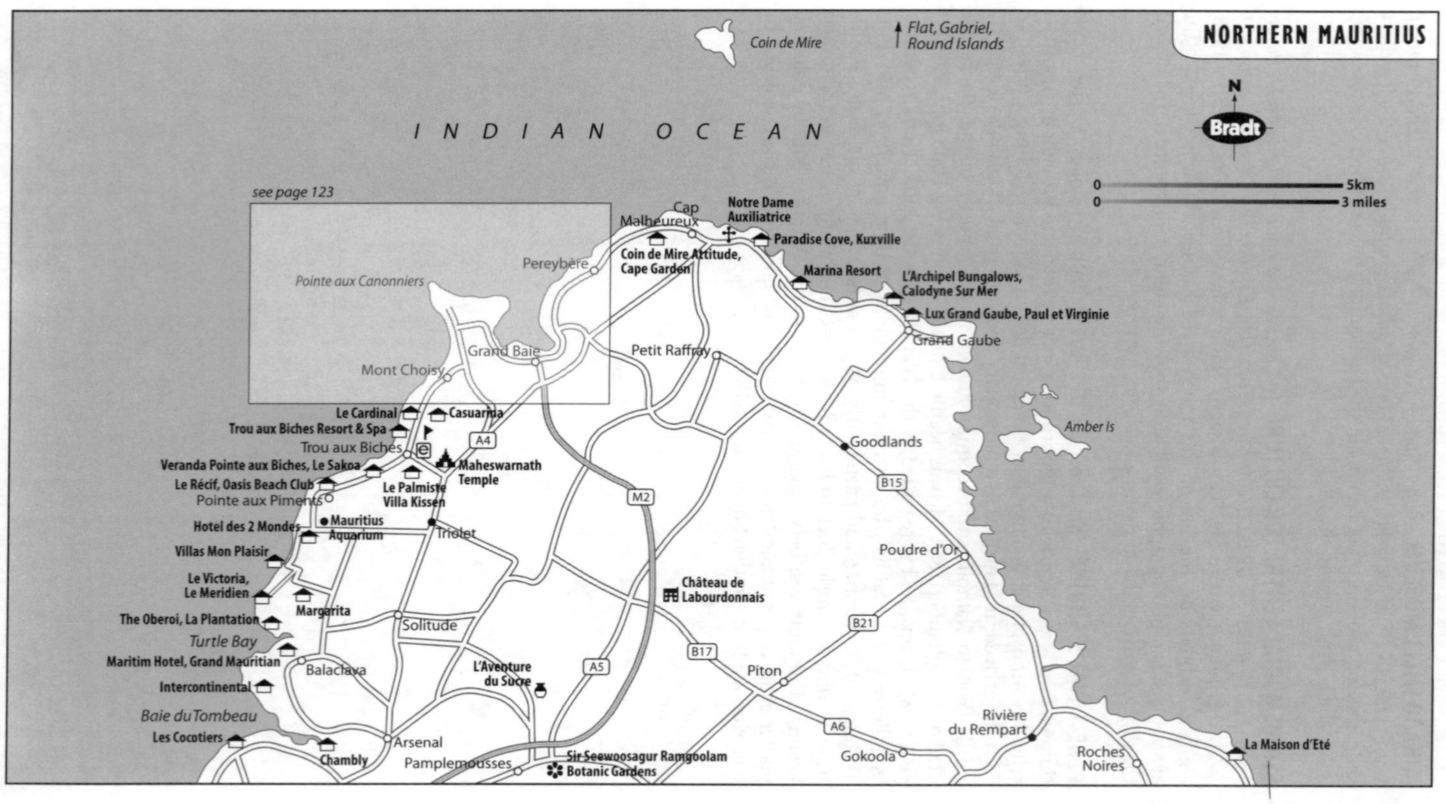
NORTHERN MAURITIUS
N
Bradt
0 5km
0 3 miles
Coin de Mire
Flat, Gabriel, Round Islands
INDIAN OCEAN
see page 123
Pointe aux Canonniers
Pereybère
Cap Malheureux
Notre Dame Auxiliatrice
Coin de Mire Attitude, Cape Garden
Paradise Cove, Kuxville
Marina Resort
L'Archipel Bungalows, Calodyne Sur Mer
Lux Grand Gaube, Paul et Virginie
Grand Gaube
Grand Baie
Mont Choisy
Petit Raffray
Amber Is
Le Cardinal
Casuarina
Trou aux Biches Resort & Spa
Trou aux Biches
A4
Veranda Pointe aux Biches, Le Sakoa
Maheswarnath Temple
Le Récif, Oasis Beach Club
Le Palmiste
Villa Kissen
Pointe aux Piments
Goodlands
B15
M2
Hotel des 2 Mondes
Mauritius Aquarium
Triolet
Villas Mon Plaisir
Poudre d'Or
Le Victoria, Le Meridien
Château de Labourdonnais
Margarita
The Oberoi, La Plantation
Solitude
B21
Turtle Bay
B17
Maritim Hotel, Grand Mauritian
Balaclava
L'Aventure du Sucre
A5
Piton
Intercontinental
Baie du Tombeau
Rivière du Rempart
A6
Les Cocotiers
Arsenal
Chambly
Pamplemousses
Sir Seewoosagur Ramgoolam Botanic Gardens
Gokoola
Roches Noires
La Maison d'Eté

5

Northern Mauritius

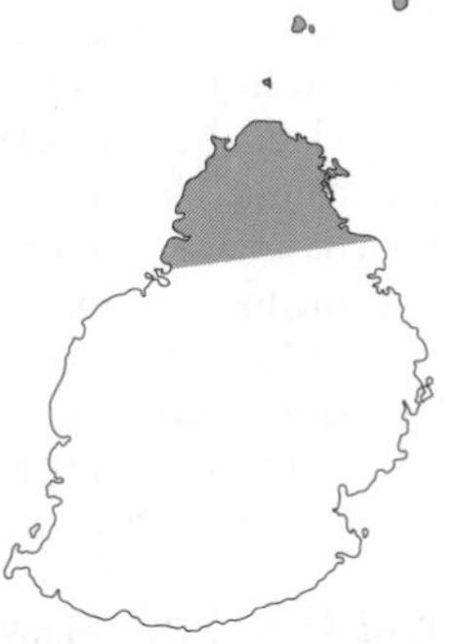

Northern Mauritius is divided into two districts: Pamplemousses in the west and Rivière du Rempart in the east.

The coast of Pamplemousses is largely given over to tourism and includes the lively resort of Grand Baie. Its boundary is the mountain range encircling Port Louis, with Crève Coeur, behind Pieter Both, as its southernmost village. It cuts through the sugar plantations east of Pamplemousses town and runs northwards to the coast at Pointe aux Canonniers.

Rivière du Rempart is a compact district of contrasts, encompassing the tourist hot spots to the east of Grand Baie, the industrial/agricultural area of Goodlands and the rugged northeast coast around Poudre d'Or. The town of Rivière du Rempart is in the east of the district, originally named Rampart River for its steep banks.

The importance of sugar in the north of Mauritius gave rise to the construction of the island's first railway line in 1864. The Northern Line, which connected Port Louis to Pamplemousses and Flacq, was used to transport sugar to Port Louis. It stopped carrying passengers in 1956 and was closed down completely in 1964.

BAIE DU TOMBEAU TO POINTE AUX PIMENTS

The elbow of land just north of Port Louis is named **Baie du Tombeau** (Tomb Bay), in memory of George Weldon, an English merchant who was drowned there in 1697. He was not alone in his fate and treasure hunters are convinced that treasure lies in this bay, a legacy of the many ships wrecked in its waters. If ferreting for treasure doesn't interest you, then there is little to keep you in Baie du Tombeau.

Back on the main road from Port Louis to the north, you pass through the village of **Arsenal**. Although locals are quick to point out the link with the English football team of the same name, the name actually comes from the munitions stores which the French had here.

Inland from Arsenal is the small village of **Pamplemousses**, which is home to the **Sir Seewoosagur Ramgoolam Botanic Gardens**, one of Mauritius's best-known tourist attractions (see *What to see in Northern Mauritius*, pages 133–5).

The **Church of St François** in the village of Pamplemousses was built in 1743 and is one of the oldest on the island. Its cemetery contains the tomb of Abbé Buonavita (1752–1833), who was Napoleon's almoner (distributor of alms) on St Helena. He settled in Mauritius after Napoleon's death in 1821. Villebague, Governor of Mauritius from 1756 to 1759, is also buried here. Behind the primary school in Pamplemousses is the **Bassin des Esclaves** (Slave Pond), where it is said slaves were washed before being sold.

Not far from Pamplemousses are two sites that evoke the area's agricultural history: **L'Aventure du Sucre** tells the story of the island's sugar industry (see page

134), while the restored 19th-century **Château de Labourdonnais** gives an insight into the life of a wealthy sugar-estate owner.

Back on the coast near **Balaclava, Turtle Bay** is a marine park which offers good snorkelling. The coast here is naturally largely rocky, although the hotels lining the coast have each created their own beaches. From the coast you can see ships queuing to enter Port Louis harbour. The ruins of an 18th-century **French arsenal** are here and, further north, at **Pointe aux Piments**, lie the remnants of the **Batterie des Grenadiers**. Some of the most impressive ruins are within the grounds of the Maritim Hotel. Non-residents can obtain permission to visit them at the security hut by the entrance.

WHERE TO STAY Many of the hotels that line this area of coast, particularly the luxury and upmarket ones, are fairly isolated, wedged between cane fields and the sea. Most have excellent facilities and are within walking distance of other hotels but there is no popping out to local shops and bars on foot.

Luxury

The Oberoi (48 rooms, 28 villas) Turtle Bay, Balaclava; 204 3600; f 204 3625; e reservations@oberoi-mauritius.com; www.oberoihotels.com. This hotel, which is a member of 'Leading Small Hotels of the World', prides itself on excellent service & guest privacy. Thoughtful architecture uses natural materials to recreate the charm of a village set in 20 acres of tropical gardens. The luxurious accommodation includes 18 sumptuous villas with private pool. Interior design is natural elegance with memorable touches like the woven sugarcane headboards, sunken marble bath & small private tropical garden with outdoor shower. It'll leave you planning to redecorate when you get home! Rooms are equipped with everything you could possibly need. There are stunning swimming pools, tennis courts, a watersports centre (even water skiing is free) & a dive centre. The spa offers all sorts of pampering, including free yoga & t'ai chi classes. The food is, of course, excellent. It's a romantic, relaxation-focused retreat rather than a family hotel. **$$$$$**

Upmarket

Intercontinental Mauritius (210 rooms) Balaclava; 261 1200; f 261 2101; e sales@icmauritius.com; www.intercontinental.com. A new hotel typical of this large international chain. The hotel has good conference facilities & is well set up for children with family rooms & a kids' club. Rooms are on the small side but have all the features you would expect of an Intercontinental. There are 5 restaurants & a small spa. In some ways it lacks soul – it could be a large international hotel anywhere. Some will enjoy watching the ships heading into Port Louis, others will find it off-putting. **$$$$**

Le Victoria Hotel (254 rooms) Pointe aux Piments; 204 2000; f 261 8224; e victoria@bchot.com; www.levictoria-hotel.com. A Beachcomber property whose rooms are some of the most spacious on the island (standard rooms are 60m2). It also has suites & family apartments. All are equipped with AC, TV, phone, minibar, safe, tea/coffee facilities & balcony/terrace. There are 3 restaurants, including 1 Italian. There are the usual free watersports, a dive centre, floodlit tennis courts, a large swimming pool & a kids' club. Guests can use the golf course at Trou aux Biches Resort & Spa. Being such a large hotel, it can feel a little impersonal but the beach here is good & the facilities & room sizes make it ideal for families. The all-inclusive package is popular. **$$$$**

Maritim Hotel (215 rooms) Turtle Bay, Balaclava; 204 1000; f 204 1020; e info.mau@maritim.de; www.maritim.com. This large hotel stands in 25ha of tropical gardens containing 18th-century French ruins. The rooms & suites are equipped with AC, TV, phone, minibar, safe & balcony/terrace. Bathrooms are rather small. There is a choice of restaurants & bars, plus a spa, 9-hole golf course, watersports, dive centre, tennis & horseriding. Decent standards without too many frills. Many guests find the AI option good value for money. The clientele is predominantly German & it is popular for weddings. Dbl/sgl from €295/195 BB.

The Grand Mauritian (193 rooms) Turtle Bay, Balaclava; 204 1400; f 204 1401; e info.

thegrandmauritian@luxurycollection.com; www.thegrandmauritian.com. This impressive addition to the area opened in 2008. It is a large property, with beautifully decorated & particularly spacious rooms with balcony/terrace. If you can, it is worth paying the extra for a sea-view, rather than a pool-view, room. The spa suites have an adjoining private spa treatment room. Surprisingly for a hotel of this calibre, the broadband connection in the guestrooms is payable. There is, however, a business centre with free internet access. There is a spa, 2 pools, 3 restaurants & a kids' club. The cuisine here is creative, varied & of an excellent standard. **$$$$**

Mid range

Chambly Hotel (42 rooms) Port Chambly Village, Terre Rouge; 405 3000; f 405 3001; e info@portchambly.com; www.portchambly.com. Small hotel within a Mediterranean-village-style complex of private apartments & a few shops. Set on an estuary with views out to sea, around 15mins' drive from Port Louis; there is no beach. Rooms are modern & have all you need but don't aim to be luxurious. They are en suite (shower no bath) with AC, TV, phone & safe. The suites are considerably larger than the standard rooms but only the 2 executive suites have a balcony. Kayaks are available to explore the waterways & there is a boat shuttle to the beach. The pool area is very pleasant, although rather overlooked by the rooms, there is an Italian restaurant (see page 118) & concerts are held here. Self-catering apartments in the complex are also available, & if you really like it here you can purchase an apartment under the ERS scheme. **$$$**

La Plantation Resort & Spa (270 rooms) Turtle Bay, Balaclava; 204 3000; f 261 5709; e resa.plantation@apavou-hotels.com; www.apavou-hotels.com/laplantation. Set in 8 acres at the centre of the bay. This is one of the older hotels on the island &, although it is regularly renovated it does feel more tired than its competitors. The rooms & suites, which have AC, TV, phone, safe & balcony/terrace, have been redecorated in a trendy, modern style. There are 4 rooms equipped for the disabled. There are 3 restaurants, including 1 on the beach. There is a choice of bars, pool, spa, watersports, a dive centre, tennis courts, a small fitness centre, nightclub & a kids' club. **$$$**

Le Meridien (265 rooms) Village Hall Lane, Pointe aux Piments; 204 3333; f 204 3304; e resa@lemeridien.mu; www.lemeridien.com/mauritius. A large hotel, popular with families. The rooms & suites are in 3 blocks of 3 storeys on either side of an impressive lobby area. The buildings aren't particularly pretty but rooms are spacious, with room for children. There are 5 restaurants & bars, 2 pools, tennis courts, a gym & spa, as well as the usual free watersports. Children are well catered for with a kids' club & babysitting service. I have heard reports of poor service. **$$$**

Le Récif (70 rooms) Coastal Rd, Pointe aux Piments; 261 0444; f 261 5247; e resa@recif-hotel.com; www.lerecif.com. The hotel is located on a good stretch of beach (although a little rocky), & guests can step straight from the pool onto the sand. Rooms are en suite & equipped with AC, TV & phone. They have a clean, modern feel. Facilities include 2 restaurants, a bar, watersports (inc free water skiing), a small spa (sauna, steam room & massage) & kids' club. **$$$**

Les Cocotiers (48 rooms) Le Goulet, Baie du Tombeau; 247 4222; f 247 4211; e resweb@apavou-hotels.com; www.apavou-hotels.com. A 2-star equivalent hotel 15mins from Port Louis. All rooms are en suite with AC, TV, phone, safe, minibar & balcony/terrace. The rooms are simply decorated. There is a restaurant, bar & pool. There are relatively few activities/facilities included in the price, & the immediate surrounds have little to offer. The hotel provides a free shuttle service to Mont Choisy Beach 3 days per week, & to Port Louis once per week. **$$$**

Veranda Pointe aux Biches Hotel (115 rooms) Royal Rd, Pointe aux Piments; 265 5901; f 265 5905; e resa@veranda-resorts.com; www.veranda-resorts.com. An informal family-friendly hotel on the beach. The architecture is rustic but modern & features sand floors, including in the reception & beach bar. Rooms have en suite, AC, TV, safe, minibar & balcony/terrace. The 44 family rooms have a separate children's bedroom area. There is also a wing for couples, with its own pool, beach restaurant & bar. There is a small spa & kids' club. There are limited watersports here but guests can use the watersports facilities at other Veranda hotels. **$$$**

Villas Mon Plaisir (48 rooms) Coastal Rd, Pointe aux Piments; 261 7471; f 261 6600; e villasmp@intnet.mu; www.villasmonplaisir.com. One of those small hotels independent travellers on a budget hope to find & seldom do.

In a quiet cul-de-sac with direct access to the beach, the hotel has cosy en-suite rooms with AC, including 3 family rooms. All have TV, phone, safe & balcony/terrace overlooking the pool. There is a bar & a restaurant with sea view. Some non-motorised watersports are free & there is a dive centre next door. Internet is available at reception for a small fee. Prices increased significantly following renovations in 2007 but it is still good value. **$$$**

Budget

Margarita Hotel (19 rooms) Coastal Rd, Pointe aux Piments; 261 3969; **f** 261 8238; **e** margarita@intnet.mu; www.lamargaritahotel.com. A small hotel opened by the owners of Villas Mon Plaisir in 2007, which aims to be equivalent to 2-star. It is about 200m inland from Villas Mon Plaisir & the beach, on the coastal road. Set behind high walls, it doesn't look like much from the outside. However, behind the austere exterior hides clean, modern, but simple accommodation in a 3-storey building around a small pool. Rooms are en suite & have AC, TV, safe & balcony/terrace. There is a restaurant & guests can use the facilities at Villas Mon Plaisir. There are some unsecured parking places by the road. **$$**

Shoestring

Oasis Beach Club (22 apts) Coastal Rd, Pointe aux Piments; 265 5808; **f** 265 5207; **e** info@oasisbeachclub.com; www.oasisbeachclub.com. Simple self-catering studios & apartments equipped with AC & kitchenette (fridge, cooker, etc). The stark, white, 2-storey units face the sea & are fronted by a pool. There is a restaurant, bar, entertainment & a decent beach. Excursions & diving can be arranged. Run by Italians & popular with Italian tourists. **$**

WHERE TO EAT There is a small supermarket in Pointe aux Piments and numerous snack vendors. Most of the hotels in this area have restaurants which are open to non-residents.

La Table du Château Château de Labourdonnais, Mapou; 266 9533; 09.00–17.00, Sat dinner. Cuisine: Creole, French. A clean, modern restaurant & tea room in the grounds of the mansion, with views of the impressive chateau built in 1859 (see pages 134–5). Nicely presented dishes, many of which use fruit from the orchard. **$$$**

Le Fangourin L'Aventure du Sucre, Beau Plan; 243 7900; 09.00–17.00 daily. Cuisine: Creole, French. Set in the grounds of the old Beau Plan sugar factory, which now houses a sugar museum. Dining is indoors or outdoors, overlooking attractive gardens &, in the distance, Pieter Both mountain. The menu is diverse & sophisticated with seafood, meat & vegetarian dishes as well as light snacks. Meals are beautifully presented, as well as in any fine-dining restaurant. The fabulous desserts are made with special, unrefined sugar from the estate. The dark chocolate fondant gateau with vanilla ice cream is incredible. **$$$**

Mona Lisa Port Chambly Village, Terre Rouge; 405 3000; for lunch & dinner daily. Cuisine: Italian. Within the Port Chambly apartment & hotel complex, dining is indoors or on a terrace overlooking the estuary, It has a real Italian piazza feel. Substantial main courses are priced from Rs450 but pizza & pasta dishes start at around Rs280. **$$$**

Café Valse de Vienne Powder Mill Rd, Pamplemousses; 243 0560; 09.00–20.00 daily. Cuisine: Austrian, German. Near the main entrance to the gardens, opposite the Church of St François. Has a pleasant atmosphere & serves excellent pastries. **$$**

Le Brisant Resto Coastal Rd, Pointe aux Piments; 261 5923; for lunch & dinner daily. Cuisine: Creole, seafood. A great little restaurant next to the aquarium (see page 135). There is no shortage of rustic charm – tables are on a covered terrace with a floor of waste coral, lampshades made from woven pandanus hats & a bar made from old oil drums. The owner works with local fishermen to get the best seafood. Grilled lobster is a speciality & the crispy calamari is very tasty. Wi-Fi is free. **$$**

Villas Mon Plaisir Coastal Rd, Pointe aux Piments; 261 7471; for lunch & dinner daily. Cuisine: Creole, Chinese. Unpretentious restaurant with views of the ocean. Good value for money. **$$**

TROU AUX BICHES TO POINTE AUX CANONNIERS

From Pointe aux Piments the coast road runs parallel to the main road, through the extended hamlet of **Trou aux Biches** (Hole of the Does), so named because there is supposed to have been a small watering hole here frequented by female deer. In contrast, Trou aux Cerfs (Hole of the Stags) at Curepipe was said to be used by the males of the species.

Despite falling victim to extensive tourism development, Trou aux Biches retains much of its Mauritian charm. A far quieter alternative to Grand Baie, it features a good beach, excellent snorkelling and a range of accommodation and restaurants. The northern end of Trou aux Biches seems to almost blend into **Mont Choisy**, which has one of the best beaches in the area. The beach curves around a large bay lined with casuarina trees, stretching to **Pointe aux Canonniers**. On the weekends the beach is crowded with Mauritians; buses bring them down from the large population areas around Port Louis and in the central plateau. Families set themselves up under the casuarinas trees, makeshift shops selling inflatable creatures and other beach paraphernalia spring up and by the afternoon there is usually singing and dancing.

Inland from Trou aux Biches is **Triolet**, which boasts the largest **Hindu temple** in Mauritius. It is an amalgamation of seven temples added to the original Maheswarnath Temple, built in 1857. As soon as you arrive, an elderly gentleman will probably appear out of nowhere to give you a guided tour. A donation to the temple is usually all that is required in exchange. He may seem eccentric but he appears to know his stuff.

WHERE TO STAY

Upmarket

Le Cardinal (13 rooms) Coastal Rd, Trou aux Biches; 204 5200; **f** 265 6111; **e** info@lecardinalresort.intnet.mu; www.lecardinalresort.com. A new boutique hotel finished to a very high standard. The hotel is on a small stretch of beach & all rooms face the sea. Rooms are spacious with modern fixtures & fittings. There are 2 penthouses, one of which has its own pool. The hotel markets itself as a couples' retreat but there is a duplex suitable for families. Room facilities include AC, TV, minibar, safe & Wi-Fi. There is an à la carte restaurant, bar, pool & a massage room. Guests can use the gym, tennis courts & spa at Casuarina Hotel. **$$$$**

Trou aux Biches Resort & Spa (333 rooms, including 27 villas) Trou aux Biches; 204 6800; **f** 204 6868; **e** trouauxbiches@bchot.com; www.trouauxbiches-resort.com. This old favourite, on one of the island's best beaches, was completely knocked down & rebuilt in 2009. The new hotel opened in 2010 & the result is astounding. It is a large resort but thankfully the rooms are arranged in crescents, each with a swimming pool in the centre, to ensure an intimate feel. The rooms are exceptionally modern & spacious, especially in the beachfront suites. All accommodation, apart from junior suites, has an outdoor shower. The upstairs beachfront suites have a decent-sized plunge pool, while those downstairs have a tiny pool, more like an outdoor bath. They are also visible from the beach. Free Wi-Fi throughout the resort, including in rooms, is a bonus. There are 6 restaurants offering a variety of cuisine, watersports facilities, a large spa, gym, kids' & teens' clubs. The hotel was built with eco-friendly aims; for example, used water is collected & stored under the 6 tennis courts. **$$$$**

Mid range

Bois d'Oiseaux (10 apts) Coastal Rd, Trou aux Biches; 265 5341; **f** 265 7070; **e** hitie@boisdoiseaux.com; www.boisdoiseaux.com. Self-catering accommodation of a good standard on the seafront. The 2 villas have 3 or 4 bedrooms & private pool, & the 8 duplexes have 2 bedrooms. The accommodation is well equipped, internet access is available & daily maid service is included. There is a pool overlooking the ocean, & a dive centre & deep-sea fishing nearby. **$$$**

Casuarina Hotel (109 rooms) Trou aux Biches; 204 5000; f 265 6111; e casuarina@intnet.mu; www.hotel-casuarina.com. Across the road from the beach, the hotel is a mass of white, thatch cottages, round like toadstools. The rooms are comfortable but not outstanding with AC, TV, minibar & balcony/terrace. The 15 apartments have 2 bedrooms, a living/dining area, kitchenette & bathroom. They sleep up to 2 adults & 4 children (1 room with 2 sets of bunk beds), although 6 may be a bit of a squeeze. Kitchens are well equipped. There is a restaurant, bar, 2 pools, tennis court, kids' club & many watersports are included. **$$$**

Hotel Le Canonnier (247 rooms) Pointe aux Canonniers; 209 7000; f 263 7864; e canonnier@bchot.com; www.beachcomber-hotels.com. This is a large, family-friendly hotel, set on a peninsula surrounded by sea on 3 sides. The rooms have sleek, modern décor, AC, TV, minibar, safe & balcony/terrace. There are some interesting ruins in the 7ha of tropical gardens: a lighthouse (now housing the kids' club), cannons & an old fortress. Extensive facilities, always something going on & very child friendly. The all-inclusive is popular. **$$$**

Hotel le Palmiste (81 rooms) Morcellement les Mascareignes, Impasse le Palmiste, Trou aux Biches; 265 6815; f 265 6811; e info@hotel-lepalmiste.com; www.hotel-lepalmiste.com. A 3-star equivalent, 200m from the beach. Heading towards Pointe aux Piments on the coast road, take the road on the left after the police station. Accommodation is in 3-storey buildings around a pool area. Rooms are equipped with en suite, AC, TV, phone, safe, minibar Wi-Fi & balcony/terrace; there are 12 family rooms. There are 2 restaurants, a bar, a nightclub, 2 pools, watersports & a spa. If you don't mind not being on the beach, this is a good option. **$$$**

Hotel Mont Choisy (88 rooms) Mont Choisy; 265 6070; f 265 6749; e mont_choisy@intnet.mu; www.montchoisyhotel.net.The beach immediately in front of the hotel is pretty but small, although the fabulous beaches of Mont Choisy & Trou aux Biches are nearby. Close to amenities – shops, bank, taxis & restaurants. The rooms are in colourful 2-storey units, they are small & unfussy, but clean (as you'd expect from a 3-star hotel, which is how this property is marketed). The rooms are en suite with AC, TV, phone, minibar & safe but no tea/coffee facilities. There are 3 restaurants, 2 bars, pool, tennis courts, watersports, dive centre & kids' club. A lively hotel on a lively stretch of beach – the constant whining of speedboats being the inevitable downside. **$$$**

Le Sakoa (16 apts) Coastal Rd, Trou aux Biches; 265 5244; f 265 8910; e info@sakoa-management.com; www.lesakoa.com. A small, homely hotel, which is fast earning a very good reputation among independent travellers. Accommodation is in 2-storey thatched buildings, located in a well-maintained tropical garden on a decent stretch of beach. Rooms are en suite, with kitchenette, AC, TV, phone, safe & balcony/terrace. There is a restaurant, pool, daily maid service & regular evening entertainment. Pedaloes & kayaks are available. Wi-Fi is free & there is a computer at reception for guest use. **$$$**

Budget

Grand Baie Travel & Tours Holiday Rentals Coastal Rd, Grand Baie; 454 4038; f 454 4038; e resagbtt@intnet.mu; www.gbtt.com. Offers self-catering accommodation at several complexes around Mont Choisy. They are well maintained, have a pool & prices include linen & daily maid service but no meals. Bookings can be made at the GBTT address above. They also organise airport transfers & excursions. **$$**

Hotel des 2 Mondes (16 rooms) Coastal Rd, Mont Choisy; 265 7777; e contact@hoteldes2mondes.com; www.hoteldes2mondes.com. A new hotel set back across the road from the ocean; at the top end of the budget category in terms of price & quality. Rooms are simply furnished but comfortable, with en suite, AC, flat screen TV with DVD player, phone, safe & balcony/terrace. There is also a 2-bedroom apartment. The public areas are pleasantly decorated with an African theme. There is a Creole restaurant, a small pool & a very small, basic spa area. **$$**

Les Filaos Village (12 studios) Club Rd, Pointe aux Cannoniers; 263 7482; f 263 7916; e nathanfilao@intnet.mu; www.filaosvillage.8k.com. Cosy self-catering accommodation 2km from the centre of Grand Baie. En-suite studios with AC, TV, phone, kitchenette & sea-facing balcony/terrace. Facilities include a restaurant, bar, pool, maid service & internet access. **$$**

Le Grand Bleu Hotel (64 rooms) Coastal Rd, Trou aux Biches; 265 5812; f 265 5842; e lgbtab@intnet.mu; www.legrandbleu.com.

A small hotel across the road from the beach. Accommodation is in smallish, basic rooms, huddled around a little pool, with another pool under construction at the time of our visit. Rooms are en suite (shower but no bath) & have AC, TV, phone, safe, fridge & balcony/terrace. Family rooms are available. There is a restaurant & internet is available in reception for a fee. **$$**

Seapoint Beach Bungalows (13 apts) Pointe aux Canonniers; 696 4804; **f** 686 7380; **e** nakaloo@intnet.mu; www.seapointbungalows.com. In a good location on the beach. Simple self-catering accommodation in studios, apartments & bungalows for up to 5 people. Some have sea view. AC is available for a fee. Daily maid service included. **$$**

Sous le Badamier (12 rooms) Coastal Rd, Pointe aux Canonniers; 263 4391; **f** 263 1552; **e** info@souslebadamier.com; www.souslebadamier.com. A charming little hotel around a courtyard with a badamier tree in the centre. The ensuites are nicely decorated, with AC, TV, safe & minibar. The open-air restaurant serves Creole cuisine. Free internet access on the ground floor. The beach is a few metres away but the hotel offers a shuttle service (payable) to Mont Choisy Beach. Good value for money. **$$**

Shoestring

Cosi Hotel (14 rooms & 5 apts) Coastal Rd, Mont Choisy; 265 5104; **f** 265 5103; **e** cosihotel@gmail.com; http://cocoteraie.amltd.net. Across the road from the Hotel Mont Choisy & 5mins' walk from the beach. 14 basic double rooms & 5 studios & apartments, most of which have simple self-catering facilities. Rooms have a safe, most have balcony/terrace & some have AC. TV on request. Rates include a daily maid service & linen. Next door are a Creole restaurant & bar/pizza restaurant (see below). There is a small pool on site. **$**

Villa Kissen (6 rooms, 4 studios) Trou aux Biches; 265 5523; **f** 283 7313; **e** sandonna@intnet.mu; www.villa-kissen.com. Simple but clean accommodation in a residential area, 150m from the beach. The rooms are basic with en suite, AC, TV, safe, minibar & balcony. There is a restaurant, pool & daily maid service is included. **$**

WHERE TO EAT For self-caterers there's the **Choisy Royal supermarket**, in a colourful building at the southern end of the main road through Mont Choisy (Coastal Road); also **Chez Popo** at the Pointe aux Piments end of Trou aux Biches.

Caprice Coastal Rd, Mont Choisy; for lunch & dinner daily. Cuisine: Italian. On the way to Trou aux Biches, across the road from the beach. A very pleasant restaurant with indoor & outdoor dining, as well as a lounge area. Good quality homemade pasta, pizza & seafood dishes. **$$$**

La Bay des Pirates Coastal Rd, Mont Choisy; 265 5104; 10.00–late daily. Cuisine: pizza, pasta, bar. A new open-air bar next to the Cosi Hotel. **$$$**

La Cravache d'Or Coastal Rd, Trou aux Biches; 265 7021; for lunch & dinner Mon–Sat. Cuisine: French, Creole, seafood. On the seafront at the southern end of Trou aux Biches. Upmarket with excellent seafood & exceptional views. Reservation recommended. **$$$**

Le Pescatore Coastal Rd, Mont Choisy; 265 6337; for lunch & dinner daily. Cuisine: Creole, European, seafood. A good upmarket option right on the seafront with superb seafood. **$$$**

Wakamé Coastal Rd, Pointe aux Canonniers; 263 9888; www.wakamerestaurant.com; for lunch & dinner Wed–Mon. Cuisine: Asian. A stylish, modern restaurant serving fine Asian cuisine à la carte, including sushi & a range of vegetarian options. Reservation recommended. **$$$**

Café de la Paix Coastal Rd, Mont Choisy; 265 5335; 09.00–15.00 & 18.00–22.30 daily. Cuisine: Creole, Chinese, seafood. A great little restaurant between the Casuarina & Mont Choisy hotels,serving good food at reasonable prices. The décor is simple, with tables on a covered terrace or small indoor area. There is a good selection of vegetarian dishes. The shrimps in garlic butter & the sweet & sour chicken are particularly good. They also serve some decent cocktails, including a very good planter's punch. **$$**

Cosi Mont Choisy; 265 5104; for lunch & dinner daily. Cuisine: Creole. Relaxed atmosphere, clean restaurant & outdoor dining. They serve a good prawn & chicken curry. Tasty, reasonably priced food. **$$**

✂ **Patch 'n' Parrot** Hidden Reef Garden, Coastal Rd, Pointe Aux Canonniers; ☎ 269 0374; ⏱ 10.00–late. Cuisine: European, bar/pub. A large South African-run pub popular with expats & tourists. It can become crowded, especially when big sporting matches are shown on the big screen.

OTHER PRACTICALITIES

Money and banking There is a branch of MCB and an ATM near the public beach in the centre of Trou aux Biches. The new **police station** is opposite the bank.

Communications There are payphones at Trou aux Biches public beach. **Cyber Punk** around 200m inland from the Trou aux Biches Police Station (☎ *988 3688*) offers **internet access**. There is a post office in the centre of Trou aux Biches.

GRAND BAIE

Just within the boundaries of Rivière du Rempart, **Grand Baie** gapes inland beyond **Pointe aux Canonniers**, providing a deep and sheltered bay, often as calm as a lake. It is the place for watersports, self-catering accommodation, and a selection of hotels and restaurants that are among both the worst and best in the island. It is the only area blatantly devoted to mass tourism and consequently has earned the affectionate nickname of 'The Mauritian Côte d'Azur'.

Grand Baie is the safety valve of Mauritius – the place where ordinary tourists, and locals, can go to let off steam without having to pretend to be wealthy jetsetters. Unfortunately, over the years this has resulted in a lowering of the usual excellent standards of the hospitality industry in Mauritius. While Grand Baie has developed, with many bars and restaurants, into a fun place to stay if you like a lively after-beach life, courtesy, warmth and style have been sacrificed to some degree. Petty crime is also a by-product of the development, so visitors are advised to be vigilant.

However, there is plenty to do in Grand Baie. All manner of excursions and watersports can be arranged by one of the many activity operators with offices here, and the bars and restaurants which line the bay make it a great place for an evening out.

At the western end of Grand Baie is a very colourful **Tamil temple** covered with statues of gods. If you like temples, it is one of the best Tamil examples on the island.

GETTING THERE AND AWAY The **bus stop** in Grand Baie is on the coastal road, just outside La Jonque Restaurant. Buses operate regularly between here and the Immigration Square bus station in Port Louis, including an express service which departs every hour. Non-express buses also link Grand Baie to the other coastal villages of the north and east, including Pereybère, Cap Malheureux, Mont Choisy and Trou aux Biches.

TOURIST INFORMATION There is no tourist office as such but there are countless travel agencies who arrange excursions and who can give advice. Everyone in Grand Baie is very keen to share their wisdom on hotels, boat trips and tours but remember that they are wise to tourists and that their cousin almost certainly owns the hotel, boat or tour company which they recommend. The warning to be vigilant about purchasing tours from unlicensed operators is more pertinent in Grand Baie than any other part of the island.

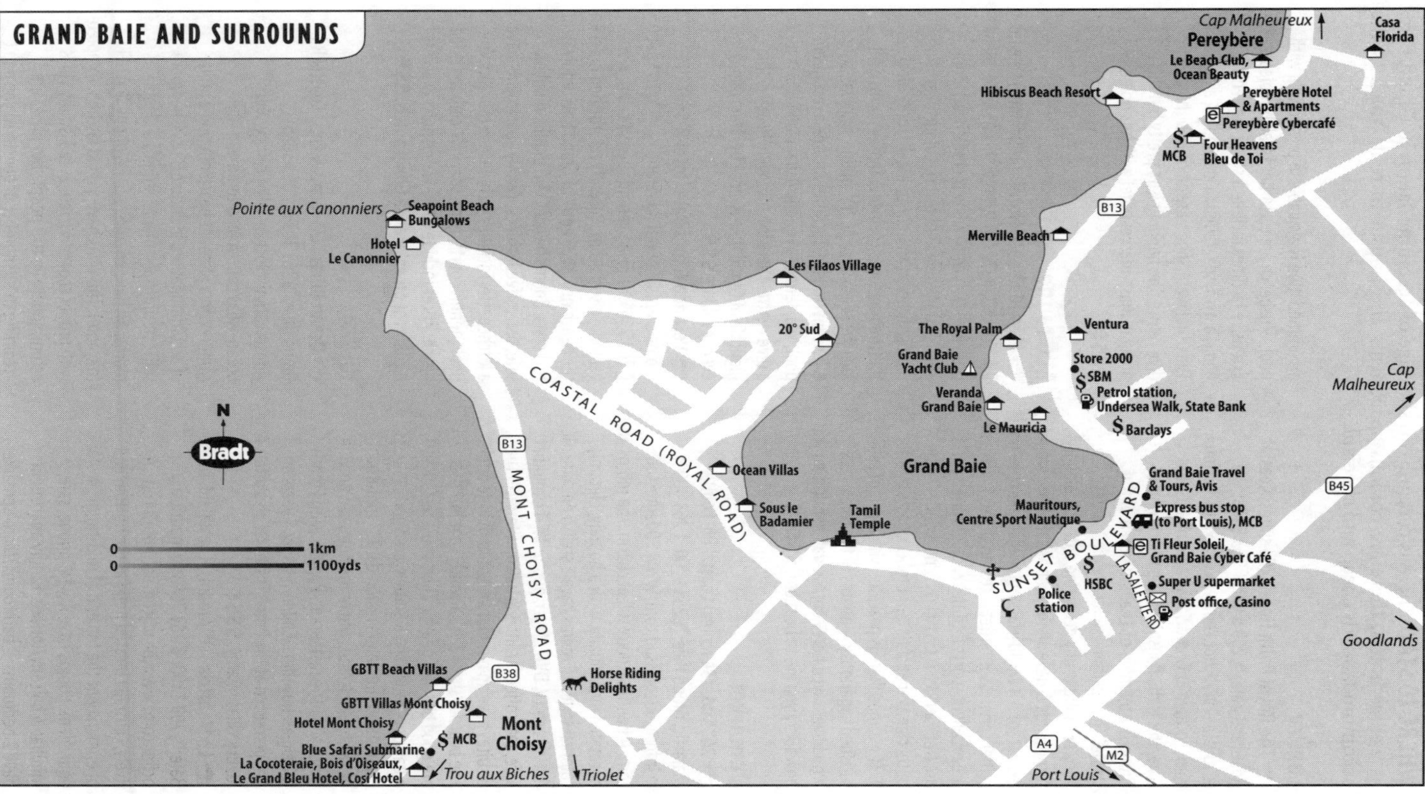
GRAND BAIE AND SURROUNDS
Cap Malheureux
Pereybère
Casa Florida
Le Beach Club, Ocean Beauty
Hibiscus Beach Resort
Pereybère Hotel & Apartments
Pereybère Cybercafé
MCB
Four Heavens
Bleu de Toi
Pointe aux Canonniers
Seapoint Beach Bungalows
Hotel Le Canonnier
B13
Merville Beach
Les Filaos Village
20° Sud
The Royal Palm
Ventura
Store 2000
SBM
Grand Baie Yacht Club
Veranda Grand Baie
Petrol station, Undersea Walk, State Bank
Le Mauricia
Barclays
Cap Malheureux
N
Bradt
COASTAL ROAD (ROYAL ROAD)
Ocean Villas
Grand Baie
Grand Baie Travel & Tours, Avis
B45
Mauritours, Centre Sport Nautique
Express bus stop (to Port Louis), MCB
Sous le Badamier
Tamil Temple
Ti Fleur Soleil, Grand Baie Cyber Café
0 1km
0 1100yds
SUNSET BOULEVARD
HSBC
LA SALETTE RD
Super U supermarket
Police station
Post office, Casino
MONT CHOISY ROAD
Goodlands
GBTT Beach Villas
B38
Horse Riding Delights
GBTT Villas Mont Choisy
Hotel Mont Choisy
Mont Choisy
MCB
Blue Safari Submarine
La Cocoteraie, Bois d'Oiseaux, Le Grand Bleu Hotel, Cosi Hotel
Trou aux Biches
Triolet
A4
M2
Port Louis

WHERE TO STAY There is certainly no shortage of accommodation in Grand Baie; as well as hotels, there are copious apartments and houses to rent. Much of the accommodation is cheap and cheerful.

Luxury

The Royal Palm Hotel (84 suites) Coastal Rd, Grand Baie; 209 8300; f 263 8455; e royalpalm@bchot.com; www.royalpalm-hotel.com. Located at Grand Sable, adjoining Grand Baie, this is the flagship of the Beachcomber Group & a member of 'Leading Hotels of the World'. The luxurious suites are on 3 storeys. They're thoughtfully decorated with colonial-style furnishings & have all the features that you would expect from a world-class hotel, including personal butler service & internet access in the suites. There are excellent sports facilities & most watersports are free. Service is first-class & no wonder – the hotel claims that staff outnumber guests by 3 to 1. The atmosphere is peaceful with an air of self-satisfied superiority – photos of the celebrities who have stayed here adorn a wall, reminding you how lucky you are to be there. **$$$$$**

Upmarket

20° Sud (34 rooms) Coastal Rd, Pointe Malartic, Grand Baie; 263 5000; f 263 4000; e info@20degressud.com; www.20degressud.com. A boutique hotel full of charm. The rooms are decorated individually, with a homely, elegant, colonial style. All rooms have a stylish en suite, AC, flat-screen TV, DVD player, phone, Wi-Fi, minibar, safe, tea/coffee facilities & balcony/terrace. The 6 suites have an outdoor jacuzzi or plunge pool. The beach is small & it's a windy spot but there are good beaches nearby. There are 2 restaurants, a bar, pool, small spa & some watersports. Guests can dine on the hotel's restored 1929 motorboat or sail to Flat Island, where the hotel can provide lunch at a little restaurant. Popular with French & Belgian travellers. Children under 5 years are not permitted at the hotel. The hotel also offers 4 luxury villas nearby. **$$$$**

Le Mauricia (197 rooms) Coastal Rd, Grand Baie; 209 1100; f 263 7888; e mauricia@bchot.com; www.beachcomber-hotels.com. A lively, centrally located hotel at the bottom end of upmarket or the top end of mid-range, 4-star equivalent. Rooms have AC, TV, phone, safe, minibar & balcony/terrace. Family apartments have 2 bedrooms, 2 bathrooms. More upmarket accommodation is available in private villa with pool. The beach area is rather small but pleasant. Extensive facilities include a shopping centre, 2 pools, a gym, spa, tennis, a kids' club & a nightclub. The usual watersports are on offer & there's a dive centre. The building isn't pretty but this is a popular, mass-market hotel with lots going on. **$$$$**

Mid range

Merville Beach Hotel (169 rooms) Coastal Rd, Grand Baie; 209 2200; f 263 8146; e info@mervillebeach.com; www.mervillebeach.com. A good 3-star equivalent resort. Colourful en-suite rooms, either in an uninspiring 3-storey block or thatched cottages (deluxe & family rooms). All face the sea & have AC, TV, phone, minibar, safe & balcony/terrace. Facilities include a restaurant, pool, spa, tennis, gym, the usual watersports & a dive centre. There is a nice wide beach & the nightlife of Grand Baie is close by. Entertainment every evening. **$$$**

Veranda Grand Baie Hotel & Spa (94 rooms & apts) Coastal Rd, Grand Baie; 209 8000; f 263 7369; e resa@veranda-resorts.com; www.veranda-resorts.com. Recently refurbished hotel on the beach near the centre of Grand Baie, equivalent to 3 stars. Rooms have AC, TV, phone, minibar, safe, tea/coffee facilities. Family apartments have a kitchenette. Facilities include 2 restaurants, 2 pools, tennis courts, gym, spa, kids' club & a good beach. Prices include some watersports & access to facilities at other Veranda Group hotels. **$$$**

Budget

Ocean Villas (31 rooms & apts) Coastal Rd, Grand Baie; 263 3039; f 263 3055; e reservations@ocean-villas.com; www.ocean-villas.com. A Mediterranean-style complex on a pleasant beach offering a range of accommodation, including 3- & 4-bedroom self-catering apartments, studios & double rooms. All have en suite, AC, TV, phone & Wi-Fi (payable). The villas have a good kitchen, complete with proper cooker & oven. 2- & 3-storey villas accommodate up to 9 people but prices are according to the number of guests, so you don't pay for 6 when there are only 2 of you. There's a nice pool, restaurant, barbecue facilities & maid service. Excursions & watersports can be arranged (payable). Worth considering if you are a large family or group. **$$**

Ti Fleur Soleil (18 rooms) Coastal Rd, Grand Baie; 269 3380; **f** 263 7060; **e** tifleursoleil@intnet.mu; www.tifleursoleil.com. No-frills accommodation across the road from the beach in the centre of Grand Baie. Rooms are simple & colourful, with en suite, AC, TV, safe, tea/coffee facilities, fridge & balcony. Massage & beauty treatments are available. The bar & restaurant on the ground floor are modern & trendy. Also helpful are the free Wi-Fi in the rooms, daily maid service, beach towels & free 15-minute welcome massage. Close to shops, nightlife & watersports but not suitable for those looking for a peaceful retreat. **$$**

Ventura Hotel (28 rooms) Coastal Rd, Grand Baie; 263 6030; **f** 263 7479; **e** info@hotelventura.net; www.hotelventura.net. Behind a row of shops, with the main road, private bungalows & large gardens between it & the beach. The rooms, studios & 2-bedroom family units are in small 2-storey blocks grouped around a pool. All come with en suite, AC, TV & phone, & most have a balcony/terrace. There is a good Indian/Creole restaurant here. **$$**

WHERE TO EAT Diners are spoilt for choice in Grand Baie, with restaurants offering a variety of cuisine to suit all budgets. Most are open daily for lunch and dinner but prices and standards vary greatly.

For self-caterers there is a **Store 2000 supermarket** (*07.30–19.30 Mon–Sat, 07.30–12.00 Sun & public holidays*) on the coastal road at the Pereybère end of town. A little further into Grand Baie is the **Epicerie Gourmande** (*269 1123; 09.30–19.00 Mon–Thu, 09.30–20.00 Fri/Sat, 09.00–12.00 Sun*), which sells a range of fine food and treats. There is also a large and well-stocked **Super U supermarket** (*09.00–20.30 Mon–Thu, 09.00–21.00 Fri/Sat, 09.00–13.00 Sun & public holidays*), which is clearly signposted and just inland from the centre of Grand Baie.

Here is a selection of Grand Baie's restaurants:

La Langouste Grisée Coastal Rd; 263 1035; **f** 263 1034; 10.00–22.00 daily. Cuisine: seafood, French. Award-winning upmarket seafood restaurant. **$$$$**

La Villa Garden Chemin 20 Pieds; 262 7552; for dinner Mon–Sat, lunch Tue–Sat. Cuisine: French. Between Grand Baie & Pereybère. A sophisticated restaurant serving French gastronomic dishes, with a relaxing lounge bar/walled garden area & a small art gallery. Regular live music & easy parking. **$$$$**

Le Capitaine Coastal Rd; 263 6867; for lunch & dinner daily. Cuisine: seafood. Well-regarded restaurant in a romantic setting overlooking the bay. Superb seafood platter. Reservation recommended. **$$$$**

Cocoloko Coastal Rd; 263 1241; daily 09.00–late. Cuisine: European, light lunches. An inviting bar/restaurant next to the Ti Fleur Soleil, across the road from the bay. A good spot for pizza & other light lunches. Free Wi-Fi. **$$$**

Happy Rajah Coastal Rd; 263 2241; for lunch & dinner Mon–Sat. Cuisine: Indian. Popular with locals & tourists alike for its authentic Indian dishes. **$$$**

La Terrasse Coastal Rd; 263 6391; 10.00–14.00 & 17.30–22.00 Wed–Mon. Cuisine: Creole, French, Chinese, seafood. A relaxed restaurant around 1km north of the centre of Grand Baie. The 1st-floor dining area is above a fairly busy road but does have sea views. Consistently good, unpretentious dishes. **$$$**

Le Bistrot de Bacchus Ventura Complex, Coastal Rd; 263 3203; for lunch & dinner daily. Cuisine: French & wine shop. Has a true French bistro atmosphere. Good, reasonably priced food & a huge selection of wines from around the world. **$$$**

Mamma Mia Coastal Rd; 422 4269; for dinner Wed–Mon, lunch Sat–Sun. Cuisine: Italian. Across the road from the bay but with good sea views. A popular pasta & pizza joint, which also does take-away. **$$$**

Rendez Vous Café Coastal Rd; 263 4589; 07.30–late daily. Cuisine: Creole, French. A varied menu from pizza to carri. There is a lounge, bar & Wi-Fi. **$$$**

✕ **Sakura** Coastal Rd; ☎ 263 8092; ⏲ for lunch & dinner, closed Sun lunch. Cuisine: Japanese. Take-away available. Good food, particularly the tepanyaki. Reservation recommended for weekends. $$$

✕ **Tutto Bene** La Cuvette, Grand Baie; ☎ 263 3000; ⏲ 10.00–15.30 & 18.00–late daily. Cuisine: Italian, Creole. A large, modern restaurant serving well-presented dishes. Near The Royal Palm Hotel. Reservation recommended. $$$

✕ **Don Camillo** Coastal Rd; ☎ 263 8540; ⏲ for lunch & dinner daily. Cuisine: Italian. Take-away available. This Grand Baie classic continues to impress with tasty pasta & pizza dishes. $$

✕ **Luigi's** Coastal Rd; ☎ 269 1125; ⏲ for dinner Tue–Sun, lunch Sat. Cuisine: Italian. Just north of town, next to Epicerie Gourmande. Owned & run by an Italian family. Offers plenty of choice, from homemade pizza & pasta to sumptuous seafood dishes with a Mediterranean twist. Good food at reasonable prices. Wi-Fi available. $$

✕ **Sunset Café** Sunset Bd; ☎ 263 9602; ⏲ 08.30–19.00 daily. Cuisine: European snacks & light lunches. European atmosphere, right on the seafront. $$

NIGHTLIFE Most hotels in the mid-range and upmarket categories organise evening entertainment in the form of live bands, *séga* nights or themed evenings. However, for nightlife outside of the hotels, Grand Baie is the place to go in the north. Most nights of the week you will find something going on, although Sundays are a little quieter. Entry to nightclubs is typically around Rs100–150 or free, and is more likely to be free for females than males.

Bars, like **Banana Café** (☎ *263 8540*), with loud music and sand on the floor, are open all day until late, closing only when they feel like it. Banana Café has been around for years and soon becomes a favourite for most visitors to Grand Baie. Lounging in comfy chairs and twiddling your feet in the sand certainly has its appeal. **Cocoloko** (☎ *263 1241*) restaurant/bar draws a good crowd. The décor is very pleasant, there are big screens for sports fans and free Wi-Fi. **Bay Lounge** (☎ *258 1700;* ⏲ *10.00–late daily*) across the road from the ocean has plenty of atmosphere – comfy chairs are dotted around a courtyard with a coral floor and there is a dance floor inside for party animals. Crêpes, pizzas and light meals are available. **Beach House Bar** (☎ *263 2599*) to the north of town is another trendy restaurant/bar on the beach. South African-run pub/restaurant **Patch 'n' Parrot** at Pointe aux Canonniers (☎ *2269 0374;* ⏲ *10.00–late*) opened in 2009, and expats and tourists flock there for the tropical pub atmosphere, dancing and a variety of sports on the big screen.

The nights for clubbing in Grand Baie are typically Wednesday, Friday and Saturday. Popular dance spots are **Les Enfants Terribles** (☎ *263 8117*) on the road to Pointe aux Canonniers and **Takamaka** (☎ *747 4563*) on the coastal road. Les Enfants Terribles has several bars and attracts a slightly older crowd than some of the other nightspots. **Zanzibar** (☎ *263 3265;* ⏲ *23.00–late Mon–Sat*), is an old favourite for many. Other options include the **Godfather Club** (☎ *263 3000*) on the beach near the Royal Palm; it has several rooms each with different types of music, and is popular with locals and tourists. **N'Gyone**, to the north of the town centre, has a modern, European feel and next door is **Buddha Bar** (☎ *263 7664*).

OTHER PRACTICALITIES

Money and banking Perhaps because there are so many opportunities to spend money in Grand Baie, there are several bank counters that are open outside normal bank hours, enabling visitors to change travellers' cheques or to withdraw cash. Most are open 08.00–18.00 Monday–Saturday, 09.00–14.00 Sunday. There are numerous ATMs in Grand Baie, mostly along the coastal road.

Communications The **post office** (⌚ *08.15–16.00 Mon–Fri, 08.15–11.45 Sat*) is in the Richmond Hill Complex next to the Super U supermarket on La Salette Road. There are numerous **payphones** in Grand Baie.

The post office has **internet access**, or you can try **Grand Baie Cyber Café** near the Ti Fleur Soleil Hotel.

PEREYBERE

The coastal road from Grand Baie to Cap Malheureux passes through **Pereybère**, which offers a pleasant bay and beach, popular with locals at weekends. It is quieter than Grand Baie but is growing rapidly and with just 2km separating the two it probably won't be long before they meet in the middle.

WHERE TO STAY Most of the accommodation in the area is aimed at budget travellers. There is a particularly healthy population of self-catering apartments.

Mid range

Four Heavens (4 villas) Pereybère; 263 1340; **f** 263 1274; **e** resa@myvillas.mu; www.myvillas.mu. Modern 2-storey villas in a gated residence a few mins' walk from the beach. Villas have 3 bedrooms, 2 bathrooms, AC, TV, equipped kitchen, Wi-Fi (payable), & daily maid service. There is a pool, pleasant gardens & room to park next to each villa. A deposit of €125 is payable on arrival, refundable on departure subject to inventory check. **$$$**

Hibiscus Beach Resort & Spa (36 rooms) Coastal Rd, Pereybère; 263 8554; **f** 263 8553; **e** hibisvv@bow.intnet.mu; www.hibiscushotel.com. In a pretty garden on the seafront. The rooms are spacious & newly refurbished, with AC, TV, phone, minibar & balcony/terrace. There are 2 restaurants, 1 on the water's edge, & there is a private manmade beach with sunloungers to make up for the lack of natural beach. There is a good pool, watersports, a dive centre, small spa & kids' club. **$$$**

Ocean Beauty (9 rooms) Pointe d'Azur Lane, Pereybère; 263 3039; **f** 263 3055; **e** info@ocean.mu; www.ocean-beauty.com. A boutique hotel on the beach at Pereybère, opened in 2005. The en-suite rooms & suites are modern, tastefully furnished & equipped with AC, TV, safe, minibar, tea/coffee facilities, Wi-Fi & balcony/terrace. The double rooms have a microwave. Some suites have a 2nd bedroom, & some have a kitchenette. There is a pool with sea view & some watersports are free. There is no restaurant (breakfast is served in your room) although for independent travellers this offers the opportunity to sample local eateries. The hotel can arrange dinner on the beach for special occasions. **$$$**

Budget

Bleu de Toi (8 rooms) Coastal Rd, Pereybère; **f** 269 1761; **e** info@hotelbleudetoi.com; www.hotelbleudetoi.com. Charming guesthouse accommodation in a large villa, at the entrance to Pereybère coming from Grand Baie. Rooms are modern & tastefully decorated, equipped with en suite, AC, TV, safe, minibar & Wi-Fi. Some rooms have a balcony. There is a restaurant & a pool. While there may not be many facilities or activities at the guesthouse, it is close to touristy spots where all manner of entertainment can be arranged. A great budget option if you don't mind a 5min walk to the beach. **$$**

Casa Florida (80 rooms & apts) Mont Oreb Lane, Pereybère; 263 7371; **f** 263 6209; **e** florida@intnet.mu; www.casaflorida.net. Basic accommodation set back down a lane 5mins' walk from the beach & the centre of Pereybère. The rooms, self-catering studios & 2-bedroom apartments are set in an attractive garden, & equipped with TV, fan, safe, tea/coffee facilities & balcony/terrace. AC & kitchenette cost extra. There is a restaurant, a pool, small spa & tennis courts (racquets & balls aren't supplied). **$$**

Le Beach Club (16 apts) Coastal Rd, Pereybère; 263 5104; **f** 263 5202; **e** beachclub@intnet.mu; www.le-beachclub.com. Clean, colourful (think tangerine walls ...) studios & apartments on the seafront, by a small, unimpressive beach. Accommodation is equipped with en-suite facilities, AC, TV, kitchenette, safe

& balcony/terrace. Rooms are cleaned daily & all linen is provided. There is a bar/restaurant, pool table & table tennis. There is no pool but the sea here is suitable for swimming/snorkelling. Breakfast is available. Well located for self-caterers, a short walk from the supermarket. **$$**

Pereybère Hotel & Apartments (21 rooms & apts) Coastal Rd, Pereybère; 263 8165; **f** 263 6353; **e** pereyberehotel@intnet.mu; www.pereyberehotel.com. A range of AC accommodation across the road from the beach. 14 en-suite rooms with TV, phone, minibar, tea/coffee facilities & balcony. 2 studios with bathroom, phone & kitchenette. 5 2-bedroom apartments with kitchenette, living area, TV & balcony. There's also a 2-bedroom suite with dining room, living area, TV, stereo, kitchen, jacuzzi & balcony. The restaurant specialises in seafood & there is a pool & small spa. **$$**

WHERE TO EAT

Sea Lovers Coastal Rd; 263 6299; for breakfast, lunch & dinner daily. Cuisine: French, seafood, Creole, Chinese, Japanese. Upmarket restaurant in a converted seafront home at the northern end of the public beach. Elegant indoor & outdoor dining – the tables on the huge terrace have great sea views. There is an excellent choice of wines & a relaxing bar. The best place in the area to treat yourself to a memorable meal. Incorporates a Chinese dining room, Japanese room & the trendy Redcat Beach Lounge, where a lively beach party is held on the last Sun of the month, *séga* show on Tue & Sat evening. **$$$$**

Nirvana Coastal Rd; 262 6711; for lunch & dinner Mon–Sat. Cuisine: Indian. About 1km north of Pereybère. Excellent food in elegant surroundings. Pricey but worth it. Reservation recommended. **$$$**

Wangthai Beach Hse, Coastal Rd; 263 4050; for lunch Tue–Sat, for dinner daily. Cuisine: Thai. Tasty, authentic Thai cuisine. **$$$**

Pereybère Café Coastal Rd; 263 8700; for lunch & dinner daily. Cuisine: Chinese, Creole, European. Also take-away. **$$**

NIGHTLIFE Pereybère is less lively than Grand Baie by night but it does have one claim to fame – a karaoke bar. **Julie Bar** on the coast road (*269 0320*) caters not only for frustrated sopranos but also for sports fans with a large television screen. On Saturday evenings there's a *séga* show. The Redcat Beach Lounge is at the heart of the area's bar scene.

OTHER PRACTICALITIES

Communications Internet access is available at the Pereybère Cybercafé (*263 2866*) and **Hardrive Cybercafé** (*263 1076*) on the coastal road.

CAP MALHEUREUX TO GRAND GAUBE

Cap Malheureux is the most northerly point of Mauritius, 22km from Port Louis. It was there that the British landed in 1810, although no monument marks the site. From Cap Malheureux, the view of **Coin de Mire** (Gunner's Quoin) shows the wedge shape that gave the island its name (the quoin was the wedge used to steady a cannon). There is a picturesque, much-photographed, bright red Roman Catholic chapel close to the beach, **Notre Dame Auxiliatrice**. Services are held on Saturdays at 18.00 and Sundays at 09.00. During the week from about 13.00, cheerful fishermen gather round a set of scales near the church, weighing, sorting and selling their catch of colourful fish.

Heading east from Cap Malheureux, the coastal road turns inland through stone-encrusted patches of cane, touching the coast again briefly at **St François** before reaching **Grand Gaube**. *Gaube* or *goab* is the local word for an inlet or bay. This small village is still very much a fishing community and groups of fishermen can be seen relaxing in the evenings with a game of *boules* or dominoes by the beach. As yet largely untainted by tourism, there is an atmosphere of the 'real Mauritius'.

Grand Gaube is somewhat isolated, but the industrial town of **Goodlands** is not far inland. **Historic Marine**, makers of wooden ship models, is on the St Antoine Industrial Estate. Visitors can watch the models being made in the workshop (weekdays only) and buy the finished products on site (see page 132).

WHERE TO STAY

Upmarket

Le Paradise Cove Hotel & Spa (67 rooms) Anse La Raie, Cap Malheureux; 204 4000; f 204 4040; e pcove@intnet.mu; www.paradisecovehotel.com. Enjoys an enviable position on a peninsula, which means the beaches are essentially private. Accommodation is in 2- & 3-storey complexes around a small cove with a glittering white beach. The rooms, refurbished in 2008 with an Indian theme, are equipped with AC, TV, phone, internet access, safe, minibar & balcony/terrace. There are tennis courts, a pool, spa, gym, watersports & a dive centre. Plenty of little luxuries without going overboard. Being small it has a cosy feel, & no ugly scrums for the buffet as in some of the larger resorts. **$$$$**

Lux Grand Gaube (198 rooms) Grand Gaube; 204 9191; f 288 2828; e reservation@luxislandresorts.com; www.luxislandresorts.com. A good-quality hotel in a quiet location, within easy reach of the north's attractions. There are 6 room categories, meaning everyone should find something to suit their needs. Rooms & suites are well equipped, with AC, TV, phone, Wi-Fi, safe, minibar, tea/coffee facilities & balcony/terrace with sea view. There is a 2-bedroom villa with private pool & beach area. There are 5 restaurants, 3 pools, a spa, watersports, dive centre, tennis courts, golf driving range, gym & kids' & teenagers' clubs. It is the only hotel on the island to have a private cinema. Certainly no shortage of entertainment for the family, & there is a good beach. **$$$$**

Mid range

Calodyne sur Mer (82 rooms) Mirabelle Av, Calodyne; 288 2590; f 288 4595; e resa@calodynehotel.com; www.calodynesurmerhotel.com. At the end of a residential street on a quiet part of the coast near Grand Gaube with views of Coin de Mire. Rooms are simply but comfortably furnished, with AC, TV, phone, safe & balcony/terrace. Family apts have 2 or 3 bedrooms & a kitchenette. There are 2 restaurants, regular evening entertainment, a pool, massage rooms & a kids' club. Kayaks, lasers & pedaloes are available free of charge. There aren't many hotels or attractions nearby & you would need a bike or car to explore the area. **$$$**

Cape Garden (34 studios, 68 apts) Bain Boeuf; 263 1340; f 263 1274; e resa@myvillas.mu; www.myvillas.mu. Super modern, well-equipped studios & 2-bedroom duplex apartments 50m from the beach. Accommodation has AC, TV, equipped kitchen, Wi-Fi (payable), linen & daily maid service. There is a pool, gym, parking & 24hr security. A deposit of €125 is payable on arrival, refundable on departure subject to inventory check. **$$$**

Coin de Mire Attitude (118 rooms) Coastal Rd, Bain Boeuf, Cap Malheureux; 204 9900; f 262 7305; e info@coindemire-hotel.com; www.coindemire-hotel.com. A 3-star equivalent hotel across the road from a small beach & a pretty lagoon. Rooms have been thoughtfully renovated & have AC, phone, TV, safe & balcony/terrace. There are 2 pools, limited free watersports, tennis court, a restaurant, small spa & small kids'club. Wi-Fi zone available. The pool area suffers from some road noise & can feel crowded. **$$$**

Paul et Virginie Hotel (81 rooms) Coastal Rd, Grand Gaube; 288 0215; f 288 9233; e veranda@veranda-resorts.com; www.veranda-resorts.com. A well laid-out hotel, with thatched blocks of 2 & 3 storeys housing clean, comfortable en-suite rooms. All rooms have AC, TV, phone, minibar, safe & balcony/terrace. There are 2 restaurants overlooking the sea, 2 pools, a small spa & a floodlit tennis court (across the road). A good range of non-motorised watersports are free & bikes can be hired. Guests can play at the Heritage Golf Club in the south of the island for a fee. Although rooms can accommodate a child, the hotel is aimed at couples, rather than families.

Budget

Kuxville (25 apts) Coastal Rd, Cap Malheureux; 262 7913; f 262 7407; e kuxville@intnet.mu; www.kuxville.de. Self-catering bungalows (3 bedrooms), studios & apartments with bathroom, kitchen, AC. In addition to the original beachside accommodation, there are new bungalows in a garden setting across the road from the beach. There is no restaurant but staff can prepare meals for you. There is a daily maid service. Some watersports, a dive centre & kitesurfing are available. Run by a German family with a conspicuously German atmosphere. **$$**

L'Archipel Bungalows (11 apts) Mirabelle Av, Calodyne; 288 9518; f 288 7910; e archipel@intnet.mu; www.larchipel-bungalows.com. In a residential area on an undeveloped part of the coast. Basic self-catering apartments with 1, 2 or 3 bedrooms, AC & sea view. They are grouped in Creole-style buildings around a pool, in a pleasant garden. The coast is rocky here but there is a small beach & views of Coin de Mire, Flat Island & Round Island. Kayaks, pedaloes & windsurfing are free. You can catch a speedboat to Cap Malheureux for a fee. It is quite isolated & you would need a bike or car to get around. **$$**

WHERE TO EAT

Restaurant Amigo Royal Rd, Cap Malheureux; 262 6248; for lunch & dinner Mon–Sat. Cuisine: Creole, European, seafood. On the B45 road which heads inland from Cap Malheureux towards Port Louis. The seafood dishes are particularly good. Sooner or later the owner is bound to boast to you that Jacques Chirac has been there, so I'll spoil the surprise & tell you now. **$$$**

Le Coin de Mire Cap Malheureux; 262 8070; 10.30–22.00 daily. Cuisine: Creole, seafood. In a lovely position opposite the red church. The fish is as fresh as it gets – bought directly from the fishermen who come ashore next to the church. **$$**

NORTHERN OFFSHORE ISLANDS

COIN DE MIRE This distinctively shaped island, a nature reserve, lies 4km from the north coast and can be visited on excursions arranged by hotels or travel agents, although landing is tricky (see *What to do in Northern Mauritius*, page 131). There is a cave on the island called **Madam's Hole**, which was used by the British navy in the 19th century for target practice. Graceful white *paille en queues* (tropic-birds) can be seen soaring around the black cliffs.

FLAT, GABRIEL, ROUND, SERPENT AND AMBER ISLANDS Off the northern coast beyond Coin de Mire are Flat, Gabriel, Round, Serpent and Amber islands, which are all uninhabited.

The most visited of these are **Flat Island** (L'île Plate) and **Gabriel Island** (L'îlot Gabriel). Flat Island has a lighthouse built in 1855, which is still operating, and there is good snorkelling around both islands. Although excursions to these islands are becoming increasingly popular, they do not have the sometimes crowded feel of Ile aux Cerfs in the east. (For further details of excursions, see *What to do in Northern Mauritius*, page 131.)

Round Island (L'île Ronde) cannot be visited without a permit, since it is a nature reserve. The island, which is kidney-shaped, not round, and about 1.5km^2 in area, is some 22km from Mauritius. Its flora and fauna are fascinating as much of it is rare, having evolved in isolation without the attentions of the early colonists (see also pages 15–19).

Neighbouring **Serpent Island** (L'île aux Serpents), a large barren rock with no serpents or snakes, is a sanctuary for birds, and so not open to the public.

Amber Island (L'île d'Ambre) is so called because of the ambergris which used to be found there. It is largely surrounded by mangroves. The ill-fated *St Géran* was wrecked on the Amber Island reefs in 1744 with heavy loss of life. The tragedy inspired the Mauritian love story of *Paul et Virginie*, written by Bernadin de St Pierre. A monument commemorating the disaster was erected at Poudre d'Or in 1944 and artefacts recovered from the ship can be seen at the National History Museum in Mahébourg (see page 159). Amber Island is a popular picnic spot for Mauritians on weekends, and can be visited by tourists on excursions arranged locally (see *What to do in Northern Mauritius*, below).

POUDRE D'OR TO RIVIERE DU REMPART Poudre d'Or is an unspoilt fishing village with a sturdy building built in 1864 as a chest hospital. The name could have derived from gold found in the region or, more likely, from the golden powder sands found here. Virginie, the fictional heroine of St Pierre's novel, *Paul et Virginie*, is supposed to have been washed ashore on this coast, prompting Mark Twain to observe wryly that it was 'the only one prominent event in the history of the island, and that didn't happen'.

The road down the east coast passes between cane and tobacco fields to reach **Rivière du Rempart**. This town has many cyclone-proof concrete houses as well as two old wooden mansions, opposite each other, that have managed to survive all of the progress and storms.

WHAT TO DO IN NORTHERN MAURITIUS

Most hotels offer or can arrange excursions, activities and watersports, as do the numerous travel agents in Grand Baie. Cruises to the nearby islands and deep-sea fishing are particularly popular. For more information on the activities listed below, see *Chapter 3, Activities*, pages 85–96.

ISLANDS OF THE NORTH Excursions depart from many of the hotels in the north and from Grand Baie. They typically sail to two or more of the islands and include snorkelling and a picnic lunch. White Sand Tours (☎ *208 5424*) offers a full-day catamaran cruise visiting **Flat Island** and **Coin de Mire**, with swimming, snorkelling and a barbecue lunch. Easy Days (☎ *252 4266;* e *info@ezzydays.com; www.ezzydays.com*) operates trips to Flat Island, with a barbecue lunch and the option of guided walks to see the flora and fauna. For the more energetic, Yemaya Adventures (☎ *752 0046*) offers half-day and full-day sea kayak excursions to **Amber Island**.

SPORTS

Scuba diving The reefs off the northern coast and the islands off Cap Malheureux offer some of the best diving in Mauritius. There are many scuba-diving operators in the north of the island catering for all levels and experience (see pages 89–92).

Snorkelling The best snorkelling in northern Mauritius is in the lagoons at Turtle Bay, Trou aux Biches, Pereybère, Grand Baie and around Flat and Gabriel islands. There are numerous half- and full-day cruises around the north and east that include snorkelling, such as the White Sand Tours full-day catamaran cruise (see above).

Other undersea experiences Those who don't want to dive can experience underwater life on an undersea walk or in a submersible, such as the Blue Safari Submarine or a submersible scooter (see page 93). The north is where these activities take place.

Deep-sea fishing Although the west coast is reputed to be the best for deep-sea fishing, several companies offer trips from the northern coast.

Watersports The north of the island, Grand Baie in particular, has the island's greatest range of watersports. If your hotel does not have watersports facilities, there are operators in Grand Baie, such as Centre Sport Nautique (*263 8017*).

Golf There is a nine-hole course at **Trou aux Biches Resort and Spa** (see page 119).

Horseriding Most hotels and tour operators can arrange horseriding. One of the island's better riding stables is **Horse Riding Delights** at the Mont Choisy Sugar Estate (*265 6159; www.horseidingdelights.com*) near Grand Baie (see page 87).

Hiking and adventure sports

Yemaya Adventures Grand Gaube; 752 0046. Based in Grand Gaube & offers hiking, mountain biking & sea kayaking (see also page 95).

SPA TREATMENTS

Grand Baie Gym & Hydrospa X Club Rd, Grand Baie; 263 4891; **f** 263 9291; **e** info@grandbaiegym.com; www.grandbaiegym.com; 06.00–21.00 Mon–Fri, 07.30–19.30 Sat, 09.00–13.00 Sun & public holidays; spa closed Sun. Offers a gym, pool, spa, beauty treatments, weight-loss programmes, hairdresser & a range of group classes, such as martial arts, dance & aerobics. Decent café on site. Temporary membership of the gym is from Rs1,398 per week, Rs690 per day. Expect to pay around Rs1,900 for a 60-minute massage.

Surya Coastal Rd, Pereybère; **f** 263 1637; **e** info@spasurya.com; www.mauriweb.com/surya; 09.00–20.00 daily. This Ayurvedic spa between Grand Baie & Pereybère offers a range of relaxing massages & treatments. As well as one-off treatments, programmes lasting from 3 days to 3 weeks are available. Yoga classes are also available.

Trou aux Biches Beach Spa Coastal Rd, Trou aux Biches; 256 2012

CASINO There is a **Ti Vegas** casino at the Super U complex in Grand Baie (*269 1448*).

SHOPPING **Grand Baie**, and Sunset Boulevard in particular, is crammed with boutiques, reminiscent of any touristy beach resort. Some of the jewellery shops here are duty free.

At **Historic Marine** in Goodlands (*283 9404;* **f** *283 9204;* **e** *info@hismar.mu; www.historic-marine.com;* *09.00–17.00 Mon–Fri, 09.00–12.00 Sat/Sun*), visitors can tour the model-ship workshop and buy finished models in the shop. Prices range from €50 to €4,500.

The **Saga World** complex (*09.00–18.00 Mon–Sat, 09.00–15.00 Sun*) opposite the botanical gardens at Pamplemousses has a number of upmarket shops selling rugs, clothing and jewellery.

There are several commercial art galleries in the north, including **Galerie du Moulin Cassé** in Pereybère (*727 0672;* *10.00–18.00 Fri*), in a converted 19th-century sugar mill. It has permanent exhibitions by Diane Henry, natural world photographer, and Malcolm de Chazal (1902–82), Mauritian artist. Seebaluck Art Gallery in Pointe aux Canonniers (*263 6470;* *09.30–19.00 Mon–Sat*) has local and international art.

WHAT TO SEE IN NORTHERN MAURITIUS

SIR SEEWOOSAGUR RAMGOOLAM BOTANIC GARDENS (*Pamplemousses;* ☎ *243 9401; gardens* ⏰ *08.30–17.30 daily; admission Rs250*) Formerly known as the Royal Botanic Garden, this is one of the island's most popular tourist attractions, located 11km northeast of Port Louis. Most hotels and travel agents offer tours to the gardens and they are easily accessible from Port Louis by bus from the Immigration Square bus station or from Grand Baie (bus route 216). There are also buses from the coastal towns of the north. Buses stop on the main road and the garden is a five-minute walk away. On Sundays it is popular with picnickers.

The garden covers 60 acres so a guide or good map is essential to get the most out of it. Official guides (with a badge) are available (for a small fee) by the main gate and the entrance from the car park. It is by no means obligatory to have a guide and their sales pitch can sometimes be rather pushy. Unofficial guides (no badge) operate within the garden and may approach you. The booths at the main gates, which are only open on weekdays, sell comprehensive guidebooks on the gardens (Rs225) but the leaflets, which have a good map, are sufficient to find your way around.

The fence and gates at the entrance are scrolled in wrought iron and gained a first prize in the International Exhibition at London's Crystal Palace in 1862. The gate was a gift from François Liénard, a Frenchman, born in India in 1783, who lived in Mauritius. There is a memorial obelisk to him in the garden.

The garden's origins go back to 1729 when a French colonist acquired about half the present site, then called Mon Plaisir. Mahé de Labourdonnais bought it in 1735 and created a vegetable garden (to the left of the present main entrance) beside his own residence, Château de Mon Plaisir, to supply vegetables to his household, the town and visiting ships. The garden was also used as a nursery for plants imported from Europe, Asia and South America. Mulberry bushes were planted in the hope of starting a silkworm industry but were replaced by *bois noir* (*Albizia lebbeck*), to be turned into charcoal for use in the manufacture of gunpowder for the island's defence.

When, in 1770, the garden became the private property of Pierre Poivre, administrator of the island, Pamplemousses flourished. He cultivated spices such as nutmeg and cloves, as well as ornamental trees. In 1810, the garden reverted to government ownership and was neglected by the British until James Duncan was appointed director in 1849. He introduced many of the palms including the royal palms (*Roystonea regia* and *Roystonea oleracea*), which add a majestic splendour to the main avenue. Thousands of eucalyptus trees were planted in the garden after the malaria epidemic of 1866, for transplanting in swamps to dry them out and reduce mosquito-breeding grounds. Since 1913 the garden has been under the control of the Ministry of Agriculture.

Today the garden boasts 500 species of plant, of which 80 are palms and 25 are indigenous to the Mascarene Islands. The numerous highlights include the impressive giant water lilies (*Victoria amazonica*), which float like giant baking tins in a rectangular pond. Their flowers open for two days only, from the late afternoon to the following morning. On the first day they are cream-coloured with a heady fragrance, on the second they are pink. Another pond contains the white and yellow flowers of the lotus (*Nelumbo nucifera*), which is held in veneration by Hindus. The betel nut palm (*Areca cathecu*) grows nearby. Its orange fruit contains the betel nut which is sliced, mixed with lime paste, wrapped in the leaf of the vine (*Piper betel*) and chewed. It's a cancer-causing stimulant which depresses the appetite and stains the gums and lips an alarming red. The talipot palms (*Corypha umbraculifera*) are said to flower once every 40 to 60 years with over 50 million tiny blooms, reaching a height of 6m above the tree. After waiting so long to flower just once, the tree dies.

The **Château de Mon Plaisir** looks impressive but lightweight, perhaps because it is not the original home of Labourdonnais but an English-built office mansion, now used for administration and exhibitions. The nearby **sugar mill** is also a reconstruction. Former prime minister and governor general Sir Seewoosagur Ramgoolam was cremated outside the mansion and his ashes scattered on the Ganges, in India. In front of the chateau are trees planted by visiting royal and political dignitaries, such as Nelson Mandela.

The **tortoise pen** houses Aldabra tortoises, first brought to the gardens in 1875 from Aldabra Island to protect them from being wiped out by seabirds (when young) or being eaten by humans (when older). The **stag park** contains the *Cervus timorensis russa* deer, first introduced in 1639 from Batavia.

Animals to be seen at liberty include the indigenous fruit bat (*Pteropus niger*), two species of rat (the brown Norway rat and the black arboreal Asiatic rat), and the Madagascar tenrec (*Centetes* spp.). The large, black butterfly with blue windows on its wings is the *Papilio manlius*.

Indigenous birds include the moorhen (*Gallinula chloropus pyrrhorrhoa*), with its red bill, and the green-backed heron (*Butorides striatus rutenbergi*). The small greyish bird in groups with a 'tip-tip-tip' call is *l'oiseau Manioc* (*Malacirops borbonicus mauritianus*). Species of the *Phelsuma* lizard may be seen on palm trees.

There are several **monuments** in the garden including a stone slab which the sentimental believe marks the grave of the fictitious lovers, Paul and Virginie. Their creator, Bernadin de St Pierre, is remembered with a bust.

L'AVENTURE DU SUCRE (*Beau Plan, Pamplemousses;* ☎ *243 7900;* **f** *243 9699;* **e** *aventure.sucre@intnet.mu; www.aventuredusucre.com;* 🕘 *09.00–17.00 daily; admission adult/child Rs350/175*) In 1999, the Beau Plan sugar factory, which had been operating since 1895, closed down. In October 2002, it was converted into a fascinating high-tech museum covering the history of sugar, the history of Mauritius and the process of sugar production. The exhibits on slavery and the treatment of slaves and runaways are particularly thought-provoking. In fact, the museum provides one of the most comprehensive and digestible histories of Mauritius available on the island. The visit culminates in a tasting of export-quality sugars and rums. Sugar products and other souvenirs are on sale at the shop. Allow approximately two hours for self-guided tours, including tasting. There is a restaurant, Le Fangourin, which serves delicious meals and special sugar desserts (see page 118).

CHATEAU DE LABOURDONNAIS (*Mapou;* ☎ *266 9533;* **f** *266 6415; www.unchateaudanslanature.com;* 🕘 *09.00–17.00 daily; admission adult/child Rs350/175*) A Creole mansion built in 1859 at the heart of an agricultural estate. A private home until 2006, the house had fallen into disrepair but was carefully restored and opened to visitors in 2010. Although some French experts were called in, much of the restoration work was done by local artisans, including the wonderful metal railings along the veranda. A video tells the fascinating story of the restoration and audio in the various rooms reflecting family life (currently only in French) brings the place alive. The wallpaper in the dining room, which features countryside scenes of deer and birds in a forest, is the original, painstakingly restored. There is no disabled access but disabled guests can view a virtual tour on a screen on the ground floor. You cannot wear high-heeled shoes or take photographs in the chateau. After visiting the house you can explore the 150-year-old orchards and at the end of the tour you can taste fruit juice, rum and fruit jelly made on the estate. There is a modern restaurant in the grounds (see page 118), a shop and a few tortoises in a pen.

MAURITIUS AQUARIUM (*Coastal Rd, Pointe aux Piments;* ☎ *261 4561;* **f** *261 5080;* **e** *info@mauritiusaquarium.com; www.mauritiusaquarium.com;* ⏲ *09.30–17.00 Mon–Sat, 10.00–15.00 Sun & public holidays; admission adult/child/family (2 adults, 2 children) Rs250/125/650*) Opened in 2004, the aquarium has filled an important gap in the island's attractions. It is small but thoughtfully designed and offers a good opportunity to see some of the creatures you'll observe while snorkelling or diving off Mauritius, except in the aquarium they have handy labels. Favourites include the Picasso triggerfish (*Rhinecanthus aculeatus*), Moorish idol (*Zanclus cornutus*), domino fish (*Dascyllus aranus*), white tip reef sharks (*Triaenodon obesus*) and green sea turtles (*Chelonia mydas*). There are freshwater fish too, such as the carp caught locally by the manager. Children will enjoy the touch pool. There is a small souvenir shop and snack bar. The fish are fed daily at 11.00.

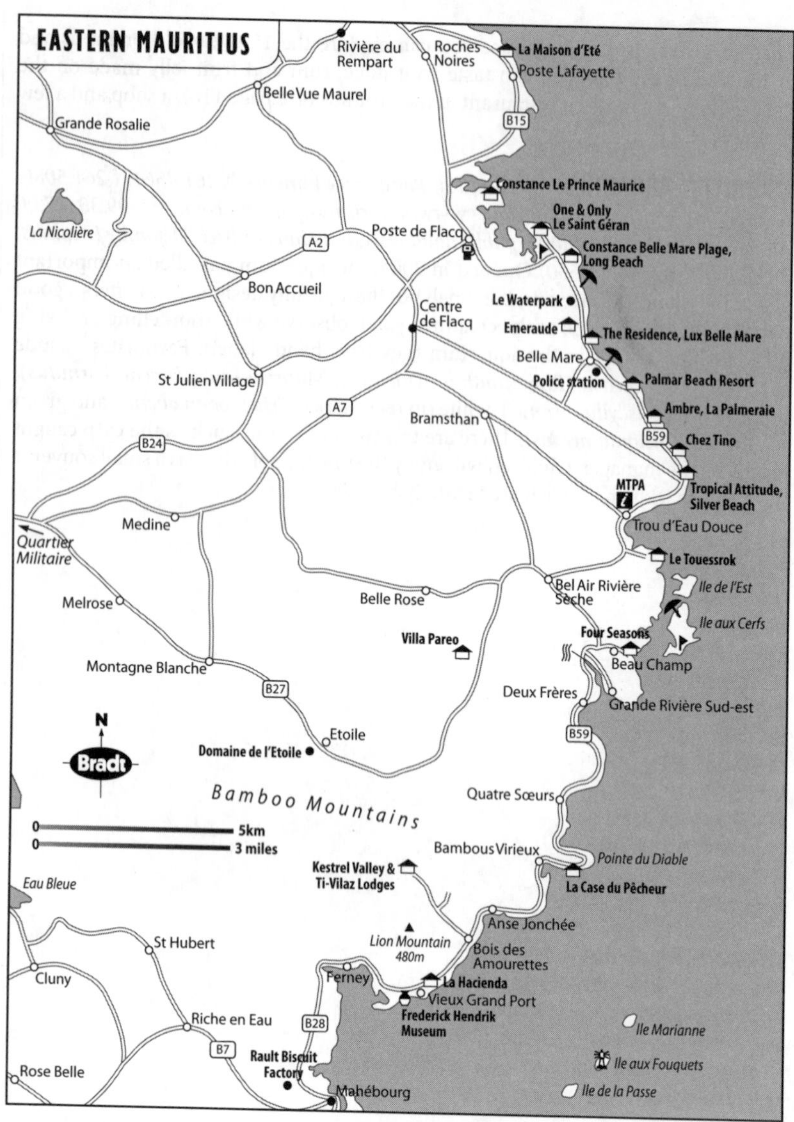
EASTERN MAURITIUS
Rivière du Rempart
Roches Noires
La Maison d'Eté
Poste Lafayette
Belle Vue Maurel
Grande Rosalie
B15
Constance Le Prince Maurice
La Nicolière
One & Only Le Saint Géran
Poste de Flacq
A2
Constance Belle Mare Plage, Long Beach
Bon Accueil
Centre de Flacq
Le Waterpark
Emeraude
The Residence, Lux Belle Mare
Belle Mare
St Julien Village
Police station
Palmar Beach Resort
A7
Ambre, La Palmeraie
Bramsthan
B24
B59
Chez Tino
MTPA
Tropical Attitude, Silver Beach
Medine
Quartier Militaire
Trou d'Eau Douce
Le Touessrok
Melrose
Belle Rose
Bel Air Rivière Sèche
Ile de l'Est
Ile aux Cerfs
Four Seasons
Villa Pareo
Montagne Blanche
Beau Champ
B27
Deux Frères
Grande Rivière Sud-est
N
Etoile
Domaine de l'Etoile
B59
Bradt
Bamboo Mountains
Quatre Sœurs
0
5km
0
3 miles
Bambous Virieux
Pointe du Diable
Kestrel Valley & Ti-Vilaz Lodges
La Case du Pêcheur
Eau Bleue
Anse Jonchée
Lion Mountain 480m
St Hubert
Bois des Amourettes
Cluny
Ferney
La Hacienda
Vieux Grand Port
Frederick Hendrik Museum
Riche en Eau
B28
Ile Marianne
B7
Rault Biscuit Factory
Ile aux Fouquets
Rose Belle
Mahébourg
Ile de la Passe

Eastern Mauritius

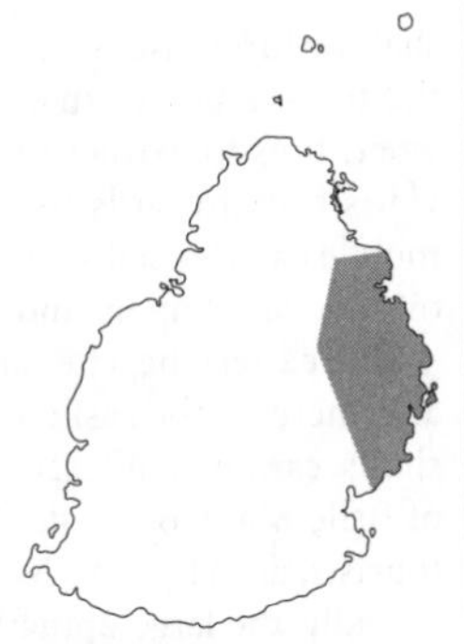

The district of Flacq occupies most of the east of the island, which for our purposes extends from Roches Noires in the northeast down to Bois des Amourettes in the southeast.

Much of eastern Mauritius was covered with ebony forest when the Dutch settled here in the 17th century, but it didn't take them long to start felling the trees to make a road northwards from their settlement at Grand Port. The French continued attacking the forests, using the timber to build ships and houses. The land is now primarily devoted to sugarcane.

The beaches around Belle Mare are glorious, if a little windy in winter, and have attracted a string of upmarket hotels. However, there is still mid-range and budget accommodation to be found. The area is popular with golfers, who come to take advantage of the two Constance Belle Mare Plage courses (see page 86).

The uninhabited Ile aux Cerfs, off Trou d'Eau Douce, is one of the best-known tourist attractions of the east, with its miles of beaches, copious watersports facilities and championship golf course belonging to Le Touessrok Hotel. The area south of Trou d'Eau Douce is largely undeveloped owing to the lack of beaches. Driving along this coast is a real pleasure, with the road sandwiched between the sea and unspoilt fishing villages.

ROCHES NOIRES TO BELLE MARE

South of Rivière du Rempart is the bulge of **Roches Noires**, with weekend houses – *campements* – facing the turquoise sea. The term *campement* originally referred to a weekend house made of *ravenala* and straw. Nowadays the word is applied to the ever-multiplying concrete villas.

In summer, this coast is pleasant, but it suffers from strong southeast winds in winter. Peddlers on motorbikes, loaded with goods of every description, travel the roads selling their wares to women working in the fields who can't go to town to shop.

From Roches Noires the road trickles down the east coast, passing through **Poste Lafayette**. The coast is lined with casuarinas, bent by the winter winds. There are some beaches but the sea is rougher than in other areas and they don't compare to those further south, although you may sometimes have a beach to yourself here. The town of **Poste de Flacq** is little more than a road junction, although there is a petrol station.

The heart of the Flacq district is **Centre de Flacq**, a town of about 15,000 inhabitants. Its courthouse and post office are housed in a well-maintained, French-style colonial building, listed as a national monument.

Belle Mare, **Palmar** and the surrounding area offer some of the island's best beaches. Belle Mare Beach is true postcard material, with a long white-sand beach, shallow turquoise waters and a border of casuarina trees. The old **lime kiln** among the trees is one of many along this coast, where coral was burnt over casuarina wood fires to extract the lime. You can climb the steps to the top of the kiln for views back towards the mountains of the centre or out to sea. Among the trees, mobile eateries sell *samoussas* and other light bites, while hopeful pineapple sellers on mopeds chug up and down the beach looking for customers.

The eastern beaches are not easily reached by bus, but a taxi is inexpensive from anywhere on the east coast. The village of Belle Mare is small but has a few touristy shops, car hire and excursions companies and a **police station**. At the northern end of Belle Mare, opposite Belle Mare Plage Hotel, are a few modern shops aimed at tourists, an ATM and MCB currency exchange counter.

Sadly, the large upmarket hotels which have come to dominate this area of coast have brought with them jet skis, banana boats and water-skiing tourists. At times, you strain to hear the gentle lapping of the ocean over the wailing of outboard motors.

One of the best things about the area is that whilst there are hotels on the beach side of the road, the opposite side is still the domain of small farmers, who seem to tend their modest crops at all hours of the day. Vegetables such as onions, chillies and aubergines are the main crops, grown for sale at local markets.

WHERE TO STAY

Luxury

Constance Le Prince Maurice (89 suites) Poste de Flacq; 402 3636; **f** 413 9130; **e** info@princemaurice.com; www.princemaurice.com. A luxury hotel in a quiet location on a pretty bay. 76 junior suites, 12 senior suites & 1 'princely suite', some of which are on stilts over the water. All are very private & superbly appointed with large en suite, balcony/terrace & free Wi-Fi. 9 senior suites have a private pool. The main pool is brilliantly designed & when viewed from the hotel foyer seems to flow into the sea. There are 3 restaurants, including Le Barachois, a small floating restaurant. There is a very impressive Guerlain spa & a wide range of free watersports. Other amenities include a gym, squash, tennis, library, kids' club & free access to the golf courses of Constance Belle Mare Plage Golf (see page 86). The service is discreet & you really do feel pampered. **$$$$$**

One&Only Le Saint Géran (163 rooms) Poste de Flacq; 401 1688; **f** 401 1668; **e** info@oneandonlylesaintgeran.mu; www.oneandonlyresorts.com. This member of 'Leading Hotels of the World' boasts 148 luxurious junior suites, 14 ocean suites & 'The Villa', an extravagant 2-bedroomed monument to self-indulgence. The junior suites have a view of either the sea or lagoon & come with butler service, as well as everything else you'd expect from a first-class hotel. 1 junior suite is suitable for disabled guests. There are 3 lavish restaurants, including the Spoon des Iles, which serves innovative international cuisine at heart-stopping prices. Facilities include a casino, a Gary Player-designed 9-hole golf course & a Givenchy spa, which offers such vital services as 'herbal wraps', 'skin peeling' & 'special lifting objectives'. Free watersports include water skiing & small-game fishing. There are 5 tennis courts, a gym offering personal training & a dive centre. As well as a kids' club, there is 1 for teenagers. The hotel prides itself on its service & is the only hotel on the island to offer a beach concierge service. **$$$$$**

Upmarket

Constance Belle Mare Plage (256 rooms) Belle Mare; 402 2600; **f** 402 2626; **e** info@bellemareplagehotel.com; www.bellemareplagehotel.com. This sprawling resort stretches along a pristine beach. Although this is a big hotel, there is plenty of space so it doesn't tend to feel too crowded. As well as 235 rooms & suites, there are 20 luxurious 2- & 3-bedroom villas & a presidential villa. There are 2 rooms with disabled facilities. The accommodation is stylish & comfortable, with the usual upmarket amenities. The villas are impressive, each with private pool & butler service. There are 7 restaurants, including the first-class Blue Penny Café (see page 140) & those at the golf courses. A popular hotel with golfers, who take advantage of the 2 18-hole championship courses (see page 86). Also available are a choice of 4 pools, a fitness centre, spa, tennis, watersports & a kids' club. Good value for money. **$$$$**

La Palmeraie (60 rooms) Coastal Rd, Belle Mare; 401 8500; f 415 1804; e resa@palmeraie-hotel.com; www.hotel-palmeraie.com. A boutique hotel with a Moroccan theme, on a nice stretch of beach. The abundance of concrete means it is rather less attractive than its thatched competitors. The en-suite rooms have AC, TV, phone, minibar, safe & balcony/terrace. There are 2 restaurants (1 Moroccan), a spa, watersports & kids' club. Free Wi-Fi in the bar & reception. At the bottom end of the upmarket range in terms of price but the facilities are closer to mid-range. **$$$$**

Long Beach (255 rooms) Belle Mare; 401 1919; f 401 1999; e info@longbeach.mu; www.longbeachmauritius.com. A new concept from Sun Resorts featuring ultra modern, urban architecture. It is on the site of the old Coco Beach Hotel & care was taken to protect the environment during the knock-down-rebuild process – 1.5 million plants were removed & replanted & the new hotel was designed to use green energy, in particular solar. The 5 restaurants, bars & a nightclub sit around a central plaza, giving a village feel. The dining options are excellent & include Chinese, Japanese & Italian. The sports facilities are extensive & include a pool, tennis courts, watersports (non-motorised are free), pitch & putt & a climbing wall. **$$$$**

Lux Belle Mare (174 rooms, 12 villas) Belle Mare; 402 2000; f 415 2020; e reservations@luxislandresorts.com; www.luxislandresorts.com. Located on a good stretch of beach is this large resort hotel (formerly Beau Rivage), whose rooms & suites are in 3-storey buildings with thatched roofs. Rooms are spacious & equipped with AC, TV, phone, safe, minibar & balcony/terrace. The luxury villas are delightful & have kitchenette, dining room, butler service, sumptuous bathroom, private garden & plunge pool. The hotel has a spa, an impressive pool with palm trees seemingly growing in it, tennis courts, a gym & kids' club. Free watersports include water skiing. Aside from the main restaurant, there is a Mediterranean beach restaurant, a seafood one & a very nice Indo-Chinese one (see page 140). HB & AI packages available. **$$$$**

The Residence (163 rooms) Belle Mare; 401 8888; f 415 5888; e info-mauritius@theresidence.com; www.theresidence.com. The entrance is suitably grand for a hotel which is impressive in every way. The style is intended to be that of a colonial palace. The rooms & suites are spacious & beautifully decorated, equipped with everything you need, including butler service. The bathrooms deserve special mention – they are superb. Surprisingly for a modern luxury hotel, not all the rooms face the sea but those with a view of the garden are cheaper. There are 4 restaurants, including the unforgettable La Plantation (see page 140) right on the beach. Facilities include an excellent kids' club, tennis courts, many free watersports (inc water skiing) & a fabulous spa. Reasonable value for money. **$$$$**

Mid range

Emeraude Hotel (61 rooms) Coastal Rd, Belle Mare; 401 1400; f 415 1109; e info@hotelemeraude-mauritius.com; www.emeraudebeachhotel.com. Across the road from the northern end of the beach, 2-storey white cottages with thatched roofs are scattered in a garden. The hotel changed hands in 2010 & underwent an extensive renovation. All rooms are en suite but with shower only, no bath. They are clean & simply furnished with AC, TV & phone. The hotel sets up a bar on the beach during the day so its guests don't have to run back across the road for drinks. Guests can also get a boat to Ile aux Cerfs from sister hotel, Le Tropical at Trou d'Eau Douce. There are 2 small pools, a tiny spa offering massage & beauty therapies, a restaurant & a bar with sand floor. Diving & kitesurfing are available. Glass-bottom boat & snorkelling are included. The all-inclusive package is good value. **$$$**

Hotel Ambre (297 rooms) Coastal Rd, Belle Mare; 401 8188; f 401 8099; e info@ambre.mu; www.apavou-hotels.com. At the time of writing, the hotel had just been bought by Sun Resorts & was under renovation, due to re-open in October 2012 as a 4-star equivalent hotel. Rooms have contemporary décor, AC, TV, phone, minibar, safe & balcony/terrace. Family units have 2 bedrooms. There are 3 restaurants, 2 bars, a nightclub, pool, spa, gym, extensive watersports, tennis courts, kids' club & teenagers' club. Internet & Wi-Fi access is available. It is on a great stretch of beach. **$$$**

Palmar Beach Resort (76 rooms) Coastal Rd, Belle Mare; 402 3500; f 415 1043; e resa@veranda-resorts.com; www.veranda-resorts.com. An informal Veranda Group hotel on a superb stretch of beach. The nicely decorated en-suite rooms are equipped with AC, TV, phone, minibar, safe & balcony/terrace. There are 2 restaurants (one on the beach), 2 bars, a pool, spa, kids' club & a good choice of free watersports. Bike hire is available & guests have use of the facilities at other Veranda hotels. **$$$**

Budget

La Maison d'Eté (10 rooms) Coastal Rd, Poste Lafayette; **\f** 410 5039; **e** info@lamaisondete.com; www.lamaisondete.com. A great find for those wanting the option of self-catering. Beautifully decorated throughout with great attention to detail, it feels modern & clean, yet warm & cosy. There are 4 en-suite rooms & 6 bungalows with kitchenette. All rooms have a generous bathroom/dressing area & are equipped with fan, safe, emergency button (now compulsory in guesthouses) & minibar. There is room to dine either in the room or on your terrace, & there is also a good restaurant on site (see below). There are 2 pools & the owners have made an inviting private beach area with loungers, plus there is the option of the adjacent public beach. There are no motorised watersports here, which makes it very peaceful, but kayaks & snorkelling equipment are available free of charge, as are bikes. Excellent value for money. **$$**

WHERE TO EAT

Blue Penny Café Constance Belle Mare Plage; 402 2600; 19.30–22.00 Mon–Sat. Cuisine: European. Far from being a café – this is an exclusive restaurant which is likely to offer you one of the finest dining experiences of your life. It is worth ordering tea at the end of your meal just to see the elaborate preparation, where the leaves are meticulously weighed at your table in hand-held scales. Reservation recommended. **$$$$$**

Deer Hunter The Legend Golf Course, Belle Mare; 402 2600; for breakfast, lunch & dinner daily. Cuisine: Creole, European. If you've seen enough of the beach, this may be the restaurant for you, with its sweeping views of the golf course. You may even spot a deer drinking at one of the lakes. Traditional Creole dishes are given a creative twist. **$$$$**

Indouchine Lux Belle Mare, Belle Mare; 402 2000; for dinner daily. Cuisine: Indochinese. An upmarket restaurant within the hotel, with sea views. Carefully crafted, beautifully presented dishes with a southeast Asian flavour. If you struggle to choose a wine from the wide selection, the highly qualified sommelier can provide invaluable advice. **$$$$**

La Plantation The Residence Hotel, Belle Mare; 401 8888; for lunch & dinner daily. Cuisine: Creole, seafood. Built in the style of a planter's house, perched on the beach away from the main body of the hotel. A great place to treat yourself. The food is as fantastic as the setting & the service is both friendly & slick. Reservation recommended. **$$$$**

East Side Restaurant & Bar Coastal Rd, Belle Mare; 415 1254; 12.00–22.30 daily. Cuisine: Creole, Chinese, European. Set up by a couple of veterans of the Mauritian tourism industry with extensive experience in some of the island's most prestigious hotels. Authentic 'grandma-style' Creole dishes & good-value lobster. Main courses start at Rs260. Take-away available. **$$$**

Symon's Tropical Restaurant Coastal Rd, Belle Mare; 415 1135; 11.00–midnight daily. Cuisine: Creole, Chinese, Indian, seafood. An old favourite around these parts. Also does take-away & there's a lively bar. **$$$**

Chez Manuel St Julien Village; 418 3599; for lunch & dinner Mon–Sat. Cuisine: Creole, Chinese. Inland, just off the A7 between Centre de Flacq & Quartier Militaire. A nice escape from the coast. Offers plenty of choice & has a good reputation among locals. **$$**

Maison d'Eté Coastal Rd, Poste Lafayette; 410 5039; for lunch & dinner Tue–Sat, dinner Mon. Cuisine: Mediterranean, Creole. A clean, cosy restaurant in the guesthouse with a well-deserved reputation for great food. Reservation recommended. **$$**

TROU D'EAU DOUCE

The fishing village of **Trou d'Eau Douce** is an early Dutch settlement. The **Puits des Hollandais**, meaning 'Wells of the Dutch', is an extinct crater well still used for fresh water and Trou d'Eau Douce refers to this freshwater spring although, since it is often pronounced *Tro do-doo*, some historians have assumed it is named after the dodo, which lived in this region.

In the centre of Trou d'Eau Douce is a large black **church** of volcanic rock, Notre Dame des Bon Secours. The black rock, combined with the church's blue windows, gives it an unusual, sombre atmosphere.

Opposite the tourist information office in Trou d'Eau Douce are the remains of a **lime kiln** on the waterfront. You can climb it for views over the bay but take care as there is no hand rail and the stone steps are uneven.

Off Trou d'Eau Douce lies **Ile aux Cerfs**, an uninhabited island which has been transformed into a tourist attraction, with miles of beaches, numerous watersports and a handful of restaurants. It is marketed as a 'paradise island' and is a popular excursion but many travellers find it too touristy and overpriced. The island has a total area of 300ha, much of which has been transformed into the superb Le Touessrok Golf Course (see *Chapter 3, Golf*, page 86).

If you walk far enough around from the boat landing area, you should be able to find a quiet spot on the beach. Once you've settled down, it probably won't be long before a passing gentleman offers you a pineapple or coconut. It's almost worth the Rs100 just to watch him expertly hack the pineapple into the classic ice-cream-cone shape (see also *What to do in Eastern Mauritius*, pages 144–5).

TOURIST INFORMATION There is an MTPA tourist information office in Trou d'Eau Douce (*Coastal Rd, La Pelouse; ☎ 480 0925; ⌚ 09.30–18.00 Mon–Sat*).

WHERE TO STAY

Luxury

Le Touessrok (203 rooms) Trou d'Eau Douce; ☎ 402 7400; **f** 402 7500; **e** info@letouessrok.mu; www.letouessrokresort.com. This hotel has long been one of the most luxurious on the island & a member of 'Leading Hotels of the World'. It is set on a pristine, shallow bay, ideal for swimming. There is a range of first-class accommodation, including 98 suites on a private island, linked by a bridge to the mainland. The rooms are luxuriously appointed with all mod cons, including broadband internet, & have superb sea views plus 24hr butler service. There are 3 sumptuous 3-bedroom villas with private pools. There are 3 restaurants, including the excellent Barlen's on the beach. The kids' & teenagers' clubs are outstanding. There is a Givenchy spa & guests enjoy free use of the hotel's golf course on Ile aux Cerfs (see page 86). There are regular free boat transfers to Ile aux Cerfs (popular for watersports) & the hotel's exclusive Ilot Mangénie, a small sand island. As with the main hotel beach, guests who cannot face moving from their sunbeds will be indulged by smiley waiters on hand to deliver food & drink, & polish sunglasses. The hotel states it aims for the highest standards of service in the world, & it has certainly gone a long way towards achieving that. **$$$$$**

Mid range

Silver Beach (60 rooms) Coastal Rd, Trou d'Eau Douce; ☎ 419 2600; **f** 419 2604; **e** silverbeach@intnet.mu; www.silverbeach.mu. A fairly unattractive building but it is on a beautiful stretch of beach. 30 comfortable sea-facing rooms & 30 garden-view bungalow rooms with AC, TV, phone, minibar, safe & balcony/terrace. The bungalows are cheaper & sleep 2 adults & 2 children. Facilities include a restaurant, pool, regular evening entertainment & some free non-motorised watersports. Free Wi-Fi at reception. Priced at the lower end of mid-range. **$$$**

Tropical Attitude (62 rooms) La Pelouse, Trou d'Eau Douce; ☎ 480 1300; **f** 698 422; **e** resa@tropical-hotel.com; www.letropicalhotel.com. A cosy, friendly hotel with 60 sea-view rooms & 2 garden-view family units. All are pleasantly decorated & equipped with AC, TV, phone, minibar, safe & balcony/terrace. The restaurant, like the rest of the hotel, has wonderful sea views & there is a pool. Non-motorised watersports are free & there is a dive centre nearby. **$$$**

Budget

Villa Pareo (1 villa) Coastal Rd, Trou d'Eau Douce; ☎ 480 1345; **e** patrice.hardy@

myvillasmauritius.com; www.myvillasmauritius.com. Modern villa on the coastal road, around 50m from the beach. The villa was built in 2008 & has 3 bedrooms, each with its own bathroom; it can sleep up to 10 people. It is spacious, modern & equipped with everything you could need – a real home away from home. There is a shared garden, private terrace & pool. Excursions can be arranged. Good value for money, especially for large families or groups. **$$**

Shoestring

Chez Tino (3 studios) Coastal Rd, Trou d'Eau Douce; 480 2769. These basic studios above the restaurant (see below) come with en suite, fan, TV & balcony. 1 room has a kitchenette. AC is available for a supplement. **$**

WHERE TO EAT

Le Café des Arts Victoria Rd, Trou d'Eau Douce; 480 0220; for lunch & dinner Mon–Sat. Cuisine: Creole, European, seafood. Set in a former sugar mill, this restaurant has been beautifully restored & displays an impressive art collection. A creative menu & thoughtfully prepared dishes using local ingredients. **$$$$**

Le Four à Chaux Coastal Rd, Trou d'Eau Douce; 480 1036; for lunch daily, for dinner Fri/Sat. Cuisine: Creole, seafood. Smart seafood restaurant at the northern end of the village, across the road from the beach & above some shops. It is signed. Has a good reputation & a creative menu. **$$$**

Chez Gilda Coastal Rd, Trou d'Eau Douce; 480 1253; 08.30–22.30 Mon, Wed–Sat, 14.00–22.30 Sun. Cuisine: Creole, European, seafood. Charming restaurant & bar in an old, stone building & with a terrace out the back overlooking the bay. Gilda had a good apprenticeship, growing up as the daughter of Tino of Chez Tino fame. Serves croissants & patisserie for breakfast, as well as pizzas, panini & full main courses later in the day. Pizza from Rs200, main courses from Rs300. Free wi-fi. Good value. **$$**

Green Island Beach Restaurant Coastal Rd, Trou d'Eau Douce; 515 0240; for lunch & dinner Tue–Sun. Cuisine: Creole, European, Chinese, seafood. Across the road from the ocean. Is not cheap but offers plenty of variety. **$$**

Sous le Manguier Coastal Rd, Trou d'Eau Douce; 419 3855; for dinner on reservation. Cuisine: Creole. Tiny *table d'hôte* restaurant opposite the church, offering traditional, home-cooked food. A set menu will cost you Rs750 plus tax (15%) & includes aperitif, starter, main course, dessert, wine & a digestif (after-dinner drink). **$$**

Chez Tino Coastal Rd, Trou d'Eau Douce; 480 2769; 09.30–14.30 & 19.00–21.30 Mon–Sat, 09.30–14.30 Sun. Cuisine: Creole, Chinese, seafood. Unassuming but popular restaurant on the first floor, with sea views. Offers a wide choice of inexpensive dishes. **$**

OTHER PRACTICALITIES

Communications There is a **post office** in the centre of Trou d'Eau Douce, which offers **internet access**; **Chez Gilda Café** (see above) has Wi-Fi access.

SOUTH OF TROU D'EAU DOUCE TO BOIS DES AMOURETTES

Travelling south from Trou d'Eau Douce, the road heads inland and passes through the village of **Bel Air Rivière Sèche** before turning back towards the coast and crossing over the **Grande Rivière Sud-est**.

At the mouth of the river is a charming fishing village. There is a small waterfall where the river dives into the sea, which is often visited during tourist boat trips. It can also be reached on foot. Follow the signs marked GRSE to the parking area and it's a 15-minute walk.

Across the river is the village of **Deux Frères** (Two Brothers), with another village, puzzlingly called **Quatre Sœurs** (Four Sisters), a little further on. The scenery along this road is beautiful, with sugarcane clinging to the impossibly steep slopes of the **Bamboo Mountains** on one side and fishing boats huddling together in turquoise water on the other.

The mountain range descends to the sea at the headland of **Pointe du Diable** (Devil's Point), where the ruins of French batteries are listed as a national monument. Cannons here date from 1750–80 and were used to guard two wide gaps (North and Danish passages) in the reef. The devil of this point was said to be responsible for upsetting the magnetic compasses of ships passing the headland.

The road follows the coast around the edge of the peninsula, from where **Ile aux Fouquets** and **Ile de la Passe** are visible. An unmanned lighthouse on Ile aux Fouquets marks the rocks at the southern entrance through the reef into Grand Port. During the battle for Grand Port, Ile de la Passe was captured by the British, who kept the French flag flying to lure in French vessels. Ruined fortifications remain on the island.

At **Anse Jonchée** is **Kestrel Valley**, part of an estate formerly known as Domaine du Chasseur. In 2007 the estate teamed up with the Mauritian Wildlife Foundation to aid in the preservation of the Mauritius kestrel, so watch out for the sandy-coloured birds hovering in the area. Before you reach Domaine de l'Ylang Ylang, where ylang ylang is grown and essential oil distilled, you will pass a rather smaller enterprise of a similar ilk. A bright orange kiosk outside a modest home on a sharp bend opposite the sea, is where Laurianne Ghansseeram sells **essential oils** and candles. The oils include ylang ylang, frangipani, eucalyptus, peppermint and cinnamon. With over ten years' experience in oil distillation, Laurianne is very knowledgeable on their various medicinal uses. Prices start at Rs350 for 10ml.

Legend says that French soldiers used to duel over the girls they met at **Bois des Amourettes** (Young Lovers' Wood). Swords have been found in the vicinity of the cave and rock known as **Salle d'Armes** down on the sea's edge.

WHERE TO STAY

Luxury

Four Seasons Resort Mauritius at Anahita (123 rooms) Beau Champ; 402 3100; **f** 402 3120; **e** reservations.mas@fourseasons.com; www.fourseasons.com. The hotel opened in Oct 2008 as part of a village-style Integrated Resort Scheme (IRS), which includes residential villas & a range of facilities. The hotel emphasises its lush, tropical surrounds rather than being a traditional beach resort, as this area of coast is known for its mangroves & lack of sandy beaches. There are, however, 3 manmade beaches. Hotel accommodation is divided between the resort's private island & the mainland. Rooms are beautifully decorated & come complete with private garden, plunge pool & outdoor shower. There are 4 restaurants, a main pool, tennis, a spa & kids' club. One of the hotel's main draw cards is a stunning 18-hole golf course, designed by Ernie Els (see *Chapter 3*, *Golf*, page 86). **$$$$$**

Budget

La Case du Pecheur (16 rooms) Anse Bambous; 634 5643; **/f** 634 5708; **e** jeanfrancois.lazare@gmail.com. Rustic accommodation near Pointe du Diable. En-suite rooms in thatched buildings on the water with AC & a small terrace. The coast here is far from the idyllic beaches for which Mauritius is known; instead mangroves grow at the water's edge & there is no lagoon. This in itself has its attractions: tranquillity & natural beauty. Shellfish are farmed here, some of which are served in the restaurant (see below). There is also a small pool. Nature trails through the mangrove forest start here. **$$**

Ti-Vilaz Lodges (7 bungalows) Kestrel Valley, Anse Jonchée; 634 5011; **f** 634 5261; **e** ledomaine@intnet.mu; www.ledomaine.mu. Back-to-nature-style accommodation in this estate in the mountains above Vieux Grand Port. Simply furnished bungalows with 1 bedroom, a bathroom & a balcony. Le Panoramour Restaurant boasts superb views (see below). Those of a sensitive disposition should avoid the hunting season. (See also *What to see in Eastern Mauritius*, below). **$$**

WHERE TO EAT

Le Panoramour Kestrel Valley; 634 5011; for lunch daily. Cuisine: Creole, European, game, seafood. An open-sided thatched restaurant high in the Bamboo Mountains; diners enjoy superb views down to the coast. Specialities include dishes using every imaginable part of the estate's deer & wild boar. They do a good wild boar curry. **$$$$**

La Case du Pecheur Anse Bambous; 634 5643; for lunch daily. Cuisine: Creole, seafood. Specialises in crabs, oysters & lobsters, which are farmed on site. They also do a good venison curry. You can walk off your lunch on the nature trail. **$$$**

WHAT TO DO IN EASTERN MAURITIUS

MARKETS There is a market in **Centre de Flacq** on Wednesdays and Sundays.

ILE AUX CERFS For those whose hotels don't provide trips to Ile aux Cerfs, there are other ways of getting there. Almost every second person you pass in Trou d'Eau Douce will offer to take you there but be wary as their service may not be reliable, particularly when it comes to bringing you back again. Operators with good reputations include Vicky Tours (*754 5597; www.bateauxvicky@yahoo.com*) and the Trou d'Eau Douce Co-operative Ferry (*519 0452*), both located at the northern end of Trou d'Eau Douce. Expect to pay around Rs300 per person return by ordinary boat, which takes around 15 minutes, or around double those prices by speedboat, which only takes around five minutes. Boats leave at regular intervals, usually every 30 minutes between 09.00 and 16.30 but you should confirm with your particular operator the time of the last trip back to the mainland. The departure point is clearly marked in Trou d'Eau Douce and you can buy tickets on the spot.

A number of operators, such as White Sand Tours (*208 5424*) and Vicky Tours, offer full-day group excursions to Ile aux Cerfs, which usually include a barbecue and a visit by boat to the small waterfall at Grande Rivière Sud-est. Such excursions cost around Rs1,000 per person.

Buy essential oils The east of the island is the place to buy essential oils. **Laurianne Ghansseeram** sells oils and candles from her small kiosk in Anse Jonchée (see page 143).

THEME PARK

Le Waterpark and Leisure Village (*Coastal Rd, Belle Mare; 415 2626;* **f** *415 2929;* **e** *lewaterpark@intnet.mu; www.lewaterpark.intnet.mu; 10.00–17.30 daily; admission adult/child Rs450/250*) An amusement park with numerous waterslides and fairground rides, located amidst the agricultural land opposite the public beach.

YACHTING/CATAMARAN CRUISES Catamaran cruises and sailing trips frequently depart from Trou d'Eau Douce, usually stopping off at Ile aux Cerfs. For details, see *Chapter 3, Sailing*, pages 93–4.

DEEP-SEA FISHING While the east coast is not as highly regarded for deep-sea fishing as the west coast, fishing trips are available. For details, see *Chapter 3, Deep-sea fishing*, pages 88–9.

GOLF Some of the island's best golf courses are on the east coast. For details, see *Chapter 3, Golf*, pages 86–7.

WHAT TO SEE IN EASTERN MAURITIUS

KESTREL VALLEY (*Anse Jonchée;* ☎ *634 5011;* **f** *634 5261;* **e** *ledomaine@intnet.mu; www.kestrelvalley.com;* ⏱ *08.30–16.30 Mon–Fri; hiking without guide Rs150, hiking with guide Rs300*) A stony track leads from the coast road to the estate. Nature trails wind through the forest on the slopes of the Bamboo Mountains, home to Javanese deer, wild boar, monkeys, hare and the famed Mauritius kestrel. The area can be explored on foot by following one of the marked trails (2–6km) or with a guide. Hunting is also available, with guns and guides provided (see *Chapter 3, Hunting*, page 88). There is a good restaurant (see page 144) and rustic accommodation is available (see pages 143–4). Wear sturdy shoes, plenty of insect repellent and suncream.

7

Southern Mauritius

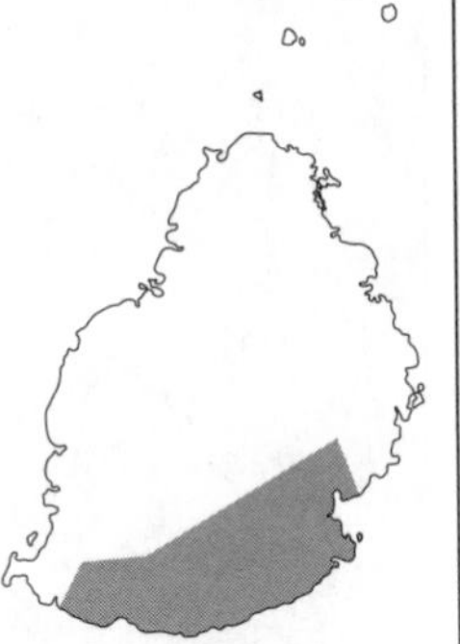

The south extends from historic Vieux Grand Port in the southeast to Baie du Cap River, on the border between the districts of Savanne and Black River, in the southwest.

Saved by a lack of beaches, the south of Mauritius has avoided much of the tourist development that has taken place elsewhere. The southeast is most visitors' first experience of the island, having arrived at the international airport at Plaisance. Many simply pass through the area, returning only to catch another flight, yet there is so much for the visitor to see.

The ruins and monuments around Vieux Grand Port attest to its dramatic past: the first landings of the Dutch in 1598 and the naval battle between the English and French in 1810. Nearby is the south's main town, Mahébourg, a sleepy fishing community crammed with colourful old houses.

There is a small beach resort around Pointe d'Esny and Blue Bay, with a good selection of accommodation. Just off the coast here is Ile aux Aigrettes, a nature reserve run by the Mauritian Wildlife Foundation, which is well worth a visit.

Savanne is the southernmost district of Mauritius, stretching westwards from the sugar-growing village of Savannah along a coast that is the island's most rugged. Cane fields interspersed with fishing villages dominate the coast, while the interior around Grand Bois is tea-growing country. In 2004, this area changed forever when the Bel Ombre Sugar Estate, prompted by the downturn in the sugar industry, allowed three upmarket hotels to be built on some of its coastal land. Thankfully the hotels were built in such a way as to minimise any negative impact on the local area and the community. For visitors looking for tranquillity, the area now offers a peaceful alternative to the north and east coasts.

VIEUX GRAND PORT AND MAHEBOURG

Vieux Grand Port was named Warwyck Bay in 1598 by the Dutch, who made two attempts to establish a colony here before they left in 1710. The French named the bay Port Bourbon and planned to have the headquarters of the French East India Company there, although after a feasibility study they chose Port Louis instead.

Port Bourbon then became Port Sud-est and slipped into decline. Governor Decaen visited the harbour in 1804 and sensed its vulnerability. He abandoned the manning of the old Dutch posts and built a new town on the opposite side of the bay. Mahébourg, after Mahé de Labourdonnais, was his original name for this new town but he soon changed it for reasons of diplomacy to Port Imperial. He renamed Port Louis at the same time, as Port Napoleon.

When the British tried to take Grand Port in August 1810 they were soundly beaten. Both sides used subterfuge but the French were more successful. They

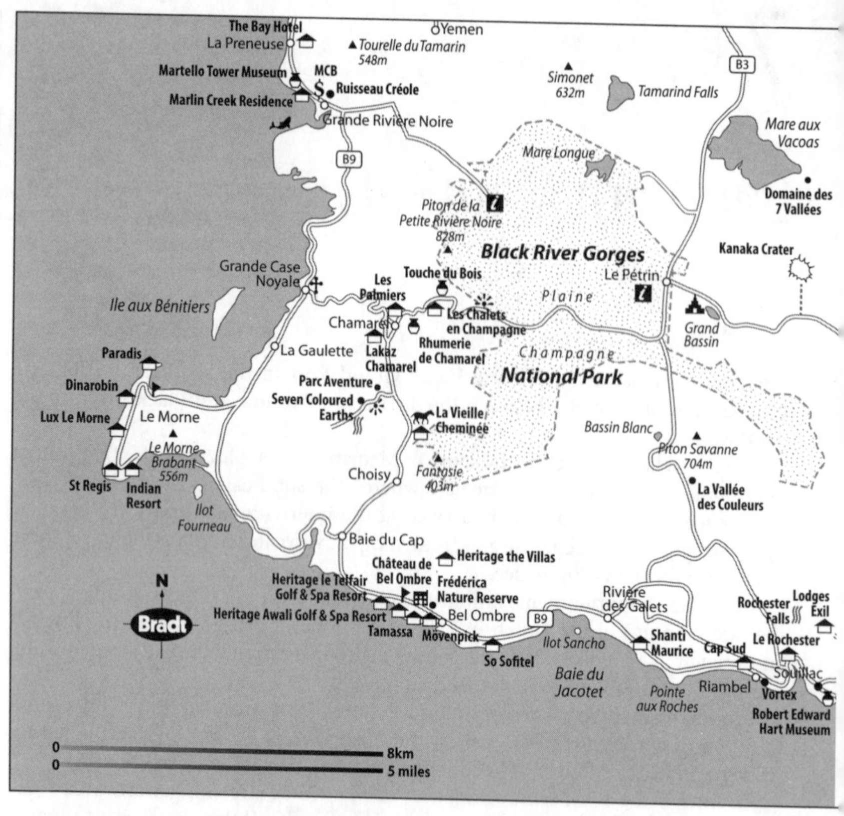

managed to move the buoys marking the passage through the reef, causing British vessels to run aground. The victory of the French is recorded at the Arc de Triomphe in Paris. Four months later, however, the island capitulated and Port Imperial became Mahébourg again.

The crouching lion of **Lion Mountain** (480m) guards the bay around **Vieux Grand Port**, the site of the first Dutch settlement. Some of the oldest buildings in Mauritius, with foundations dating back to the 17th century, are to be found in this town. The ruins of the Dutch **Fort Frederick Hendrik** are located in a park at the northern end of the town. The park also contains the **Frederick Hendrik Museum**, which tells the story of the Dutch on the island (see *What to see in Southern Mauritius*, page 159).

About 3km from Vieux Grand Port, on the coastal side of the road at **Ferney**, is an obelisk, erected on 20 September 1948, to commemorate the landing of the Dutch 350 years before to the day. Bodies of the Dutch settlers are buried at the foot of Lion Mountain.

Mahébourg (pronounced *My bore*) is the main town in the south of the island, a laid-back fishing community of some 20,000. Its development suffered through the malaria epidemic in 1866 which drove coastal town-dwellers to the hills.

However, Mahébourg has prospered since it was described in a 1973 guide as 'a down-at-heel town lined with small shops where friendliness of service has to substitute for sophistication of goods'. Rue Shivananda has acquired a rather smart **promenade** (Esplanade Sir Charles Gaetan Duval), which, provided it's one of Mahébourg's rare non-windy days, is a good spot from which to watch the fishermen.

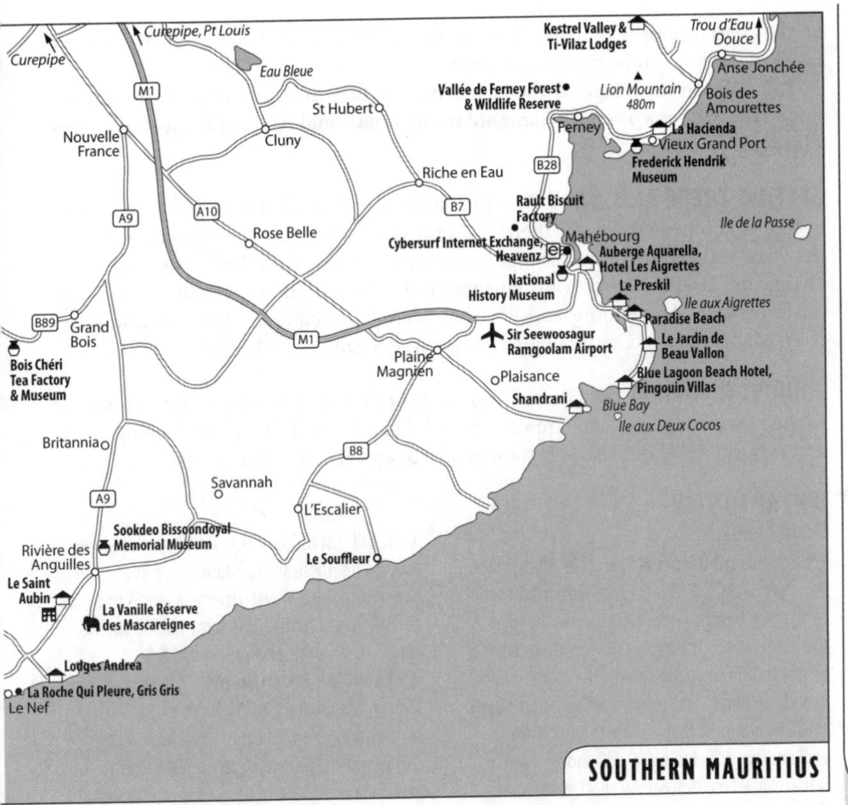

The **market** is between Rue de la Colonie and Rue des Hollandais, at the northern end of town (see *What to do in Southern Mauritius*, page 157). The **police station**, **banks** and **petrol station** are on Rue des Créoles, which is a continuation of Royal Road.

The **National History Museum** (formerly the Mahébourg Naval and Historical Museum) lies about 1km south of Mahébourg on the main road (see *What to see in Southern Mauritius*, page 159). About 1km north of Mahébourg is the Rault Biscuit Factory, which has been producing manioc biscuits since 1870. The short guided tour is fascinating (see *What to see in Southern Mauritius*, page 000).

On a headland at the northern end of Rue Shivananda is Pointe des Régates, where there is a memorial to the French and English killed 'during the engagement off Ile de la Passe 20–28 August 1810'. This was erected in 1899 and lists the names of the vessels that took part.

Further north, at Pointe Canon is a memorial to slavery, a column crowned with a stone disk showing fists breaking the shackles that bound them.

To the south of Mahébourg lies Ile aux Aigrettes, an island nature reserve managed by the Mauritian Wildlife Foundation. Many of the plants found there grow nowhere else and there is a good chance of seeing pink pigeons, one of the rarest birds in the world (see also pages 19 and 158).

Blue Bay, to the south of Mahébourg, offers a good beach, fabulous turquoise lagoon and a range of accommodation. An area off the coast was declared a protected marine park in 1997, the water is clear and the snorkelling excellent. Just off the coast, opposite the Shandrani Hotel, is Ile aux Deux Cocos, which is run by Lux Resorts but can be visited (see page 157).

The only disadvantage to the hotels here is that they can suffer from aircraft noise. The **Sir Seewoosagur Ramgoolam International Airport** lies just inland, at **Plaisance** (see pages 52–3).

GETTING THERE AND AWAY The **bus station** in Mahébourg is at the northern end of Rue Shivananda and there is a **taxi stand** nearby. Buses operate regularly between Mahébourg and Curepipe, via the airport and Rose Belle. Passengers can change in Curepipe for onward journeys to Port Louis and the north coast. Direct buses between Mahébourg and Port Louis are less frequent. There are also buses from Mahébourg to Centre de Flacq, Blue Bay, Souillac and Le Val.

TOURIST INFORMATION There is no tourist office in either Vieux Grand Port or Mahébourg but the people are very friendly and helpful. If you are staying in the area, your hotel should be able to offer advice and arrange excursions.

WHERE TO STAY

Upmarket

Shandrani Resort & Spa (327 rooms) Blue Bay; 603 4343; **f** 637 4313; **e** shandrani@bchot.com; www.beachcomber-hotels.com. The road to the hotel follows the airport runway then twists & turns through sugarcane fields. The rooms, which include 36 family apartments, are spread through spacious grounds. They all face the sea & are well equipped, including AC, TV, phone, minibar & tea/coffee facilities. Family apartments are thoughtfully designed, with a separate en-suite bedroom with TV for up to 3 children under 12. Those with restricted mobility should note that there are 2 steps in superior rooms. There are 5 restaurants, a pitch & putt golf course, 2 pools, tennis, watersports, bike hire, kids' club & a spa. More recent additions are a dive centre, sailing school & kitesurfing school. Interestingly, there are 3 types of beach: bay, lagoon & ocean. Lots of facilities & endless activities, but you do get some aircraft noise. The hotel's AI package 'serenity plus' has been well received by travellers – included in the price are all meals & drinks, watersports (inc unlimited waterskiing), & a massage. **$$$$**

Mid range

Blue Lagoon Beach Hotel (72 rooms) Pointe d'Esny, Blue Bay; 631 9046; **f** 631 9045; **e** blbhotel@intnet.mu; www.bluelagoonbeachhotel.com. In pleasant gardens overlooking the lagoon, just 10km from the airport. Rather plain en-suite rooms with AC, TV & phone; some have balcony/terrace. A fridge in your room will cost Rs50 per day. Only superior rooms have a safe. There are 2 restaurants, a pool, some free non-motorised watersports, a tennis court & a small fitness centre. Gets some noise from the airport. Seems rather overpriced. **$$$**

Le Preskil Beach Resort (156 rooms) Pointe Jérome, Mahébourg; 604 1000; **f** 631 9603; **e** reservation@lepreskil.mu; www.lepreskil.com. The location is stunning & very private – on a peninsula with views to Ile aux Aigrettes across a shallow, protected turquoise lagoon. Rooms have sea view & are en suite with AC, TV, phone, Wi-Fi (payable), minibar, safe & tea/coffee facilities. There is 1 room with disabled facilities. The standard rooms are smallish but well decorated. The cottages are lovely but try to get 1 with direct beach access if you can. There are 2 pools, 3 restaurants, tennis, a gym & a spa offering massage. The selection of free watersports is impressive & includes water skiing. The hotel is popular as a base for windsurfing & kitesurfing, & as a departure point for trips to Ile aux Aigrettes. Aircraft noise does not seem to be such an issue here – aircraft can be seen in the skies above the area but are usually too high to be heard at the hotel. **$$$**

Lodges Andrea (10 lodges) Relais des Lodges, Rivière des Anguilles; 471 0555; **f** 626 2541; **e** resa@relaisdeslodges.mu; www.relaisdeslodges.com. The lodges are set on a cliff top among the cane fields of the Union Sugar Estate east of Souillac. They each accommodate 2 people, are modern, private & have sea view, fan, safe & tea/coffee facilities. They aren't luxurious but they are nicely done. There is a restaurant serving breakfast & dinner (lunch on request) & a pool. Quad biking can be arranged & guests can join in the activities at Lodges Exil. **$$$**

Lodges Exil (10 lodges) Relais des Lodges, Rivière des Anguilles; 471 0555; **f** 626 2541 **e** resa@relaisdeslodges.mu; www.relaisdeslodges.com. Rural lodges for 2 people, in the forest near Rivière des Anguilles. It is around a 2–3hr walk to a waterfall, where guests can swim. As getting away from it all is the aim, there is no TV in the rooms but guests can walk, cycle (Rs200 pp per day) or birdwatch in the forest. Quad biking can be arranged. Guests can use the pool at Lodges Andrea. There is a restaurant serving breakfast & dinner (lunch on request). **$$$**

Paradise Beach (12 apts) Pointe d'Esny; 452 1010; **f** 452 2057 **e** reservations@paradisebeach.mu; www.paradisebeach.mu. Upmarket, modern, well-maintained self-catering apartments in a 3-storey building on a beautiful part of the coast. The 8 3-bedroom apartments & 2 4-bedroom penthouses are equipped with everything you need, including a modern kitchen, espresso machine, TV, DVD player, Wi-Fi & iPod docking station. The grounds are beautifully maintained, with a pool & inviting sun lounges. Bike, kayak & car hire can be arranged. Watersports & shuttle to nearby shops on request. Maid service 6 days a week &, for a fee, a local chef will come & cook for you in your apartment. Entry to the complex is controlled by a security guard, which is reassuring. Ground-floor apartments cost a little more than those on the first floor. A superb self-catering option. In high season a deluxe apartment costs around £290/€345 per night for 4 people. **$$$**

Budget

Auberge Aquarella (10 rooms) 6 Rue Shivananda, Mahébourg; 631 2767; **f** 631 2768; **e** aquarellaamu@email.com. Simple but spotless accommodation in the gardens of the Borsato family home on the seafront. 8 double rooms, 1 family room & 1 'suite' for up to 4 people. The rooms have en-suite shower & balcony but only the 'suite' has a TV. 4 rooms have AC. 1 thatched bungalow is particularly cute – the one that's almost dipping its toes in the water. Breakfast is served in the dining room overlooking the bay, & there is a pool. Traditional Mauritian evening meals can be provided if booked in advance. Good value for money & friendly service. **$$**

La Hacienda (4 villas) Vieux Grand Port; 263 0914; **f** 263 5202; **e** lahacienda@orange.mu; www.lahacidendamauritius.com. Rustic but modern villas in attractive grounds on a hillside overlooking the coast. There are 3 1-bedroom villas & 1 with 2 bedrooms. Each has AC, TV, safe, Wi-Fi & fully equipped kitchen. There is a pool & breakfast is provided. 24hr security. The nearest good beach is Blue Bay, around 11km away. The estate offers pleasant walks, including to Lion Mountain, bike hire & excursions can be arranged. **$$**

Le Jardin de Beau Vallon (3 rooms) Beau Vallon; **f** 631 2850; **e** beauvallon.fvl@Intnet.mu; www.lejardindebeauvallon.com. Charming guesthouse accommodation & *table d'hôte* in a pretty garden. The rooms are thoughtfully decorated in a colonial style, with en suite, AC, safe, minibar & Wi-Fi. The pavillion is the most spacious & has a TV. The guesthouse is away from the coast but there is a bus stop around 100m from the entrance, & there is a pool on site. **$$**

Pingouin Villas (5 apts, 2 studios) 94A Daurades Rd, Blue Bay; 758 3837; **f** 637 3051; **e** resa@pingouinvillas.com; www.pingouinvillas.com. Around 200m from the beach & beautiful Blue Bay. Simple, clean self-catering accommodation with TV, phone, Wi-Fi, safe, fan (no AC) & balcony/terrace. Apartments sleep up to 6 people. **$$**

Shoestring

Hotel les Aigrettes (20 rooms) Cnr Rue Chaland & Rue des Hollandais, Mahébourg; **f** 631 9094; **e** saidadhoomun@hotmail.com; www.hotellesaigrettes.com. Close to the centre of town, a block from the seafront. Rooms are uninspiring but clean & have AC, TV, phone & sea view. There is a restaurant, pool & jacuzzi. **$**

WHERE TO EAT There are a dozen or more snack vendors around the bus station in Mahébourg and in front of the nearby vegetable market.

La Belle Kréole Coastal Rd, Pointe d'Esny; 631 5017; 10.00–15.00 & 18.00–22.30 daily. Cuisine: Creole. A wonderful restaurant on the banks of the La Chaux River. The thatched roof

& rustic décor using local antiques complement the authentic Creole cuisine, which is cooked the old-fashioned way – on a wood fire. Try a tasty wild boar dish & some of the rather unusual rums, such as chilli or onion flavour. There is a band every evening & a *séga* show on Fri/Sat evenings. Reservation recommended. $$$

✕ **Le Jardin de Beau Vallon** Beau Vallon; ☎/f 631 2850; e beauvallon.fvl@intnet.mu; ⊕ 09.00–22.00 daily. Cuisine: Creole, European. A *table d'hôte* restaurant in a refurbished colonial house set in pleasant, peaceful gardens between the SSR International Airport & Mahébourg. Reservation recommended. $$$

✕ **Les Copains d'abord** Rue Shivananda, Mahébourg; ☎ 631 9728; ⊕ 10.00–15.00 & 18.00–23.00 daily. Cuisine: European, Creole, seafood. Near the junction with Rue Suffren, opposite the promenade, with views of the bay. The menu is extensive & varied. Game is a speciality. As well as venison & wild boar in numerous guises (from curry to roast), there is a good selection of pasta, Creole & French dishes. It is also a piano bar & attracts a lively crowd on Sat evenings. $$$

✕ **Auberge Aquarella** 6 Rue Shivananda, Mahébourg; ☎ 631 2767; ⊕ for dinner daily. Cuisine: Creole. Simple fare served in the guesthouse dining room, which overlooks the ocean. $$

✕ **Monte Carlo** Rue de la Passe, Mahébourg; ☎ 631 7449; ⊕ for lunch & dinner daily. Cuisine: European, Chinese, seafood. Relaxed restaurant near the bus station. $$

✕ **Chez Patrick** Royal Rd; ☎ 631 9298; ⊕ for lunch & dinner daily. Cuisine: Creole, Chinese, Italian. Popular with locals for its traditional Creole dishes. Reservation recommended. $

OTHER PRACTICALITIES

Communications The **post office** is on Rue des Créoles and offers **internet access**, as does **Cybersurf Internet Exchange** on Rue Labourdonnais (☎ *631 4247*) or **Heavenz** on Royal Road (☎ *762 6340*).

SOUTH OF BLUE BAY TO SOUILLAC

Heading southwest towards Souillac from the busy area around the airport, you step back into a far more traditional, rural Mauritius of cane fields and small village communities.

The village of **L'Escalier** takes its name from Baron Daniel l'Escalier, a French officer. There is a road here, which winds through sugarcane fields to **Le Souffleur**, a blowhole formed in the rocks of the coast. (See *What to see in Southern Mauritius*, page 160).

Rivière des Anguilles (Eel River) has the atmosphere of a country village. It has all the essentials: petrol station and ATMs, plus plenty of fruit and vegetable stalls and pavement vendors. Just south of the town is **La Vanille Réserve des Mascareignes**, formerly known as the La Vanille Crocodile and Tortoise Park (see *What to see in Southern Mauritius*, pages 159–62).

North of Rivière des Anguilles is the immaculately maintained **Britannia Sugar Estate**. The odour of warm sugar pervades the air and workers swathed in protective clothing tend the sugar crop. Just north of here is a turning to the village of Camp Diable and the **Tookay Temple**, an impressive colourful temple in the midst of the cane fields.

Further north on the main road (A9) is the turning to **Grand Bois**, which is surrounded by fields of tea bushes belonging to the **Bois Chéri Tea Estate**. One can only marvel at the women who work in the fields plucking the tea leaves with mechanical precision and dropping them into their wicker baskets. Their speed and dexterity is even more amazing when you consider how meagre the rewards are. They work from 04.00 to midday and are paid about Rs5 per kilogram picked; on a good day they can pick around 60–80kg. The leaves they pick are transported to the nearby Bois Chéri Tea Factory, which has produced tea since 1892. It is worth taking a guided tour of the factory and museum, followed by a tea tasting. (For details, see *What to see in Southern Mauritius*, pages 159–62.)

Off the road to Souillac, 2km south of Rivière des Anguilles, is **Le Saint Aubin**, an attractive colonial house built in 1819, which has been transformed into a wonderful restaurant (see opposite). You can learn about vanilla, sugar and rum production and enjoy the tropical gardens. The anthuriums grown here are of the *andreanium* type and have been grown in the region for nearly 200 years, but it is only during the past 30 years that the growing of anthuriums has become the first horticultural industry in Mauritius. The wax-like leaf (actually the flower spathe) is normally pink although some varieties are blood red and others white. The plants, which bloom all year, are grown in humid, warm conditions under vast awnings of netting.

The fishing town of **Souillac** lies midway between the east and west corners of the island. It is named after Vicomte de Souillac, Governor of Mauritius from 1779 to 1787, who encouraged settlers to develop the south of the island. There is a ponderous, black stone Roman Catholic church here dedicated to St Jacques. It was built between 1853 and 1856, and restored in 1997.

On the coast in the town are the **Telfair Gardens**. Charles Telfair was a British planter who arrived with Governor Farquhar in 1810 and took over the sugar factory at Bel Ombre. He published pamphlets on his enlightened treatment of slaves which only won him censure from abolitionists. He was a keen amateur botanist. The garden bearing his name is mostly lawn, badamier (Indian almond) and banyan (*Ficus benghalensis*) trees, and drops steeply down to the sea. It is a popular picnic spot for locals, but bathing in the sea below is dangerous because of currents.

Across the road from the ocean, the building that houses the **police station** was used in the 18th century to accommodate slaves working on the sugar plantations, who every morning would walk down to the wharf at Port Souillac. After the opening in 1878 of the Rose Belle/Souillac branch of the Port Louis to Mahébourg railway line, the building was used for train passengers. The railway closed in 1954.

A little further along the coast, is the site of the house where **Robert Edward Hart**, half-French, half-Irish Mauritian poet and writer, spent his last years. In 1967, the house was turned into an evocative free **museum**. In 2002, the Mauritius Museums Council was forced to rebuild the house because of its poor condition, but it has been kept as close to the original as possible. (See *What to see in Southern Mauritius*, pages 159–62.)

Hart is buried in the cemetery on the point across the bay. He shares it with a number of British and French soldiers and drowned seamen whose tombs have been defaced by the fierceness of the elements. Bones were scattered around the graveyard by the cyclone of 1962.

Inland from Souillac are **Rochester Falls**. The falls are signed from the main road just west of Souillac and reached on foot by following signposts through cane fields. Fed by water flowing down from the Savanne Mountains, they are not high but reveal vertical columns created in the rocks by the constant pounding of the falling water.

Also inland from Souillac, about 10km north of the town, is **La Vallée des Couleurs**, an exposed area of the stratum under the earth's crust, similar to the Seven Coloured Earths at Chamarel (see *What to see in Southern Mauritius*, page 159).

On the coast just beyond Le Nef is **Gris Gris**, a viewpoint where black cliffs drop away sharply. There is a beach where swimming is dangerous, despite the apparent shallow lagoon formed by the reef that runs close to the shore. The name *Gris Gris* is associated with local witchcraft. There are deep chasms in the cliffs surrounding the beach which lead to a distinctive headland known as **La Roche Qui Pleure** (The Crying Rock), so called because one of the rocks here is said to resemble a crying man. You can walk out on the headland to look for the face but take care, as the path is steep and the rocks uneven. The rock that you're looking for is on the furthest point, facing out to sea. When the waves roll in water drenches his face and he is then crying.

WHERE TO STAY

Budget

Auberge de St Aubin (3 rooms) Royal Rd, St Aubin, Rivière des Anguilles; 625 1513; **f** 626 2558; **e** lesaintaubin@intnet.mu; www.staubin.mu. Guesthouse accommodation in a 1908 Creole cottage in the grounds of the St Aubin estate, a few kilometres north of Souillac. The rooms are beautifully furnished, in keeping with the historic surrounds. The *table d'hôte* meals are a good opportunity to compare experiences & exchange recommendations with other guests. There is a pool; bikes are available but it would also be handy to have a car if staying here. Priced at the top end of the budget category. **$$**

Shoestring

Le Rochester (3 rooms) Coastal Rd, Souillac; 625 4180; **f** 625 8429; **e** lerochester@hotmail.com. Above the restaurant (see below), basic en-suite rooms, 2 of which have AC. **$**

WHERE TO EAT

Le St Aubin Rivière des Anguilles; 625 1513; for 09.00–17.00 Mon–Sat. Cuisine: Creole, seafood. In the historic St Aubin planter's mansion. The *table d'hôte* menu uses homegrown ingredients to create delicious local dishes, such as heart of palm salad, freshwater prawns with watercress, chicken with vanilla & pineapple mousse. A good selection of wines is available too. The Route du Thé includes lunch here (see *What to see in Southern Mauritius*, page 162). **$$$$**

Le Batelage Village des Touristes, Coastal Rd, Souillac; 625 6083; 12.00–17.00 & 18.00–21.30 daily. Cuisine: European, Creole, seafood. Very good food in an open-air restaurant overlooking the water. It turns into a piano bar on Fri evenings & features a *séga* show on Sat. Dinner on reservation only. **$$$**

Le Bois Chéri Grand Bois; 507 0216; for lunch daily. Cuisine: Creole, European. In a lovely setting within the Bois Chéri Tea Estate, on a hill with views to the coast. Serves excellent Creole dishes & some tea-flavoured specialities. Main courses from Rs345. You may be asked to pay a Rs100 entry fee to the grounds if you have not been for a tour of the tea factory. **$$$**

Rochester Restaurant Coastal Rd, Souillac; 625 4180; **f** 625 8429; 11.00–15.00 & 18.00–21.30, closed Tue dinner. Cuisine: Creole, Indian, European, seafood. The sort of restaurant every traveller hopes to find. In Dec 2004, Mr & Mrs Appadu converted the front room of their home into a tiny restaurant (6 tables), which has been so successful it has now expanded significantly. It is clean, nicely decorated, has a well-stocked bar & serves a wide range of delicious traditional food. The old stone building adds interest. **$$$**

RIAMBEL TO BAIE DU CAP

The village of **Riambel** marks the beginning of a long rugged beach that stretches up to **Pointe aux Roches**. Swimming here is dangerous because of currents and rocks – the signs on the beach leave you in no doubt, 'if you bathe here, you may be drowned'.

Riambel has an unusual claim to fame: it is said to be the home of an energy **vortex**, one of only 14 in the world. The site opened to the public in 2007 and is now visited by those wanting to replenish their energy stores (see page 162).

Just off Pointe aux Roches, in **Baie du Jacotet**, is **Ilot Sancho**. During the preliminary forages of the British in 1810, the French battery on this coral islet was captured and a French colonist taken hostage in exchange for supplies. Rumours of treasure buried on the island have never been proved. It is now covered in scrub.

As you continue along the coast, you enter the domain of the **Bel Ombre Sugar Estate**. The Bel Ombre factory has now closed, although sugarcane is still grown here and transported to other factories for processing. In 2004, the estate allowed luxury hotels to be built on some of its coastal land, along with a championship **golf course** (see page 86). The development of this area has included a new road, making this part of the island more accessible. The **Château de Bel Ombre**, a colonial house across the road from the coast, has been converted into an excellent restaurant (see page 157). Although there was some objection from local communities to the tourism development of the area, this appears to have been controlled by a government policy of compensation and a requirement for the hotels to recruit at least 40% of their staff from the area.

The road continues along the coast, passing through yet more cane fields and fishing villages. Opposite the **St Martin Cemetery** is a cairn monument recalling the landing of survivors from the wreck of the steamer *Travessa*, which foundered in 1923 on its way to Australia. The cigarette-tin lid, which was the measure for the daily water ration of the survivors during their ordeal at sea, is an exhibit at the National History Museum (see *What to see in Southern Mauritius*, pages 159).

Hills roll down to the scruffy beach at **Baie du Cap**. A church on a hillock overlooks the sea here, which is shallow for a long way out. Baie du Cap is a quiet beachside village, whose inhabitants work in the cane fields or as fishermen. By the sea there is a monument to Matthew Flinders, who left the UK in 1801 on a scientific voyage of discovery to New Holland (Australia). On the way back to the UK in 1803 he stopped at Baie du Cap and was detained by the French governor, Decaen. He was released in 1810 and his book *A Voyage to Terra Australis* (which gave Australia its name) was published in 1814, the day before he died.

On the road to **Choisy**, a village in the hills behind Baie du Cap, there are good views of the sea; look back before you get to **Chamarel**.

WHERE TO STAY

Luxury

Heritage the Villas Bel Ombre; 605 5000; f 605 5300; e info@heritagethevillas.mu; www.heritagethevillas.mu. Luxury 2, 3- & 4-bedroom villas on the Domaine de Bel Ombre, on a hillside overlooking the coast. Villas are luxuriously appointed & have infinity pool. A golf cart is allocated to each villa; guests receive unlimited green fees at the Heritage Golf Club, daily maid service & free Wi-Fi. They are some distance from the beach, being located behind the golf club. Guests have access to the facilities of the 2 Heritage hotels (Heritage Le Telfair & Heritage Awali, plus C Beach Club adjacent to Heritage Le Telfair; see page 156). For a fee you can have meals & spa treatments in your villa. Villas can either be purchased as art of an IRS scheme, or rented short term. **$$$$$**

Shanti Maurice (61 rooms) Rivière des Galets, Chemin Grenier; 603 7200; f 603 7250; e reservations@shantimaurice.com; www.shantimaurice.com. Far more than a hotel, this is the ultimate health & relaxation retreat – a destination spa. The emphasis is on balancing mind, body & spirit through tailored cuisine, meditation, yoga & spa treatments. The setting is peaceful – no noisy watersports here, although they can be arranged nearby. The suites are large & beautifully decorated, & there are sumptuous villas with private pool. A range of packages is available, including weight management, stress management & detox. Ayurveda, an ancient Indian healing system, is important here. Guests can have a consultation with an Ayurvedic doctor, & there are Ayurvedic treatments & cuisine on offer. If you think it sounds too New Age for you, do not fear: none of the relaxation activities is compulsory – you can simply enjoy the tranquillity, the excellent cuisine & service. **$$$$$**

Upmarket

Heritage Awali Golf & Spa Resort (160 rooms) Coastal Rd, Bel Ombre; 601 1500; f 601 1515; e info@heritageawali.mu; www.

heritageawali.mu. The African-inspired design is used to great effect throughout, from the bedrooms to the spa. There are 154 rooms, 5 suites & 1 villa with private pool. One room has disabled facilities & wheelchair access around the resort is generally good. The standard rooms are spacious & well equipped, with a large balcony/terrace. Facilities include 3 restaurants, 2 pools, tennis, gym, watersports, a hairdresser, a kids' club & a nursery. Being part of the Domaine de Bel Ombre, 11 restaurants are available, including those at Heritage Le Telfair & Château de Bel Ombre. The spa offers all manner of pampering – massage, relaxation areas, pools, steam rooms & a sauna. For golfers, the stunning Heritage Golf Club opposite the hotel will be hard to resist (see page 86). Excursions to the Frédérica Nature Reserve are also popular with guests (see page 159). A premium AI package is available, which includes wine & spirits, a massage at the spa, one free green fee per day & an excursion to Frédérica. Guests also have access to C Beach Club, adjacent to Heritage Le Telfair (see opposite). If you plan to indulge yourself while in Mauritius, the AI package could be a very economical way of doing so. **$$$$**

Heritage Le Telfair Golf & Spa Resort (158 rooms) Coastal Rd, Bel Ombre; 601 5500; **f** 601 5555; **e** info@heritageletelfair.mu; www.heritageletelfair.mu. The hotel is part of the Domaine de Bel Ombre (the Bel Ombre Sugar Estate). Everything about this hotel evokes colonial times, giving the impression you are a guest at the vast home of a wealthy, 19th-century sugar baron. The hotel, which is built on either side of the Citronniers River & spread over 15ha, is a member of Small Luxury Hotels of the World. The rooms are housed in 2-storey villas of 6 or 8 rooms, which means the hotel is unlikely to feel crowded. All the rooms are enormous & unusually light & airy; they feature AC, TV, DVD, phone, safe, minibar & balcony/terrace. There are 3 impressive restaurants on site, but diners also have access to all restaurants within Domaine de Bel Ombre (which inc those at Heritage Awali & Château de Bel Ombre), making a total of 11 restaurants Don't miss the sophisticated Cavendish Bar, complete with pianist, cigar lounge & reading area. The facilities are first class: a large spa, tennis, gym, watersports & kids' club. Surprisingly, Wi-Fi is not free in the rooms but can be used in the bar free of charge. Rates include green fees for the Heritage Golf Club (see page 86). Opposite the hotel is the Frédérica Nature Reserve, with hiking, 4x4 & quad biking available (see page 159). A new addition to the Heritage collection is the neighbouring C Beach Club, a trendy, modern restaurant, bar & pool on the beach. **$$$$**

Mövenpick Resort & Spa (181 rooms) Allée des Cocotiers, Bel Ombre; 623 5000; **f** 623 5001; **e** resort.mauritius@moevenpick.com; www.moevenpick-hotels.com. This hotel has an atmosphere of grandeur & is reminiscent of a Moorish palace, thanks to the Arabic & Portuguese theme used in the design. The rooms & suites have AC, TV, phone, minibar, safe & balcony/terrace. The hotel is family friendly – there are family rooms, over 50% of rooms are interconnecting & there is a kids' club. The spa is impressive & continues the Arabic/Portuguese theme. There are 3 restaurants, several pools, tennis courts, the usual free watersports, minigolf & gym. **$$$$**

So Sofitel (92 rooms) Coastal Rd, Bel Ombre; 605 5800; **e** h6707@sofitel.com; www.sofitel.com. The 84 suites & 8 villas within an Integrated Resort Scheme, where foreigners can buy luxury villas. A new hotel with a completely modern, urban décor. Rooms look like the London flat of a 20-something banker, rather than evoking Mauritius. One drawback of the rooms is that the only bath in the suites is outside – lovely in good weather but this part of the coast tends to be rather windy. On the plus side, the beds are exceptionally comfortable. There are 2 restaurants, 2 bars, a pool, small spa, gym & kids' club. The hotel was suffering some teething problems after it opened in 2011 but hopefully is set to improve. While it may have the 'designer touch' (the marketing material goes on & on about the architect), the concept doesn't seem to have taken account of some practical considerations. **$$$$**

Tamassa (214 rooms) Coastal Rd, Bel Ombre; 698 9800; **f** 698 4222; **e** reservation@luxislandresorts.com; www.tamassaresort.com. A hotel designed to appeal to a young clientele, with a trendy, modern feel, an emphasis on sport & a party atmosphere. The architecture is not to everyone's taste, being dominated by fairly charmless red-roofed buildings reminiscent of a Spanish resort village. Rooms face the sea & are equipped with AC, TV, phone, Wi-Fi, minibar, safe & balcony/terrace. There are 2 restaurants, 3 pools, a spa, watersports, a dive centre, tennis, a nightclub, kids' club & teenagers' club. **$$$$**

Shoestring

Cap Sud (4 rooms) Coastal Rd, Riambel; 625 5268. Very basic accommodation at the restaurant of the same name (see below). There are 2 simple rooms with en suite, 2 with shared bathroom. It is a fair walk across the road to a rather dangerous beach. Only worth considering if you need to be in the south but are on a very tight budget. **$**

WHERE TO EAT

Gin'ja Le Telfair Hotel, Bel Ombre; 601 5500; for lunch & dinner daily. Cuisine: Asian, seafood. A stylish, modern restaurant overlooking the ocean, with tables in the sand. Refined, exotic cuisine with an Asian twist. Reservation recommended. **$$$$$**

Château de Bel Ombre Bel Ombre; 623 5620; www.domainedebelombre.mu; for lunch, afternoon tea & dinner Mon–Sat. Cuisine: European, Creole. Creative cuisine in the refined setting of the beautifully restored chateau, which dates from the early 1800s & overlooks the Golf du Château. Ideal for a special occasion. Reservation recommended. **$$$$**

Cap Sud Coastal Rd, Riambel; 625 5268; from 10.00 until late daily. Cuisine: Creole, seafood. Opened in 2008, tables are arranged under a covered area in the grounds of this former private house. There is also a swimming pool. **$$**

Mo Filaos Coastal Rd, Baie du Cap; 796 6160; 11.00–22.00 Tue–Sun. Cuisine: Chinese, seafood. A neat little restaurant in this tiny village, overlooking the park & ocean. **$$**

WHAT TO DO IN SOUTHERN MAURITIUS

MARKET **Mahébourg** market is on Mondays. It's near the bus station, between Rue de la Colonie and Rue de Labourdonnais. There are stalls selling fresh fruit and vegetables, household goods, clothing and handicrafts.

ILE AUX DEUX COCOS This small sand island off the coast at Blue Bay is run by Lux Island Resorts but is open to residents and non-residents of the company's hotels. A very pleasant day can be spent on the island, lounging on the sand, snorkelling in the bay, taking a glass-bottom boat trip and indulging at the restaurant and bar. If it weren't for the fabulously attentive service, excellent food and luxurious lounge chairs, it would feel as if you were on a desert island. There is a Moroccan-style villa on Ile aux Deux Cocos, built in 1920 for the then British governor, who used it for lavish parties. Most visitors opt for a day excursion to the island but you can rent the two-bedroom villa overnight and have the whole island to yourself. It is also a popular spot for weddings. Thankfully there is a limit to the number of people allowed on the island at any one time, so it doesn't tend to feel crowded. Visits to Ile aux Deux Cocos can be booked at Lux Island hotels or through tour operators. A full day (10.00–16.00) on an all-inclusive basis (including boat transfer) costs around €120 per person.

SPORTS

Golf The Golf du Château at Bel Ombre is one of the best courses on the island. For more information, see *Chapter 3, Activities*, page 86.

Scuba diving Several hotels around Blue Bay offer diving. For more information, see *Chapter 3, Activities*, pages 89-92.

Sailing/catamaran cruises For details of companies offering cruises and yacht charter in the area see *Chapter 3, Activities*, pages 93–4.

Deep-sea fishing The south is less well known for deep-sea fishing than other areas. For more information, see *Chapter 3, Activities*, pages 88–9.

Kitesurfing Le Shandrani Hotel has a kitesurfing school catering for all levels of experience and ability. For more information, see *Chapter 3, Activities*, page 94.

Ziplining Domaine de Chazal (*Chamouny; ☎ 422 3117; www.incentivepartnersltd.com*) has a circuit of 13 ziplines over Rivière des Galets, ranging from 60m to 250m in length. You can stop for a swim at the base of a waterfall during the circuit and have a Creole meal at the end. For more information, see *Chapter 3, Activities*, page 95.

NATURE RESERVES

Ile aux Aigrettes (*Excursions arranged directly with the Mauritian Wildlife Foundation, via tour operators or your hotel; ☎ 631 2396 or e reservation@mauritian-wildlife.org (reservations); www.mauritian-wildlife.org; admission adult/child Rs800/400*) This coral islet is a nature reserve managed by the Mauritian Wildlife Foundation (MWF). Conservationists are working to restore it to its original state, by clearing exotic species of plants and replacing them with native ones. Endangered endemic birds and reptiles have been re-introduced to the island which is a safe haven for them away from introduced species such as rats, cats and monkeys which predate their young. Visitors have a good chance of spotting rare pink pigeons, olive white-eyes, Mauritius fodies, Guenther's geckos and Telfair's skinks as well as discovering fascinating plants, giant Aldabra tortoises roaming free in the wild and cannons left by the British after World War II,

The tour starts with a short boat trip to the island, leaving from Pointe Jérome, about 500m south of Le Preskil Hotel at Blue Bay. One of the MWF rangers will take you on a guided tour of the island and talk you through the flora, fauna and history. Being a coral island, it is very hot and do remember to take a hat, water and mosquito repellent with you. There is a small exhibition on the extinct fauna of the Mascarenes, to highlight what has been lost already from the islands and the importance of the MWF conservation work (for more information see page 19).

Tours start at 09.30, 10.00, 10.30 and 13.30, 14.00 and 14.30 (mornings only on Sundays) and last about two hours. It is money well spent as not only is the tour a fascinating insight into what the coastal forests of Mauritius would have looked like around 400 years ago, but part of the tour fee goes directly towards the continuation of MWF's work. There is also a small shop on the island, where the money you spend benefits MWF's conservation projects.

Vallée de Ferney Forest & Wildlife Reserve (*Ferney; ☎ 253 1050; e cieletnature@drbc-group.com; www.cieletnature.com; 🕘 09.00–16.00 daily; hikin g (3km) adult/child non-guided Rs345/207, guided Rs575/345; 4x4 (1 hr) adult/child Rs1095/655, with lunch Rs1,525/915*) A 200ha reserve with conservation at the heart of everything it does. It is an initiative of the government and a not-for-profit organisation, so by visiting you are doing your bit to contribute to the conservation efforts. Under the expert guidance of conservation manager, Pricila Iranah, the team is working to restore native forest and eradicate invasive species, such as traveller's palm and goyavier. The visitor's centre has informative exhibits on the flora and fauna of the area.

Visitors can hike around the reserve with or without a guide; guided tours (on reservation) depart at 10.00 and 14.00. 4x4 tours are on reservation. Keen-eyed visitors have a chance of seeing tropic birds, olive-white eyes, Mauritius fodies, Mauritius kestrels and pink pigeons. A former hunting lodge has been converted into a rustic restaurant serving Creole cuisine and specialising in game. Bring sturdy shoes and mosquito repellent.

Frédérica Nature Reserve (*Bel Ombre;* ☎ *623 5615;* **f** *623 5616;* **e** *frederica@domainedebelombre.mu; www.domainedebelombre.*mu) A nature reserve (and deer farm) of 1,300ha bordering the Black River Gorges National Park, and which offers fantastic scenery and the opportunity to see deer, fruit bats, monkeys and native plants. If you are particularly lucky you may see a Mauritius kestrel or echo parakeet. Visitors can explore the area via guided hiking, quad biking and 4x4 tours; commentary on the flora and fauna is provided. Bookings can be made through most tour operators, preferably two–three days in advance. Long trousers are recommended for quad biking. The following minimum age requirements apply: 18 years for a double quad bike, 16 years for a single quad bike, 12 years for a quad-bike passenger.

WHAT TO SEE IN SOUTHERN MAURITIUS

FREDERICK HENDRIK MUSEUM (*Vieux Grand Port* ☎ *634 4319;* 🕘 *09.00–16.00 Mon, Tue, Thu, Fri, Sat, 09.00–12.00 Sun, closed public holidays; admission free*) This small museum charts the history of the Dutch on the island. In the grounds are the remains of the first Dutch settlement, Mauritius's earliest colonial structures. The ruined buildings you see today were the bakery (closest to the sea) and a store/prison (near the road). Just south of the museum is a tower known as the Tour des Hollandais, the Tower of the Dutch.

THE NATIONAL HISTORY MUSEUM (*Royal Rd, Mahébourg;* ☎ *631 9329;* 🕘 *09.00–16.00 Mon, Wed–Sat, 09.00–12.00 Sun & public holidays; admission free*) On the main road just south of Mahébourg is the French colonial mansion built in 1722, which houses the museum formerly known as the Mahébourg Naval and Historical Museum. It is here that, in 1810, wounded British and French naval commanders, Willoughby and Duperré, were brought for medical treatment. The battle is described in the museum, which contains relics from numerous ships that have been wrecked off Mauritius over the years, including *Le Saint Géran*. The tragedy was the inspiration for the love story ***Paul et Virginie***, by Bernardin de St Pierre. Paul attempts to save his beloved but, for the sake of modesty, she refuses to remove her heavy clothing and is drowned. Accounts of the shipwreck tell of other women making the same terminal decision.

In the grounds of the museum are the wooden huts of the **Village Artisanal**, run by the Ministry of Arts, Culture, Leisure and Reform Institutions. The idea is that local artisans can be seen at work but sadly the huts are often empty; a range of handicrafts is on sale.

BISCUTERIE H RAULT (BISCUIT FACTORY) (*Mahébourg;* ☎ *631 9559;* **e** *manioc@intnet.mu; www.raultmaniocbiscuit.com;* 🕘 *09.00–15.00 Mon–Fri; admission adult/child Rs175/125*) Quaint, quirky and well worth a visit. Since 1870, this small, family-run business has been producing biscuits made from manioc (a local root vegetable). The business is now in the hands of the fourth generation of the family. A fascinating guided tour explains the process from raw vegetable to finished biscuit. The nine staff still do everything by hand. The ingredients are weighed on a fabulous set of scales made in Liverpool, UK, in 1869 and the biscuits are cooked over burning sugarcane leaves. The tour culminates in a tasting of the biscuits in various flavours – chocolate, coconut, custard and cinnamon. If you want to stock up, they are very reasonable: Rs65 per pack.The factory is about 1km north of Mahébourg: follow the brown tourist attraction signs after Cavendish Bridge (don't be put off by the narrow residential streets lined with corrugated iron).

LE SOUFFLEUR (*07.00–16.00 Mon–Fri, 07.00–12.00 Sat; admission free*) The sea used to spout spectacularly from this blowhole at high tide. Erosion has deprived it of the power it had 150 years ago when a writer remarked that 'it roared furiously to a height of fully sixty feet', though it still roars a little when the tide is high.

LA VANILLE RESERVE DES MASCAREIGNES (*Senneville, Rivière des Anguilles; 626 2503; f 626 1442; e crocpark@intnet.mu; www.lavanille-reserve.com; 09.30–17.00 daily; admission adult/child Rs330/180 weekdays, Rs220/100 weekends & public holidays*) Located just south of the town of Rivière des Anguilles, the park was created in 1985 by an Australian zoologist as a crocodile farm. Nile crocodiles are still bred here for their skins (there are some 2,000 of them) but the park has grown into a mini zoo with macaques (*Macaca fascicularis*), iguanas, deer, wild boar and freshwater fish. A favourite with visitors are the giant Aldabra tortoises (*Geochelone gigantea*), which roam in a large open space where visitors can walk freely amongst them. Visitors can also walk through the Rodrigues fruit bat (*Pteropus rodericensis*) enclosure. In the insectarium over 23,000 species of butterflies and beetles are displayed. The cool, shady walkways through the lush forest make this an ideal excursion on a hot day. Because spraying would upset the ecology, there are mosquitoes too, but repellent can be bought at the shop, which also sells crocodile-skin goods. There is a licensed restaurant, where crocodile meat is the main feature of the menu. The meat comes from the tail of three-year-old crocodiles and is part of the commercial side of the park.

Feeding time (see the crocs leap out of the water for chicken carcasses) is on Wednesday and Saturday at 11.30. Guided tours are on the hour, every hour. Some of the park is wheelchair-accessible, including the tortoise area.

SOOKDEO BISSOONDOYAL MEMORIAL MUSEUM (*Royal Rd, Tyack, Rivière des Anguilles; 626 3732; www.mauritiusmuseumscouncil.com; 09.00–16.00 Mon, Tue, Thu, Fri; admission free*) Sookdeo Bissoondoyal was a prominent figure in Mauritian politics until his death in 1977 and was a key figure during the transition to independence in 1968. The house where he was born has been made into a small museum telling the story of his life.

ROBERT EDWARD HART MEMORIAL MUSEUM (*Autard St, Souillac; 625 6101; 09.00–16.00 Mon & Wed–Fri, 09.00–12.00 Sat; admission free*) This museum on the site of Hart's home offers the visitor a very personal insight into the life and work of this well-known Mauritian poet. In 2002, the original house was destroyed for safety reasons and a replica built in its place. The interior has been left, as far as possible, as it was when Hart died. Quotes from Hart's work are displayed, as are personal belongings such as photographs, a pith helmet, his OBE (1949) and his *Légion d'honneur* (1950). The museum is next to Telfair Gardens; follow the signs and don't be put off by the route through narrow residential streets.

BOIS CHERI TEA FACTORY (*Bois Chéri, Grand Bois; 507 0216; 08.30–16.30 Mon–Fri, 08.30–14.30 Sat; factory tour plus tea tasting adult/child Rs400/250; tea tasting only Rs200*) This working tea factory turns 40 tonnes of tea leaves into ten tonnes of tea per day. Guided tours take you through the whole process, from the drying of the leaves when they are first received through to the flavouring of the tea and finally the packaging. Tours take place every 30 minutes in the mornings and in winter the factory usually operates only on a Wednesday, due to the reduced harvest. There is also a museum which charts the history of tea and exhibits various machines which have become obsolete over the 115 years that the factory has been in production. A short drive brings you to a chalet where you can taste a number of the teas produced in the factory, such as vanilla, coconut and mint flavours, while enjoying magnificent views down to the coast. There is also a good restaurant here (see page 154). Packets of tea are on sale in the shop and make a good souvenir. Tour buses seem to arrive around 11.00 and it can get busy at this time. It may be wise to phone ahead. See also *La Route du Thé*, below.

LE SAINT AUBIN (*Rivière des Anguilles;* **t/f** *625 1513;* **e** *lesaintaubin@intnet.mu;* ⌚ *Mon–Sat 08.30–16.00; admission adult/child Rs700/350*) At the heart of a sugar estate, a picturesque colonial house, built in 1819 using wood taken from ships. Visitors can learn about some of the island's main agricultural and horticultural

MEHENDI (HENNA TATTOOING)

The art of *mehendi*, or henna tattooing, has been practised for thousands of years and is very much a part of Hindu and Muslim tradition, particularly in marriage ceremonies. Immigrants to Mauritius brought their tradition and skills with them, and visitors to the island are likely to see young Mauritian women with their hands and feet beautifully decorated. There is now a growing number of skilled henna artists offering *mehendi* to tourists wanting to follow the trend set by numerous celebrities, such as Madonna and Naomi Campbell.

The origins of *mehendi* are unclear, although it is believed to have originated in Mesopotamia before being introduced to India in the 12th century. The leaves of the henna bush (*Lawsonia inermis*) are harvested, then dried and crushed to make a fine powder. It is then mixed with rosewater or essential oils, cloves and water to make a paste. The henna paste seen in Mauritius uses plants grown on the island. The henna artist applies the paste to the skin in intricate patterns. After a few hours the paste crumbles away, leaving the skin temporarily stained in a shade between orange and brown. The tattoo gradually fades and usually disappears completely between one and three weeks later. The trick to prolonging the life of the tattoo is to ensure the paste remains moist while on the skin. This is done by spraying it with water or a mixture of lemon juice and sugar.

Mehendi is typically applied to the hands and feet and almost any design can be drawn by a skilled henna artist. Indian and Pakistani designs are often very ornate, giving the appearance of a lace glove or stocking. They traditionally reflect nature and include leaves, flowers and birds. Middle Eastern designs are mostly made up of floral patterns, while north African *mehendi* is typified by geometric shapes. Today these styles are often mixed, and some artists now use Chinese and Celtic symbols.

For weddings, it is traditional for the female friends and family of the bride-to-be to spend several hours, or even days, preparing her *mehendi* and discussing the forthcoming marriage. The *mehendi* is intended to charm and seduce the bridegroom, and in Hindu tradition his initials may be hidden among the designs for him to find on the wedding night.

Mehendi can be organised via many hotels, and there are often artists at markets and shopping centres. Prices range from Rs300 to Rs5,000 depending on the size and intricacy of the design.

activities here: vanilla, sugar, rum and anthurium production. The production of vanilla is immensely complicated and the short video and exhibits on the processes involved are fascinating – in total it takes around 18 months to produce the vanilla pods we see in our supermarkets. The method of pollination by hand was discovered by a slave on neighbouring Réunion Island and allowed the vanilla orchid, which is native to Mexico, to be grown outside that country. In 2011, a new attraction focusing on sugar production was being built, along the lines of Aventure du Sucre near Pamplemousses, in the island's north. The rum distillery and tasting are fun and there is a small shop selling souvenirs, including vanilla, sugar, rum and tea. The restaurant here is excellent (see page 154) and accommodation is available in a cottage on the estate (see page 154). See also *La Route du Thé*, below.

LA ROUTE DU THE (THE TEA ROUTE) (*626 1513; e lesaintaubin@ intnet.mu; www.larouteduthe.mu; adult/child Rs1,700/850, inc lunch*) A combined tour, allowing you to visit three sites linked to the Bois Chéri Tea Estate. Unless you are on an organised tour, transport is not provided between the three points and you must make your own way. The route begins at Domaine des Aubineaux near Curepipe, a colonial mansion built in 1872 as the home of the estate's owner. The interior contains furniture and photographs from the period (see page 188). The second stop is Bois Chéri Tea Factory for a guided tour and tasting (see pages 160–1). Finally, you visit Le Saint Aubin, where lunch is provided (see pages 161–2). All three are interesting sites and the obvious advantage of the combined tour is that it works out cheaper than visiting the three separately.

VALLEE DES COULEURS (*Chemin Grenier; 251 8666; e info@lavalleedescouleurs.com; www.lavalleedescouleurs.com; 09.00–16.30 daily; adult/child rs150/75*) About 10km north of Souillac lies this multi-coloured exposed area of earth, similar to the seven coloured earths of Chamarel. It is less visited than Chamarel and claims to have 23 colours of earth as opposed to seven. It is within a pleasant forested area with good views of the coast. A walking circuit takes you past areas of endemic plants, a few animals (deer, ducks, tortoises, etc) and waterfalls, as well as the coloured earth. Quad biking, ziplining and pedaloes are available for the energetic. There is a café on site.

SPIRITUAL CENTRE OF RIAMBEL – THE VORTEX (*Coastal Rd, Riambel; 736 9038; 09.00–17.00; free admission*) The vortex is signed from the main road. It is reputed to be one of 14 energy centres on earth. The vortex is marked by a ring of stones and around it are areas set aside for each of the body's chakras. People come here to meditate and restore their inner balance. There is usually a volunteer on hand to show you what to do. It gets particularly busy on weekends.

8

Western Mauritius

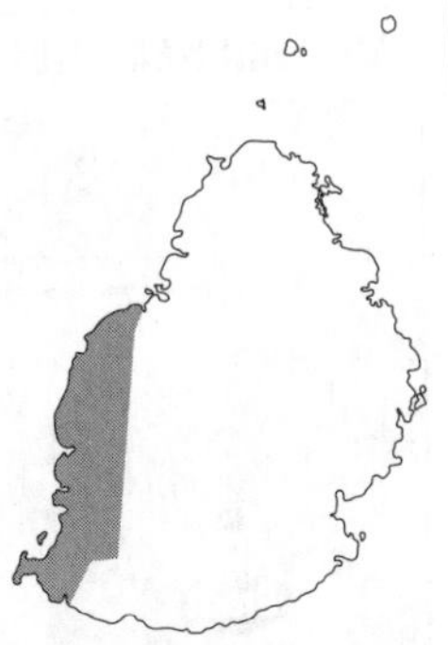

The district of Black River covers the west coast of Mauritius, extending from the southwest, by Baie du Cap, northwards to the boundary of Port Louis. It was called Zwarte River by the Dutch and Rivière Noire by the French, who created the district in 1768. The river itself is not black, so the name probably refers to the black rocks of its bed and banks.

Black River is mostly mountainous and sparsely populated, its inhabitants employed in fishing, tourism and sugar. The southwest has no towns, only village communities, and is the most 'African' part of the island. Creole lifestyle dominates, with Catholic churches rather than Hindu temples providing the focal point for communities. The region is also famed for its *séga* music and dancing.

The Black River Gorges National Park is by far the island's largest nature reserve. For walkers and nature lovers, the park offers spectacular scenery and wildlife. For details see pages 12–14.

The west is the driest and sunniest of the island's coasts and it boasts dramatic sunsets. Its climate, combined with some superb beaches, makes this a popular weekend escape for Mauritians. There is also plenty of accommodation for visitors, particularly around Flic en Flac and Le Morne.

The west is the best coast for deep-sea fishing. This is particularly so around the area of Grande Rivière Noire, where the ocean floor drops away to a great depth, attracting large predators to feed on smaller fish.

MORNE BRABANT TO TAMARIN

The sheer cliff of the square-shaped **Morne Brabant** (556m) rises dramatically out of the southern peninsula, dominating the west coast of the island with its looming presence. Runaway slaves fled to Le Morne during the 18th and early 19th centuries, taking refuge in its caves. On 1 February 1835, fearing that the police party sent to tell them slavery was abolished had come to capture them, the slaves threw themselves off the summit to their deaths. A sadness haunts the mountain still. A community for freed slaves was set up at the southern foot of Le Morne but was later moved to the present location of Le Morne village. Their descendants still live there today and regard Le Morne, which came to symbolise the suffering of the island's slaves, as sacred. In 2008 Le Morne was declared a UNESCO World Heritage Site and the following year UNESCO unveiled a memorial at the foot of Le Morne, as part of its Slave Route Project. The **International Slave Route Monument** (🕘 *09.30–16.00 Tue–Sat, 09.30–12.30 Sun*) lies just beyond the Dinarobin Hotel, across the road from the public beach. At its centre is a black granite block engraved with the image of a slave, around which are a series of stones and sculptures symbolising the countries from which the slaves came. In front of the memorial is

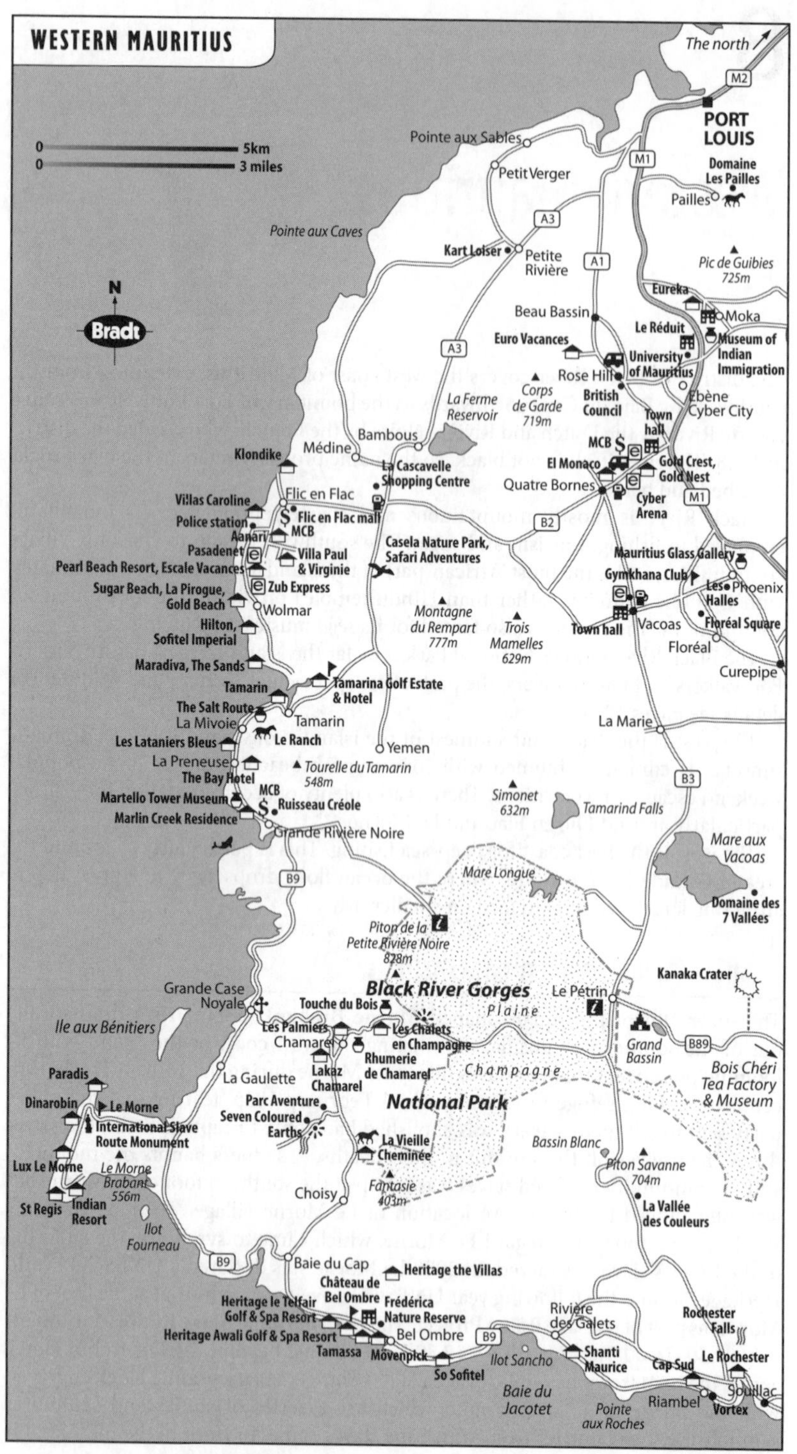

WESTERN MAURITIUS
0 5km
0 3 miles
Bradt
The north
M2
PORT LOUIS
Domaine Les Pailles
Pailles
Pointe aux Sables
Petit Verger
M1
A3
Pointe aux Caves
Kart Loiser
Petite Rivière
A1
Pic de Guibies 725m
Eureka
Moka
Beau Bassin
Le Réduit
Museum of Indian Immigration
Euro Vacances
University of Mauritius
Rose Hill
Ebène Cyber City
Corps de Garde 719m
La Ferme Reservoir
British Council
Town hall
Bambous
MCB
Médine
Klondike
La Cascavelle Shopping Centre
El Monaco
Gold Crest, Gold Nest
Quatre Bornes
Cyber Arena
Flic en Flac
Villas Caroline
Flic en Flac mall
Police station
Aanari
MCB
B2
Pasadenet
Villa Paul & Virginie
Casela Nature Park, Safari Adventures
Mauritius Glass Gallery
Pearl Beach Resort, Escale Vacances
Gymkhana Club
Zub Express
Les Halles
Phoenix
Sugar Beach, La Pirogue, Gold Beach
Wolmar
Montagne du Rempart 777m
Trois Mamelles 629m
Town hall
Vacoas
Floréal Square
Hilton, Sofitel Imperial
Floréal
Maradiva, The Sands
Curepipe
Tamarin
Tamarina Golf Estate & Hotel
The Salt Route
La Mivoie
Tamarin
Les Lataniers Bleus
Le Ranch
La Marie
Yemen
La Preneuse
Tourelle du Tamarin 548m
The Bay Hotel
B3
Martello Tower Museum
MCB
Simonet 632m
Ruisseau Créole
Marlin Creek Residence
Tamarind Falls
Grande Rivière Noire
Mare aux Vacoas
Mare Longue
B9
Domaine des 7 Vallées
Piton de la Petite Rivière Noire 828m
Kanaka Crater
Grande Case Noyale
Black River Gorges
Le Pétrin
Plaine
Touche du Bois
Ile aux Bénitiers
Les Palmiers
Les Chalets en Champagne
Chamarel
Grand Bassin
B89
Rhumerie de Chamarel
Lakaz Chamarel
Champagne
Bois Chéri Tea Factory & Museum
La Gaulette
Paradis
National Park
Dinarobin
Le Morne
Parc Aventure
Seven Coloured Earths
International Slave Route Monument
La Vieille Cheminée
Bassin Blanc
Lux Le Morne
Le Morne Brabant 556m
Piton Savanne 704m
Fantasie 403m
St Regis
Indian Resort
Choisy
La Vallée des Couleurs
Ilot Fourneau
B9
Baie du Cap
Heritage the Villas
Château de Bel Ombre
Heritage le Telfair Golf & Spa Resort
Frédérica Nature Reserve
Rochester Falls
Rivière des Galets
Heritage Awali Golf & Spa Resort
Bel Ombre
B9
Tamassa
Movenpick
Shanti Maurice
Le Rochester
Cap Sud
Ilot Sancho
So Sofitel
Souillac
Baie du Jacotet
Riambel
Vortex
Pointe aux Roches

inscribed in Creole, French and English, a verse of the poem 'Le Morne. Territoire Marron!' by Sedley Assone:

> There were hundreds of them, but my people the maroons
> chose the kiss of death over the chains of slavery.
> Never must we forget their noble deed,
> written in the pages of history for the sake of humanity.

Large hotels and some upmarket homes now lie at the foot of Le Morne; it is a breathtaking setting between the austere cliff and the gentle beaches. Between the hotels, there is access to the pleasant public beach and a large, shallow lagoon. On weekends families of Mauritians come here to picnic and it is popular with kitesurfers.

The foothills of the island's highest mountain, **Piton de la Petite Rivière Noire** (Little Black River Mountain – 828m), reach down to the road near **La Gaulette**. A French soldier called Noyale retired to the area on the coast now known as **Case Noyale**. He was renowned for his hospitality and built a resthouse at **Petite Case Noyale**, but was murdered by runaway slaves.

There is a turning next to the church at **Grande Case Noyale** that leads to **Chamarel** and into the **Black River Gorges National Park**. It is a steep, winding road with spectacular views of the coast, Le Morne Brabant, **Ile aux Bénitiers** and the countless colours of the lagoon. About 6km from the coast is the village of **Chamarel**, which lies amidst fields of pineapples and sugarcane. There are two popular restaurants in the vicinity: Le Chamarel, just before the village, and the Varangue Sur Morne, a further 4km towards the national park. Both have splendid views. (See *Where to eat*, page 168.

Taxi drivers repeat the words '**seven coloured earths of Chamarel**' as a litany that will bring them business. There is, indeed, an exposed heap of colourful clinker on a private estate just south of Chamarel village. The piles are remarkable for being an exposed part of the stratum under the earth's crust. The 'seven colours' are best seen with the sun on them. Some people marvel at them whilst others are disappointed having heard so much hype. Also on the estate is a waterfall, which plunges 100m down a sheer cliff face. (See *What to see in Western Mauritius*, page 176.) Chamarel is known for its **coffee**, although buying a sample is not as easy as you may think as most is sold to hotels or Curepipe supermarkets. There is a shop at Le Chamarel restaurant which sells it, as does the souvenir shop at the 'seven coloured earths'.

On the main road through Chamarel, 3km from the village in the direction of Grand Bassin, is **La Rhumerie de Chamarel**, which explains the process of producing rum from sugarcane. (See *What to see in Western Mauritius*, page 176.)

The Chamarel road continues up to the forest plateau of **Plaine Champagne**, at 737m above sea level. Off this road is a viewpoint overlooking the Black River Gorges National Park and a second viewpoint with views of **Alexandra Falls** and the coast. The area is part of the nature reserve and glimpses of deer, monkeys and mongoose are likely.

Returning to the coast road, mountains are the main feature of the landscape on the drive towards Port Louis. Beyond the Black River mountain range is **Simonet** (632m), in the Vacoas mountain range, overlooking the plain between Montagne du Rempart and Yemen to the sea at Tamarin. By the coast is **Tourelle du Tamarin** (548m), but it is the profiles of the upturned, udder-like **Trois Mamelles** (629m) and the mini Matterhorn, **Montagne du Rempart** (777m), which are so impressive.

In the village of **Grande Rivière Noire**, the Black River Aviary is hidden away near the wooden Creole building which houses the **police station**. Visitors are not allowed, except by arrangement, as this is a sponsored scientific project run by the Mauritian Wildlife Foundation to encourage the breeding of rare species of birds which might otherwise become extinct. However, Mauritius kestrels can sometimes be seen flying around the area having ventured from their nesting boxes. There is a visitor's centre for the Black River Gorges National Park just inland from Grande Rivière Noire on Les Gorges Road.

Between Grand Rivière Noire and Tamarin is the popular **Ruisseau Creole** shopping centre, with over 50 shops and numerous restaurants (see page 172). The modern shopping centres and housing developments in the area are indicative of the recent influx of foreigners to the area, particularly South Africans.

The road to **Tamarin** runs beside salt pans, where seawater flows through a series of pools and via evaporation produces salt. Salt pans were introduced to Mauritius during French rule (1715–1810) and the ones you see here have been producing salt for over 175 years. In the early morning, ladies can be seen shovelling the salt and carrying it on their heads to the salt stores. If you think they look too heavily dressed for the weather, in their wellington boots and long skirts, the clothing is necessary to protect their skin from the salt. Guided tours explaining salt production are available (see *The Salt Route*, *What to see in Western Mauritius*, page 174).

The beach at Tamarin has waves, unlike many of the northern and eastern beaches, and so is popular with surfers.

WHERE TO STAY

Luxury

Dinarobin Hotel Golf & Spa (172 rooms) Le Morne Peninsula; ☎ 401 4900; f 401 4901; e dinarobin@bchot.com; www.dinarobin-hotel.com. A brilliantly designed all-suite Beachcomber hotel. The suites are arranged in crescents, each with a pool at the centre. The emphasis is on relaxation & luxury. The junior suites have a light, airy bedroom & sitting area, plus a huge bathroom. The senior suites have a separate sitting room with dining area. All suites have a large covered veranda looking out to sea. Rooms have everything you'd expect from a top hotel, including internet access. There are 4 excellent restaurants, numerous pools, tennis & a fitness centre. There is a Clarins spa, which also offers Ayurvedic treatments. If the calm here becomes too much you can head next door to the livelier Paradis & use the facilities or eat at one of the restaurants; there is a regular shuttle service. Watersports take place here & at Paradis. Guests have access (payable) to the Paradis Golf Academy, Heritage Golf Club & the course at Tamarina Golf Estate & Beach Club. **$$$$$**

Paradis Hotel & Golf Club (299 rooms) Le Morne Peninsula; ☎ 401 5050; f 450 5140; e paradis@bchot.com; www.paradis-hotel.com. This huge Beachcomber resort boasts an 18-hole golf course, deep-sea fishing, dive centre & 4 restaurants (see page 168). The hotel is fronted by 5km of beach & uses lots of traditional materials, like wood & thatch. Rooms have the usual upmarket facilities & are particularly spacious; there are also 13 luxury villas. Sports are free, except golf, scuba diving, deep-sea fishing & mountain biking. The tennis facilities are exceptional – 6 floodlit courts. There are 4 restaurants, a spa & kids' club. Guests can use many of the facilities, including the restaurants, at the Dinarobin Hotel. Great for families & sports enthusiasts.

Upmarket

Indian Resort (167 rooms) Le Morne Peninsula; ☎ 401 4200; f 450 4011; e resa.indian@apavou-hotels.com; www.apavou-hotels.com. The hotel lies at the end of the peninsula in a windy spot, making it popular with kitesurfers & windsurfers but not suitable if you want to lounge on the sand. Rooms are equipped with AC, TV, minibar & safe; they are large but unappealing & feel in need of refurbishment. 4 rooms have disabled facilities. Facilities include 3 pools, kids' & teenagers' clubs, a fitness centre & spa. Overall the service, decor & cuisine fall short of most upmarket hotels. **$$$$**

Lux Le Morne (149 rooms) Le Morne Peninsula; ☎ 401 4000; f 450 5248; e reservation@luxislandresorts.com; www.luxislandresorts.com. Popular hotel on a beautiful stretch of beach. Rooms & suites are in 2-storey colonial-style villas. They

above Réunion is home to a number of striking waterfalls, such as La Cascade de Grand-Galet at Langevin (AR) page 301

below Rodrigues is drier and more rugged than Mauritius but is surrounded by a spectacular lagoon. A navigable channel, La Passe, snakes through the coral reef (G/A) page 197

left The ornate day gecko remains common on Mauritius (B/GG/FLPA) page 10

below There are seven species of sea turtle left in the world and five are found around Réunion. Pictured, a green sea turtle (AR) page 327

bottom Dolphin watching is a popular activity in the waters surrounding the Mascarene Islands (AR) page 94

above left In 1973 the Mauritius kestrel was named the rarest bird in the world, but now there are estimated to be between 400 and 500 on the island (B/GG/FLPA) page 9

above right The rare pink pigeon is thriving on Ile aux Aigrettes (NS) page 8

right The giant Aldabra tortoises at François Leguat Giant Tortoise and Cave Reserve in Rodrigues are related to the species that once roamed the Mascarenes (NS) page 226

below Bébour-Bélouve rainforests, Réunion: these luxuriant forests constitute the single-most important stop in Réunion for naturalists (TG/A) page 329

above **The colonial house of the administrator in Port Mathurin, Rodrigues, was built in 1873** (NS) page 217

left **Now a UNESCO World Heritage Site, Aapravasi Ghat was built in 1849 to receive indentured labourers** (AR) page 111

below **Le Morne Brabant in the southwest of Mauritius is regarded as a symbol of resistance to slavery** (SS) page 163

above **The much-photographed Notre Dame Auxiliatrice at Cap Malheureux** (AR) page 128

right **Colourful Tamil temples are dotted throughout Mauritius** (AR) page 38

below **The annual Maha Shivaratree festival at the sacred Grand Bassin draws in hundreds of Hindu worshippers** (AR) page 72

left **Fishermen in Rodrigues use traditional lobster pots made from vacoas leaves** (NS) page 33

below **Tea-picker at Bois Chéri Tea Estate, Mauritius** (AR) page 160

bottom **The Rault Factory, near Mahébourg, has used the same methods to make its manioc biscuits since 1870** (AR) page 159

above Colourful handicrafts are a feature of the weekly market in St-Pierre, Réunion (AR) pages 264–5

right After settling down on a beach it won't be long before a gentleman on a bicycle offers you a pineapple or a coconut (AR)

below The *tisane*-seller at Port Louis market sells plants to cure all manner of ailments (AR) page 110

bottom right Hats handmade from vacoas leaves are sold at Port Mathurin market (AR) page 217

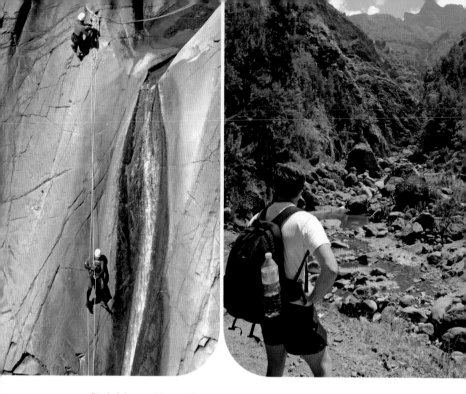

above left **Réunion's innumerable waterfalls and spectacular gorges are ideal for canyoning** (NS) page 272

above right **Réunion's cirques offer world-class hiking. Pictured here, Cirque de Cilaos** (AR) page 333

below **Like many of Mauritius's rural estates, Domaine de l'Etoile can be explored on a quadbike tour** (AR) page 188

are nicely decorated with AC, TV, minibar, safe, free Wi-Fi & sea-facing balcony/terrace. There are 3 restaurants, 3 bars, 3 pools, a spa, numerous free watersports, a dive centre, gym & tennis courts. There are both kids' & teenagers' clubs. **$$$$**

Mid range

Lakaz Chamarel (11 villas) Pinot Canot, Chamarel; 483 5240; f 483 5253; e lakazchamarel@intnet.mu; www.lakazchamarel.com. Elegant boutique accommodation in 11 villas for 2 or 3 people, set in a stunning tropical garden. The rooms have an air of luxury & encourage relaxation with thoughtful inclusions like the outdoor shower. There are 3 suites with private pool & garden. There is a TV room, small spa, 2 pools & a restaurant serving breakfast & dinner. A wonderful, private retreat. **$$$**

Les Lataniers Bleus (3 villas, 2 rooms) La Mivoie, Rivière Noire; 483 6541; f 483 6903; e latableu@intnet.mu; www.leslataniersbleus.com. A good budget option but priced at the bottom end of mid-range. The clean, simple villas, each with 2 to 5 bedrooms, are set in pretty gardens. You can either rent the whole villa or just 1 en-suite bedroom. The location is quiet – on the beach. Villas have a living room, kitchen, dining area, AC, TV & phone. There is a pool, Wi-Fi access & a good *table d'hôte* restaurant. **$$$**

Tamarin Hotel (71 rooms) Tamarin; 483 6927; f 483 6581; e resaweb@hoteltamarin.com; www.hoteltamarin.com, www.blue-season-hotels.com. The hotel sports a 1970s theme, so prepare to be amazed by colours you never knew existed. Rooms have en-suite facilities, AC, phone, safe & balcony/terrace. The 2-bedroom villas also have TV & minibar, while the suites have a separate living room. There are 2 restaurants, a pool & a kids' club. The hotel is known for its kitesurfing school, & other watersports are available nearby (payable). **$$$**

Tamarina Golf Estate & Hotel (50 rooms) Tamarin Bay; 404 0150; f 415 1804; e resa@tamarinahotel.com; www.tamarinahotel.com. A 4-star equivalent hotel on the beachfront within the Tamarina Golf Estate. Rooms are nicely furnished with all the facilities you would expect of a 4-star resort. The hotel is not designed to accommodate young children – there are no communicating rooms, no extra bed in the rooms & no kids' club. As well as the 18-hole championship golf course, there are 2 restaurants, tennis, watersports, 4 pools & a spa. The hotel's AI package includes green fees, 1 golf lesson, a spa treatment, entrance to Casela (see pages 174–5). **$$$**

The Bay Hotel (16 rooms) Cocotiers Av, La Preneuse; 483 6525; f 483 6332; e thebayhotel@intnet.mu; www.the-bay-hotel-mauritius.com. A lovely little hotel featuring traditional thatched buildings, on the beach at La Preneuse. Rooms are modern, clean, nicely decorated & have AC, TV, phone, safe, Wi-Fi (free) & minibar. Superior rooms & suites face the sea & have tea/coffee facilities & balcony/terrace. The public areas have a fresh, beachy feel; there is an open-air restaurant overlooking the pool & the sea. A yoga/pilates teacher offers sessions at the hotel, as well as massages & natural therapies. There are a few watersports available at a fee. **$$$**

Budget

La Vielle Cheminée Chamarel; 483 5249; f 483 5250; e caroline@laviellecheminee.com; www.laviellecheminee.com. Delightfully rustic self-catering accommodation on a working farm, which grows pineapples, sugarcane & palm trees. There is a 3-bedroom house & 2 cottages with 1 bedroom each. The 1-bedroom cottages have AC, while the 3-bedroom house has fans. The large house & one of the cottages have a fireplace on the terrace for cool winter evenings; each has a garden area. There are no TVs, no internet, just a wonderful opportunity for total relaxation. The décor is rustic but very nicely done in traditional Creole style. The farm is on a hill with views of the surrounding countryside. Guests can wander the farm on foot or on a guided horseride from the well-run stables (see page 87). There is a small pool with a little bar on a hill in the middle of the property, a very peaceful spot. This is one of few Mauritian properties which takes recycling seriously & does what it can to limit its impact on the environment. Dbl/sgl from €86/65 RO, breakfast can be provided for €6 pp, dinner for €12 pp. **$$**

Les Chalets en Champagne (3 villas) 110 Route Plaine Champagne, Chamarel; 483 6610; f 483 5410; e varangue@intnet.mu; www.leschaletsenchampagne.com. Pretty wooden mountain lodges with 2 or 3 AC bedrooms, living/dining area, fireplace, TV & kitchenette. Guided hikes of the surrounding forests are available, & guests can fish for berry rouge in the lake. A pleasant mountain escape. **$$**

Les Palmiers (5 rooms) Chamarel; ☎ 483 8364. Simple accommodation in the hills of Chamarel, above the restaurant of the same name (see below). Dbl from €35 BB. $$

Marlin Creek Residence (15 rooms) 10 Colonel Dean Av, Rivière Noire; ☎ 491 9727; e speleca@yahoo.fr; www.ilemauricelocation.fr. Rooms are in a thatched 3-storey building facing the pool & colourful garden. They have a modern feel & are equipped with trendy en suite, AC, TV, safe & minibar. Also 2 self-catering bungalows available. Breakfast is served near the pool; there are 2 bars but no restaurant, although there are plenty nearby. Wi-Fi available. Not on the beach but near the marina from where catamaran & deep-sea fishing excursions leave. It would be wise to have a car if staying here so you can get to the beach at Flic en Flac & try the local eateries. A great budget option.

WHERE TO EAT

Big Willy's Route du Barachois, Tamarin; ☎ 483 7400; ⌚ 14.00–02.00 Tue–Fri, 09.00–02.00 Sat, 11.00–21.00 Sun. Cuisine: Creole, European. A popular new pub in a garden setting with a lively nightlife. $$$$

La Varangue sur Morne Coeur Bois; ☎ 483 5710; www.varanguesurmorne.com; ⌚ for lunch daily, dinner by arrangement. Cuisine: Creole, European, game, seafood. If you can get a table on the open side of the restaurant or outside there are wonderful views of the surrounding mountains & down to the coast. You do need to book for lunch. It is a popular stop for organised tours, which tend to arrive at about 13.30. There are usually no tour groups on weekends. Expect to pay around Rs1,200 for a 3-course set menu. Next to the restaurant is a small wood museum. $$$$

Le Chamarel Chamarel; ☎ 483 6421; www.lechamarelrestaurant.com; ⌚ for lunch daily. Cuisine: Creole, European, game, seafood. You feel perched on the edge of the world as you sit on the veranda overlooking forest, plain & sea. The menu is extensive. It's advisable to book, & tour groups stop here from about 13.00 on Wed & Sat. There is a small souvenir shop. $$$$

Bistrot du Barachois Route du Barachois, Tamarin; ☎ 483 7594; ⌚ for lunch & dinner Tue–Sat. Cuisine: French, seafood. On a privately owned hunting estate, dining is on a covered terrace overlooking a river. An upmarket European menu with a Mauritian twist – prawns with garlic butter, duck with raspberry sauce, pineapple tart. $$$

Zucca Ruisseau Creole, Rivière Noire; ☎ 483 7005; ⌚ for lunch & dinner daily. Cuisine: Italian, seafood. The Italian chef prepares a good range of dishes, including homemade pasta. $$$

Embafilao Le Morne Peninsula; ☎ 401 4085; ⌚ 08.30–15.30 daily. Cuisine: Creole, Chinese, seafood. On the public beach near Les Pavillions Hotel. Casual outdoor dining at reasonable prices. Expect to pay around Rs150 for a grilled fish skewer. Take-away available. $$

La Bonne Chute La Preneuse; ☎ 483 6552; ⌚ for lunch & dinner Mon–Sat. Cuisine: European, Creole, seafood, game. It may not look like much from the outside but this restaurant has a reputation for good food, although some travellers report an air of nonchalance. $$

Les Palmiers Chamarel; ☎ 483 8364; ⌚ 10.00–17.00 daily. Cuisine: Creole. Mrs Beehary has turned part of her home in the village of Chamarel into a cosy restaurant. Traditional Creole food, made using homegrown ingredients, is served on banana leaves. Great value. $$

Pizzadelic Ruisseau Creole, Rivière Noire; ☎ 483 7003; ⌚ for lunch & dinner daily. Cuisine: Italian. Also take-away. Wide range of homemade pizzas. $$

Epicerie Gourmande Royal Rd, Tamarin; ☎ 483 8735; ⌚ 08.30–18.30 Mon–Sat. Cuisine: European. An upmarket delicatessen selling a good range of tasty treats, most of which originate from France.

NIGHTLIFE Most hotels in the mid-range and upmarket categories organise evening entertainment in the form of live bands, *séga* nights or themed evenings. **Big Willy's** (*Route du Barachois, Tamarin; ☎ 483 7400; ⌚ 14.00–02.00 Tue–Fri, 09.00–02.00 Sat, 11.00–21.00 Sun*) is at the heart of the nightlife scene outside the hotels. This pub/restaurant with a dance floor is in a garden setting and is the haunt of the growing South African expat community in the area.

WOLMAR AND FLIC EN FLAC TO PORT LOUIS

A few kilometres off the main road to Port Louis (A3), Wolmar and Flic en Flac have seen considerable development over recent years with hotels and holiday houses multiplying at an alarming rate. The village of **Wolmar** has largely disappeared and luxury hotels now dominate this stretch of coast, giving it an air of exclusivity. **Flic en Flac** has a broader range of accommodation and all the trappings of a tourist resort: restaurants, travel agents and souvenir shops.

Despite the rows of Spanish Costa-style holiday homes opposite, the Flic en Flac public beach remains relatively unspoilt. Mauritians flock here on weekends and picnic among the casuarinas trees around the old lime kiln.

The name 'Flic en Flac' is thought to come from Old Dutch, an onomatopoeic word for the sound of hands slapping goatskin drums. Say it quickly.

TOURIST INFORMATION The outlets you see in Flic en Flac advertising tourist information are not MTPA tourist information offices; rather they are private companies. While they can provide information on excursions, bear in mind they will be trying to sell their own products. One such outlet is the Flic en Flac Tourist Agency (☎ *453 9389*; **e** *ffagency@intnet.mu; www.fftourist.com*).

WHERE TO STAY

Luxury

Maradiva Hotel (65 villas); Wolmar; ☎ 403 1500; **f** 453 5555; www.maradiva.com. The epitome of luxury. Believe it or not, the most basic accommodation here is a 163m² villa with private pool, outdoor dining area, open-air garden shower, plasma TV, DVD/CD, internet, minibar, safe & 24hr butler service. There are 2 restaurants, including 1 specialising in pan-Asian where you can marvel at the skills of the tepanyaki chef. The spa is superb & offers a range of treatments, including Ayurvedic therapies. There is a lovely outdoor heated pool & the treatment rooms have a sauna & shower attached. There are the usual watersports, beautiful pools, tennis, free use of bikes & a kids' club. A hotel designed for romantic relaxation rather than family fun. **$$$$$**

St Regis (173 rooms) ☎ 403 9000; **e** stregismauritius@stregis.com; www.stregismauritius.com. A new luxury hotel designed to evoke a bygone, colonial era. Beautifully decorated suites & villas with all the bells & whistles, including 24hr butler service. There are 6 upmarket restaurants, a spa, pool, gym, tennis, watersports & everything else you would expect from a luxury hotel. **$$$$$**

Upmarket

Hilton Mauritius Resort & Spa (193 rooms) Wolmar; ☎ 403 1000; **f** 403 1111; **e** info_mauritius@hilton.com; www.hilton.com. Forget all images that you have of Hilton hotels as concrete monstrosities in smoggy city centres. This is an architecturally striking hotel with grand gardens & public areas. It is particularly beautiful at night when flaming torches are lit around the grounds with great ceremony at 19.00 by members of staff who may normally go unseen, such as boat house, gardening & kitchen staff. The sea-facing rooms & suites include 2 rooms with disabled facilities. Rooms have all that you'd expect from a first-class hotel & are decorated in warm colours. There are lots of activities during the day & entertainment 3 evenings per week. The 4 restaurants include 1 excellent Thai (see page 171). The spa offers all manner of pampering & there are plenty of land & watersports available, many of which are included. There is a kids' club & gorgeous pools. A popular hotel for conferences, which are most common between May & Sep, should you wish to avoid them. **$$$$**

La Pirogue (248 rooms) Wolmar; ☎ 403 3900; **f** 403 3800; **e** info@lapirogue.mu; www.lapirogue.com. This large hotel first opened in 1976 but renovations have kept it up to date. The rooms are in thatched bungalows spread over a large area dotted with palm trees, & there is a beautiful beach. All rooms are ground floor & have AC, TV, minibar, phone, safe & terrace. Superior rooms are closer to the ocean. There is a room equipped for the disabled. There is a choice of bars & restaurants, including the romantic Paul et Virginie seafood restaurant (see page 172), & plenty of entertainment. A huge, winding pool is the centrepiece of the hotel. The sports facilities are impressive & include tennis courts, a gym with martial arts area, a wide range of watersports & a dive centre. Kids' & teenagers' clubs are on offer. Guests can use some of the facilities at neighbouring Sugar Beach, such as the spa. **$$$$**

Sofitel Imperial Hotel (191 rooms) Wolmar; 453 8700; f 453 8320; e h1144@sofitel.com; www.sofitel.com. The hotel looks like a Thai temple from the outside & there is a serenity within. The recently renovated rooms & suites have all the facilities of an upmarket hotel, including free internet access. The beds here are Sofitel's 'my bed' & are particularly comfortable. There are 5 restaurants, a pool, gym, tennis, watersports, a dive centre & an Asia-inspired spa. The hotel is popular with families & there is a kids' club. It is worth noting the family suites overlook the garden & not the sea. The Wine Corner restaurant allows you to sample a different, suggested wine with each course. **$$$$**

Sugar Beach Resort (258 rooms) Wolmar; 453 9090; f 453 9100; e info@sugarbeachresort.mu; www.sugarbeachresort.com. Colonial-style architecture & manicured lawns create the desired impression of an elegant sugar estate. Renovated in 2008, the hotel represents great value for money & the service is excellent. The rooms, suites & beach villas are beautifully furnished & well equipped, with en suite, AC, TV, phone, minibar, safe, Wi-Fi (payable) & balcony/terrace. The interconnecting rooms are ideal for families. The 3 restaurants, including 1 Italian (see page 171), offer an excellent variety of cuisine. There are 2 pools, a gym, watersports, kids' club & teenagers' club. One of the pools is designated as 'quiet' which means you shouldn't be bothered by other people's children. The spa is impressive – the large hammam is wonderful & can be booked for 30mins free usage. The hotel is spread along 500m of beautiful beach & there is a wonderful feeling of space, so however full the hotel may be it is unlikely to feel crowded. The sunsets are fabulous. Guests can use some of the facilities at neighbouring La Pirogue. **$$$$**

The Sands Resort (91 rooms) Wolmar; 403 1200; f 453 5300; e thesands@intnet.mu; www.thesandsresort.mu. Less luxurious than many of its exclusive neighbours (a 4-star equivalent rather than 5), but very comfortable & welcoming. The rooms are modern & particularly large, with huge en-suite bathrooms (with bath & shower), AC, TV, phone, minibar & safe. All rooms face the sea. The pool is fairly small but there is a good stretch of beach. The hotel targets couples & there is a spa but no kids' club. There are 3 restaurants, a bar, dive centre & some watersports are included. Unusually for a hotel of this type, the Sands welcomes outsiders, including locals, to their entertainment evenings. Fri night dinner, entertainment & dancing are particularly popular with locals, who mingle with the hotel guests. **$$$$**

Mid range

Pearle Beach Resort & Spa (74 rooms) Coastal Rd, Wolmar; 401 6300; f 453 8405; e pearle@intnet.mu; www.pearle-beach.com. A complete renovation has significantly improved this hotel. All but 10 of the rooms face the pool/sea, so try to get 1 that does. The rooms are nicely decorated with en suite, AC, flat-screen TV, phone, internet access (payable), safe, minibar & tea/coffee facilities. There is only 1 restaurant but in a hotel of this small size that isn't really an issue & there are plenty of restaurants nearby. There is a pool, small spa, watersports & evening entertainment. There is no kids' club but babysitting can be provided (payable). Considering the location, this is reasonable value for money. **$$$**

Gold Beach Resort (31 rooms) Coastal Rd, Wolmar; 453 8235; e goldbeach@intnet.mu; www.goldbeachresort.com. A small property on a good stretch of beach. The architecture is unusual – a series of round, white cottages. Rooms have en suite, AC, TV, phone, safe & tea/coffee facilities. There is a restaurant, pool, gym & entertainment 3 evenings per week. Watersports are available nearby (payable). I have heard reports of poor service. **$$$**

Aanari Hotel & Spa (50 rooms) Pasadena Village, Coastal Rd, Flic en Flac; 453 9000; f 453 5696; e reservations@aanari.com; www.aanari.com. Across the road from the beach in the Pasadena shopping complex, which houses the Spar supermarket, bars, restaurants & nightclubs. The location isn't very appealing but the rooms are modern with en suite, AC, TV, phone, safe & minibar. There is a Chinese restaurant. There is a very small spa area with 2 massage cabins but only guests in club rooms can use the jacuzzi & sauna free of charge. Not for those seeking a relaxing retreat. **$$$**

Budget

Escale Vacances (12 apts) Coastal Rd, Flic en Flac; 453 5002; f 453 5082; e ffagency@intnet.mu; www.fftourist.com. Across the road from the beach in the centre of Flic en Flac. Simple but clean self-catering duplexes with 1 bedroom, shower, living room with sofa-bed & equipped kitchenette (microwave, fridge, etc), AC, TV & balcony/terrace. 6 have sea view & are slightly more expensive, but they also get some road noise. Facilities include a good pool, private parking & daily maid service. Internet access is available. Renovated in 2011. **$$**

Klondike Hotel (31 rooms) Coastal Rd, Flic en Flac; 453 8333; f 453 8337; e info@klondikehotel.com; www.klondikehotel.com. At the northern end of Flic en Flac. Cottages house 20 rooms with AC, TV, safe, phone & minibar. There are also 11 bungalows with kitchenette (4–8 people). There is a good pool & a newly created beach, as well as a restaurant & bar. Regular live entertainment including a *séga* show on Sat. Some free watersports, a dive centre & tennis court. Popular with German guests. The hotel is looking rather tired & there are better options around. **$$**

Villa Paul et Virginie (12 rooms) Sea Breeze Lane, Flic en Flac; 453 8537; f 453 8159; e info@villa-paul-et-virginie.com; www.villa-paul-et-virginie.com. A cheap & cheerful guesthouse in a quiet spot in the village of Flic en Flac, a 5min walk from the beach. There are 11 bright en-suite rooms with AC & phone, each with a different décor. There is also an en-suite family room with kitchen (up to 6 people). The hotel has a pool, a TV room & a restaurant serving Creole, French & Italian cuisine (see page 172). **$$**

Villas Caroline (74 rooms) Coastal Rd, Flic en Flac; 453 8411; f 453 8144; e caroline@intnet.mu; www.carolinegroup.com. Has expanded over the years to 68 rooms & 6 self-catering bungalows for either 2 or 4 people. Rooms are simply furnished & have AC, TV, phone, safe, minibar & balcony/terrace. Superior rooms have a nicer, less spartan feel. Bungalows also have a well-equipped kitchen. Public areas are very pleasant, with a pool, open-air international restaurant, speciality Indian restaurant, bar & shop. There is a fantastic beach that is separated from the main strip of beach. Live music daily except Sun & a barbecue & *séga* show on Sat. Limited free non-motorised watersports & there is a dive centre, where English & German are spoken. **$$**

WHERE TO EAT For self-caterers there is a **Spar supermarket** in the Pasadena Village Complex near Flic en Flac Beach (*08.00–20.00 Mon–Sat, 08.00–17.00 Sun*) and a new supermarket within La Cascavelle shopping centre on the road into Flic en Flac. There is also a small supermarket on the coast road and another in the group of shops beyond the Flic en Flac Mall, on the way out of town.

Ginger Thai Hilton Resort; 403 1000; for dinner Tue–Sun. Cuisine: Thai. The Thai chef here conjures up excellent dishes. Elegant setting with tables indoor & out. Very plush with prices to match. Reservation necessary. **$$$$$**

The Cilantro Maradiva Hotel, Wolmar; 403 1500; for dinner daily. Cuisine: Asian. A fine-dining restaurant serving pan-Asian cuisine. Dinner at the tepanyaki counter, watching the skilled chefs perform, is entertaining. **$$$$$**

Citronella Café Sugar Beach Resort, Wolmar; 453 9090; for lunch Tue–Sun, for dinner Mon–Sat. Cuisine: Italian. Upmarket Italian restaurant on the beachfront. Diners can watch the chefs prepare delicious pizza in the wood-fired oven. The service here is excellent. There are inexpensive options on the menu, with main courses priced from Rs350. **$$$$**

Domaine Anna Flic en Flac; 453 9650; www.domaineanna.net; for lunch & dinner Tue–Sun. Cuisine: European, Chinese, seafood. Turn right from the road into Flic en Flac coming from the main Port Louis–Tamarin road (A3). Elegant dining in a colonial-style building surrounded by forest & lakes; you can also dine in thatched pavillons on the edge of the lakes. Lobster is the chef's speciality. Reservation necessary. 3-course set menus from Rs1,450. **$$$$**

Hippocampe Kalimaye Rd, Flic en Flac; 453 8227; www.hippocampe.mu; 11.00–late

Thu–Sun. Cuisine: Creole, Indian, European, pub. Behind the Pasadena Village. A trendy bar/restaurant/patisserie. Think tapas, cocktails & nicely presented, modern dishes. Cakes & pastries are available in the afternoon, even scones are on the menu. Free Wi-Fi. $$$$

✕ **Les Coquillages** Hilton Resort; ☎ 403 1000; ⌚ 12.00–17.00 daily. Cuisine: European, Creole, seafood. Informal but upmarket restaurant right on the beach, with tables on the sand. Excellent food, service & views. $$$$

✕ **Paul et Virginie Restaurant** La Pirogue Hotel; ☎ 453 8441; ⌚ for lunch daily, for dinner Mon–Wed & Fri/Sat. Cuisine: seafood. Upmarket open-air dining on the beach. $$$$

✕ **Black Steer** Pasadena Complex, Flic en Flac; ☎ 453 8590; ⌚ 08.45–22.30 daily. Cuisine: European, steakhouse. Serves mostly grilled meat, chicken, & some salads. $$$

✕ **Le Mirador** Casela Nature & Leisure Park, Royal Rd, Cascavelle; ☎ 452 0845; ⌚ 10.30–16.00 daily. Cuisine: Creole, French. A good-quality restaurant on a hill with wonderful views of the west coast. Serves tasty Creole dishes. $$$

✕ **Villa Paul et Virginie Restaurant** Sea Breeze Lane, Flic en Flac; ☎ 453 8537; ⌚ for lunch & dinner daily. Cuisine: Italian, Creole, French. Also take-away. A good option with tasty pizzas, grilled fish & paella. Live music Wed & Sat evening. Reservation recommended. $$$

✕ **Chez Leslie** Coastal Rd, Flic en Flac; ☎ 453 8172; ⌚ for lunch & dinner Tue–Sun. Cuisine: Creole, Chinese. Inexpensive, friendly restaurant at the northern end of Flic en Flac. $$

✕ **Le Papayou** Flic en Flac Mall; ☎ 453 9826; ⌚ 09.00–22.00 Mon–Sat. Cuisine: Creole, Chinese, pizza, snacks. Also take-away. Simple but modern & spotless with good-value food. $$

✕ **Zub Express** Coastal Rd, Flic en Flac; ☎ 453 8868; www.zub-express.com; ⌚ 10.00–22.00 daily. Cuisine: Indian, Chinese. Casual café across the road from Flic en Flac Beach. Lunch & dinner are served at the usual times but the café remains open all day. Also has internet facilities (payable). Main courses from Rs150. Take-away available. $$

NIGHTLIFE Flic en Flac's nightlife has grown rapidly in recent years and there are now plenty of options outside the hotels. There is a **casino** and several bars across the road from the beach, around the Pasadena Village shopping complex. Many of the bars are open from mid-morning until late. **Hippocampe** on Kalimaye Road, Flic en Flac (☎ *453 8227;* ⌚ *11.00–late Thu–Sun*) is a modern bar/restaurant/patisserie with inviting lounge bar and free Wi-Fi. **Shout (Shotz)** (☎ *453 5607*) has comfy chairs on a wooden deck, plus indoor and outdoor dance floors. **Teasers** and **AK47** are two more bars open until late. **Kenzi Bar** near Villa Paul and Virginie gets a good crowd on the dance floor.

SHOPPING Flic en Flac has lots of touristy shops, selling cheap clothing and souvenirs. There are two shopping malls: the Flic en Flac Mall at the northern end of town and the new Pasadena Village opposite the police station near Flic en Flac Beach. The abundance of tourists in the area means that shopkeepers tend to try it on when it comes to price. A few words of Creole usually do the trick (see *Appendix 1, Language*, pages 347–8).

Beyond Flic en Flac Mall, on the way out of town on the right, there are two model ship shops. **Pirate Ship Models** (☎ *453 9028;* ⌚ *09.30–17.30 Mon–Sat*) has lots of choice. The smaller **Superbe Ship Shop** is almost next door.

Ruisseau Creole (☎ *483 8000;* **e** *contact@ruisseaucreole.com; www.ruisseaucreole.com; shops* ⌚ *09.30–18.30 Mon–Sat*) is a large shopping centre at Rivière Noire, which targets the tourist market and well-heeled Mauritians. It opened in June 2005 and has around 50 shops selling jewellery, clothing, handicrafts and art, as well as restaurants (see page 168) and bars. There is also a bank with ATM and free parking. A free shuttle is available from most hotels on the west coast.

Another large shopping complex, **La Cascavelle**, was recently built on the road into Flic en Flac. As well as boutiques, it contains a supermarket and food court.

OTHER PRACTICALITIES There is a **petrol station** on the road into Flic en Flac, and a **pharmacy** in the Pasadena Village. The **police station** is on the main road into Flic en Flac, opposite the Pasadena Village.

Money and banking The Flic en Flac Mall has a Mauritius Commercial Bank with an ATM. There is also a State Bank ATM at the Pasadena Village.

Communications The **post office** is across the road from the Pasadena Village, behind the police station; **internet access** is available. The **Pasaden Internet Café** at the Spar supermarket in Flic en Flac (☎ *453 8226*) offers fax, scanning, photocopying, CD burning and international phonecards, as well as internet access. **Flic en Flac Tourist Agency** (☎ *453 9389*; **e** *ffagency@Intnet.mu; www.fftourist.com*) has internet access, fax, photocopying and a photolab. **Zub Express** (☎ *453 8868; www.zub-express.com;* ⌚ *10.00–22.00 daily*), across the road from the beach, is a restaurant with internet facilities.

WHAT TO DO IN WESTERN MAURITIUS

SPORTS

Deep-sea fishing The island's first deep-sea fishing clubs were set up around the area of Grande Rivière Noire as the deep waters here provide ideal conditions. There is now a good choice of operators based in the southwest of the island. This is where you will find Le Morne Anglers' Club (*www.morneanglers.com*). For more information, see *Chapter 3, Activities*, pages 88–9.

Scuba diving The southwest and west coasts have excellent diving sites for all levels of experience, including a number of shipwrecks. There is a good choice of diving operators to choose from around Flic en Flac and Le Morne. For more information, see *Chapter 3, Activities*, pages 89-92.

Kitesurfing Le Morne Peninsula has ideal conditions for kitesurfing and several of the hotels in the area offering kitesurfing for a fee. For more information, see *Chapter 3, Activities*, page 94.

Golf The 18-hole course at Paradis Hotel is open to non-residents. Many of the hotels on the west coast can also arrange for guests to play at the 18-hole course at the Tamarina Golf Estate and Beach Club on the Médine Sugar Estate. For more information, see *Chapter 3, Activities*, pages 86–7.

Go-karting/quad biking Available at **Kart Loisir** at Petite Rivière (☎ *233 2223*; **f** *233 2225*; **e** *kartloisir@intnet.mu;* ⌚ *from 09.00 daily*). Go-karting costs from Rs300 per person for ten minutes, quad biking costs from Rs1,380 per person for one hour.

Horseriding Available at **La Vieille Cheminée** at Chamarel and **Le Ranch** near Rivière Noire. For more information, see *Chapter 4, Activities*, pages 87–8.

Parc Aventure (*Chamarel;* ☎ *234 5385;* **f** *234 5866;* **e** *parcaventure@intnet.mu; www.parc-aventure-chamarel.com;* ⌚ *Thu–Tue; reservation necessary*) An elaborate **obstacle course** through the forest, with rope bridges, climbing nets, etc. The course takes around two hours to complete. Wear long trousers, trainers, gloves and insect repellent. There is a minimum age requirement of six years. Also on offer are **mountain biking**, **hiking**, **kayaking** and **canyoning**.

SPA TREATMENTS Outside the hotels there are a few small spas in the Flic en Flac area, such as **Om Spa** (*Complex Les Flamboyants, Coastal Rd, Flic en Flac;* ☎ *769 2676;* 🕘 *09.15–17.30 Tue–Sat, 09.15–13.00 Sun & public holidays*), which offers traditional and Ayurvedic massage, plus beauty treatments.

WHAT TO SEE IN WESTERN MAURITIUS

THE SALT ROUTE (LA ROUTE DU SEL) (*Mont Calme, Royal Rd, Tamarin;* ☎ *483 8764;* **f** *483 8798;* **e** *montcalme@intnet.mu;* 🕘 *08.30–17.00 Mon–Sat; admission adult/child Rs200/100*) The salt pans at Tamarin have been producing salt for over 175 years. Today the pans yield around 1,300–1,400 tons of salt per year. Guided tours of around 15 minutes explain the process of salt production. Seawater is pumped into the pools, of which there are 1,586, and then flows through a series of pools at different temperatures. Between five and ten days later it reaches the last pool, the water evaporates and it crystallises into salt. The hardworking ladies of the salt pans collect the salt and carry it in tubs or baskets on their heads to one of nine salt stores, where it is dried. Each tub of salt weighs around 20kg and sometimes you can see women carrying two or even three tubs on their heads. If you want to see the ladies in action you will need to be there before 09.30 as they typically work in the early morning to avoid the heat. Culinary and cosmetic products made from the salt are on sale in the small shop.

MARTELLO TOWER MUSEUM (*La Preneuse Rd, Grande Rivière Noire;* ☎ *583 0178;* **e** *foemau@intnet.mu;* 🕘 *09.30–16.30 Tue–Sat, 09.30–13.30 Sun; admission adult/child Rs70/40*) In the 1830s, the British built five Martello Towers, with sturdy walls and cannon, to protect the island. They were in the process of negotiating the abolition of slavery, a proposition which faced hefty resistance from the French sugarcane planters, who relied on slave labour. The British feared a rebellion by the planters might be followed by a French invasion and so built the towers, which have come to symbolise the abolition of slavery. The tower at Rivière Noire has opened as a museum, where a short video is followed by a guided tour. On display are cannon, coins and military paraphernalia from the period.

CASELA NATURE AND LEISURE PARK (*Royal Rd, Cascavelle;* ☎**f** *452 2828;* **f** *452 0694;* **e** *caselaresa@medine.com; www.caselayemen.mu;* 🕘 *May–Sep 09.00–17.00 daily; Oct–Apr 09.00–18.00 daily; admission adult/child Rs325/200*) Access is off the Black River road between Tamarin and the turning to Flic en Flac. There are 1,500 birds of 150 different species, as well as tigers, monkeys, wallabies and other zoo favourites. Well-known residents include the rare pink pigeon. The park is well laid out, with shaded walks through the 85 aviaries, and there is a petting zoo area with farm animals. A safari-park-style area, with resident zebra, ostrich, deer, wild pigs and giant tortoises, can be explored in a safari bus (Rs85 for one hour), on a Segway (Rs1,100 for one hour) or on a quad bike (Rs2,160 for one hour). It is the zebra which make this worthwhile. Casela also offers ziplining (flying-fox) over the ravines surrounding the sugarcane fields (Rs880 for one hour, Rs2,420 for a full day) and canyoning (Rs2,810 for a full day). Tilapia fishing (Rs80 for 30 minutes) and minigolf (Rs75). The tigers are fed at 11.30. There is a restaurant with views of the coast (see *Where to eat*, page 172).

SAFARI ADVENTURES (*Casela Nature and Leisure Park, Cascavelle;* ☎ *452 5546;* **f** *452 5574;* **e** *safari-adventures@intnet.mu; www.safari-adventures-mauritius.com;* ⏰ *09.00–16.00 Mon–Sat*) Located at the Casela Nature and Leisure Park, Safari Adventures Mauritius was established in 2006 by renowned wildlife experts Graeme and Julie Bristow from Zimbabwe. It offers the chance to interact with lions and/or cheetahs and/or tigers. All of the interactions are wonderful, memorable experiences, or if you don't fancy getting too close you can simply observe the big cats from a platform or take a safari-style drive-through and watch them from a

KAYA

In the early hours of the morning of Sunday 21 February 1999, Joseph Reginald Topize, better known as Kaya, was found dead in a high-security police cell.

His death brought Mauritius to a standstill but, more importantly, it revealed how important it is for the government to address potential racial tension.

Kaya was a popular Rastafarian singer, an important Creole figure known throughout the Indian Ocean islands and beyond. His group, Racinetatane, was responsible for launching *séggae*, a blend of reggae and *séga*, in the late 1980s.

In early 1999, the Mouvement Républicain (MR) began a campaign for the decriminalisation of cannabis smoking. On 16 February, a concert was held in support of the campaign and Kaya was asked to perform.

The following day, he and eight others were arrested for smoking cannabis in public. All but Kaya denied the charge and were released. Kaya admitted it and was sent to a high-security cell at Line Barracks, known locally as Alcatraz.

He was granted bail of Rs10,000 but his family could not raise the money. Surprisingly, the MR did not attempt to pay the bail, although Kaya had performed for free at their concert.

When his body was found in the cell, it was clear that he had died of head injuries and an autopsy later confirmed this. News of Kaya's death, apparently a result of police brutality, swept through the island. Groups of protesters gathered, and by the afternoon there were widespread riots. Severe rioting continued for three days. Police stations were attacked and buildings set alight all over Mauritius. Hundreds of police officers and rioters were injured during the unrest, many by gunshot wounds. Several people were killed.

News of Kaya's death spread to Réunion too, where I was living at the time, and I vividly remember the anger amongst the Creole population there.

The unrest in Mauritius began to take on a political and racial tone. Creoles vented their frustration at what they considered to be their disadvantaged position in society and rebelled against the Indo-Mauritian-dominated authorities.

Something positive did come out of Kaya's death – it forced politicians to acknowledge the discontent of the Creole community and a government department was set up to address their concerns. The events were a reminder that Mauritius's ethnic cocktail, which is an asset in so many ways, can also be an explosive mixture. It seems that politicians have learnt their lesson and realise that constant efforts must be made to listen to and involve all communities.

vehicle.The pick of the options has to be 'walking with lions'. In a small group and accompanied by guides you take the lions for a walk around the reserve (no leads, they're free, but far more obedient than my dogs). In recent years, the Bristows have also added the opportunity to walk with a lion and a tiger. It is an unforgettable experience and I'd recommend it to any animal lover. You'll need comfortable walking shoes and ideally long trousers and mosquito repellent. Photographs and video are taken during the walk, which you can buy on DVD as a souvenir. Reservation recommended. There is a minimum height requirement of 1.5m for all interactions and walks, and a minimum age of 15. Approximate prices are 30-minute observation from a platform Rs100, 15-minute interaction Rs500, drive-through Rs250, walking with lions Rs2,500 per person, walking with a lion and tiger Rs3,000 per person. You will also need to pay the Casela Nature and Leisure Park entrance fee.

THE SEVEN COLOURED EARTHS (*Mare Anguilles, Chamarel;* ☎ *622 6177;* 🕘 *07.00–17.00 daily; admission adult/childRs125/75*) Signed from the village of Chamarel, a track through the private estate leads first to the waterfall then on to the coloured earths. Both attractions involve parking the car for a short walk. The track is lined with the Arabica coffee plants for which the area is known and 'heart of palm salad trees'. The Chamarel Waterfall is the island's highest and tumbles 100m down a sheer cliff face. The track continues to the second car park. A viewing platform allows you to see the denuded earth from on high. Specimens of the coloured earths in glass tubes are on sale in the small shop. There is also a snack bar.

RHUMERIE DE CHAMAREL (*Royal Rd, Chamarel;* ☎ *483 7980;* **e** *infos@rhumeriedechamarel.com; www.rhumeriedechamarel.com;* 🕘 *10.00–17.00 Mon–Sat; admission & guided tour adult/child Rs350/175*) On the main road through Chamarel, 3km from the village in the direction of Grand Bassin. The *rhumerie* was purpose built as an attraction in 2008. Admission includes a 30-minute guided tour explaining the process of producing rum from sugarcane, followed by a rum tasting. There is a shop selling rum and souvenirs, and an upmarket restaurant serving local produce (open for lunch).

TOUCHE DU BOIS (*Coeur Bois;* ☎ *483 5710;* **e** *varangue@intnet.mu;* www.varanguesurmorne.com; 🕘 *11.00–15.00 daily; admission Rs100*). This small but fascinating museum is on the site of the Varangue sur Morne restaurant and was created by the owner, a keen woodworker. It has been nicely put together and shows the various uses of wood, past and present, including in religion, sport, music and medicine.

9

Central Mauritius

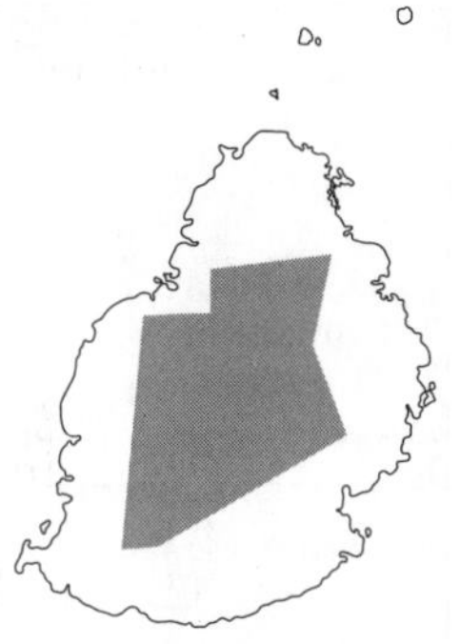

Two districts make up central Mauritius: Plaines Wilhems to the south and west of centre and Moka to the north and east.

At around 600m above sea level, the centre of the island is noticeably cooler and wetter than the coast. Temperatures are generally 3–5°C lower so a visit to the centre can be a welcome break from the heat of the beaches.

The central plateau is characterised by extinct volcanic craters, lakes, rivers and waterfalls. Some of the island's most spectacular scenery lies within the Black River Gorges National Park, which protects Mauritius's remaining forests and offers good opportunities for hiking.

Another attraction which draws tourists to the centre is the abundance of discount clothing and souvenir shops in the plateau towns. These towns are largely residential, linked to each other and to Port Louis by the motorway that cuts through the centre of the island.

PLAINES WILHEMS

Although Plaines Wilhems has had settlers since 1690, officially it only became an inhabited district in 1877. Since then it has burgeoned into the island's most densely populated region, with at least 30% of Mauritius's population living in the plateau towns of Beau Bassin, Rose Hill, Quatre Bornes, Phoenix, Vacoas, Floréal and Curepipe.

The district begins as a thin wedge between the Port Louis and Black River districts. It follows the motorway southwards, widening gradually around the plateau towns. In the south, beyond Curepipe, it borders the districts of Grand Port and Savanne. The northern part of Plaines Wilhems is largely residential, while the south is characterised by tea plantations, forests and reservoirs.

Plaines Wilhems was sparsely populated until 1861, when a cholera epidemic caused the first exodus from Port Louis of people seeking a healthier climate and swelled the population to 28,020. The malaria epidemic of 1866–68 accelerated the drift. This migration resulted in ghettos. Whereas Port Louis had been a cosmopolitan mixture, the races here divided to form new towns. Those of French origin settled in Curepipe, whilst the upper class of the Indian and Creole population chose Rose Hill. The division between social/ethnic groups was emphasised by the trains, which had three separate classes, and were used by the plateau town dwellers to commute every day to Port Louis. Now the settlements from Beau Bassin to Curepipe have merged into a single, built-up area, but the divisions remain by tradition.

BEAU BASSIN AND ROSE HILL Beau Bassin and **Rose Hill** are intertwined, largely residential, sister towns that hold little interest for the average tourist. Although

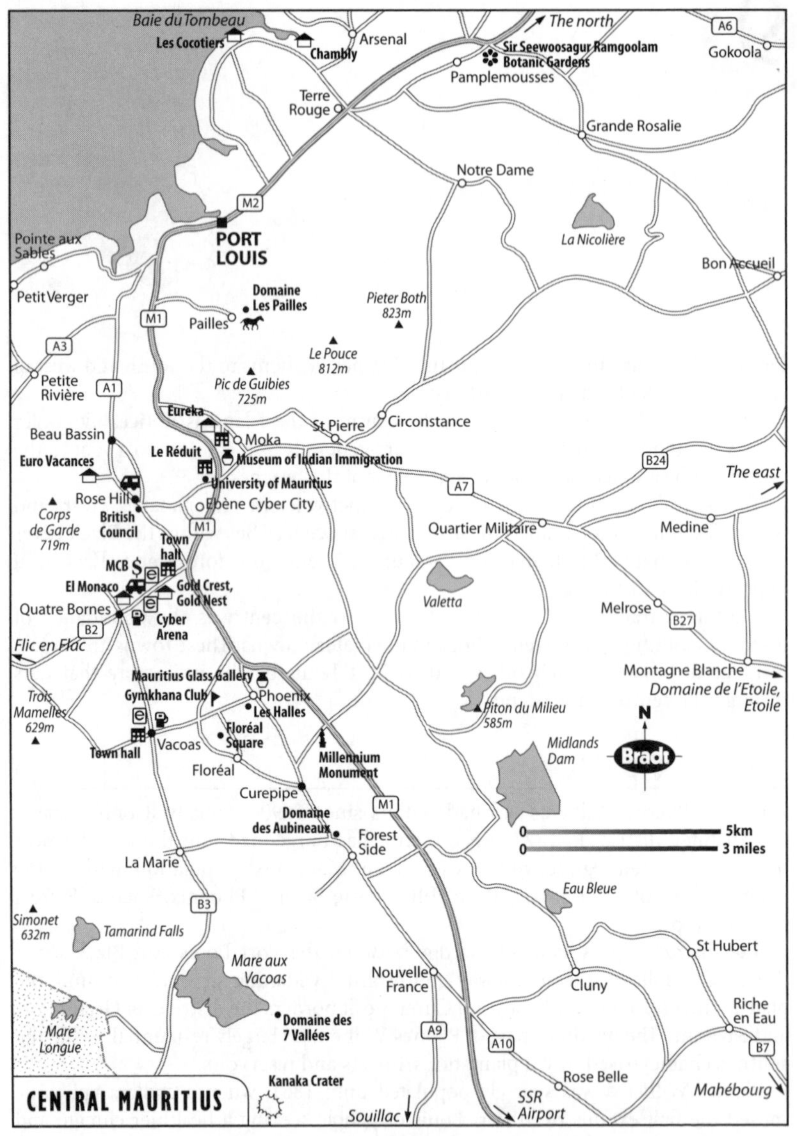

Beau Bassin/Rose Hill was declared a town in 1896, it was not until 1927 that it was decided to build its **town hall**. This resulted in the series of linked, two-tiered pavilions that lie off the main road just outside the centre of Rose Hill. As well as the town hall, the complex includes the **Plaza Theatre**, with an extravagant rococo interior of gold leaf and maroon plush. It was originally built as a cinema (1929–32) but on 12 June 1934 the Mauritius Dramatic Club performed an inaugural play, *The Last of Mrs Cheney*.

Beau Bassin has a small municipal park, **Balfour Gardens**, overlooking the **Plaines Wilhems Gorge**, where there is a waterfall. Across this valley is Le Réduit (see *Around Le Réduit*, pages 186–7). **La Tour Blanche**, a white manor house built in 1834, lies to the south of the garden. This is where Charles Darwin stayed during his visit in 1836. At the other side of the town are the island prisons, the police training school and the college of education.

In Rose Hill a number of solid Victorian buildings have been preserved amidst the lock-up shops and apartment blocks of this bustling town. Some say its name comes from the rosy glow of sunset on Corps de Garde Mountain behind it, whilst others claim the town, being on a hill, was named after Rose, the mistress of the landowner. **Corps de Garde** mountain (719m) won its name because a French military post was established on it to control the bands of runaway slaves in the region.

Getting there and away The **bus station** in Rose Hill is at Place Margéot. There are regular buses from Victoria Square in Port Louis to Rose Hill, and some continue via the other plateau towns to Curepipe. There are also buses linking Rose Hill and Centre de Flacq.

Where to stay If you really need to stay in the Beau Bassin/Rose Hill area and don't have friends or relatives who can put you up, you may struggle for options.

Budget

Euro Vacances (24 rooms) 8 Rue Poivre, Beau Bassin; 466 3524; f 465 1022; e eurovacances@intnet.mu; www.eurovacanceshotel.com. Basic, uninspiring en-suite rooms with fan, TV & phone; some have AC, minibar & balcony. A room with kitchenette is available on request. There is a restaurant & pool.

Where to eat

Le Pékinois 4 Ambrose St, Rose Hill; 454 7229; for lunch & dinner Tue–Sun. Cuisine: Chinese, grills. $$

Other practicalities Royal Road is the main street, on which you'll find **banks**, **ATMs**, **shopping malls** and **payphones**.

QUATRE BORNES The main road from Rose Hill (Royal Road) takes you to the St Jean's Church roundabout, where you can either continue to Phoenix and Curepipe or turn right to Quatre Bornes. The town was so named as four former sugar estates (Bassin, La Louise, Palma and Beau Séjour) shared a common four-point boundary.

With a population of over 80,000, Quatre Bornes has developed on either side of the main road as the centre of five residential communities. The emergence of a large middle class in the area is apparent from the presence of modern shops, supermarkets and good-quality restaurants and snack bars.

The **market** is centrally located on St Jean Road, the main road through the town. The markets on Thursday and Sunday are reputed to be the island's best for clothing, handicrafts and household items; on Wednesday and Saturday there are fruit and vegetable markets. There are plenty of discount clothing shops on the same road, especially in the **Orchard Centre**, which is just west of the market. The shopping centre is relatively modern and has a food court, where Wi-Fi is available. A little further on is the **police station**, near the Total **petrol station**.

Getting there and away The **bus station** is roughly in the middle of St Jean Road, near the junction with Victoria Avenue. There are regular buses to and from Port Louis via Rose Hill and Beau Bassin. Buses also depart from Quatre Bornes for Curepipe, Baie du Cap and Wolmar (via Flic en Flac).

Where to stay

Budget

El Monaco (93 rooms) 17 St Jean Rd; 425 2608; f 425 1072; e elmo@intnet.mu; www.el-monaco.com. Set back from the main road in attractive gardens, the hotel is a warren of en-suite rooms of different vintages (the hotel was begun in 1971), with fan (no AC), TV & phone. It has a restaurant, pool & conference room. A basic hotel catering largely for tour groups from Réunion. $$

Gold Crest Hotel (59 rooms) Georgetown Bldg, St Jean Rd; 454 5945; f 454 9599; e crestel@intnet.mu; www.goldgrouphotels.com. In the centre of town above a shopping complex. The unfussy en-suite rooms have AC, TV & phone, & overlook the central plaza. It has a restaurant (see below) & a conference room. $$

Gold Nest Hotel (33 rooms) Cnr St Jean Rd & Orchidées Av; 466 3100; f 466 2393; e goldnest@intnet.mu; www.goldgrouphotels.com. Clean, comfortable en-suite rooms with AC, TV, phone & safe. There is an Indian restaurant & a conference room. $$

Where to eat

For self-caterers there is a supermarket within the Orchard Centre.

Happy Rajah St Jean Rd; 427 1400; for lunch & dinner daily. Cuisine: Indian. The sister of the restaurant of the same name in Grand Baie. Good, authentic Indian cuisine. $$$

Gold Crest Hotel St Jean Rd; 454 5945; for lunch & dinner daily. Cuisine: Indian, Chinese, Creole, European. Pleasant AC restaurant serving a wide range of dishes. $$

Golden Spur The Orchard Ctr; 424 9440; 11.00–late daily. Cuisine: Mexican, steakhouse. Modern restaurant with a fast-food feel. $$

King Dragon La Louise; 424 7888; for lunch & dinner Wed–Mon. Cuisine: Chinese. At the west end of St Jean Rd. $

Le Bon Choix St Jean Rd; 465 3856; for lunch & dinner daily. Cuisine: Creole. Popular restaurant serving reasonably priced food. $

Other practicalities

Communications **Cyber Arena** (*427 7295*) on the second floor of the Orchard Centre has **internet access**. There is also an internet café in the library at the **town hall** on St Jean Road (*454 8054*) and internet access is available at the **post office**. The food court in the Orchard Centre has Wi-Fi.

Money and banking The banks are mostly on St Jean Road, including a branch of Mauritius Commercial Bank with an **ATM**, opposite the market. There is also a branch of HSBC on the corner of Avenue des Rosiers and Avenue des Palmiers, near the market. The Barclays is near the Shell petrol station.

VACOAS AND PHOENIX South of Quatre Bornes lies another residential area, **Vacoas** (pronounced 'Vak-wa'). It was named 'Les Vacoas' in the 18th century after the pandanus trees (known locally as vacoas) that grew in the region.

Residential and agricultural, it produces mainly vegetables and has some light industry. The heart of the town is a crossroads with a **taxi stand**, a **public toilet**, a **petrol station** and the **municipality building**.

The British presence in Mauritius lingered on at Vacoas with a land-based communications station on St Paul Avenue, and with British instructors training the men of the Special Mobile Force, which has its headquarters in Vacoas. The frightfully British **gymkhana club** on Suffolk Road originally opened in 1849 as a polo club for officers. It now has an 18-hole golf course (see page 86), tennis courts, swimming pool, squash courts, gym, snooker table and a modern clubhouse with a view of the golf course. It also has a restaurant with a stage, a lounge bar and library. The atmosphere is of a well-run establishment with dedicated, long-serving staff. Temporary membership is available to visitors on a daily or monthly basis.

Phoenix is an industrial area, with Mauritius Breweries producing their Phoenix and Stella beers at **Pont Fer**. Pont Fer also has a **Mauritius Glass Gallery** workshop, where bottles, lamps and ornaments are made from recycled glass (see *What to see in Central Mauritius*, page 187). In recent years, one of the island's largest shopping centres, **Les Halles**, was built just outside Phoenix. It is slick and modern and has shops selling clothing, cosmetics, home wares and electronics; there is a decent food court with free Wi-Fi.

Where to eat On the road to Floréal from Phoenix there is a **Continent supermarket**.

Mandarin Restaurant Royal Rd, Vacoas; 696 4551; for lunch & dinner daily. Cuisine: Chinese. Popular restaurant with tables around a dance floor. $$$

FLOREAL Members of the diplomatic corps live in Floréal, in country houses set in large gardens on leafy lanes. Floréal is a comparatively new community, having been begun by Governor Hesketh Bell during his tenure (1916–24).

Bargain-hunting is probably the visitor's main reason for stopping here. Of particular interest to shoppers is the **Floréal Knitwear Factory**, which has a boutique in Mangalkhan, selling export-quality, locally made knitwear.

Floréal Square on John Kennedy Street houses shops (mostly clothing, but also jewellery, art and carpets) and a café (see below).

More expensive, but just as popular, are the duty-free diamond shops, such as Adamas in Mangalkhan (see also pages 74–5).

Where to eat

La Clef des Champs Queen Mary Av, Floréal; 686 3458; for lunch Mon–Sat. Cuisine: French with a Creole accent. An upmarket restaurant in a converted house, which caters for Floréal's diplomatic residents & well-heeled gourmets. Reservation recommended. $$$$

Floréal Café Floréal Sq, 1 John Kennedy St, Floréal; 698 8040; 09.30–17.30 Mon–Fri, 09.30–16.00 Sat. Cuisine: European. Homemade meals, light snacks & pastries. $$$

Epicerie Gourmande Royal Rd, Floréal; 697 5429; 08.30–18.30 Mon–Sat. Cuisine: European. A branch of the upmarket chain of delicatessens, which sells a good range of tasty treats, most of which originate from France.

CUREPIPE Many writers have seen Curepipe as a dismal place. Mark Twain described it as 'the nastiest spot on earth'. Michael Malim, writing in the 1950s book *Island of the Swan*, which caused a stir in Mauritius when it was published, said, 'it seems drowned in some immemorial woe … stricken and inconsolable'. Mauritians themselves say there are two seasons in Curepipe: 'the rainy season and the season of rains'. In fact, its annual rainfall matches London's. It can be humid ('God – the dankness of it all,' wrote Malim) and temperatures as low as 7°C have been known there.

Perhaps its off-putting publicity is a campaign by the 80,000 or so residents to keep visitors away. They like their privacy. The avenues of the residential areas are lined with tall bamboo hedges, hiding the old, French-style, verandaed villas, wooden cottages and concrete, cyclone-proof houses. Streets have no names displayed, nor numbers on the houses, so only those familiar with the town will find their way around. It is not a welcoming place, with its grim market building of upturned culverts. The town seems to have no heart, either geographically or spiritually.

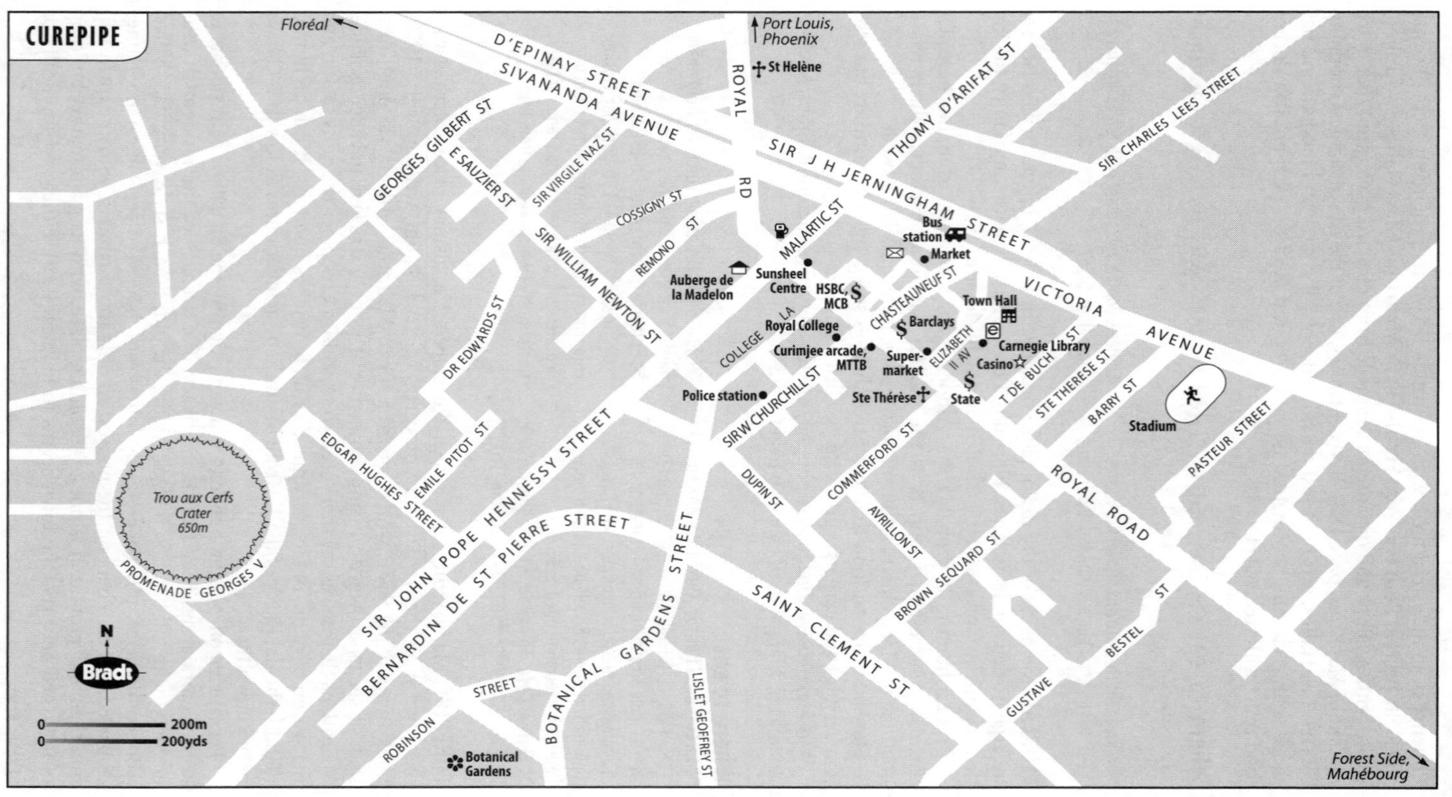

CUREPIPE
Floréal
Port Louis, Phoenix
St Helène
ROYAL RD
D'EPINAY STREET
SIVANANDA AVENUE
SIR J H JERNINGHAM STREET
THOMY D'ARIFAT ST
SIR CHARLES LEES STREET
GEORGES GILBERT ST
E SAUZIER ST
SIR VIRGILE NAZ ST
COSSIGNY ST
REMONO ST
SIR WILLIAM NEWTON ST
MALARTIC ST
Bus station
Market
Auberge de la Madelon
Sunsheel Centre
HSBC, MCB
CHASTEAUNEUF ST
VICTORIA AVENUE
Town Hall
LA COLLEGE
Royal College
Barclays
Curimjee arcade, MTTB
Super-market
ELIZABETH II AV
Carnegie Library
Casino
T DE BUCH ST
STE THERESE ST
BARRY ST
Stadium
DR EDWARDS ST
Police station
SIR W CHURCHILL ST
Ste Thérèse
State
PASTEUR STREET
EDGAR HUGHES STREET
EMILE PITOT ST
SIR JOHN POPE HENNESSY STREET
DUPIN ST
COMMERFORD ST
ROYAL ROAD
Trou aux Cerfs Crater 650m
PROMENADE GEORGES V
BERNARDIN DE ST PIERRE STREET
BOTANICAL GARDENS STREET
AVRILLON ST
BROWN SEQUARD ST
SAINT CLEMENT ST
BESTEL ST
GUSTAVE
N
Bradt
0 200m
0 200yds
STREET
ROBINSON
Botanical Gardens
LISLET GEOFFREY ST
Forest Side, Mahébourg

Its origins go back to the 18th century when it was a halt for travellers from one side of the island to the other. The usual story is that travellers stopped to smoke there, after which they would clean (cure) their pipes. However, its name is more likely to have come from a village in France.

The **town hall** overlooks a large compound of open square and gardens with the **Carnegie Library** and the former railway station, now used by the Central Water Authority, close to it. Close by are the Roman Catholic **Ste Thérèse Church** and the **casino**. The formal **gardens**, with lawns, flowerbeds and pathways, soften the administrative square and provide relief from the chaos of the open-air market nearby. The gardens include a memorial to Abbé de la Caille, the 18th-century surveyor of the island, and a romantic statue of Paul and Virginie, which is a bronze replica of Mauritian sculptor Prosper d'Epinay's original. There are other listed national monuments in Curepipe, notably the grim stone building of **Royal College**, the island's most prestigious school, and the **war memorial** in front of it.

It is tempting to wonder if the **market** building will ever be declared a national monument; it is certainly a unique feature of Curepipe's skyline, with its ugly concrete pipes pointing upwards. The **public toilets** are closed for cleaning every day, 06.00–06.30, 10.30–10.45, 15.00–15.15 and 17.15–17.30. Be warned.

Curepipe is another popular town for shopping. As well as the usual discount clothing and duty-free jewellery shops, there are numerous handicraft outlets, including several model ship shops.

Curepipe has its own small **botanical gardens** to the southwest of the centre. The **Forestry Department** (*675 4966*) offices next door are where permission can be sought to visit the nature reserves of the interior.

The unsightly spread of Curepipe can be seen from the hills around the extinct volcanic crater of **Trou aux Cerfs**, at 650m above sea level. To get there from the centre of Curepipe, follow Sir John Pope Hennessy Street for about 800m, then turn right into Edgar Hughes Street. It is a short climb to the crater. The inside of the crater is wooded and it is possible to climb the 85m to the bottom. If you've been to Réunion you won't be overly impressed by the crater, but the views are far-reaching. The panoramic view takes in the plateau towns and the mountains to the north and northwest, including the three cones of **Trois Mamelles** (629m). There is a meteorological station of futuristic design poised by the crater, as though mooning for its architectural soulmate, the market complex.

On the road from Curepipe to the motorway is the **Millennium Monument**, an 18m-high tower made of no fewer than 3,500 dark blue basalt stones, some six or seven million years old. It was erected by the Ministry of Arts and Culture to 'celebrate the passage of the Republic of Mauritius into the third millennium'.

Getting there and away The **bus station**, which adjoins the market on Sir J H Jerningham Street, is the island's busiest. Buses from Port Louis to Curepipe leave from the Victoria Square bus station. There are regular buses to Mahébourg, via Rose Belle and the airport. Buses also depart from Curepipe for Centre de Flacq, Souillac, Grand Bassin (via Bois Chéri) and Wolmar (via Flic en Flac). The best place to find a **taxi** is on Chasteauneuf Street. If you are in your own **car**, be aware that Curepipe is one of the towns where street parking coupons (bought at petrol stations) are required.

Tourist information There is no tourist office in Curepipe. There are some travel agents that may be able to help, provided your query is pretty simple. You could also try logging onto www.curepipe.org for information on the town.

Where to stay

Budget

Auberge de la Madelon (25 rooms) Sir John Pope Hennessy St; t 676 1520; f 676 2550; e madelon@intnet.mu. Just north of the town centre. Simple but clean en-suite rooms with fan, TV & phone. There is a restaurant, small pool & Wi-Fi. $

Where to eat

The **Prisunic supermarket** near the town hall stocks all the essentials. For cheap snacks, try the stalls around the market.

La Nouvelle Potinière Hillcrest Bldg, 18 Sir Winston Churchill St, Curepipe; t 676 2648; ⌚ for lunch Mon–Sat, for dinner Thu–Sat. Cuisine: French, crêpes, Creole, snacks. Claims to be the oldest restaurant in Mauritius. Has a sophisticated summery atmosphere. Reservation recommended. $$$

Le Gaulois Dr Ferrière St, Curepipe; t 675 5674; ⌚ 11.00–17.00 Mon–Sat. Cuisine: Creole, French. Great for people-watching because of its corner location on the road leading to the post office & bus station. *Table d'hôte* & à la carte menus. Plenty of plastic but clean. $$

Other practicalities

Communications The **post office** is near the market and offers poste restante and internet access. **Internet access** is also available at the cybercafé behind the **Carnegie Library**.

Money and banking Banks, including branches of Barclays, HSBC and Mauritius Commercial Bank, are found on Royal Road, in the centre of town.

BLACK RIVER GORGES NATIONAL PARK AND AROUND Access to the Black River Gorges National Park from Curepipe and Vacoas is via **La Marie**. There is a memorial here to the hapless English adventurer Matthew Flinders who, having helped explore and map Australia, stopped off in Mauritius in 1803, unaware that the British and French were at war. He was arrested by the French and imprisoned on Mauritius for six years.

Along the road (B3) to the national park are two important bodies of water. The reservoir of **Mare aux Vacoas** is the largest in Mauritius, a mountain lake at 600m above sea level, surrounded by pine forest and traveller's palms. Unlike many of the reservoirs it can be visited by road and is a popular spot for local fishermen. Further on through the forest, where deer abound, there is a motorable track leading to **Mare Longue**, another reservoir. The track passes through the shorn terrain of tea plantations and through woods where monkeys leap excitedly out of the way of the occasional car. It is possible to hike from the main road on forest trails to reach the seven cascades of **Tamarind Falls**. This is a restricted area so permission is required from the Forestry Department in Curepipe.

The main road continues southwards, passing into the Black River Gorges National Park, and reaches a crossroad at **Le Pétrin**. This is on the eastern edge of the park and there is a visitors' information centre here with picnic facilities.

Black River Gorges is the largest national park in Mauritius (6,574ha) and protects the remaining native forests on the island. It is home to many of the rare endemic plants and birdlife, and offers spectacular natural scenery and excellent walks. However, some areas where conservation projects are in progress are off-limits to visitors. These areas are clearly marked. (For detailed information, including a map of the national park, see *Chapter 1, Black River Gorges National Park*, pages 12–14.)

At Le Pétrin, the turning to the east leads to **Grand Bassin**, a natural lake in the crater of an extinct volcano at 702m above sea level. It is regarded as sacred by Hindus, who come here regularly to leave offerings of fruit and incense on small pedestals on the lake's edge. Japanese macaque monkeys and birds watch carefully from a distance, before raiding the fruit left for the gods. The lake is also known as **Ganga Talao** (Lake of the Ganges) as the Hindus believe that it is linked to the Ganges by an underground stream. There are temples around the lake, containing ornate statues of gods.

Sadly, Grand Bassin now features on the itineraries of all tour operators and coaches of tourists tend to arrive from late morning and throughout the afternoon. Scores of tourists line up for a Hindu blessing, each returning to the coach proudly sporting a token *tika* (red dot) on their forehead. Early morning and late afternoon are the best times to visit. Shoes should be removed before entering any of the temples.

During the festival of **Maha Shivaratree**, in honour of the god Shiva, is when Grand Bassin really comes into its own. For several days during February/March hundreds of thousands of Hindus make the journey to the lake, where they leave offerings for Shiva and take holy water from the lake to purify their bodies. Traditionalists make the pilgrimage following an all-night vigil, dressed in white and carrying the *kanwar*, a highly decorated wooden structure which they make themselves. Nowadays it is not unusual to see families making the journey by car but the number of pilgrims on foot lining the roads is still an incredible sight.

The nearby **Kanaka Crater** can only be reached by hiking along a trail off the road that goes beyond Grand Bassin towards **Bois Chéri**. This is the entrance to tea-growing country, with hills up to 500m above sea level covered with the close-cropped bushes. This area is covered in *Chapter 7, Southern Mauritius*.

MOKA

This district is part of a plateau of scrub, sugarcane and, in the midlands area, tea. It caters for the educational overspill of Port Louis, with the University of Mauritius and the Mahatma Gandhi Institute, and also contains the president's official residence at Le Réduit.

Coffee was planted here when it was introduced from Al Makha in Yemen, hence the name 'Moka'. Its boundary runs along the mountains ringing the south of Port Louis to Pieter Both, then skirts below La Nicolière Reservoir, across Nouvelle Découverte Plateau – embracing the agricultural centre of the island – to the outskirts of Curepipe and Rose Hill.

The approach to Moka is by the two-lane motorway that links Port Louis with the residential plateau towns. After crossing the St Louis Stream, the road passes through **Pailles**, a suburban community with a church, temple and mosque overshadowed by **Pailles Hill** (225m) and the peaks of the **Moka mountain range**.

Pailles has become widely known since the opening of **Domaine Les Pailles**, an extraordinary creation by a Mauritian who has converted previously unutilised land into a kind of educational theme park. A whole day can be spent there discovering the old ways of living via a series of exhibits that recreate old traditions. There are four upmarket restaurants on the estate (see below), a riding stables and a casino. (For details see page 188.)

Further south along the motorway, a road branches off to the left beneath **Junction Peak** to the residential sprawl of **Moka, St Pierre** and **Circonstance**. The motorway continues, skirting around the university and leaving the Moka district at the Cascade Bridge. The range of hills between Moka, St Pierre and Port Louis consists of the bush-covered **Guiby**, **Berthelot**, **Junction** and **Mount Ory** peaks, rising to 500m.

Off to the right, just after the road to Moka crosses the rubbish-clogged Moka River, is a lane leading to **Eureka**, a colonial house open to the public and where accommodation is available. Although it has a French colonial appearance with its 109 doors and windows and encircling veranda, it was built by an Englishman, with the help of a French carpenter, at the beginning of English colonisation. It gained its name when Eugène Leclézio, a wealthy lawyer and planter, cried 'Eureka' as his bid to buy the house at auction in 1856 was accepted. See also *What to see in Central Mauritius* (pages 188–9), *Where to stay* and *Where to eat* (below).

WHERE TO STAY

Mid range

Eureka (3 rooms) Moka; 433 8477; f 433 4951; e eurekamr@intnet.mu; www.eureka-house.com. Accommodation is available in 3 guesthouses in the grounds of Eureka, a colonial house built in 1830. They are equipped with double bedroom, bathroom & kitchenette. If you want to escape the heat of the coast for a few days, then this is a good option. Priced at the bottom end of mid range. **$$$**

WHERE TO EAT

Domaine les Pailles Les Guibies, Pailles; 286 4225. Has the following 4 restaurants, each beautifully decorated & serving excellent food.

Clos St Louis for lunch Mon–Sat, for dinner Fri/Sat. Cuisine: Creole, European. **$$$**

La Dolce Vita for lunch 11.00–17.00 & for dinner on Wed, Fri, Sat & Sun. Cuisine: Italian. Less formal than the others with a terrace overlooking a swimming pool. **$$$**

Fu Xiao for lunch & dinner daily, closed Sat lunch. Cuisine: Chinese. **$$$**

Indra for lunch & dinner Mon–Sat. Cuisine: Indian. **$$$**

Escale Creole Moka; 433 1641; for lunch on reservation. Cuisine: Creole. Delicious traditional *table d'hôte* menus are prepared using only fresh ingredients. Meals must be booked a day in advance. Spices are also on sale here. **$$**

Le Ravin Eureka, Moka; 433 4501; f 433 4951; e eurekamr@intnet.mu; www.maisoneureka.com; for lunch Mon–Fri. Cuisine: Creole, French. Smart restaurant, which also serves light meals & snacks. Decorated in a colonial style, with some seating by the river. **$$$**

AROUND LE REDUIT Although many Mauritians aspire to studying at an overseas university, they do have an option locally. The **University of Mauritius** at Le Réduit was created in 1965 with the help of a £3 million grant from the British Government. Together with a large school of agriculture, the university has faculties of engineering, science, law and management, as well as social studies and humanites. The **Mahatma Gandhi Institute**, for the study of Indian and African cultures, is within walking distance of the Le Réduit campus. The institute contains the **Museum of Indian Immigration** (see page 189).

In 1748, the French governor built a small wooden fort, surrounded by a ditch and stone walls, on a 290m-high bluff between two rivers. It was to serve as a redoubt (*réduit*) for women, children and valuables of the French East India Company if ever the island was invaded. It became the official residence of the French, and then the British, governors of the island and was extended several times to create a rather grand house. The gardens are equally impressive, filled with a mixture of native and exotic plants.

Today, Le Réduit is the president's official residence and is therefore only open to the public two days a year. Apparently the president is not keen on tourists strolling around his backyard, scrutinising his flowerbeds.

The eastern part of the Moka district is sparsely populated, with **Quartier Militaire** on the main road (A7) the only settlement of any size. It was once a military post offering protection to travellers against attacks by runaway slaves. After passing through Quartier Militaire the road continues to Centre de Flacq and the east coast.

WHAT TO DO IN CENTRAL MAURITIUS

HIKING The Black River Gorges National Park provides the island's best opportunities for hiking and seeing wildlife. For more information, see *Chapter 1, Black River Gorges National Park*, pages 12–14 and *Chapter 4, Hiking and adventure sports*, pages 95–6.

HORSERIDING **Domaine les Pailles**, just off the motorway between Port Louis and Moka, **Domaine de l'Etoile** at Moka and **Domaine des 7 Vallées** near Mare aux Vacoas offer horseriding. Treks are an ideal way to see the dramatic surrounding countryside. For more information, see *Chapter 3, Activities*, pages 87–8.

OTHER SPORTS The **Mauritius Gymkhana Club** (*Suffolk Rd, Vacoas;* ☎ *696 1404;* e *recep.mgp@intnet.mu; www.mgc.intnet.mu*) has an 18-hole golf course (see page 00), tennis courts, pool, squash courts, gym, snooker table and a modern clubhouse with a view of the golf course. It also has a restaurant, bar and library. Temporary membership is available to visitors on a daily or monthly basis.

QUAD BIKING Available at Domaine des 7 Vallées and Domaine de l'Etoile (see page 188).

CASINOS The **Casino de Maurice** (☎ *602 1300;* ⌚ *21.00–04.00 Mon–Fri, 13.00–04.00 Sat/Sun*) is near the town hall in Curepipe. **Le Grand Casino** (☎ *286 0405*) at Domaine les Pailles is open every evening. There is a **Ti Vegas** casino at St Jean Road, Quatre Bornes (☎ *454 8800*).

SPA TREATMENTS **Spa Viva** at 102 St Jean Road, Quatre Bornes (☎ *467 8907;* e *spaviva@intnet.mu*) offers massages and beauty treatments.

SHOPPING The towns of the centre are now well known to tourists in search of bargain clothing and souvenirs. Quatre Bornes and Curepipe are known for their markets and bargain shops, Floréal for its knitwear and two of the island's largest, new shopping centres are in the area, Bagatelle at Moka and Les Halles at Phoenix. For more information, see *Chapter 2, Shopping*, pages 73–6.

WHAT TO SEE IN CENTRAL MAURITIUS

MAURITIUS GLASS GALLERY (*Pont Fer, Phoenix;* ☎ *696 3360;* e *mgg@intnet.mu;* ⌚ *08.00–17.00 Mon–Sat; admission free*) The workshop at Pont Fer produces handmade glass ornaments from recycled glass and aims to promote environmental awareness. Glass-blowing demonstrations take place throughout the day except 12.00–13.00 and there is a shop selling the products.

BOTANICAL GARDENS (*Curepipe;* ⌚ *06.00–18.00 daily; admission free*) The botanical gardens in Curepipe are a miniature Pamplemousses. There is a small lake in which nandia palms can be seen growing. It is a pleasant place in which to recover from the cacophony of Curepipe.

DOMAINE DES AUBINEAUX (*Curepipe;* ☎ *676 3089;* **f** *626 1535;* **e** *lesaintaubin@intnet.mu;* ⏲ *08.30–16.30 Mon–Fri, 08.30–13.30 Sat; admission adult/child Rs350/175*) An attractive colonial house built in 1872 as the home of the owners of the Bois Chéri Tea Estate. Visitors can take a guided tour of the interior, which contains much of the original furniture and family photographs. The guide will explain the history of the family and the estate, as well as significant events in the island's past. There is a small gift shop, selling locally made soap, rum and tea. Domaine des Aubineaux can be visited as part of the Route du Thé, which also includes a visit to the Bois Chéri Tea Factory and lunch at Le Saint Aubin (see page 162).

DOMAINE LES PAILLES (*Les Guibies, Pailles;* ☎ *286 4225;* **f** *286 4226;* **e** *domaine.sales@intnet.mu; www.domainelespailles.net;* ⏲ *09.00–17.30 daily; guided tour of the domaine adult/child Rs190/95, guided tour plus horse-carriage ride adult/child Rs270/135*) Just 3km from Port Louis, this place offers a great day out. The *domaine* gives visitors an insight into the island's past, with its recreation of an 18th-century ox-driven sugar mill, a working rum distillery from 1758 and other exhibits, such as aloe weaving and coffee grinding. There is also a spice garden and a tropical forest. It has four fantastic restaurants, as well as a shop, swimming pool and the island's biggest casino. The vast reserve can be explored on horseback or in a 4x4, whilst shorter journeys are made by horse-drawn carriage or the estate's train.

DOMAINE DE L'ETOILE (*Royal Rd, Moka;* ☎ *729 1050;* **e** *resa.cieletnature@drbc-group.com; www.cieletnature.com;* ⏲ *09.30–16.30 daily*) The estate lies on the Grande Rivière Sud-est. The forests, which are home to deer and many species of bird, can be explored on foot (Rs670), horseback (1½hrs with lunch adult/child Rs2,660/1,865), quad bike (2½hrs with lunch Rs2,530 per person on a double quad) or mountain bike (Rs670). Archery is also available (Rs670), using animal-shaped targets dotted around the forest. The estate has some beautiful scenery, including views of the coast from its hilltops. There is a good restaurant serving Mauritian cuisine and some of the packages include lunch there. Wear full-length trousers and bring mosquito repellent and suncream. Reservation recommended for all activities.

DOMAINE DES 7 VALLEES (*Line Barracks, Mare aux Vacoas;* ☎ *631 3336;* **f** *631 3198;* **e** *dchasseur@intnet.mu; www.domainedes7vallees.com;* ⏲ *09.00–17.00 daily*). A 4,000ha estate known for its deer and wild boar hunting. Also offers quad biking, mountain biking, 4x4 tours, hiking, horseriding and archery. Reservation recommended.

EUREKA (*Moka;* ☎ *433 8477;* **f** *433 4951;* **e** *eurekamr@intnet.mu; www.maisoneureka.com;* ⏲ *09.00–17.00 Mon–Sat, 09.00–15.30 Sun; admission adult/child Rs250/125 (house & garden)*) A Creole mansion, built in 1830, which is now open to the public and also offers accommodation in cottages in its grounds. It is set in pleasant gardens overlooked by the Moka mountain range and crossed by the Moka River. The house is decorated in colonial style with antique furniture, some of which was produced by the French East India Company. Every detail is designed to take you back to that era. For an additional fee you can follow a trail through the grounds to a waterfall for a swim. A typical Creole lunch can be provided. See also *Where to stay* and *Where to eat*, page 186.

MUSEUM OF INDIAN IMMIGRATION (*Le Réduit;* ☎ *433 1277;* 🕘 *09.00–16.00 Mon–Fri; admission free*) Holds records relating to the indentured labour scheme and Indian immigration. They can help visitors trace ancestors who came to Mauritius as indentured labourers.

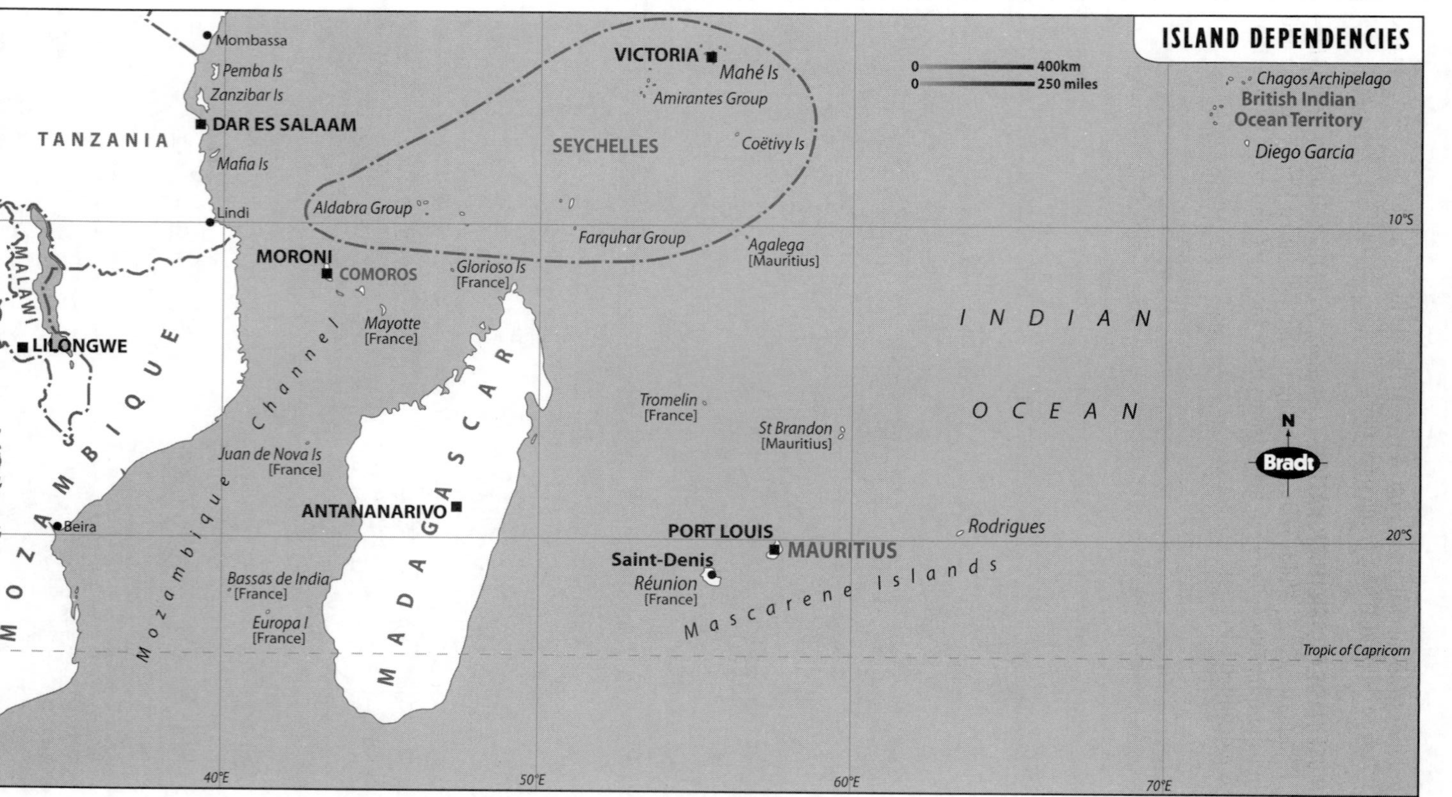

ISLAND DEPENDENCIES
0 400km
0 250 miles
Chagos Archipelago
British Indian Ocean Territory
Diego Garcia
Mombassa
Pemba Is
Zanzibar Is
DAR ES SALAAM
TANZANIA
Mafia Is
Lindi
MALAWI
LILONGWE
MOZAMBIQUE
Beira
VICTORIA
Mahé Is
Amirantes Group
SEYCHELLES
Coëtivy Is
Aldabra Group
Farquhar Group
Agalega [Mauritius]
MORONI
COMOROS
Glorioso Is [France]
Mayotte [France]
Mozambique Channel
Juan de Nova Is [France]
MADAGASCAR
ANTANANARIVO
Bassas de India [France]
Europa I [France]
Tromelin [France]
St Brandon [Mauritius]
INDIAN
OCEAN
N
Bradt
Rodrigues
PORT LOUIS
MAURITIUS
Saint-Denis
Réunion [France]
Mascarene Islands
10°S
20°S
Tropic of Capricorn
40°E
50°E
60°E
70°E

10

Island Dependencies

AGALEGA

Agalega is situated between the Seychelles and Mauritius, west of the Mascarene Ridge, about 1,206km north of Mauritius and 563km south of the Seychelles. There are actually two islands (North and South), separated by a sandbank which can be forded at low tide. Taken as one, the island is 24km long but not more than 3.25km wide.

The islands were named by the Portuguese after the nationality of their discoverer, Juan de Nova, who was a Spanish Galician serving the King of Portugal. At the time of the British takeover they were occupied by the captain of a French privateer, licensed by General Decaen to cultivate and harvest coconuts, using slaves from Madagascar.

There are nearly 300 people living on Agalega, which is administered by the Outer Islands Development Corporation as an island plantation producing coconut oil. It is almost entirely covered with coconut palms and some casuarinas. North Island has the main coconut mill on it; pear-shaped South Island is used as the administrative centre.The resident manager is responsible for a working population of 180 to 200, including administration staff, police, meteorologists, teachers, medical personnel and approximately 150 labourers. Wives and children make up the additional population.

ST BRANDON

In Mauritius, reference to '**Les Iles**' means the St Brandon Archipelago, also known as the Cargados Garayos Islands. These lie 395km northwest of Mauritius, forming an arc from south to north, its convex side facing towards the east. There are 22 low-lying islands, parts of which are sometimes submerged, as well as numerous reefs and sandbanks. The largest of the islands are named **Cocos**, **Albatross** and **Raphael**, which is the administrative centre and home to a privately owned commercial fishing station.

From 1546, the islands were shown on Portuguese charts as São Brandao, which is puzzling since St Brandon is an Irish saint. The Portuguese also called them Cargados Garayos, deriving the name from Coroa dos Garajãos, meaning 'reef of seabirds'.

The islands abound with birds and in the past guano was the main export. In 1862, cotton was tried, without success. Cyclones, problems with fresh water, and the harsh conditions of life (no women) also affected the islands' development. Since the 1830s, the richness of the fishing grounds has been exploited and in 1910 there were 100 fishermen based in the islands.

Fish is salted and dried for export to Mauritius. Fishermen are engaged by the Outer Islands Development Corporation, which manages St Brandon, on a four to six months' contract. Their working day begins at dawn and by 07.00 they are at sea.

After they have returned with their catch, the fish have to be gutted, cleaned and put in the salt beds.

The fishermen, several dozen of them from Mauritius, Rodrigues and the Seychelles, lodge in barracks. Raphael (Establishment) Island has a modest chapel, a house for the administrator and his staff, a hangar for the salt fish, a community hall and a shop.

TROMELIN

Mauritius and the Seychelles claim sovereignty over Tromelin but France owns it and Madagascar wants it. It is a flat, sandy, barren place, less than 2km long and about 640m wide. It lies between the St Brandon Archipelago and Madagascar, actually closer to Madagascar than Port Louis, which is 482km away.

Mauritius's claim to ownership is based on the capitulation terms of 1810, as Tromelin was regarded then as a dependency of Mauritius. In 1954, the British allowed the French to build a meteorological station and landing strip on the island. France and Mauritius agreed a co-management treaty in 2010.

Tromelin is an important seabird nesting site, in particular for masked and red-footed boobies.

It was known in the 18th century as Ile aux Sables or Sandy Island. In 1761, a French vessel was shipwrecked on the reef which extends from its southern point. The whites in the crew built a boat and reached Madagascar safely. They left 80 blacks on the island, promising to return. It was 15 years before a French chevalier, M Tromelin, landed and found seven women living there. They were the only survivors, having existed on shellfish, turtle and brackish water. He took them to Mauritius.

THE CHAGOS ARCHIPELAGO

The Chagos Archipelago, together with Desroches, Farquhar and Aldabra, formerly part of the Seychelles group, now constitute the British Indian Ocean Territory (BIOT). They lie 1,930km northeast of Mauritius, south of Gan in the Maldives. Visits by individuals are difficult to arrange.

SIX ISLANDS This group of six low islands arranged in a horseshoe shape is 109km from Diego Garcia. When they were dependencies of Mauritius, they were harvested for coconuts as well as supplying pigs, poultry and fat-tailed land crabs. They are connected by shoals and access is difficult because of the reefs and breakers.

PEROS BANHOS A cluster of a score of small islands which form the largest group of the Chagos Archipelago, Peros Banhos forms a basin of 29km in length, north to south, and 19km in breadth from east to west. The main one, Ile du Coin, is about 3km long. They were also known as the Iles Bourdés after a M de Bourdé, who is credited with discovering them after the Portuguese had named them.

In the 18th and 19th centuries, the islands were home to up to 500 people employed in the coconut plantations and fishing station. In 1970, the British Government removed the entire population to Mauritius. Part of Peros Banhos is now a nature reserve.

SALOMON ISLANDS Known as Les Onze Iles, being 11 in number, the Salomons were named after a ship called *Salomon*. They form a basin with a safe anchorage for vessels of small draught. Their soil is rich in coconut trees, which used to be harvested by resident Mauritians.

In the last century, these islands were noted for a rare tree called *faux gaiac*, which grew to a height of 40m, and was a deep chocolate colour, with sound wood when old. Fresh water could be obtained from wells. Turtles used to be found here but, owing to the presence of seals, not so many fish.

TROIS FRERES Actually four small islands, connected by shoals. Coconuts grow on all of them and fish, turtles and fresh water are all to be found. Nearby, between this group and Six Islands, are **Eagle** and **Danger** islands. All used to provide coconut oil for the Mauritius market.

DIEGO GARCIA The name of the Chagos Archipelago used to be Bassas de Chagos, after the largest island of the group, which was known as Chagos, or Gratiosa, as well as by the name which has survived today, Diego Garcia.

Diego Garcia is in the form of a serpent bent double, its interior forming a broad, steep, coral wall standing in the ocean. This encompasses a lagoon which is a large natural harbour and safe anchorage. The island is $28.5km^2$ in area with a steep coral reef all around, except at the entrance to the lagoon.

The French exiled leprous slaves to Diego Garcia from Mauritius claiming that the turtle, which would be their sole diet, would restore them to good health. In 1792, an English merchant ship sent two Indian crew members ashore for water and some of the leper residents – women as well as men – met them and showed them to a well. When the master of the ship learned of the encounter he made the seamen stay on the island and sailed away as fast as he could.

After the British takeover in 1810, the exiling of leprosy sufferers was discontinued and some 300 migrants, including Europeans, went voluntarily from Mauritius to set up a saltfish trading company and to plant and harvest coconuts. The settlement flourished peacefully for 150 years. Produce was ferried to Mauritius, whence came the imported goods the settlers needed to live.

By 1965, the population of the entire Chagos Archipelago had grown to some 900 families, representing 2,000 inhabitants. The islands were dependencies of Mauritius and the *îlois* – the Creole term for the Chagos islanders – conducted trade with Mauritius through an irregular ferry link. They were content with their simple and presumably happy existence.

In the countdown to independence, Britain decided to detach Diego Garcia and the nearby islands from Mauritius, virtually taking them over a second time. The politicians in Mauritius were obliged to agree because, being a colony, they had little choice and gaining independence was their priority.

Three million pounds in development aid was the reward while Mauritius stipulated two conditions for letting Britain keep Diego Garcia: it would be used for communication purposes only, and the atoll would be returned to Mauritius if Britain no longer needed it.

Having signed the agreement, Britain created a new colony: the British Indian Ocean Territory. The Chagos islanders were bemused, but the future soon became clear. The ferry service linking them to Mauritius was stopped, the sole employer of labour was bought out by the British and the copra plantation was closed down. Work ceased, and so did food imports. Many of the *îlois* had to leave to survive.

Less than a year later, in 1966, Diego Garcia was leased to the United States of America for 'defence purposes'. The 1,500 *îlois*, 500 of whom lived on Diego Garcia, were removed to Mauritius and the Seychelles. Foreign Office documents reveal one British official wrote, 'unfortunately, along with the birds go some few Tarzans and Man Fridays whose origins are obscure and who are hopefully being wished on to Mauritius'. The lease to the US is for 50 years, with an option for a further 20 years, which both parties must agree by December 2014.

Now Diego Garcia is the main US military base in the Indian Ocean, with superb port facilities, the latest in communications systems and a 3,600m runway capable of handling, and fuelling, B52 bombers. A key launch pad for bombing attacks into Iraq and Afghanistan, the island's coconuts have been replaced with a nuclear arsenal.

When politicians in Mauritius realised what had happened, a cyclone of protest and controversy raged. After years of angry negotiations, Britain acknowledged that the Chagos islanders, who had been forcibly displaced from their homes, were entitled to better treatment than being abandoned in the backstreets of Port Louis. Compensation was paid in 1982, but mainly to the Mauritian Government, who had to accommodate the islanders.

In November 2000, the *îlois* won an historic victory in the English High Court, which upheld their right to return to their homeland. However, the British Government declared that this ruling had to be balanced with their treaty obligations to the US and affirmed that the right to return excluded Diego Garcia. Furthermore, the UK and US both said it was not their responsibility to arrange for the Chagos islanders to return.

In June 2002, the British Foreign and Commonwealth Office completed a feasibility study into resettlement of the islands and concluded that it would be difficult, precarious and costly. Harvard resettlement expert, Jonathan Jenness, commented that the study's conclusions were 'erroneous in every assertion'.

In June 2004, the British Government used the Royal Prerogative – effectively a decree by the government in the name of the Queen – to enforce the continued exile of the *îlois*. The Chagos islanders challenged the government's order and, in 2006, High Court judges ruled in their favour, granting them the right to return to the islands and describing the government's order as 'repugnant'.

The Court of Appeal upheld the decision in 2007, but, on 23 October 2008, the British Government won its appeal to Britain's highest court, the House of Lords, against the previous rulings allowing the Chagos islanders to return home. British Foreign Secretary, David Miliband, welcomed the ruling. On behalf of the government he expressed regret for the way the resettlement of the Chagos islanders was carried out, but noted: 'the courts have previously ruled that fair compensation has been paid and that the UK has no legal obligation to pay any further compensation.'

In April 2010, the British Government established a marine reserve around the Chagos Islands. While the marine environment around the islands certainly merits protection, the motivation behind the creation of the reserve was called into question when a cable released by Wikileaks revealed that a Foreign Office official had told a US counterpart that 'establishing a marine park would, in effect, put paid to resettlement claims of the archipelago's former residents'.

Part Three

RODRIGUES

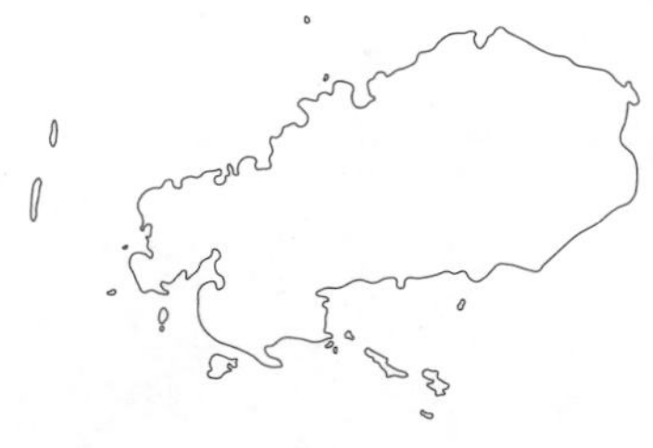

RODRIGUES AT A GLANCE

Country An integral part of Mauritius, with its own regional assembly
Location 560km northeast of Mauritius
Size Rodrigues has an area of 108km^2; it is 18km long (west–east) and 8km at its widest point (north–south). It is roughly equivalent in size to the British Channel Island of Jersey and is surrounded by 14 satellite islets.
History Discovered by Arabs, then Portuguese explorer Diego Rodriguez, in 1528. Some believe Diego Fernandez de Pereira got there first in 1507. The first settlers were French Huguenots fleeing France, who arrived in 1691. The French colonised the island in 1725; the British took it in 1809. A dependency of Mauritius until 1968, when Mauritius gained independence, Rodrigues has remained part of Mauritius. In 2002, Rodrigues took steps towards autonomous administration with the creation of the Rodrigues Regional Assembly.
Nature Valleys and forest with rare wildlife, rugged coastline, beaches and coral reefs
Climate Generally warmer and drier than Mauritius. In summer (November to April), temperatures range from 29°C to 34°C, and in winter (May to October) from 15°C to 29°C. Subject to drought, winds from the southeast and prone to cyclones.
Capital Port Mathurin
Population Approximately 38,000 (July 2011); 98% of Creole origin
Economy Based on subsistence agriculture and fishing. Tourism and handicraft production are growing.
Language Creole is the everyday language; French is widely spoken and English much less so
Religion 97.5% of the population is Roman Catholic. Anglicans, Adventists, Hindus, Muslims and Rastafarians form a minority.
International telephone code +230
Time GMT+4
Electricity 220 volts

11

Background Information

OVERVIEW

Rodrigues is remote, a part of Mauritius but 560km further northeast.

There's something stark about the island and things are decidedly low key. It is not a tropical paradise but those in search of something offbeat will find it a fascinating, peaceful place to explore, with a people whose shy friendliness is genuine. Life here is slow and uncomplicated. Being such a small community, it has a delightful intimacy and sense of security. After just a few days on the island, I began to bump into people whom I had already met and no-one was ever too busy to stop for a chat.

As they are administratively linked, much of the information about Mauritius in *Chapters 1–3* is relevant to Rodrigues.

GEOGRAPHY

Like the other Mascarenes, Rodrigues is of volcanic origin. Its landscapes of steep hills, plunging valleys and scattered rocks create the impression that it is much larger than it is. The two highest points are Mont Limon, a mere 398m, and Mont Malartic at 386m.

There are no impressive mountains and no imposing rock formations. Large rivers and lakes are also absent, and there are only a few really attractive beaches. But where Rodrigues wins hands down is in the quality of its marine environment. The island is entirely surrounded by reefs, which offer some of the best underwater experiences available in the Indian Ocean. A vast lagoon (200km^2) shelters some of the best beach and reef areas. Among its many coral caves is the often-visited, 795m-long Caverne Patate, near Plaine Corail, and those within the François Leguat Giant Tortoise and Cave Reserve.

Much of the island features grass or scrub-covered slopes, some of which are rocky with black cliffs. At Plaine Corail, in the southwest, the landscape is especially harsh and barren. The remaining woodlands are severely degraded and cover only certain hillsides around the Solitude–Citronelle–Cascade Pigeon area. The higher reaches of the hilly interior are often covered by mist, at which time the surrounds take on a dreamy, sultry ambience.

The tumbling Cascade Pigeon River offers some of the island's more attractive scenery. While much of the coast features rocky shores, there are also some pleasant, sandy beaches on the east coast, like St François and Trou d'Argent.

NATURAL HISTORY AND CONSERVATION

FLORA AND FAUNA When the first settlers arrived on Rodrigues, they found an island largely swathed in woodland and populated by a bizarre ensemble of

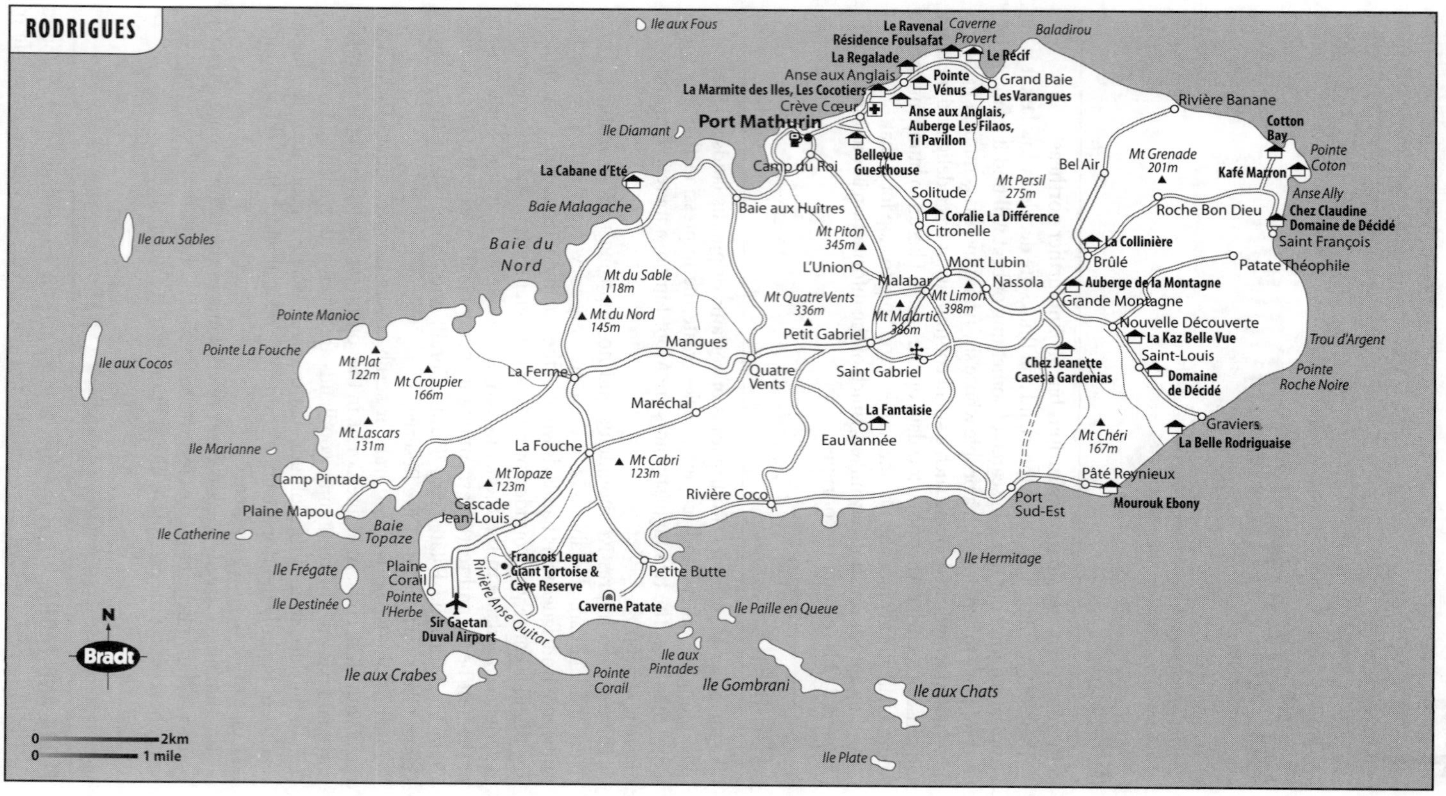
RODRIGUES
Ile aux Fous
Le Ravenal
Résidence Foulsafat
Caverne Provert
Baladirou
La Regalade
Le Récif
Anse aux Anglais
Pointe Vénus
Grand Baie
La Marmite des Iles, Les Cocotiers
Les Varangues
Crève Cœur
Anse aux Anglais, Auberge Les Filaos, Ti Pavillon
Ile Diamant
Port Mathurin
Bellevue Guesthouse
Rivière Banane
Cotton Bay
Pointe Coton
Kafé Marron
Camp du Roi
Bel Air
Mt Grenade 201m
Mt Persil 275m
La Cabane d'Eté
Solitude
Anse Ally
Roche Bon Dieu
Chez Claudine
Domaine de Décidé
Baie Malagache
Baie aux Huîtres
Coralie La Différence
Citronelle
Saint François
Ile aux Sables
Mt Piton 345m
La Collinière
Brûlé
Baie du Nord
L'Union
Mont Lubin
Patate Théophile
Mt du Sable 118m
Malabar
Nassola
Auberge de la Montagne
Mt Quatre Vents 336m
Mt Limon 398m
Grande Montagne
Pointe Manioc
Mt du Nord 145m
Mt Malartic 386m
Nouvelle Découverte
Petit Gabriel
La Kaz Belle Vue
Trou d'Argent
Pointe La Fouche
Mangues
Ile aux Cocos
Mt Plat 122m
Chez Jeanette Cases à Gardenias
Saint-Louis
Mt Croupier 166m
La Ferme
Quatre Vents
Saint Gabriel
Pointe Roche Noire
Domaine de Décidé
Maréchal
La Fantaisie
Mt Lascars 131m
Graviers
Eau Vannée
Mt Chéri 167m
La Belle Rodriguaise
Ile Marianne
La Fouche
Mt Cabri 123m
Mt Topaze 123m
Pâté Reynieux
Camp Pintade
Rivière Coco
Port Sud-Est
Mourouk Ebony
Cascade Jean-Louis
Plaine Mapou
Baie Topaze
Ile Catherine
Francois Leguat Giant Tortoise & Cave Reserve
Ile Hermitage
Ile Frégate
Plaine Corail
Petite Butte
Pointe l'Herbe
Ile Destinée
Caverne Patate
Ile Paille en Queue
N
Sir Gaetan Duval Airport
Rivière Anse Quitar
Bradt
Ile aux Pintades
Ile aux Crabes
Pointe Corail
Ile Gombrani
Ile aux Chats
0 2km
0 1 mile
Ile Plate

animals. These included two species of giant tortoises, fruit bats, herds of dugong in the lagoons and a variety of endemic birds.

Most conspicuous of these were the Rodrigues solitaire (*Pezophaps solitaria*), the island's answer to the Mauritian dodo. These extraordinary creatures shared their Mauritian cousins' fate and were soon exterminated. Trade in the two species of giant tortoise began in 1736. By the turn of the 19th century, they too were extinct.

Of 17 endemic species of vertebrate, just three remain: the Rodrigues warbler (*Acrocephalus rodericanus*), Rodrigues fody (*Foudia flavicans*) and the Rodrigues fruit bat (*Pteropus rodericensis*).

The two surviving endemic bird species are both threatened. The greyish Rodrigues warbler is classed 'endangered'. A survey in 1974 recorded just 32 warblers, by 1999 the number had climbed to 150, and in 2010 the population was at 4,000. The increase is largely the result of habitat restoration by the Mauritanian Wildlife Foundation.

The pretty yellow and orange Rodrigues fody is classed as 'vulnerable' but is in line to be reclassified as 'near-threatened' after a survey in 2010 revealed a population of around 8,000. This is a marked improvement on the numbers from 1974, when there were just 30 individuals.

To see the endemic birds, go to the Grand Montagne Nature Reserve, the areas along the island's central ridge, the woods around Cascade Pigeon River or Solitude, not too far from Port Mathurin. You should find both species within half an hour.

The endemic Rodrigues fruit bat is the last remaining indigenous mammal. As a result of conservation efforts, the population of Rodrigues fruit bats numbered around 10,000 in 2011. Once, these famed 'blonde bats' were on the verge of oblivion. They were down to a population of fewer than 100 during the mid 1970s when the late Gerald Durrell and the Jersey Wildlife Preservation Trust (now the Durrell Wildlife Conservation Trust) undertook a collecting expedition to Rodrigues and Mauritius (see box *The Durrell Wildlife Conservation Trust in the Mascarenes*, pages 200–1). Thanks to the intensive captive-breeding efforts which followed the JWPT expedition, along with habitat creation and restoration and sensitisation campaigns throughout Rodrigues by the Mauritian Wildlife Foundation, the bat population has increased substantially. Bats can be seen any time of the day, roosting in trees but they are easiest to spot from about 16.00 when they fly from their daytime rest sites. The best places to see them include Solitude, between Port Mathurin and Mount Lubin, or near Malabar.

Owing to continuous reforestation work, the outlook for the Rodrigues fody, Rodrigues warbler and Rodrigues fruit bat is bright, provided that their forest habitat is safeguarded.

ENDANGERED FLORA Most of the 49 endemic plant species are rare with fewer than five wild plants found throughout the island. These include the madrinette (*Hibiscus liliiflorus*), a hibiscus endemic to Rodrigues, which has been saved from extinction. This was done after only two were found to remain on Rodrigues itself. One of the world's rarest plants, 'café marron' (*Ramosmania rodriguesii*), is Rodriguan. A lone specimen remains in the wild on the island, just off the road near Mont Plaisir, where it is carefully fenced in. In 1986, cuttings were sent to Kew Gardens, where one took root. Several have also been produced in Rodrigues since the 1990s and there are now hundreds at Kew. Many of the island's indigenous plants are shared with the other Mascarenes, where they are usually more numerous.

The critically endangered shrub, 'figue marron' (*Obetia ficifolia*), is extinct on Mauritius but is shared with Réunion, where it is known to be pollinated by a single, endangered species of butterfly. Another rare shrub is the 'bois cabris' (*Clerodendron laciniatum*); growing to 3–4m high, it bears small clusters of white flowers. The hardwood tree 'bois d'olive' (*Cassine orientalis*), which attains a height of 20m, was once used to make furniture.

REFORESTATION The Mauritian Wildlife Foundation (MWF) has been doing marvellous work in Rodrigues, with help from the Rodrigues Regional Assembly. A nursery has been established at Solitude, where all the native Rodriguan plant species are being propagated.

Even the local pandanus, which are endemic and which appear plentiful, are threatened because of extensive rat damage. Like many of the threatened plant species, it has been used for centuries by Rodriguans in their daily lives. Whilst many of the plants have a medicinal purpose, the leaves of the pandanus are used

THE DURRELL WILDLIFE CONSERVATION TRUST IN THE MASCARENES

When Gerald Durrell founded Jersey Zoo in 1959, he chose the dodo as the trust's symbol, vowing that its tragic story would never be repeated. He also had the conservation of species in the wild as his main goal, a concept that we now accept as normal, but something that was a radical departure for a zoo 50 years ago. Since that time, Jersey Zoo has become the Durrell Wildlife Conservation Trust. Building on Gerald's legacy, their mission is saving species from extinction. Conservation efforts are delivered through the three pillars of the Trust, the wildlife park in Jersey, the field programmes around the world and the training programmes that provide the conservationists of the future with the skills they need to save species.

When Gerald first visited Mauritius and Rodrigues in 1976, indigenous birds had been reduced to 13 species, including the world's rarest pigeon, falcon and parrot all teetering on the brink of extinction. Off the Mauritian coast, Round Island was the bleak, barren home of eight species of reptiles, including the world's two rarest snakes. Nearby Rodrigues had suffered drought and cyclones in addition to manmade indignities. The Rodrigues fruit bat was considered the world's rarest bat, and only two endemic species of native land birds remained. Small conservation efforts were under way but the international zoological community largely regarded the Mascarenes as paradise lost – it seemed that the legacy of the dodo would continue. With the encouragement of the Mauritian Government and the support of the International Council for Bird Preservation (now Birdlife International), Durrell mounted an intense conservation campaign to save some of these species. This effort led to the establishment of the Mauritian Wildlife Foundation (MWF). Since that time MWF has become the leading non-government environmental organisation in Mauritius, championing the cause for biodiversity conservation and restoration in the islands. Durrell's commitment to encouraging and supporting local expertise continues.

With species such as the Mauritius kestrel and pink pigeon on the very edge of extinction, not only were drastic steps needed but the team had to develop new techniques and skills to ensure the last remaining individuals did not disappear. With only four kestrels and nine pigeons left, a combined response involving captive breeding and extensive field work was needed to start turning numbers around. Now there are over 300 kestrels and pink pigeons in the wild. As a result of these joint achievements, the Mauritian Government have set

for weaving. The MWF has undertaken community projects to boost the numbers of such plants, with the help of villagers who take responsibility for the young plants. In the long term, both the plants and the villagers will benefit.

Very noticeable in the remaining Rodriguan woods is the high proportion (97%) of exotic vegetation. In particular, eucalyptus, sisal and lantana have taken over large tracts of land. However, the MWF is hard at work, weeding out the alien vegetation and replanting saplings of other fast-growing native trees.

Visiting a nursery like the one at Solitude or the nature reserves is certainly encouraging, and well worth the effort if you want to see the endemic and indigenous flora up close. When seeing the extent of the reforestation programmes and the commitment of the MWF staff and volunteers, one can't help but feel positive about the future of Rodriguan flora and fauna.

up a national park in the last remaining natural forest, Black River Gorges. Similar successes were achieved for the echo parakeet which went from around 12 individuals to now more than 500 and the Rodrigues fruit bat which now numbers over 10,000 individuals. The skills developed with these species have been applied to conservation projects around the world and hundreds of students and researchers have studied the recovery of these populations, contributing greatly to our knowledge of threatened species recovery.

Developing from the restoration of these species was the concept of rebuilding Mauritius's highly threatened ecosystems, starting with some of the offshore islands and one in particular, Round Island. Round Island was used by sailors as a dumping ground for goats and rabbits and soon these animals grazed out the native vegetation, sending the native flora and fauna almost to extinction. After a major programme of eradication for the goats and rabbits it was possible to start working on the restoration of the plants and animals. Almost immediately the island's flora started to recover. Intensive work started on the endemic reptiles and together with management on the other offshore islands populations of Telfair's skink, Guenther's gecko and the Round Island boa have been shown to recover. Recently non-native tortoises have been introduced to the island to replicate the grazing functions carried out by now extinct native species and studies have shown how native plant species benefit from this, while introduced plants do not.

We have now extended this model to work on a number of the smaller islands off Mauritius. We are currently restoring the native reptiles to these islands and working with the National Parks and Conservation Service, a government agency, to restore vegetation and remove invasive species.

The world-renowned Durrell Wildlife Conservation Trust has enjoyed spectacular success with its Mascarene-related projects.

Donations may be made to the Mauritius Programme of Durrell Wildlife Conservation Trust, which works with the MWF, by sending a cheque in any currency to Durrell Wildlife Conservation Trust (*Les Augrès Manor, La Profonde Rue, Trinity, Jersey JE3 5BP, Channel Islands;* 01534 860000; f *01534 860001;* e *info@durrell.org; www.durrell.org*). To find out more about the Durrell's fascinating work or to become a member, contact them at the same address or via their website.

Abundant seabirds on offshore islands The idyllic Ile aux Cocos is an island sanctuary and breeding ground for huge populations of seabirds. Common noddies (*Anous stolidus*) and lesser noddies (*A. tenuirostris*) are present in their thousands, nesting on casuarina ('filao') trees wherever space permits. The sooty tern (*Sterna fuscata*) and the graceful fairy tern (*Gygis alba*) are also present. Part of Ile aux Cocos is fenced off to protect the ground-nesting sites of bridled terns.

Nearby Ile aux Sables is a nature reserve and closed to the public. It is home to fairy terns, common noddies and lesser noddies. According to Ian Sinclair and Olivier Langrand, who co-authored the excellent field guide *Birds of the Indian Ocean Islands*, common tern (*Sterna hirundo*) and wedge-tailed shearwater (*Puffinus pacificus*) are also seen there.

For information on excursions to Ile aux Cocos, see page 226.

HISTORY AND POLITICS

Rodrigues shares its history with Mauritius although it was discovered later, in 1528, and retained the name of its Portuguese discoverer, Diego Rodriguez, throughout Dutch, French and British colonisation. Some historians maintain that it was discovered earlier, in 1507, by another Portuguese seafarer, Diego Fernandez de Pereira.

The Dutch paid little attention to Rodrigues and the first known settlers were French, although they came during the Dutch period. These were nine French Protestants fleeing from France, led by François Leguat. They had actually been trying to reach Ile Bourbon (Réunion) but stumbled upon Rodrigues in 1691 and found the island covered in luxuriant vegetation, with an abundance of birds and tortoises. After two years, the settlers made it to Mauritius, where Leguat was arrested on the orders of the Dutch governor and charged with amber trafficking.

In 1725, France decided to colonise Rodrigues in the name of Louis XV and sent eight soldiers, 13 planters and 15 slaves. The colonisation was unsuccessful, although some of the slaves remained when the French left. The French noted that Rodrigues suffered from more cyclones and higher winds than Ile de France, and had a difficult approach through rocks and shoals to the harbour they called Port Mathurin.

The first permanent settler was a master mariner, Germain le Gros, who arrived in September 1792 to engage in fishing and trading. He was followed in 1793 by Michel Gorry and Philibert Marragon, who had visited previously in 1791. Marragon and his wife lived at L'Orangerie until both died on Rodrigues in 1826. They, and several slaves, are buried at L'Union, near a monument to the slaves (see also page 221).

In the time-honoured manner of expatriates living on a small island, the three French settlers distrusted each other and soon fell out. Marragon was civil agent for the French Government, a position that did not deter him from entertaining and welcoming the crews of British ships when they put in for water and food, much to Le Gros's annoyance.

The fraternisation of the settlers on Rodrigues with the British made the new governor of Ile de France, General Decaen, keen to replace Marragon and the others with his own island's unwanted lepers. The plan failed. Marragon remained and the lepers went to Diego Garcia.

Marragon conducted a census in 1804 which shows the island's population as 22 whites (about half of them actually of mixed race) and 82 slaves. The majority of the slaves were from Mozambique, yet nearly a third (24) were born in Rodrigues.

In 1794, Britain decided to capture Ile de France, but their attempts were limited to foraging expeditions to Rodrigues. They wanted to take Rodrigues too, and concentrated on building up good relations with the settlers by paying for their supplies instead of looting. By August 1809, they had no qualms about making their intentions known and landed the first of the forces being assembled to capture Ile de France: 200 infantry and 200 sepoys (Indian soldiers trained by the British).

The occupation of Rodrigues began enthusiastically, with Colonel Keating, who was in command, writing home: 'These are some of the most delightful valleys I ever saw and the soil naturally rich in one of the finest climates in the world capable of producing every sort of vegetation and there is a sufficient quantity of land already cleared for cultivation and the feeding of cattle.' Keating imported cattle and slaves from Madagascar as more British troops assembled.

In July 1810, a force of 4,000 left Rodrigues and went on to capture Ile Bourbon (Réunion) from the French. Following their unexpected defeat at Vieux Grand Port in August, the British gathered a large force in Rodrigues for their successful assault on Ile de France in December 1810. After that, the British occupied Rodrigues until April 1812 when they withdrew, leaving behind most of the 300 slaves they had imported. British rule of Rodrigues was confirmed by the Treaty of Paris in May 1814.

The first British settler was a young man called Thomas Robert Pye, a lieutenant of the marines at a loose end, who was sent by Governor Farquhar in 1821. He stayed only two years. When slavery was abolished, those slaves who had not emancipated themselves already promptly left their owners and squatted on crown land. They finally settled in the mountains where their descendants still live today.

In the mid 19th century, several Europeans or near-Europeans settled in Rodrigues, mostly in the lowlands. They included shipwrecked sailors and minor British civil servants who liked the island. Some of the British married Rodriguan women while others had affairs with them and, as the saying goes in Rodrigues, 'left one or two portraits behind'.

The portraits and the mixed-blood population were centred on Port Mathurin, Baie aux Huîtres, Grand Baie and La Ferme. When the first steamer arrived in the 1890s, so did more settlers, including Indian and Chinese traders. By 1970, the Chinese owned 90% of all the shops on the island.

The growth of the population was rapid. As there were more men than women at first, most women had several partners, their children being raised as the children of the man of the moment. At the end of the 19th century, the population was 3,000. Twenty years later this had become 6,573. The population almost doubled in subsequent 20-year periods, becoming 11,385 in 1944, 18,587 in 1963 and 32,000 in 1981.

Rodrigues was administered as a dependency of Mauritius during the 158 years of British rule. Like a poor relation, it was mostly forgotten or neglected, with occasional official reports warning of the consequences of too large a population.

Since 1968, it has been an integral part of Mauritius. For many years Rodrigues sought greater autonomy over its affairs and on 12 October 2002 the newly created Rodrigues Regional Assembly met for the first time. The Assembly is made up of 21 members, plus its chairperson. At present the Organisation du Peuple Rodriguais (OPR) has a majority of ten members. While the assembly may initiate legislation, this must pass through the Mauritian National Assembly to become law. For further information, visit the Assembly's website http://rra.gov.mu.

ECONOMY

Fishing and agriculture provide the livelihood of Rodriguans although the young hanker for employment either with government or in commerce. There is little vibrant private sector, in contrast to Mauritius.

Onions and garlic are grown for export to Mauritius and maize and chicken are produced for home consumption. Livestock (cattle, pigs, sheep) are also reared for the Mauritian and local markets. Octopus is dried and fish salted for export.

The traditional system of farmers growing maize and beans, helping each other with harvesting and existing on a barter basis has died out. People have become money and subsidy minded. As a district of Mauritius, social benefits filter through to the island from central government and international aid agencies.

A decline in agriculture over the last decade has resulted in a boom in small handicraft units, which is being encouraged by the growth of tourism.

The island's fishing industry is organised on a co-operative basis under the auspices of the Rodriguan Fishermen's Cooperative Federation. Fish is delivered to the area co-operative for distribution and sale on the island or for cold storage at the plant in Port Mathurin. Training in fishing methods, assistance with boat and equipment purchase, catch monitoring and marketing, and foreign aid funding are all provided under various schemes to sustain a viable fishing industry.

The tourism industry in Rodrigues is gradually being developed and has the potential to become one of the island's greatest income earners. The airport has been expanded and several mid-range hotels have been built, some of which are managed by groups with hotels in Mauritius. Rodriguans have, by and large, reacted positively to the establishment of tourism, with many families opening their homes to offer guesthouse-style accommodation. However, according to locals in 2011, tourism in Rodrigues was off to a slow start and the island was not receiving the number of visitors that had been expected.

It is vital that tourism in Rodrigues is developed gradually and thoughtfully. The Rodriguan way of life will be vulnerable to overdevelopment and the island's already stretched resources, water and waste disposal in particular, will be further

SHOALS RODRIGUES

Sabrina Meunier

Shoals Rodrigues is a non-governmental organisation, which developed from the Shoals of Capricorn Programme, a three-year initiative led by the Royal Geographical Society.

The new organisation was established in September 2001 to continue the marine research, education and training activities on Rodrigues. With the combination of these three disciplines good progress is being made towards discovering more about the seas around Rodrigues and promoting sustainable resource use and marine conservation.

The Shoals Centre is based at Pointe Monier, on the outskirts of Port Mathurin, alongside the government agencies which have responsibility for the sea, such as the Coastguard, the Fisheries Protection Service and the Fisheries Research and Training Unit. Our work focuses on collecting information about the Rodrigues lagoon and seas, which can be used to improve the management of the important fishery resources and protect the biodiversity and health of the marine ecosystem. Our most recent project is the establishment of marine reserves around Rodrigues. We have just finalised a draft management plan for four northern marine reserves to aid the sustainability of the fisheries sector and the viability of alternative livelihoods for those who depend on fishing.

The Shoals Rodrigues Centre is run by a committed group of young Rodriguans with the help of a newly established board of trustees. Our work on the reef fisheries, zooplankton populations and the effect of land-based

tested. Rodrigues will never compete with Mauritius's beaches, luxury hotels and first-class service. Nor should it try to. It has a charm of its own, which will attract visitors who will relish the island as it is.

PEOPLE

Travellers coming to Rodrigues from Mauritius are often surprised by how different the population looks. Rodrigues has a predominantly Roman Catholic Creole population, descended from African and Malagasy slaves. Rodriguans sometimes feel closer to the Seychelles than to the Indo-Mauritian-dominated Mauritius. That's a contention visitors are often made aware of as Rodriguans speak freely about the neglect of their isolated backwater.

LANGUAGE AND EDUCATION

Creole is the everyday language but educated Rodriguans also speak French. Although English is the official language and is used in school and official communication, it is less spoken on Rodrigues than in Mauritius.

The secondary school in Port Mathurin is a joint venture between the Roman Catholic and the Anglican churches. There are five state secondary schools on the island, at Maréchal, Le Chou, Mont Lubin, Grande Montagne and Terre Rouge.

RELIGION

The Roman Catholic faith is very strong and is the religion of the majority. Other active religions are Anglicanism, Adventist, Islam and Hinduism.

sediments has been developed in collaboration with foreign experts. We have been carrying out an extensive programme of coral reef surveys to monitor the health of the reef ecosystem and now have ten years' worth of data on the reefs of Rodrigues.

With training in the scientific collection and analysis techniques this local team is working towards building up important long-term data sets. Many new skills and techniques have been taught to a wide range of people on the island. These range from first aid, lifesaving and diving qualifications to marine tourist guide training. We also regularly visit fishing villages to give first aid and swimming training to fishermen and to discuss marine ecology and resource use.

Shoals Rodrigues is also a thriving centre for young people who come to learn more about the marine environment through 'Club Mer'.

The work of Shoals Rodrigues is supported by private donations, as well as a variety of organisations in Mauritius and abroad: the Decentralised Cooperation Programme, the Indian Ocean Commission, North of England Zoological Society, the United Nations Development Programme, GEF-SGP, the British and Australian high commissions, Barclays Bank, the US National Fish and Wildlife Foundation and the Sea Trust, as well as many others.

Visitors are welcome to come and see the work of the organisation at Pointe Monier. Contact Jovani Raffin (☎ *831 1225*). If you would like to help or find out more please see our website at www.shoals-rodrigues.net.

Creoles and Chinese form the Roman Catholic community, although some Chinese are members of the Anglican Church. There are no Buddhists. The Muslim community is small, mostly traders, but supports a mosque in Port Mathurin. There are a few Rastafarians in the interior village communities.

Witchcraft is also practised in the traditional Afro-Creole manner of believing in the efficacy of certain potions, charms, herbs, fortune telling and the warding off of evil.

CULTURE

Rodriguans pride themselves on their hospitality and refer to their remote haven as the 'anti-stress' island. It's certainly worth taking time to see some of the towns, villages and scenery and to get a feel for Rodriguan lifestyle.

Most of the people live either off the sea or the land. The crops cultivated – onions, garlic, chillies, potatoes and maize – are not the same as on Mauritius. As a result, the countryside bears no resemblance to that of Mauritius, but reminds many of the Transkei in southern Africa, with deep green valleys, cultivated lands, and herds of livestock (cattle, goats and pigs).

Maize cobs are left to dry on roofs, which is very reminiscent of Africa and something that is not seen in Mauritius. Sausages, left to cure in the sun, are also often seen on rooftops. The rather uninspiring but neatly built square houses one sees so much of in the countryside are government subsidised, built using coral bricks and designed to be cyclone-proof.

Water is very scarce in Rodrigues. Although there is a mains water supply, most houses have water tanks for collecting and storing water.

In late afternoon, fishermen can be seen sailing to shore in their pirogues and bringing in their nets, whilst at low tide groups of women wade out to the reefs to fish for octopus. This requires a great deal of skill as the octopus are well camouflaged.

One of the highlights of the week for most people is the market at Port Mathurin on Wednesday and Saturday, where much of the home produce is sold.

On weekend evenings the island vibrates to the sound of traditional music at nightclubs, hotels, community 'balls' and private celebrations. Dancing is a vital part of the Creole culture but the European influence is obvious: the *Scottish*, *polka*, *laval* (the waltz) and *quadrille* are still danced today, mainly by the older generation. The traditional *séga-tambour* has its roots in Africa and Madagascar. The *séga* of Rodrigues is said to be closer to its original form than that of Mauritius, thanks to its isolation from external influences. It is also known as the *séga coupé* because the only couple on the dance floor is continually separated by other male and female partners cutting in.

The European influence can also be seen in the musical instruments, namely the accordion, which gave rise to the *séga-kordion*. However, there is now concern amongst the older generation that the tradition of accordion playing is at risk, as few young people are learning to play the instrument. With the help of the European Union, a programme to teach the accordion to youngsters has been established. The Franco-Malagasy legacy to the Rodriguan folk group is a series of simple instruments, such as the drum, the *maravanne* (a small box filled with dry seeds), the triangle and the *bobre* (musical bow).

FESTIVALS One of the highlights of the Rodriguan calendar is **Fish Day** on 1 March, when celebrations throughout the island mark the first day of the dragnet fishing season. *Banané*, or New Year (from *Bonne Année*), is also a time for festivities, which typically last for a week. Families eat their fattened pigs and there is a drinking contest known as *Le Roi boire*.

On 12 October the island celebrates **Autonomy Day**, marking the day in 2002 when Rodrigues gained autonomy.

The recently created **Corn Festival** (April/May) acknowledges the important role of this crop in the island's culture and cuisine.

The **Kreol Festival** at the beginning of December remembers the island's history and showcases its culture. Music and dancing are, as usual, at the centre of the celebrations.

Accordion Day coincides with the Roman Catholic Assumption of the Virgin Mary on 15 August. The accordion has been central to the island's musical tradition since the 19th century and musicians from around the island gather to show-off their skills.

12

Practical Information

HIGHLIGHTS

As part of its campaign to promote Rodrigues as a destination to appeal to sensitive travellers, the MTPA has produced a glossy leaflet with a section on what to do and see. The list is short but pinpoints some of the charms of the island. The activities can be organised by a tour operator or hotel.

- Hiking/trekking/mountain biking
- Rod and line fishing or accompanying fishermen when they pick up lobsters, crab and octopus from the *casiers* left overnight in the lagoon
- Visit Caverne Patate (the cave) at Plaine Corail; guide essential
- Visit local people in their homes. It is possible to stay with them and sample home cuisine.
- Boat trip to Ile aux Cocos, a haven for seabirds
- Experience the *séga-tambour*, the island's folkloric dance
- Enjoy Rodriguan fish and seafood in local restaurants

I would add to that list a visit to the François Leguat Giant Tortoise and Cave Reserve (see page 226); and a walk along the east coast between Graviers and St François stopping off at beautiful, isolated beaches such as Trou d'Argent (see page 231).

TOURIST INFORMATION

For information before you go, contact the Mauritius Tourism Promotion Authority (MTPA), either in your home country or in Mauritius (for contact details, see page 44). The Rodrigues Tourism Office, which opened in 2006, is on Rue de la Solidarité, Port Mathurin (*832 0866; f 832 0174; e info.rodrigues@intnet.mu; www.tourism-rodrigues.mu; 08.00–16.00 Mon–Fri, 08.00–12.00 Sat*). Its website contains plenty of useful information and it publishes some helpful brochures on the island.

TOUR OPERATORS

The sense of going somewhere 'off the beaten track' begins as soon as you try to get to Rodrigues. As yet, few tour operators feature the island.

UK

Partnership Travel White Lion Hse, 64a Highgate High St, London N6 5HX; 020 8347 4020; e info@partnershiptravel.co.uk; www.partnershiptravel.co.uk

Rainbow Tours 305 Upper St, London N1 2TU; 020 7666 1250; e info@rainbowtours.co.uk; www.rainbowtours.co.uk

Tribes Travel 12 The Business Centre, Earl Soham, Woodbridge, Suffolk IP13 7SA; 01728 685971; www.tribes.co.uk

AUSTRALIA

Mauritius Holidays 439 North Rd, Ormond, VIC 3204; ☎ +61 3 9597 9877; e travel@mauritiusholidays.com.au; www.mauritiusholidays.com.au

FRANCE

Nouvelles Frontières various offices; www.nouvelles-frontieres.fr

GERMANY

Trauminsel Reisen Summerstrasse 8, D–82211 Herrsching, Munich; ☎ +49 8 1529 3190; e info@trauminselreisen.de; www.trauminselreisen.de

ITALY

Best Tour Via Tito Speri 8, 20154 Milan; ☎ +39 2 336 33310; e mho@besttours.it; www.besttours.it

SOUTH AFRICA

Origin Tours & Safaris 3 Sir Lowry St, Gordons Bay, Western Cape; ☎ +27 21 856 5851; www.origintours.co.za

USA

Aardvark Safaris 312 South Cedros Av, Suite 315, Solana Beach, California CA 92075; ☎ +1 888 776 0888; e info@aardvarksafaris.com; www.aardvarksafaris.com

RED TAPE

Entry requirements as for Mauritius (see pages 45–8).

HELP

CONSULAR HELP Only Britain and France have honorary consulates in Rodrigues. For other countries the relevant high commission, embassy or consulate in Mauritius has responsibility for Rodrigues (pages 48–9).

UK

Mrs Suzanne Auguste CARE-Co Centre, Camp du Roi; ☎ 832 0120; e brhonconrod@intnet.mu

France

Mr Benoît Jolicoeur Jean-Tac; ☎ 831 1760; f 831 1072; e benjos@intnet.mu

EMERGENCY SERVICES

Police emergency ☎ 999
Police station Port Mathurin; ☎ 831 1536
Ambulance Queen Elizabeth Hospital; ☎ 831 1628
Fire station Port Mathurin; ☎ 831 1588

GETTING THERE AND AWAY

BY AIR Air Mauritius flies regularly between Mauritius and Rodrigues, with at least four flights per day in peak season and two per day in low season.

Demand for flights from Mauritius is high and reservations need to be made well in advance, and reconfirmed. The return airfare from Mauritius is expensive for non-citizens at around Rs4,500 return. However, it is possible to include Rodrigues on an Air Mauritius ticket from Europe to Mauritius at a reduced add-on rate, if it is bought prior to flying to Mauritius. Alternatively, tourists can soften the blow by buying the air ticket from a travel agent in Mauritius (instead of from Air Mauritius or overseas), when it comes lower as part of a package that includes accommodation.

For non-Mauritian passport holders, the check-in procedure at Sir Seewoosagur Ramgoolam Airport for flights to Rodrigues is as for international flights. Passports must be shown even though this is a domestic flight, although there is no departure tax to pay. It is advisable to check in early, otherwise your seat may be given to someone on standby. The luggage allowance is just 15kg.

Flying time between Mauritius and Rodrigues is 1 hour 30 minutes. The ATR42 has 48 seats and not much leg or arm space, so keep your hand baggage small.

Air Mauritius can be contacted at the airport (☎ *832 7700;* **f** *832 7321*) or at their office in the ADS Building on Rue Max Lucchesi in Port Mathurin (☎ *831 1558;* **f** *831 1959;* **e** *mkrodrigues@airmauritius.com*).

BY SEA The *Mauritius Pride* links Mauritius and Rodrigues three times a month. The journey takes about 36 hours to Rodrigues but only 24 hours on the way back. There are two classes: *loisirs* (seats) and *excellence* (cabins). Expect to pay from around Rs3,500 per person return for a seat and Rs5,000 per person return for a cabin. Children under 12 receive a 50% discount. The *Mauritius Trochetia* makes one journey per month between Mauritius and Rodrigues. Prices for second-class cabins start from Rs5,500 per person return. For information on either service, contact the Mauritius Shipping Corporation in Mauritius (☎ *208 5900*) or Rodrigues (☎ *831 0640*).

ON ARRIVAL/DEPARTURE

The first sight of Rodrigues, in the dry season, is of parched hillsides with cactus-like vegetation and box-type houses dotted all over an inhospitable landscape. Arriving by air, the views of the surrounding lagoon are spectacular.

The Sir Gaetan Duval Airport is on the coast in the southwest of the island. When I first visited Rodrigues in 2002, the airport terminal was a tiny, one-storey building, with spectators waiting obediently behind the perimeter fence where jeeps and buses were parked. The person at the immigration desk had a hand-written list of the passengers due to arrive on each flight, and he checked the names off one by one. However, things have changed in the last few years. There is now a smart, new terminal building with a small duty-free shop, and immigration and customs procedures have been formalised in line with those in Mauritius (see pages 45–8).

GETTING TO YOUR HOTEL Most hotels and guesthouses will provide airport transfers for a fee, usually around Rs500–800. If you haven't pre-arranged transport you can take a bus or one of the jeeps or vans that come to pick up hotel guests. The Supercopter bus that operates between the airport and Port Mathurin for arrivals and departures costs around Rs150.

If you are planning to hire a car, there is an Avis (☎ *832 8100*) desk at the airport, open whenever a flight arrives or leaves (see page 213 for further details).

HEALTH AND SAFETY

There is no malaria on Rodrigues so you need not take prophylaxis. The advice on inoculations for Mauritius (see *Chapter 2, Health*, pages 53–6) applies equally to Rodrigues.

Insect repellent is necessary as mosquitoes are abundant. Strong sunblock is essential. Water is drinkable in hotels but, as in Mauritius, can cause upsets. It is advisable to drink bottled water.

There is one **hospital** on the island, the Queen Elizabeth Hospital (☎ *831 1628*) at Crève Cœur on the outskirts of Port Mathurin. In emergencies they will send an ambulance. Medical care is also available at the Mont Lubin Clinic (☎ *831 4403*) and La Ferme Clinic (☎ *831 7202*). There is a **pharmacy** (☎ *831 2279;* ⊕ *07.30–16.30 Mon–Sat, 07.30–11.30 Sun*) in Rue de la Solidarité, Port Mathurin.

A huge plus factor on Rodrigues is safety: crime, it would appear, is virtually absent. There are three prison cells, which are hardly ever occupied. Nevertheless, caution cannot be a bad thing, especially for women.

WHAT TO TAKE

Take light, casual cotton clothing. Bathing costumes and T-shirts are acceptable everywhere. Remember beach shoes to protect your feet against sea urchin spines whilst swimming. Pack some long trousers or similar for the more upmarket hotels and restaurants in the evenings. Comfortable trainers with a sturdy grip are sufficient for the hiking trails.

Paul Draper of CARE-Co gave me a handy tip for travellers to Rodrigues: take a second form of photo identification, other than your passport. If you lose your passport on Rodrigues, you will need a new one before you can board a flight back to Mauritius. Unfortunately, there are no embassies or consular officers on Rodrigues and the honorary consuls cannot issue passports, you need to go to Mauritius for that and to go to Mauritius you need a passport. So, you could well end up stranded in Rodrigues while your home country's authorities try to solve the conundrum.

MONEY AND BANKING

Hotels and most guesthouses and restaurants accept the major credit cards. Opening hours for banks are typically 09.15–15.15 Monday–Friday, and in some cases 09.15–11.15 Saturday.

$ **Barclays Bank** Rue de la Solidarité, Port Mathurin; ☎ 831 1553
$ **Mauritius Commercial Bank** Rue Max Lucchesi, Port Mathurin; ☎ 831 1833
$ **SBI Mauritius** Rue François Leguat, Port Mathurin; ☎ 831 1591
$ **State Bank** Rue Max Lucchesi, Port Mathurin; ☎ 831 1642

There are also **ATMs** in Mont Lubin and La Ferme.

GETTING AROUND

INBOUND TOUR OPERATORS The following agencies can provide transfers, excursions and activities, as well as car hire:

2000 Tours Rue Hajee Bhai Fatehmamode, Port Mathurin; ☎/f 831 1894; e 2000trs@intnet.mu; www.rodrigues-2000tours.com
Beraca Tours Baie aux Huîtres; ☎ 831 2198; e tropicalguy17@caramail.com
Ebony Tours Mourouk Ebony Hotel; ☎ 832 3351; f 832 3355; e ebony@intnet.mu; www.mouroukebonyhotel.com
Rotourco Pl François Leguat, Port Mathurin; ☎/f 831 0747; e rotourco@intnet.mu; www.rotourco.com

DRIVING During the 1990s, roads were improved and many more vehicles imported, although there are still relatively few cars on the island. Regulations for drivers are as for Mauritius, except for the speed limit, which is 50km/h. Take care as there are many steep, windy, narrow roads which are not lit at night. 4x4 vehicles are common and are best suited to the conditions. There is no coastal road around the island; you have to keep climbing back up to the centre to get almost anywhere. There is only one petrol station on the island, in Port Mathurin, so keep an eye on the fuel gauge. Should you run out of fuel, most of the tiny village shops dotted around the island will sell you a couple of litres of petrol in a soft-drink bottle.

In addition to the inbound tour operators above, the following offer **car hire**:

Avis Sir Gaetan Duval Airport Plaine Corail; 832 8100; f 832 8075; e avis@avismauritius.com; www.avismauritius.com

Chez M et Mme Poupon Pointe Monier; 877 4292

Scooters, motorbikes and **bicycles** can also be hired. However, be wary – some people hire out these vehicles without having the necessary permits.

The following offers **motorcycle hire**:

Chez M et Mme Poupon Pointe Monier; 877 4292

TAXIS There is just a handful of taxis on the island and they do not drive around looking for clients. Your best chance of finding one is at the bus station in Port Mathurin. The tourist office can provide a list of taxi drivers and their contact details. Here is a selection:

Port Mathurin

J D Payendee 876 4144
J S Edouard 875 2215
M J Limock 875 2387

Baie aux Huîtres

J B Meunier 976 7086
J P Meunier 875 3583

Grand La Fouche Corail/airport

J M Botte 875 8509
S Prudence 875 4511

Mont Lubin/Grande Montagne

J R Casimir 875 6818

Pointe Coton

M J Félicité 875 2184

BY BUS The **bus station** is on the outskirts of Port Mathurin at the east end of Rue de la Solidarité. It's on the seafront beyond the Winston Churchill Bridge. On one side are buildings housing snack bars and stalls selling an array of goods. The bus stops are on the other side, with the bus number and destination marked on each. The network is far-reaching as much of the population is without a car, but timetables are pretty 'flexible' and buses stop running at about 17.00. Travelling by bus is inexpensive: the maximum price for a ticket is usually around Rs30. Don't forget to raise your hand or clap in order to stop the bus.

HITCHHIKING Hitchhiking around Rodrigues is an absolute pleasure, because it's the 'done thing' to pick up anyone thumbing for a lift. You should, however, exercise due caution when accepting a lift from a stranger.

ACCOMMODATION

Although there are much-discussed plans to further develop tourism in Rodrigues, the industry is in its infancy. There are just a few small hotels and numerous guesthouses on the island and no tourism training school, so if you are hoping to find accommodation and service of mainland Mauritian standards, you will be disappointed.

However, visitors who are looking to experience a unique and simple island way of life will be delighted. Perhaps the best way to achieve this is to stay with a family or rent a house from a local, or at least eat a home-cooked meal at one of the many *table d'hôte* restaurants. Plenty of Rodriguans now offer this type of accommodation and dining, and a full list can be obtained from the tourist office.

Details of many of the establishments are given in the following *Where to stay* and *Where to eat* sections in *Chapter 13*.

Lack of crime and limited accommodation mean that opportunities for camping holidays are still many. Some of the best spots are around the beaches of the east coast.

Please note that as water is so scarce in Rodrigues, all of the hotels ask you to limit the amount that you use.

EATING AND DRINKING

Rodriguan food tastes fresh and healthy, perhaps because many of the ingredients are organically grown on the island. The chickens you see wandering free-range all over the island could well end up on your plate, usually in the form of a *cari poulet*. The *caris* are similar to those eaten in Mauritius, and are typically made from octopus, chicken or pork. Rodrigues is well known for its octopus, which is usually hand-fished by ladies walking through the lagoon at low tide and left to dry by the sea.

Maize is a staple part of the islanders' diet and is often eaten as maize soup. Other specialities include locally produced honey, kidney beans, sausages, chillies, papayas and limes.

If you choose to eat with a local family in one of the island's *table d'hôte* (see page 224), you may well find that the entire meal was prepared on a wood fire as this is how many Rodriguans cook.

As in Mauritius, rum is a popular drink, particularly after meals as a *digestif*.

PHOTOGRAPHY

It is best to buy photography paraphernalia before you arrive in Rodrigues; choice on the island is limited. Film, development and digital photography services are expensive in Rodrigues and are available at Citronelle Fotolab in the Rogers Centre on the corner of Rue Max Lucchesi and Rue Mamzelle Julia in Port Mathurin (☎ *831 1555*).

RODRIGUAN RECIPE

Translation by Alexandra Richards

This recipe comes from *Les Délices de Rodrigues* by Françoise Baptiste, owner of Auberge de la Montagne and La Belle Rodriguaise (see page 222).

RODRIGUAN FISH CURRY

Ingredients (serves 6):

2kg of fish (firm, white fish is best)
5–6 tomatoes (diced)
2 onions (diced)
3 cloves of garlic
crushed ginger
sprig of thyme
sprig of parsley
30g of saffron powder
salt and pepper to taste

Method: Cut the fish into slices. Add salt and pepper and leave to rest for 15 minutes. Heat the oil in a large frying pan, then fry the fish until golden. For the sauce, fry the garlic, ginger, onion, tomatoes and saffron, then add a pinch of salt and one teaspoon of lemon juice. Put the slices of fish into the sauce one at a time. Add the thyme and parsley and half a glass of hot water. Simmer for ten minutes. Serve with rice.

COMMUNICATIONS

POST The main post office is at the eastern end of Rue de la Solidarité, Port Mathurin (☎ *831 2098*; ⌚ *08.15–16.00 Mon–Fri, 08.15–11.45 Sat*). There are small post offices in Grande Montagne, La Ferme, Rivière Coco and Mont Lubin.

TELEPHONE To call Rodrigues from overseas, after dialling the international access code dial 230 followed by the seven-digit number beginning with 831. From Mauritius, dial 095 followed by the seven digits.

There are a few coin-operated payphones in Rodrigues – at the airport, in Port Mathurin and also some villages, like La Ferme, Quatre Vents, Mont Lubin and Port Sud-est. Cardphones are now fairly widespread throughout the island.

Phone calls can be made and faxes sent at Mauritius Telecom in Rue Johnston, Port Mathurin (☎ *831 1816*; ⌚ *09.00–16.00 Mon–Sat, 09.00–12.00 Sun*). You can also buy phonecards (*télécartes*) here. Many hotels and guesthouses now have fax machines.

Mobile-phone coverage is pretty good in Rodrigues, even beyond Port Mathurin.

Useful telephone number

Administration office Port Mathurin; ☎ 831 1515

INTERNET ACCESS/EMAIL There is a shortage of internet cafés and many of those that have opened in recent years have had a very short lifespan. The only internet café in Port Mathurin is currently **Rodnet Cybercafé** (*Patricio Bldg, Pl François Leguat*; ☎ *831 0747*; ⌚ *08.30–16.30 Mon–Fri, 08.30–13.00 Sat*). Internet access costs around Rs3 per minute or Rs300 for five hours. Scanning, faxing, CD/DVD burning and photocopying are also available.

Internet access and Wi-Fi are available at the library in Port Mathurin, in the Alfred North-Coombs Building on the corner of Hajee Bhai Fatehmamode and François Leguat streets (⌚ *09.00–16.30 Mon–Fri, 09.00–14.00 Sat*).

Internet access is also available at the post office in Port Mathurin and Mauritius Telecom.

Wireless internet is available at many of the guesthouses and hotels, if you have a laptop with you. It is also available in the grounds of the Rodrigues tourist office in Port Mathurin.

13

Exploring Rodrigues

PORT MATHURIN

The island's tiny capital is neatly laid out with a grid system of streets running parallel and perpendicular to the sea.

While it is small it is not as easy as you may think to find your way around. Few of the streets are signed and you will find even the locals don't know the street names, largely because they change with every change of administration. If asking directions, it is therefore best to use landmarks. The town is best explored on foot, partly because it allows you to avoid the puzzling one-way system.

Rue de la Solidarité runs the length of the town and emerges to cross over reclaimed land and on to the seaside village of **Anse aux Anglais** (English Bay).

A walk down Rue de la Solidarité leads past the colonial **house of the administrator** (built in 1873), with a cannon outside the gates. This now houses the **Rodrigues Tourism Office** (*832 0866;* **f** *832 0174;* **e** *info.rodrigues@intnet.mu; www.tourism-rodrigues.mu;* *08.00–16.00 Mon–Fri, 08.00–12.00 Sat*), which has Wi-Fi facilities as well as information on the island. The offices of Discovery Rodrigues are opposite.

Just near the tourist office, on the corner of Rue de la Solidarité and Rue Hajee Bhai Fatehmamode, is **Barclays Bank**. Behind the bank is the large, modern Alfred North-Coombs building, which houses the **library**. Here you can use computers and access Wi-Fi free of charge. In a courtyard in front of the library are kiosks, where members of the **Association Rodrigues Entreprendre au Féminin** (an association for local businesswomen) sell their wares, including delicious honey and pickles. Opposite Barclays Bank on Rue de la Solidarité, and almost hidden by one-storey houses, are the six miniature minarets of the **Noor-ud-Deen Mosque**, rebuilt in 1979–81.

Running parallel to Rue de la Solidarité, along the seafront, is Rue Wolphart Harmensen. This leads to the **port**, **customs office** and the offices of the **Rodrigues Regional Assembly**. At the port, opposite Rue Hajee Bhai Fatehmamode, is a **war memorial** with three rifles forming a tripod and two cannon shafts beside them. The inscription reads: '*Aux engagés volontaires Rodriguais 1914–18, 1939–45*' (For the Rodriguans who served 1914–18, 1939–45).

At the western end of Rue Wolphart Harmensen is the slaughterhouse, where the white-painted buildings are marked PORC, CABRIS and BOEUF (pigs, goats and cattle). The street outside the slaughterhouse was traditionally where the market took place every Wednesday and Saturday morning. However, when I visited in 2011 a new **market** building was under construction at the eastern end of Rue de la Solidarité, just before Winston Churchill Bridge. The market is crammed with stalls selling all manner of homemade and homegrown goodies: chutneys, drinks, woven baskets and hats, fruit and vegetables. For many locals this is the highlight of their week and a chance to catch up on the island's gossip.

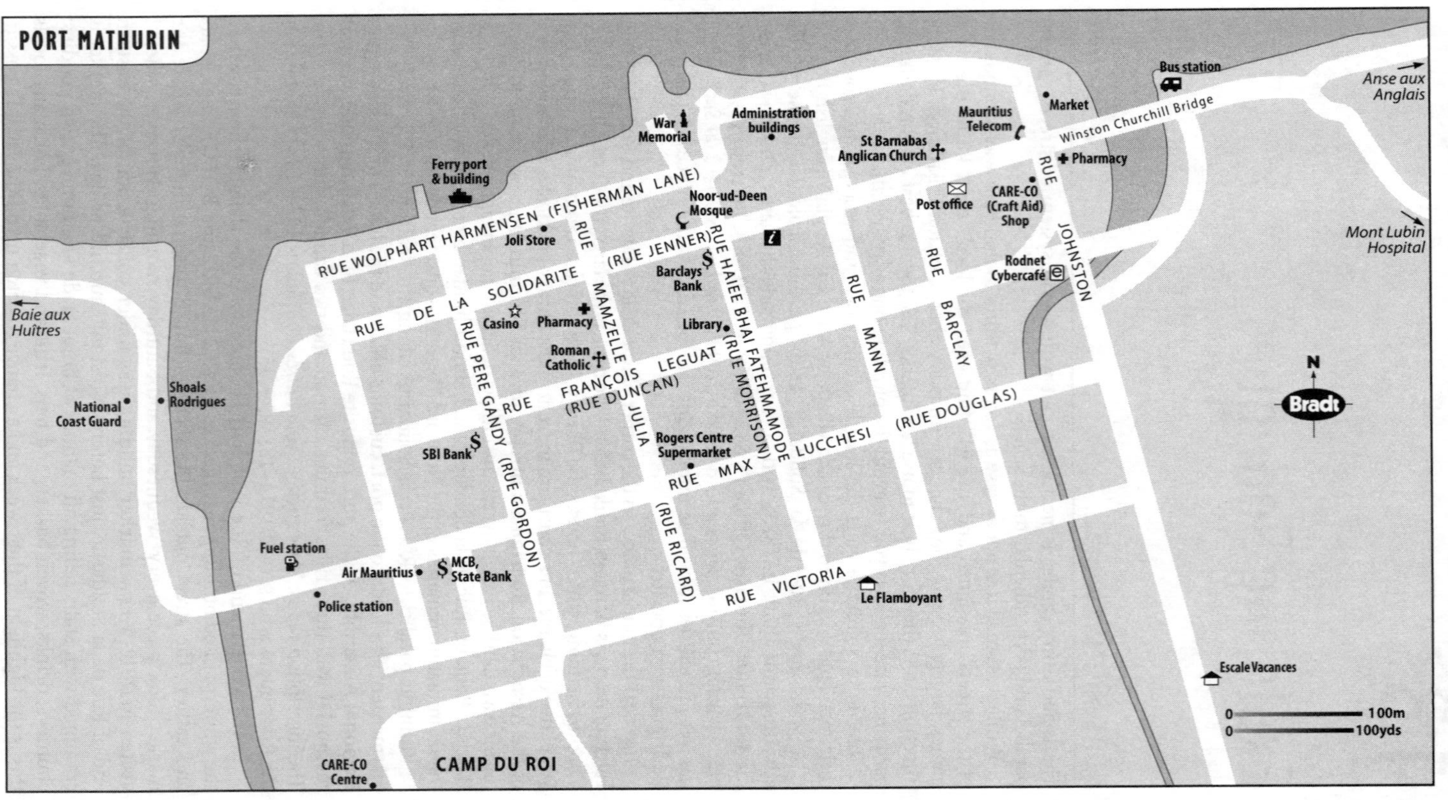
PORT MATHURIN
Ferry port & building
War Memorial
Administration buildings
St Barnabas Anglican Church
Mauritius Telecom
Market
Bus station
Anse aux Anglais
Winston Churchill Bridge
Pharmacy
Post office
CARE-CO (Craft Aid) Shop
Noor-ud-Deen Mosque
Mont Lubin Hospital
RUE WOLPHART HARMENSEN (FISHERMAN LANE)
Joli Store
RUE MAMZELLE JULIA
(RUE JENNER)
Barclays Bank
RUE HAIEE BHAI FATEHMAMODE
(RUE MORRISON)
RUE MANN
RUE BARCLAY
Rodnet Cybercafé
RUE JOHNSTON
Baie aux Huîtres
RUE DE LA SOLIDARITE
Casino
Pharmacy
Library
RUE PERE GANDY (RUE GORDON)
Roman Catholic
RUE FRANÇOIS LEGUAT
(RUE DUNCAN)
N
Bradt
Shoals Rodrigues
National Coast Guard
SBI Bank
Rogers Centre Supermarket
RUE MAX LUCCHESI
(RUE DOUGLAS)
(RUE RICARD)
Fuel station
Air Mauritius
MCB, State Bank
RUE VICTORIA
Le Flamboyant
Police station
Escale Vacances
0 100m
0 100yds
CARE-CO Centre
CAMP DU ROI

It's worth getting up early to see the market at its busiest, around 08.00. If you are going to buy souvenirs at the market it is worth seeking out those made in Rodrigues. When it comes to woven pandanus items, the ones made in Rodrigues tend to be the plain, non-coloured ones, while the brightly coloured bags, hats and drums are usually made overseas. Watch out for a stall selling jewellery made from local pearls and shells – the initiative of a new local co-operative which farms oysters near Anse aux Anglais.

On Rue Mamzelle Julia is the incredible **Joli Store**, a small bright blue store crammed with a staggering array of items from modern electronic goods to toys that seem to have been hanging in the shop since the 1970s.

The **St Barnabas Anglican Church** and **Rodrigues College** school complex is at the eastern end of Rue de la Solidarité. The church is contemporary in style (built in 1977) with an interior tower. The simple, white **Roman Catholic church** is in Rue Mamzelle Julia. Mass is celebrated on Saturdays at 17.00 and Sundays at 07.00. There is a **pharmacy** just north of the church on Rue Mamzelle Julia and another one at the eastern (Anse aux Anglais) end of Rue de la Solidarité.

The **court house**, **police station**, **Air Mauritius office** and the island's only **petrol station** are at the western (Baie aux Huîtres) end of Rue Max Lucchesi.

The **bus station** is over the **Winston Churchill Bridge** at the far eastern end of Rue de la Solidarité. To prevent tailbacks at the petrol station, a brightly painted petrol tanker, which looks more like an ice-cream van, is used to fill up the buses at the bus station. Just beyond the bridge the road divides into two; one leads inland to Mont Lubin, whilst the coast road leads to Anse aux Anglais.

WHERE TO STAY

Mid range

Escale Vacances (23 rooms) Fond la Digue, Port Mathurin; ☎ 831 2555; f 831 2075; e escal.vac@intnet.mu; www.escalesvacanes.com. Opened in Apr 1997, in a quiet area on the outskirts of Port Mathurin. The en-suite rooms have AC, TV & minibar; some have a phone. It has a bar, pool & terrace with table tennis & snooker tables. There is also a comfortable TV lounge with a small library. Free Wi-Fi is available in some areas of the hotel. The restaurant here is highly regarded (see below). **$$$**

Budget

La Marmite des Iles Baie Lascars; ☎ 832 1279; e timais-resto@orange.mu. On the beach at the eastern end of Port Mathurin. Clean, new rooms with AC, TV & sea view. There is a good restaurant here (see below). **$$**

Le Flamboyant Hotel (27 rooms) Rue Victoria, Port Mathurin; ☎ 832 0082; e resa@hotelflamboyant.com; www.hotelflamboyant.com. Small, simple rooms with en suite, TV & minibar. There is a restaurant & a little pool. Dbl/sgl €35/20 BB. **$$**

WHERE TO EAT

There is a small supermarket in the Rogers Centre on the corner of Rue Max Lucchesi and Rue Mamzelle Julia. Snack vendors are dotted all over town. There is a good one next to Safari Bar on the way to Anse aux Anglais. The market on Wednesdays and Saturdays is great for fruit and vegetables.

Aux Deux Frères Patriko Bldg, Pl François Leguat; ☎ 831 0541; ⏰ from 08.30 daily. Cuisine: French, pizza, Rodriguan. The menu consists largely of French dishes & pizza, with a few Creole dishes also on offer. Mains from Rs245, pizza from Rs215. Also take-away. **$$$**

Escale Vacances Hotel Fond la Digue; ☎ 831 2555; ⏰ for lunch & dinner daily. Cuisine: Rodriguan, Chinese, European, seafood. Good standards of food & service. **$$$**

La Marmite des Iles Baie Lascars; ☎ 832 1279; e timais-resto@orange.mu. Cuisine: Rodriguan, European, seafood. A clean, new restaurant on the beach at the eastern end of Port Mathurin. **$$**

Le Nouveau Capitaine Rue Johnston; ☎ 831 1581; ⏰ 10.00–15.00 & 17.00–22.00 Mon–Sat.

Cuisine: Rodriguan, European, seafood. It may not look much from the outside but the chef here cooks up some of the best seafood dishes around. The service is professional & friendly, although it can be a little slow. The portions are generous, making this good value for money. **$$**

✕ **Restaurant du Quai** Rue Wolphart Harmensen; ☎831 2840; ⌚ for lunch & dinner Tue–Sun. Cuisine: Rodriguan, Chinese, Mauritian, seafood. Small but extremely popular, especially for its seafood. Reservation recommended. **$$**

✕ **Paille en Queue** Rue François Leguat; ☎831 1616; ⌚ for lunch & dinner daily. Cuisine: Creole, Chinese. Also take-away. Popular with locals, many of whom seem to be sleeping off a hangover. Wouldn't win any prizes for hygiene. **$**

AROUND RODRIGUES

The island's fish shape has its head in the east and its forked tail in the west. The bay at **St François** is its mouth. The road from the airport at the western corner of Rodrigues to Port Mathurin winds over the spine of mountains in the island's centre. These spines run north to south with deep ravines between them and offer breathtaking views down to the coast.

The Sir Gaetan Duval Airport is at **Plaine Corail**. The quickest route to Port Mathurin and the east is via **La Fouche**, **Quatre Vents** and **Mont Lubin**. From La Fouche you can also head north or south to the coastal roads. The north coast road takes you through **Port Mathurin** as far as **Grand Baie**, whilst the southern equivalent ends at the Mourouk Ebony Hotel in **Pâté Reynieux**. Both offer picturesque drives through villages and smallholdings, where cattle and pigs can often be seen rummaging on the seashore. Mangroves have been replanted along both coasts and can be seen in various stages of development.

The road from Mont Lubin in the centre of the island down to **Anse Mourouk** is steep and winding, with 52 bends, giving you time to admire the spectacular view of the lagoon. The deep blue channel you can see snaking through the reef is known as La Grande Passe. Dotted through the lagoon you can also see the islands of Hermitage, Ile aux Chats, Ile Plate and Ile Gombrani. At **Port Sud Est** is the tiniest hairdressing saloon I have ever seen, Pierette Coiffeur, consisting of one small room in an unassuming concrete box on the hillside but with million dollar views.

Beyond Port Mathurin is **Crève Cœur**, where there is a **Hindu temple** dedicated to Shiva. Further along the coast is the pretty bay of **Anse aux Anglais**, which has a sandy beach and plenty of places to stay. Scores of local ladies can often be seen walking out into the lagoon to catch octopus.

Almost all the island's roads lead to **Mont Lubin** before branching off in different directions. On the road from Port Mathurin to Mont Lubin, the **Queen Elizabeth Hospital** is on the right and the **meteorological station** is on the left. Opposite the meteorological station is a shrine to the Virgin Mary, **La Reine de Rodrigues**, built in 1954, with magnificent views over Port Mathurin and out to sea. Nearby is a cannon, placed there by the British to defend the island. On the same road around the area of **Solitude**, you're likely to see rare **Rodrigues fruit bats** in the late afternoon.

In the centre of the island is **Mont Limon**, Rodrigues's highest point at 398m. From the road there is a short path leading to the summit, which offers far-reaching views around the island. Nearby, just south of the main road, is **St Gabriel**, which boasts the island's largest church. It was built from limestone blocks from 1934 onwards by devoted parishioners who carried the coral, sand and cement on foot.

To the north of the main road is the tiny village of **L'Union**, where there is a low-key, pyramid-shaped **monument to the island's slaves**. According to its inscription, in 1736 the island's population was two whites and six black slaves. Nearby small stones mark the graves of unnamed slaves. This is also where you will find the **tomb of Philibert Marragon** and his wife – in contrast to the slaves' graves, rather elaborate. Marragon was one of the island's first permanent settlers, arriving in 1793. He was a farmer and the island's first civil agent for the French Government (see also page 202).

There is no road along the east coast but this is where the island's best **beaches** are found, including the much-photographed **Trou d'Argent**. They can be reached on foot and are almost always deserted (see page 231). A protected marine area stretches along the south of the island from Pointe Roche Noire in the east to Plaine Corail in the west.

Travelling west from Port Mathurin the road hugs the coast; octopus can often be seen hanging out to dry in the sun. At **Pointe la Guele**, is the island's only (usually empty) **prison**, an unassuming blue and white building with fantastic sea views. At **La Ferme**, a school and church serve scattered dwellings. It was at this unassuming church that Pope John Paul II celebrated Mass on 15 August 1989.

The west is the driest part of the island and is sprinkled with small rural settlements. The lagoon is wide here and provides memorable views. In the community of **Baie Topaze** Mme Grandcourt (*831 7535*) sells honey and homemade pickles at the door. In 2011, a church in the shape of a boat was built at **Camp Pintade**; before its construction the residents of this part of the island had to travel to the church at La Ferme.

WHERE TO STAY

Mid range

Cases à Gardenias (3 rooms, 3 villas) Mt Bois Noir; 832 5751; f 832 5751; e casesagardenias@hotmail.com; www.casesagardenias-rodrigues.com. An unusual accommodation option for Rodrigues, with a sophisticated, European feel. This is probably because the owners, Mr & Mrs Verbeek Comarmond (a Belgian man married to a Mauritian) lived in France for many years. Marie-Line Comarmond is well known for her homemade jams, honey & chutneys (Marie Island Products), which you will have the chance to taste at breakfast. The house & grounds are beautifully maintained & the European-style furnishings create an atmosphere of elegance. There are 3 en-suite rooms around the main house plus a new section of rooms & villas in a separate complex, known as Les Pavillons. Les Pavillons allows families to have separate rooms within the same villa; the villas are around a central courtyard with pool & bar area. **$$$**

Cotton Bay Hotel (48 rooms) Pointe Coton; 831 8001; f 831 8003; e reservation@cottonbay.intnet.mu; www.cottonbayhotel.biz. The en-suite rooms & 2 suites are housed in sea-facing 2-storey buildings. Rooms are spacious & have AC, TV, phone, minibar & small safe. It has a pool, restaurant, games room, tennis court, kids' club, good dive centre & watersports, including kitesurfing (payable). There are pleasant, albeit rocky, beaches in the area but it's an unattractive, windswept location & by Rodriguan standards is a long way from anywhere (30mins from Port Mathurin & 45mins from the airport). **$$$**

Le Réci (8 rooms) Caverne Provert; 831 1804; f 831 0760; e ebony@intnet.mu; www.lerecifhotel.com. Overlooking the beach at Caverne Provert, not far from Port Mathurin. The 6 rooms & 2 apartments with kitchenette are clean, spacious, comfortable & have sea views. They are equipped with AC, TV & balcony. There is a restaurant serving Rodriguan meals & *séga* shows on the weekends. A range of excursions & activities can be arranged. **$$$**

Les Cocotiers (32 rooms) Anse aux Anglais; 831 1058; e lescocotiers@intnet.mu. In a good location, on the beach just outside Port Mathurin. Simply furnished en-suite rooms with AC, TV & phone. There are 2 family apartments with kitchenette. The restaurant is one of the better ones on Rodrigues. From the pool area you can walk directly onto the beach. Reef shoes are advisable as it is stony. Wi-Fi available. **$$$**

Mourouk Ebony Hotel (30 rooms, 1 villa) Pâté Reynieux, Mourouk; 832 3351; f 832 3355; e ebony@intnet.mu; www.mouroukebonyhotel.com. Perched on a hillside facing a vast lagoon &

Ile aux Chats, this is a very popular hotel so book well in advance. The rooms are housed in neat, red-roofed chalets set in beautiful gardens. Rooms are simply furnished with en-suite facilities, AC, fridge & small terrace. There are no phones or TV. The villa is in a separate building with its own small pool; 2 bedrooms upstairs, kitchen & sitting room downstairs. There is a good restaurant (see page 225) with a bar, & a small pool overlooking the ocean. There are mountain bikes for hire, a dive centre & a very well-equipped windsurfing, sailing & kitesurfing school – Kite for Fun (see page227). The hotel organises a range of excursions & evening entertainment. **$$$**

Pointe Vénus Hotel & Spa (54 rooms) Mont Vénus; 832 0104; **f** 832 0101; **e** resa@otentik.intnet.mu. Opened in 2004, this is, in theory, the island's most upmarket hotel, claiming to offer the equivalent of 4-star accommodation & facilities. However, consistently scathing reports on the service & food have plagued the hotel. It is about 3km from Port Mathurin, overlooking the town & the ocean. The rooms are comfortable & clean, with AC, TV, phone, minibar, safe, tea/coffee facilities (payable) & balcony/terrace. For families, there are apartments designed to take 2 adults & 2 children. There are 2 restaurants, a bar, 2 pools (1 for children), gym, massage rooms, dive centre & kids' club. Activities such as deep-sea fishing can be organised. There is no beach to speak of in front of the hotel but there is a good beach about 500m away. **$$$**

Budget

Auberge de la Montagne (3 rooms) Grande Montagne; /**f** 831 4607; **e** villa@intnet.mu; http://aubergedelamontagne.net.tc. This large house on a hill in this small village offers 3 self-catering studios with en suite & kitchenette. Owner, Françoise Baptiste, is a superb chef & author of the Rodriguan cookbook, *Les Délices de Rodrigues*. She can prepare delicious *table d'hôte* meals on request. **$$**

Coralie La Différence (5 rooms) Solitude; 832 1072; **f** 831 6306; **e** brigilou13@hotmail.fr. Opened in 2008 as Le Bois d'Olive. Accommodation at the top of the hill overlooking Port Mathurin, which is less than a 5min drive away. Rooms are en suite & have TV, phone & minibar. The restaurant here is excellent (see page 224) & has panoramic views of the coast. **$$**

Domaine de Décidé (4 rooms, 6 studios, 1 villa) Batatrana, Nouvelle Découverte & St François; 831 8752; **e** domainededecide@hotmail.com; www.villarodrigues.com. Comfortable self-catering accommodation & en-suite rooms, in Creole-style houses within a quiet park off the road to Gravier, in the southeast. The island's best beaches are within walking distance. Excursions can be arranged. RO, BB & HB available. **$$**

Kafé Marron (4 rooms) Pointe Coton; 706 0195; **e** dorothy@kafemarron.com; www.kafemarron.com. A large, modern house in a quiet location in the island's northeast & within walking distance of the beach. The rooms are spacious & thoughtfully decorated with doors leading onto the balcony that runs around the house. Only 2 of the rooms are en suite, 2 have shared bathroom. AC is available for a supplement of Rs300 per room per day. Accommodation is on a HB basis & is priced from around €70 per room per night. **$$**

La Belle Rodriguaise (12 rooms) Graviers; 832 4040; **e** villa@intnet.mu; www.labellerodriguaise.com. In 2009, Françoise & Laval Baptiste, owners of Auberge de la Montagne, opened their new small hotel on the coast at Graviers. It is in a fantastic location, completely off the beaten track on a hill overlooking the beach & with some wonderful coastal walks nearby. The sea-facing, en-suite rooms are in 2-storey buildings. They are warmly decorated in tropical colours & feel new & clean. There is a pool, an excellent little restaurant with wonderful ocean views & a small spa. Excursions & activities, such as a Creole cookery course with Françoise, can be arranged. **$$**

La Cabane d'Eté (2 apts) Baie Malgache; 831 0747; **e** phanuel@rotourco.com; www.lacabanedete.com. The 2-bedroom apartments have AC, TV & shared kitchen, & overlook the ocean. New, clean & comfortable. Can be booked on a self-catering or HB basis. **$$**

La Collinière (4 rooms) Brûlé; /**f** 831 8558; **e** lelangoustier@intnet.mu. A French couple runs this comfortable guesthouse with beautiful tropical gardens & views of the ocean. The rooms are simply furnished & clean. All have en-suite facilities & 3 have a balcony. There are good walks in the area & the *table d'hôte* restaurant serves excellent Creole & seafood dishes. Closed Jul/Aug. **$$**

La Fantaisie (4 rooms) Eau Vannée; 832 6100; **f** 831 6634; **e** fantaisie@intnet.mu; www.

fantaisierodrigues.com. Overlooking the Mourouk lagoon, a house with 2 simple en-suite bedrooms, kitchenette & sitting/dining room, an apartment with en-suite room & kitchenette, & a charming Creole 'kaz' (rustic house) with a double en-suite room & sun deck. There is a pool with panoramic views. BB, HB & FB options are available. **$$**

La Kaz Belle Vue (1 villa) Coromandel; 727 6773; e contact@bellevue-rodrigues.com; www.bellevue-rodrigues.com. A recently built 2-bedroom *gîte* at the eastern end of the island with an additional en-suite room. It stands on a hill in pleasant gardens, overlooking the lagoon. It is nicely finished inside & out. There is a pool with fabulous views of the ocean. A good self-catering option. **$$**

Les Varangues (1 villa, 3 apts) Grand Baie; 832 0022; e lesvarangues@intnet.mu; www.lesvarangues.com. Close to the pretty beach at Grand Baie. Offers a fully furnished 3-bedroom villa with AC, 2 studios & a 2-bedroom apartment. Accommodation is simply furnished but comfortable & clean. Paintings by local artists hang on the walls. Can be booked on BB or HB basis. **$$**

Résidence Foulsafat (2 rooms, 3 villas) Jean Tac; 831 1760; f 831 1072; e benjos@intnet.mu; http://residencefoulsafat.com. There are 2 en-suite rooms attached to the house, & 3 self-catering villas with 1, 2 or 3 bedrooms. The 1- & 2-bedroom villas are more rustic than the larger one, & the 1-bedroom villa has a kitchenette rather than full kitchen. *Table d'hôte* meals are served on the terrace, overlooking the pretty garden. **$$**

Ti Pavillon (9 rooms, 2 studios, 1 apt) Anse aux Anglais; 875 0707; f 831 2825; e tipavillon@intnet.mu; www. tipavillon.com. Just up from Auberge Anse aux Anglais, around 150m from the beach. Comfortable, colourful guesthouse accommodation in the grounds of the family home. Most of the rooms feel reassuringly new. Accommodation is en suite & has AC (payable). The studios & apartment have a kitchenette & TV. Meals are taken on the terrace, which is decorated with colourful local art. Wi-Fi is free for guests. **$$**

Shoestring

Auberge Anse aux Anglais (21 rooms) Anse aux Anglais; 831 2179, f 831 1973; e aubergehung@yahoo.com; www.aubergehung.free.fr. Coming from Port Mathurin, turn right after Seth mini market & the hotel is on your left. The simply furnished rooms have en-suite facilities & phone, AC or fan, & 2 have a mini fridge. Rooms are spacious with whitewashed walls & a small balcony/terrace. Facilities include a restaurant, an open-air TV lounge & a pool. **$**

Auberge Les Filaos (14 rooms) Anse aux Anglais; 831 1644; f 831 2026; e filaos@intnet.mu; www.filaosetravenal.com. Opposite Auberge Anse aux Anglais, a 10min walk from Port Mathurin. The location is quiet & the gardens are a good place to relax; the beach is about 30m away. There are 10 en-suite rooms & 4 with shared bathroom. Rooms are stark but spacious with ceiling fan & balcony/terrace. There is a simple, clean restaurant & a pool. **$**

Bellevue Guesthouse (8 rooms) Crève Cœur; 831 1665; e gerard07@intnet.mu; www.gitebellevue-rodrigues.com. Set on a hill just east of Anse aux Anglais, overlooking Port Mathurin. M & Mme Edouard offer carefully decorated guesthouse accommodation in the grounds of their home. All rooms have en-suite facilities, kitchenette, & fan or AC. There is a TV in the dining room. The owners are incredibly enthusiastic & eager to please their guests, & Mme Edouard prepares delicious Rodriguan meals. **$**

Chez Claudine (4 rooms) St François; /f 831 8242; e cbmoneret@intnet.mu. In a tranquil spot on one of the island's best beaches. Fantastic views of the ocean & there are some great coastal walks in the area. Rustic rooms with shared bathroom. There is a TV lounge & the *table d'hôte* meals are delicious. Dbl/sgl from €40/20 HB. **$**

Chez Jeanette (Le Tropical) (8 rooms) Mt Bois Noir; 724 2119; f 831 5860; e letropicalchezjeanette@yahoo.com; www.gite-letropical.com. Guests at Chez Jeanette are guaranteed a warm Rodriguan welcome & superb, authentic local cuisine cooked on a wood fire. The house is on a hill overlooking farmland &, in the distance, the ocean. Accommodation is in comfortable, clean en-suite rooms or there is a large house available for rent in the grounds. There is a small disco here, popular with locals. A great option for those seeking a genuine experience of life in Rodrigues. Good value, priced from €30 pp HB. **$**

La Regalade (5 rooms) Anse aux Anglais; 713 8831; e laregalade.mailhos3@gmail.com. Basic accommodation above the restaurant across the road from the sea. Some rooms have space for children, all have en-suite shower room. Breakfast is on the terrace overlooking the ocean & the restaurant is good. The restaurant is also a piano bar so the rooms have the potential to be noisy. **$**

Le Ravenal (5 rooms) Jean Tac; 831 0644; **f** 831 2288; **e** ravenal@intnet.mu; www.filaosetravenal.com. A great accommodation option & excellent value for money, 5min walk from Caverne Provert Beach. A choice of en-suite rooms & 1- & 2-bedroom apartments, all with ocean view & veranda. All rooms are finished to a high standard, especially when compared with many of its competitors. Wi-Fi is free for guests. Home-cooked meals are provided on the terrace of the main house, & excursions can be organised. The pretty garden, panoramic ocean views & pool are an added bonus. **$**

WHERE TO EAT

All villages have a small general store, where you can buy essentials. Larger shops stocking food can be found in Anse aux Anglais, La Ferme and Port Mathurin.

Bear in mind that some restaurants and tables d'hôte may only open for dinner if they have received half a dozen or more reservations.

In family homes

There is nothing like good old home cooking and, luckily for us, some Rodriguan families have opened up their homes for *table d'hôte* dinners. The following will serve up a traditional gastronomic delight if you reserve beforehand. Expect to pay around Rs300 per person for lunch or dinner.

Cases à Gardenias Mt Bois Noir; 832 5751

Chez Claudine St François; 831 8242

Chez Jeanette (Le Tropical) Mt Bois Noir; 831 5860

La Collinière Brûlé 831 8241

Restaurants

Chez Madame Larose Pointe Coton; 876 1350; for lunch daily, dinner on reservation. Cuisine: Rodriguan, seafood. A charming, informal little restaurant just before the Cotton Bay Hotel. Dolly Larose prepares delicious, authentic Rodriguan dishes. **$$**

Coralie La Différence Solitude; 832 1071; 09.00–22.00 daily. Cuisine: Rodriguan, seafood. A smart, modern restaurant, opened in 2008, perched on the hill above Port Mathurin & with spectacular views of the coast. The restaurant prides itself on its seafood dishes & the prawns with garlic butter are a particular favourite. **$$**

Domaine La Détente Eau Claire; 831 2179; for lunch daily, dinner on reservation. Cuisine: Rodriguan, Chinese, seafood. A large restaurant set on a hill with fantastic views of the lagoon & Ile Hermitage. **$$**

John's Resto Mangues; 831 6306; for lunch daily, dinner on reservation. Cuisine: Rodriguan, Chinese, seafood. This well-known restaurant has moved next door to where it used to be. It is nicely decorated & feels modern & clean. Good seafood & generous portions. The *bol renversé* (upside down bowl) crammed with egg, rice & stir fried meat, chicken or seafood is a hearty meal. Main courses from Rs180. **$$**

La Belle Rodriguaise Graviers; 832 4040; www.labellerodriguaise.com. Cuisine: Rodriguan. The restaurant of this small hotel sits on a hill overlooking the ocean. Owner, Françoise Baptiste, is a well-known Rodriguan cook & author of cookery books. *Table d'hôte* meals are prepared using fresh, local ingredients & traditional recipes. Creole cookery courses with Françoise, can be arranged. Reservation recommended. **$$**

La Marmite Resto Crève Cœur; 831 1689; for lunch & dinner daily. Cuisine: Rodriguan, Mauritian & Indian. The owner of this cheerfully decorated restaurant is a schoolteacher during the day & chef by night, cooking with his wife. Good friendly service & great food – most people come back for more. **$$**

La Regalade Anse aux Anglais; 713 8831; **e** laregalade.mailhos3@gmail.com; for lunch & dinner daily. Cuisine: Rodriguan, French. A new (2011) restaurant & bar cross the road from the beach. There is musical entertainment every evening as the French owner, Bernard, is a musician. **$$**

✕ Le Récif Caverne Provert; ☎ 831 1804; ⌚ for lunch & dinner Thu–Tue. Cuisine: Chinese, Rodriguan. Popular, smart place with evening entertainment on the weekends. **$$**

✕ Les Trésors de la Buse Anse aux Anglais; ☎ 876 3534; ⌚ 10.00–15.00 & 17.00–22.00, Tue–Sat, 09.00–12.30 Sun. Cuisine: French, pastries. Not far from Ti Pavillon guesthouse, around 250m from the seafront. In the grounds of a family home. Meals can be eaten on site or taken away. Main courses from Rs200. **$$**

✕ Mourouk Ebony Hotel Pâté Reynieux, Mourouk; ☎ 832 3351; ⌚ daily for lunch & dinner. Cuisine: Rodriguan, seafood. The restaurant at this hotel has a well-deserved reputation for excellent traditional food. Diners can enjoy the panoramic view of one of the prettiest parts of the coast & lagoon. If you are planning a dinner here, consider combining it with one of the hotel's Rodriguan entertainment evenings. **$$**

✕ Valerie's Citronelle; ☎ 832 4350; ⌚ 09.00–18.00 Mon–Sat (except Thu – closed), 09.00–13.00 Sun. As well as selling homemade jams & chutneys, Valerie serves cakes & tea/coffee on her patio overlooking the garden & the ocean. In the afternoon Rodrigues fruit bats fly around the area. **$$**

NIGHTLIFE On weeknights Port Mathurin is transformed into what resembles a ghost town by about 20.30.

There is regular live entertainment (traditional music and dance) at most of the mid-range hotels. The *séga* nights at **Mourouk Ebony** on Wednesday and Saturday are a highlight of a visit to the island.

Safari Bar (☎ *832 1168;* ⌚ *16.00–22.00 Tue–Thu, 21.30–late Fri & Sat*) just east of Port Mathurin is at the heart of the island's nightlife. During the week it is a pub, where people play pool, sing karaoke and catch up with friends. On the weekend the dance floor is the centre of the action. **Waves** nightclub, not far from the airport at Cascade Jean-Louis, is also popular with locals.

SHOPPING Rodrigues is not a souvenir hunter's paradise. That said, there has been a recent growth in the handicraft industry, which today provides employment for some 700 Rodriguans. They're involved in basketry, hat-making, textile-based crafts like embroidery, coconut crafts and jewellery. The Rodrigues branch of the national handicraft centre acts as co-ordinator and facilitates the development of the industry by hosting workshops, seminars and training sessions.

The hats you can buy in Rodrigues are made from fibre of vetyver, pandanus, coconut or latanier leaves. Basketry also utilises bamboo or sisal. Other items made from these materials include cradles, baskets, briefcases, tablemats, lampshades, letter holders and so on. In Port Mathurin, as well as the market, there are several roadside kiosks and curio shops which sell local handicrafts and food preserves, including hellishly hot chillies, mango and tamarind.

When doing your souvenir shopping, bear in mind that it is well worth supporting **CARE-Co** (see box *CARE-Co*, page 230).

WHAT TO SEE AND DO

CAVERNE PATATE There are many caves in the west of the island but Caverne Patate, near Petite Butte, is the largest. The cave is 1,040m long and 18m below sea level. It takes around 45 minutes to do a guided walk through the maze of contorted stalactites and stalagmites. There is no boardwalk, handrail or lighting (torches are available) and the surface is uneven and, in parts, slippery. You will be given a hard hat to wear. When the cave was discovered many bones of the extinct Rodrigues solitaire were found.

Comfortable clothes and sturdy shoes should be worn. The cave is not suitable for those with limited mobility. Guided tours depart daily at 09.00, 11.00, 13.00

and 15.00. Tickets are available on site or from **Discovery Rodrigues** (*Rue de la Solidarité, Port Mathurin;* ☎ *832 1062;* e *discoveryrodrigues@intnet.mu*), which organises excursions to Ile aux Cocos for €3. If you go on an organised excursion, this should be handled for you.

FRANCOIS LEGUAT GIANT TORTOISE AND CAVE RESERVE (*Anse Quitor;* ☎ *832 8141;* f *832 8142;* e *info@torti.intnet.mu; www.tortoisecavereserve-rodrigues.com;* ⏲ *09.00–17.00 daily; admission adult/child Rs155/75 (reserve), Rs280/140 (cave & reserve)*) Guided tours depart at 10.30, 12.30 and 14.30. A popular attraction for Rodrigues, established by the owners of La Vanille Réserve des Mascareignes in Mauritius. Visitors can walk among the giant Aldabra tortoises (*Dipsochelys elephantina*), which roam in plenty of space. There are also Radiata tortoises from Madagascar (*Dipsochelys radiata*). In September 2011, 1,015 baby tortoises had been born at the reserve since January 2008, making a total of around 1,500 tortoises at the reserve. Visitors can sponsor a baby tortoise and receive regular updates on its progress. The reserve is planting native and endemic plants in the area, with the help of the Mauritian Wildlife Foundation. Guided tours through the cave are informative (although can be rather too long); there is a boardwalk, handrail and lighting, but you'll have to negotiate some very narrow gaps during the walk and climb some steep steps. The reserve plans to open another cave more suited to those with limited mobility. There is an excellent museum here, which tells the story of Rodrigues, as well as that of the various extinct species of the Mascarenes. There is a small souvenir shop and a café. You will need to allow around 2½ hours for the reserve and cave visit.

OFFSHORE AND COASTAL EXCURSIONS The excursion to **Ile aux Cocos**, around 4km off the west coast, is unquestionably the most popular day trip available and should cost around Rs700 (including the permit fee for the island). It is a shallow sand bar with coconut palms, casuarina trees and colonies of terns and noddies.

Most hotels and tour operators organise full-day trips, which include a barbecue lunch. Apart from admiring the seabirds you can relax on the unspoilt beach and swim and snorkel in the shallow lagoon.

Certain areas of the island are bird nesting sites and so are off-limits to visitors.

On the return trip the boats head into the wind and the crossing can be long, wet and cold. Some boats now come ashore at Pointe Diable to meet a minibus, which is a more comfortable option.

Discovery Rodrigues (*Rue de la Solidarité, Port Mathurin;* ☎ *832 1062;* e *discoveryrodrigues@intnet.mu*) organises excursions to Ile aux Cocos.

An operator who is regularly recommended as being very flexible and accommodating is **Andy Albert** (☎ *875 8457;* e *andyspirit7@yahoo.com; www.kiterodrigues.skyblog.com*).

Ile aux Chats (Cat Island) is an uninhabited islet in the vast lagoon fronting the Mourouk Ebony Hotel. A full-day excursion there organised by the hotel or a tour operator costs around Rs800 and includes a beach barbecue. You can stop off for diving/snorkelling at Gouzoupa *en route* (see page 229).

SPORTING ACTIVITIES The companies listed in the *Inbound tour operators* section, page 212, can arrange activities such as hiking, fishing and bike rental.

Hiking

There are several possible trails into the interior, where gorges, hills and deep valleys beckon keen hikers. No special skills are required, as grading is mostly moderate or easy.

Some trails commence near the hotels, such as behind the Mourouk Ebony Hotel (Anse Mourouk). The hotels and tour operators will advise keen hikers on routes and can organise local guides.

A 5km trail starts at Anse Mourouk and runs uphill to Grande Montagne. First the trail leads to Montagne Chéri, a viewpoint over the vast lagoon to one side and the Mourouk Gorge on the other. Continue further uphill through a small village, with a few houses and herds of goats and cattle. The last part of the trail covers wooded terrain and ends at the broad, paved road leading to the Grande Montagne police station. The trail can be done in reverse for those who don't want to walk continuously uphill. Public bus services are available at either end of the trail.

Mount Limon and Mount Malartic offer good opportunities for hiking, while the pristine beach of Trou d'Argent is a fairly easy 30-minute walk from the coastal village of St François. Other good walks include Port Mathurin to Grand Baie and on to Pointe Coton and Port Mathurin to Baie du Nord.

Guided hikes can be organised by the inbound tour operators (see page 212). Eco-évasion (for contact details see page 212) offers guided hikes in the island's nature reserves for Rs250 per person.

Mountain biking Mount Limon and Mount Malartic offer good mountain biking. For bike hire, contact **Club Osmosis** (*Mourouk Ebony Hotel, Pâté Reynieux;* ☎ *832 3051;* **f** *832 3355;* **e** *osmosis@intnet.mu; www.osmosis-rodrigues.com*).

Ziplining A series of ziplines span the ravines in the southeast of the island and offer spectacular views of the lagoon. The approach doesn't fill you with confidence, being through a field and with a meeting point under a pandanus tree but rest assured the course was created by an experienced Frenchman, who has installed similar ziplines in Mauritius. Tour operators and hotels can arrange ziplining or you can call direct (*Tyrodrig;* ☎ *499 6970; www.ican.ws/pages/tyrodrigpag.html;* ⏲ *09.00–17.00 daily*).

Windsurfing/kitesurfing Available through **Club Osmosis** (for contact details, see *Mountain biking* above).

Tryst Kitesurfing Safari (Andy Albert) ☎ 875 8457; **e** andyspirit7@yahoo.com; www.kiterodrigues.skyblog.com.

Deep-sea fishing Rodrigues can now claim three fishing world records, including a 561.5kg Pacific blue marlin caught there in January 2007.

BDPM Mont Fanal; ☎/**f** 831 2790; **e** birgit.dirk@intnet.mu

Blue Water Fishing Anse aux Anglais; ☎ 831 0919; **e** bluewater@intnet.mu

Rod Fishing Club Johnston St, Port Mathurin; ☎ 875 0616; **e** contact@rodfishingclub.com; www.rodfishingclub.com

Glass-bottom boat (☎ *777 0475*) Departs from Anse Enfer, near Mourouk. Costs from Rs1,500 including lunch.

Scuba diving and snorkelling Having never been affected by industrial pollution, the reefs around Rodrigues offer rewarding scuba diving and snorkelling. Many people believe that the underwater experiences to be had there are superior even to those around the outer Seychelles or Maldives. Furthermore, some insist that divers need not even use scuba gear, because even without it they can see such a stunning array of underwater life.

Snorkelling excursions can be arranged by many of the island's hotels and cost around Rs200 per person. This includes boat trips to and from the reefs.

The island's dive sites and dive centres are best suited to qualified divers with a reasonable amount of experience. Rodrigues lacks the shallow, clear, sandy-bottomed sites which beginners need and the instructors at the dive centres tend to focus on leading rather than teaching. However, some of the dive centres do offer resort courses for beginners.

Warning to divers Scorpionfish, lionfish (firefish) and stonefish are all common around Rodrigues and are highly venomous. Striped catfish and banded eels are present too. Wear gloves as protection from anemones on wrecks and watch out for black-spined sea urchins.

Dive centres The dive centres below offer a range of diving options and packages. The following is a rough guide to the prices you can expect to pay:

Single dive	Rs920 (qualified)
Beginner's resort course (pool lesson and sea dive)	Rs1,400
Night dives	Rs2,000
Five-dive package	Rs5,400

These rates include equipment.

Bouba Diving Centre Mourouk Ebony Hotel, Pâté Reynieux; ☎ 832 3351; f 832 3355; e ebony@intnet.mu. Run by NAUI instructor Benoît de Baize. Fully equipped to cater for 6 divers at a time.

Cotton Dive Centre Cotton Bay Hotel, Pointe Coton; ☎ 831 8001; f 831 8003; e diverod@intnet.mu; closed Jul/Aug. Run by Jacques & Marie-Jose Degremont (CMAS 2-star instructor & CMAS-3 star diver, respectively); both are PADI dive masters. A well-run outfit with well-maintained equipment & good safety awareness. Caters for 8 divers at a time. Prices on request from the dive centre.

Eco-évasion Pointe Monier, Port Mathurin; ☎ 875 8481; e rpayandee@hotmail.com; www.rodrigues-eco-evasion.com. Run by Richard Payandee, a CMAS 2-star instructor & PADI dive master. Offers diving & snorkelling trips, boat trips to the outlying islands & guided nature walks.

Rodriguez Diving Anse aux Anglais; ☎ 831 0957; e rodiving@hotmail.com; www.rodriguez-diving.com

Top dive sites

Grande Paté Near Port Mathurin, this site is outstanding for its coral gardens at depths of 8–28m.

Grand Bassin Beyond the waters of the pass, there are some superb sites at around 20–25m with large table corals. Occasional sightings of white-tipped reef sharks, large groupers and jacks are reported. The two islets of **Ile aux Sables** and **Ile aux Cocos** lie within an extensive fringing reef and can be visited at high tide. Both offer good diving and snorkelling, but go with skippers familiar with the area or else the chances of being shipwrecked are alarming here.

Pointe Coton At depths of 4–5m the diving is spectacular.

Off Port Sud-est People dive in the passage near the entrance to the barrier reef. Diving is best along the cliff, at 4–18m.

Gouzoupa Opposite Mourouk Ebony Hotel, this is an excellent site (depth 2–17m). There is a good chance of seeing large shoals of jacks, parrotfish and surgeonfish,

CORALS OF RODRIGUES

Tom Hooper

The corals on the reef slopes of Rodrigues are in very good condition, with around 140 different species of coral represented. Compared with places such as Indonesia or the Great Barrier Reef, this biodiversity is quite low. A coral reef is made up of countless individual animals called polyps. These invertebrate animals manufacture their skeleton from calcium in the seawater.

The following species are commonly found in Rodrigues:

ACROPORA This is the fastest-growing coral. With a very light and delicate skeleton the fingers of some branching shapes can grow 10cm a year. This group has a wide variety of shapes with forms which are branching, mounds, fingers and flat plates.

FAVIA This coral grows in huge mounds known as 'massive' formations. When alive it is a brown or green colour. Its polyps are translucent and come out at night to feed. They are very sensitive and can quickly retract back into the skeleton if they sense movement such as a fish about to take a nip of their tentacles.

FUNGIA These are called mushroom corals as they resemble field mushrooms with their disc shapes and radiating vanes. This coral has only one polyp with many bright green tentacles. Unlike other corals, this one does not stay cemented to the reef, but is free living and will be moved around by the waves.

GONIASTREA This is one of the toughest corals and is often found in places where other corals cannot survive. It can tolerate long exposure to the sun and muddy conditions. The skeleton looks a bit like honeycomb.

PAVONA Has a form which resembles leaves. The corallites are on both sides and have a very clear spider shape. They are brown in colour and are often found in muddy habitats such as around the channel at Port Mathurin, which is quite unusual for corals.

POCILLOPORA This is a coral with very fine branches. Sometimes these corals are a beautiful pink colour. Their bumpy corallites can look like popcorn!

PORITES This group are often large, rounded and dense balls. They are very slow growing, with a coral taking up to 50 years to reach the size of a football. Some huge colonies which reach the size of a car are thousands of years old and are sometimes cored to yield climatic information.

STYLOPHORA These corals live all around the tropics. Their larvae can travel for hundreds, if not thousands, of miles.

and the area is rich in branching and other formations of coral. There are currents, so the site is best visited when there is little tide and conditions are calm.

Grand Baie Has excellent varieties of coral and fish (depth 2–20m).

Shipwrecks There are many wrecks around the reefs which ring Rodrigues. Those around the southern reefs include *Quatre Vingt Brisants*, *Clytemnesra* (1870)

CARE-CO (RODRIGUES)

CARE-Co, formerly known as Craft Aid, is a non-profit, non-government organisation with a centre for handicapped people (blind, deaf and physically handicapped) founded in 1989 by Paul Draper MBE, one of two British expats living on the island.

The project's aim is to provide creative and remunerative employment, as well as education, for people with disabilities. There are no shareholders in the organisation, and profits are shared among the workforce. Surplus is reinvested.

Suzanne Auguste, originally from Scotland, is the second British expat living on the island and runs the educational aspect of the project, the Gonzague Pierre-Louis Centre. The school, which opened in 1994, is privately run for hearing and visually impaired children who, because of their handicap, are unable to benefit from the formal education offered by their local primary school. The centre also provides the island's only hearing and sight tests. Suzanne is qualified to carry out hearing tests, but since there is no optician on the island specialists must come over from Mauritius. All the equipment, books and stationery are financed by private donation.

After completing their education, the youngsters are employed in the CARE-Co workshop and receive all the conditions of employment that anyone else would.

The only items made on Rodrigues which are sold further afield than Mauritius are the jewellery made at the CARE-Co Centre. The items are made from coconut and include a variety of necklaces, hair slides, bracelets, earrings (for pierced and non-pierced ears), brooches, key rings and pendants. They are all very striking. Fencing, souvenirs, handicrafts and furniture are also made.

Latest on the agenda is a project involving Rodriguan honey. The honey has already had huge success and won second prize at the international London Honey Show in 2000 and third prize in 2001. With 45 employees, CARE-Co is one of the island's largest private-sector employers. Production activities are carefully chosen to fit in with the ability of the handicapped people to manage the work. The human benefits of CARE-Co both to individuals and Rodriguan society are evident but immeasurable.

To arrange to visit the CARE-Co workshop at Camp du Roi in Port Mathurin contact Beverley Betsy or Suzanne Auguste (☎ *831 1766;* **f** *831 2276*). There are two CARE-Co shops where you can purchase jewellery and souvenirs, one adjoining the workshop and one in Johnston Street. The shops and the workshop are both open 08.00–16.00 Monday–Friday, while the Rue de la Solidarité shop is also open 08.00–12.00 Saturday (closed Sunday and public holidays).

For further details of how you can help CARE-Co's vital work, see *Chapter 2, Travelling positively*, pages 83–4.

and *Nussur Sultan*. Northwest of Port Mathurin are the *White Jacket* (1871) and *Traveller*.

BEACHES Aside from **Ile aux Cocos** and **Ile aux Chats**, the best beaches on Rodrigues itself are on the east coast at **Pointe Coton**, **Mourouk** and around **St François**.

The coastline between St François and **Graviers** is dotted with beaches, which are usually deserted. There are no roads in this part of the island and a walk along this coast is perfect for those in search of solitude, privacy and relaxation. To walk from St François to Graviers takes around three hours. You will need sturdy shoes: it is hilly in parts and involves some clambering over rocks.

You can get to the long, unspoilt beach of St François by bus or car, from where a 30-minute walk through the casuarina trees will take you to the small scallop-shaped cove of **Trou d'Argent** ('Silver hole'). This scallop-shaped beach sheltered on either side by black rock appears in just about all the island's tourism marketing material. The path continues south of Trou d'Argent to another beautiful cove, **Anse Bouteille**, which, as its name suggests, is in the shape of a bottle. This coast can be windy and the sea is often rough but the sheltered Trou d'Argent and Anse Bouteille are usually calm enough for swimming.

Part Four

REUNION

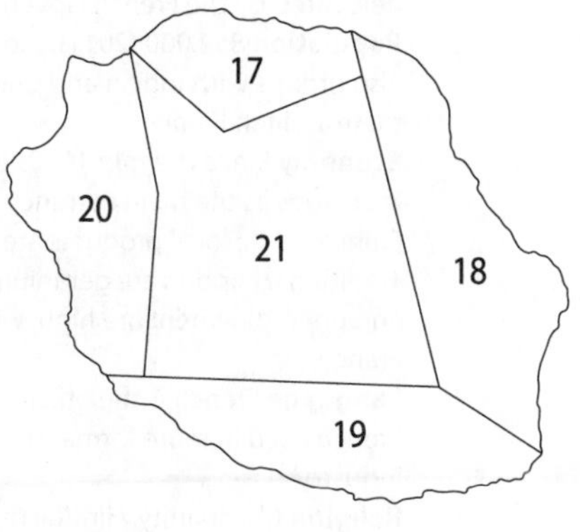

REUNION AT A GLANCE

Country An overseas department of France
Location Island in the western Indian Ocean, south of the Equator and north of the Tropic of Capricorn
Size 2,512km^2
History Discovered by Arab and Malay sea traders around the 10th century, then by the Portuguese. In 1642, it was annexed for France but remained uninhabited. The first settlers were exiled from Madagascar in 1646. After Napoleon Bonaparte surrendered to Britain in 1810, Britain received Réunion but showed no interest in the island and never assigned a governor to it. The island was handed back to France after the Treaty of Paris in 1814. In 1848, the island's name was changed from Ile Bonaparte to Réunion. On 19 March 1946, Réunion was declared a Département d'Outre-Mer (overseas department) and it remains one of France's last colonies.
Climate The island features some 200 microclimates. Broadly speaking, the climate around the coast is tropical while in the mountainous uplands it is temperate. The hot and rainy summer lasts from November to April, while the remaining months are cooler and drier. Cyclones may occur from January to March.
Nature Réunion has the highest mountains in the Indian Ocean, one of the world's most active volcanoes, more remaining natural forests than on the other Mascarenes, black volcanic beaches in the south and east, white sandy beaches on the west coast, coral reefs, rare birds and waterfalls in abundance.
Visitors 471,268 tourists in 2011, 81% from France. Visitors come all year round; busiest times coincide with French school holidays.
Capital St-Denis
Government The island is administered by a *préfet* (prefect), who is delegated by the French Government
Population 852,000 (2011), mostly Creole (blend of Franco-Africans, but also groups with Indian and Chinese origins). Substantial community of metropolitan French.
Economy Since the mid 1990s tourism has taken over from traditional industries as the main currency earner. Most goods are imported from France, while local products are exported to France by agreement. Traditional exports are geranium and vetyver oils, sugar and vanilla. Inflation and unemployment are high, with rates exceeding those of mainland France.
Language French is the official language. Creole spoken in daily life but French used in more formal situations. English barely spoken outside tourist industry.
Religion Christianity, Hinduism, Islam, Buddhism. Some islanders adhere to tribal lore.
Currency The euro (€)
Rate of exchange £1=€1.27, US$1=€0.81, Rs38=€1 (August 2012)
International telephone code +262
Time GMT+4
Electricity 220 volts
Weights and measures Metric system

14

Background Information

GEOGRAPHY

Réunion is situated in the western Indian Ocean, 700km east of Madagascar. Mauritius, the nearest of the Mascarenes, lies 200km to its northeast.

Réunion's volcanic birth is estimated to have started some 2½ million years ago. First to rise up from the Indian Ocean floor was its oldest and highest peak, the formidable Piton-des-Neiges (Snow Peak – 3,069m), said to have become extinct about 500,000 years ago. It is the highest mountain in the western Indian Ocean but, despite its name, snow is very rarely seen on its peak.

More recently (about 380,000 years ago), the aptly named Piton-de-la-Fournaise (Furnace Peak) evolved. It stands at 2,631m and is one of the world's most active volcanoes. Since 1998, the volcano has erupted almost every year. The lava tends to flow down the eastern slope of the volcano, spilling into the sea and modifying the coastline with every eruption. The 2007 eruption, one of the largest recorded, added some 200ha to the island's area.

The two mountain ranges and three vast natural amphitheatres known as 'cirques' (Cilaos, Mafate and Salazie) account for much of the island's rugged interior. Converging at the 2,991m summit of Le Gros Morne, the amphitheatres give Réunion its wildly dramatic appearance, as well as breathtaking hiking trails, waterfalls, forests and gorges. Its landscapes are remarkable and over 40% of the island has been designated a UNESCO Natural World Heritage Site.

Réunion retains more original forest than do the other Mascarenes. Where there are accessible tracts of arable land, fields of geranium, vetyver and sugarcane are cultivated. Tucked away between the ravines, on small patches of level ground called *ilets*, are vineyards and lentil fields.

The inhospitable interior means that the majority of the population is concentrated in towns along the narrow coastal plains. Réunion does not have the abundance of wide sandy beaches that Mauritius enjoys but there are both black- and white-sand beaches along the west and south coasts. Coral reefs and lagoons are also dotted along the west and south of the island.

CLIMATE

The island lies in the path of moist tropical weather pattern circulations, rainfall being highest in the eastern region. In fact, a world record for rainfall of over 12m in a year was claimed in the 1980s for Takamaka, a gorge in Réunion's interior uplands.

Waterfalls are numerous and a prominent feature of the scenery, especially in the many steep ravines. In the amphitheatre of Salazie, for example, there are around 100 waterfalls, plunging like silvery ribbons down sheer, green cliffs.

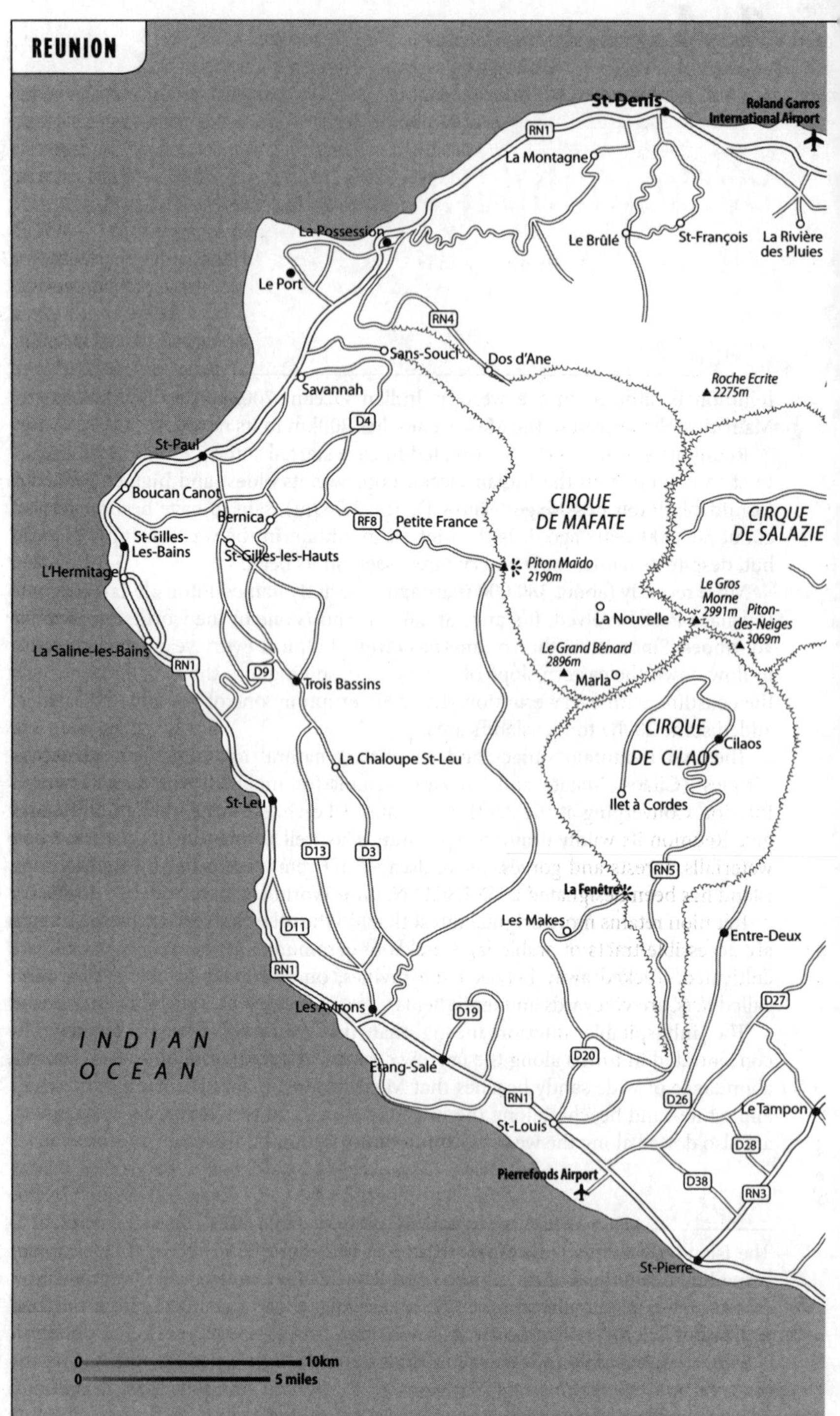
REUNION
St-Denis
Roland Garros International Airport
RN1
La Montagne
La Possession
Le Brûlé
St-François
La Rivière des Pluies
Le Port
RN4
Sans-Souci
Dos d'Ane
Roche Ecrite 2275m
Savannah
D4
St-Paul
Boucan Canot
CIRQUE DE MAFATE
CIRQUE DE SALAZIE
Bernica
RF8
Petite France
St-Gilles-Les-Bains
St-Gilles-les-Hauts
Piton Maïdo 2190m
L'Hermitage
Le Gros Morne 2991m
Piton-des-Neiges 3069m
La Nouvelle
La Saline-les-Bains
RN1
Le Grand Bénard 2896m
D9
Trois Bassins
Marla
CIRQUE DE CILAOS
Cilaos
La Chaloupe St-Leu
St-Leu
Ilet à Cordes
D13
D3
RN5
La Fenêtre
Les Makes
D11
Entre-Deux
RN1
D27
Les Avirons
D19
INDIAN OCEAN
Etang-Salé
D20
RN1
D26
Le Tampon
St-Louis
D28
Pierrefonds Airport
D38
RN3
St-Pierre
0 10km
0 5 miles

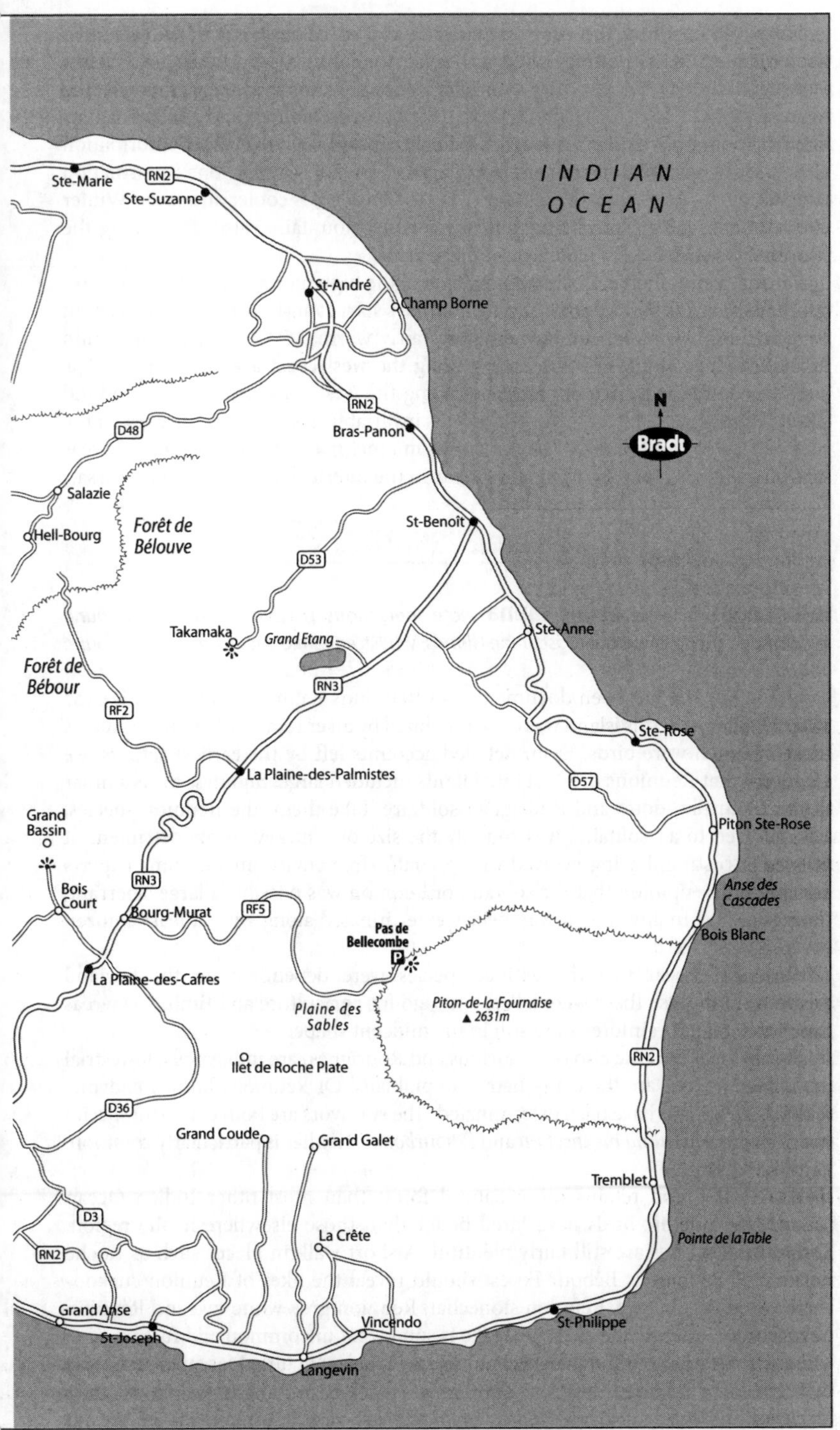
INDIAN OCEAN
Ste-Marie
RN2
Ste-Suzanne
St-André
Champ Borne
RN2
Bras-Panon
D48
Salazie
Hell-Bourg
Forêt de Bélouve
D53
St-Benoît
N
Bradt
Takamaka
Grand Etang
Ste-Anne
Forêt de Bébour
RN3
RF2
Ste-Rose
La Plaine-des-Palmistes
D57
Grand Bassin
Piton Ste-Rose
RN3
Bois Court
Anse des Cascades
RF5
Bourg-Murat
Bois Blanc
Pas de Bellecombe
P
La Plaine-des-Cafres
Plaine des Sables
Piton-de-la-Fournaise
▲ 2631m
RN2
Ilet de Roche Plate
D36
Grand Coude
Grand Galet
Tremblet
D3
La Crête
Pointe de la Table
RN2
Grand Anse
St-Joseph
Vincendo
St-Philippe
Langevin

The weather along the coast is pleasant almost all year round, although in winter the southeasterly trade winds can make the south coast unbearably blustery. Summer, which is hot and humid, is from November to April with rains peaking from January to March. Cyclones may strike between January and March, as they may in the whole of the western Indian Ocean region. (For more information on cyclones in the Mascarenes, see pages 4–5. For the cyclone information telephone line, see page 251.) Winter (May to October) is cooler and drier. Winter temperatures, aside from being very low in the mountains, also drop along the windward east coast.

During winter nights, frost and ice occur in the high mountains as temperatures fall to freezing point. In the interior, winter days start at around 4°C, rising to about 15°C by midday, whilst summer days are fairly warm, 15°C in the morning and up to 25°C by midday. Temperatures along the west coast average around 21°C in winter to 31–35°C in summer. Skies along the west coast are usually clear and sunny, whereas a blanket of mist and clouds invariably descends over the rest of the island in the mid-afternoon. The numerous microclimates mean that when there is rain on the coast it can be completely clear in the interior uplands, and vice versa.

NATURAL HISTORY AND CONSERVATION

FAUNA

Indigenous and endemic fauna

Note 'indigenous' pertains to something found in Réunion and on the other Mascarene Islands, whilst 'endemic' means something found only in Réunion.

Surprisingly little has been documented of Réunion's natural history. Just like the other Mascarenes, this island was once inhabited by an ensemble of animal oddities, most of which were birds. From detailed accounts left by the earliest settlers, we can glean that Réunion's original inhabitants included large, flightless birds similar to the Mauritian dodo and Rodriguan solitaire. Like them, the Réunion species, also referred to as 'solitaire', was roughly the size of a turkey. To its detriment, it was very trusting, having evolved in a predator-free environment. Some experts are now of the opinion that the solitaire of Réunion was possibly a large, aberrant, terrestrial ibis. In any case, it was swiftly exterminated along with at least a dozen other endemic birds.

It would appear that the extinct species were dependent on the lowland rainforests, because these were felled long ago for agriculture and timber, whereas Réunion's upland rainforests are still in magnificent shape.

Absent (as is the case also on Mauritius and Rodrigues) are indigenous, terrestrial mammals; neither are there any native amphibians. Of Réunion's known endemic reptiles, all but two have been exterminated. The survivors are both colourful species of day gecko: *Phelsuma inexpectata* and *P. bourbonas*. Neither is particularly common.

Birds As Réunion retains more natural forest than most other Indian Ocean islands, its endemic birds have fared better than those elsewhere in the region. Today, nine species are still fairly plentiful. A short walk in places such as Roche Ecrite or the fabulous Bébour Forest should reveal the likes of Réunion cuckoo-shrike, Réunion bulbul, Réunion stonechat, Réunion grey white-eye and Réunion olive white-eye. Only the cuckoo-shrike is somewhat uncommon and furtive.

Easier to see in Réunion than on Mauritius is the elegant little Mascarene paradise flycatcher. The land bird best known to locals is the Réunion harrier, a handsome black-and-white raptor often seen soaring over lush vegetation in search of prey. It is also found on Madagascar but is less common there. Locally, it is known as the *papangue*. Also shared with Mauritius is the Mascarene swiftlet, flocks of which can be seen wheeling energetically around their nesting caves.

Two small, threatened seabirds are high on the lists of visiting birders: the Réunion black petrel (*Pterodroma atterima*) and the Barau's petrel (*Pterodroma baraui*). Both are virtually confined to Réunion and breed in the inhospitable heights of Piton-des-Neiges, which they leave just before dusk for nocturnal foraging jaunts far out at sea.

Sometimes, however, fledgling petrels which are not familiar with artificial lights in coastal buildings fly into the buildings. Many are killed in this way and a campaign is under way to foster an awareness of the petrels' plight. People are requested, if they find injured petrels, to bring them to local experts who then treat and release the birds back into the wild. Owing to their rarity, the precise nesting locations of these petrels are kept secret, known only to a few dedicated ornithologists.

A third highly localised, small seabird is the Mascarene shearwater (*Puffinus atrodorsalis*), thought to inhabit only the Mascarenes and Comoros.

The national bird is the white-tailed tropic-bird, or *paille en queue*, often seen flying gracefully in the vicinity of its sheer nesting cliffs.

FLORA Nobody who visits the lush montane forests in places such as Bébour-Bélouve, La Roche Ecrite, Cilaos (Plateau du Matrum), Salazie and Maïdo can fail to leave impressed. The same applies to the heathlands higher up, such as those of Brûlé de St-Paul, Maïdo and Grand Bénard, at about 1,600–2,400m.

Thanks to the inaccessibility of most of the interior uplands, large tracts of Réunion's original forest still remain intact. The habitat types which have suffered most at the hands of man are lowland evergreen rainforests (everywhere, but especially in the eastern half) and the much drier scrub and woodlands of the west. Some 98,972ha of forest are under the care of the Office National des Forêts (ONF), which controls about 39% of Réunion. The French state presides over the coastal environment. The island's only nature reserve is Mare Longue.

Réunion has some 700 indigenous plant species, of which 161 are endemic. There are several impressive botanical gardens around the island, where endemic and indigenous plants can be seen. At the Conservatoire Botanique Nationale deMascarin, above St-Leu, visitors can enjoy guided walks around the gardens with experienced botanists or ecologists (see page 327).

A USEFUL PEST: GOYAVIER

Considering the large number of invasive exotic plants which have run rampant in Réunion, it is refreshing to note that one of these pests, the goyavier (*Psidium cattleyanum*), is actually extremely useful.

Introduced from eastern Brazil, the goyavier is a fairly nondescript shrub which grows to a height of 8m. Its deep red fruit somewhat resembles a miniature guava. It is an excellent source of vitamin C.

After being picked, the fruit tastes quite acidic, but innovative Réunionnais have found many uses for it.

For starters, goyavier cocktails are hallucinatory! Alternatively, try the exceedingly potent rum punch flavoured with it. Goyavier jam, too, is really tasty. So significant has this fruit become in Réunion, that there is even a two-day Goyavier festival, held every June in La Plaine-des-Palmistes.

Commonly seen on the forest floor in humid places is the fern *Marattia fraxinea*. It is shared with Mauritius, Madagascar and the Comoros. Much more impressive is the tree fern *Cyathea borbonica*, which dominates the 5,146ha Bébour-Bélouve forest area. It attains a height of 10m and is also found in Mauritius. One bamboo, *Nastus borbonicas*, is endemic and easily identifiable by its papyrus-like clusters of leaves.

In dry western Réunion are two endemic succulents, although they aren't common. The one you're most likely to see is the aloe, *Lomatophylum locrum*, which bears yellow and dull-orange flowers.

There are many orchids endemic to the western Indian Ocean islands and, of these, some seven species are unique to Réunion. Most are now very rare. Indigenous orchids tend to have white blooms, with many flowering from December to March. *Angraecum mauritanium* is also found in Mauritius and, like other 'comet' orchids, it features a very long spur. Presumably, it is pollinated by hawk moths as other 'comet' (angrecoid) orchids are. *Aeranthes arachnites* is less showy and is shared with the other Mascarenes. The diminutive *Bonniera appendiculata* is extremely rare and endemic, with blooms shaped like a very thin starfish.

Some of the palms local to the Mascarenes are on the verge of extinction. An exception is the attractive *Hyophorbe indica*, endemic to Réunion. Today, it's still quite plentiful. The same applies to the large, endemic 'latanier rouge' (*Latania lontaroides*), which has fan-shaped leaves with a distinct reddish hue. However, the 'white palm' (*Dictosperma album*, also found in Mauritius) is virtually extinct in the wild, because it is often used for heart of palm salad. That said, it has been cultivated very successfully.

Hibiscus are well represented in the Indian Ocean islands. Two rare species are unique to Réunion and Mauritius. Both are now protected. *Hibiscus boryanus* has scarlet or orange-red flowers, while those of *H. columnarus* are a bright yellow.

The shrub *Ruizia cordata* is possibly Réunion's best-known endemic, because it is used as a 'flagship' species, to educate the public about the plight of endangered life forms. It is highly endangered and its silvery leaves are used in certain Tamil rituals. Unfortunately, researchers have not yet determined what the shrub's pollinators are.

Foetidia mauritanium is an endemic hardwood used for construction. Its pungent wood is apparently not attacked by termites, hence its popularity, and as a consequence, its rarity. The silvery endemic tamarind, *Acacia heterophylla*, is abundant and it is the preferred wood for furniture production.

Two endangered shrubs – *Pouzolia laevigata*, used for treatment of fever, and *Obetia ficifolia*, which is shared with Rodrigues – are known to have their own, specific pollinator butterfly species. The extreme rarity of these shrubs means that their pollinator butterflies are also endangered.

HISTORY

From about the 10th century, Arab and Malay traders occasionally stopped by on Réunion. They never settled because the island lacked a large harbour and protected lagoons, which featured so prominently on Mauritius.

The Portuguese were the next to arrive. First was explorer Tristan da Cunha, who accidentally landed in the area in 1507 and named the island Santa Apollonia. In 1512, Pedro de Mascarenhas renamed it Mascareigne, the name still applied to the island group as a whole. The Portuguese did not settle.

The first French arrival was in 1642, when a French East Indiaman landed, planted the French flag and departed. The French, meanwhile, had claimed nearby

Madagascar, where they established several ill-fated settlements, notably in the giant island's southeast at Fort Dauphin.

It was from Fort Dauphin that Réunion's first settlers came, in 1646. The then governor of Madagascar, Sieur Pronis, exiled a dozen-odd troublesome Frenchmen to Réunion. They were left there to fend for themselves and lived in caves around what is now St-Paul.

A fleet of five French ships brought more settlers in December 1649. The island's name was then changed to Ile Bourbon, after Colbert Bourbon, who had founded the French East India Company. Twenty French volunteers and 42 Malagasy slaves, under Etienne de Regnault, established the island's first permanent settlement.

By the late 1600s, Réunion had become a prominent pirate base, as international seafaring riff-raff realised the island was conveniently removed from the French military machine. Well-known pirate captains (including the likes of Captain William Kidd) ruled that no weapons were to be brought ashore and that no treasure was to be buried on the island. In 1713, the French East India Company arrived in full force, sinking many of the pirate vessels. Aiming to make the island profitable, they set up a garrison and brought in hundreds of African and Malagasy slaves from 1715 to 1730, despite contravening their own regulations by doing so. The slaves were put to work on coffee, cotton and spice plantations.

In 1735, Bertrand Mahé de Labourdonnais arrived in the Mascarenes to administer Ile Bourbon and Ile de France (Mauritius) simultaneously, on behalf of the French East India Company. He was responsible for a mini industrial revolution in Réunion, building schools, roads, clinics and a successful export

THE ABOLITION OF SLAVERY: A UNIQUE CASE

Abolition of slavery on this particular French colony proved to be a convoluted process. Initially, slavery had been banned outright in 1794 by the First French Republic. But slave owners balked, maintaining that one stroke of a pen could not simply eliminate all their investments involved in labour purchases (at least not without compensation). Napoleon therefore reinstated slavery.

When the French monarchy was abolished in 1848 and the Second Republic came into being, the question of banning slavery arose once again in the light of the French motto – 'Liberty, Equality , Fraternity'.

So on 27 April 1848, slavery was abolished for a second time, but with the necessary compensation to slave owners. When the French commissioner arrived on 13 October to announce the new law, he was refused permission to set foot on the island. The following day, he declared that although slavery had been abolished according to the law passed in April, slaves would have to return to work and finish harvesting the crops; only after that was their freedom to be discussed.

This situation was strikingly different from those in Martinique and Guadeloupe, where slaves heard about the new law on 22 May and immediately demanded instant freedom, announcing that they would never again work as slaves. To drive the point home, they promptly set about burning down some of their (former) owners' houses and business premises.

Eventually, on 20 December 1848, slavery on Réunion was abolished in practice. Former slaves were not only granted liberty, but France also gave them equality, as citizens with full civil rights.

infrastructure. Labourdonnais held his position until 1746, when he left for India. In June 1764, the French East India Company collapsed and the French crown assumed control of its assets. Ile Bourbon was virtually forgotten during the French Revolution. It then fell under the jurisdiction of the Colonial Assembly and, in 1794, was finally renamed Ile de la Réunion. Slavers who had not been ousted from their feudal landlord positions insisted on referring to it as Ile Bonaparte, after Napoleon.

In 1806, Réunion's agriculture was devastated by a cyclone and the island was rendered wholly dependent on France. Four years later, after Napoleon surrendered to British forces, Réunion was ceded to Britain. On 9 July 1810, the British navy arrived and set about establishing a Royal Marine garrison. They did not assign a governor to Réunion, preferring to invest effort and resources in Mauritius and the Seychelles. Following the signing of the Treaty of Paris (1814) by the British and the French, Réunion, then known as Ile Bonaparte once again, was handed back to France.

France invested heavily in the island: towns were established, the sugar industry was developed and immigration was actively encouraged. With the birth of the Second French Republic in 1848, the name 'Réunion' was reinstated. Slavery was abolished in 1848, spelling the liberation of some 63,000 slaves (see box *The abolition of slavery: a unique case*, page 241). The subsequent lack of labour meant that the Colonial Assembly indentured Indians, Chinese and Arabs between 1848 and 1855.

From 1850 to 1870, the island flourished and the economy boomed, thanks to the sugar industry and the island's location on the trade routes between Europe, India and the Far East. This period of prosperity was followed by a dramatic decline, attributable to two main causes. Firstly, the opening of the Suez Canal in 1869 removed the need for ships to circumnavigate Africa in order to reach the Far East. Secondly, the use of sugarbeet in Europe, in lieu of expensive imported sugar, dealt a severe blow to the sugar industry. An exodus to Europe ensued.

The two world wars drained Réunion significantly. In World War I, about 15,000 Réunionnais left to fight in Europe. During World War II, Nazi Germany blockaded the French island colonies. Consequently, nothing left or arrived in Réunion for two years and the island declined into a state of famine. By the end of 1942, that abominable blockade was broken. On 9 March 1946, the French Government officially declared Réunion a Département d'Outre-Mer. Today Réunion remains a department of France and thereby a member of the European Union.

GOVERNMENT AND POLITICS

Réunion, together with Martinique, Guadeloupe, French Guiana and Mayotte, is a French Département d'Outre-Mer (DOM), or overseas department. It is administered by a *préfet* (prefect), who is appointed by the French Government. The island elects five deputies to the National Assembly and three representatives to the Senate. General and Regional councils for Réunion are elected every six years.

As in Mauritius, the white and Indian communities are substantially better off than the Creole population, which causes underlying socio-economic tensions. The economic well-being of Réunion and containment of these tensions depends heavily on continued financial assistance from France. Although there are groups who would like to see independence for Réunion, the majority of the population is aware that this would mean forfeiting the significant financial benefits of their association with France, something which they are not prepared to do.

ECONOMY

In many ways Réunion is similar to Hawaii in terms of its economic history, although unlike Réunion, Hawaii had a native population when it was discovered by Westerners. Réunion was first settled by a small group of Europeans, who subsequently brought in large numbers of slaves to work plantations of coffee and spices. Attention was then turned to sugar.

Following the abolition of slavery in 1848, Tamil labourers were recruited. In the late 19th century, Chinese and Muslim (Gujarati) immigrants came. Like Hawaii, Réunion began exporting sugar and fruit, particularly pineapples. Floriculture (notably of anthuriums) was developed, as were fisheries and tourism. Today, the fishing and tourism industries are still growing, not yet having been developed to their full potential.

FISHERIES Réunion's fishing industry has benefited greatly from the fact that stocks in the Indian Ocean are in better condition than in other waters. Tuna and swordfish are filleted and exported by airfreight to France, Italy and the UK. Red tuna is exported to Japan, a new market for the island. Réunion also has some barren islets around which Patagonian toothfish and lobsters are caught and frozen for export.

SUGAR The only agricultural industry in Réunion which has been developed to its full potential (in terms of land usage and technology) is the sugar industry. It accounts for around 25% of the island's agricultural production and provides income for some 5,000 small-scale farmers. The island's mountainous interior means that only a narrow strip of land between the coastline and interior is suitable for agriculture – around 20% of the island's land area. The sugarcane grown on these slopes plays an important part in reducing erosion. Réunion sells its sugar above world market prices, which is possible because the industry is heavily subsidised.

TOURISM The target that Réunion hoped to achieve by the year 2000 was only 500,000 tourists per annum. They fell slightly short with 430,000 arrivals and the number was down to 380,500 in 2007. The fall was largely attributed to the follow-on effect of the chikungunya virus outbreak of 2006 (see box on page 58). In 2011, 471,268 tourists landed in Réunion. Of the total number of visitors, almost half stayed with friends or family. Despite efforts to encourage more English-speaking and German tourists, the vast majority (81%) are from metropolitan France.

At present, tourism is the industry which holds the largest potential for growth. The limited amount of English spoken on the island is a stumbling block, although attempts are being made to increase English teaching in Réunion and to expose Réunionnais students to anglophone countries by sending them on exchange visits. And I have to say, in the 15 years that I have been visiting Réunion the amount of English spoken by those working in tourism has noticeably increased.

Also standing in the way of tourism development is the limited number of airlines flying to Réunion. Almost all long-haul flights are via France or Mauritius. Réunion is very under-marketed in the anglophone world and in the Far East; few people outside France even know of its existence.

FOOD Réunion's food industry is flourishing. Foodstuffs exported are largely tropical fruits, spices and rum. Business is booming for the local gift parcel courier service, Colipays, which delivers parcels of fruit, sweets and flowers around the world. Most are sent to France, either by Réunionnais who have relatives there or by expatriate French.

Concerns like Coca-Cola arrived in the 1950s, to be followed later by other soft drinks, alcoholic beverages and a range of dairy products. Many are now manufactured locally under French patents.

UNEMPLOYMENT There is a very high rate of unemployment in Réunion, currently around 30% but as high as 60% in the 15–25 age bracket. According to the French Catholic dictum, the lowest economic strata in society must not be left in the lurch. So even if people don't have jobs, they are still provided with homes and are accorded a set minimum revenue (the Revenue Minimum d'Insertion), which enables them to survive. This leads to many people not really needing or wanting to work and increasingly those who do go out and find jobs do so for the sake of dignity, not finances. That said, almost half the population lives below the poverty line. One sees fewer people out on the streets in Réunion than is the case in Europe, not simply thanks to the RMI but also because there is still a strong sense of family solidarity in Réunion. People will take in the homeless.

In February 2012 riots broke out across the island, protesting unemployment, high fuel prices and the high cost of living. Buildings were damaged, cars set on fire and police injured; riot police were flown in from mainland France.

PEOPLE

The faces of today's Réunionnais attest to the racial diversity of their ancestors. About 40% of the population is Creole (of mixed African/European origin), while Europeans make up around 35%, Indians 20% and Chinese 3%.

It is often hard to pinpoint the ethnic origin of Réunionnais, but colloquial terms are freely used by the locals to describe themselves: a *Cafre/Cafrine* is a black man/woman of African origin, a *Malbar/Malbaraise* is an Indian man/woman,a *Yab* is a white Creole, usually from the interior, and *Zarab* refers to a Muslim. The locals refer to the white French who live on and visit the island as *Zoreilles*, which literally means 'ears' in Creole. The word is thought to originate from the French slavers straining to understand the Creole spoken by their slaves. Some believe in a less palatable explanation – that the French used to cut off the ears of their slaves, who therefore referred to the whites as *Zoreilles*.

LANGUAGE

As in Mauritius, the Creole language is a powerful unifying force amongst Réunionnais of every ethnic origin. French is the island's official language and is spoken by the majority of the population in formal situations, but amongst friends and family the user-friendly Creole is favoured. It is not identical to the Creole of neighbouring Mauritius but there are similarities as both derive largely from French with some African, Malagasy and local terms thrown in. There is no grammar and the language is written phonetically, according to the writer's whims.

Réunionnais have been battling for some time to have Creole recognised as a language and taught in schools. When I taught in Réunion it was very clear that the pupils confused Creole and French without realising it, thereby dragging their marks down when it came to examinations (which are all taken in French). Many people campaigned for Creole to be taught in schools so that children would grow up treating it as a separate language from French. Thankfully, in 2002, the first trainee teacher of Creole qualified at the University of St-Denis and Creole is now an optional subject on the school curriculum.

Although it is taught in schools, very little English is spoken in Réunion. Anglophone visitors are still a novelty, so locals patiently make every effort to help and to understand those who struggle to communicate in French.

For some handy Creole phrases see *Appendix 1, Language*, page 347.

RELIGION

The majority of the population (about 86%) is Roman Catholic. Many of the island's towns are named after saints, and roadside shrines line every route. However, many Réunionnais follow more than one religion. For this reason, Tamil festivals, such as Cavadee, and Hindu festivals, like Dipavali, are celebrated with great enthusiasm. Chinese New Year is also welcomed with a great deal of noise and festivities.

Some descendants of the Malagasy still practise ancient rites, like summoning the spirits via a living family member, particularly on All Saints' Day, the Christian festival. You may come across people who have been baptised into the Roman Catholic Church and who go to Mass, but seek help from a Malagasy spirit or Hindu god in times of trouble.

Sorcery (*gris gris*) is also practised on the island. In St-Pierre, the grave of the famous sorcerer and murderer, Sitarane, continues to be visited by those seeking his assistance (see box *Le Sitarane*, page 309).

Roadside shrines where the colour red dominates are a familiar sight in Réunion. They are dedicated to Réunion's national saint, Saint Expédit, who is usually depicted as a Roman legionnaire. The saint is revered by Réunionnais of all faiths, who generally turn to Saint Expédit when they want revenge or to put a curse on someone. It is fascinating how an originally Christian concept has been distorted to incorporate beliefs in sorcery and superstition (see box *Saint Expédit*, page 343).

EDUCATION

The education system is on the French model, with primary schools, *collèges* (10–15 years) and *lycées* (15–18 years). State-run schools in Réunion suffer from the same problems as those in mainland France (*la Métropole*), such as overcrowded classes, underfunding and poor morale amongst teachers. Both teachers and pupils follow French counterparts by striking at regular intervals.

The University of St-Denis gained university status in 1982 and offers a good range of courses, including modules in Creole studies, Creole-language classes and tropical environment studies. There are around 12,000 students at the university.

It is possible for foreign students to study at the University of St-Denis on an exchange programme, although competition for places can be fierce. The ERASMUS programme allows students already at university in the European Union to study for a year in another European university, which of course includes St-Denis. Speak to your university or contact the University of St-Denis (*0262 938322;* **f** *0262 938006;* **e** *contact@univ-reunion.fr; www.univ-reunion.fr*). The International Student Exchange Programme provides similar opportunities for students in the US. For more information visit www.isep.org.

CULTURE

While Réunionnais are quite happy to refer to themselves using terms linked to their ethnicity (see *People*, page 244), ethnic and cultural distinctions are more blurred on Réunion than they are in Mauritius, largely because mixed marriages have long been practised. Ubiquitous alongside the African and Indian cultures are elements of French culture. However, while Réunionnais may support France in sporting events, there is a degree of resentment towards '*les métropolitains*' or '*zoreilles*' (French mainlanders).

Music and food are important elements of Creole culture, and loyalty to family and friends is highly valued.

MUSIC Music is an important part of life in Réunion and enjoys considerable government funding aimed at keeping Creole culture alive. The main traditional styles are *séga* and *maloya*, which stem from the island's African roots. These are often blended with modern European styles. The *séga* is shared with Mauritius, although each island has its own variations.

Séga blends tropical rhythms with European instruments like violin, accordion and the banjo. The songs usually deal with slavery, island life and romance. *Maloya* was born in the slave communities of the 18th century, and the lyrics traditionally express misery and anger. The rhythm is African and the instruments are percussion. Vocals tend to be plaintive and repetitive, and the style is often compared to the blues. For many years it was forbidden to sing *maloya* in public but those days are gone and recently *maloya* has enjoyed a surge in popularity. The best-known *maloya* artists include the late Gramoun Lele and Daniel Waro. Leading popular bands who combine *maloya* with other (Western) styles are Ti Fock (jazz *maloya*), Baster and Ousa Nousava (electric *maloya*), and Natty Dread (local reggae).

Séga and *maloya* are combined with reggae to produce *séggae* and *maloggae* respectively. Popular Mauritian musician Kaya was a pioneer of *séggae* until his controversial death in 1998 (see box *Kaya*, page 167). *Zouk*, from the Caribbean islands, is also popular and frequently played in nightclubs. It has a slower rhythm than *séga* and *maloya* and romance is usually the theme.

Réunion regularly hosts music festivals combining performances by foreign and local artists. Best known of these is KabaRéunion, held each October over ten days to celebrate the World Music Movement. Visitors may also have the opportunity to attend one of the numerous concerts simply entitled '*Kabar*', which are organised by associations, clubs, neighbourhoods or private individuals. These are normally free and feature mostly unknown musicians from Réunion. The atmosphere is decidedly 'underground'.

ARCHITECTURE European settlers brought with them European styles of architecture, which can now be seen side by side with traditional Creole buildings. In some cases, the two styles are blended in the one building. Both Mauritian and Réunionnais Creole architecture utilise the *lambrequin*, a carved wooden or metal fringe adorning the roof.

Thanks to energetic conservation efforts on the part of the French Government, Creole architecture tends to be better preserved in Réunion than it is in Mauritius. Particular efforts have been made to restore and maintain Réunion's many delightful *'ti cases*, the humble dwellings of ordinary Creole families. These are typically small, single-storey, wooden homes painted in bright colours, featuring shuttered windows, a corrugated-iron roof and decorative *lambrequin*. The best examples of these are found in Hell-Bourg, Entre-Deux, Cilaos and Rivière St-Louis.

15

Practical Information

WHEN TO VISIT

Cyclone season, January to March, is best avoided. Even if a cyclone does not strike, rains are plentiful at this time. If hiking is on your itinerary, you may prefer to visit in winter (April to October) as trails can become impassable after the heavy rains of summer. Accommodation for hikers becomes very booked up during the winter, so try to book well in advance.

The other factor to consider is the French school holidays. Flights and hotels tend to be very full at any time which coincides with school holidays in mainland France (*la Métropole*): Christmas, Easter and from July to September.

HIGHLIGHTS

Unlike most island destinations, it is Réunion's interior, not its coastline, that draws visitors back year after year.

HIKING For many, hiking is *the* reason for visiting Réunion, which boasts over 1,000km of well-maintained trails. The island's three **cirques**, formed by the collapse of ancient volcanic craters, are a hiker's dream, with spectacular mountainous scenery punctuated by thundering waterfalls. **Mafate** is the most remote of the cirques and only accessible on foot or by helicopter. It can, however, be seen from the spectacular viewpoint at **Piton Maïdo**. For non-hikers the cirques are still a 'must-see', not least for their spectacular scenery and cool, clean mountain air. The cirques of **Cilaos** and **Salazie** can be reached by road. The pretty town of Cilaos is set in a basin surrounded by mountains and is known for its thermal springs. Salazie is the wettest and greenest of the cirques, with numerous waterfalls and pretty Creole villages, such as **Hell-Bourg**, rated one of the most beautiful in France.

High on your list of things to do in Réunion should be hiking around **Piton-de-la-Fournaise**, one of the world's most active volcanoes – provided it's not erupting at the time, of course. Keen hikers will also enjoy the two-day climb of **Piton-des-Neiges**, which can be timed so you arrive at the summit to watch the sun rise over the Indian Ocean.

If hiking doesn't appeal or you are short of time, you needn't miss out on seeing the interior – **helicopter rides** over the island are becoming increasingly popular.

ADVENTURE SPORTS Réunion offers all manner of adventure sports and **activities** – climbing, canyoning, mountain biking, horseriding and paragliding to name but a few. For water-based activities try **scuba diving** at St-Gilles-les-Bains or **surfing** at St-Leu.

CULTURE Those seeking culture will be spoilt for choice. The **Creole people** are incredibly friendly and only too happy to share aspects of their culture with visitors. Music and dance are central to Creole life. Head to a nightclub in St-Pierre, or a live show, and locals will be glad to teach you to dance the *séga*, *zouk* or *maloya*. You can't leave Réunion without sampling the delicious **Creole cuisine** – try *cari ti-jacques* or *rougail saucisses*. Follow your meal with a *rhum arrangé* (fruit-infused rum). There are festivals all year round: highlights include **Tamil fire walking** ceremonies and the **Abolition of Slavery** celebrations on 20 December.

SUGGESTED ITINERARIES

Thanks to the well-maintained coastal road, you can drive around the island in one day but there is plenty to see along the way so allow more time if you can. A one-week stay will suffice for most visitors, especially those combining Réunion with another destination, such as Mauritius or Madagascar. However, if you are planning to spend several days hiking, or a few days relaxing on the beach at the end of your visit, you will need to allow two weeks.

ONE WEEK Most visitors will arrive at the airport in **St-Denis**, where you can pick up a hire car and begin exploring. If you are willing to brave the traffic, have a quick look around the capital, which offers a European café culture in a tropical setting and some good examples of colonial and Creole **architecture**. Continue on to the beach resort of **St-Gilles-les-Bains** for two nights, making sure you get the chance to snorkel in the lagoon at L'Hermitage. Get up early on the first morning and drive up to **Piton Maïdo** for spectacular views of the **Cirque de Mafate**.

Head to **Cilaos** – the long, hair-raising drive means you will need to spend at least one night. The following morning, hike one of the shorter trails, such as Bras Rouge, which takes you to a waterfall. If you have longer than one week on the island, hikes up the extinct **Piton des Neiges** start here and you can spend a night at the *gîte* at the base of the summit before getting up early to climb to the top in time for sunrise.

From Cilaos head back down to the coast and spend the night at **St Pierre**, the hub of the south coast. It has a lively nightlife, some great **restaurants** and the daily **markets** are one of the best places on the island to pick up souvenirs. If you can time your visit to include the large Saturday morning street market, all the better.

From St Pierre head up towards the volcano, **Piton-de-la-Fournaise**, and spend the night at one of the nearby hotels ready for an early start and a climb to the rim of the crater.

Return to St Pierre and head eastwards, through **St Joseph** and along the east coast. Between **St-Philippe** and **Ste-Rose** is where you will see the remnants of past **lava flows** and the path they took down the eastern face of Piton-de-la-Fournaise to the sea. The coast in this area is rugged – lava cliffs constantly pounded by the ocean. Don't miss **Piton Ste Rose**, where lava has skirted around the church.

Spend two nights in the **Cirque de Salazie**, at the delightful village of **Hell-Bourg**. Take in the fresh mountain air, explore the cirque and perhaps have a go at canyoning.

Returning to the coast, continue north back to St Denis, stopping off at **St-André** to learn about **vanilla** production.

TOURIST INFORMATION

Marketing the island as a tourist destination is the responsibility of Ile de la Réunion Tourisme, based in St-Denis at Place du 20 Décembre 1848 (*0262 210041;* **f** *0262 210021;* **e** *resa@reunion-nature.fr; www.reunion.fr*).

Ile de la Réunion Tourisme works in conjunction with French tourist offices abroad, which should be able to give you information and advice on Réunion prior to departure.

It publishes numerous useful information booklets on the island, including the invaluable *Run Guide*, which contains contact details of hotels, restaurants, tourist attractions, activity operators, etc. Its website (*www.reunion.fr*) is also packed with information. (For other useful websites see *Appendix 2, Further information*, pages 349–52). Everyday enquiries during your stay on the island should be directed to the regional tourist offices. There are 17 of these, located in each of the major towns on the island (see *Tourist information* in the relevant town description).

FRENCH TOURIST OFFICES Information about any of the following tourist offices can be found on www.franceguide.com.

UK Lincoln Hse, 300 High Holborn, London WC1V 7JH; +44 90 6824 4123; **f** +44 20 7061 6646; **e** info.uk@franceguide.com

Australia Level 13, 25 Bligh St, Sydney NSW 2000; +61 2 9231 5244; **f** +61 2 9221 8682; **e** info.au@franceguide.com

Canada 1800 Av McGill College, Suite 1010, Montreal, Quebec H3A 3J6; +1 514 288 2026; **f** +1 514 845 4868; **e** canada@franceguide.com (office not open to the public)

Germany Postfach 100128, D-60001 Frankfurt **f** +49 69 7455 56; **e** info.de@franceguide.com (office not open to the public)

South Africa Block C, Morningside Cl, 222 Rivoniq Rd, Johannesburg; +27 1 02 05 02 01; **f** +27 1 02 05 02 03; **e** info.za@atout-france.com

Spain C/Serrano, 16–3 Izq, 28001 Madrid; +34 93 302 0582; **f** +34 91 541 2412; **e** info.es@franceguide.com

USA **e** info.us@franceguide.com

TOUR OPERATORS

Tour operators specialising in the Indian Ocean islands are able to secure special low-cost airfares to Réunion, as well as competitive rates on accommodation. Many offer a stay in Réunion combined with a visit to Mauritius, the Seychelles or Mayotte. Unfortunately, there are few tour operators outside France that offer package holidays to Réunion. Some of these are listed below.

UK

Onyx Travel 26 Woodford Cl, Caversham, Reading RG4 7HN; 0118 947 2830; **f** +44 118 946 3104; **e** information@onyxtravel.co.uk; www.onyxtravel.co.uk

Partnership Travel White Lion Hse, 64a Highgate High St, London N6 5HX; +44 20 8347 4020; **e** info@partnershiptravel.co.uk; www.partnershiptravel.co.uk

Rainbow Tours 305 Upper St, London N1 2TU; +44 20 7666 1250; **e** info@rainbowtours.co.uk; www.rainbowtours.co.uk

AUSTRALIA

Beachcomber Tours 10/5 Canopus St, Bridgeman Downs, Queensland 4034; +61 7 3353 6204; **f** +61 7 3353 6214; **e** info@beachcomber.com.au; www.beachcomber.com.au

FRANCE

Kuoni various offices; www.kuoni.fr

Nouvelles Frontières various offices; www.nouvelles-frontieres.fr

GERMANY

Alizee Kirschbaümleboden 30, D-79379 Mühlleim; ☎ +49 7 641 954 8890; **f** +49 7 6311 0721; **e** info@alizee-reisen.de; www.alizee-reisen.de

Trauminsel Reisen Summerstr 8–82211, Herrsching; ☎ +49 8 1529 3190; **f** +49 8 1529 31920; **e** info@trauminselreisen.de; www.trauminselreisen.de

ITALY

Cormorano Via de Santis SNC, 58015 Orbetello; ☎ +39 5 6486 0309; **f** +39 5 6486 3848; **e** info@cormoranoviaggi.eu; www.cormoranoviaggi.eu

SOUTH AFRICA

Animal Tracks & Island Ventures 17 David Pl, Glendower, Edenvale 1610; ☎ +27 11 454 0543; **f** +27 11 454 2365; **e** info@animaltracks.co.za; www.animaltracks.co.za

Sun & Sandals PO Box 2513, Edenvale 1610, Johannesburg; ☎ +27 11 616 4825; **f** +27 110866725965; **e** info@sunandsandals.com; www.sunandsandals.com

RED TAPE

ENTRY REQUIREMENTS The entry requirements for Réunion are the same as those for France. Holders of European Union passports do not need a visa for a stay of up to three months but do need to carry a valid passport or identity card. Other nationalities require a visa. The French Embassy or Consulate in your home country will be able to provide up-to-date information and handle visa applications. All visitors must be in possession of a return ticket.

STAYING ON Those who do not need a tourist visa but who wish to stay longer than three months should apply for a *carte de séjour* (residence permit). French bureaucracy makes this far harder than it should be and applications are usually only accepted if you have been offered a job on the island or cannot leave for medical reasons. You will need to go to the *Préfecture* in St-Denis armed with copious documents, including certified translations of your birth certificate, a letter from your potential employer, passport photos, etc. The requirements change regularly so it is best to check with the Service d'Etat Civile et des Etrangers at the *Préfecture* (☎ *0262 407777; www.reunion.pref.gouv.fr;* 🕘 *08.00–13.00 Mon–Fri*).

IMMIGRATION There are two channels – one for European Union passport holders and one for all other nationalities. Staff are generally efficient.

CUSTOMS Incoming visitors are permitted to import free of duty the following:

Cigarettes	200
Spirits	1 litre
Wine	2 litres of wine, ale or beer
Perfume	50g of perfume and 25cl of eau de toilette
Coffee	500g
Tea	100g
Medicines	Quantities corresponding to the duration of stay

Plants and animals The importation of plant material, dairy and meat products is prohibited.. For enquiries, contact the Direction des Services Vétérinaires (☎ *0262 486132*); they also handle requests for the importation of pets. Cats and dogs must be microchipped, have a valid anti-rabies certificate and health certificate. Other requirements vary depending on the country of origin.

HELP

CONSULAR HELP As Réunion is not an independent country, few countries have diplomatic representation on the island. The following are honorary consulates:

Germany 9c Rue de Lorraine, 97400 St-Denis; ☎0262 216206; f 0262 217455; e h.mellano@wanadoo.fr

India 266 Rue Maréchal Leclerc, 97400 St-Denis; ☎0262 417547; f 0262 210170; e congendia@guetali.fr

Mauritius 20 Rue Tessan, 97490 Ste-Clotilde; ☎/f 0262 296305

Netherlands 135 Av Principale, 97450 St-Louis; ☎0262 548418; f 0262 269149

Norway 43 Rue Paul Verlaine, BP111, 97823 Le Port; ☎0262 433048; f 0262 432248

Switzerland 107 Chemin Crève-Cœur, 97460 St-Paul; ☎/f 0262 455574; e poldestpol@wanadoo.fr

UK St-Denis; ☎0262 347576; f 0262 348015

In the event of a serious problem, British and American visitors should contact their respective embassies in Paris. The country code for telephoning France is +33.

UK 35 Rue du Faubourg, St-Honoré, 75383 Paris; ☎01 44 51 31 00; f 01 44 51 31 27

USA 2 Av Gabriel, 75008 Paris; ☎01 43 12 22 22; f 01 42 66 97 83

EMERGENCY SERVICES

Police ☎17 (emergency); ☎0262 907474 (non-emergency)
Ambulance ☎15
Fire service ☎18
Coastguard ☎0262 434343
Mountain rescue ☎0262 930930

OTHER USEFUL TELEPHONE NUMBERS

Directory enquiries ☎12
Weather forecast ☎3250 (from a land line); ☎0892 680808 (from a mobile phone)
Cyclone information ☎0897 650101
Volcano information ☎0262 275292; ☎0262 275461 (recorded message)
Hiking trail information ☎0262 373839
Traffic information ☎0262 972727

GETTING THERE AND AWAY

BY AIR The majority of visitors arrive by air, from Africa, Europe or other Indian Ocean islands. The main airport is Roland Garros International Airport, which is 11km east of the main town, St-Denis (see pages 252–3). The airport at Pierrefonds, in the south of the island, only handles flights within the Indian Ocean. For more information, see page 253.

From Europe

From Europe The only direct flights from Europe to Réunion are from France and take 11 hours from Paris. A number of airlines have introduced flights from regional airports in France. These flights are considerably more expensive during high season, ie: French school holidays. If you are travelling from any other part of Europe you will need to fly to France to connect with an onward flight. However, most airlines offer special fares for the flight to Paris if you are carrying on to Réunion. Alternatively, you could fly to Mauritius and on to Réunion from there.

Air France Twelve flights per week from Paris to St-Denis.

Air Austral Eleven flights per week from Paris, two flights per week from Lyon, Bordeaux, Nantes and Marseille.

Corsairfly Daily flights from Paris.

From Africa

Air Austral Up to two flights weekly from Johannesburg. Also flights from Madagascar (Antananarivo, Nosy Be, Dzaoudzi and Tamatave).

Air Madagascar Several flights per week from various destinations in Madagascar, including Antananarivo, Nosy Be and Tamatave.

From the Indian Ocean islands

Air Austral Several flights daily between Mauritius and St-Denis. Daily flights from Mauritius to Pierrefonds. Also ten flights per week from Mayotte and two from the Comoros (Moroni) to St-Denis; one flight per week from the Seychelles.

Air Mauritius Several flights daily between Mauritius and St-Denis. Daily flights from Mauritius to Pierrefonds.

From the US To Paris by any airline and then as above. Air Mauritius can arrange visits of two to three days to Réunion as extensions to holidays in Mauritius. For Air Mauritius details, see pages 50–2.

From Australia Weekly flights with **Air Mauritius** to Mauritius from Melbourne and Perth, then on to Réunion. **Air Austral** offers flights from Sydney to Paris via St-Denis, two or three times weekly.

Airline offices in Réunion

Air Austral 4 Rue de Nice, 97400 St-Denis; ☎ 0262 909090; f 0262 909091; e reservation@air-austral.com; www.air-austral.com. Also at 14 Rue Archambaud, 97410 St-Pierre; ☎ 0262 962696; f 0262 354649; e saintpierre@air-austral.com.

Air France Indian Ocean Office, 7 Av de la Victoire, BP 845, 97477 St-Denis; ☎ 0820 820820; f 0262 403840; www.airfrance.re. Also at 73 Rue Luc Lorion, 97410 St-Pierre; ☎ 0820 820820.

Air Madagascar 31 Rue Jules Auber, 97461 St-Denis; ☎ 0892 680014; f 0262 218568; e contact@airmadagascar.com; www.airmadagascar.com

Air Mauritius 13 Rue Charles Gounod, 97400 St-Denis; ☎ 0262 948383; f 0262 412326; www.air-mauritius.com. Also at 7 Rue François de Mahy, 97410 St-Pierre; ☎ 0262 960600; f 0262 962747.

Corsairfly 2 bis Rue Maréchal Leclerc, 97400 St-Denis; ☎ 0820 042042; f 0262 488013; www.corsairfly.com

BY SEA Few cruise ships stop off at Réunion, although the number is rising. Lots of glamorous French yacht owners keep their vessels in St-Gilles-les-Bains and may be looking for crew if you're lucky. Try asking at the local tourist office or around the port, where everyone seems to know each other.

For details of regular sea links between Mauritius and Réunion, see page 53.

ON ARRIVAL/DEPARTURE

ROLAND GARROS INTERNATIONAL AIRPORT The airport, which is named after a French aviator born in Réunion (1888–1915), is 11km east of St-Denis (☎ *0262 488068;* e *arrg.dir@reunion.cci.fr; www.reunion.aeroport.fr. For flight information,* ☎ *0262 281616*). Although relatively small, this is a well-organised airport. There are souvenir shops, a post office, a bank and ATMs in the entrance hall of the terminal building. The bank and post office are open on weekdays and Saturday mornings, but close for lunch. There is also a very helpful tourist information desk with lots of leaflets, including the invaluable *Run Guide*. Next to the desk is a touch-screen information point – follow the instructions on the screen and it gives you details of hotels (which you can then telephone free), transport, entertainment, etc. The restaurants and bars are upstairs, and there is rather pricey internet access and free Wi-Fi. The departure lounge has a duty-free shop and snack bars. The main car-hire companies, including Budget, Avis, Hertz and Europcar, are represented at the airport, with offices in a separate building on the right-hand side of the car park as you exit the terminal building. See *Car hire*, pages 56–7 for further details.

Luggage Baggage reclaim is located just beyond immigration. For a trolley you will need a €1 coin, which you will get back when you return it.

Getting to your hotel There is a shuttle-bus service (*navette*) between Roland Garros International Airport and St-Denis city centre, which makes around 12 return trips daily between 07.00 and 19.45. The journey takes around 20 minutes and costs from €4.

A taxi to the centre of St-Denis costs from €20. Fares are higher after 20.00. If you can't find a taxi, which may be the case on a public holiday or at night, ☎ 0262 488383.

PIERREFONDS AIRPORT The south of the island is now conveniently linked to neighbouring Indian Ocean islands by flights to and from Pierrefonds Airport, 7km west of St-Pierre (☎ *0262 968000;* e *info@pierrefonds.aeroport.fr; www.grandsudreunion.org. For flight information,* ☎ *0262 967766*).

A regular bus service connects the airport to St-Louis and the main bus station in St-Pierre; the journey takes 20 minutes and costs €5. Buses leave St-Pierre 1½ hours before each flight departs and leave the airport one hour after each flight arrives. Taxis between the airport and St-Pierre cost around €15.50. Car rental can also be arranged in the terminal building.

HEALTH

Although there are mosquitoes on Réunion, they are not malarial so you don't need prophylaxis. However, watch out for malarial symptoms developing if you've just arrived from a malarial area such as Madagascar.

No inoculations are compulsory but medical practitioners may recommend those for hepatitis A, typhoid, tetanus, diphtheria and polio.

Medical care is excellent, conforming to French standards throughout the island. For hospital treatment you need to be referred by a doctor – ask at your hotel or look in the *Yellow Pages* (*Pages Jaunes*). You can usually turn up at a doctor's surgery and be seen fairly promptly without an appointment. Medical care is expensive and European visitors should carry a European Health Insurance Card in order to take advantage of reciprocal agreements and to claim refunds of fees. The form can be obtained from post offices in your home country or online (*www.ehic.ie*).

Water is officially safe to drink throughout the island but can cause minor upsets. It's best to stick to mineral water, which costs around €1.20 per two-litre bottle, and avoid ice in drinks. You should be particularly careful to avoid tap water after heavy rains or cyclones, as the supply can be contaminated. As with any tropical country, try to peel or wash fruit before eating it.

As in Mauritius, there is an uncomplicated attitude to sex, and AIDS has arrived on the island.

SAFETY

Violent crime is rare. However, there are some nasty tales of hikers disappearing in the cirques, particularly Mafate. If you plan to hike it is best to go in a group and make sure that you tell someone what route you are taking and how long you expect to be away. Be wary in bars and nightclubs as a large number of both locals and visitors tend to drink excessively, which can lead to tension. As in Mauritius, stray dogs can be a problem, particularly as they tend to hang around in packs. As well as being a potential danger to pedestrians, they can cause traffic accidents, so be wary whether on foot or in a vehicle. There are usually one or two shark attacks off the coast of Réunion each year and the number is on the rise, so avoid swimming alone or at the mouths of rivers. Lagoons are the safest places.

WOMEN TRAVELLERS

Women attract a lot of unwanted attention in Réunion. A pair of sunglasses can be very helpful as it enables you to avoid eye contact. Women should not walk alone at night. Knowledge of French or Creole helps in such situations and a few firm but polite words are usually sufficient. There have been incidences of women being attacked on quiet stretches of beach (even during the day), so try to remain within sight of other people.

DISABLED TRAVELLERS

Réunion is better equipped than neighbouring Mauritius for disabled travellers. By law, all hotels of a certain size and classified three star or above must have some rooms equipped for the disabled. However, some hotels with fewer than three stars also have rooms for the disabled.

GAY/LESBIAN TRAVELLERS

In recent years the island's tourism board has instigated a big push for Réunion to become more gay friendly. Many tourism companies, in particular hotels, have signed Réunion's Gay Friendly Charter and carry a gay-friendly certification, which can assist gay and lesbian travellers in choosing their accommodation. There are plenty of gay-friendly bars and nightclubs, particularly in St-Denis, St-Pierre and St-Gilles-les-Bains. In the broader community, however, homophobia exists and travellers should avoid public displays of affection.

TRAVELLING WITH KIDS

Unlike Mauritius, only a handful of hotels have kids' clubs but most of the hotels are child friendly and some offer a baby-sitting service. Accommodation designed for hikers is less likely to be kitted out for children. Being part of France, the infrastructure is good, and there are large supermarkets stocking baby paraphernalia. The main car-hire companies can supply car seats at additional cost.

WHAT TO TAKE

Don't forget that Réunion is part of France so visitors from EU countries should carry a European Health Insurance Card (see *Health*, page 253).

Credit cards are widely accepted and travellers' cheques and cash easily changed at the many banks. You should be able to buy everything that you need in Réunion, although it is likely to be more expensive than in your home country. Mosquito repellent and suncream are essential. Sockets take two-pin continental plugs, so carry an adaptor if necessary.

Take light, comfortable clothing, with a smart-casual outfit for dinner in hotels. Include beachwear for the coast, not forgetting beach/swimming shoes to protect your feet from sea-urchin spikes and sharp coral. Some warm clothing will come in handy for the evenings, particularly in the interior. For the mountains (which can get very cold) you'll need rain gear and really warm clothing; and also good hiking boots if you plan to explore the trails.

As ever, travel insurance is essential. If you plan to partake in any of Réunion's many activities, such as canyoning or paragliding (see *Chapter 16, Activities*, pages 269–77), make sure your travel insurance covers this.

MAPS Tourist maps of the island are available at tourist offices (see page 249 for contact details); many hotels also have a supply. Tourist maps, including ones showing the main hiking trails and *gîtes*, are available online (*www.reunion-nature.com,* under *infos pratiques/cartes*). For hikers, map 4402 RT is widely available in Réunion and should be sufficient for most routes. However, if you want detailed maps for hiking, it's best to get them in advance: contact the Institut Géographique National, 107 Rue de la Boétie, 75008 Paris, France. For more information, see *Hiking*, pages 269–72.

MONEY

The main French banks, such as Crédit Agricole and BNP Paribas, have branches in all the main towns. Banks are generally open 08.00–16.00 Monday–Friday. ATMs are widespread on the coast and you can withdraw money using Visa, MasterCard, Cirrus and Eurochèques. Credit cards are widely accepted in shops, restaurants and hotels. If you're travelling to the interior, take sufficient cash with you as there are very limited banking facilities.

The currency exchange rates in August 2012 were as follows: £1=€1.27, US$1=€0.81, Rs38=€1.

BUDGETING

Réunion is an expensive destination because so many goods are imported but with careful planning travelling costs can be kept down. Markets and roadside stalls sell fruit, vegetables and handicrafts at very reasonable prices. Eating out in restaurants is not cheap but *camions bars* (mobile snack bars) are a good option for those on a budget, serving everything from *samoussas* to pizzas.

You can keep accommodation costs low by staying in *meublés de tourisme* (self-catering holiday rentals, referred to in Réunion as 'furnished flats'), *chambres d'hôtes* and *gîtes* (see *Accommodation*, pages 259–61). There is an excellent, inexpensive bus service. *Taxis collectifs*, which take passengers until the car is full, are far cheaper than ordinary taxis as you pay a proportion of the fare.

If you are staying in one of the island's more upmarket hotels, expect meals and drinks to be pricey. Bars and nightclubs are also expensive: most clubs charge around €12–15 for entry and drinks are often around €8.

Finally, you are bound to be tempted to try some of the many outdoor activities on offer in Réunion, so allow for some extra expenses.

INBOUND TOUR OPERATORS Inbound tour operators meet visitors on behalf of hotels and overseas tour operators. They can arrange transport, accommodation, excursions and activities with multi-lingual guides. Here is a selection.

Bourbon Tourisme 14 Rue Rontaunay, 97463 St-Denis; ☎ 0262 330870; **f** 0262 330879; **e** bourbon.tourisme@travel-run.com; www.bourbontourisme.com

Comptoir Corail 12 Pl des Coquillages, Boucan-Canot, 97434 St-Gilles-les-Bains; ☎ 0262 338838; **e** comptoircorail@orange.fr; www.comptoircorail.com

Connections Réunion 53 Route de Domenjod, 97490 Ste-Clotilde; ☎ 0262 931398; **f** 0262 931399; **e** resa@connections-reunion.com; www.connections-reunion.com

Mille Tours 9 bis Rue Sarda Garriga, 97460 St-Paul; ☎ 0262 225500; **f** 0262 456590; **e** milletours.individuel@wanadoo.fr; www.milletours.com

Nouvelles Frontières Résidence Claire, 31 Pl Paul Julius Bénard, 97434 St-Gilles-les-Bains; ☎ 0262 331199; **f** 0262 331198; **e** receptif.run@nouvelles-frontieres.fr

Objectif 46 Bd Hubert Delisle, St-Pierre; ☎ 0262 330833; **f** 0262 242680; **e** objectif.reunion@wanadoo.fr

COACH TOURS

Transports Souprayenmestry 2 Chemin Souprayen, Ravine à Marquet, 97419 La Possession; ☎ 0262 448169; **f** 0262 449162; **e** transports-souprayenmestry@wanadoo.fr. Offers guided tours in comfortable, AC coaches. They leave early in the morning, picking up passengers from all the main towns along the west coast, from St-Pierre to St-Denis. There are various tours offered each week, such as Salazie, Piton-de-la-Fournaise, Cilaos & the island tour. Ask at the nearest tourist office or contact them directly.

Groupe Transports Mooland ZI Bel-Air, BP24, 97899 St-Louis; ☎ 0262 913939; **f** 0262 913938; **e** s.fontaine@transports-mooland.fr; www.groupetransportsmooland.fr. Offers a good range of tours.

Moutoussamy et Fils Rue des Limites, 97412 Bras-Panon; ☎ 0262 729080; **f** 0262 729081; **e** moutoussamyetfils@wanadoo.fr. Also offers a good range.

DRIVING Réunion's roads are overcrowded. Driving through towns such as St-Denis and St-Pierre during peak hours can be exasperating. The coastal road between St-Leu and St-Gilles-les-Bains is prone to very heavy traffic and there are invariably long queues around L'Hermitage. In 2009, a new road was constructed between St-Paul and L'Etang-Salé-les-Bains, designed to bypass the towns of the west coast and alleviate the traffic pressure on the area. It has achieved that to a certain extent, but this area still sees a lot of traffic.

Driving is on the right and road markings are as in France. The roads are well maintained but the standard of driving is frighteningly bad at times. Every year over 100 people are killed on the island's roads and the situation is not improving. For many young Réunionnais a car is a status symbol and they seem to believe that the faster they drive, the more their image benefits. The speed limit on the dual carriageway that runs along much of the west coast is 110km/h, although you wouldn't know it. Drink-driving is a real problem and some people even smoke *zamal* (locally grown marijuana) whilst at the wheel. Stray dogs also cause their fair share of accidents, so keep your eyes peeled. Don't be put off hiring a car! It is one of the best ways to see the island and gives you valuable independence. Just be vigilant.

Car hire Most visitors will hire cars for at least one day whilst on the island. Car hire can be arranged either through your hotel, tour operator or directly. The main car-hire companies have desks at Roland Garros Airport. Cars can be hired on a daily basis plus mileage or for longer periods with unlimited mileage. Air conditioning may cost extra but is a real blessing in the summer.

The requirements vary but the minimum age for car hire is usually 21 years and you must have held a driving licence for two years. You will be asked to pay in advance and provide a deposit. Do check that the insurance cover that comes with the car is fully comprehensive (*tous risques*). Some car-hire companies may try to tell you that no firm offers fully comprehensive insurance – not true. Make sure you know what 'excess' you will have to pay if you cause an accident; some companies keep costs down by scrimping on insurance.

Expect to pay around €50–55 per day (one–three days) for a Peugeot 206 or about €100–110 per day for a 4x4. As noted above, air conditioning may be extra.

Car-hire companies

ADA Location 3 Rue de la Croix Rouge, ZAE La Mare, 97438 Ste-Marie; 0262 527253; airport, 0262 488183; e info@ada-reunion.com; www.ada-reunion.com

Avis Réunion 83 Rue Jules Verne, BP 8, 97821 Le Port; 0262 421599; airport, 0262 488185; 82 Rue Marius et Ary Leblond, 97410 St-Pierre; 0262 350090; e resa@avis-reunion.com; www.avisreunion.com

Budget 2 Rue Pierre Aubert, ZI du Chaudron, 97490 Ste-Clotilde; 0262 289200; airport, 0262 280195; 2 Chemin des Anglais, Zac des Mascareignes, 97420 Le Port; 0262 4548716; e budget.run@caille.com; www.budget-reunion.com

Europcar Gillot la Ferme, 97438 Ste-Marie; 0262 931415; airport, 0262 282758; e europcar-reunion@wandoo.fr; www.europcar-reunion.com

Hertz Locamac 1 Rue de la Pépinière, ZAE La Mare, 97438 Ste-Marie; 0262 532255; airport, 0262 280593; e reservations@hertzreunion.com; www.hertzreunion.com

ITC Tropicar 27 Av de Bourbon, 97434 St-Gilles-les-Bains; 0262 240101; e contact@itctropicar.com; www.itctropicar.com

National Citer 65 Bd du Chaudron, 97490 Ste-Clotilde; 0262 974974; airport, 0262 488377; e contact@foucque.fr; www.citer.re

Motorbike/moped hire Take extra care on the roads on a motorbike or moped, as drivers are not courteous. Hire is by the day and usually includes unlimited mileage, with reduced rates for seven days or more. You will need to leave a deposit and, as with cars, check that you are happy with the insurance cover provided.

EXPLORING REUNION WITHOUT A CAR

Hilary Bradt

If you rent a car you feel you should use it each day – such a pity in a lovely island like Réunion, where the hiking is superb and the bus service excellent. In the two weeks that we were there we travelled by bus, hitchhiking and on foot, and saw everything we wanted to see.

The yellow buses, or *cars jaunes*, are great. Each bus stop displays the timetable (so it is easy to plan your day), buses arrive on time, their destination is clearly displayed on the front, and the driver will make an unauthorised stop if you are caught out between official bus stops.

The only problem with buses is that they are infrequent on some routes (about every two hours around St-Philippe, for instance) so hitchhiking is a useful alternative. We (two women) found it easy and fun – and very good for our French, even if the Creole accent put a strain on our understanding.

Expect to pay around €35 per day for a 125cc moped (one–seven days) and €65–70 per day for a 600cc motorbike (one–seven days).

Locascoot 162 Rue du Général de Gaulle, 97434 St-Gilles-les-Bains; t/f 0262 255698; e locascoot@wanadoo.fr; www. locascoot.com. Also mountain-bike hire.

Max Moto 10 Av Gaston Monerville, 97400 St-Denis; t 0262 211525; f 0262 214566; e maxmoto.run@wanadoo.fr

974 Motoloc 3 bis Rue Georges Pompidou, 97436 St-Leu; t 0692 694842; e manu7.bertin@laposte.net; www.974motoloc.com

Runtwin 43 Rue Ruisseau des Noirs, 97400 St-Denis; t 0262 509973; e contact@rutnwin.re; www.runtwin.re. Offers Harley-Davidson hire & tours of the island from €110 per day.

TAXIS Taxi stands are usually situated in town centres, often near the bus station. Taxis are numerous but quite expensive. They don't tend to hang around looking for passengers in the evening, so you'll probably need to order one and there is a surcharge after 20.00. Most taxis have meters but it's not a bad idea to negotiate a fare beforehand, otherwise you may be charged 'tourist rates'. A cheaper option is a *taxi collectif* (shared taxi). The driver waits until the car is full before leaving, then each passenger pays a proportion of the fare. The only disadvantage is that you could be waiting a while in quieter areas for the taxi to fill up, and they only run during the day.

Taxi firms

In & around St-Denis

Roland Garros Airport Taxis t 0262 488383
Allo Taxi m 0692 854134
Taxis Express t 0262 417890
Taxis GTD t 0262 213110
Taxis Paille-en-Queue t 0262 292029
Taxis Plus t 0262 283774

St-André

Taxis Léopards t 0262 460028

St-Benoît

Taxis les Marsouins t 0262 505558

St Philippe

Taxi Hoareau m 0693 319394

St-Pierre

Taxis Saint-Pierrois t 0262 385484

Le Tampon

Taxi rank t 0262 271169

St-Louis

RUN Taxis m 0692 663061

Etang Salé

Solutions Taxi m 0693 860727

St-Leu

Taxi rank t 0262 348385

St-Paul

Taxi rank t 0262 456434
Taxis de St-Paul m 0692 863996

Cilaos

Taxi Figuin t 0262 391945

BY BUS Travel between towns is provided by the excellent bus service (*cars jaunes*). Buses are a reliable, easy and cost-effective way to get around the island. *Cars jaunes* are easily distinguished from the buses which operate within towns because, as the name indicates, they are bright yellow.

Cars jaunes tickets cost €1.40, €2.80 or €4.20, depending on the distance travelled. For example, a ticket from St-Denis to Le Port costs €1.40, St-Denis to St-Paul costs €2.80, and St-Denis to St-Pierre costs €4.20. Local bus etiquette dictates that you should get on at the front and off at the back. Don't forget to validate your ticket by putting it in the machine as you get on, and keep hold of it as on-the-spot checks are frequent. Stops are mostly on request, so you will need to clap your hands to signal that you want to get off.

Listed below are bus routes with the duration of each journey. On the main routes buses are regular (every one to two hours) and service is from around 05.00 to 18.30. On quieter routes (like the east coast) buses are less frequent and operate from around 07.00 to 17.30. Fewer buses run on Sundays and public holidays. Each bus stop displays a timetable so planning is easy. The French for bus station is *gare routière*.

Line A	St-Denis to/from St-Pierre (express): 2hrs
Line A2	St-Denis to/from St-Leu: 2hrs 10mins
Line B	St-Denis to/from St-Pierre (coastal road): 1hr 40mins
Line B1	St-Pierre to/from St-Leu: 50mins Mon–Sat, 2hrs Sun & public holidays
Line C	St-Denis to/from St-Pierre (inland): 3hrs
Line C1	St-Pierre to/from St-Leu: 1hr
Line C2	St-Denis to/from St-Paul: 1hr
Line D	St-Denis to/from St-Paul: 1hr
Line E	Chaloupe St-Leu to/from St-Pierre: 2hrs
Line F	St-Denis to/from St-Benoît (express): 1hr
Line G	St-Denis to/from St- Benoît: 1hr 30mins
Line H	St-Benoît to/from St-Pierre via les Plaines: 2hrs
Line I	St-Benoît to/from St-Pierre via St-Philippe: 2hrs 45mins
Line I2	St-Joseph to/from Le Tampon: 1hr
Line L	St-Pierre to/from Entre-Deux: 45mins
Line Z'éclair 1	St-Denis to/from St-Pierre (minibus): 1hr 40mins
Line Z'éclair 2	St-Denis to/from St-Benoît (minibus): 50mins

If you need more information, current fares, schedule updates or timetables, contact *Cars Jaunes* (*0810 123974; www.cg974.fr*)

HITCHHIKING Hitchhiking in Réunion is relatively easy but women should not attempt it alone. It's an excellent way of meeting the locals, practising your French and learning more about the island. You may end up doing a fair amount of walking but on such a beautiful island this is no hardship.

ACCOMMODATION

As there are only a limited number of hotels on Réunion, accommodation should preferably be booked well in advance, particularly if you are travelling during peak season (November–January, March and April, July–October). Try to book at least six weeks prior to departure.

Accommodation in Réunion is divided into 'classified' and 'unclassified', with a star rating system applied to the classified hotels. It is this star system, devised by the French Government, which is reflected in this guide. Star ratings are allocated by the *préfet*.

Price brackets have been supplied as a guide only – rates do change regularly, according to season and demand. It is therefore better to judge a hotel by its description than by the price. In any case, if the hotel is booked as part of a package holiday including flights, the public rate is never what you, the guest, actually pay. Even for those who make their own hotel bookings direct, there could be significant discounts on the public rates at luxury, upmarket and mid-range properties. The vast majority of hotels offer considerable discounts for children and infants are

ACCOMMODATION PRICE CODES

Double room per night on HB:

Luxury	$$$$$	£450; US$711; €549
Upmarket	$$$$	£200–450; US$316–711; €244–549
Mid range	$$$	£100–200; US$158–316; €122–244
Budget	$$	£50–100; US$80–158; €62–122
Shoestring	$	up to £50; US$80; €62

often accommodated free of charge. It is worth visiting the websites of hotels as many, particularly the larger ones, publish special offers on the internet.

The price brackets are based on the hotels' public rates for a standard double room, per room per night during high season on half board, based on two people sharing. However, budget and shoestring properties are likely to be sold on a bed and breakfast or self-catering (room only) basis.

A tax (*taxe de séjour*), calculated on the room rate and the duration of your stay, is payable when you settle your account. As in Mauritius, the board basis is indicated, either all-inclusive (AI), full board (FB), half board (HB), bed and breakfast (BB) or room only (RO). (For definitions of these terms, see page 67.)

There is only one five-star hotel on Réunion and the service does not compare to that in Mauritius, but accommodation with plenty of character is easy to find. As well as hotels there are guesthouses (*gîtes de France*), self-catering holiday rentals (*meublés de tourisme*, also known as furnished flats), rural farm inns (*fermes auberges*), mountain huts/lodges (*gîtes de montagne*), guesthouses/huts on hiking trails (*gîtes d'étape*), 'VVF' holiday villages and youth hostels (*auberges de jeunesse*).

GITES DE FRANCE Classified guesthouses of reasonable standard, found throughout Réunion. Can be booked as per *gîtes ruraux* (see below).

GITES RURAUX (*For bookings, contact Centrale Régionale de Réservation de la Réunion, 5 Rue Rontaunay, 97400 St-Denis;* ☎ *0810 160 000;* **f** *0262 418429;* **e** *resa@reunion-nature.com; www.reunion-nature.com, www.gitesdefrance.re;* 🕘 *09.00–17.00 Mon–Fri, 09.00–16.00 Sat*) Self-catering accommodation, with owners living on the property but not in the house itself. They carry the 'Gîtes de France' label. Prices are typically between €230 and €1,200 per *gîte* per week for between two and 14 people.

CHAMBRES D'HOTE Bed and breakfast-style accommodation. These are not self-catering and the owner lives in the house; some also offer *table d'hôte* meals. Staying in such accommodation can be a marvellous experience as the owner and guests usually all dine together. Double rooms cost from €25 per night on BB. *Table d'hôte* meals start at around €18 (very worthwhile). Can be booked as per *gîtes ruraux* (see above).

MEUBLES DE TOURISME There are 189 furnished flats and villas, classified from one to four stars. Guides to these self-catering holiday rentals, published annually, are available at tourist offices. Those that are categorised *Clé Vacances* are regularly inspected and have been awarded an additional mark of quality. The Réunion Island tourism website (*www.reunion-nature.com*) contains a list of *meublés de tourisme* under *Où dormir/types hébergement* (Where to sleep/types of accommodation).

Most owners insist on a minimum stay of at least two nights. Rates often depend on length of stay. No meals are provided. You can book directly with the owners.

GITES DE MONTAGNE AND REFUGES DE RANDONNEE (*For bookings, contact Centrale Régionale de Réservation de la Réunion, 5 Rue Rontaunay, 97400 St-Denis;* 📞 *0810 160 000;* **f** *0262 418429;* **e** *resa@reunion-nature.com; www.reunion-nature.com;* ⏱ *09.00–17.00 Mon–Fri, 09.00–16.00 Sat*) There are 31 of these, mostly on hiking trails. Expect to pay from €14.50 per person per night.

GITES D'ETAPE Often in small villages; those with the Gîtes de France label are usually better in quality. Dinners and breakfasts prepared by hosts. No self-catering. Can be booked as per *gîtes de montagne*, see above.

REFUGES (rest huts) Basic. No self-catering, as meals (dinners, breakfasts) are prepared by host.

CAMPSITES There are very few campsites in Réunion and camping in state forests (just about all forests) is frowned upon.

VVF VILLAGES VACANCES FAMILLES (FAMILY HOLIDAY VILLAGES) (*Village de Corail, 80 Av de Bourbon, 97434 St-Gilles-les-Bains;* 📞 *0262 242939;* **f** *0262 244102;* **e** *contact@villages-des-australes.com; www.villages-des-australes.com*) There is one in St-Gilles- les-Bains offering 129 fairly basic self-catering flats. You need to become a member of the VVF organisation to stay here but you can arrange this at the time of booking. Reservations are made direct with the VVF. Self-catering studio flats cost from €51 RO.

AUBERGES DE JEUNESSE There are three youth hostels on the island, in Hell-Bourg (📞 *0262 474131*), Entre-Deux (📞 *0262 395920*) and Bernica, above St-Gilles-les-Bains (📞 *0262 228975*). To use these you need to buy a membership card, which can be done at the hostel or by contacting Auberges de Jeunesse Ocean Indien, 2 Place Etienne Regnault, 97400 St-Denis (📞 *0262 411534;* **f** *0262 417217;* **e** *ajoi@wanadoo.fr; www.auberge-jeunesse-reunion.com*). Expect to pay around €15 for a dormitory bed.

See also *Chapter 16, Hiking*, pages 269–72.

EATING AND DRINKING

Eating in Réunion is a pleasure. There is such variety, with Creole, Chinese and French restaurants in almost every town. Surprisingly, Indian cuisine is harder to find.

Traditional Creole food is slightly spicy and includes elements from French and Indian culinary styles. The mainstay of Creole cuisine is the *cari* – fish, meat or poultry in a tasty sauce packed with spices. It is eaten with rice and *grains* (beans or lentils) and accompanied by *rougail*, a kind of spicy chutney often made with tomatoes, onions and chillies. Tuna, shark and swordfish make delicious *cari*, as do *camarons* (large freshwater prawns). *Cari poulet* (chicken *cari*) and *rougail saucisses* (a spicy pork sausage in a tomato-based stew) are a good inexpensive option. *Cari ti-jacques* (curried young jackfruits) is very traditional, as are duck with vanilla and *cabri massalé* (masala spiced goat stew). If you're feeling adventurous, look out for *cari tang* (curried tenrec – similar to a hedgehog), although this is rarely seen on menus nowadays.

TWO POPULAR CREOLE RECIPES

Translated by Alexandra Richards

Here are two of the most popular examples of Creole cuisine, as prepared by culinary wizard Mamie Javel, author of Creole cookbook, *La Réunion des Mille et une Saveurs*. Mamie Javel used to run one of the island's top restaurants, Relais des Cîmes in Hell-Bourg (see page 342), where meals are still prepared according to her famous recipes.

COCONUT CHICKEN

Cooking time = 30 minutes
Ingredients (serves 4):

1 chicken (1.5kg)
6 ripe tomatoes
3 large onions
5 cloves of garlic
1 sprig of thyme
25cl fresh or tinned coconut milk
100g grated coconut
½ teaspoon turmeric
20 peppercorns
3 cloves
4 tablespoons of oil
salt to taste

Method: Cut chicken into pieces. Finely chop the onions and tomatoes. Crush the garlic, peppercorns and cloves. Heat the oil in a large pan and lightly brown the chicken pieces. Add the onions, garlic, peppercorns and cloves. When the onions have softened, add the tomatoes. Cook until the mixture has reduced, then add the turmeric. Stir continuously and add a glass of water. Cover and allow to simmer for 20 minutes. Finally, add the coconut milk. Serve sprinkled with grated coconut.

VANILLA TROUT

A speciality in Hell-Bourg, Cirque de Salazie, where you can also catch your own trout which will then be prepared for you.

Cooking time = 20 minutes
Ingredients (serves 4):

4 trout, each weighing 200g
50cl crème fraîche
½ vanilla pod
2 cloves of garlic
butter to taste
soya sauce
salt and pepper to taste

Method: Clean trout, salting the insides. Grill fish for five minutes on each side. Just before they are cooked, sprinkle a few drops of soya sauce over each fish, turn and heat again for two minutes. Meanwhile, prepare the vanilla cream.

Crush the garlic cloves. Cook in butter on low heat. Add cream, making sure that it doesn't stick to the pan. Slice the vanilla pod lengthways, using the knife to scrape the vanilla seeds from the pod into the sauce. Then add the rest of the pod to the mixture. Stir continuously. Season with salt and pepper.

Presentation: Pour the vanilla cream on to the plates and place the trout on top. Pour a tablespoon of heated rum over each trout and light. Serve with mixed vegetables.

RESTAURANT PRICE CODES

Average price of a main course:

Expensive	$$$$$	£30+; US$48+; €36+; Rs1,380+
Above average	$$$$	£20–30; US$32–48; €24–36; Rs920–1,380
Midrange	$$$	£10–20; US$16–32; €12–24; Rs460–920
Cheap and cheerful	$$	£5–10; US$8–16; €6–12; Rs230–460
Rock bottom	$	£0–5; US$0–8; €0–6; Rs0–230

For traditional food in a family atmosphere, try a *table d'hôte*. If you're on a tight budget, there is a very healthy population of *camion bars* (mobile snack bars) on the island, serving inexpensive filled baguettes, *samoussas* and other light meals.

Most towns have fish sellers on the seafront. If you have access to a kitchen, there is nothing better than cooking freshly caught tuna or shark. Try to buy it in the morning though, because the stalls are not refrigerated and fish that has sunbathed for eight hours is more than a little risky.

Whilst there are plenty of tasty options for seafood lovers, vegetarians are not well catered for on the island. Restaurants with a French flavour usually serve a variety of salads, whilst vegetarian Creole fare includes *achards* (spicy, pickled vegetables) and *brèdes* (a mixture of greens). If you would like a vegetarian meal, you may well have to ask for a dish to be prepared specially, and then politely decline when the waiter offers to add some ham to make it more interesting! The French for vegetarian is *végétarien*, vegan is *végétalien*.

On Sundays Réunion goes for a picnic. We're not talking a wicker hamper filled with a few Scotch eggs and some cheese sandwiches. This is picnicking on the grandest scale, a real family affair. Réunion is equipped with excellent picnic facilities, not merely tables but also barbecue areas. From the beaches to the forests, people can be seen picnicking, some arriving as early as 10.00 to claim their favourite spot and prepare their *cari*. If you are ever invited to join in, don't miss the opportunity.

As in Mauritius, rum – as a by-product of the sugar industry – is big business. *Rhum arrangé* is made by adding fruit and spices to white rum and allowing it to ferment for several months. You are likely to be offered a *rhum arrangé* at the end of your meal in most restaurants or alternatively a *punch* (pronounced 'ponsh'), which also has rum as the main ingredient but is more fruity and less powerful.

When in a bar you may hear people ordering '*une Dodo*'. This is not as ridiculous as it sounds – the local brand of beer is called 'Dodo'. It is usually the cheapest beer on offer and is very popular. Just take care not to order '*un dodo*'; not even the most skilled of barmen can produce one of those.

To assist you in choosing a restaurant, we have provided a rough indication of the price using codes to represent the average price of a main course.

WORKING HOURS

Offices are typically open 08.00–12.00 and 14.00–18.00 Monday–Friday. Shops open 08.30–12.00 and 14.30–18.00 Monday–Saturday. Some food shops are open on Sunday mornings. State administrative offices are a law unto themselves, many opening for very limited hours. For example, the *Préfecture* in St-Denis opens 08.00–13.00 Monday–Friday.

PUBLIC HOLIDAYS

New Year's Day	1 January
Easter Monday	variable (March/April)
Labour Day	1 May
1945 Victory	8 May
Ascension Day	variable (May)
Whit Sunday	variable (May)
Bastille Day	14 July
Assumption	15 August
All Saints' Day	1 November
1918 Armistice	11 November
Abolition of Slavery	20 December
Christmas Day	25 December

FESTIVALS

JANUARY/FEBRUARY/MARCH

Fête du Miel (honey), La Plaine-des-Cafres, January (duration: seven days)
Thaipoosam Cavadee (Tamil festival), January/February (variable)
Chinese New Year, January/February (variable)
Tamil fire walking ceremonies, throughout the island, January/February

APRIL/MAY/JUNE

Varusha Pirappu (Tamil New Year), April
Fête du Vacoas, St-Benoît, April (duration: seven days)
Fête de la Vanille, Bras-Panon, May (duration: ten days)
Sacred Heart (Roman Catholic pilgrimage), St-Leu, June
Fête des Goyaviers, Plaine-des-Palmistes, June (duration: two days)
Festival of Music, main towns, 21 June
Comedy festival, main towns, June
Fête de la Randonnée (hiking), throughout the island, June

JULY/AUGUST/SEPTEMBER

Bastille Day, throughout the island, 14 July
Tamil fire walking ceremonies, August
La Salette (Roman Catholic pilgrimage), St-Leu, August

OCTOBER/NOVEMBER/DECEMBER

Flower show, Le Tampon, October (duration: two weeks)
Dipavali (Hindu Festival of Light), November
Fête du Curcuma (turmeric), St-Joseph, November
Fête des Lentilles (lentils), Cilaos, November
Foire de St-Pierre, St-Pierre, December (duration: ten days)
Fête des Letchis (lychees), St-Denis, December (duration: seven days)

SHOPPING

Réunion is not a bargain-hunter's paradise. Clothing here tends to be imported from France and is therefore expensive. Parts of St-Denis and St-Gilles and, to a lesser extent, St-Pierre are reminiscent of fashionable Parisian streets with their chic boutiques and effervescent French sales assistants.

The only bargains to be had are in the wonderful local markets. St-Paul claims to have the biggest and best weekly market, which takes place on Fridays. The markets in St-Pierre are also worth a visit. Sadly, few of the handicrafts on sale are made in Réunion. The majority come from Madagascar and even Indonesia. A lot of work has recently been put into promoting Réunionnais handicrafts and they are gradually becoming more readily available, both in small souvenir shops and the markets. The French for handicrafts is *artisanat.*

Worthwhile souvenirs include geranium oil, rum, vanilla and products made from woven pandanus (*vacoas*) leaves. Vanilla grown on the island can be bought direct from producers or tourist offices. The vanilla sold in the markets is often from Madagascar; it is cheaper but is said to be of inferior quality.

MARKETS

St-Denis	Grand Marché daily, Petit Marché daily except Sunday
St-Benoît	05.00–12.00 Saturday
St-Pierre	covered market daily, street market 05.00–12.00 Saturday
St-Louis	daily
St-Leu	07.00–12.00 Saturday
St-Gilles-les-Bains	07.30–12.00 Wednesday
St-Paul	06.00–18.00 Friday, 05.00–12.00 Saturday

ARTS AND ENTERTAINMENT

Local tourist offices should be able to tell you what's going on while you're in Réunion. I also recommend obtaining a copy of *L'Attitude*, a glossy lifestyle magazine published bi-monthly and sold in newsagents. It has sections on music, theatre, restaurants, exhibitions and sport, as well as a regular slot on tourism, reviewing worthwhile excursions and activities. Also useful is the free monthly publication *Pages Noires*, which is widely available in bars. It is devoted to nightlife and has details of the coming month's concerts, as well as what the bars and nightclubs will be offering. *Kwélafé* is a similar publication, which covers live music, shows, cinema, exhibitions, etc.

THEATRE AND DANCE The arts in Réunion have benefited greatly from financial grants from France. Cultural events happen throughout the year – plays, music, dance, and even stand-up comedy. Several theatre troupes are well established on the island: Théatre Vollard, Théatre Talipot and Compagnie Act 3 are the best known. Théatre Talipot has participated in the Edinburgh Festival and in South Africa's Grahamstown Arts Festival.

To find out who is performing when you're in Réunion, contact the ODC (local cultural office) (*0262 419300; www.odcreunion.com*). There are numerous theatres, including the open-air theatre in St-Gilles-les-Bains, a wonderful setting. Most publish a programme for the coming season, which you can get hold of at the tourist offices.

ART GALLERIES The best of Réunion's many galleries is the Musée Léon Dierx, at 28 Rue de Paris in St-Denis (*0262 202482*) (see page 287). The focus of the permanent exhibition is modern and contemporary art, including works by the likes of Gauguin, Picasso, Bernard, Maufra, Erro and Chen Zen. At 26 Rue de Paris is Artothèque du Département, which is also worth a visit.

There are numerous commercial art galleries selling art, particularly in St-Denis, such as Galerie Cadre Noir at 11 Rue de Paris in St-Denis (*0262 214488*).

LITERATURE Despite the work of organisations such as ADER (Association for the Promotion of Réunionnais Authors) and MCR (Cultural Movement of Réunion), Réunion's literature is little known beyond the Mascarene Islands.

The first novel written by a Réunion-born author and set on the island was *Les Marrons* by Louis-Timagène Houat, published in Paris in 1844. Houat was an abolitionist and *Les Marrons* provides a detailed portrait of Réunion society in 1833, condemning slavery and racism. As do many later Réunionnais novels, *Les Marrons* explores the themes of runaway slaves and romance between a black slave and a white woman.

'Colonial novels' thrived at the height of colonial expansion (1920–30), when authors such as Marius-Ary Leblond attempted to exalt the virtues of the colony. Marius-Ary Leblond was the pseudonym used by two cousins, George Athenas and Aimé Merlo, who published 20 novels and over 250 articles under that name. *Ulysse Cafre* (1924) tells the story of a slave who goes in search of his son, revealing the clash between black magic and Christianity.

The 1970s saw the birth of what is known as the 'Réunionnais novel', dealing with Creole issues throughout the island's history. Well-known authors publishing from the 1970s to the present include Anne Cheynet, Axel Gauvin, Agnès Gueneau and Jean-François Sam-Long. Sam-Long's novel *Madame Desbassyns* draws on the life story of the plantation owner of the same name, who is said to have been a particularly cruel woman. The true story of Madame Desbassyns is told at the Musée de Villèle at her former estate near St-Gilles-les-Hauts (see pages 327–8).

The poet Leconte de Lisle is undoubtedly the best known of Réunion's literary figures. He was born in St-Paul in 1818 and went on to be admitted to the prestigious Académie Française. He is buried in the seafront cemetery in St-Paul. If you are able to read French, you can find his works, and many more, in any of the island's bookshops.

NIGHTLIFE St-Denis, St-Gilles-les-Bains and St-Pierre are the three towns where people head for a night out. St-Pierre wins hands down as far as I'm concerned – it is the only town with lots of bars and clubs that still offer a genuine local, tropical flavour. If French Riviera is more your style, then St-Gilles-les-Bains has exactly what you want. The numerous nightclubs there cater almost exclusively for French holidaymakers. St-Denis has a real mixture and you're likely to bump into English-speaking students from the university. Wherever you go out, prepare to dance to an eclectic mixture of musical styles, likely to include *séga*, *zouk*, reggae and *maloya*, as well as French, British and American chart music. (For more information on local music see *Chapter 14, Culture*, page 246.)

Throughout the island there are bars offering regular live music. To find out what's going on when, pick up a copy of *Pages Noires* from a bar (see page 265).

Casinos are popular with locals and are found in St-Denis, St-Gilles-les-Bains and St-Pierre. Going out in Réunion is not cheap. Entry to nightclubs is expensive, typically around €12, and drinks are costly too.

PHOTOGRAPHY

Réunion offers superb opportunities for the amateur photographer, in particular its stunning landscapes. It is courteous to ask people before taking their photo and it is particularly important to do so when you visit the island's interior, where people are less accustomed to the eccentricities of tourists. Film, digital memory cards and developing are readily available but tend to cost more than in Europe.

MEDIA AND COMMUNICATIONS

MEDIA Local newspapers and magazines are in French. You may be able to find international newspapers on sale in St-Denis's larger bookshops. The island's main newspapers are *Le Quotidien* (*www.lequotidien.re*) and *Le Journal de l'Ile de la Réunion* (*www.clicanoo.re*). Both offer free classified advertising on certain days of the week.

Télé 7, *Télé Mag* and *Visu* all have weekly television and radio guides. There are two state television channels run by Réseau France Outre-Mer, RFO1 and RFO2, which include programmes from France. Independent channels are Antenne Réunion, Canal Réunion, TV4 Réunion and TV Sud. Almost all programmes are in French but RFO1 broadcasts the news in Creole at 12.30 on Saturdays.

There are two RFO state radio stations, plus numerous others, such as Kreol FM and Radio Arc-en-Ciel.

MAIL All towns of any size have a post office which is open 08.00–12.00 and 14.00–17.00 Monday to Friday, and until midday on Saturday. Poste restante is handled at the main post office in St-Denis, on the corner of Rues Juliette Dodu and Maréchal Leclerc. The postal codes for the main towns are as follows:

St-Denis	97400	St-Gilles-les-Bains	97434
St-Benoît	97470	St-Paul	97460
St-Philippe	97442	La-Plaine-des-Cafres	97418
St-Joseph	97480	La-Plaine-des-Palmistes	97431
St-Pierre	97410	Cilaos	97413
Le Tampon	97430	Salazie	97433
St-Leu	97436		

TELEPHONE Telecommunications are straightforward. To call Réunion from abroad, use the IDD code 262 followed by the local number minus the initial zero. All land line numbers begin with 0262 and mobile numbers begin 0692/3. There are public payphones and most take phonecards (*télécartes*), which are sold in post offices, newsagents and shops displaying the sign.

By far the cheapest way to make international calls is to buy an international phonecard, available at newsagents. You can make calls from any touchtone phone by first dialling a freephone number, then the code on the back of the card. If you own a mobile phone you should be able to use it in Réunion, via the local networks, SFR and Itinéris. You should confirm with your service provider before travelling that your phone will work. Parts of the interior have very patchy reception.

FAX There are plenty of offices offering fax services and hotels will usually send/receive them on your behalf for a fee.

INTERNET ACCESS/EMAIL Although increasingly used in homes, schools and businesses, public internet facilities are surprisingly rare. Wi-Fi access is gradually becoming available at hotels and in some public places, such as tourist offices, libraries and certain cafés. If you are resident on the island, your local *médiathèque* should provide free internet access but you'll need to prove that you live in the surrounding area. Prices at internet cafés vary but you can expect to pay €7–12 per hour.

You will see throughout the island a number of *Cyber Bases*. These were created by local government to increase internet usage by Réunionnais. They offer computer and internet classes, and free internet access. However, the *Cyber Bases* encourage tourists not to use their facilities, but rather to go to an internet café, leaving the *Cyber Bases* facilities for locals.

BUSINESS

While not being a viable alternative for labour-intensive concerns because of the high cost of labour, Réunion is suitable for capital-intensive businesses. A range of tax incentives and grants are available to investors and it is worth noting that anything manufactured in Réunion gets the prestigious 'made in France' label.

The Agence de Développement de la Réunion (☎ *0262 922492; www.adreunion.com*) can provide advice on investing in or setting up a business in Réunion, as well as long-term assistance for businesses.

There are incentives for such investors, who are assisted by tax elimination schemes and direct subsidies.

Those who wish to learn more about investment opportunities might want to obtain copies of *L'Eco Austral*, a bimonthly economic newspaper, or visit the website of the Agence de Développement de la Réunion (*www.adreunion.com*).

BUYING PROPERTY

The regulations around buying property in Réunion are as for buying property in France. There is an abundance of information available online, including at www.buyingahouseinfrance.info.

CULTURAL ETIQUETTE

Although beachwear is fine for a coastal resort, it may be frowned upon away from the beach. For women, it will also attract unwanted attention. If visiting temples or mosques, dress conservatively and remove your shoes before entering. For women, it is a good idea to carry a long-sleeved top and sarong, just in case. You may be asked to remove leather items when visiting Hindu temples and you may be requested to cover your head at certain mosques.

The large number of young, single mothers in Réunion is likely to shock most visitors. Sadly, the pregnancies are all too often the result of incest and sexual abuse. Domestic violence is also a problem and frequently goes undetected.

If you see strange objects on the side of the road, such as red pieces of material, coconut, or parts of chickens, resist the temptation to interfere with them. They are often left by people practising black magic and are part of a spell. Keep your eyes on the road as many local drivers will swerve to avoid such objects, for fear of being cursed.

It is perhaps also useful to know that, for some superstitious Réunionnais, various actions must be avoided in order to prevent attracting bad spirits. These include burning hair, burning a shoe or putting wood in a cross shape on the fire.

16

Activities

Réunion's beaches may not be world class but its list of sporting activities certainly is. Activities have become big business in Réunion, so there are usually several operators to choose from, and it is good to know that reputable operators must adhere to French safety standards.

MULTI-ACTIVITY COMPANIES

Below are the contact details of a few multi-activity operators and an indication of the kinds of activities that they can arrange.

Centrale de Réservation Loisirs Accueil Nature et Campagne 5 Rue Rontaunay, 97400 St-Denis; ☎ 0262 907878; f 0262 418429; e resa@reunion-nature.com; www.reunion-nature.com; ⏲ 09.00–17.00 Mon–Thu, 09.00–16.00 Fri, 09.00–12.00 Sat. This snappily named organisation is the central reservations office used by many activities companies & should be able to help with most queries. Can arrange hiking, canyoning, climbing, horseriding, mountain biking, rafting, hang gliding, 4x4 excursions & helicopter trips.

Alpanes 14 Rue Simon Pinel, 97419 La Possession; m 0692 777530; e contact@alpanes.com; www.alpanes.com. Hiking & canyoning.

Austral Aventure 16 Av Amiral Lacaze, Hell-Bourg, 97433 Salazie; ☎ 0262 324029; m 0692 875550 e austral-aventure@wanadoo.fr; www:creole.org/austral-aventure/index.html. Hiking, canyoning, white-water rafting, climbing, paragliding & mountain biking.

Ducrot Daniel 30 Chemin des Trois Mares, 97413 Cilaos; m 0692 659067; e ducrotd@wanadoo.fr; www.canyoning-cilaos-reunion.com. Hiking, canyoning & mountain biking.

Evasion Kréol 32 Rue de l'Amiral Decaen, St-Denis; ☎ 0692 613455; e contact@evasionkreol.com; www.evasionkreol.com. Hiking, canyoning.

Jean-Yves Hervet 26 Av des Moutardiers, Plateau Caillou, 97460, St-Paul; ☎/f 0262 324568; m 0692 766643; e jyhervet@wanadoo.fr. Hiking, white-water rafting & mountain biking.

Parc du Maïdo Route du Maïdo, 97423 Petite France; ☎ 0262 325252; f 0262 325200. Hiking, mountain biking, mini bobsleigh & archery.

Ric à Ric 15 Chemin Clément Fossy, S-Leu; m 0692 865485; e ricaric@canyonreunion.com; www.canyonreunion.com. Canyoning, white-water rafting & climbing.

Run Evasion 23 Rue du Père Boiteau, 97413 Cilaos; ☎ 0262 318357; f 0262 318072; 69 Rue Marius & Ary Leblond, 97410 St-Pierre; ☎ 0262 964684; www.run.evasion.voici.org. Hiking, canyoning, climbing & mountain biking.

Vincent Terrisse 131 Rue du Four à Chaux, 97410 St-Pierre; m 0692 245658; e iles.d.aventures@wanadoo.fr; www.ilesdaventures.org. Hiking, climbing & canyoning.

HIKING

Réunion's rugged interior makes it the best hiking destination in the western Indian Ocean. More than 1,000km of trails criss-cross the island's mountains.

Opened in 1997, the **Maison de la Montagne** (Mountain House) in St-Denis is the central reservations office for accommodation in rural areas. Here visitors can obtain all the necessary information about hiking trails, accommodation along the routes, grading of routes and other activities on offer in rural areas. As yet, their literature is available only in French; however, the maps are useful and the staff speak English. They also provide itineraries, which can be booked as packages. (For contact details see *Accommodation for hikers* opposite.) The trails are well managed and marked according to the official French system. The two **Grande Randonnées hiking trails** (GR R1 and GR R2) are marked with red and white paint. Other footpaths are indicated in red and yellow. The **GR R1** trail, known as Le Tour du Piton-des-Neiges, is a complete circle, which covers the north of Cirque de Cilaos, passes through Hell-Bourg and around Cirque de Salazie, then into Mafate and back to Cilaos via the Col du Taïbit. **GR R2**, or La Grande Traversée de l'Ile, cuts across the island from St-Denis to the coast near St-Philippe, via the cirques, Entre-Deux, the Plaines and Piton-de-la-Fournaise. The trails classified as Sentiers Marmailles are easy walks of less than three hours, designed to be suitable for children. There are 42 listed in a book, *Sentiers Marmailles*, published by the Office Nationale des Forêts (for details of other publications on hiking, see *Appendix 2, Further information*, page 351).

Even for organised hikes, you must bring along your own backpack, sleeping bag, torch, Swiss army knife, crockery, cutlery, toiletries (including loo paper), warm clothing, appropriate footwear (sturdy hiking boots), rain gear, sun protection and any personal medication.

If you are hiking independently, it is advisable to ring the Maison de la Montagne beforehand to check that your proposed route is open. A good **map** is essential: 4402 RT is ideal for most hikes as it covers Cirque de Mafate, Cirque de Salazie and the northern part of Cirque de Cilaos, including the whole of the GR R1 trail. It is widely available from the Maison de la Montagne and tourist offices. To obtain maps prior to travel, contact the Institut Géographique National, 107 Rue de la Boétie, 75008 Paris. (See also the map of the cirques on page 334.)

Always let someone know where you are going and how long you plan to be away. Avoid hiking alone. Do check the weather forecasts and make sure that you are well prepared and equipped. If the worst does happen, the following are the official **distress signals** (helicopters do fly across the island regularly):

- Arms raised above your head in a 'V' shape
- Red flare
- Red square and a white circle

The *gendarmerie nationale* has a 24-hour emergency line (☎ *0262 930930*).

(See also box *Day hikes around Hell-Bourg*, page 340. For literature on hiking see *Appendix 2, Further information*, page 269.)

GUIDED HIKES There are a number of state-certified guides and organisations operating in the mountains.

Expect to pay around €40–60 per person per day for a guided hike with the following companies or the multi-activity companies listed on page 269.

Allon' Bat' a Pat' Rando 45 Impasse Gustave Courbet, 97430 Le Tampon; ☎ 0262 574407; **m** 0692 879516; **e** allonbatapat@orange.fr; www.allonbatapat-rando.fr

Kokapat Rando 109 Chemin Farjeau, Trois Mares, Le Tampon; ☎ 0262 333014; **e** kokapat.rando@hotmail.com; www.kokapatrando-reunion.com

Rando Run 2 Impasse des Acacias, 97427 Etang-Salé-les-Bains; ☎/f 0262 263131; m 0692 852256; e gilbert.aureche@wanadoo.fr; www.randorun.com

Rando Trek Réunion 139 Bd de l'Océan, Manapany les Bains; ☎ 0692 015956; e randotrekreunion@gmail.com; www.randotrek-reunion.com

ACCOMMODATION FOR HIKERS There are numerous options open to hikers but remember to book well in advance. Most can be booked through the Maison de la Montagne in St-Denis (*5 Rue Rontaunay, 97400 St-Denis;* ☎ *0262 907878;* **f** *0262 418429;* **e** *resa@reunion-nature.com; www.reunion-nature.com;* ⏲ *09.00–17.00 Mon–Thu, 09.00–16.00 Fri*). The following types of accommodation are available in rural areas: *gîtes de montagne, gîtes d'étape, gîtes ruraux, chambres d'hôte, fermes auberges* and *refuges* (rest huts). For details, see *Chapter 15, Accommodation*, pages 259–61.

Gîtes de montagne/gîtes d'étape

These mountain houses/huts are the most plentiful type of accommodation on hiking routes and are often the only option in remote outposts. Thanks to the central reservations system you can book them in advance, at the following offices:

- **Maison de la Montagne** in St-Denis (see contact details above)
- **All tourist offices**

Reservations must be made well in advance to avoid disappointment (they prefer it if people book six months before travelling, particularly for high-season months), with payment preferably two weeks before arrival. Late reservations may be accepted, as there are often last-minute cancellations. Meals can be arranged through the caretakers, at least a day in advance, by phone. Pay for your meals directly, in cash.

Note that *gîtes de montagne* and *gîtes d'étape* are basic, dormitory-type accommodation. Some visitors have arrived to find that other guests have hogged all the blankets and pillows for themselves, but this is rare. Most do not have hot water and a few don't have showers, so they really are only suitable as overnight stops.

All *gîtes* provide two blankets, a pillow and two sheets per person. Some kitchen utensils and a gas cooker are provided as well (speak to caretakers). Lighting in *gîtes* is usually by means of solar power.

Below is a selection of mountain *gîtes*. Expect to pay around adult/child €16/12, breakfast €6, dinner €19.

Piton-de-la-Fournaise

Volcan (57 beds) Mr Picard; ☎ 0692 852091; f 0262 591662; www.legiteduvolcan.com

Roche Ecrite

Plaine des Chicots (36 beds) Mr Bonald; ☎ 0262 439984

Basse Vallée

Basse Vallée (16 beds) Mr Bénard; ☎ 0262 373625

Piton-des-Neiges

Bélouve (30 beds, 2 dbl rooms) Mrs Rosset; ☎ 0262 412123; e gite.belouve@wanadoo.fr

Caverne Dufour (48 beds) Mr Dijoux; ☎ 0262 511526

Rivière des Remparts

Roche Plate (31 beds) Mrs Morel; ☎ 0262 591394

Cilaos

La Roche Merveilleuse (14 beds, 4 dbl rooms) Mr Payet; ☎ 0262 318242

⌂ **Route de Cilaos** (13 beds, 1 dbl room) Mr Ethève; ☎ 0262 450816; e etheve.eric@sfr.fr. Between St-Louis & Cilaos.

Mafate

⌂ **Aurère** (14 beds, 3 dbl rooms) Mr Boyer; ☎ 0262 550233

⌂ **Aurère** (16 beds) Ms Charlemagne; ☎ 0262 433683

⌂ **Grand Place Cayenne** (16 beds, 2 dbl rooms) Mr C Thomas; ☎ 0262 438542

⌂ **Ilet à Bourse** (16 beds, 2 dbl rooms) Mrs M Thomas; ☎ 0262 434393

⌂ **Marla** (16 beds, 4 dbl rooms) Mrs Hoareau; ☎ 0262 437831

⌂ **La Nouvelle 1** (12 beds, 5 dbl rooms, 10 4-person bungalows) Mr A Begue; ☎ 0262 436177

⌂ **La Nouvelle 2** (12 beds, 1 dbl room) Mrs Oréo; ☎ 0262 435857

⌂ **Roche Plate** (24 beds) Mrs Thiburce; ☎ 0262 436001

Salazie

⌂ **La Mandoze** (24 beds, 3 dbl rooms) Mr Manoro; ☎ 0262 478965

⌂ **Relais des Gouverneurs** (20 beds, 1 dbl room) ☎ 0262 477621; e calouboyer@wanadoo.fr

CANYONING

Canyoning, or abseiling down waterfalls, is becoming increasingly popular amongst thrill-seekers in Réunion. The island, with its innumerable waterfalls and spectacular gorges, boasts the ideal landscape. Canyoning starts at around €45 per half day, €55 per full day. For details of multi-activity operators that organise canyoning, see page 269.

MOUNTAIN BIKING

Mountain bikes are all the rage in Réunion and are available for hire in most activity centres. The island has over 1,400km of marked trails, which meet French Cycling Federation standards. Popular trails are around Maïdo, Entre-Deux, Cilaos, Salazie, Piton-de-la-Fournaise and the coast around Ste-Rose.

The French for mountain bike is *VTT* (*vélo tous terrains*) (pronounced 'vay-tay-tay'). The Centrale de Reservation Loisirs Accueil Nature et Campagne in St-Denis can supply information on the many routes throughout the island and arrange bike hire (for contact details, see page 282). You will also see suggested routes marked on large boards in many tourist areas.

Once a year, usually in November, Réunion plays host to one round of the Mega Avalanche international series of downhill mountain-bike races. The races in this series are unusual for the downhill discipline as they are mass-start races of up to 25km. Packages which include flights, accommodation and bike transport are available from mainland France. For more information visit www.avalanchecup.com.

The going rate for hire is around €5 per hour, €10–12 per half day, €20 per day. Helmets and gloves are extra. Some companies organise group rides, which cost around €40 per half day and include instructor, gear and insurance.

Descente VTT Télénavette 3 Rue Ste-Alexis, 97434 St-Gilles-les-Bains; ☎ 0262 245026; m 0692 211111; e telenavette@oceanes.fr; www.telenavette.com

Locascoot 162 Rue du Général de Gaulle, 97434 St-Gilles-les-Bains; ☎/f 0262 255698; e locascoot@wanadoo.fr; www. locascoot.com

Rando Réunion Passion 13 Rue du Général de Gaulle, 97434 St-Gilles-les-Bains; ☎ 0262 242619; e randoreunion@wanadoo.fr; www.vttreunion.com

Services Cycles 17 Rue Amirale Lacaze, 97410 St-Pierre; ☎ 0262 702193; e iougy@live.fr

VTT Réunion 404 Chemin de la Ravine Sèche, 97427 Etang-Salé; ☎ 0262 380197; e vttreunion@gmail.com; www.vtt-reunion.com

HORSERIDING

On horseback is the ideal way to explore Réunion's rugged interior. Rides can be arranged for just an hour, a half day, a full day or several days. Some of the establishments around La Plaine-des-Cafres offer rides to the volcano, Piton-de-la-Fournaise.

Riding schools vary considerably in standard, although instructors are usually qualified. Although most establishments are affiliated to the French Equestrian Federation, many are reluctant to loan hats, even if they have them. If you insist, you will usually get one, which is important as the terrain in the interior is invariably rocky and uneven. An hour's ride will usually cost around €20–30, a half day €45–50, a full day €90–115.

Alti Merens 120 Rue Maurice Kraft, 97418 La Plaine-des-Cafres; ☎ 0262 591884; m 0692 041238; e centreequestre.alti-merens@orange.fr. A very picturesque place to ride & the 8 Merens horses from the Pyrenees are ideally suited to the rough ground. Can offer a 2-day ride to the volcano, with accommodation & meals, if booked in advance.

Centre Equestre de la Fenêtre 31 Route de Mont Plaisir, 97421 Les Makes; ☎ 0262 378874

Centre Equestre de la Montagne 50 Chemin Couilloux, St-Bernard, 97417 La Montagne; ☎ 0262 236251; e cem@runedit.com; www.equimontagne.com

Centre Equestre du Cap 124 Route Hubert Delisle, 97416 Chaloupe St-Leu; ☎ 0262 547617; m 0692 823576; e ceducap@orange.fr; www.ceducap.com

Centre Equestre du Maïdo 350 Route du Maïdo, 97423 Le Guillaume; ☎/f 0262 324915; m 0692 675447. Plenty of well-cared-for horses & equipment.

Club Hippique de L'Hermitage Zac Hermitage, Chemin Ceinture, 97434 St-Gilles-les-Bains; ☎ 0262 244773; f 0262 330048; ⏲ Tue–Sun. Lots of very chic French regulars, so it feels a bit cliquey. You can ride along the beach.

Ecuries d'Eldorado 22 Chemin Band'colons, 97427 Etang-Salé-les-Hauts; m 0692 877448; e ecuries.eldorado@gmail.com; www.eldorado.re. Forest & beach rides.

Ecuries de Notre Dame de la Paix 37 Chemin de la Chapelle, Notre Dame de la Paix, 97418 La Plaine-des-Cafres; ☎ 0262 593449; m 0692 614679; e antoine-patrick.lauret@wanadoo.fr

Ecuries du Relais 75 Chemin Léopold Lebon, Manapany-les-Hauts, 97429 Petit-Ile; ☎ 0262 567867

Ecuries du Volcan 9 bis Domaine de Bellevue, 97418 La Plaine-des-Cafres; m 0692 666290; f 0262 355445

Ferme Equestre Auberge du Pont-Neuf 59 ter, CD 11 Pont Neuf, 97425 Les Avirons; ☎/f 0262 380940; e ferme.pontneuf@caramail.com

Ferme Equestre du Grand Etang RN3, Pont Payet, 97470 St-Benoît; ☎ 0262 509003; m 0692 868825; e riconourry@wanadoo.fr; www.fermequestre.re. A wide range of rides offered, including treks of up to 6 days. Mountain biking is also available.

Pony Club Equirun 37 Allée Montignac, 97427 Etang-Salé; ☎ 0262 265252;. More of a riding school than a trekking centre, but it does offer rides through Etang-Salé Forest.

GOLF

Although not a popular sport amongst locals, Réunion boasts a few beautiful courses. All the clubs offer trolley and club hire, as well as lessons. In all cases, the green fees shown for weekends also apply on public holidays. Lessons cost in the region of €20 for 30 minutes.

Bassin Bleu Country Club 75 Rue Mahatma Gandhi, Villèle, 97435 St-Gilles-les-Hauts; ☎ 0262 700300; e golf@bassinbleu.fr; www.golfbassinbleu.com; ⏲ daily. 18-hole par-72 course. Has a restaurant serving lunch, bar & pool. Green fees €60 (18 holes), €35 (9 holes).

Golf Club du Bourbon 140 Les Sables, 97427 Etang-Salé; ☎ 0262 263339; e golfclubbourbon@wanadoo.fr; www.golf-bourbon.com; ⏲ daily except Mon morning. Beautiful 18-hole par-72 course with hordes of tropical plants. Attractive clubhouse with a restaurant (closed Mon) & swimming pool. Green fees €48 for 18 holes weekdays, €60 weekends; €27 for 9 holes weekdays, €35 weekends.

Golf du Colorado 52 Zone de Loisirs du Colorado, 97417 La Montagne; ☎ 0262 237950; e gcc4@wanadoo.fr; www.golfclubcolorado.fr; ⏲ daily except Mon morning. 9-hole par-68 course. Snack bar. Green fees for 18 holes €23 weekdays, €35 weekends.

4X4 EXCURSIONS

The going rate for excursions in 4x4 vehicles is around €90–95 per person per day (usually including lunch).

Kréolie 4x4 4 Impasse des Avocats, 97414 Entre-Deux; ☎/f 0262 395087; m 0692 865226; e kreolie4x4@wanadoo.fr; www.kreolie4x4.com

MICROLIGHTING

Microlighting offers a bird's-eye view of some of the island's greatest assets. The French for microlight is *ULM* (*Ultra Léger Motorisé*) (pronounced 'oo-el-em').

Felix ULM RUN Bas ULM Cambaie, 97460 St-Paul; ☎ 0262 430259; m 0692 873232; f 0262 4556308; e felixulm@wanadoo.fr; www.felixulm.com. Lagoon €65, Cirque de Mafate €65, Mafate/Salazie/Cilaos €145, Mafate/Salazie/Cilaos/volcano €170.

Mascareignes Airlines Chemin de l'Aerodrome, 97410 St-Pierre; ☎ 0262 325325; m 0692 725160; e mascareignes@gmail.com; www.mascareignes.fr. Volcano €90, Mafate/Salazie/Cilaos/Trou de Fer/lagoon €130.

Papangue ULM 10 Allée Belynted, Chemin Segret 97419 La Possession ☎ 0692 088586; www.papangue-ulm.fr. Cirque de Salazie from €80.

Les Passagers du Vent Base ULM, ZI de Cambaie, 97460 St-Paul; ☎ 0262 429595; m 0692 687055; f 0262 422234; e contact@ulm-reunion.com; www.ulm-reunion.com. Introductory flight €40, Cirque de Mafate €70, Mafate/lagoon €110, Mafate/Salazie/Cilaos/Trou de Fer €145.

PARAGLIDING

Paragliding is very popular, particularly in the hills above St-Leu. Beginners glide in tandem with an instructor. The French for paragliding is *parapente*. Expect to pay around €75 for an introductory flight over the lagoon (a descent of about 800m).

Air Lagon Parapente 67 Rue Jean-Baptiste de Villèle, Les Colimaçons, 97436 St-Leu; ☎ 0262 247817; m 0692 875287; e airlagon@wanadoo.fr; www.airlagon-parapente.fr

Azurtech 3 Impasse des Plongeurs, La Pointe des Châteaux, 97436 St-Leu; ☎ 0262 349189; m 0692 850400; f 0262 380186; e contact@azurtech.com; www.azurtech.com

Bourbon Parapente 4 Rue Haute, BP 12 97898 St-Leu; ☎/f 0262 341834; m 0692 875874; e master@bourbonparapente.com; www.bourbonparapente.com

Modul'Air Aventure 26 Ruelle des Bougainvilliers, 97434 St-Gilles-les-Bains; **m** 0692 040404; **f** 0262 338449; **e** nicodid@wanadoo.fr; www.modulair-parapente.com

Parapente Réunion 103 Rue Georges Pompidou, 97436 St-Leu; ☎ 0262 248784; **m** 0692 829292; e info@parapente-reunion.fr; www.parapente-reunion.fr

BUNGEE JUMPING

Bungee jumpers leap from the Pont d'Anglais Suspension Bridge between Ste-Anne and Ste-Rose. The organisers (*www.elasticjump.com*)need to have a group of people jumping on each occasion, so you may not be able to jump until several days, or even weeks, after your initial enquiry. Jumps take place on weekends and cost around €60.

HELICOPTER RIDES

If your time on Réunion is limited, a helicopter ride is a great way to see the island. The most popular flights cover the island's main attractions: the volcano, the cirques, the coast, Trou de Fer, etc. Prices are in the range €85–300 per person, depending on the itinerary. A short, 15-min flight will start from around €85, while a 45-min flight is around €240.

Corail Helicoptères Aéroport de Pierrefonds, 97410 St-Pierre; ☎ 0262 222266; **m** 0692 006666; **e** info@corail-helicopteres.com; www.corail-helicopteres.com

Helilagon Altiport de l'Eperon, 97467 St-Paul; ☎ 0262 555555; **e** heliglagon@helilagon.com; www.helilagon.com

SURFING

Surfing is very popular in Réunion and an international championship competition is held annually at St-Leu. Surfers should seek the advice of locals before leaping into the water as the majority of shark attacks are on surfers. Stand-up paddle is the latest craze to hit Réunion and you will see plenty of people giving it a go in the lagoons. For more information contact the Surf League (☎ *0262 243310*).

Expect to pay around €30 for a one-hour individual surfing lesson or €20 for a group lesson. The following surf schools cater for all levels, from children to competition training.

Ecole de Stand-Up Paddle du Lagon et de Surf des Roches-Noires 19A Lot des Charmilles, 97434 St-Gilles-les-Bains; ☎/**f** 0262 246328; **m** 0692 860059; **e** bertrand.surf@wanadoo.fr; www.ecole-surf-reunion.com

Ecole de Surf Bourbon Réunion 25 Rue Amirale Lacaze, St-Pierre; ☎ 0692 661673; **e** ecolesurfbourbonreunion@gmail.com; www.ecolesurfbourbonreunion.com

Ecole de Surf Extreme Sud & Surf Shop 67 Rue Octave Bénard, 97427 Etang-Salé-les-Bains; ☎/**f** 0262 266702; **m** 0692 644514; **e** valverde-postigo@wanadoo.fr

Ecole de Surf de St-Leu 22 Chemin des Tourterelles, St-Leu; ☎ 0692 654492; www.surf-reunion.com

WATER SKIING

Ski Club de St-Paul 1 Rue de la Croix, 97460 St-Paul; ☎ 0262 454287; **f** 0262 212288; www.skiclubdelareunion.com; ⏲ 10.30–18.00 Mon, Wed & Thu, 09.00–18.00 Sat/Sun. Caters for all levels of ability.

OTHER WATERSPORTS

Oasis Eaux Vives 38 Ilet Coco, St-Benoît; ☎ 0692 001623; e rvpiaut@wanadoo.fr; www.oasisev.com. White-water rafting.

Planch'Alizé 25 Rue des Mouettes, 97434 La Saline-les-Bains; ☎ 0262 246261; www.planchalize.net. Hire of windsurfers, kayaks, pedaloes & snorkelling equipment.

THIM Nautique 165 bis Rue du Général de Gaulle, 97434 St-Gilles-les-Bains; ☎ 0262 242324; e thim.loc@wanadoo.fr. Boat & jet-ski hire, water skiing.

SAILING

The majority of private yachts are kept in the marinas at St-Gilles-les-Bains and St-Pierre, where you may be able to organise sailing trips on an ad hoc basis. Alternatively, contact one of the following companies:

Batoloc Port de Plaisance, 97434 St-Gilles-les-Bains; ☎/f 0262 334867; e www.batalocs@wanadoo.fr; www.rj73.com/batoloc. Boat hire, fishing.

Bleu Indien 7 Rue Andromède, Le Mont Roquefeuille, 97434 St-Gilles-les-Bains; m 0692 853753; e bleu_indien@hotmail.com; www.bleuindien.com. Boat hire, plus fishing, wakeboarding & scuba-diving gear.

Compagnie des Pirates 4 Rue Générale de Gaulle, 97434 St-Gilles-les-Bains; ☎ 0692 700277; e oceandream@live.fr; www.lacompagniedespirates.com. Sailing, cruises.

SCUBA DIVING

The best diving is on the west coast, around St-Leu and St-Gilles-les-Bains. It is not as good as the diving in the other Mascarenes but is worth trying nonetheless.

All dive centres cater for all levels. Expect to pay around €60 for an introductory dive of about 20–30 minutes. Dives for those with experience cost around €40 or €250 for six dives. Snorkelling trips, with equipment supplied, can usually be arranged by dive centres for around €20.

If you don't speak French, check before you book that the dive centre can provide an English-speaking instructor as it's essential that you understand the safety instructions.

Abyss Plongée 17 Bd Bonnier, 97436 St-Leu; ☎/f 0262 347979; e plongeurs@abyss-plongee.com; www.abyss-plongee.com

Bleu Marine Réunion Port de Plaisance, 97434 St-Gilles-les-Bains; ☎ 0262 242200; e bleu-marine-run@wanadoo.fr; www.bleu-marine-reunion.com

Bleu Océan 25 RN1, 97436 St-Leu; ☎/f 0262 349749; e bleuocean2@wanadoo.fr; www.bleuocean.fr

Corail Plongée Port de Plaisance, 97434 St-Gilles-les-Bains; ☎ 0262 243725; e info@corail-plongee.com; www.corail-plongee.com

O Sea Bleu Enceinte Portuaire, 97434 St-Gilles-les-Bains; ☎ 0262 331615; e osea.bleu@reunion-plongee.com; www.reunion-plongee.com

Réunion Plongée 13 Av des Artisans, 97436 St-Leu; ☎/f 0262 347777; e clubhouse@reunionplongee.com; www.reunionplongee.com

Sub Excelsus 1 Impasse des Plongeurs, ZA Pointe des Châteaux, 97436 St-Leu; ☎/f 0262 347365; e contact@excelsus-plongee.com; www.excelsus-plongee.com

DEEP-SEA FISHING

In 2003, a female fishing world record was achieved in the waters off Réunion, when Catherine Lavit caught a blue marlin weighing 551kg. Other fish caught off Réunion include bonito, tuna, wahoo, dorado, shark and swordfish.

The French for deep-sea fishing is *la pêche au gros*. Expect to pay around €80–90 per person per half day and €50 for those who don't want to fish but just go along for the ride. Drinks and light refreshments are often included.

Albacore Port de Plaisance, St-Gilles-les-Bains; ☎ 0262 330441; www.albacorefishingclub.com
Alpha Port de Plaisance, St-Gilles-les-Bains; ☎ 0262 240202
Blue Marlin Port de Plaisance, St-Gilles-les-Bains; m 0692 652235
Maevasion Port de Plaisance, St-Gilles-les-Bains; ☎ 0262 333804
Pêche Passion Sud St-Pierre m 0692 444477
Pêche Sud Evasion St-Pierre; m 0692 700518; e pechesudevasion@hotmail.com; www.pechesudevasion.fr
Réunion Fishing Club 10 Enceinte Portuaire, 97434 St-Gilles-les-Bains; ☎ 0262 243610; m 0692 761728; e reunion.fishing.club@wanadoo.fr; www.reunionfishingclub.com

GLASS-BOTTOM BOATS

These are a good way for non-divers to see the marine environment and are suitable for children of any age.

Grand Bleu Port de Plaisance, 97434 St-Gilles-les-Bains; ☎/f 0262 332832; e info@grandbleu.re; www.grandbleu.re. 2 large boats & a bubble boat, all with underwater viewing. Trips last 1½hrs & depart at least 5 times daily. Dolphins are often seen in the early morning. The large boats can feel a bit crowded. Adult from €18.

Visiobul Réunion Port de Plaisance, 97434 St-Gilles-les-Bains; ☎ 0262 243704; m 0692 852346; e visiobulreunion@wanadoo.fr; www.visiobul-reunion.com; ⏲ from 08.00 daily. 4 smaller boats with trips lasting 30mins. Adult/student/child €12/10/7.

DOLPHIN WATCHING

Dauphin Safari Port de St-Gilles-les-Bains; ☎/f 0262 332832; www.dauphinsafari.com. Dolphin-watching cruises departing from St-Gilles-les-Bains, with a trained guide. 2hr cruises depart at 08.00 & 10.00; there are also lunchtime & sunset cruises. 2hr cruise adult/child from €29/17. Reservation essential. Lunch cruise with snorkelling, kayaking & swimming adult/child from €36/25, sunset cruise adult/child from €30/20.

17

Northern Réunion

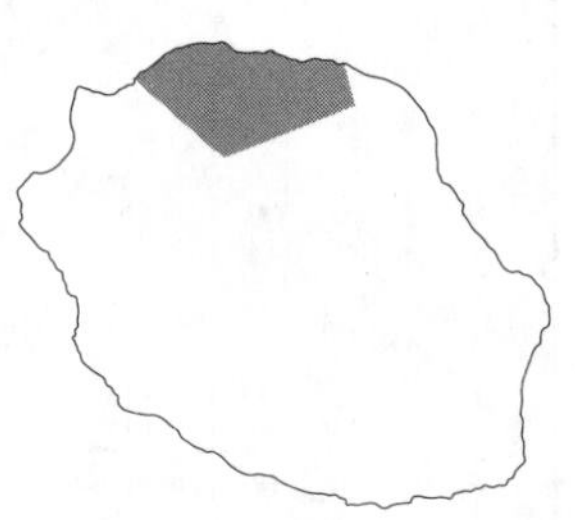

As the Roland Garros International Airport and the department's main city, St-Denis, are located on the north coast, it is the start (and end) point of most Réunion holidays. The far north of Réunion is generally defined as the area around St-Denis, extending inland to St-François, Plaine d'Affouches and the wonderful hiking area of Roche Ecrite, on the northern edge of the Cirque de Salazie.

ST-DENIS

Founded in 1668, this attractive coastal city in northern Réunion is home to around 140,000 inhabitants. St-Denis took over as capital from St-Paul in 1738, after being declared as such by the then governor Mahé de Labourdonnais. Understandably, people refer to St-Denis (pronounced 'san de-nee') as the capital, and it is the administrative capital of the island, but Réunion's status as a *département d'outre-mer* means that Paris is the true capital.

St-Denis is bordered by the sea to the north and backed by high, green mountains to the south, so its setting is very appealing. Although it sits on a tropical island, its trendy cafés and French shops give it a European flavour. The simple grid system makes it an easy place to explore.

It is possible to see the town's main attractions in a day's walkabout. The seafront promenade known as **Le Barachois**, once a port, is a good place to start, with its cannons left over from the days of war with the British. The bars and restaurants in the area really come to life in the evenings. At **Place Sarda Garriga** (named after the governor who published the decree abolishing slavery) you'll see the statue of Roland Garros, a famed St-Denis-born aviator after whom the international airport is named.

St-Denis is perfect for lovers of history and architecture, with a wealth of old buildings. The ***Préfecture***, the island's administrative offices near Le Barachois, is in an attractive former French East India Company building, constructed in 1735. On Avenue de la Victoire is the Tuscan-style **Cathédrale de St-Denis**, which was begun in 1829. Further along is the impressive **old town hall**, lighting up the street with its sunflower-yellow exterior. In front of it is the **Monument aux Morts**, erected in 1923 in honour of the Réunionnais casualties of World War I. **Rue de Paris** is lined with wonderful **colonial buildings**, many of which are 19th-century Creole mansions built for those made wealthy by the sugar industry. The attractive **Maison Carrère**, at 14 Rue de Paris, dates from 1820 and now houses the **tourist office**. On the corner of Rue Félix Guyon stands the opulent, much-photographed Creole **mansion of the Secretary General**. Rue de Paris is also where most of the town's **museums** are found.

The main **market** (*grand marché*) and its smaller counterpart (*petit marché*) are both on Rue Maréchal Leclerc, which also boasts a fine Creole building, the home of former French prime minister, Raymond Barre. In the same street is the city's

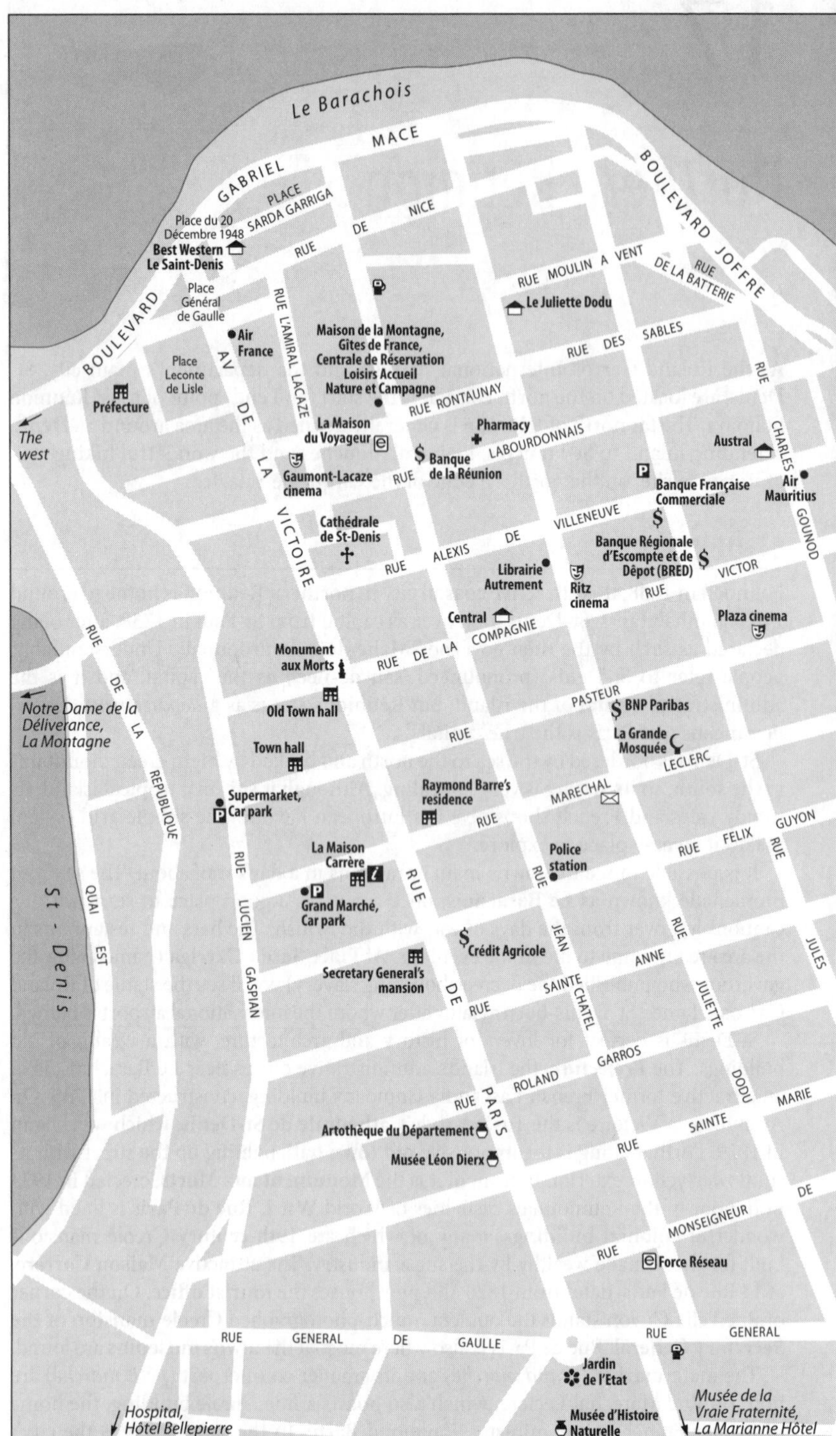

Le Barachois
BOULEVARD GABRIEL MACE
BOULEVARD JOFFRE
PLACE SARDA GARRIGA
Place du 20 Décembre 1948
Best Western Le Saint-Denis
RUE DE NICE
RUE MOULIN A VENT
RUE DE LA BATTERIE
Place Général de Gaulle
RUE L'AMIRAL LACAZE
Le Juliette Dodu
Air France
Maison de la Montagne, Gites de France, Centrale de Réservation Loisirs Accueil Nature et Campagne
RUE DES SABLES
Place Leconte de Lisle
AV DE LA VICTOIRE
Préfecture
RUE RONTAUNAY
The west
La Maison du Voyageur
Pharmacy
RUE LABOURDONNAIS
Banque de la Réunion
Austral
RUE CHARLES GOUNOD
Air Mauritius
Gaumont-Lacaze cinema
Banque Française Commerciale
Cathédrale de St-Denis
RUE ALEXIS DE VILLENEUVE
Banque Régionale d'Escompte et de Dépot (BRED)
Librairie Autrement
Ritz cinema
RUE VICTOR
Central
Plaza cinema
RUE DE LA COMPAGNIE
Monument aux Morts
RUE DE LA REPUBLIQUE
Notre Dame de la Déliverance, La Montagne
Old Town hall
RUE PASTEUR
BNP Paribas
La Grande Mosquée
Town hall
RUE MARECHAL LECLERC
Raymond Barre's residence
Supermarket, Car park
RUE FELIX GUYON
La Maison Carrère
Police station
RUE DE PARIS
St - Denis
QUAI EST
RUE LUCIEN GASPIAN
Grand Marché, Car park
RUE JEAN CHATEL
RUE JULIETTE DODU
JULES
Crédit Agricole
Secretary General's mansion
RUE SAINTE ANNE
RUE ROLAND GARROS
RUE SAINTE MARIE
Artothèque du Département
Musée Léon Dierx
RUE MONSEIGNEUR DE
Force Réseau
RUE GENERAL DE GAULLE
RUE GENERAL
Jardin de l'Etat
Hospital, Hôtel Bellepierre
Musée d'Histoire Naturelle
Musée de la Vraie Fraternité, La Marianne Hôtel

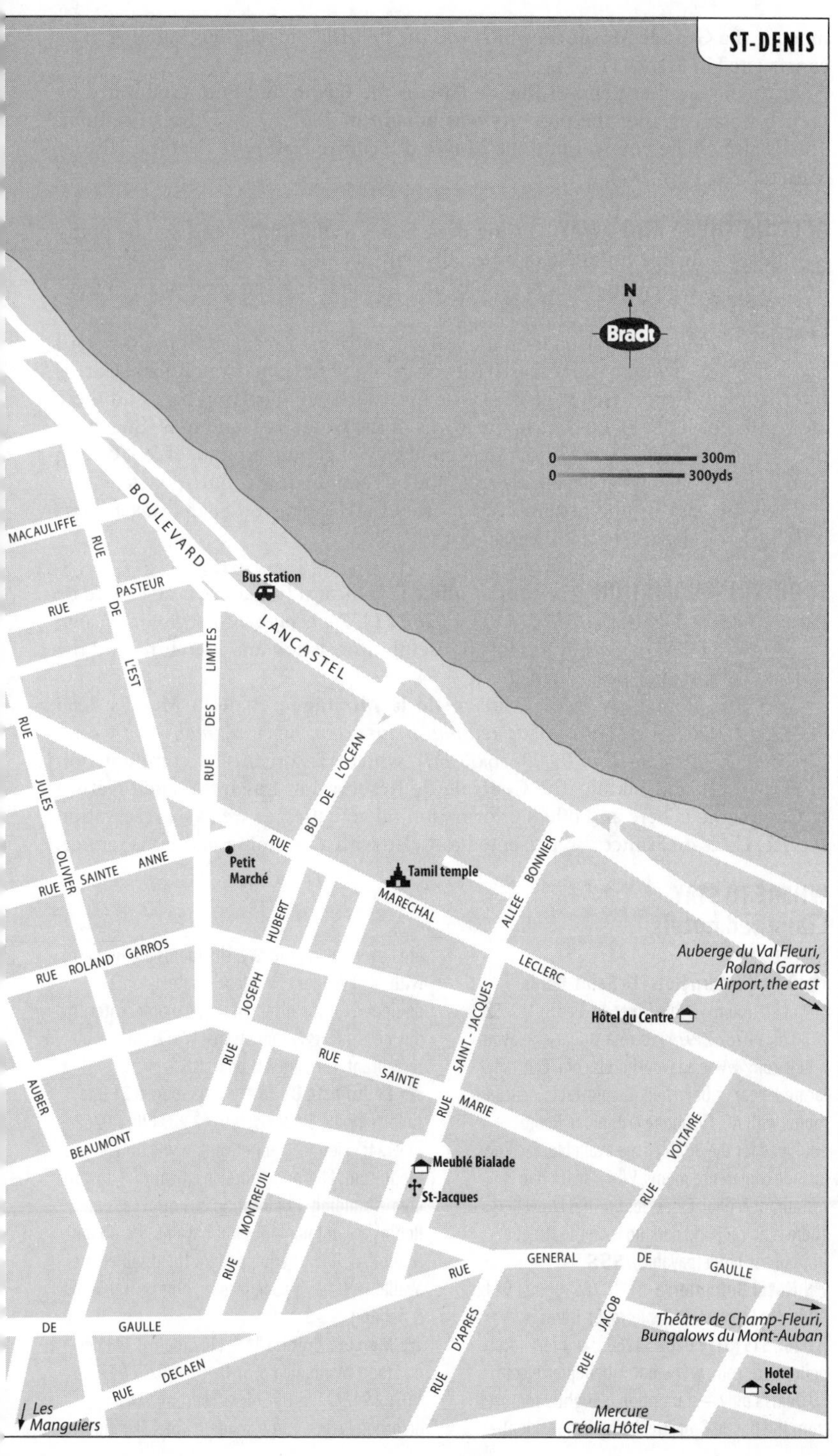
ST-DENIS
N
Bradt
0 300m
0 300yds
BOULEVARD
LANCASTEL
Bus station
MACAULIFFE
RUE PASTEUR
RUE DE L'EST
RUE DES LIMITES
RUE JULES OLIVIER
BD DE L'OCEAN
RUE MARECHAL LECLERC
Petit Marché
Tamil temple
RUE SAINTE ANNE
ALLEE BONNIER
RUE ROLAND GARROS
RUE JOSEPH HUBERT
RUE SAINT - JACQUES
Auberge du Val Fleuri, Roland Garros Airport, the east
Hôtel du Centre
RUE SAINTE MARIE
AUBER
BEAUMONT
RUE VOLTAIRE
Meublé Bialade
St-Jacques
RUE MONTREUIL
RUE GENERAL DE GAULLE
DE GAULLE
RUE JACOB
Théâtre de Champ-Fleuri, Bungalows du Mont-Auban
RUE D'APRES
RUE DECAEN
Hotel Select
Les Manguiers
Mercure Créolia Hôtel

mosque, **La Grande Mosquée**, which was the first Islamic religious building to be constructed in France (1905).

At the far southern end of Rue de Paris is the **Jardin de l'Etat**, established by French botanists after the property was bought in 1767 by an Officer Cremont. This is also where you will find the **Musée d'Histoire Naturelle** (Natural History Museum; see page 287).

GETTING THERE AND AWAY During peak hours traffic in St-Denis can be pretty intimidating for the uninitiated, especially with its intricate one-way system. The town is small enough to explore on foot and Le Barachois is a good place to leave your car.

The *cars jaunes* **bus station** is on the seafront and can be reached from Boulevard Lancastel. This is where you will arrive if you get the shuttle bus from Roland Garros International Airport (see page 253). The bus routes are displayed here and there are regular buses to St-Pierre, via the towns of the west coast, and to St-Benoît on the east coast. St-Denis city buses are a good way of getting around, except during rush hour. Timetables are available from the bus station or the tourist office.

Taxis are easy to find at the bus station but are expensive. Shared taxis (*taxis collectifs*) also depart from the bus station.

TOURIST INFORMATION The **tourist office** (Syndicat d'Initiative) is at 14 Rue de Paris, 97400 St-Denis; *0262 418300;* **f** *0262 213776;* **e** *info@ot-nordreunion.com; 09.00–18.00 Mon–Sat*). It has lots of useful information and literature, and the staff are helpful and speak English.

At 5 Rue Rontaunay is the **Maison de la Montagne et de la Mer** (*0262 907890;* **f** *0262 418429;* **e** *resa@reunion-nature.com; www.reunion-nature.com; 09.00–17.00 Mon–Thu, 09.00–16.00 Fri*), which can organise accommodation in rural areas and hiking. The **Centrale de Réservation Loisirs Accueil Nature et Campagne** is here and offers information on activities, as well as a reservation service. **Gîtes de France** is represented too, also with a central reservations service.

WHERE TO STAY

Classified hotels

Mid range

Best Western Hotel Le Saint-Denis *** (118 rooms) 2 Rue Doret, St-Denis; 0262 218020; **f** 0262 219741; **e** resa.stdenis@apavou-hotels.com; www.apavou-hotels.com. Centrally located, near Le Barachois. Comfortable, spacious rooms with AC, TV, phone & minibar. Rooms equipped for the disabled are available. Facilities include conference rooms, Wi-Fi, snack bar, restaurant & pool. Caters for business travellers. There is no car park, parking is on the street in front of the hotel (payable). **$$$**

Hôtel Bellepierre **** (85 rooms) 91 bis Allée des Topazes, Bellepierre, St-Denis; 0262 515151; **f** 0262 512602; **e** info@hotel-bellepierre.com; www.hotel-bellepierre.com. St-Denis's only 4-star option is slightly removed from the hustle & bustle, being in a residential area overlooking the city. The rooms are modern, with AC, TV, phone, minibar & safe. Rooms equipped for the disabled are available. Caters for business guests & there is free Wi-Fi. There is a restaurant, car park & a pool. **$$$**

Le Juliette Dodu *** (43 rooms) 31 Rue Juliette Dodu, St-Denis; 0262 209120; **f** 0262 209121; **e** jdodu@runnet.com; www.hotel-jdodu.com. Charming hotel in a beautiful, historic Creole building. The location is central yet quiet. Rooms are not luxurious but have AC, TV, phone & minibar. Rooms equipped for the disabled are available. It has a pool, jacuzzi, library, free Wi-Fi & parking. **$$$**

Mercure Créolia *** (107 rooms) 14 Rue du Stade, Montgaillard, St-Denis; 0262 942626; **f** 0262 942727; **e** H1674@accor.com; www.accorhotels.com. Large, modern hotel 3km from the centre with impressive views of the city & ocean. Rooms have AC, TV, phone, minibar & superior rooms have a safe. Rooms equipped for the disabled are available. Facilities include a large pool, jacuzzi, sauna, conference room, free Wi-Fi & car park. The restaurant specialises in Creole & French food. **$$$**

Budget

Austral Hotel *** (53 rooms) 20 Rue Charles Gounod, St Denis; 0262 944567; f 0262 211314; e hotel-austral@wanadoo.fr; www.hotel-austral.fr. In the centre of town. Unremarkable but comfortable en-suite rooms with AC, TV, phone, Wi-Fi & minibar. Rooms equipped for the disabled are available. Facilities include underground parking, a small pool & a restaurant serving breakfast only. B/fasts (buffet €11 pp) are good. **$$**

Central Hotel ** (57 rooms) 37 Rue de la Compagnie, St-Denis; 0262 941808; f 0262 216433; e central.hotel@wanadoo.fr; www.centralhotel.re. Functional, no-frills accommodation in the centre of town. Rooms have en suite, AC, TV, phone, & safe; some have minibar. There is a small car park & plenty of competition for spaces. Be warned, there is no lift & you could find yourself dragging your luggage up 3 flights of stairs. **$$**

Hotel Select ** (55 rooms) 1 bis Rue des Lataniers, St-Denis; 0262 411350; f 0262 416707; e hotelselect@wanadoo.fr; www.runweb.com/hotelselect. Comfortable, clean en-suite rooms with AC, TV & phone. It has a small pool, parking & Wi-Fi. There are rooms suitable for the disabled. **$$**

La Marianne ** (24 rooms) 5 Ruelle Boulot, St-Denis; 0262 218080; f 0262 218500; e hotel-la-marianne@wanadoo.fr. Close to the town centre. Rooms are plain with en suite, AC, TV, phone & minibar. 3 of the rooms are equipped with kitchenette & are more expensive. There is an underground car park. **$$**

Unclassified accommodation

Shoestring

Hôtel du Centre (35 rooms) 272 Rue Maréchal Leclerc, St-Denis; 0262 417302; e hotelducentrerun@wanadoo.fr; www.hotelducentrerun.com. Centrally located, close to plenty of restaurants. Simple, small, colourful rooms with AC & TV; some have en suite. There is a small car park. Breakfast is taken on a pleasant patio. En-suite dbl from €35, sgl with shared bathroom from €25 RO. **$**

Les Manguiers (20 apts) 9 Rue des Manguiers, St-Denis; 0692 919292; f 0262 202223; e manguiers@wanadoo.fr; www.runweb.com/manguiers. Self-catering apartments, including 2 equipped for the disabled. All have 1 double room, bathroom, sitting area, kitchenette, AC, TV, phone & balcony. Good option for businesspeople staying for lengthy periods. **$**

Self-catering holiday rentals

Bungalows du Mont-Auban ** (3 bungalows) 27 bis Chemin Montauban, La Bretagne, Ste-Clotilde; 0262 525008; e loc.974@wanadoo.fr. About a 30mins' drive from the centre of St-Denis. Each bungalow has 2 bedrooms, bathroom, sitting area, kitchenette & terrace. Bungalow from €370 per week (2 people), €470 (4 people).

Meublé Bialade * (1 apt) 6 Rue Magallon, St-Denis; 0262 202891; e bialade.gerard@wanadoo.fr. Close to the town centre. 1-bedroom apartment for up to 4 people with AC. Apt from €260 per week (2 people).

WHERE TO EAT For self-caterers, there is a **Continent hypermarket** between St-Denis and Roland Garros Airport, as well as several smaller supermarkets in town. For eating out, there are numerous restaurants, street vendors, snack bars, bistros, brasseries and cafés, which are part and parcel of St-Denis's café society. However, finding a restaurant that's open Sunday lunchtime can be a challenge. Below is a cross-section of St-Denis's eateries:

✕ **Atelier de Ben** 12 Rue de la Compagnie; ☎0262 418573; ⏲ for lunch Tue–Fri & dinner Tue–Sat. Cuisine: French. Has a good reputation for creative cuisine. $$$$

✕ **Bordeaux** 1 bis Av de la Victoire; ☎0262 901727; ⏲ for lunch & dinner Tue–Fri, closed Sat lunch, Sun & Mon evening. Cuisine: French. A small restaurant near Le Barachois, serving traditional dishes from the Bordeaux region of France. $$$

✕ **Chez Piat** 60 Rue Pasteur; ☎0262 214576; ⏲ for lunch & dinner Tue–Fri, closed Sat lunch, Sun & Mon evening. Cuisine: French. It may not look like much from the outside but within lies a stylish restaurant with a romantic atmosphere. The restaurant has been going for 25 years & has a healthy number of regulars. $$$

✕ **Le Clos St-Jacques** 5 Ruelle Edouard; ☎0262 215909; closed Sat lunch, Sun & Mon evening. Cuisine: French. An upmarket restaurant in an attractive Creole house next to the cathedral & close to the university. A good option for a special occasion. $$$

✕ **Le Roland Garros** 2 Place du 20 décembre 1848; ☎0262 414437; ⏲ 07.00–midnight daily. Cuisine: French, Creole. Handy location at Le Barachois, European feel. $$$

✕ **O Bar Resto** 32 Rue de la Compagnie; ☎0262 413888; ⏲ 10.00–00.30 Mon–Sat. Cuisine: French. A trendy, modern bar/restaurant in the centre of town, opposite Hotel Central. There is a tempting cocktail menu. $$$

✕ **Via Veneto** 151 Rue Jules Auber; ☎0262 219271; ⏲ for lunch Mon, for dinner Tue–Sat. Cuisine: Italian, French. $$$

✕ **La Récré** 21 Rue de la Victoire; ☎0262 238341; ⏲ 09.00–15.00 Mon/Tue, 09.00–22.00 Wed–Sat. Cuisine: French, Creole. Tables are in a covered outdoor eating area – an informal atmosphere. $$

✕ **Le Pavillon d'Or** 224 Rue Maréchal Leclerc; ☎0262 214986; ⏲ for lunch & dinner Mon–Sat. Cuisine: Chinese. Relaxed atmosphere. Main courses from €9.50. $$

✕ **Les Délices de l'Orient** 59 Rue Juliette Dodu; ☎0262 414420; ⏲ for lunch & dinner Tue–Sat. Cuisine: Chinese. Large, popular restaurant with a relaxed atmosphere. $$

✕ **L'Eté Glacé** 19 Rue de la Compagnie; ☎0262 201401; ⏲ 10.30–14.30 Mon, 10.30–18.00 Tue–Sat. Very French tea rooms offering a wide variety of teas & coffees, plus homemade pastries & ice cream. Art is exhibited & on sale. $$

✕ **L'Igloo Glacerie** Cnr Rues Jean Chatel & Compagnie; ☎0262 213469; ⏲ 11.00–midnight Mon–Sat, 15.00–midnight Sun. Cuisine: light meals, ice cream. 2 separate shops on either side of the road offering a huge range of ice creams, sorbets & crêpes, plus light meals. $$

✕ **Mumbai** 79 Rue Pasteur; ☎0262 300672; ⏲ for lunch & dinner Mon–Sat. Cuisine: Indian. Good-quality Indian food. $$.

✕ **Oasis** Le Barachois; ☎0262 218020; ⏲ 07.00–midnight daily. Cuisine: French, Creole. $$

✕ **Boulanger Castel** 43 Rue de la Compagnie; ☎0262 212766; ⏲ 06.00–14.00 & 15.30–19.00 Tue–Sat, 07.00–12.00 Sun. Cuisine: French, bakery, tea rooms. A large, traditional bakery with a well-deserved reputation for fine breads & patisserie. Eat in or take-away. $

✕ **Massalé** 30 Rue Alexis de Villeneuve; ☎0262 217506; ⏲ 10.00–20.00 Mon–Thu & Sat, 14.00–20.00 & 11.00–20.30 Sun. Cuisine: Indian snacks. Eat-in or take-away. Tiny establishment selling a tempting variety of delicious *samoussas*, *bonbons piments* & other tasty bites. *Samoussas* cost just 50c & you can easily make a full meal of the treats on offer. $

NIGHTLIFE The European theme continues into the night in St-Denis, with lots of bars and ice-cream parlours open until late. The **bar** of the moment appears to be **Les Récréateurs** (*2 Pl Etienne Regnault; ☎0692 490493; www.lesrecreatures.info; ⏲ 17.30–02.30 Tue–Sun*). **Moda Bar** (*75 Rue Pasteur; ☎0262 587614*), has a trendy, modern atmosphere. **Le Zanzibar** (*41 Rue Pasteur; ☎0262 200118*), a restaurant/bar, is very popular and customers hit the dance floor later in the evening. Nightclubs include the gay-friendly **Le Boy's** (*108 Rue Pasteur; m 0692 662553*), **Le Gin Jet** (*9 Bd Vauban; m 0692 361561*) and **Le First** (*8 Av de la Victoire; ☎0262 416825*). Clubs really only get going after 23.00. As in most towns, entry is around €12.

The **Casino de Saint-Denis** is in Le Barachois (☎*0262 413333; slot machines ⏲ from 10.00 daily & the tables 21.00–02.00 Mon–Thu, 21.00–03.00 Fri/Sat, 21.00–01.00 Sun*).

ENTERTAINMENT

Cinema There are three cinemas in St-Denis, usually showing international films dubbed into French: **Ritz** (*53 Rue Juliette Dodu; ☎ 0262 902270*), **Plaza** (*79 Rue Pasteur; ☎ 0262 210436*) and **Gaumont Lacaze** (*cnr Rues Amiral Lacaze & Rontaunay; ☎ 0262 412000*). Tickets cost around €7.

Theatre The tourist office can provide information on forthcoming productions.

Centre dramatique de l'Océan Indien 2 Rue Maréchal Leclerc; ☎ 0262 203399; www.cdoi-reunion.com

Théâtre de Champ-Fleuri 2 Rue du Théâtre, St-Denis; ☎ 0262 419315; www.theatreunion.com

SHOPPING

In St-Denis, both **Le Grand Marché** (main market) and **Le Petit Marché** (small market) are on Rue Maréchal Leclerc. The main market (*daily*) sells mostly handicrafts. The small market (*06.00–18.00 Mon–Sat, 06.00–12.00 Sun*) has mostly fruit, vegetable, flower and spice stalls. There are markets in **Le Chaudron** on Wednesday and Sunday mornings, **Le Moufia** on Saturday morning, **La Source** on Thursday morning and **Les Camélias** on Friday morning. You'll find a range of handicrafts at the markets, as well as in the **Galerie Artisanale** at 75 Rue du Karting in the suburb of Ste-Clotilde (☎ *0262 295666*), but prices around St-Denis may be higher than in smaller towns.

Librairie Autrement (*82 Rue Juliette Dodu; ☎ 0262 209480*) is an excellent bookshop, and stocks a host of books on the Mascarene Islands.

Chic French clothing shops are popping up all over St-Denis. They are not cheap but stock some very appealing, good-quality clothes.

OTHER PRACTICALITIES

Money and banking Many French banks are represented in St-Denis. Currency and travellers' cheques can be changed at all the banks and most have ATMs.

$ Banque de la Réunion 27 Rue Jean Chatel; ☎ 0262 400123

$ Banque Française Commerciale 60 Rue Alexis de Villeneuve; ☎ 0262 405555

$ Banque Nationale de Paris Paribas (BNPP) 67 Rue Juliette Dodu; ☎ 0820 840830

$ Banque Régionale d'Escompte et de Dêpot (BRED) 33 Rue Victor MacAuliffe; ☎ 0262 901560

$ Caisse d'Epargne de la Réunion 55 Rue de Paris; ☎ 0262 948000

$ Crédit Agricole 18 Rue Félix Guyon; ☎ 0262 909100

Communications There are a number of **post offices** in the capital. The main post office (☎ *0262 211212; 07.30–18.00 Mon–Fri, 08.00–12.00 Sat*) is on the corner of Rue Maréchal Leclerc and Rue Juliette Dodu. It also handles poste restante.

Public **telephones** are widespread and, as throughout the island, the majority take phonecards (*télécartes*). These can be bought at post offices, newsagents and shops displaying the sign.

For **internet access** try **La Maison du Voyageur** (*18 Rue Rontaunay*), which also offers fixed line overseas call facilities, post box rental, photocopying and assistance with seeking accommodation. Alternatively, head to **Force Réseau**, 148 Rue Jean Chatel (☎ *0692 380738*).

Medical care The main **hospital** is on Allée des Topazes, Bellepierre (☎ *0262 905050*) and there are numerous medical practitioners. There are plenty of **pharmacies** – a good starting point is Rue Maréchal Leclerc.

AROUND ST-DENIS

East of St-Denis is the booming district of **Ste-Clotilde**, where the University of Réunion campus is found. **St-François** is a residential area in the mountains overlooking St-Denis, with a mild climate and lush vegetation. Higher up, at 800m, is **Le Brûlé**, a starting point for hikes on the **Plaine-des-Chicots**, which rises to the **Roche Ecrite** (2,275m). This overlooks the Cirque de Salazie. **La Montagne** is another residential area west of St-Denis, praised for its pleasant climate. The winding road lined with flamboyant trees features some excellent viewpoints.

About 12km east of St-Denis city centre is the village of **Ste-Marie**. There is little to see in the village itself but nearby **Rivière des Pluies** is known for its statue of the **Black Virgin (La Vierge Noire)**. The statue stands in a tall white shrine to the left of the village church, surrounded by an explosion of flower arrangements and row upon row of candles. People arrive in droves to pray to her for good health, prosperity and protection. The story goes that a runaway slave fled to the place where the shrine now stands. There, the Black Virgin appeared to him, instructing him to hide under a flimsy bush. The slave complied, although the bush was much too small to conceal him properly. Just before the slave hunters reached the spot, the Black Virgin instantly increased the size of the bush, thereby completely covering the runaway. To honour her, the slave then carved the statue and, subsequently, the shrine was erected.

WHERE TO STAY

Classified hotels

Budget

Auberge du Val Fleuri ** (8 villas) 91 Route de la Roche Ecrite, St-Denis; 0262 230107; e aubergevalfleuri@orange.fr; www.aubergevalfleuri.fr. In a park setting around 30mins by car from St-Denis, near Roche Ecrite & good hiking country. The wooden chalets are well equipped. There is a restaurant overlooking the countryside. A sauna/hammam, jacuzzi & bikes are available at no extra charge.

WHAT TO DO IN NORTHERN REUNION

ORGANISED TOURS The **tourist office** (*14 Rue de Paris, 97400 St-Denis; 0262 418300*) offers organised tours of St-Denis, Ste-Marie and Ste-Suzanne.

HIKING On the outskirts of St-Denis and beyond you'll find picturesque hamlets in breathtaking surroundings. There are plenty of options in terms of hiking trails.

Inland from Roland Garros Airport, southeast of St-Denis, is the waterfall of **Le Chaudron**. Its name comes from the cauldron-like formation into which it plunges. Getting there entails an 8km hike, which takes around two to three hours (grading: moderate).

Hiking trails around **Roche Ecrite** ('written rock') are some of the island's best. The Roche Ecrite forest road is also where you can see most of the island's endemic birds. A 10km, four-hour hike (grading: difficult) takes you to the remote **Bassin du Diable** (Devil's Pond). Alternatively, you could try the 9km, four-hour walk (grading: easy) to **Piton Laverdure**, an extinct volcanic peak, which features a mass of flowers in October and November. A popular and easily reached picnic spot is **Cascade Maniquet** (30 minutes' walk).

The Roche Ecrite walk itself is wonderful, though quite challenging, and can be done in a day. It is, however, recommended that you stay overnight at the Plaine-des-Chicots *gîte*, which you can book at Maison de la Montagne. If you have a car, you can leave it at the Mamode Camp forest road car park but there have been reports of cars being stolen or damaged here. The first leg, which is the part covered by birding tour groups, involves the three-hour walk to the *gîte* on the **Plaine-des-Chicots** path (5km), through tamarind and bamboo forest. The second leg is on the Roche Ecrite path (4km, 1½ hours). Do this early in the morning for the best weather. From a rocky spur covered with inscriptions (the 'written rock'), you can see the magnificent amphitheatres of Salazie and Mafate. On the way back, stop off at the **Soldiers' Cave (Caverne des Soldats)**, overlooking Rivière des Pluies. Another path leads to **Mare aux Cerfs (Stags' Pond)**.

The energetic (and fairly fit) can continue from Roche Ecrite, west to **Plaine d'Affouches**, which means a three-hour hike past a disused prison, Ilet à Guillaume. You can continue even further, to **Dos d'Ane** village, by taking the path branching off after Ilet à Guillaume. Ardent hikers can confront the steep trail into the Cirque de Salazie. Bring warm clothing since night temperatures are often around freezing point.

GOLF There is a nine-hole course at La Montagne, called **Golf du Colorado**. For details, see *Chapter 16, Activities*, page 274.

HORSERIDING The **Centre Equestre de la Montagne** is at La Montagne. For details, see *Chapter 16, Activities*, page 273.

WHAT TO SEE IN NORTHERN REUNION

JARDIN DE L'ETAT (*Place de Metz, St-Denis; ⌚ 06.00–18.00 daily; admission free*) At the southern end of Rue de Paris is this botanical garden, which features 2,000 species from around the world. It was originally created in 1773 by the French East India Company. It is a beautiful, tranquil place in which to spend a few hours. Guided visits start at 09.30, 11.00, 13.00, 14.45 and 16.30 Monday to Friday.

MUSEE D'HISTOIRE NATURELLE (*1 Rue Poivre, St-Denis; ☎ 0262 200219; e museum@cg974.fr; ⌚ 09.30–17.30 Tue–Sun; admission adult/child €2/1*) Natural history museum housed in a colonial building in the Jardin de l'Etat. Exhibits extinct and rare species of the western Indian Ocean, including the solitaire, Réunion's dodo-like bird.

MUSEE LEON DIERX (*28 Rue de Paris, St-Denis; ☎ 0262 202482; e musee.dierx@cg974.fr; www.cg974.fr; ⌚ 09.30–12.00 & 13.00–17.30 Tue–Sun; admission €2*) The museum opened in 1911 in the former bishop's residence. Well worth a visit, it houses original works by the likes of Gauguin, Maufra, Erro, Chen Zen and even Picasso. There is wheelchair access in Rue Ste-Marie.

MUSEE DE LA VRAIE FRATERNITE (*28 Bd de la Providence, St-Denis; ☎ 0262 210671; ⌚ 09.00–17.00 Wed & Sat; admission adult/child €2/1*) Exhibits are designed to represent the island's different communities and cultures throughout their history.

LA MAISON CARRERE (*14 Rue de Paris, St-Denis; ☎ 0262 418300; f 0262 213776; e maisoncarrere@lebeaupays.com; www.lebeaupays.com; ⌚ 09.00–18.00 Mon–Sat; admission adult/child €3/1.50*) Self-guided or guided tours (guided tours every hour) of the attractive Creole mansion which now houses the tourist office. The house was originally built in 1820 as a simple, single-storey wooden building. In 1905, Raphaël Carrère, who had made his fortune in the sugar industry, moved into the house with his wife and five children. They extended the house and added the upper floor. The house has been carefully restored and is decorated as it would have been during the days of the Carrère family.

JARDIN DE CENDRILLON (*48 Route des Palmiers, 97417 La Montagne;* ☎ *0262 418300;* **m** *0692 817010;* **e** *lejardindecendrillon@wanadoo.fr; tours last 1½hrs & cost adult/child €8/4*) Pleasant private garden in the hills above St-Denis, created in 1935. The orchids are a particular feature. Guided tours must be booked in advance.

ST-DENIS DES RELIGIONS (☎ *0692 863288;* **e** *contact@guid-a-nou.com; www.guid-a-nou.com; guided tours on Sat, €15*) A guided tour of places of worship of the various religions represented in St-Denis, including the Noor-e-Islam Mosque, a Buddhist temple and a Roman Catholic Church.

ARTOTHEQUE (*26 Rue de Paris, 97400 St-Denis;* ☎ *0262 417550;* 🕘 *09.30–17.30 Tue–Sun*) This contemporary art gallery exhibits work from regional artists.

18

Eastern Réunion

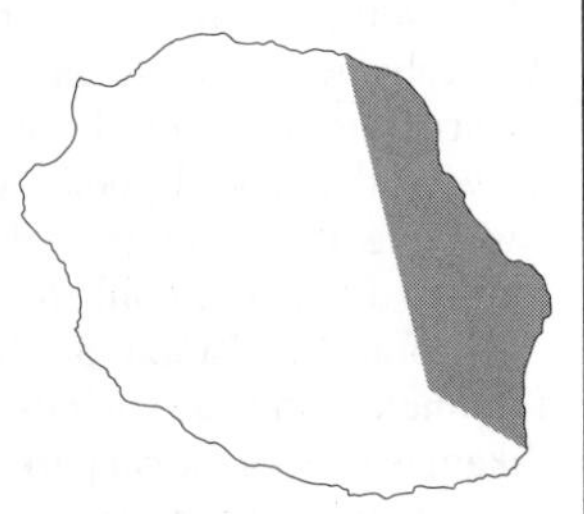

The sparsely inhabited eastern region stretches from Ste-Suzanne in the north through St-André and Bras-Panon to St-Benoît, continuing southwards to La Pointe de la Table. It is a lush area of sugarcane, lychee fields and vanilla. In fact, a visit to one of the vanilla estates is one of the highlights of the east. The region includes the awe-inspiring active volcano, Piton-de-la-Fournaise.

Although it is the south which has earned the adjective *sauvage* (wild), it could equally be applied to the unspoilt east coast. This is the region which receives the most rain and it is the one into which violent cyclones tear when they rage in the western Indian Ocean between January and March. Most of the east coast consists of black volcanic rock or cliffs, against which rough seas lash continuously. The regular activity of Piton-de-la-Fournaise constantly adds to Réunion's surface area, as lava flows out of the crater towards the eastern coast, solidifying as it hits the ocean.

STE-SUZANNE TO BRAS-PANON

The colonial houses and flowery gardens of **Ste-Suzanne** render the atmosphere somewhat more pleasant than is the case in bustling St-André. It is one of the island's oldest settlements, dating from 1667, and is best known for its **lighthouse**, at the western end of town.

Nearby **Cascade Niagara** is signposted from the southern end of town. The short drive takes you through cane fields and you can park right at the foot of the falls. Although far less impressive than its Canadian namesake, it is a pretty waterfall, 30m high.

St-André is a large industrial town with factories galore. It is the centre of Réunion's Tamil community and therefore the best place to see awe-inspiring **Tamil ceremonies and festivals** such as fire walking and Cavadee (see pages 71–2).

On the coast, a few kilometres from the centre of St-André among sugarcane fields, is **Parc Nautique du Colosse** (*www.cycloparc.com*). The park features boutiques, eateries, picnic areas and a children's playground, you can also hire bikes and go-karts here. The park is home to the local **tourist office**.

About 2km south of St-André is the turning to **Salazie** and **Hell-Bourg** (see *Chapter 21, The Interior*, pages 339–44).

Continuing south along Route Nationale 2 (RN2), you come to **Bras-Panon**, the centre of the vanilla industry. Worth a visit is **Pro Vanille**, which explains the production of vanilla (see *What to see in Eastern Réunion*, pages 296–7). The nearby village of **Rivière des Roches** is where much of the island's *bichiques* are fished, a small sprat-like fish usually served in *cari*. In the village is a turning to two beautiful natural pools beneath wooded waterfalls: **Bassin La Paix** and **Bassin La Mer**. About 3km from the RN2, you come to a track that leads to Bassin La Paix, where you can leave your car. It is a short walk through lush woods to the *bassin*. A sizeable waterfall plunges into the deep pool, where a quick dip offers welcome respite from the tropical sun. If you continue uphill for another 30 minutes, you'll arrive at the second pool, Bassin La Mer, arguably even more attractive than the lower one. It's in this area (the tumbling river between the two pools) that people come to do 'water hiking', in other words hiking upstream in the river itself.

Beyond Bras-Panon, on the RN2 to St-Benoît, is a turning to the viewpoint at **Takamaka**. The road winds gradually upwards for about 15km before reaching Takamaka. From the car park, there is a wonderful view of a semicircle of mountains painted with the thin strips of waterfalls. It is the starting point for a walk of 6.5km to the Electricité de France platform at Bébour.

TOURIST INFORMATION The **tourist office** in Ste-Suzanne is at 18 Rue du Phare (*0262 521354;* **f** *0262 521363; 09.00–12.30 & 13.30–17.00 Mon–Sat*). There is also a tourist office in **St-André**, at Maison Valliamée, 1590 Chemin du Centre (*0262 461616;* **f** *0262 465216; 09.00–17.00 Mon–Sat*).

WHERE TO STAY There are no classified hotels in the area but there are *gîtes ruraux* and *chambres d'hôtes*, which can be booked through the Centrale Régionale de Réservation de la Réunion or through the tourist offices in Ste-Suzanne and St-André (see *Chapter 15, Accommodation*, pages 259–61).

Unclassified accommodation

Shoestring

Au P'tit Coin Exotique (3 rooms) 460 Ruelle Virapatrin; 0262 464607; **e** leonce.patou-parvedy@wanadoo.fr. Clean, comfortable guesthouse accommodation 3km from the centre of St-André. **$**

Auberge de Quartier Français (5 rooms) 58 Rue Raymond Verges, Quartier Français, Ste-Suzanne; 0692 235900; **e** contact@aubergemoise974.com; www.aubergemoise974.com. Comfortable en-suite accommodation & a good *table d'hôte* restaurant with 3-course menus from €17. Dbl/sgl from €40/25 RO. B/fast from €5 pp. **$**

Pharest (4 bungalows, 1 dbl room) 22 Rue Blanchet, Ste-Suzanne; 0262 989110; **e** pharest-reunion@wanadoo.fr; www.pharest-reunion.com. Well-maintained bungalows of varying sizes which sleep 1–7 people. All have TV, AC costs an extra €4 per day. There is a room equipped for those with limited mobility. There is a restaurant & pool. Wi-Fi is free. **$**

Self-catering holiday rentals

Les Gîtes Ango (3 houses) 140 Commune Ango, Ste-Suzanne; 0262 521900; **f** 0262 521788; **e** gitesango@wanadoo.fr; www.gites-ango.com. The 3 *gîtes* are grouped around a pool, 2 sleep 4 people & the third sleeps 8. The houses are Creole style with modern, comfortable interiors. They are nicely furnished & well maintained, each with their own garden. Only the largest house has AC. All 3 *gîtes* have access to the sauna, hammam & jacuzzi on site. A great self-catering option. 2-bedroom *gîte* from €525 per week, 4-bedroom *gîte* from €920 per week.

WHERE TO EAT

La Cuisine de Clémencia 18 Chemin des Glaïeuls, Bras Pistolet, Ste-Suzanne; 0262 475278; on reservation. Cuisine: Creole. Good quality *table d'hôte* serving traditional Creole meals cooked over a wood fire. **$$$**

Le Beau Rivage Vielle-Eglise, Champ-Borne; 0262 460866; 10.00–23.00 Tue–Sat, for lunch Sun. Cuisine: Creole, French. In a pleasant location on the seafront, beside the ruined church. Fairly smart & very popular. **$$$**

Le Beauvallon Route du Stade, Rivière des Roches; 0262 504292; 09.00–15.00 daily, for dinner Fri/Sat. Cuisine: Creole, Indian. A great place to try local specialities such as *cari bichiques*.

Reservation recommended. Main courses from €12. $$$

Le Bec Fin 66 Route National, Bras-Panon; 0262 515224; daily for lunch, for dinner Thu–Sat. Cuisine: Creole, Chinese. Has earned an excellent reputation thanks to its good food & friendly service. Main courses from €7. $$$

Vani-La Pro Vanille, Bras-Panon; 0262 517102; 11.30–15.00 Mon–Fri. Cuisine: Creole, European. A fascinating menu with most of the dishes incorporating vanilla. $$$

ST-BENOIT

Originally built almost entirely of wood, St-Benoît was flattened by a fire in the 1950s and then rebuilt in brick and cement. The town itself is not particularly inspiring; most tourists simply pass through *en route* to the attractions inland.

Rivière des Marsouins runs through the town and *bichiques* are caught at the mouth of the river. The **tourist office** and **banks** (**Crédit Agricole** and **Banque de la Réunion**) are found on Rue Georges Pompidou. About 10km southwest of the town on the RN3 (towards La Plaine-des-Palmistes) is the turning to **Grand Etang**, a lake once considered sacred by slaves, who would conduct rituals on its shores. There are some pleasant walks here and it is a very popular picnic spot, particularly on weekends. On the same road is the pretty village of **La Confiance**, about 6km from St-Benoît.

GETTING THERE AND AWAY Getting to St-Benoît is not difficult: *cars jaunes* (buses) run regularly to and from St-Denis (Line G) and there are buses to and from St-Pierre, either along the coast road (Line I) or inland via La Plaine-des-Palmistes (Line H).

TOURIST INFORMATION The **tourist office** (*0262 470509; 09.00–12.00, 13.00–17.30 Mon–Sat*) is at Place de l'Eglise in Ste-Anne. The staff are very helpful and speak some English.

WHERE TO STAY

Unclassified accommodation

Shoestring

L'Orangeraie (1 room, 1 bungalow) Pont Payet, St-Benoît; 0262 509760; e orangeraie@hotmail.fr; http://monsite.orange.fr/orangeraie. A friendly guesthouse set in beautiful gardens. Tasty homemade cuisine using produce grown on site. Comfortable, clean accommodation in a peaceful location.

Self-catering holiday rentals

Logani's Lodge (1 house) 95 Chemin Harmonie, l'Abondance; 0692 768452; e contact@loganilodge.com; www.loganilodge.com. Modern house in a quiet, rural setting 4km from St-Benoît. The house, which can sleep up to 6 people, is nicely furnished, fully equipped & has a pleasant garden. Wi-Fi access available. From €100 RO.

WHERE TO EAT There are large **Cora** and **Champion supermarkets**, both signed from the RN2.

Le Vieux Domaine 204 Route Nationale 2, St-Benoît; 0262 509050; for lunch Sun–Fri, for dinner Tue–Sun. Cuisine: Creole, European. Excellent food in a peaceful setting. $$$

Les Letchis 42 Ilet Danclas, Ilet Coco, St-Benoît; 0262 503977; www.lesletchis.re; Tue–Sat for lunch & dinner, Sun lunch. Cuisine: French, Creole. In a pleasant garden setting on the banks of the Rivière des Marsouins. Elegant surroundings & sophisticated dishes. **$$$**

✕ **Dauphin Gourmand** 2 bis Rue Amiral Bouvet, St-Benoît; ☎ 0262 504282; ⏲ for lunch Sun–Fri, for dinner Tue–Sun. Cuisine: Italian, French, Creole. Small, clean & pleasant. **$$**

OTHER PRACTICALITIES

Communications The **post office** is on Rue Georges Pompidou. **Le Web Kafé** (*Pl Antoine Roussin;* ☎ *0262 929672*) is a well-equipped internet café with a non-alcoholic bar. It's in the centre of town, behind the church and next to the *mediathèque*.

STE-ANNE

About 5km south of St-Benoît on RN2 lies Ste-Anne, a pretty village that has proudly preserved many of its Creole houses.

Just off the main road is the village's highly unusual **church**. The original building, dating from 1857, was rebuilt by Father Daubenberger and his parishioners from 1892. The result is an extravagant pastel pink building embellished with rather odd stone carvings. Near the church is a small shop called Ilôt Savons, which sells locally made soap.

Just north of Ste-Anne on the RN2 is **La Grotte de Lourdes**, a shrine to the Virgin Mary. It is said that in 1862 a tidal wave hit the area, but the locals hid in a cave and were saved. They built the shrine, which still attracts many pilgrims, as a symbol of their gratitude to the Virgin.

STE-ROSE AND SURROUNDS

On the way from Ste-Anne to Ste-Rose, you pass a large suspension bridge, **Le Pont d'Anglais**, which was built in 1894. Adrenalin junkies now practise bungee jumping from the bridge over the **Rivière de l'Est**. This is also one of many favoured spots for the customary Sunday family picnic.

Surrounded by endless sugarcane fields, **Ste-Rose** is on the shoulder of the Piton-de-la-Fournaise volcano. There's something savage about the coastline here, with its black, rocky cliffs and wild, wild seas. Swimming is not on, but I am told by those in the know that the scuba diving offshore is excellent. (If you do this, make sure you go with very experienced people as the sea is potentially murderous.) In terms of sporting activities, the area is possibly best known for its **mountain-biking** trails (see page 295).

Ste-Rose is essentially a fishing village which has grown up around the harbour. At the harbour is a monument in honour of the defeated British naval commander, Corbett, who died in a battle with the French in 1809. The **post office** is at 184 Route Nationale 2. **Pharmacie Boyer** is at 447 RN2 in Piton-Ste-Rose.

Ste-Rose's big claim to fame is the church of **Notre Dame des Laves**, which is actually at **Piton-Ste-Rose**. On 12 April 1977, Piton-de-la-Fournaise blew its top once again, spewing out a wall of molten lava that rushed directly towards Piton-Ste-Rose. Everything in its path was destroyed: houses, trees and crops. The lava began crossing the road in front of the church. And then the unbelievable happened. The lava separated exactly at the church's front door and forked around it, flowing on either side until the two halves met on the other side of the church and continued towards the sea. Locals thought it was a miracle. Going inside the church and examining the framed photographs and newspaper clippings depicting that incredible event, you can see why. You'll also see a painting of Christ halting the lava. Some strange things have happened on this island.

Heading south of Ste-Rose, you'll arrive at **Pointe des Cascades**, Réunion's easternmost point. Just below it is **Anse des Cascades**, a beautiful quiet bay, backed on three sides by very high, very steep cliffs. The 'cascades' referred to plummet down the green cliffs into a pool. This is a popular area for local fishermen and colourful fishing boats lie in neat rows along the shore. There's a dense palm grove with several picnic spots and a small restaurant. The bay has a surreal feel and people come here from all over the island to enjoy the natural beauty and remote surrounds. Needless to say, it becomes packed on weekends. Once again, swimming is not safe.

GETTING THERE AND AWAY Ste-Rose lies on the St-Pierre–St-Benoît coastal bus route (Line I) and there is a stop almost directly outside Notre Dame des Laves.

WHERE TO STAY

Unclassified accommodation

Budget

Hotel La Fournaise (23 rooms) 154 RN2, Ste-Rose; 0262 270340; e hotellafournaise2@wanadoo.fr; www.hotellafournaise.fr. A relatively new accommodation option. Fresh, clean, unfussy en-suite rooms with AC, TV & phone, & wooden, Creole-style furniture. Some rooms have a view of the sea. There is a good restaurant & a pool. **$$**

Shoestring

Auberge du Poisson Rouge (7 rooms) 503 RN2, Piton-Ste-Rose; 0262 473251. Simply furnished, clean rooms. **$**

Le Joyau des Laves (4 rooms) Piton Cascades, RN2, Piton-Ste-Rose; 0262 473400; f 0262 472535; e spielmann@joyaudeslaves.com; www.joyaudeslaves.com. This chambre d'hôte is in a wonderful setting on a hillside overlooking the sea, south of Ste-Rose. The comfortable rooms have en-suite facilities & 1 is designed to be accessible to the disabled. Rooms 1 & 3 have a phone. **$**

WHERE TO EAT

Gingembre Combava Hotel La Fournaise, 154 RN2, Ste-Rose; 0262 470340. for lunch & dinner daily. Cuisine: Creole, French, seafood. A clean, fairly smart restaurant. *Table d'hôte* meals from €25. Reservation recommended. **$$$**

Anse des Cascades Restaurant Anse des Cascades, Piton-Ste-Rose; 0262 472042; for lunch Sat–Thu. Cuisine: French, Creole, seafood. Popular restaurant in an idyllic setting. Dinner on reservation. Dish of the day from €10. **$$**

Auberge du Poisson Rouge 503 RN2, Piton-Ste-Rose; 0262 473251; for lunch Tue–Sun, for dinner Tue–Sat. Cuisine: Creole, French, Chinese, seafood. Casual atmosphere. Good reputation for fish dishes. Main courses from €10. **$$**

Bel Air 480 RN2, Piton-Ste-Rose; 0262 472250; 08.00–14.00 daily. Cuisine: Creole. Informal restaurant, popular with locals. Dinner on reservation. Set menus from €12. **$$**

Deux Pitons RN2, Piton-Ste-Rose; 0262 472316; for dinner Thu–Tue. Cuisine: Creole, French. Heart of palm salad & fish *cari* are specialities. Main courses from €9. **$$**

Joyau des Laves Piton Cascade, RN2, Piton-Ste-Rose; 0262 473400; for dinner daily. Cuisine: Creole. Reservation only. *Table d'hôte* meals from €16. **$$**

Le Corail RN2, Piton-Ste-Rose; 0262 237536; 09.30–18.00 daily. Cuisine: Creole. Take-away available. Casual restaurant serving tasty local dishes. **$$**

Restaurant 168 RN2 Ste-Rose; 0262 472041; for lunch Tue–Sun, dinner on reservation. Cuisine: Creole, Indian. **$$**

NIGHTLIFE On Saturday nights, the energetic might want to try the disco **Roz d'Zil** (*317 RN2, Ravine Glissante; 0262 473606*).

SOUTH TO LA POINTE DE LA TABLE

From the road between Ste-Rose and St-Philippe (RN2) you can see the **lava flows** which attest to the fact that Piton-de-la-Fournaise is one of the world's most active volcanoes. Each flow is marked with the date of the eruption from which it originated.

One of the first lava flows you come to as you drive south from Ste-Rose is that of the April 2007 eruption, one of the biggest ever recorded. A viewing platform has been built just off the main RN2 road. Walking on the solidified lava gives you a chance to admire the coiled patterns of rope lava and appreciate the beauty and drama of this extraordinary place. Do take care, though, as lava is very uneven, sometimes fragile and can be very sharp.

The lava flows from the 1970s and 1980s have been colonised by pioneer plants such as sword ferns, lichens, mosses and a few small herbaceous plants.

The lava cliffs around **Pointe de la Table** are a perfect example of how the volcano has added tens of hectares to the island's surface area. The views are breathtaking and the furious sea seems locked in a constant battle against the intruding lava.

South of **Bois Blanc** is **La Vierge au Parasol** (the Virgin with the Umbrella). She is easily recognisable, dressed in blue and carrying a blue umbrella, designed to help her in her struggle to protect the local families and crops from the fury of the volcano. The local mayor had the Virgin removed just prior to the January 2002 eruption, for fear that she would be destroyed. Local residents were furious and still claim that had she been left there, she would have diverted the lava and they would have had a miracle to rival that of Piton-Ste-Rose. After the 2002 eruption she was re-positioned next to Notre Dame des Laves Church at Piton St-Rose but in 2010 was moved back to her current position, beside the lava flows near Bois Blanc. She is invariably surrounded by a range of offerings from locals of all religions who seek her protection.

PITON-DE-LA-FOURNAISE

Most people consider this to be Réunion's single most striking attraction. **Piton-de-la-Fournaise** (Furnace Peak) is one of the world's largest and most impressive shield volcanoes, reaching 2,631m. It is also one of the world's most active, having erupted a number of times in recent years. As activity can last for two weeks or more, the eruptions draw crowds of spectators (at least 20,000 came to see the eruption that began on 8 March 1998). In-depth information on the volcano can be found at the **Maison du Volcan** in La Plaine-des-Cafres (see *What to see in La Plaine-des-Cafres*, page 333).

When Piton-des-Neiges was still active, some 300,000 years ago, Piton-de-la-Fournaise rose up to its southeast and the successive layers of lava from both the volcanoes created the eerily lunar Plaine des Sables.

The drive to the volcano is an adventure in its own right. From La Plaine-des-Cafres you climb through an Alpine landscape dotted with cows sporting cowbells, which look as if they should be advertising Swiss chocolate. There are several spectacular viewpoints, including the panorama of Piton-des-Neiges looming over La Plaine-des-Cafres, and perhaps most striking of all, the view of La Vallée de la Rivière des Remparts at **Nez de Boeuf**. This valley, which stretches for 23km, is lined by cliffs rising up to 1,000m and looks almost tunnel-like as you peer down into it. And then you catch sight of a lone village on the valley floor, **Roche Plate**, and are left wondering how people manage to live in such isolation. Certainly, according to the information board at the viewpoint, life is not easy for those villagers, who battle cyclones and landslides on a regular basis.

The landscape becomes gradually stranger until you begin your descent to the barren moonscape that is **La Plaine des Sables**, preceding the volcano crater. Then it's an uphill stretch to **Pas de Bellecombe** (2,311m), which offers a fantastic view of the volcano and outer crater. There is a kiosk (⌚ *07.30–16.00 daily*) displaying information on the volcano and the walks, which is worth reading before you set off as it indicates the routes and their level of difficulty. The building also contains toilets and sells drinks. You can leave your car in the car park whilst you walk. It is best to set off as early as possible in the morning when the skies are clear because in the afternoon the clouds roll in like a thick fog. You will walk across solidified lava, so take care and make sure you have suitable footwear. Water, some food, suncream and a sunhat are essential, as is some warm clothing. For safety reasons, it is important that you stick to the marked paths.

From Pas de Bellecombe the walk starts with a descent via steep steps to the floor of the outer crater. Various routes are marked with paint, some shorter and easier than others. The most popular takes you straight across the outer crater towards the classically cone-shaped volcano directly in front of you. Since the eruption of December 2010, the walk is rather more arduous than it was and to reach the crater takes around seven hours return. Don't be surprised if you are passed by eager Frenchmen in Lycra running the path, just for fun. On the way to the crater you will come across some distinctive formations, such as Formica Leo, a scoria cone formed in 1753, and a natural cavern in the lava known as Chapelle de Rosemont.

The fit and energetic can try one of the many hiking trails that lead up to the volcano from various other parts of the island. Grading on all of them is difficult. Alternatively, you could see it from the air, as part of an unforgettable helicopter ride over the island. Whichever you choose, don't miss out on seeing the volcano: it is a mind-boggling, primal experience. There is a *gîte* at Pas de Bellecombe (one of the island's better mountain houses), where visitors can stay overnight. It is also a handy place to have lunch after walking to the crater.

WHAT TO DO IN EASTERN REUNION

MOUNTAIN BIKING There are eight mountain-bike trails around Ste-Rose, which vary from 5km to 44km and are graded according to difficulty. The trails are marked on a large signboard at the Marina Snack Bar, which you'll find at a conspicuous viewpoint near groves of pandanus trees. Most of the trails start at the four grey reservoirs you'll see up on the slopes above Ste-Rose.

HORSERIDING

Ferme Equestre du Grand Etang RN3, Pont Payet, St-Benoît; ☎ 0262 509003. Offers some very picturesque rides, including treks to the volcano. For details, see *Chapter 16, Activities*, page 273.

HIKING There are various hikes around Piton-de-la-Fournaise (see above and *Chapter 16, Activities* pages 269-72).

THEATRE

Théatre Conflore Chemin Champ Borne, St-André; ☎ 0262 582875

Théâtre Les Bambous 29 Av Jean Jaurès, St-Benoît; ☎ 0262 503863; www.lesbambous.com

CINEMA

Salle Multimédia Guy Alphonsine 270 Rue de la Gare; 0262 580900

SHOPPING There are **markets** in **St-André** on Friday morning, **Bras-Panon** on Thursday afternoon and **St-Benoît** on Saturday morning. Roadside stalls selling delicious, locally made honey, jam and vanilla are a common sight in the east.

WHAT TO SEE IN EASTERN REUNION

TAMIL TEMPLES There are some impressive, ornate and colourful Tamil temples around St-André. Two of the most visited are Le Colosse at Champ-Borne and Le Temple du Petit Bazar in St-André. Guided tours of the latter (**m** *0692 674725/147507*) are available Monday–Saturday and cost €4.

BOIS ROUGE SUGAR FACTORY/SAVANNA DISTILLERY (*2 Chemin Bois-Rouge, St-André;* *0262 585974;* **e** *sucreriesbourbon@bois-rouge.fr; www.distilleriesavanna.com;* *Jul–Dec 09.00–20.00 Mon–Fri, 09.00–18.00 Sat, Jan–Jun 10.00–18.00 Mon–Sat; combined tour: admission adult/child €8/5.50; distillery only: adult/child €3.50/2; children under 7 are not allowed at the sugar factory; reservation essential*) Just north of St-André, the Bois Rouge sugar factory offers guided tours from July to mid-December. Tours of the Savanna Distillery, exploring rum production and ending with a tasting, are available all year except mid-December to mid-January. Both tours can be provided in English. Combined tours of the sugar factory and the distillery are possible from July to December.

MUSEE DAN TAN LONTAN (*2208 Chemin du Centre, St-André;* *0262 584789;* *09.00–17.00 Mon–Sat; admission adult/child €4/2*) A collection of local antique objects. Guided tours on reservation.

MAISON VALLIAME (*1590 Chemin du Centre, St-André;* *0262 469163; guided visits 09.30, 10.45, 13.45 & 15.00 Mon–Sat; admission adult/child €3/1.50*) Guided visits of the impressive wooden Creole mansion which houses the St-André Tourist Office. Built in 1925, it was classified an historic building in 1983. Guided visits last around 45 minutes.

PRO VANILLE (*21 RN2 Bras-Panon;* *0262 517102;* **e** *provanille@wanadoo.fr;* *09.00–12.00 & 13.30–17.00 Mon–Sat; admission €5*) This vanilla co-operative was created in 1968 and is now made up of 120 producers. Tells the story of vanilla via a guided tour of the factory and a film on the history of vanilla production. The fascinating tours last about 45 minutes and are available in English if arranged in advance. They start at 09.00, 10.30, 14.00 and 15.30. There is a shop selling vanilla products and a restaurant open for lunch (see page 291).

LE DOMAINE DU GRAND HAZIER (*5 Le Grand Hazier, Ste-Suzanne;* *0262 523281;* **f** *0262 522312; admission adult/child under 12 €5/free; reservation essential*) A sugar plantation since the early 20th century. Guided tour of the 18th-century planter's house, surrounded by a large garden of fruit trees and endemic species.

LA VANILLERAIE (*Domaine du Grand Hazier, Allée Chassagne, Ste-Suzanne;* *0262 230726; www.lavanilleraie.com;* *09.00–12.00 & 14.00–17.00 Mon–Sat; admission* *adult/child €5/3*). Tells the story of the history of vanilla production. Guided tours lasting 40 minutes start on the hour from 09.00.

LA PLANTATION DE VANILLE ROULOUF (*470 Rue Deschanets, St-André;* ☎ *0692 108715;* e *plantationvanille@orange.fr; www.lavanilledelareunion.com;* ⏲ *guided tours 11.00, 14.00, 15,00, 16.00 Mon–Sat; tours €4*). Guided tours of this working vanilla plantation last around 1 hour.

RIVIERE DU MAT DISTILLERY (*Chemin Manioc, ZI Beaufonds, St-Benoît;* m *0692 674641;* e *visitedistillerie@gqf.com; www.gqf.com;* ⏲ *Mar–Dec morning Tue–Sat; on reservation only; admission adult/child €5/3*) Historic rum distillery on the Beaufonds sugar estate. One-hour tours of the distillery include a film on rum production and rum tasting.

LE DOMAINE COCO (*Impasse Marco, Ste-Anne;* ☎ *0692 277519;* e *contact@domaine-coco.com; www.domaine-coco.com;* ⏲ *tours 10.30, 14.30 daily, reservation essential on weekends; tours adult/child €7/4*) Agriculture-themed guided tours explain sugar production and the cultivation of tropical fruit trees, spices and medicinal plants.

19

Southern Réunion

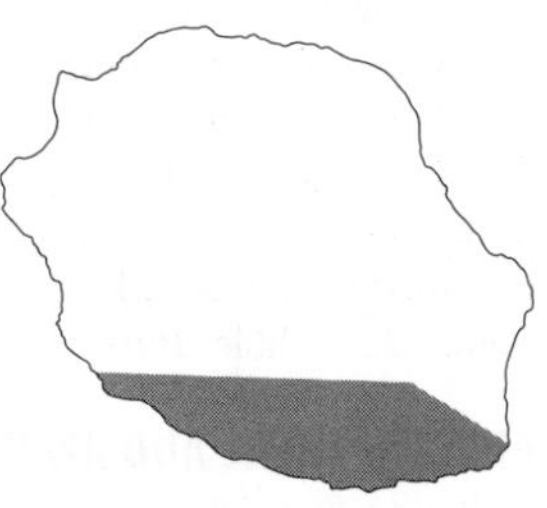

The southern part of the island stretches from the town of St-Philippe in the southeast up to Le Tampon and from there down to Etang-Salé-les-Bains in the southwest.

The bustling coastal town of St-Pierre has deservedly earned the unofficial title of 'capital of the south' and is the gateway to the *sud sauvage* (the wild south), the name given to the rugged southeast coast. This is an area which lies in the shadow of Piton-de-la-Fournaise, with a coastline of black volcanic cliffs, the remains of lava flows stopped in their tracks by the sea. By contrast, there are some good white-sand beaches further west around St-Pierre and a large, black-sand beach at Etang-Salé-les-Bains.

The southern towns have plenty of charm and character, generally featuring small, neat Creole-style homes surrounded by colourful gardens. Creole gardens characteristically serve more than just a decorative purpose, containing flowers, medicinal plants, tropical fruit and vegetables intentionally bunched together in each flowerbed. There is a flourishing cottage industry in this region, including Creole furniture, lacework, honey, pâté and cheeses.

ST-PHILIPPE AND SURROUNDS

St-Philippe is small, peaceful and few tourists spend any time here. This makes it worth staying for a night or two. The town, which is a vanilla and fishing centre, has a backdrop of sugarcane and forested mountains.

St-Philippe has the basic necessities: a few restaurants, a **pharmacy**, a **post office** and a **petrol station**, although no banks. There is a small **supermarket** but the prices tend to be exaggerated, so locals recommend shopping in St-Joseph.

A few kilometres west of St-Philippe is **Le Baril**, where you will find a pandanus-lined coast and two adjacent swimming pools, one fresh water and one which is a corralled area of sea. The best rock-pooling area is to the east of the swimming pool, where colourful fish are often trapped in pools in the volcanic rocks. This is the place to watch rock-skippers (or mud-skippers), an amphibious species of goby. This fish has evolved large, powerful pectoral fins to enable it to escape potential predators by leaping from the sea to the safety of rocks.

The charm of St-Philippe and Le Baril is not the designated sights, of which there are few, but the lava flows and coastal and forest walks. Between St-Philippe and Le Baril is the **Réserve Naturelle de Mare Longue**. Incorporated into this forest area is the *sentier botanique*, a path through a beautiful section of primary forest where the indigenous trees are labelled. A clearly marked Grande Randonnée hiking trail runs straight up the mountainside but you can also take the longer forest road which is easier on the legs and excellent for birdwatching. Bring a picnic and enjoy the flora, fauna and views of this lush region.

For the best views of pounding waves, craggy headlands and graceful tropical birds visit **Cap Méchant**, about 2km west of Le Baril. From here you can walk along the headland, through casuarina trees and vanilla plantations. This is also where you will find **Les Puits des Français** (the wells of the French), the southernmost of a series of mysterious holes in the lava coastline. The origin and purpose of these apparently manmade holes is unknown. Similar holes are at Le Baril (**Puits des Anglais**), La Pointe de la Table (**Puits des Arabes**) and Le Tremblet (**Puits du Tremblet**).

GETTING THERE AND AWAY St-Philippe is easily reached by bus as it lies on the St-Pierre–St-Benoît coastal route (Line I).

TOURIST INFORMATION The **tourist office** (*0262 977584;* **f** *0262 370233;* **e** *officedutourismesaintphilippe@yahoo.fr;* *09.00–12.00 & 13.00–17.00 Mon–Fri, 10.00–12.00 & 13.00–17.00 Sat*) in St-Philippe is next to the town hall at 62 Rue Leconte Delisle, the main coastal road.

WHERE TO STAY

Classified hotels

Budget

Hotel Le Baril * (13 rooms) 62 RN2, Le Baril; 0262 370104; **f** 0262 370762; **e** lebaril@wanadoo.fr; www.lebaril-reunion.com. A cosy, family-run hotel, perched on a typically wild stretch of coast. With limited accommodation in the area, this hotel gets busy so try to book well in advance. The en-suite rooms (1 with disabled facilities) are fairly simple & a little dark, but some have spectacular views of the pounding sea. Only some have AC. TVs are available in some rooms on request & there is a TV lounge. There is also a small pool & a good restaurant overlooking the sea (see below). Sea-view supplement €5.

Unclassified accommodation

Budget

La Vague du Sud (6 rooms) 77 RN2, St-Philippe; 0262 415785; **f** 0262 685786; **e** lavaguedusud@orange.fr. Simple but clean & comfortable accommodation across the road from the sea. Rooms have en suite, sea view, TV & AC. Free internet access. There is a good restaurant.

WHERE TO EAT

Marmite du Pêcheur RN2, Ravine Ango, St-Philippe; 0262 370101; for lunch Thu–Tue. Cuisine: Creole, French, seafood. Tucked away among houses, signed from the main road through St-Philippe. It may not look very special from the outside but this restaurant has a reputation for superb seafood dishes. **$$$**

Etoile de Mer Cap Méchant, Basse Vallée; 0262 370460; daily 11.30–22.00. Cuisine: seafood, Creole, Chinese. Large restaurant known for its excellent seafood. **$$**

Hotel Le Baril RN2, Le Baril; 0262 370104; for lunch & dinner daily. Cuisine: Creole, Chinese. A large menu with lots of local specialities. Informal with friendly service & a sea view. **$$**

La Vague du Sud 77 RN2, St-Philippe; 0262 415785; for lunch & dinner daily. Cuisine: Creole, French. Pleasant restaurant across the road from the sea. **$$**

Le Cap Méchant Basse-Vallée; 0262 370061; for lunch Tue–Sun. Cuisine: Creole, Chinese. Very popular seafront restaurant. Reservation recommended. **$$**

ST-JOSEPH AND SURROUNDS

The area around St-Joseph is known for its production of turmeric, an important ingredient in *cari*, and for the weaving of pandanus fronds to produce baskets, hats and bags.

Between St-Philippe and St-Joseph is the village of **Vincendo**. There is usually a black-sand beach at La Marine de Vincendo, although its presence depends on the tide.

Further west on the RN2, before you reach St-Joseph, is the turning to **Rivière Langevin**. This is a magical spot. The drive takes you through the village of Langevin, with its colourful Creole houses facing the river. Female residents can often be seen doing their washing on the rocks, whilst the men play dominoes in little huts on the riverbank. The road is lined with picnic tables and there are several restaurants serving Creole food.

You pass a hydro-electric station, then small banana and pineapple plantations. On the left is an adorable little chapel built around a cave, with a shrine to Saint Expédit, typically painted red.

It is a picture-perfect river shrouded by trees, with water bubbling around boulders, pausing in pools and then setting off again towards the sea. You can park and walk a short distance to **Le Trou Noir**, a pool beneath a waterfall, ideal for a refreshing dip. Further along the road, after a steep and winding climb, you can get a close-up view of some more beautiful falls, **La Cascade de Grand-Galet**. The road ends in the pretty village of **Grand-Galet**, above the falls.

St-Joseph is an attractive little town astride the **Rivière des Remparts**. However, it doesn't hold much interest for tourists, other than being an occasional stopover point for people heading eastwards. The **banks**, a **post office**, numerous restaurants, a **pharmacy** and a **medical centre** are on Rue Raphael Babet. To the east of St-Joseph is **Manapany-les-Bains**, a seaside village with a protected natural swimming pool and a beach.

TOURIST INFORMATION There is a **tourist office** at Manapany-les-Bains (*15 Allée du Four à Chaux*; *0262 373711*; **f** *0262 373715*; **e** *pat.sudsauvage@wanadoo.fr*; *www.sudsauvage.com*; *09.00–17.00 Mon–Fri, 10.00–17.00 Sat*). You can book accommodation here or gather information on activities in the area.

WHERE TO STAY There are no classified hotels in St-Joseph but there are plenty of furnished flats and houses in the area, some of which are listed below.

Unclassified accommodation

Budget

La Plantation (4 rooms) 124 Chemin de Jean Petit, St-Joseph; 0262 560886; **e** info@laplantation.net; www.laplantation.net. Beautifully decorated en-suite rooms with TV, in a modern house. The suite has a sitting area & kitchenette. There is a beautiful pool overlooking St-Joseph & the ocean, & a jacuzzi. Dbl from €75 BB.

Self-catering holiday rentals

La Case ** (6 apts, 3 rooms) 2 Rue Jean Bart, St-Joseph; 0262 560750; **f** 0262 236339; **e** contact@case.fr; www.case.fr. Comfortable studios & apartments with AC, TV, shared pool & sea views. The rooms are en suite & simply but nicely furnished. Room from €37 per night (2 people) RO, studio from €50 (2 people), apartment from €300 (5 people).

La Villa du Barrage ** 21 Route de Grand-Galet, Langevin, St-Joseph; 0262 314268; **e** Maillot.Franck@wanadoo.fr. The owner rents out the ground floor of his home in a very pleasant, peaceful location overlooking Rivière Langevin. It's a steep climb to the village & you'll need a car to get there. From €330 per week (4 people).

L'Eau Forte ** 137 bis, Bd de l'Océan, Manapany-les-Bains; 0262 563284; **e** eau-forte@wanadoo.fr; www.eau-forte.fr. An apartment for 2 people overlooking the bay. From €250 per week (2 people).

WHERE TO EAT St-Joseph has the usual well-stocked **supermarkets** (in this case, **Score** and **Champion**), which are just west of the town on either side of the RN2. There is also a Leader Price supermarket in the centre of town.

Le Bel Air 39 Rue Lesquelin, Les Lianes, St-Joseph; 0262 375466; for lunch & dinner daily, on reservation 48hrs in advance. Cuisine: Creole. A farmhouse in the hills above St-Joseph, with sea views. Meals are prepared using fresh ingredients from the farm. $$$

Restaurant Le Tagine 23 Chemin de la Marine, Vincendo, St-Joseph; 0262 373251; for lunch & dinner Mon–Sat, closed Wed evening. Cuisine: Moroccan. Unremarkable décor but good food. $$$

Chez Jo 143 Bd de l'Océan, Manapany-les-Bains; 0262 314883; winter 09.00–18.00 Fri–Wed, summer 09.00–20.00 Fri–Wed. Cuisine: Creole, French, Chinese, snacks. Casual snack-bar-style eatery with tables on a covered terrace. $$

La Bonne Idée 172 Route de la Passerelle, Langevin; 0262 562076; 10.00–18.00 Wed–Mon. Cuisine: Creole, Chinese. Laid-back atmosphere & a varied menu. Also a dance hall. $$

L'Hirondelle 83 Bd de l'Océan, Manapany-les-Bains; 0262 315711; for lunch Mon–Sat, for dinner Tue–Sat. Cuisine: Creole, Chinese, seafood. The décor may not be particularly fancy but the owner prides himself on the quality of his homemade cuisine & only fresh ingredients are used. $$

L'Orient Express 132 Rue Raphaël Babet, St-Joseph; 0262 562838; for lunch & dinner daily. Cuisine: Chinese, Creole. Plenty of choice. $$

Pizzeria la Gondole Rue Raphael Babet, St-Joseph; 0262 561612; for lunch & dinner Wed–Sun. Cuisine: Italian. On the main road, just to the west of town. Cosy restaurant serving excellent pizzas & other Italian fare. Good value for money. $$

Chez Jim 194 Route de la Passerelle, Langevin; 0262 565601; for lunch daily. Cuisine: Creole, snacks. Also take-away. Informal & friendly, across the road from the river. $

ST-PIERRE AND SURROUNDS

On the RN2 between St-Joseph and St-Pierre is the turning to **Grande Anse**. This is a stunning bay surrounded by densely wooded slopes, with a wonderful white-sand beach. Swimming, however, is only safe in the purpose-built pool. It's a perfect place for a picnic, with barbecue areas scattered amongst the palm trees. Unfortunately, this means it can be unpleasantly crowded on weekends. There is a cave in the cliffs around which clouds of Mascarene swiftlets wheel and scream excitedly. From the hillside you can see Réunion's only outlying island, **Petit Ile**, a nesting site for birds.

St-Pierre is the largest town in the south, home to some 70,000 people. To call this town bustling is putting it mildly. St-Pierre is especially popular with Réunionnais holidaymakers, who prefer to come here while the French head for glitzy St-Gilles.

The focal point of the town is **Boulevard Hubert Delisle**, the road along the seafront. It is strewn with restaurants, ice-cream parlours and bars, as well as a casino. Across the road from the casino is a stretch of white, sandy **beach** – nothing to write home about, but adequate nevertheless. The park in front of the beach has undergone a makeover and it is now a very pleasant place to sit, although it still attracts the odd drunk in the evenings. During winter the strong winds around St-Pierre can make the beach a no-go zone. Snorkelling in the lagoon just off the beach is very rewarding and you'll invariably see many people doing just that.

The **harbour**, which is to the east of the beach, has also been expanded and smartened up, with a little help from the European Union. It now boasts a wide promenade and brand-new shops. Nearby, opposite the Café de la Gare, is the **Bassin de Radout**, a dry dock preserved since the 19th century.

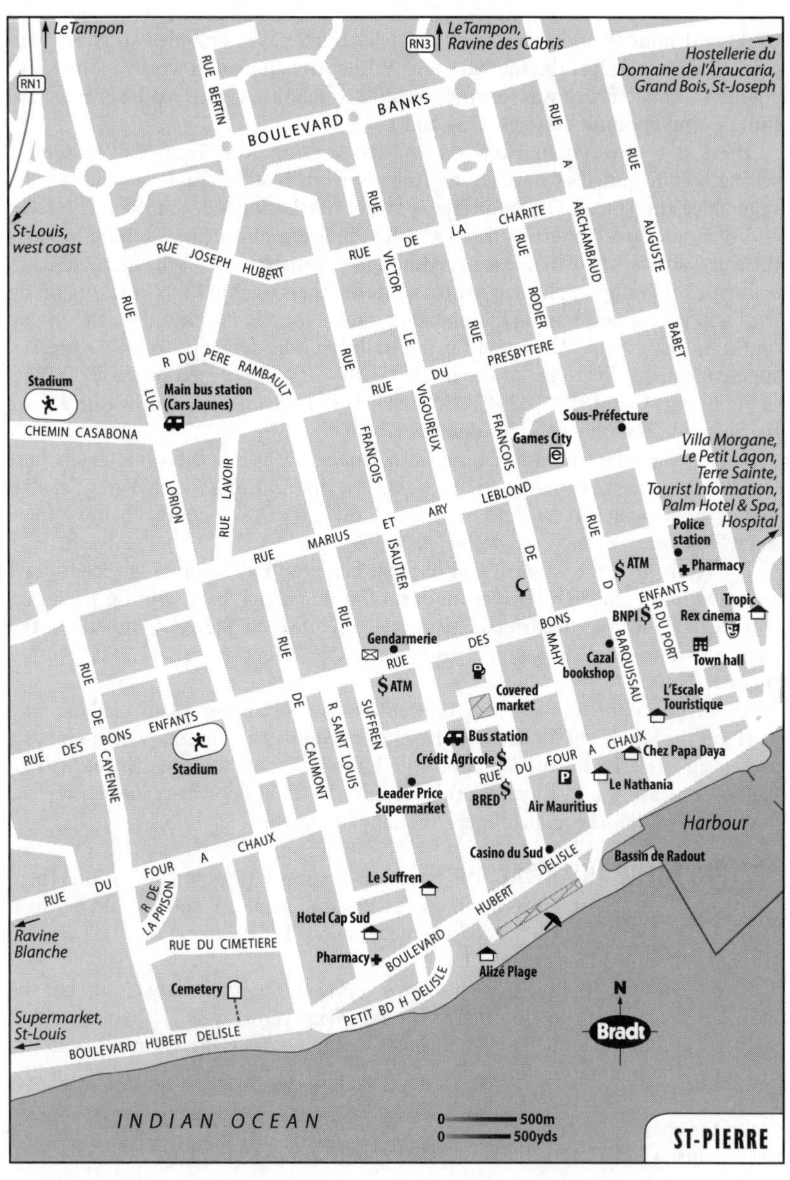

The area around the seafront is gradually acquiring a mildly European feel, with designer clothing shops creeping in, but as you climb the hill into the main part of the town that European ambience fades. The town centre, with its numerous (particularly Chinese and Indian) clothing stores, boutiques, bars and restaurants, brings to mind images of urban southeast Asia or Mauritius, rather than Europe. Despite all the recent 'smartening up', St-Pierre remains a Réunionnais town and the people are genuinely welcoming and helpful.

As you head up Rue François de Mahy, away from the seafront, you'll pass an ornate **mosque**. Provided you dress respectfully, you are welcome to visit between

09.00 and midday and from 14.00 to 16.00 (material is provided to cover your legs). The **town hall** at the southern end of Rue Archambaud is worth a look for its colonial architecture. It was formerly a coffee warehouse owned by the French East India Company, built between 1751 and 1773.

There is a **covered market** (*marché couvert*) on Rue Victor le Vigoureux, selling a good range of handicrafts (mostly from Madagascar), as well as fruit, vegetables and spices. On Saturdays, a **street market** operates at the far western end of Boulevard Hubert Delisle (which is blocked off to cars), selling more of the same and is well worth a visit. Although the market now sells many touristy souvenirs, it is a great place to see locals doing their weekly shop, stocking up on fruit and vegetables, buying live chickens, and – equally important – catching up on the week's gossip. Watch out for the stall that sells delicious, freshly squeezed sugarcane juice. Try to get to the market early – it's all finished by noon. Talking of shopping, **Cazal** (☎ *0262 353535; www.librairiecazal.com*), at 39 Rue Désiré Barquisseau, is a very good **bookshop**.

Also at the western end of Boulevard Hubert Delisle is the **cemetery**, where Hindu, Chinese and Christian graves lie side by side. The most-visited grave of all is that of the African sorcerer and murderer, Simicoundza Simicourba, better known as **Le Sitarane**. (See box *Le Sitarane*, page 309).

The seafront at the western end of town has been redeveloped in recent years and now has a children's playground, funfair and snack bars. Out on the water you are likely to see kitesurfers, particularly on one of St-Pierre's windy days. The Centre Commercial du Grand Large has a large supermarket, as well as other smaller shops.

About 10km north of St-Pierre on the RN3 is **Le Tampon**. Many of those who work on the south coast choose to live in or around Le Tampon, which enjoys a cooler climate. The town itself is of little interest, except that it is *en route* to La Plaine-des-Cafres, and therefore the volcano. Le Tampon is best known for the flower festival (Florilège) held there annually in October.

GETTING THERE AND AWAY The main **bus station** is on Rue Luc Lorion. There are regular buses between St-Denis and St-Pierre (Lines A, B and C), and between St-Benoît and St-Pierre via the coast (Line I) and via Les Plaines (Line H). There are also buses to Entre-Deux (Line L).

It's quite a walk (uphill) from the town centre to the main bus station, but the local *bus fleuri* buses do stop there. The *bus fleuri* (flowery bus) operates within St-Pierre and to the outlying villages, such as **Ravine des Cabris**, **Grand Bois** and **St-Louis**. The bus station for the *bus fleuri* is next to the covered market, on Rue François Isautier. **Taxis** are found at both bus stations.

On the coast 7km west of St-Pierre is **Pierrefonds Airport**, with flights to/from neighbouring Indian Ocean islands. (For details, see page 253.)

TOURIST INFORMATION The **tourist office** (*26 Rue Amiral Lacaze, Terre Sainte;* ☎ *0262 250236;* **f** *0262 258276;* ⌚ *09.00–12.00 & 13.00–16.45 Mon–Fri, 09.00–12.00 & 13.00–15.45 Sat*) is at the far eastern end of the seafront on the corner heading to Terre Sainte. Staff will be very happy to assist with the booking of *gîtes* and local guided tours on your behalf, often with an historical or cultural focus (on foot or by bike), and which cost adult/child from €5/3. There is no guarantee that there will be English-speaking staff, but several of them can 'get by' in English. There are books and postcards available for sale on the island but the staff specifically asked me to mention they do not sell stamps!

WHERE TO STAY

Classified hotels

Upmarket

Palm Hotel & Spa **** (48 rooms) Rue des Mascarins, Grande Anse; 0262 563030; e info@palm.re; www.palm.re. The only 4-star option in the south. The hotel opened in 2007, in a quiet location perched on the cliffs above Grande Anse. The beach at Grande Anse can be reached via a forest path; it takes about 5mins from the hotel & there is a shuttle bus to bring you back up. Rooms are finished to a high standard (comparable with those seen in Mauritius), with en suite, AC, TV, phone, safe & minibar. There are 2 good restaurants, 2 pools & a fitness centre. The hotel's trump card is an elegant spa. The beach at Grande Anse is not suitable for swimming & there are no shops or restaurants nearby – for these you can head into St-Pierre which is about 7mins away by car. **$$$$**

Mid range

Alizé Plage ** (7 rooms) Bd Hubert Delisle, St-Pierre; 0262 352221; f 0262 258063; e alizeplage@ilereunion.com; www. alizeplage. com. The best location in town, right on the beach. Clever use has been made of little space to create simple, comfortable rooms. Each is equipped with en-suite facilities, AC, TV, phone, Wi-Fi & balcony. Facilities include a good restaurant (see page 307), a bar with regular live music & some free watersports, such as kayaks & pedaloes. The regular central location, live music & lively restaurant mean this is not a relaxing retreat but it is a convenient place to lay your head after enjoying the town's famous nightlife. **$$$**

Domaine des Pierres *** (41 rooms) 60, CD26, Route de l'Entre-Deux, St-Pierre; 0262 554385; f 0262 554390; e domainedespierres@ wanadoo.fr; www.domainedespierres.com. Near Pierrefonds Airport, within easy reach of the hustle & bustle of St-Pierre, if you have a car. The en-suite rooms are in bungalows scattered in a garden. They are tastefully decorated, clean & have AC, TV, phone, safe & terrace. Rooms equipped for the disabled are available. Facilities include a restaurant, bar & pool. Guests are entitled to one free entry to the Park Exotica (see page 313). **$$$**

Budget

Hostellerie du Domaine de l'Áraucaria ** (8 rooms) 2 Chemin de l'Araucaria, Mont Vert les Bas; 0262 311010; f 0262 315339; e hotel.hda@ orange.fr; www.hotelhda.com. A small hotel in an inland village around 20mins from St-Pierre, with views to the coast. Simple en-suite rooms with TV, phone, Wi-Fi, some have balcony. There is a restaurant, pool & jazz club. Free shuttle to Pierrefonds Airport. **$$**

Hotel Cap Sud ** (16 rooms) 6 Rue Caumont, St-Pierre; 0262 257564; f 0262 252219; e hotel-capsud@orange.fr; www.hotel-capsud-reunion.com. About 300m from the beach & town centre in a plain 3-storey building. En-suite rooms with AC, TV & phone. They're spartan but clean. A modern 2-bedroom self-catering apartment is also available. **$$**

Hotel Outre-Mer * (35 rooms) 8 Rue Bourbon, Le Tampon; 0262 573030; f 0262 572929; e hotel.outremer@orange.fr. Unremarkable, basic but clean rooms with en suite, AC, TV & phone. Rooms equipped for the disabled are available & there is a restaurant. **$$**

Unclassified accommodation

Mid range

Villa Morgane (8 rooms) 334 Rue Amirale Lacaze, Terre Sainte; 0262 258277; e hoteldecharme@villamorgane.re; www. villamorgane.re. Upmarket guesthouse accommodation in a large house in the residential area of Terre Sainte, a 15min walk from St-Pierre. There are 3 double rooms & 5 suites, each lavishly decorated with a different theme, some Asian, some Italian. Suite Alexandra is my favourite, not just for the name but because it's a little more understated than those with floor-to-ceiling frescoes. For lovers of Botticelli, the suite named after him offers the opportunity to sit in the bath under the watchful gaze of Venus. There is a pretty garden, pool & jacuzzi but no secure parking. **$$$**

Budget

Le Suffren (17 studios) 14 Rue Suffren, St-Pierre; 0262 855902; e lesuffren@orange. fr; www.hotelsuffren.com. A few mins' walk from the beach & main attractions. Very large but rather soulless studios equipped with AC, TV & phone; most have a minibar & all but 1 have a balcony. **$$**

Le Victoria (16 rooms) 8–10 Allée des Lataniers, Grand-Bois; ☎ 0262 509567; **f** 0262 980146; **e** reservation@levictoria.re; www.levictoria.re. This small hotel, around a 5min drive from St-Pierre, has undergone numerous changes of management. It has potential, being located on the seafront (no beach here, just rugged black rock), but so far it has not been made into all it could be. The rooms are in bungalows around a small pool, & are equipped with AC, TV & phone. Free Wi-Fi. **$$**

Shoestring

Chez Papa Daya (17 rooms) 27 Rue du Four à Chaux; ☎/**f** 0262 256487; **e** chez.papa.daya@wanadoo.fr; www.chezpapadaya.com. Excellent central location, not far from the beach. Cheerful, spotless rooms, with AC & fridge, some with en-suite facilities. There's a well-equipped shared kitchen, as well as a TV lounge & a small garden. Wi-Fi is available. Security is good & there are 5 parking spots (not secure) for residents. Popular choice for those on a budget & the best of its kind in town. En-suite dbl/sgl from €35/25, dbl/sgl with shared bathroom from €25/16. **$**

Le Nathania (14 rooms) 12 Rue François de Mahy, St-Pierre; ☎ 0262 250457; **f** 0262 352705; **e** hotel.le.nathania@wanadoo.fr; www.hotel-nathania-reunion.com. Centrally located about 150m from the seafront & the main bar & restaurant strip. All rooms have a TV & fan, some have en-suite facilities & most have AC. Facilities include parking & use of a shared kitchen & laundry. Wi-Fi is available. A good location & not bad value for money. **$**

L'Escale Touristique (14 rooms) 14 Rue Désiré Barquisseau, St-Pierre; ☎ 0262 352095; **f** 0262 351532; **e** escaletouristique@izi.re. No-frills accommodation centrally located, around 200m from the seafront. All rooms have TV & fridge, some have en-suite facilities & some have AC. A well-equipped kitchen & a laundry area are available for use by guests. There is also secure parking. Wi-Fi is free for guests. **$**

Sud Hotel (44 rooms) 106 Rue Marius et Ary Leblond, Le Tampon; ☎ 0262 270790; **f** 0262 270239; **e** sudhotel@ilereunion.com. Centrally located in Le Tampon with comfortable en-suite rooms with TV & phone. It has a restaurant, bar, pool, pleasant public areas & parking. **$**

Tropic Hotel (14 rooms) 2 Rue Auguste Babet, St-Pierre; ☎ 0262 259070; **e** tropic.hotel@wanadoo.fr. Backpacker-style accommodation. Basic rooms some with AC, some with en suite. Does get some road noise & some lively guests visiting St-Pierre for the nightlife. Car rental is also available here. **$**

Self-catering holiday rentals

Case Paradis ** 194 bis Impasse Poudroux, Route Ligne Paradis, St-Pierre; ☎ 0262 254928; **e** www.caseparadis.com. A studio & 2 apartments for up to 6 people, a 10min drive from St-Pierre. There is a pleasant garden, parking & Wi-Fi. From €190 per week (2 people).

Le Petit Lagon * 79 Rue Amiral Lacaze, Terre Sainte; ☎ 0262 391396; **e** lepetitlagon@wanadoo.fr; www.lepetitlagon.com. A simply furnished Creole house with 6 bedrooms near the seafront at Terre Sainte & within walking distance of the centre of St-Pierre. From €400 per week (2 people).

Oasis Terre Rouge *** 41 Chemin Mézino, Terre Rouge; ☎ 0692 312880; **e** contact@oasisdeterrerouge.com; www.oasisdeterrerouge.com. Beautifully furnished accommodation with pool, to the east of St-Pierre. There are 4 1-bedroom apartments & a 3-bedroom villa with AC & everything you need for a self-catering stay. There is a pleasant garden, barbecue & secure parking. From €1,185 per week (6 people).

WHERE TO EAT There is a well-stocked **Score Jumbo hypermarket** on the way out of town, at the Centre Commercial du Grand Large, at the far western end of Boulevard Hubert Delisle. There are smaller supermarkets in the town centre. St-Pierre is packed with restaurants to suit all budgets. Just opposite the main beach, on the corner of Boulevard Hubert Delisle and Rue Victor le Vigoureux is a collection of *camions bars* (snack bars). They serve a great range of inexpensive, tasty food, such as *samoussas*, filled baguettes and *bombons piments*.

I suppose I should also add that just at the entrance to St-Pierre from St-Louis is a branch of McDonald's (they really are everywhere, aren't they?).

Here are some recommended restaurants including a cross-section of culinary styles:

La Baie des Anges 28 Av François Mitterand, Terre Sainte; 0262 351840; www.labaiedesanges.re; for lunch & dinner Mon–Sat, closed Thu dinner & Sat lunch. Cuisine: French, seafood. In a charming blue & white Creole house, nicely decorated inside. On the menu are traditional French dishes & plenty of seafood. Local ingredients are used wherever possible, although the beef comes from France. $$$$

Le Jardin Réunionnais 9 Petit Bd Hubert Delisle; 0262 256680; for lunch & dinner Tue–Sun. Cuisine: French, Creole. A neat little place at the eastern end of Petit Bd Hubert Delisle. Dining is either in the walled garden or inside in the cosy, colourful restaurant. There is also a trendy little bar. The dishes are of high quality & very professionally presented. $$$$

Les 3 Brasseurs ZI 2, Basse Terre; 0262 963060; www.les3brasseurs.com; 08.30–late. Cuisine: French, German. Out of town, in an industrial estate. One for beer lovers – a micro-brewery, beer retailer & restaurant. Has that chain-restaurant feel. Regular evening entertainment. $$$$

Alizé Plage Bd Hubert Delisle; 0262 352221; for lunch & dinner 10.00–22.00 daily. Cuisine: French, Creole, seafood. St-Pierre's best location – on the seafront. Good food overlooking the beach. Tables on the terrace are romantic, provided it's not one of St-Pierre's windy days. $$$

Bambou 15 bis Rue Archambaud; 0692 309602; for lunch Tue–Sat, for dinner Mon–Sat. Cuisine: European, Creole, Italian. There's nothing special about the location but this restaurant serves good pizzas, salads & crêpes.

Belo Horizonte 10 Rue François de Mahy; 0262 223195; for lunch daily, for dinner Thu–Sat. Cuisine: European, Creole. Unpretentious restaurant with a pleasant courtyard area. A broad menu, including pizza, seafood, paella & even kangaroo. $$$

Carpe Diem 47 Bd Hubert Delisle; 0262 254512; for lunch & dinner Mon–Sat. Cuisine: French. At the western end of the boulevard. Spacious restaurant with additional tables in the courtyard garden area. Creative menu using local ingredients to prepare dishes such as dorado with grapefruit & prawns with chilli & pineapple. $$$

DCP 38bis Bd Hubert Delisle; 0262 322171; for lunch & dinner daily. Cuisine: French, seafood. Comfortable restaurant with contemporary décor. Serves fresh fish straight from local boats. $$$

La Table est Mise Cnr Rues du Four à Chaux & Désiré Barquisseau; 0262 350215; closed Sat/Sun lunch, all day Wed. Cuisine: French, Italian. Tasty food, reasonable value for money. $$$

Le Cabanon 28 Bd Hubert Delisle; 0262 257146; for lunch & dinner Tue–Sun. Cuisine: Italian, French, grills. Fairly large with pleasant décor, popular for pizza. $$$

Le Cap Méchant d'Abord Bd Hubert Delisle; 0262 917199; for lunch & dinner Tue–Sat, for lunch Sun. Cuisine: Creole, Chinese. Popular, impressive restaurant at the far eastern (Terre Sainte) end of Bd Hubert Delisle. One of very few restaurants on the seafront side of the road, overlooking the harbour. Excellent *caris*, especially prawn (*camarons*), served with the traditional accompaniments. Reservation recommended, especially on weekends. $$$

Le Castel Glacier 38 Rue François de Mahy; 0262 229656; 11.00–18.00 Mon/Tue, 11.00–23.00 Wed/Thu, 14.00–23.00 Fri/Sat, 14.00–23.00 Sun. Cuisine: ice cream, light meals. Offers a wide range of ice cream, salads & crêpes. Free Wi-Fi. Modern & comfortable.$$$

Le Marin Bleu 45 Rue Amirale Lacaze, Terre Sainte; 0262 356165; for lunch & dinner Mon–Sat. Cuisine: Creole, French, seafood. Quiet location opposite the seafront in Terre Sainte. Well known for its seafood. $$$

Le Moana 25 Bd Hubert Delisle; 0262 327338; for lunch & dinner daily, but occasionally closes on a Sun for no obvious reason. Cuisine: French, Creole, Italian. Pleasant restaurant with an airy, tropical feel. Menu offers plenty of choice. $$$

Utopia 68 Rue M et A Leblond; 0262 351583; for lunch & dinner Mon–Sat. Cuisine:

European. In an old, atmospheric Creole house, with tables inside & in the garden. Upmarket food, a creative menu & vast portions. $$$

✕ L'Eté Indien 46 Bd Hubert Delisle; ☎ 0262 255752; ⏱ 11.30–22.00 daily. Cuisine: European, ice cream, snacks. Has been there for at least 10 years & is still as popular as ever. 3-course set menu from €15. $$

✕ La Jonque 2 Rue François de Mahy; ☎ 0262 255778; ⏱ for lunch daily, for dinner Wed–Mon. Cuisine: Chinese. Remains popular, although the apparent lack of cleanliness is off-putting. $$

✕ Restaurant Thai 54 Rue Caumont; ☎ 0262 353095; ⏱ for lunch Tue–Sun, for dinner Tue–Sat. Cuisine: Thai. Offers good, traditional Thai food & a change from Creole & French cuisine. $$

NIGHTLIFE *with Dominique Vendôme and Richard Thesée*

From my point of view, St-Pierre's nightlife is by far the best on the island. It has an abundance of bars and nightclubs open until the early hours of the morning, but perhaps the best thing about going out in St-Pierre is that it retains its Réunionnais feel and has not been transformed into a mini St-Tropez or Ibiza, as is the case in St-Gilles-les-Bains and parts of St-Denis.

There is a string of bars along Boulevard Hubert Delisle, most of which have live music several times a week. *Les Pages Noires*, stocked by most bars, will tell you which and when.

L'Endroit (☎ *0262 252696;* ⏱ *Mon–Sat*), next to the casino, has a very clean, European feel. There is a big television screen where they show sports matches and there is live music on Tuesday, Friday and Saturday. The dress code here is stricter than in most bars around town and you won't be allowed in wearing flip-flops, shorts or sleeveless tops. **Alizé Plage** (☎ *0262 352221;* ⏱ *18.00–02.00 daily*), on the main beach, has a relaxed open-air bar with regular live bands. **Le Café de la Gare** (*17 Bd Hubert Delisle;* ☎ *0262 252809*) draws a crowd day and night; it also has a nightclub (see below). For **karaoke** divas, there's **Cherwaine's** at 6 Rue Auguste Babet (☎ *0262 356949*), which also advertises itself as being 'gay friendly'.

Nightclubs don't really get going until after about 23.30 and are open until the early hours, usually Friday and Saturday and on the eve of public holidays. Some open from Wednesday to Saturday. Expect to pay in the region of €12 for entry, which usually includes one drink. The favourite club of the moment is **Africa Queen** (m *0692 383806*) in the old Café de la Gare at 17 Boulevard Hubert Delisle, opposite Rue François de Mahy. It plays a good mix of European chart music and local *séga*, *maloya* and *zouk*. **Le Zaza Club** at 16 Rue Méziaire Guignare (☎ *0262 964061*), also plays a good mixture of European and local music but it can get pretty packed.

Also out of the town centre are **Le Chapiteau** (☎ *0262 310081*) at Montvert-les-Bas and **Apollo Night** (☎ *0262 495891;* ⏱ *Sat night & Sun afternoon*) in Ravine des Cabris.

The very popular **Casino du Sud** is at 47 Boulevard Hubert Delisle (☎ *0262 252696;* ⏱ *until 02.00 Sun–Thu, until 03.00 Fri/Sat; slot machines* ⏱ *from 10.00 daily; tables* ⏱ *from 21.15 Mon–Sat, from 16.00 Sun*), next to the Sterne Beach Hotel.

For **cinemas** in St-Pierre, see *What to do*, page 312.

OTHER PRACTICALITIES

Money and banking There are plenty of banks in town, including **Banque Nationale de Paris** on Rue des Bons Enfants. **Crédit Agricole** and **BRED** are both on the corner of Rues du Four à Chaux and Victor le Vigoureux. They all have ATMs. There is also an ATM conveniently located outside the casino.

Medical Pharmacies are dotted around town, and include a particularly well-stocked and helpful one at the far western end of Boulevard Hubert Delisle, near the cemetery.

Communications The main **post office** is on Rue des Bons Enfants. There are several payphones on Boulevard Hubert Delisle, including two near the beach, outside the Alizé Plage.

Several of the cafés in St-Pierre have Wi-Fi access. **Games City** (⌚ *11.00–18.00 Mon, 10.00–18.00 Tue–Sat*) on the corner of Rue Rodier and Rue Marius et Ary Leblond has internet access, as well as computer gaming.

ST-LOUIS TO L'ETANG-SALE

St-Louis is essentially a residential and industrial town. Despite all the new buildings there, it has retained much of its Creole character and it is one of the few places where you may see bullock carts used, particularly during the sugarcane harvest.

The **Chapelle du Rosaire** here was built in 1732 by Barbe Payet and is the oldest religious building on the island. The chapel is signed from the south of the town and reached via Rue de la Chapelle.

St-Louis is the gateway to the **Cirque de Cilaos**, with buses leaving from the station at the southern end of town. Inland from St-Louis, **Entre-Deux** ('between two') is so named because it lies between two rivers, which join and become Rivière Ste-Etienne. It is a pretty village and is one of the best places to see colourful Creole houses and gardens. There is some good hiking here, including up **Le Dimitile** (1,837m) for views over the Cirque de Cilaos (see page 311). Tours by 4x4 also climb Le Dimitile.

About an hour's drive inland from St-Louis, nestled in alpine scenery, is the village of **Les Makes**. It stands at 1,200m and is home to the Indian Ocean's only

LE SITARANE

The place of Le Sitarane in Réunion's history and folklore has been assured by people's unshakable fascination with his story. It is said that he was actually quite a pleasant man, if a little simple, until he was led into crime and black magic by one St-Ange Calendrin.

They formed a gang, which began in 1907 to commit the horrific acts for which they are known. The gang forced their way into their victims' homes, murdered them and used their bodies in black-magic rituals. They also took the opportunity to burgle them.

Fear seized the population around St-Pierre and Le Tampon for two years, as the gang repeatedly evaded capture until 1909. Eventually, ten arrests were made. The three ringleaders, St-Ange Calendrin, Sitarane and Fontaine, were condemned to death. However, shortly before the execution, Calendrin's punishment was mysteriously toned down and he was deported to French Guiana. Sitarane and Fontaine were publicly guillotined in St-Pierre in 1909.

Sitarane's tomb still holds both fear and fascination for the local population. Those who dabble in *gris gris* (black magic) visit his grave to ask for assistance in their practices, whilst those who fear black magic ask for his protection. His grave, which is red and black, is almost always strewn with offerings: glasses of rum, cigarettes, pieces of red material and candles.

As you stand at the main entrance to the cemetery, the grave is on the far left near the wall, under a tree. Locals would advise you not to take photos of it, for fear of upsetting the occupant. It is also worth knowing that most locals consider it bad luck to mention Sitarane by name.

Observatory (see *What to see in Southern Réunion*, page 313). Around 10km beyond Les Makes is **La Fenêtre** (The Window), a spectacular viewpoint over the Cirque de Cilaos and a lovely spot for a picnic.

St-Louis is surrounded by fields of sugarcane. The **Gol Sugar Refinery (Sucrerie du Gol)**, which can be seen from the main road to Etang-Salé, was one of the island's first, built in 1816. It is still operational and guided tours are available during harvest season (see *What to see in Southern Réunion*, page 313).

Opposite the sugar refinery is one of the island's few identified slave cemeteries, **Le Cimtière du Père Lafosse**. Père Lafosse was a priest, an abolitionist and Mayor of St-Louis. He is buried in the cemetery, along with some of the island's earliest slaves. His tomb has become a place of pilgrimage, particularly on 20 December, the anniversary of the abolition of slavery.

L'Etang-Salé is the name given to the area encompassing the coastal village of **L'Etang-Salé-les-Bains** and, slightly inland, **L'Etang-Salé-les-Hauts**. The two are separated by the large Etang-Salé Forest.

Etang-Salé-les-Bains is largely a residential area, branching outwards from the main street. It has all the essentials: restaurants, shops, a **post office** and **ATM** facilities (opposite the Floralys Caro Beach). The vast 5km, black-sand beach is popular with locals and tourists alike, although it is noticeably quieter than the beaches around St-Gilles-les-Bains. There are designated swimming areas but the waves can be pretty powerful. Surfers, body-boarders and windsurfers flock here.

TOURIST INFORMATION The **tourist office** in Entre-Deux (*9 Rue Fortuné Hoareau;* ☎ *0262 396980;* **f** *0262 396983;* **e** *ot.entredeux@wanadoo.fr; www.ot-entredeux.com;* ⏲ *08.00–12.00 & 13.30–17.00 Mon–Sat*) organises guided tours of the village and can provide information on hiking in the area.

The **tourist office** in L'Etang-Salé-les-Bains (☎ *0892 702201;* **f** *0262 266792;* **e** *accueil.etang-sale@otisud.re; www.sud.reunion.fr;* ⏲ *09.00–12.00, 13.00–17.00 Mon–Thu, Sat*) is in a former railway station at 74 Rue Octave Bénard, the main road through town. They have plenty of literature, including lists of guesthouses and houses to let. Handicrafts are on sale and the staff are helpful.

WHERE TO STAY

Classified hotels

Mid range

Floralys Caro Beach *** (52 rooms) 2 Av de l'Océan, L'Etang-Salé-les-Bains; ☎ 0262 917979; **f** 0262 917980; **e** resa@hotel-floralys.com; www.hotel-floralys.com. In the centre of the village, across the road from the beach. The rooms are in bungalows dotted around a pleasant garden. Some are suitable for families & a few have a kitchenette. Rooms were recently refurbished & are equipped with AC, TV, phone, minibar & terrace; deluxe rooms have a safe. It has a large pool, 2 tennis courts, a restaurant & bar. Family fun is the aim here, & there is a water fun-park on site (see page 312). **$$$**

Le Dimitile **** (18 rooms) 30 Rue Bras Long, Entre-Deux; ☎ 0262 392000; **f** 0262 247011; **e** direction@dimitile.eu; www.dimitile.eu. This delightful little hotel is built around a 17th-century Creole house (*case*). It is set in pretty, tropical gardens & has an impressive mountain backdrop. The rooms are located around a pleasant pool. Rooms are well maintained & equipped with en suite, fan, TV, phone, safe & fridge. **$$$**

Unclassified accommodation

Budget

Boabab et Palmiers (5 bungalows) 36 Chemin du Cap, Etang-Salé; ☎ 0262 540276; **e** infos@baobabetpalmiers.com; www.baobabetpalmiers.com. Inland but only a few minutes from the beach by car. 4 bungalows for 2 people, 1 for 4 people. Comfortable, nicely decorated self-catering accommodation in wood cabins in a garden with pool. From €400 per week (2 people). **$$**

Self-catering holiday rentals

Chez Florelle *** & *** 26 Rue Hubert Delisle; 0262 265194; e rivierefflorelle@wanadoo.fr; http://perso.wanadoo.fr/casepei. A 2-bedroom villa & a 2-bedroom apartment. Villa from €320 per week, apt from €500 per week (5 people).

Zot case en natte *** 5 Impasse Alamandas, Etang Salé; f 0262 265773; e waro-lauret@wanadoo.fr. A typical wooden Creole house with 2 bedrooms, sitting room, dining room & kitchen. From €441 per week (4 people).

Le Fangourin ** 7 Chemin Petit Bon Dieu, La Rivière St-Louis; f 0262 391572; e elise.baret@wanadoo.fr; www.lefangourin.com. 2 self-catering apartments in a house, which sleep 2 to 6 people. From €244 per week (2 people).

Camping

Camping Municipal 58 Av Octave Bénard, L'Etang-Salé-les-Bains; 0262 917586. Facilities are basic but it's only a short walk to the beach. Tent sites from €12.50 per night.

WHERE TO EAT

L'Arbre à Palabres 29 Rue Césaire, Entre-Deux; 0262 444723; for lunch Thu–Sun, for dinner Tue, Fri, Sat. Cuisine: Creole, African, Chinese. In an adorable Creole building. Consistently good food in characterful surroundings. **$$$**

Le Bambou 56 Rue Octave Bénard, L'Etang-Salé-les-Bains; 0262 917028; for lunch & dinner Thu–Tue. Cuisine: Italian, seafood. A popular restaurant with a menu offering plenty of choice. Family friendly. Decent pizzas. **$$$**

Le Play Off Golf Club de Bourbon, 140 Les Sables, L'Etang-Salé-les-Bains; 0262 264349; for lunch Tue–Sun. Cuisine: Creole, European. Beautiful setting in stunning gardens, near the pool. Friendly service. **$$$**

La Carangue 1 Rue Roger Payet, L'Etang-Salé-les-Bains; 0262 917087; for lunch Fri–Wed, for dinner Fri–Tue. Cuisine: Italian, Chinese. Informal, small restaurant opposite the Floralys Caro Beach Hotel. **$$**

Luna Rossa Av de l'Océan, L'Etang-Salé-les-Bains; 0262 265554; for lunch & dinner daily. Cuisine: Italian. Mostly outdoor plastic seating, with an informal, 'snack bar' atmosphere. **$$**

WHAT TO DO IN SOUTHERN REUNION

HIKING Experienced, fit hikers may want to tackle the route from St-Joseph to Piton-de-la-Fournaise. It'll take two days, camping overnight or staying at the *gîte* in Roche Plate. From there, another day's hiking (grading: difficult) eastwards will have you at the Plaine des Sables, then the volcano. Along the Rivière des Remparts route you can still see some of the original wilderness (lowland forests, secluded natural pools, heathland) which once dominated southeast Réunion.

From Entre-Deux you can walk to the top of Le Dimitile (grading: difficult). It is an arduous climb and you will need a full day, or you can stay overnight at one of the *gîtes* near the summit.

GOLF **Golf Club de Bourbon** (*140 Les Sables, L'Etang-Salé; 0262 263339; e info@golf-bourbon.com; www.golf-bourbon.com*) is situated between St-Louis and L'Etang-Salé-les-Bains, easily reached from the RN1 using the Les Sables exit. Arguably the island's best golf course. A well-maintained 18-hole course with fantastic tropical vegetation. The club covers 75ha and there is an attractive clubhouse, swimming pool and restaurant. For details, see *Chapter 16, Activities*, page 273–4.

HORSERIDING There are equestrian centres in Petit-Ile, Les Makes, and L'Etang-Salé. For details, see *Chapter 16, Activities*, page 273.

BULLOCK-CART RIDES are available with **Charrette de Baster** (*54 Rue du Stade, Basse Terre;* ☎ *0693 047901;* **e** *charretteboeufreunion@yahoo.fr; www.charretteboeufreunion.com; adult/child €10/5*) Bullock carts are rarely seen in Réunion these days but they were widely used until relatively recently. Guides take you on carts through the sugarcane fields and explain (in French) the old-fashioned method of harvesting and processing the cane. A traditional meal can also be arranged.

CINEMA The **Rex** on Rue Auguste Babet (☎ *0262 250101*) is a fairly smart cinema, showing international films dubbed in French and occasionally shows foreign-language films (Spanish, Italian, etc). **Eden** is in Le Tampon, at 72 Rue Hubert Delisle (☎ *0262 571489*) and in St-Joseph is the **Cinéma Le Royal** (*8 Rue Amiral Lacaze;* ☎ *0262 565559*).

THEATRE The **Théâtre Luc Donat** (*20 Rue Victor le Vigoureux, Le Tampon;* ☎ *0262 272436;* **e** *direction@theatrelucdonat.re*) puts on regular plays, dance shows, jazz concerts and classical music recitals. During the first two weeks of June it hosts an annual comedy festival. **Sham's Theatre** (☎ *0692 704704*) in the old sugar factory at Pierrefonds also puts on productions. Etang Salé also has a theatre (*Place Fourcade;* ☎ *0262 265097*).

THEME PARK AkOatys at the Floralys Caro Beach Hotel in Etang-Salé-les-Bains (*2 Av de l'Océan;* ☎ *0262 914914;* **e** *contact@akoatys.com; www.akoatys.com; admission €9 for those under 1.4m tall, €13 for others*) has a series of waterslides and a café.

SHOPPING The **covered market** (🕘 *09.00–17.00 daily*) is on Rue Victor le Vigoureux in St-Pierre and is ideal for souvenir shopping, as is St-Pierre's busy Saturday-morning **street market** (see page 304). The markets in St-Louis are open daily.

CAHEB (*83 Rue Kervéguen, Le Tampon;* ☎ *0262 270227;* **f** *0262 273554;* **e** *caheb@geranium-bourbon.com; www.geranium-bourbon.com*) sells essential oils and custom-made perfumes created from local geranium and vetyver.

The village of La Rivière St-Louis is known for its **woodworking** artisans. Their creations can be viewed and purchased at St-Louis Artisanat Bois (*1 RN5 Bois de Nèfles Coco, La Rivière St-Louis;* ☎ *0262 261375*).

WHAT TO SEE IN SOUTHERN REUNION

ECO-MUSEE AU BON ROI LOUIS (*1 Rue de la Marine, St-Philippe;* ☎ *0262 371298;* 🕘 *09.00–12.00 & 14.00–16.30 Mon–Sat; admission adult/child €5/2; visits last 1½hrs*) Guided visits to a Creole house built around 1850, containing an assortment of antique tools, weapons, furniture, coins, documents and agricultural equipment.

LE JARDIN DES PARFUMS ET DES EPICES (*7 Chemin Forestier, Mare Longue, St-Philippe;* ☎ *0262 370636;* **m** *0692 660901;* **e** *fontaine.patrick.e@jardin-parfums-epices.fr; admission adult/child €6.10/3.10; tours daily at 10.30 & 14.30, reservation recommended*) A private garden between Le Baril and St-Philippe, which is more like a chunk of forest, where 1,500 endemic and exotic species grow side by side. Guided tours (about 90 minutes) explain the origin and use of the plants, be it medicinal, culinary or furniture making. At present tours are offered in French only.

LA SAGA DU RHUM (*Chemin Frédeline, St-Pierre;* ☎ *0262 358190;* e *sagadurhum@sagadurhum.fr; www.sagadurhum.fr;* ⊕ *10.00–18.00 daily, guided tours 10.15, 11.30, 14.30, 16.00; admission adult/child €8/4*). Housed within the Isautier rum distillery, this modern, well laid-out museum tells the story of rum making. A tasting is offered at the end of the tour and there is a shop on site. Accessible to those with limited mobility.

PARC EXOTICA (*60 CD 26, Pierrefonds, St-Pierre;* ☎ *0262 554385;* ⊕ *09.00–12.00 & 13.30–17.00 Tue–Sun; admission adult/child €6/3*) A botanical garden packed with fruit trees, orchids, anthuriums and much more. There is also a rock museum.

SUCRERIE DU GOL (*Le Camp du Gol, St-Louis;* ☎/f *0262 910547;* e *visitesucrerie@gqf.com; www.gqf.com; 1½ hr guided tours Jul–Dec at 09.00, 11,00, 13,30 & 15.30 Tue–Sat; admission adult/child €5/3; on reservation only; children aged under 7 are not allowed*) Claims to be the largest sugar refinery in the European Union. Guided tours can be organised (in French or English) during harvest season (July–December). Sugar products are on sale in the shop. Flat, enclosed shoes must be worn.

OBSERVATOIRE ASTRONOMIQUE LES MAKES (*18 Rue Georges Bizet, Plaine des Makes;* ☎ *0262 378683;* e *obs.astronomique@wanadoo.fr; www.ilereunion.com/observatoire-makes;* ⊕ *09.00–12.00 & 14.00–17.00 Mon–Fri, 09.00–12.00 Sat; guided tours 09.30, adult/child €4/2.50; night observation adult/child €7.50/4.50; on reservation only*) Observatory about one hour's drive inland from St-Louis, at an altitude of 1,000m.

CROC PARC (*1 Route Forestière, L'Etang-Salé-les-Hauts;* ☎ *0262 914041;* e *orizon.reunion@wanadoo.fr; www.crocparc.re;* ⊕ *10.00–17.30 daily; admission adult/child €8/6*) About 2km from the RN1, between l'Etang-Salé-les-Bains and l'Etang-Salé-les-Hauts. The park is home to over 165 Nile crocodiles (*Crocodylus niloticus*), which are not bred for their skin or meat, but are simply there for the benefit of the public. The gardens are pleasant (many of the plants are labelled), there are copious birds (wild and caged), as well as a small collection of farm animals, a snack bar and a souvenir shop. Crocodiles don't tend to do very much so a good time to visit is Wednesday or Sunday at 16.00 when they are fed.

20

Western Réunion

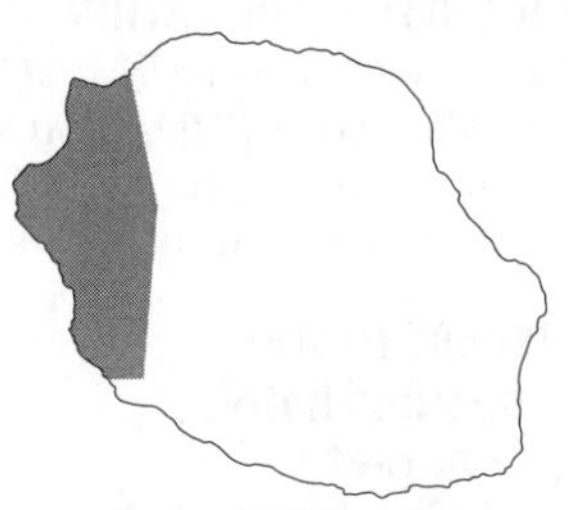

The western region stretches from Les Avirons in the southwest, all the way up to La Possession. Inland, the scenic Route Hubert Delisle links several small settlements along the western 'heights' from Les Avirons to Bois de Nèfles in the north.

The west coast is Réunion's sea, sun and sand holiday mecca, featuring 27km of beaches. It is the driest part of the island, so more often than not the weather is hot and sunny. Water temperatures generally average 20–26°C.

The coast around the historic town of St-Leu is known for its excellent surfing and black-sand beaches. There are also black-sand beaches at St-Paul but it is the clean, white-sand beaches at Boucan Canot, Roches Noires and L'Hermitage that draw the crowds.

Offshore, particularly around St-Gilles-les-Bains and St-Leu, there are colourful coral reefs, perfect for diving and snorkelling. St-Gilles-les-Bains is Réunion's main tourist resort; it has been developed with tourists in mind and while visitors may enjoy the idea of a French seaside resort in a tropical setting, those seeking an authentic Réunionnais experience will not find it here. As you head north, the coast becomes more rugged and the area around Le Port is primarily industrial. While the west of the island is best known for its coastal resorts, those who head inland will be rewarded with attractive villages, incredible viewpoints and excellent hiking country. In particular, Piton Maïdo provides unforgettable views of the Cirque de Mafate.

ST-LEU

The settlement of St-Leu was created in 1776 and soon became an important beef-rearing and coffee-growing region. By 1806, the population of this prosperous town consisted of 463 free people and 5,352 slaves. A few buildings remain from this era: the **town hall**, formerly a coffee warehouse, and the church, which was begun in 1788. The **Chapelle de Notre Dame de la Salette**, behind the church, was begun during the cholera epidemic of 1859 as a plea for St-Leu to be spared. It was, although thousands died in neighbouring towns.

Today St-Leu is surf city. You're bound to see local and visiting surfers hanging out in the street cafés and at the beach. It is also a great spot for diving and a popular area for paragliding.

St-Leu has a noticeably more relaxed air about it than St-Gilles and, although it has some good hotels, it has not been totally colonised by tourists.

Visible from the coast road south of St-Leu, is **Le Souffleur**. When the sea is rough, this blowhole is spectacular.

On the RN1, just north of St-Leu is **Kélonia**, a former turtle farm, where sea turtles are now bred in captivity and studied. It is well worth a visit (see *What to see in Western Réunion*, page 327).

TOURIST INFORMATION The **tourist office** (☎ *0262 346330;* **f** *0262 349645;* **e** *ot.stleu@wanadoo.fr;* ⌚ *13.30–17.30 Mon, 09.00–12.00 & 13.30–17.30 Tue–Fri, 09.00–12.00 & 14.00–17.00 Sat*) is on the main street through town, Rue Général Lambert, on the corner of Rue Barrelier. It has an excellent stock of leaflets and offers guided tours of the area.

WHERE TO STAY

Classified hotels

Upmarket

Le Blue Margouillat **** (14 rooms) Impasse Jean Albany, Zac du Four à Chaux, St-Leu; ☎ 0262 346400; **f** 0262 346415; **e** info@blue-margouillat.com; www.blue-margouillat.com. A spacious, elegant Creole-style mansion on the hillside above St-Leu with wonderful sea views. The 12 rooms & 2 suites are beautifully decorated, all with AC, TV, phone, free Wi-Fi, & balcony/terrace with sea view. The suites are very private & spacious, ideal for a romantic retreat or for families. There is 1 room equipped for the disabled. Meals are served around the pool or on the veranda (see below). The service is good & many of the staff speak good English. HB packages available. **$$$$**

Mid range

Iloha Seaview Hotel *** (80 rooms) Pointe des Châteaux, St-Leu; ☎ 0262 348989; **f** 0262 348990; **e** hotel@iloha.fr; www.iloha.fr. Set on a hill overlooking St-Leu. There are 14 double rooms in the main building, 2 with disabled facilities. Bungalows in the garden house 40 rooms (20 with kitchenette) & 10 family bungalows for up to 4 adults & 2 children guests (with kitchenette). As part of a renovation in 2011, 16 new 'Guetali' rooms were built to accommodate 2 adults & 2 children; they overlook a separate pool & kitchenette. All accommodation has AC, TV, phone & safe. There is a restaurant by the main pool, a second (Italian) restaurant & a small spa offering massage & beauty treatments. Not by the beach, but St-Leu is nearby & the grounds are a pleasant place to relax. A car is helpful if you want to explore from here. Reasonable value, especially for families. **$$$**

Budget

Villa Mascarine *** 396 Rue Georges Pompidou, Les Colimaçons, St-Leu; ☎ 0262 557317; **e** contact@villamascarine.fr; www.villamascarine.fr. On the hillside overlooking the coast. This attractive Creole-style guesthouse has 2 B&B rooms plus 2 self-catering studios. The rooms are clean & nicely furnished, equipped with en suite, TV, safe & fridge. The studios have a kitchenette & terrace, 1 has a sitting room. The pool & jacuzzi have far-reaching views of the coast. You will need a car if staying here. Breakfast is provided; from Sep to Jun *table d'hôte* meals are provided 3–4 evenings a month, otherwise you will need to have dinner elsewhere. Min stay 2 nights BB, 1 week self-catering. **$$**

Self-catering holiday rentals

Les Azalées **** 5 Chemin des Azalées, La Chaloupe, St-Leu; ☎ 0262 548714. A 3-bedroom apartment with living area, kitchen, TV & veranda. From €450 per week (2–4 people).

Bungalows Murat ** 273 Chemin Dubuisson, St-Leu; ☎/**f** 0262 348504; **e** bungalows.murat@ wanadoo.fr; www.bungalows-murat.re. 5 simple but comfortable bungalows for 2–4 people, on the hillside above St-Leu. From €245 per week (2 people).

WHERE TO EAT

There is a **Super U supermarket** in the centre of town.

Le Bleu Margouillat Impasse Jean Albany, Zac du Four à Chaux, St-Leu; ☎ 0262 346400; ⌚ for lunch & dinner daily. Cuisine: French, Creole. Fine food in an elegant setting. Good service. Reservation essential. **$$$$**

Iloha Seaview Hotel Pointe des Châteaux, St-Leu; ☎ 0262 348989; www.iloha.fr; ⌚ for lunch & dinner daily. Cuisine: European, Creole. The main restaurant of the hotel is by the pool, with views of the ocean. A very pleasant setting for a meal & the food is good. Reservation recommended. $$$

Tilbury Lagon 2 bis Rue du Lagon, St-Leu; 0262 347913; for lunch & dinner Wed–Mon. Cuisine: French, Creole, seafood, snacks. Tables are on a large terrace which leads directly onto the beach. $$$

La Varangue 36 Rue du Lagon, St-Leu; 0262 347926; for lunch Tue–Sun, for dinner Tue–Sat. Cuisine: Creole, grills. Upmarket restaurant on the seafront. $$$

Aux Bonnes Choses 73 Rue du Lagon, St-Leu; 0262 347626; for lunch & dinner Fri/Sat, closed Sun evening. Cuisine: Creole. On the seafront. $$

OTHER PRACTICALITIES

Money and banking There are banks on the main street through town, including **Banque de la Réunion** at 52 Rue Général Lambert.

Communications The **post office** is near the harbour on Rue de la Compagnie des Indes and has **ATM** facilities. For **faxing**, **secretarial services** and **internet access** try **Cybercafi** at 82 Rue Haute, St-Leu (*0262 348772*).

Medical Care can be obtained at the **Pharmacie de la Salette**, near which there are doctors' surgeries.

ST-GILLES-LES-BAINS AND SURROUNDS

The area around St-Gilles-les-Bains is Réunion's premier beach holiday hangout. The island's best beaches and seaside hotels are here. However, it must be said that even these beaches do not compare to those of Mauritius.

As you head north from St-Leu along the coast, you come to the largely residential area of **La-Saline-les-Bains**. There are decent beaches here, popular for snorkelling, surfing and windsurfing, and they tend to be less crowded than those in St-Gilles-les-Bains.

Continuing north, before you hit St-Gilles itself, you pass the turning to L'Hermitage – arguably the island's prettiest beach. The beach is protected by a long lagoon; the water is clear, shallow and good for swimming.

The bustling town of St-Gilles is packed with restaurants, bars, pubs and trendy nightclubs. It is a playground for hip, young, French holidaymakers, who come to enjoy the sunshine, the sea and the busy nightlife. Many travellers find it too 'commercialised' and crowded; for others it is the ideal way to unwind after hiking in the mountains. You will not get an authentic taste of Réunion in St-Gilles. It is a town built by Europeans for Europeans, a fact captured by one of my Réunionnais friends in his description of it as a *ghetto zoreilles* (white people's ghetto). Certainly, it does feel like a mini St-Tropez and traffic congestion is a real problem along this section of coast.

The **harbour** (Port de Plaisance) is also a lively place, where all manner of watersports can be arranged. This is where you'll find the excellent **Aquarium de la Réunion** (see *What to see in Western Réunion*, page 327).

About 3km inland from St-Gilles-les-Bains, on the road to St-Gilles-les-Hauts, is the starting point for the walk to three waterfalls plunging into pools (*bassins*): **Bassin du Cormoran**, **Bassin des Aigrettes** and **Bassin Bleu**. It takes about two hours and Bassins des Aigrettes and Bleu are ideal for a quick dip. You will have to take your shoes off and get your feet wet on parts of the walk, and you will need mosquito repellent.

Also on the road to St-Gilles-les-Hauts is the **Village Artisanal de l'Eperon**, where handicrafts and art produced by local artisans are on sale. The products

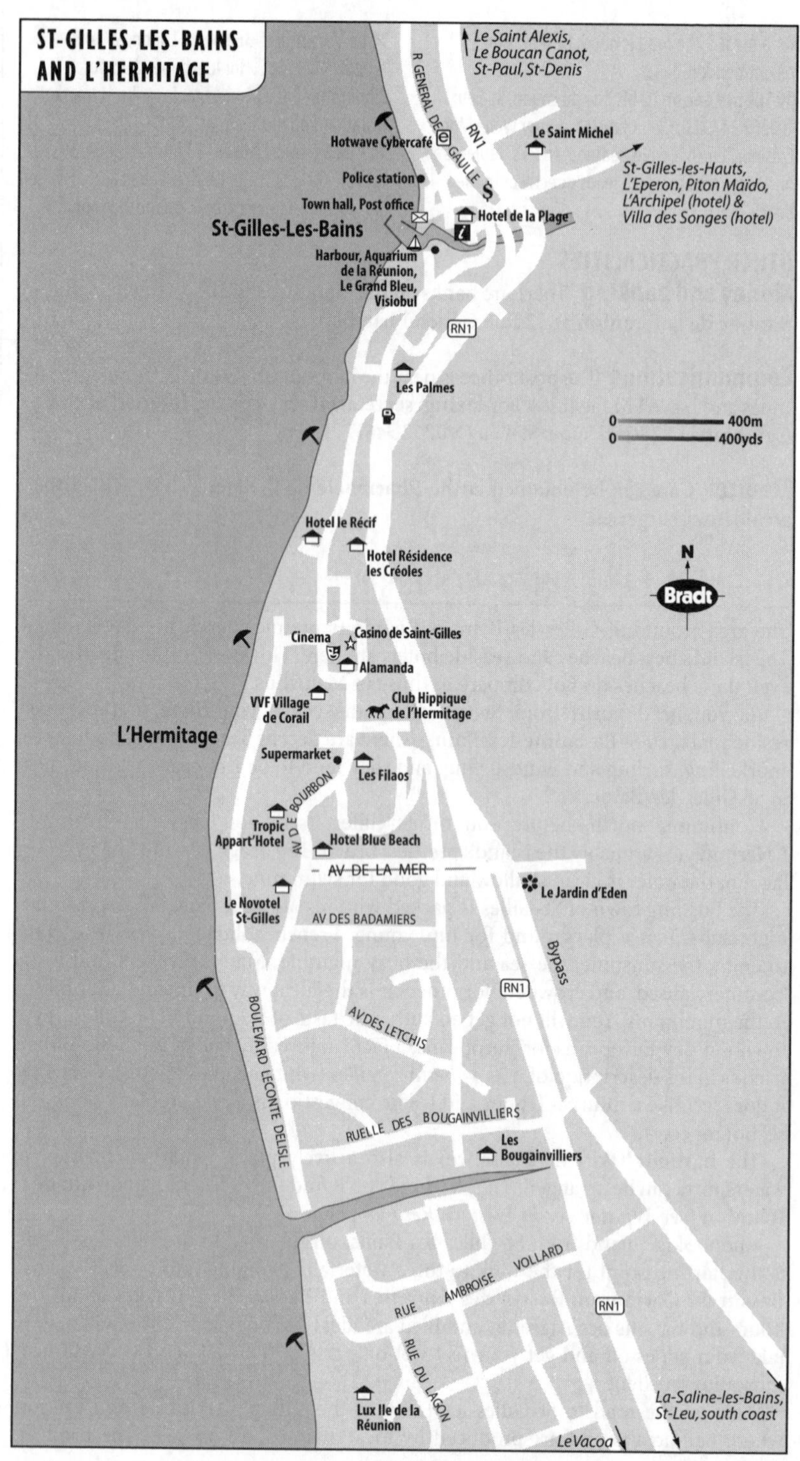

ST-GILLES-LES-BAINS AND L'HERMITAGE
Le Saint Alexis, Le Boucan Canot, St-Paul, St-Denis
R GENERAL DE GAULLE
RN1
Le Saint Michel
St-Gilles-les-Hauts, L'Eperon, Piton Maïdo, L'Archipel (hotel) & Villa des Songes (hotel)
Hotwave Cybercafé
Police station
Town hall, Post office
Hotel de la Plage
St-Gilles-Les-Bains
Harbour, Aquarium de la Réunion, Le Grand Bleu, Visiobul
Les Palmes
0 400m
0 400yds
Hotel le Récif
Hotel Résidence les Créoles
N
Bradt
Cinema
Casino de Saint-Gilles
Alamanda
VVF Village de Corail
Club Hippique de l'Hermitage
L'Hermitage
Supermarket
Les Filaos
AV DE BOURBON
Tropic Appart'Hotel
Hotel Blue Beach
AV DE LA MER
Le Jardin d'Eden
Le Novotel St-Gilles
AV DES BADAMIERS
Bypass
AV DES LETCHIS
BOULEVARD LECONTE DELISLE
RUELLE DES BOUGAINVILLIERS
Les Bougainvilliers
RUE AMBROISE VOLLARD
RUE DU LAGON
Lux Ile de la Réunion
Le Vacoa
La-Saline-les-Bains, St-Leu, south coast

include miniature Creole houses, leather goods and clothes; there are restaurants on site.

GETTING THERE AND AWAY All the towns along the west coast, including St-Gilles-les-Bains, are easily reached on the non-express St-Denis–St-Pierre buses (Lines B and C).

TOURIST INFORMATION There is a well-stocked **tourist office** (*0810 797797;* f *0262 550102;* e *info@saintpaul-lareunion.com; www.saintpaul-lareunion.com;* *10.00–13.00 & 14.00–18.00 daily, including public holidays*) at 1 Place Paul Julius Bénard, Galerie Amandine, St-Gilles-les-Bains. They can also make bookings for accommodation and activities.

WHERE TO STAY

Classified hotels

Upmarket

Hotel le Récif *** (146 rooms) 50 Av de Bourbon, L'Hermitage; 0262 700100; f 0262 700107; e reservation@luxislandresorts.com; www.hotellerecif.com. This hotel underwent a transformation in 2004 & is now a very attractive option. The rooms & suites, including 4 rooms for the disabled, are housed in 17 2-storey Creole-style buildings scattered in a large garden. Rooms have AC, TV, phone, safe, minibar & balcony/terrace. Facilities include a restaurant, bar, 2 pools, tennis & kids' club. A family-friendly hotel with an emphasis on activities. In a great location, opposite L'Hermitage Beach. **$$$$**

Le Boucan Canot **** (50 rooms) 32 Rue Boucan Canot, Boucan Canot; 0262 334444; f 0262 334445; e hotel@boucancanot.com; www.boucancanot.com. An attractive blue & white Creole-style building in a good location with direct access to Boucan Canot Beach. The rooms & suites are modern & equipped with AC, TV, phone, Wi-Fi, minibar, safe & balcony. 2 rooms are equipped for the disabled. Facilities include a restaurant overlooking the sea (see page 322), pool & regular evening entertainment. **$$$$**

Le Saint Alexis **** (60 rooms) 44 Route de Boucan Canot, St-Gilles-Les-Bains; 0262 244204; f 0262 240013; e reception@hotelsaintalexis.com; www.hotelsaintalexis.com. This hotel on the beach at Boucan Canot was extensively refurbished in 2002. All rooms & suites have AC, TV, phone, safe, spa bath, minibar & balcony/terrace. There are 2 pools, a sauna, a gym & a restaurant. **$$$$**

Lux Ile de la Réunion ***** (174 rooms) 28 Rue du Lagon, L'Hermitage, St-Gilles-les-Bains; 0262 700000; f 0262 700007; e reservation@luxislandresorts.com; www.luxislandresorts.com. Deservedly considered the most upmarket hotel on the island. It is a resort-style hotel set in gardens that run along the beach. The 23 bungalows house well-maintained rooms, including 4 with disabled facilities & 8 suites. As you'd expect, all have AC, TV, phone, minibar & safe. Plenty of activities: tennis, badminton, gym & some watersports. There are 3 restaurants, including a very good Creole restaurant on the beach, where they cook over a wood fire. Also a pool & a kids' club. The large gardens provide a feeling of space & it fronts one of the island's best beaches. **$$$$**

Mid range

Alamanda Hotel ** (58 rooms) 81 Av de Bourbon, L'Hermitage; 0262 331010; f 0262 240242; e alamanda.hotel@alamanda.fr; www.alamanda.fr. After a much-needed refurbishment, this 2-star option is now pretty good value. The hotel is close to the casino & nightlife, & 5mins' walk from the beach. En-suite rooms with AC, TV, phone & balcony/terrace overlook either the pool or small garden. It has a good restaurant, bar, gym & pool. The rooms are small but clean & modern, & it is well located. Free Wi-Fi & access to a nearby fitness centre. **$$$**

Hotel Blue Beach *** (46 rooms) 40 Av de la Mer, Les Filaos, L'Hermitage; 0262 245025; f 0262 243622; e reservation@hotelbluebeach.fr; www.hotelbluebeach.fr. Family-friendly hotel 150m from the beach. Rooms are in a 2-storey building & overlook the pool, garden or car park. They are equipped with AC, TV, phone, Wi-Fi, minibar & balcony/terrace. Standard rooms are on the small side but junior suites are ideal for families as they have a living area with sofa bed, a kitchenette & 2 bathrooms. The hotel was renovated recently & has a clean, modern feel. Facilities include a restaurant, bar, car park & pool, which feels rather overlooked by the rooms bunched around it. **$$$**

Hotel Résidence les Créoles *** (10 rooms, 22 studios, 10 apts) 43 Av de Bourbon, St-Gilles-les-Bains; ☎ 0262 265265; **f** 0262 266266; www.hotellescreoles.com. This recently renovated hotel is around 150m from the beach, amidst the bars, clubs & restaurants of L'Hermitage. Accommodation feels fresh & new & is equipped with AC, TV, phone, minibar, internet access. The studios & apartments have a well-equipped kitchenette. The buildings are attractive & grouped around a pool. The restaurant only serves breakfast (€12/8 per adult/child) but there are restaurants within walking distance. Reasonable value. **$$$**

Le Nautile *** (43 rooms) 60 Rue Lacaussade, La-Saline-les-Bains; ☎ 0262 338888; **f** 0262 338889; **e** nautile@runnet.com; www.hotel-nautile.com. Pretty hotel on the beach. The nicely decorated rooms have AC, TV, phone, Wi-Fi, minibar, safe & balcony/terrace. Facilities include a restaurant, bar, library & pool. Regular evening entertainment. Several of the staff speak English. **$$$**

Le Novotel St-Gilles *** (173 rooms) 123 Av Leconte de Lisle, L'Hermitage; ☎ 0262 244444; **f** 0262 240167; **e** H0462@accor.com; www.accor.com. Sprawling hotel spread through a 3ha garden with direct access to the beach. Rooms have views of either the mountains (& car park) or the pool. All have AC, TV, phone, safe & minibar, & most have balcony/terrace. 5 rooms have disabled facilities. It's a busy hotel, where everyone seems to take advantage of the activities – pool, tennis courts, mini golf, kayaks, pedaloes & snorkelling equipment. There's a family atmosphere, but the kids' club operates only during French school holidays. **$$$**

Le Swalibo *** (30 rooms) 9 Rue des Salines, La-Saline-les-Bains; ☎ 0262 241097; **f** 0262 246429; **e** info@swalibo.com; www.swalibo.com. A charming small hotel, 5mins' walk from the beach. Rooms are bright, colourful & spacious with AC, TV, phone, minibar, safe & balcony. Not much privacy – the balconies & small garden are overlooked by other rooms. Facilities include a restaurant, pool & jacuzzi. Beach umbrellas, kayaks & snorkelling gear are available. **$$$**

Budget

L'Archipel *** (64 studios & apts) 9 Rue de la Cheminée, Grand Fond, St-Gilles-les-Bains; ☎ 0262 240534; **f** 0262 244724; **e** reservation@archipel-residence.com; www.archipel-residence.com. On the road to St-Gilles-les-Hauts, but there is a free shuttle service to the beaches & St-Gilles-les-Bains town centre. There are 52 studios for up to 3 people & 12 apartments for up to 5 people, including 2 with disabled facilities. They are equipped with AC, TV, phone, minibar & balcony/terrace. There is a pleasant pool, snack bar & tennis. Breakfast is available but there is no restaurant for evening meals & the free shuttle to the coast stops at 17.00. **$$**

La Villa du Soleil ** (12 rooms) 54 Route Nationale, Plage de Boucan Canot; ☎ 0262 243869; **e** lavilladusoleil@wanadoo.fr; www.lavilladusoleil.com. A small hotel with simple, colourful en-suite rooms equipped with AC, TV & Wi-Fi. **$$**

Le Saint Michel ** (15 rooms) 196 Chemin Summer, St-Gilles-les-Bains; ☎ 0262 331333; **f** 0262 331338; **e** st-michel.hotel@wanadoo.fr. A small, hotel 5mins from the beach. En-suite rooms with AC, TV, phone & balcony/terrace. There is a restaurant & a pool. **$$**

Les Bougainvilliers ** (14 rooms) 27 Ruelle des Bougainvilliers, L'Hermitage; ☎ 0262 338248; **e** bougainvilliers@wanadoo.fr; www.bougainvillier.com. Around 300m from L'Hermitage Beach. Rooms are comfortable & fresh, with en suite, AC, TV & fridge. A room with a balcony costs around an extra €10 per night. There is a pool in the garden & a communal kitchen but no restaurant. Free Wi-Fi. Reasonable value for money. **$$**

Les Filaos ** (27 studios, 17 rooms) 101 Av de Bourbon, St-Gilles-les-Bains; ☎ 0262 245009; **f** 0262 242809; **e** les-filaos@wanadoo.fr; www.hotelfilaos.com. Unfortunately next to a busy road with a nightclub & supermarket in front of it but only a short walk from the beach. Small, simply furnished en-suite rooms with AC, TV, phone, & balcony/terrace; studios have a kitchenette. Rooms with disabled facilities are available. It has a bar & pool. **$$**

Les Palmes ** (21 apts) 205 Rue du Générale de Gaulle, St-Gilles-les-Bains; ☎ 0262

244712; **f** 0262 243062; **e** soresum@wanadoo.fr; www.hoteldespalmes.fr. The accommodation is in bungalows in a tropical garden, 200m from the beach. Rooms are basic & a little tired, equipped with en suite, AC, TV & phone. There is a pool. There are better value options around. **$$**

Marina ** (10 apts) 6 Allée des Pailles en Queues, Lot Champagne, St-Gilles-les-Bains; 0262 330707; **f** 0262 330700; **e** hotelmarina@wanadoo.fr; www.hotelmarinareunion.com. Rather plain self-catering studios in pretty gardens 200m from Boucan Canot Beach. Close to shops & public transport. Studios are equipped with TV, AC & phone. **$$**

Tropic Appart'Hotel *** (40 studios & apts) 102 Av de Bourbon, L'Hermitage; 0262 225353; **f** 0262 225656; **e** info@residencetropic.com; www.residencetropic.com. Comfortable self-catering accommodation 5mins' walk from L'Hermitage Beach. The studios & apartments are have AC, TV, phone, safe & internet (payable). The apartments accommodate up to 4 people. There is a decent pool & car park. **$$**

Villa des Songes ** (12 rooms) 28 Rue Joseph Hubert, St-Gilles-les-Hauts; 0262 220336; **f** 0262 550637; **e** villa.songes@wanadoo.fr. Elegant accommodation in a renovated Creole home on the hillside above St-Gilles. The rooms are beautifully decorated & equipped with all mod cons: en suite, AC, TV, phone, safe & internet access. There is a delightful restaurant serving Creole & French food (see page 322) & a hammam (payable). It is about 6km from the seafront, so you will need a car. **$$**

Unclassified accommodation

Shoestring

Hotel de la Plage (9 rooms) 20 Rue de la Poste, St-Gilles-les-Bains; 0262 240637; **f** 0262 332005. Budget accommodation 100m from Roches Noires Beach. Small, basic rooms, some with AC. En-suite dbl with TV from €45, dbl with shared bathroom from €29, sgl with fan from €26. All rates BB. **$**

Le Vacoa (16 rooms) 54 Rue Antoine de Bertin, L'Hermitage; 0262 241248; **f** 0262 246710; **e** levacoa@levacoa.com; www.levacoa.com. Simple, family-run guesthouse 300m from the beach. Rooms are comfortable & clean with en suite, AC, TV & fridge. There is a communal kitchen for guest use & a pool. Wi-Fi is available. **$**

Self-catering holiday rentals This area has plenty of apartments and villas to let to holidaymakers, many of which represent excellent value for money. Here is a selection:

At Paul & Virginie's ** Apt 8, Résidence Diane, Rue St-Alexis, St-Gilles-les-Bains; /**f** 0262 294856; **e** alonabox@wanadoo.fr. Simply furnished 1-bedroom apartment in the town centre. Apt from €360 per week (2 people).

Les Gîtes de Boucan Canot **** 255 Chemin de la Vanille, Boucan Canot; 0692 651391; **e** lesgitesdeboucancanot@orange.fr; www.lesgitesdeboucancanot.com. 8 spacious 2-bedroom & 1-bedroom wooden cabins with everything you need for a self-catering stay, including dishwasher, washing machine, Wi-Fi & satellite TV. Each has a decent-sized terrace & garden. The cabins are well spread throughout the gardens, so you have some privacy. 2 are suitable for people with limited mobility. There are 2 pools on site & the beach is around 1km away. You will need a car here. Excellent self-catering option. From €500 per week (2 people), €905 per week (4 people).

L'Ilot Vert *** (8 apts, 3 bungalows) 1 Rue des Salines, La-Saline-les-Bains; 0262 339211; **f** 0262 339212; **e** jean-pierre.fouque@wanadoo.fr; www.a-l-ilot-vert.com. A few mins' walk from the beach. Well-maintained, simply furnished apartments (2–6 people) around a small pool, all equipped with AC, TV & phone. There is a car park. Apt from €65 per night (2 people). B/fast from €8 pp.

Résidence les Boucaniers ** (9 studios, 6 apts) 27 Rue du Boucan Canot, Boucan Canot; 0262 242389; **f** 0262 244695; **e** les-boucaniers@wanadoo.fr; www.les-boucaniers.com. Across the road from Boucan Canot Beach, with AC, TV, & balcony/terrace. The accommodation is sea facing & rooms on the first floor have a good view of the coast. One room with disabled facilities is available. Clean & well situated but the kitchenettes are basic. Studio/4-person apt from €66/95.

Senteur Vanille *** (8 units) Route du Théatre, St-Gilles-les-Bains; ☎/f 0262 240488; e senteurvanille@wanadoo.fr; www.senteurvanille.com. Slightly inland amidst a wealth of tropical plants, not far from Boucan Canot Beach. Accommodation is in Creole bungalows in the garden or elegant, elevated wooden chalets with a view of the ocean. All accommodation is beautifully furnished & invites relaxation. Good value for money. Studio from €80 per night for 2 people rising to €130 per night for 6 people. Chalet from €140 per night for 2 people, €158 per night for 4 people. All prices RO.

Villages Vacances Famille (VVF): family holiday villages You must be a member of VVF to stay here. For details, see *Chapter 15, Accommodation*, page 261.

Village de Corail (129 s/c studios) 80 Av de Bourbon, 97434 St-Gilles-les-Bains; ☎ 0262 242939; f 0262 244102; e contact@villages-des-australes.com; www.villages-des-australes.com. Each studio has kitchenette, dining area & terrace. Up to 2 extra beds can be added per studio. Studio from €52 RO (2 people).

Youth hostel One of the island's three hostels is in the hills above St-Gilles, at Bernica near St-Gilles-les-Hauts (☎ *0262 228975*). To stay there you must have a membership card. For details, see *Chapter 15, Accommodation*, page 261.

WHERE TO EAT Scores of restaurants are crammed into St-Gilles-les-Bains and the surrounding area. In addition, you'll see numerous snack bars and, for those who are self-catering, well-stocked supermarkets in the centre of town (**Score**, **Champion**). There is also a **Score supermarket** in L'Hermitage and a large **Champion supermarket** in La-Saline-les-Bains.

Here is a cross-section of restaurants:

Le Cap 32 Rue Boucan Canot, Boucan Canot; ☎ 0262 334444; ⏲ for lunch & dinner daily. Cuisine: French, Creole, seafood, grills. Upmarket restaurant, overlooking the water. Specialities include heart of palm salad & grilled lobster. **$$$$**

Le St-Gilles Port de Plaisance, St-Gilles-les-Bains; ☎ 0262 245127; www.lesaintgilles.net; ⏲ for lunch & dinner Tue–Sun. Cuisine: European, seafood. Elegant restaurant in an enviable location with a terrace overlooking the marina. Excellent lobster dishes. **$$$$**

DCP 2 Place Paul Julius Bénard, St-Gilles-les-Bains; ☎ 0262 330296; www.dcp.re. Cuisine: European, seafood. It may look pretty casual but this place prides itself on preparing the freshest seafood caught in the waters around the island. **$$$**

Hacienda Cocobeach Plage de L'Hermitage; ☎ 0262 338143; ⏲ from 09.00–late daily. Cuisine: Creole, European. Trendy restaurant/bar on the beach & the place to be seen. Tables are gathered in a garden & palms give it a tropical atmosphere. A lively & popular bar but you can have a quiet meal during the day; there are actually 2 restaurants within, 1 more upmarket than the other. **$$$**

La Frigousse Villa des Songes, 28 Rue Joseph Hubert, St-Gilles-les-Hauts; ☎ 0262 220336; ⏲ for lunch Tue–Fri, for dinner Tue–Sat. Cuisine: French. Creole. Tasty food in an elegant but relaxed atmosphere. **$$$**

La Plage Lux Ile de la Réunion, 28 Rue du Lagon, L'Hermitage, St-Gilles-les-Bains; ☎ 0262 700000; ⏲ for dinner Wed–Sat, for lunch Sun. Cuisine: Creole. Very good Creole restaurant facing the beach. Traditional dishes, like *rougail saucisses*, are cooked on a wood fire. **$$$$**

Le Grand Large 42 Port de Plaisance, St-Gilles-les-Bains; ☎ 0262 278635; ⏲ for lunch daily, dinner Thu–Sun. Cuisine: European. Casual restaurant near the aquarium, overlooking the marina. Serves simple fare such as steak & chips, pizzas & crêpes. Wi-Fi available. **$$$**

Le Grilladin 21 Rue de St-Laurent, St-Gilles-les-Bains; 0262 244582. Cuisine: Creole, French. Casual restaurant near the tourist office. **$$$**

Le Toboggan Plage de L'Hermitage; ☎ 0262 338494; ⏲ for lunch daily, for dinner Thu–Sat.

Cuisine: European, Creole, snacks, ice cream. Décor isn't particularly smart but it's right on the edge of the water & the food is very good. Holds jazz evenings fortnightly on a Sat. $$$

✕ **Paul et Virginie** 15 Route de la Plage, St-Gilles-les-Bains; ☎ 0262 330453; ⏱ for lunch Wed–Sun, for dinner Tue–Sun. Cuisine: Creole, seafood. Overlooking the Roches Noires Beach. Modern décor. Known for its seafood platters. $$$

✕ **Chez Loulou** 84 Rue Général de Gaulle, St-Gilles-les-Bains; ☎ 0262 244636; ⏱ 07.00–13.00 & 15.00–19.00 daily, closed Sun evening. Cuisine: snacks, Creole, French. In a colourful Creole building in the centre of town, opposite Le Forum shopping centre. Excellent bakery which also serves a small range of meals (these vary – just look at the blackboard outside). Internet access available on site. Good value for money. $$

✕ **La Lorientaise** 1 Rue des Salines, La Saline-les-Bains; ☎ 0262 333839; ⏱ for lunch & dinner Wed–Sun. Cuisine: French. A traditional French crêperie. $$

✕ **Le Laetizia** Pl Julius Bénard, St-Gilles-les-Bains; ☎ 0262 244964; ⏱ for lunch & dinner daily. Cuisine: Italian, crêpes, snacks. Mid-range restaurant serving good food in a relaxed atmosphere. $$

NIGHTLIFE The harbour in St-Gilles and the town itself are full of bars, whilst most of the nightclubs and the casino are in L'Hermitage. The downside of nightclubbing in Réunion is that it will dent your wallet severely. In the St-Gilles-les-Bains area you can expect to pay in the region of €12–14 for entry and, on top of that, drinks are expensive. Some clubs are open only on weekends, some only on a Saturday night, but many also have a themed night on Wednesday. They tend to get going at around midnight and are open until about 05.00. Most play a mixture of music, but being St-Gilles there is less local music (*séga*, *zouk*, etc) than in St-Pierre, for example. Most clubs won't let you in wearing trainers or flip-flops.

There are various free publications, available in tourist offices, which will tell you what is going on, where and when in terms of nightlife (see page 266).

Bars are easily found on the main streets of St-Gilles and around the marina. **Cubana Club** (*122 Rue du Général de Gaulle; ☎ 0262 332491*) is usually packed. There is a well-stocked bar, a brasserie, a cigar lounge and regular events. Wednesday night is jazz night, while Thursday is salsa night. Other popular spots on Rue du Général de Gaulle include **Jungle Village** (*☎ 0262 332193*), **La Rhumerie** (*☎ 0262 245599*), **Chez Nous** (*☎ 0262 240808*) and **Mex** (*☎ 0262 330405*). At L'Hermitage, the gay-friendly **Hacienda Cocobeach** (*☎ 0262 338143*) draws a crowd day and night.

As for nightclubs, **Africa Queen** (*205 Rue du Général de Gaulle; ☎ 0262 331615*) has a tropical atmosphere and attracts a lively crowd of young, French partygoers. The ever-popular **Moulin du Tango** in L'Hermitage (*9 Av des Mascareignes; ☎ 0262 245390; ⏱ Wed & Fri/Sat nights*) is a large club, with open-air dance floors and several bars. Also in L'Hermitage is **Le Loft** (*70 Av de Bourbon; ☎ 0262 248106*).

There is also the **Casino de Saint-Gilles** at L'Hermitage (*☎ 0262 244700; ⏱ 10.00–02.00 Mon–Thu, 10.00–04.00 Fri/Sat; slot machines ⏱ from 10.00, the tables from 21.00*).

OTHER PRACTICALITIES

Money and banking The main banks have branches, with ATMs, on Rue du Général de Gaulle. There are also ATMs outside the post office, at the Score supermarket and at the casino in L'Hermitage.

Communications The **post office** is on Rue de la Poste, near Roches Noires Beach. For internet access, try **Hotwave Cybercafé** (*37 Rue du Général de Gaulle; ☎ 0262 240424*), which is set back from the main road in St-Gilles-les-Bains, or **Myly** (*163 Av de la Grande Ourse, Mont Rocquefeuil; ☎ 0262 267699*). **Chez Loulou**

(*84 Rue du Général de Gaulle, St-Gilles;* ☎ *0262 244636*) has one internet terminal in the corner of the bakery. Wi-Fi is available at **Le Forum** shopping centre on the main street, as well as several of the cafés.

ST-PAUL TO LA POSSESSION

St-Paul, the original Réunionnais capital and the site where the first settlers were abandoned, is a favoured weekend escape for residents of St-Denis, as it has the nearest beach to the capital. It's also the centre of Réunion's yachting fraternity, and international yachting events are regularly hosted here.

Of note is the seaside **cemetery**, or **Cimetière Marin**, which has become an unlikely tourist attraction. Signposts guide visitors around the tombs of the famous and infamous occupants. One of these is the notorious pirate, Olivier Levasseur, or **La Buse**, who was hanged in 1730. His tomb features a skull and crossbones. People delving into witchcraft still leave bottles of rum and cigarettes on his grave at night. Some apparently do this in order to communicate with his spirit and find out where he hid his treasure. The late and legendary treasure-hunter Bibique, who was an expert on pirate history, was positive that Levasseur's treasure is buried in Réunion somewhere. St-Paul-born poet **Leconte de Lisle** (1818–94) is also buried here. Across the road from the cemetery and to the south of town is the **Grotte des Premiers Français**, the cave in which the island's first settlers lived. They were 12 French rebels exiled from Madagascar in 1646.

There are some lovely old **colonial mansions** (now government offices) along the coastal road, Quai Gilbert. Look out for the small **park** with its old French cannons, set up to protect St-Paul but never utilised. There's also a **war memorial** for the Réunionnais soldiers who were killed in both world wars.

The most important attraction St-Paul holds for visitors is the vibrant street **market**, which residents proudly claim is the island's best. It operates on Friday and Saturday mornings. As well as souvenirs, there is plenty in the way of exotic food and the market is surrounded on three sides by snack bars.

St-Paul is also the gateway to the picturesque **Maïdo** area in the so-called 'Western Heights', overlooking the west coast. Piton Maïdo (2,190m) affords breathtaking views of the **Cirque de Mafate**. From the coast, you take winding rural roads through cane fields and vegetable plots, after which you pass by the famed **geranium fields** and finally, much higher up, forests. There are several distilleries along this road, where you can buy **essential oils**.

The forests signal a change in climate, as you enter the cool, green, high-lying area on the lip of the Cirque de Mafate. The serene **Forêt de Tévelave** makes a great spot for a picnic. On the winding RF8 road, halfway between **Le Guillaume** and Piton Maïdo, is **Petite-France**, an area where fields of geraniums (actually a pelargonium plant native to South Africa) are cultivated for their essential oil. Réunion's geranium oil is of the highest quality and so is much sought after in the pharmaceutical/essential oils industry.

It's a slow drive of 30km, but worth it. It's best to reach the viewpoint in the early morning before the clouds roll in. The peaks that you see are **Le Gros Morne** (2,991m) and **Piton-des-Nieges** (3,069m). The villages below are **Roche Plate**, **La Nouvelle** and **Ilet des Orangers**, whose combined inhabitants number some 600. It is a mind-boggling sight – a miniature world of isolated communities cupped in a deep crater, untainted by electricity pylons, roads and large buildings. The development of Réunion has passed them by, except for an unreliable water supply that was laid on in 1982. Many of the residents have never seen a car – incredible when you think that just 12km away as the crow flies, people are sitting in a traffic jam on their way to the office.

Further north on the west coast is **Le Port**, Réunion's main harbour, an uninspiring industrial town outside of which is the Nelson Mandela Stadium, where international sporting events are held. Tourists tend to pass through Le Port and **La Possession** on the way to St-Paul or St-Gilles. However, the coast road is impressive, wedged between sheer cliffs and the sea.

TOURIST INFORMATION There is a **tourist office** in La Possession (*0262 222666;* **f** *0262 222517;* **e** *possession-tourisme@wanadoo.fr; www.ville-lapossession.fr; ⌚ 09.00–16.00 Mon, 09.00–17.00 Tue–Fri, 09.00–12.00 Sat*) at 24 Rue Evariste de Parny.

WHERE TO STAY

Classified hotels

Upmarket

Roche Tamarin Lodge & Spa *** (16 rooms) 142 Chemin Bœuf Mort, La Possession; 0262 446688; **f** 0262 446680; **e** infos@villagenature.com; www.villagenature.com. Superb wooden chalets on stilts on the forested hillside above La Possession. Chalets sleep up to 3 people & are rustic yet elegant, with en suite, TV, phone, kitchenette & veranda. The 'prestige' rooms have a jacuzzi on the balcony. Facilities include a pool, small but very relaxing spa, barbecue area, restaurant, shop & conference room. A relaxing hideaway. **$$$$**

Unclassified accommodation

Mid range

La Clé des Champs (6 rooms) 154 Chemin des Barrières, St-Paul; 0262 323760; **f** 0262 324573; **e** lacledeschamps@ilereunion.com; www.lacledeschamps.re. Elegant accommodation in an impressive country house on the hillside above St-Paul, with panoramic views of the coast. En-suite rooms with a classic, country feel. 3 of the rooms have a terrace. Facilities include a lounge area, *table d'hôte* restaurant & jacuzzi. **$$$**

Self-catering holiday rentals

36 La Baie ** 36 Rue de la Baie, St-Paul; 0262 225702; **f** 0262 455916; **e** volk-hug@wanadoo.fr; www.bungalow36labaie.com. Simple 1-bedroom bungalow on the seafront. Apt from €420 per week (2 people).

Marie Cascade ** 46 Rue Frédéric Chopin, La Palmeraie 2, La Possession; /**f** 0262 322041; **e** m.cascade@soleil974.com; www.creole.org/cascade. Well-equipped apartment in owner's house with 1 bedroom & sofa-bed. Washing machine, TV, phone & small private garden. Apt from €290 (2 people).

WHERE TO EAT

There are plenty of snack bars along the seafront in St-Paul, particularly around Quai Gilbert.

Le Jardin 456 Rue St-Louis, St-Paul; 0262 450582; ⌚ for lunch Mon–Sat. Cuisine: French, seafood. One of the more elegant restaurants in the area, serving sophisticated dishes such as duck with prawns. Good, professional service. **$$$$**

Chez Doudou 394 Route du Maïdo, Petite-France; 0262 325587; ⌚ 80.00–16.00 Tue, Thu–Sun. Cuisine: Creole. Traditional Creole dishes cooked over a wood fire. Reservation recommended. **$$$**

Au Petit Gourmet Route du Maïdo; 0692 924634; ⌚ 09.30–16.00 Thu–Tue. Cuisine: Creole. Unassuming little restaurant serving authentic Creole cuisine. On the road to Piton Maïdo. **$$**

Chez Bazou 304 Route du Maïdo, le Guillaume; 0692 410892; ⌚ 11.30–16.30 daily. Cuisine: Creole. Also take-away. A great place to stop off after a visit to Piton Maïdo. This informal little restaurant serves excellent, no-fuss Creole food in generous portions. **$**

WHAT TO DO IN WESTERN REUNION

HIKING Piton Maïdo not only provides magnificent views of the cirque de Mafate; you can also hike into the cirque from here. It is a steep path and involves some clambering over rocks. Less challenging is a walk through Maïdo's beautiful tamarin forest, where you can take advantage of the tremendously clear and fresh air.

WATERSPORTS All manner of watersports can be organised along the west coast. St-Leu and St-Gilles-les-Bains are the two main areas for scuba diving; St-Leu is where surfers head and St-Paul has a water-skiing centre. For details, see *Chapter 16, Activities*, pages 275–6.

GLASS-BOTTOM BOATS Glass-bottom boat trips depart from St-Gilles-les-Bains. For details, see page 277.

DOLPHIN-WATCHING CRUISES Cruises depart from St-Gilles-les-Bains. For details, see *Chapter 16, Activities*, page 277.

HORSERIDING **Centre Equestre du Maïdo**, on the way to Piton Maïdo, is a good-quality equestrian centre in a very picturesque area. There are also riding centres in St-Leu, Les Avirons and St-Gilles-les-Bains. For details, see *Chapter 16, Activities*, page 273.

GOLF **Golf du Bassin Bleu** at St-Gilles-les-Hauts and **Golf Club du Bourbon** at Etang-Salé are popular courses. For details, see *Chapter 16, Activities*, pages 273–4.

PARAGLIDING The hills above St-Leu are the most popular area on the island for paragliding. For details, see *Chapter 16, Activities*, pages 274–5.

ACTIVITY CENTRE

Forêt de l'Aventure Route Forestière des Cryptomérias, Petite France, Maïdo; ☎ 0692 300154; e foretaventuremaido@yahoo.fr; ⏱ 09.00–17.30 daily except Tue & Thu; last entry at 15.30; admission adult/child under 16 years €20/15; reservation recommended. An activity centre in the forest with flying-fox slides & rope bridges. Minimum height of 140cm is required.

THEATRE

Le Théâtre de Plein Air Route du Théâtre, St-Gilles-les-Bains; ☎ 0262 244771; e tpa.technique@odcreunion.com. The open-air theatre takes 1,000 spectators & has regular performances, particularly of local music.

CINEMA **Grand Ecran** (☎ *0262 244666*) in L'Hermitage is rather smart.

BUYING ESSENTIAL OILS There are several distilleries on the road to Piton Maïdo where you can buy geranium and other essential oils. At **Maison du Géranium** (☎ *0692 821500;* ⏱ *08.00–16.00 Thu–Tue*) you can see their simple wood-fired still. They also offer guided tours through the forest, on reservation.

MARKETS There are markets in **St-Leu** on Saturday morning, **St-Gilles-les-Bains** on Wednesday morning and the island's largest market takes place in **St-Paul** all day Friday and Saturday morning.

WHAT TO SEE IN WESTERN REUNION

KELONIA (*Pointe des Châteaux, St-Leu; ☎ 0262 348110; f 0262 347687; e contact@kelonia.org; ⌚ 09.00–18.00 daily; guided visits at 10.00, 11.30, 14.00, 15.15 & 16.30; admission adult/child €7/5*) Formerly Ferme Corail, this conservation project used to be a farm, breeding turtles for their meat and shells, which were used to make jewellery and ornaments. Thankfully, since the international ban on this activity, the farm has become a centre for captive-breeding and release programmes and the study of the sea turtles of the Indian Ocean. There are seven species of sea turtle in the world and five are found around Réunion.

Most of the turtles here are green sea turtles (*Chelonia mydas*). Once abundant on the island, they are rare now, having been eaten almost to extinction by the early colonisers. The displays are interesting and informative; most are only in French. You may be shocked to see trinkets made from turtle shells on sale in the shop, but the shells apparently came from the remaining stock, obtained before the ban.

MUSEE DU SEL (*Pointe au Sel les Bas, St-Leu; ☎ 0262 347700; ⌚ 09.00–12.00 & 13.30–17.00 Tue–Sun; admission free*) Just south of St-Leu, this modern museum tells the story of salt production (in French only).

CONSERVATOIRE BOTANIQUE NATIONALE DE MASCARIN (*2 Rue du Père Georges, Domaine des Colimaçons, St-Leu; ☎ 0262 249227; f 0262 248563; e cbnm@cbnm.org; www.cbnm.org ⌚ 09.00–17.00 Tue–Sun; admission adult/child €6/3*) Signed from the main road just north of St-Leu. A guided walk around the grounds allows you to see and learn about the island's native flora, as well as spices and plants used for their fruit, seeds or essential oils. Well worth visiting as a one–two-hour excursion. There is a souvenir shop and a snack bar (see also *Flora*, page 239).

STELLA MATUTINA AGRICULTURAL AND INDUSTRIAL MUSEUM (*6 Allée des Flamboyants, Piton St-Leu; ☎ 0262 341624; e com.seml@wanadoo.fr; www.stellamatutina.fr; ⌚ 09.30–17.30 Tue–Sun; last entry 16.45; admission adult/child €8/5; combined ticket - Stella Matutina and Maison du Volcan* (see page 333)*: €10*) Housed in a former sugar factory, this museum tells the story of Réunion's agricultural and industrial development, covering the production of coffee, sugar, rum, spices and perfume. The turning to the museum is on the coast road south of St-Leu. There is an excellent restaurant. Audioguides, available in English, French or German, cost €2.

AQUARIUM DE LA REUNION (*Port de Plaisance, St-Gilles-les-Bains; ☎ 0262 334400; e aquarium.reunion@wanadoo.fr; www.aquariumdelareunion.com; ⌚ 10.00–18.00 Tue–Sun; last entry 17.30; admission adult/child €9/6*) Interactive displays and carefully planned tanks make this a fascinating aquarium, particularly good for children. Coral, sea horses, barracudas and all the snorkeller's favourites are to be seen in an environment that is intended to be as close as possible to their natural one. It takes at least an hour to have a good look around.

MUSEE DE VILLELE (*Domaine Panon-Desbassyns, St-Gilles-les-Hauts; ☎ 0262 556410; e musee.villele@cg974.fr; ⌚ 09.30–17.30 Tue–Sun*) A colonial estate, formerly owned by Madame Desbassyns, who is said to have been a particularly cruel plantation owner who mistreated her 300 slaves. Her story inspired Jean-François Sam-Long's novel *Madame Desbassyns* (see page 266). The Chapelle

Pointue (Pointy Chapel), where she is buried, the former slaves' hospital and the garden can be visited free of charge. Guided tours of the Chapelle Pointue and the ground floor of the house (built 1787) can be arranged and cost €2.

LE JARDIN D'EDEN *(155 RN1, L'Hermitage; ✆f 0262 338316; ⌚ 10.00–18.00 Sat–Thu; admission adult/child 7/3.50)* Exploring this 2.5ha garden, which focuses on ethnobotany, takes around 1½hrs. There are over 600 species of plant and visitors are likely to see plenty of birds and possibly a chameleon or two. Information booklets are available in English, French and German.

LE CIMETIERE MARIN (*St-Paul; ✆ 0692 863288;* **e** *contact@guid-a-nou.com; www.guid-a-nou.com; guided tour 09.00 Fri*). While you can wander around the cemetery under your own steam, this one-hour guided tour recounts the stories behind some of the more interesting occupants, such as La Buse, the pirate, and Leconte Delisle, the poet.

21

The Interior

No visit to Réunion is complete without at least a few days spent exploring the magnificent, mountainous interior.

Visitors cannot fail to be impressed by the island's three natural amphitheatres (the Cirques of Salazie, Cilaos and Mafate), with their imposing green mountains, punctuated by waterfalls plunging down steep gorges. The island's interior also boasts the highest mountain in the Indian Ocean (Piton-des-Neiges, 3,069m) and one of our planet's most active volcanoes, the monstrous 2,631m Piton-de-la-Fournaise (see *Chapter 18, Eastern Réunion*, pages 294–5).

There are also the two upland plains: Plaine-des-Palmistes is adjacent to spectacular and vast primary forests, while the much higher Plaine-des-Cafres is surrounded by dairy farms, evoking images of the Swiss Alps in summer. This noticeable resemblance to the Alps is enhanced by quaint mountain villages with charming architecture, a backdrop of imposing slopes and a reputation for producing excellent cheeses.

The best way to explore the interior, particularly the cirques, is on foot. Over 1,000km of hiking trails criss-cross the island, attracting enthusiasts from around the globe (see *Hiking* in *Chapter 16, Activities*, pages 269–72).

LA PLAINE-DES-PALMISTES

The floriferous village of Plaine-des-Palmistes, in the permanently humid uplands high above St-Benoît, is divided into Premier Village, Deuxième Village and Petite-Plaine.

The magnificent waterfall of **Cascade Biberon**, which tumbles 240m down a sheer mountainside, is easily reached from Premier Village on the RN3. It is signed from Plaine-des-Palmistes. Getting there involves an uncomplicated walk of 3km from the parking area. Most of the goyavier which grows wild in Réunion now comes from this area and, in season, you're bound to see groups of people clambering about in the forests, harvesting the small, red fruit.

The **town hall** and **post office** are on Rue de la République. There's also a **war memorial**, in honour of the soldiers who died in World War I.

South of Plaine-des-Palmistes, just beyond **Col de Bellevue** on the RN3, is a large shrine to **Saint Expédit**, with a statue of the man himself in a Roman legionnaire's outfit. A plaque tells how he was whipped and beheaded on 19 April AD303 for not renouncing Christ (see box *Saint Expédit*, page 343).

Plaine-des-Palmistes is the gateway to the fabulous primeval rainforests of **Bébour-Bélouve**. These luxuriant forests constitute the single most important stop in Réunion for naturalists.

Leaving the town for the Bébour-Bélouve forest area, you drive out along Route de la Petite Plaine, towards steep, misty slopes and ridges. *En route*, you pass dairy and vegetable farms, again very reminiscent of Switzerland, Italy or France. The road winds its way steadily uphill; turn right following the arrow pointing to Bébour-Bélouve and you'll see the first slopes swathed in evergreen montane forest.

Dominating these forests are hundreds of thousands of tree ferns, from which the name 'Plaine-des-Palmistes' was (erroneously) derived. For a short distance you then drive along a dirt road, to the sign 'Forêt de la Petite Plaine', where there is a comprehensive information board about the forests of Bébour (5,800ha of primary forest) and Bélouve (889ha of primary forest).

While no wood may be removed from Bébour, tamarind wood can be taken from Bélouve, within reason and under strict supervision. There is also a zone called Canton de Duvernay, where Cryptomeria wood may be extracted. Signs advise the following rules for all the forests: *No litter, no fires, no radios and no removing of indigenous flora.*

Continue past **Canton de Duvernay**, after which you pass the **Col de Bébour** and **Rivière des Marsouins** area to your right, and you'll arrive at another large roadside information board, where a wonderful trail commences into Bébour.

This trail, which can be walked in an hour, involves a level stretch along the mountainside (roughly 1,030m above sea level), so can be managed by almost anyone. Mosses, lichens and other epiphytes festoon the trees, clotting on the branches, like enormous, outrageous wigs. Often, these epiphytes have a yellowish or sometimes reddish hue, so the forest is really unusual in that everything appears almost golden, not green. If you search carefully among the epiphytes, you might find some of the indigenous orchids, but they're uncommon.

Also present are most of the birds unique to Réunion: Mascarene paradise flycatchers, Réunion bulbuls, Réunion stonechats, Réunion olive white-eyes and Réunion grey white-eyes. In the sky watch out for Mascarene cave swiftlets, Mascarene martins and Réunion harriers.

Along the road from here to Bélouve Forest are miles and miles of primary forest swathing steep, mist-enshrouded slopes and valleys.

When you see increasing numbers of the silvery tamarind trees, you'll know you're approaching Bélouve Forest. There is a point signposted and cordoned off, beyond which vehicles are not allowed. It's a short walk along a road flanked by impressive tamarind forest, to the Gîte de Bélouve. There's a breathtaking viewpoint at the back of the *gîte* over a wide, deep valley and a disused cable-car station.

GETTING THERE AND AWAY Plaine-des-Palmistes lies on the RN3, which links St-Pierre and St-Benoît. Buses travel the whole route about three times a day (Line H), whilst others just run between Plaine-des-Palmistes and St-Benoît.

 **WHERE TO STAY** There are several *gîtes* in the area and a *ferme auberge* (farm inn). For details, see *Chapter 15, Accommodation*, pages 259–61.

Classified hotels

Budget

Ferme du Pommeau ** (19 rooms) 10 Allée des Pois de Senteur, Plaine-des-Palmistes; 0262 514070; f 0262 513263; e la-ferme-du-pommeau@wanadoo.fr; www.pommeau.fr. Accommodation on a small farm. Comfortable Creole-style en-suite rooms with AC, TV & phone. Rooms equipped for the disabled are available. There is an excellent restaurant & bar, & tours of the farm can be arranged. **$$**

Self-catering holiday rentals

Massilia ** 9 Rue Louis Parny, Plaine-des-Palmistes; 0262 460799; e marlene.poiny-toplan@wanadoo.fr. An 8-bedroom house with large kitchen & 3 bathrooms, able to sleep up to 18 people. From €470 per weekend (8 people).

Poiny-Toplan ** 4 Rue Delmas Hoareau, Plaine-des-Palmistes; 0262 460799; e marlene.poiny-toplan@wanadoo.fr. Pretty Creole-style villa with 6 bedrooms, 2 bathrooms, living room, kitchen & large veranda. Garden & parking. From €250 per weekend (2 people).

WHERE TO EAT Supplies can be bought at the **Chez Alexis supermarket**, near the Shell petrol station in Plaine-des-Palmistes. Most of Plaine-des-Palmistes's restaurants are on Rue de la République, so finding a meal isn't difficult. Here is a selection:

Ferme du Pommeau 10 Allée des Pois de Senteur, Plaine-des-Palmistes; 0262 514070; for lunch & dinner daily, closed Sun evening. Cuisine: Creole, French. Excellent home-cooked food at the farm inn. Reservation recommended. $$$

Les Plantanes 167 Rue de la République, Plaine-des-Palmistes; 0262 513169; for lunch Tue–Sun, dinner on reservation. Cuisine: Creole, Chinese. Traditional dishes prepared with local ingredients. $$$

Café des Arts 325 Rue de la République, Plaine-des-Palmistes; m 0692 655741; 09.00–19.00 Tue–Sun. Cuisine: snacks. Informal café opposite the post office. Serves salads & sandwiches. $$

LA PLAINE-DES-CAFRES

As you drive away from Plaine-des-Palmistes in a southwesterly direction, the road takes you higher and higher, away from the forests and into a rather desolate-looking expanse featuring harsh, scrubby vegetation and grassland. You'll also see fields of dairy cattle. This is Plaine-des-Cafres, much of which is around 2,000m above sea level.

In the village of **Bourg-Murat**, just north of Plaine-des-Cafres town, is the turning which takes you onto the road to the volcano (RF5, La Route du Volcan), Piton-de-la-Fournaise. This is also where you'll find the **Maison du Volcan** (see page 333).

Many of the towns that line the RN3 between here and **Le Tampon** are named according to their distance from the sea, hence Le Dixneuvième and Le Quatorzième, etc. As well as producing cheese, the area is known for its geranium oil and honey.

The town of Plaine-des-Cafres is the starting point for some arduous trekking routes to places like Piton-des-Neiges, of which there are excellent views from here on clear mornings. On the main road you'll find a **post office** and **banks**. The area has a very laid-back atmosphere and, despite nearby attractions like the volcano, does not swarm with tourists. The climate can be pretty chilly, especially when the afternoon clouds smother the area in a cool fog.

If you take the turning towards **Bois Court** at the crossroads in Vingt-troisième, the road will take you to the viewpoint over the gorges of **Rivière des Citrons**. You'll see majestic waterfalls and, way down below, the isolated hamlet of **Grand Bassin**. The energetic can hike the 2km down to Grand Bassin, where there are several *gîtes*.

TOURIST INFORMATION The **tourist office** (*0262 274000; e officedetourismepdc@yahoo.fr; 09.00–12.30 & 13.30–17.00 Mon–Sat*) is at 160 Rue Maurice et Katia Kraft off the RN3 in Bourg-Murat.

WHERE TO STAY

Classified hotels

Budget

Hotel du Volcan ** (8 rooms) 194 Rue Maurice Kraft, PK27-RN3, Bourg-Murat, La Plaine-des-Cafres; 0262 275091; f 0262 591721; e aubvolcan@wanadoo.fr. Simple, cosy accommodation 200m from Maison du Volcan. En-suite rooms with TV, phone, heater & terrace. **$$**

L'Ecrin ** (21 rooms) PK27-RN3, Bourg-Murat, La Plaine-des-Cafres; 0262 590202; f 0262 593610; e reception@hotel-ecrin.re; www.hotel-ecrin.re. Conveniently located about 150m from Maison du Volcan & the road to the volcano. Rooms have TV, phone & heater, & most have mountain views. Family units have kitchenette. Rooms equipped for the disabled are available. It has a restaurant, sauna & mini-golf. **$$**

Les Géraniums ** (25 rooms) RN3, 24ème km, La Plaine-des-Cafres; 0262 591106; f 0262 592183; e hotelgeranium@wanadoo.fr. Commands panoramic views of Piton-des-Neiges, Bois Court & Dimitile Mountain. Comfortable, spacious en-suite rooms with TV, phone & heater. The atmosphere is peaceful & the staff are friendly. Try to get a room with a mountain view. There is good restaurant (see below). **$$**

Les Grevilleas (5 rooms, 1 villa) 7 Ter, RN3, PK20, La Plaine-des-Cafres; 0262 591797; www.grevilaire.com. Mrs Vilcourt offers guesthouse & *gîte* accommodation. The guesthouse is on the small family farm. The rooms are en suite & simply furnished. The Creole-style 3-bedroom *gîte* sleeps up 6 people & has wonderful views to the coast. Guesthouse dbl/sgl from €40/38 BB, *gîte* from €300 (2 people). **$$**

Unclassified accommodation

Shoestring

Auberge du Volcan (8 rooms) PK27-RN3 Bourg-Murat, La Plaine-des-Cafres; 0262 275091; f 0262 591721; e aubvolcan@wanadoo.fr. Co-located with Hotel le Volcan. Basic en-suite rooms with TV & heater. There is a very pretty restaurant (see below). **$**

WHERE TO EAT

Le Vieux Bardeau 24ème km, La Plaine-des-Cafres; 0262 590944; for lunch & dinner Fri–Wed. Cuisine: Creole. Elegant restaurant in a charming Creole house, set back from the main road. Superb Creole dishes with a creative twist. **$$$$**

Auberge du Volcan Bourg-Murat, La Plaine-des-Cafres; 0262 275091; 06.30–22.00, closed Sun evening & Mon. Cuisine: Creole, French. Quaint, French provincial décor & tasty food. **$$$**

La Ferme du Pêcheur Gourmand RN3, 25ème km, La Plaine-des-Cafres; 0262 592979. Cuisine: French, Creole. This small farm has a charming *table d'hôte* restaurant with a reputation for excellent, home-cooked French food. Duck is the speciality here. Many of the ingredients (including the ducks) are produced on the farm. Lunch & dinner on reservation only. **$$$**

Les Géraniums 24ème km, La Plaine-des-Cafres; 0262 591106; for lunch & dinner daily. Cuisine: Creole, French. Excellent food & wonderful views. The speciality is a sauce made from geranium mushrooms. Reservation recommended. **$$$**.

Le Panoramic PK27-RN3, Bourg-Murat; La Plaine-des-Cafres; /f 0262 593612; for lunch Fri–Wed, for dinner daily. Cuisine: Creole, French. Next to the Hotel L'Ecrin. **$$$**

Relais du Commerson 37 Rue Bois Joly Poitier; 0262 275287; 09.00–19.00 Thu–Tue. Cuisine: Creole, Chinese, grills, snacks. Cheap & cheerful. **$$$**

WHAT TO DO IN LA PLAINE-DES-PALMISTES AND LA PLAINE-DES-CAFRES

CHEESE TASTING/BUYING There are several places where you can sample and buy cheeses in the Plaines. One of the best is **Palais du Fromage** (*0262 592715; 10.00–18.00 Thu–Sun*) on the Route du Volcan in Bourg-Murat.

HORSERIDING There is some fantastic riding country around the Plaines. The equestrian centres around La Plaine-des-Cafres offer treks to the volcano (usually two days). For details, see *Chapter 16, Activities*, page 273.

WHAT TO SEE IN LA PLAINE-DES-PALMISTES AND LA PLAINE-DES-CAFRES

DOMAINE DES TOURELLES (*Rue de la République, Plaine-des-Palmistes;* ☎ *0262 514759;* **f** *0262 514764;* **e** *domainedestourelles@wanadoo.fr; www.domaine-tourelles.com;* ⏱ *09.00–17.30 Mon & Wed–Fri, 09.00–17.00 Tue, 10.00–17.00 Sat/Sun; admission free*) A wonderful Creole house, built in the 1920s, where all manner of Réunion-made handicrafts and ornaments are on sale. During the week, artisans can be seen crafting their products in the workshops on site. Visitors can also organise to do educational botanical walking tours of the area, which cost adult/child around €4/2.

MAISON DU VOLCAN (*RN3 Bourg-Murat, La Plaine-des-Cafres;* ☎ *0262 590026;* **f** *0262 591671;* **e** secretariat@*maisonduvolcan.fr; www.maisonduvolcan.fr;* ⏱ *09.30–17.30 Tue–Sun, last entry 16.45; admission adult/child €7/2.50; combined ticket – Stella Matutina* (see page 327) *& Maison du Volcan €11*) Excellent exhibitions on Piton-de-la-Fournaise and volcanoes in general, including interactive displays, models and videos. Well worth a visit before seeing the real thing, not least because there is a webcam showing what is happening around Piton-de-la-Fournaise.

THE CIRQUES

A substantial portion of Réunion's interior is taken up by three 'cirques' or gigantic natural amphitheatres, which were formed when ancient volcanic craters collapsed. Subsequent erosion by the elements completed the job. The cirques, which differ considerably from each other in scenery and climate, converge at Piton-des-Neiges.

The first inhabitants of the cirques were runaway slaves or *marrons* of Malagasy origin, who fled to the mountains to escape slave hunters. Hence many villages in the cirques have Malagasy names.

CIRQUE DE CILAOS The name 'Cilaos' is derived from a Malagasy word meaning 'the place you never leave'. This is the southernmost and driest of Réunion's cirques, covering roughly 100km^2. It lies between the island's two highest peaks: **Piton-des-Neiges** (3,069m) and **Grand Bénard** (2,896m). Where remote mountain hamlets now nestle on small, flat plots called *ilets*, runaway slaves once sought shelter.

About 10,000 people live in this cirque, where the climate is conducive to cultivation of lentils (for the nationally popular *cari* dishes), vineyards (for local wine production) and tobacco. The climate is widely renowned as the healthiest of all Réunion's microclimates and the thermal springs there are said to have healing properties (see page 338). Note that evenings, even in summer, can be very cold, whilst the days are normally pleasant, with sunny mornings. Ordinarily, a cloak of mist descends on the town by about 15.00, adding to the dreamy ambience.

Getting to the town of Cilaos, the largest settlement in the cirques and an absolutely charming place, entails the infamous uphill drive from St-Louis on the coast. I say 'infamous' because this 34km road features 200 sharp hairpin bends and you won't forget negotiating it in a hurry. The trip will take you at least two hours,

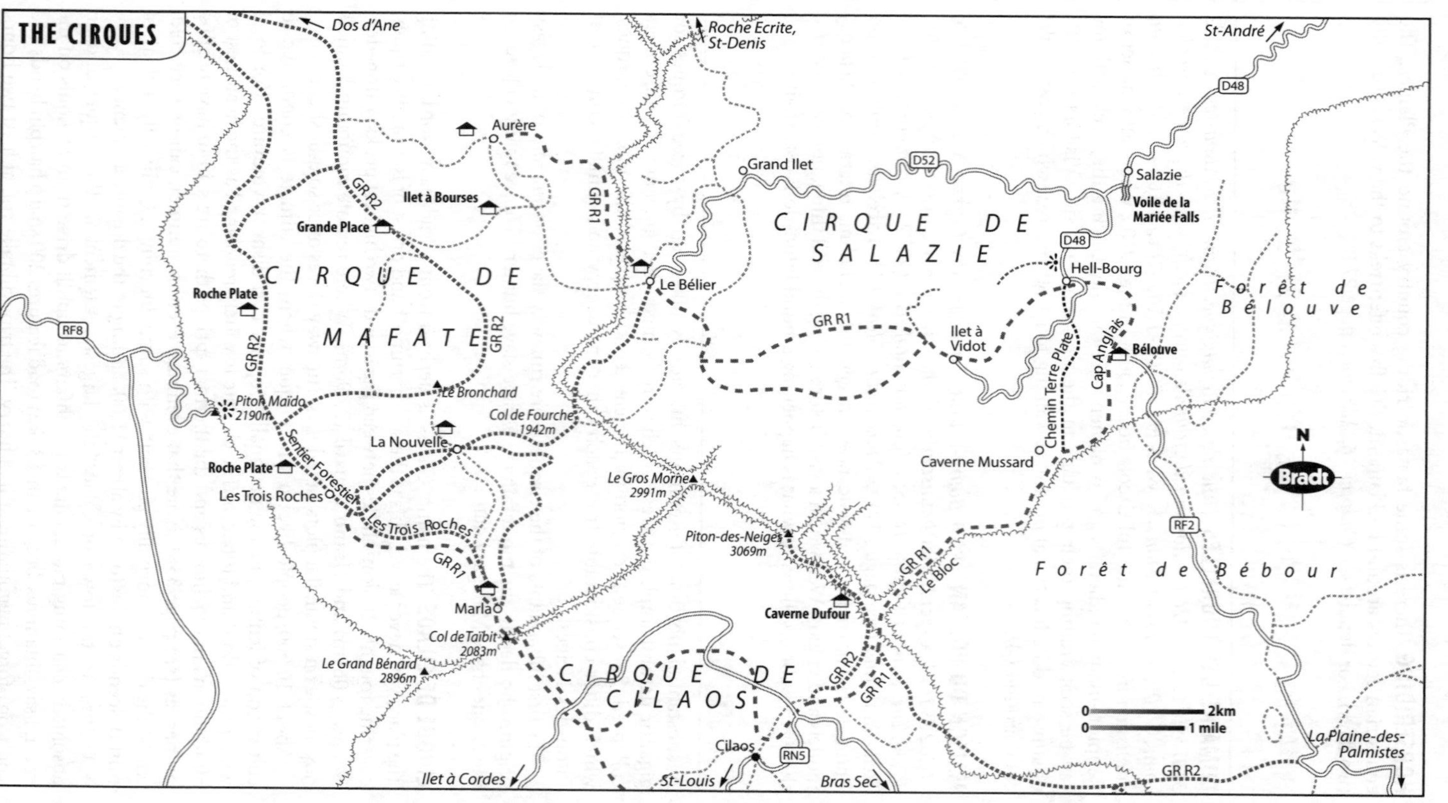
THE CIRQUES
Dos d'Ane
Roche Ecrite, St-Denis
St-André
D48
Aurère
Grand Ilet
D52
Salazie
Voile de la Mariée Falls
GR R2
GR R1
Ilet à Bourses
Grande Place
CIRQUE DE SALAZIE
Hell-Bourg
Le Bélier
Forêt de Bélouve
Roche Plate
CIRQUE DE MAFATE
RF8
GR R1
Ilet à Vidot
Bélouve
Cap Anglais
Chemin Terre Plate
Le Bronchard
Piton Maïdo 2190m
Col de Fourche 1942m
La Nouvelle
Caverne Mussard
N
Bradt
Roche Plate
Sentier Forestier
Les Trois Roches
Le Gros Morne 2991m
Les Trois Roches
RF2
Piton-des-Neiges 3069m
Le Bloc
Forêt de Bébour
Marla
Caverne Dufour
Col de Taïbit 2083m
Le Grand Bénard 2896m
CIRQUE DE CILAOS
0 2km
0 1 mile
Cilaos
RN5
La Plaine-des-Palmistes
Ilet à Cordes
St-Louis
Bras Sec

with stops at awesome viewpoints. Sadly, the road has seen many fatalities, as is evident from the presence of numerous roadside shrines.

Many visitors remark on the similarity of Cilaos's scenery to that of the western European Alps in summertime. This is mostly true of the region around the town of Cilaos itself, which is at 1,200m, but there are also some lush tropical forests.

Cilaos is known for the **embroidery** which is produced here and numerous shops sell locally made examples.

You used to be able to visit **thermal springs** in the forest just outside the town, which were discovered in 1819. Unfortunately a rock slide during a cyclone covered the springs and they can no longer be reached. Visitors can still experience the thermal waters at the Irénée Accot Thermal Centre (see *What to do in Cirque de Cilaos*, page 338).

Above the town of Cilaos is the small settlement of **Ilet a Cordes**, said to be named for the ropes that the runaway slaves used to reach the small plateau on which it sits. It is cradled within steep slopes and arriving there you feel as if you are the first to discover it. The 430 or so inhabitants are predominantly farmers; **lentils** have been grown here since 1835 and are the main crop, harvested around September and left to dry in the sun.

Getting there and away If you drive, take your time and take care. Don't be distracted by the view – you'll need all the concentration you can get! Alternatively, you can take the bus, although this may involve at least as many, if not more, heart-in-mouth moments as driving. Buses (Line K) run between St-Pierre and Cilaos, via St-Louis, about six times a day (three times on Sunday).

Tourist information The **tourist office** (*0892 270201;* **f** *0262 317818;* **e** *accueil.cilaos@otisud.re; www.sud.reunion.fr;* *08.30–12.30 & 13.30–17.00 Mon–Sat, 09.00–12.00 Sun & public holidays*) is at 2 Rue MacAuliffe. Staff can provide information on trails and local guides, and can book accommodation for any hikes you are planning. Free internet access is available in 15-minute slots.

Where to stay

Classified hotels

Mid range

Hotel les Chenêts *** (47 rooms & suites) 40E Chemin des Trois Mares, Cilaos; 0262 318585; **f** 0262 318717; **e** contact@leschenets.fr; www.leschenets.fr. Good-quality accommodation within a Creole-style building. TV, phone & minibar. Facilities include a restaurant, library, internet access, a pool, 2 saunas, a hammam (Turkish bath) & babysitting service. **$$$**

Tsilaosa *** (15 rooms) 21 Rue du Père Boiteau, Cilaos; 0262 373939; **f** 0262 373938; **e** accueil@tsilaosa.com; www.tsilaosa.com. A pretty hotel right in the centre of Cilaos. The architecture wouldn't be out of place in a French ski resort. Romantic en-suite rooms with spa bath, TV, phone & minibar. There are no tea/coffe making facilities in the room but there is a cosy tea room downstairs, from 14.00 (see page 338). There is off-road parking & guests can use the internet in reception. There is no restaurant on site but HB can be arranged in partnership with local restaurants. **$$$**

Budget

Hotel des Neiges * (31 rooms) 1 Rue de la Mare à Joncs, Cilaos; 0262 317233; **f** 0262 317298; **e** reservation@hotel-des-neiges.com; www.hotel-des-neiges.com. About 15mins' walk from the town centre. Plain but spotless rooms of varying sizes, standards & prices all with en-suite facilities & phone. Some also have TV, heating & a balcony. There is a good restaurant – Le Marla (see below). Additional facilities include internet access, a pool, jacuzzi, sauna, snooker & table tennis. Parts of the hotel are a little dark. **$$**

Le Vieux Cep ** (45 rooms) 2 Rue des Trois Mares, Cilaos; 0262 317189; **f** 0262 317768;

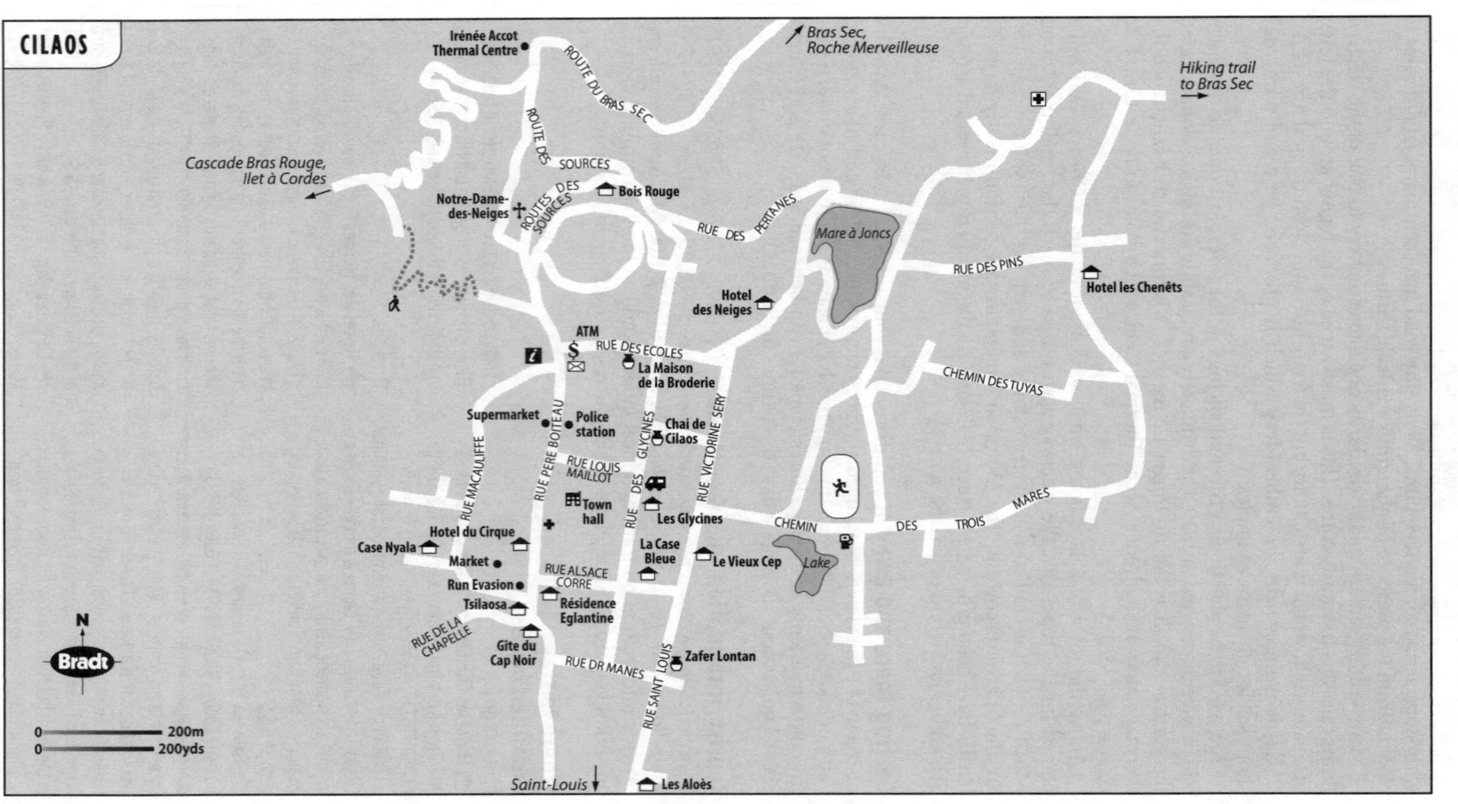
CILAOS
Irénée Accot Thermal Centre
ROUTE DU BRAS SEC
Bras Sec, Roche Merveilleuse
Hiking trail to Bras Sec
ROUTE DES SOURCES
Cascade Bras Rouge, Ilet à Cordes
Notre-Dame-des-Neiges
ROUTES DES SOURCES
Bois Rouge
RUE DES PERTANES
Mare à Joncs
RUE DES PINS
Hotel les Chenêts
Hotel des Neiges
ATM
RUE DES ECOLES
La Maison de la Broderie
CHEMIN DES TUYAS
Supermarket
Police station
Chai de Cilaos
RUE MACAULIFFE
RUE PERE BOITEAU
RUE LOUIS MAILLOT
RUE DES GLYCINES
RUE VICTORINE SERY
Town hall
Les Glycines
CHEMIN DES TROIS MARES
Hotel du Cirque
Case Nyala
La Case Bleue
Le Vieux Cep
Lake
Market
RUE ALSACE CORRE
Run Evasion
Résidence Eglantine
Tsilaosa
RUE DE LA CHAPELLE
Gîte du Cap Noir
RUE DR MANES
RUE SAINT LOUIS
Zafer Lontan
N
Bradt
0
200m
0
200yds
Saint-Louis
Les Aloès

e le.vieux.cep@wanadoo.fr; www.levieuxcep.fr. Popular, centrally located hotel with plenty of charm. The attractive, Creole-style building houses comfortable en-suite rooms with TV, phone, heater & balcony. Superior rooms have Wi-Fi access (payable). Rooms for the disabled available. Facilities include an excellent restaurant (see page 338), TV/video lounge, pool, sauna, jacuzzi & table tennis. Massage is available. **$$**

Les Aloès ** (10 rooms) 14 Rue St-Louis, Cilaos; 0262 318100; f 0262 318796; e hotel.aloes@wanadoo.fr; www.hotel-aloes.com. Charming, colourful Creole building in the centre of Cilaos. Rooms are simply furnished & have en suite, TV, phone & heater. Rooms for the disabled are available. **$**

Shoestring

Hotel Du Cirque * (11 rooms) 27 Rue du Père Boiteau, Cilaos; 0262 317068; f 0262 318046; e hotel-du-cirque@orange.fr. An unremarkable hotel, centrally located. Basic rooms, some of which have TV & phone. There is a restaurant serving Creole & Chinese food & a car park.

Unclassified accommodation

Budget

Bois Rouge (5 rooms) 2 Route des Sources, Cilaos; 0262 475757; f 0262 317536; e leboisrouge@ilereunion.com; www.ilereunion.com/leboisrouge. Charming Creole house owned by artist & sculptor, Philippe Turpin, with 5 en-suite rooms decorated by the artist. Rooms have en-suite facilities, TV, heating & terrace. There is a cosy lounge with fireplace, a great place to relax after a hard day's hiking. **$$**

Case Nyala (5 rooms) 8 Ruelle des Lianes, Cilaos; /f 0262 318957; e case-nyala@wanadoo.fr; www.case-nyala.com. A charming Creole house on a quiet street. The rooms are immaculate & beautifully decorated. The public areas are warm & inviting, in particular the dining room. Rooms have en-suite facilities, TV & heating. Guests have use of a communal kitchen. **$$**

Résidence Eglantine (7 studios) 2–4 Rue Alsace Corre, Cilaos; /f 0262 315772; e residence.eglantine@wanadoo.fr; www.residence-eglantine.fr. Well-maintained self-catering accommodation close to the main street, in a pretty Creole building. Simple but pleasant studios with kitchenette, TV & heating. There is a communal barbecue. **$$**

Shoestring

La Case Bleue (1 dbl room, dormitory – 7 beds) 15 Rue Alsace Corré, Cilaos; 0692 092730; e etheve.valerie@gmail.com; www.gitecasebleue.com. Backpacker-style accommodation in a Creole house. B/fast €6. Dormitory bed from €16.

Self-catering holiday rentals

Gîte du Cap Noir *** 19 C RN, Cilaos; 0262 317547; e j-f.grondin@wanadoo.fr. Has 3 double rooms & a mezzanine with 4 further double beds. From €406 per week.

Les Glycines (2 studios & 2 1-bed apts) 20 Rue des Glycines, Cilaos; 0262 317033; e payetjeanbaptiste@gmail.com. In the centre of town. Each has TV & parking. From €245 per week (2 people).

Where to eat There is a **supermarket** on Rue du Père Boiteau, as well as bakeries, greengroceries and butcher's shops. The covered market (*marché couvert*) on the main street (Rue du Père Boiteau) sells fruit and vegetables, meat, a variety of local jams (goyavier, papaya, etc) and sweet Cilaos wine.

Chez Miko Fils 25 Rue du Père Boiteau, Cilaos; 0262 317052; 10.30–21.00 daily except Thu (closes at 18.00) & Sun (closes at 14.00). Cuisine: Creole. Indoor & terrace dining on the main street. A selection of Creole dishes & grilled meat & fish; vegetarians may struggle. More reasonably priced than many of its competitors. Main courses (*caris* & accompaniments) from €11, 3-course menus from €16, including aperitif (house punch) & *digestif (rhum arrangé)*. **$$$**

Chez Noé 40 Rue du Père Boiteau, Cilaos; 0262 317993; 10.00–15.00 & 18.00–21.00 Tue–Sun. Cuisine: Creole. Popular restaurant in a pink Creole house in the centre of Cilaos. Traditional homemade food in an atmospheric setting, complete with log fire. **$$$**

✕ Le Cottage 2 Chemin des Saules, Cilaos; ☎ 0262 310461; ⏲ for lunch & dinner Thu–Tue, closed Sun evening. Cuisine: Creole, French. This restaurant has fine views from the edge of Mare à Joncs Lake & serves good-quality food. Outdoor dining is a pleasure in summer. **$$$**

✕ Le Vieux Cep 2 Rue des Trois Mares, Cilaos; ☎ 0262 317189; ⏲ for lunch & dinner daily. Cuisine: Creole, French. Wide range of dishes with specialities including duck *cari* with corn & the delicious home-smoked pork with Cilaos lentils. The restaurant's excellent reputation is well deserved. Reservation recommended, particularly for dinner. **$$$**

✕ Le Platane 46 Rue du Père Boiteau; ☎ 0262 317723; ⏲ for lunch & dinner, closed Wed. Cuisine: Creole, French, Italian. Neat little restaurant in a yellow & green Creole house in the centre of town. Wi-Fi available. **$$**

✕ Petit Randonneur 60 Rue du Père Boiteau; ☎ 0262 317955; ⏲ 09.00–18.00, closed Tue afternoon & Wed. Cuisine: Creole. **$$**

✕ Tsilaosa Tearooms 21 Rue du Père Boiteau, Cilaos; ☎ 0262 373939; ⏲ 14.00–17.00. The Tsilaosa Hotel serves a range of exotic teas, pancakes & homemade cakes as afternoon tea, in comfortable surroundings. The fireplace near reception is a real feature – a copper still salvaged from a sugar factory that was being demolished. **$$**

Other practicalities

Money and banking There is no bank but there is an **ATM** outside the **post office**. To be on the safe side, it is best to bring sufficient cash with you as this is the only ATM in Cilaos and it cannot always be relied upon.

Communications The **post office** is in the main street through the village (Rue du Père Boiteau), not far from the church. **Internet access** is available at **the tourist office**.

Medical The **hospital** (☎ *0262 317050*) is at Les Mares and there are two **pharmacies** on the main street, Rue du Père Boiteau.

What to do in Cirque de Cilaos

Spa treatments **Irénée Accot Thermal Centre** (*Route de Bras-Sec, Cilaos;* ☎ *0262 317227;* **f** *0262 317657;* **e** *thermes-cilaos@cg974.fr;* ⏲ *08.00–12.00 & 14.00–18.00 Mon–Sat, 09.00–17.00 Sun & public holidays, closed Wed afternoon*) Just above the town of Cilaos, the Irénée Accot Thermal Centre was opened in July 1988, its proprietors having capitalised on the combination of thermal springs and beautiful, tranquil surrounds.

Certain elements in the water, like sodium, magnesium and calcium, are apparently effective in the treatment of complications varying from rheumatism to digestive ailments.

A range of treatments is offered from spa baths (€15) and hammam (€15) to health packages lasting several days. A 30-minute massage is around €38. The combination options are good value and typically include two or more of the following: sauna, mineral spa bath, shiatsu, algae or Dead Sea salt treatment and electro-belt massage.

Hiking Needless to say, Cilaos has numerous possibilities for those into walking, hiking or lengthy treks. Even if you do only one of the short walks to nearby villages, you can still enjoy some breathtaking views. Two simple options which come to mind here are the roads to **Bras Sec** village and to the **Roche Merveilleuse**, a superb mountain viewpoint overlooking the whole cirque. You can also drive to the base of Roche Merveilleuse and a short climb up some steps takes you to the viewpoint. From the village you can walk to the impressive waterfall known as

Cascade Bras Rouge (grading: moderate). It involves walking down a steep path and, of course, back up it and takes around 2½ hours.

For the adventurous, Cilaos is the starting point for the arduous two-day trek to **Piton-des-Neiges** (for more details, see page 247).

Mountain biking Cilaos is an excellent area for mountain biking. There are two particularly popular routes: the first starts in town, then crosses **Plateau des Chênes** and ends at **Roche Merveilleuse** (grading: moderate). The other starts in **Bras Sec** village, then takes you to **Bras de Benjoin** village and on to Cilaos. **Run Evasion** has mountain bikes and helmets for hire (for contact details, see *Chapter 16, Activities*, pages 272–3).

Other outdoor activities Cilaos is a popular area for numerous other activities, especially **canyoning** and **river hiking**. Run Evasion has an outlet in Cilaos, which sells outdoor equipment and can arrange activities. For details of activities and operators, see *Chapter 16, Activities*, page 269.

What to see in Cirque de Cilaos

La Maison de la Broderie (*4 Rue des Ecoles, Cilaos; ☎ 0262 317748; e info@broderie-cilaos-reunion.com; ⏲ 09.30–12.00 & 14.00–17.00 Mon–Sat; admission* €1) An insight into the traditional **embroidery** for which the area is known. There is a demonstration workshop and exhibition. Items are on sale.

Chai de Cilaos (*34 Rue des Glycines, Cilaos; ☎ 0262 317969; e contact@lechaidecilaos.com; ⏲ 09.00–12.00 & 14.00–17.30 Mon–Sat; wine tasting €5*) Grapes were introduced by the French in 1771. Guided tours and a short film (in French) exploring the history of wine production in the Cilaos area. Visitors can taste and buy some of the Vin de Pays de Cilaos wine.

Zafer Lontan (*30 Rue de St Louis; ☎ 0262 319421; ⏲ 10.00–12.00, 13.30–17.30, closed Tue all day & Sun afternoon; admission to the art gallery is free; guided museum visit adult/child €5/4*) Within lies an interesting display of artefacts from the area, charting the history of Cilaos up to 200 years ago. Of particular interest are the recreation of a Creole kitchen and living area, slave chains and a gun used to hunt runaway slaves. There is also a projection room where you can watch 1950s cartoons, on reservation.

CIRQUE DE SALAZIE The largest of the cirques, Salazie measures about 12km by 9km and has a population of about 8,000. Its name comes from a Malagasy word meaning 'good place to stay'.

The cirque was only settled by European farmers during the mid 19th century, after a hot spring was found at **Hell-Bourg**. A military hospital was established in 1860 to treat soldiers wounded during unrest in Madagascar. Thanks to its pleasant climate, Hell-Bourg became a popular place for coastal inhabitants to visit during the hot months. In 1948, a severe cyclone somehow destroyed the hot spring and Hell-Bourg was all but deserted until 1980, when the government realised its potential value for culture and nature-oriented tourism.

Cirque de Salazie is the greenest of the cirques and has no fewer than 100 waterfalls, which drop down incredibly high, steep gorges. Réunion's best-known waterfall, the exquisite **Voile de la Mariée**, or 'Bridal Veil', is in this cirque. Salazie is the most accessible of the cirques, a picturesque 20-minute drive from St-André.

Salazie and Hell-Bourg The drive inland from St-André takes you into increasingly lush and verdant surrounds, along the Rivière du Mât (you also pass through a village of the same name). Then, looming up ahead, are the high gorges, usually shrouded in a mist mantle. You'll know you're approaching the mouth of the cirque when you see several narrow waterfalls, one of which continually showers on to the tarred road, giving you a free carwash. A signpost announces it as '*Pisse en l'air*' (I don't think that one needs translating!).

Salazie is the area where Réunion's most famed vegetable, the *chouchou* (*Sechium edule*), is cultivated. You will see many small homes surrounded by frames engulfed by this fast-growing climbing plant. The uses for it are many and menus in the area's eateries typically feature everything from *chouchou* stuffed with prawns and melted cheese to *chouchou* cake as a dessert.

The first town you'll come to in the cirque is Salazie itself, but most visitors continue to the smaller town of Hell-Bourg, quite a distance higher up. Few tourists spend any time in Salazie but it does have a **petrol station**, small **supermarket** and a **post office** complete with **ATM** and **payphone**. Both Salazie and Hell-Bourg have **pharmacies**.

DAY HIKES AROUND HELL-BOURG

Hell-Bourg is *the* centre for hiking in Réunion. Apart from its superb mountain scenery and numerous trails, it's such a pretty village that it invites a stay of a few days even for casual walkers. Be warned, however: it rains a lot in Hell-Bourg and the most popular trails are consequently very muddy. Good rain gear and waterproof hiking boots are a prerequisite.

An information sheet on the walks ('Liste des Balades dans le Cirque de Salazie') is available from the tourist office in Hell-Bourg (for contact details, see opposite). They are also marked on map 4402 RT (St-Denis) in the IGN 1:25,000 series of six maps covering Réunion. It is useful to know that the official French trail system, the Grandes Randonnées, is marked by red and white paint. Other footpaths are indicated in red and yellow.

As a warm-up try **Les Trois Cascades** (one hour there and back) where you'll find a series of waterfalls in a lovely mountain setting, or the four-hour walk (there and back) to **Source Manouilh**. More challenging is the climb up to the top of the escarpment and Bélouve Forest. Beginning at the town hall, this is a two-hour slog up a well-constructed path to the **Gîte de Bélouve** where, disconcertingly, you'll find some parked cars (it is connected by forest road to Plaine-des-Palmistes). The altitude gain from Hell-Bourg to the gîte is about 500m, so it's hard work but the views and vegetation on the way up are magnificent. The return takes only about an hour.

Once here, you can walk to the famous **Trou de Fer**, a deep pool fed by waterfalls hurtling down the sheer mountainsides that surround it. However, you should allow at least four hours for this walk (there and back). The latter part of the trail can be very muddy and difficult, and although it looks level on the map it is steeply up and down the whole way. So if you are an average hiker you need to leave Hell-Bourg early in the morning to be sure to be back before dark, and be fit enough for a seven-hour walk. It's much better, therefore, to stay in the comfortable dormitories in the gîte. Book as far in advance as possible (**Vf** *0262 412123;* **e** *gite.belouve@wanadoo.fr*).

As you continue on the winding road from Salazie to Hell-Bourg, it is worth stopping at the **Point du Jour** viewpoint for fantastic views of the cirque. There is a map indicating which peak is which.

Nearby is the sign to the lake of **Mare à Poule d'Eau**, which can be reached on foot or mountain bike. This is where the local inhabitants used to come to collect their water. The village of the same name is just a little further on, shortly beyond which are the famous **Voile de la Mariée Falls** (Bridal Veil Falls). The falls are signed and there is space to pull in and admire them from the road as they tumble into the gorge below.

As you travel between Salazie and Hell-Bourg it is worth making the 15km detour to **Grand Ilet**. It is a pretty, unspoilt village cupped by the cirque's commanding mountains. The village's **Church of St Martin** is a beautiful example of Creole architecture, with its *lambrequin* (filigree-style decoration), its light blue shutters and its tamarind shingle walls. A sign next to the bell tower, which is now in the grounds of the church, tells the building's tortured history – detailing the numerous times it has been destroyed, moved and rebuilt. In the centre of Grand Ilet is a mountain-biking station with a signboard detailing the local trails. **Grand Ilet** is the starting point for hikes to St-Denis via **La Roche Ecrite**, while nearby **Le Bélier** allows access to the hiking trails which connect Cirque de Salazie and Cirque de Mafate. The viewpoint at **Mare à Martin** provides good views of the cirque and its villages.

In contrast to Salazie, which has little charm, **Hell-Bourg** is picture-postcard-perfect. Residents will proudly tell you that Hell-Bourg was awarded the prestigious title of 'Most Beautiful Village in France' in 2000 (I know, 'in France' still seems odd, doesn't it?). It features small Creole houses with tiled roofs, intricate railings and explosions of colourful flowers in the small gardens and ubiquitous flower boxes. EU money has been made available to restore many of the **Creole houses** to their former glory. The wrought-iron *lambrequins* on the front of the eaves are typical, as are the bright colours.

Hell-Bourg is popular with tourists – there are many **souvenir shops** and numerous good Creole restaurants.

Getting there and away Salazie is easily reached by car or local bus service from St-André along a twisty but well-maintained road. Buses travel regularly between Salazie and Hell-Bourg, except on Sunday.

Tourist information Information about the area, hiking and bookings at *gîtes de montagne* are available from the **tourist office** in Hell-Bourg (*47 Rue Général de Gaulle, Hell-Bourg;* ☎ *0262 478989;* **f** *0262 478970;* **e** *info@oti-est.re;* ⏲ *09.00–12.15 & 13.00–17.00 Mon–Sat*).

Where to stay

Classified hotels

Budget

Domaine des Songes $$ (20 rooms) Chemin du Butor, Mare à Vielle Place, Salazie; ☎ 0262 463535; **e** ledomainedessonges@wanadoo.fr. Opened in 2005, the hotel appears to have resolved the teething problems that plagued it at the start. Has pleasant views & the service is good. The large, en-suite rooms are modern & equipped with TV, phone & heating. **$$**

Le Relais des Gouverneurs *** (5 rooms) 2 bis Rue Amiral Lacaze, Hell-Bourg; ☎ 0262 477621; **e** calouboyer@wanadoo.fr. In a large colonial-style house. The rooms are simply but comfortably furnished & have en suite, TV & heating. **$$**

Les Jardins d'Héva ** (10 rooms) 16 Rue Auguste Lacaussade, Hell-Bourg; ☎ 0262 478787; **f** 0262 478606; **e** lesjardinsdheva@orange.fr; www.lesjardinsdheva.com. Opened in 2006 by one of the island's leading mountain guides, Alice Deligey, this cosy hotel is sure to be a hit with visitors to the cirque. The hotel is perched above the main part of Hell-Bourg, with views of the cirque from the restaurant & the grounds. The charming en-suite rooms (with terrace & phone) are housed in 5 colourful chalets with a Creole flavour. Guests can use the mini spa (sauna, hammam, jacuzzi), which is welcome relief for tired hikers. The restaurant serves Creole food prepared with local ingredients. If you feel inspired, Creole cooking lessons are also available. Alice is very knowledgeable about Réunion & hiking, & she speaks good English. **$$**

Relais des Cîmes ** (30 rooms) 67 Rue du Général de Gaulle, Hell-Bourg, Salazie; ☎ 0262 478158; **f** 0262 478211; **e** info@relaisdescimes.com; www.relaisdescimes.com. A very popular hotel in the centre of Hell-Bourg, so book well in advance. The rooms are comfortable with en suite, TV, phone & heater; many have superb views. The new rooms are particularly appealing. The restaurant here is legendary (see below). **$$**

Unclassified hotels

L'Orchidée Rose (6 rooms) 26 Rue Olivier Manès, Hell-Bourg; ☎ 0262 478722; **e** reservation@orchideerose.net; www.orchideerose.net. On a quiet backstreet. Rooms have en-suite facilities, TV & Wi-Fi, are clean & well furnished. There is a cybercafé here. Dbl/sgl from €40.50 BB.

Self-catering holiday rentals

Chez Festin ** 3 Impasse Sisayhes, Hell-Bourg; ☎ 0262 465461. Simply furnished 3-bedroom house with terrace & parking. From €275 per week (6 people).

Youth hostel One of the island's three hostels is in Hell-Bourg at 2 Rue de la Cayenne (☎ *0262 474131*). To stay there you must have a membership card. For details, see *Chapter 15, Accommodation*, page 261.

Where to eat

There are small **general shops** in both Salazie and Hell-Bourg, where you can stock up on food for hiking. The **supermarket** in Hell-Bourg on the corner of Rues Général de Gaulle and Cayenne is probably your best bet.

Relais des Cîmes 67 Rue Général de Gaulle, Hell-Bourg; ☎ 0262 478158; ⏲ for lunch & dinner daily. Cuisine: Creole, French. Arguably the island's best Creole cuisine. This well-known restaurant was founded by Mamie Javel, author of a superb Creole cookbook titled *La Réunion des Milles et Une Saveurs*. In 2006, Mamie Javel, aged 85, finally retired to St-Denis, but her cuisine lives on at this restaurant. Meals are prepared using local products & according to Mamie Javel's famous recipes. Copies of her Creole cookbook are on sale in the restaurant. The décor is unmistakably French, with red & white checked tablecloths & curtains. The *cabri massalé* (goat curry) & the *poulet coco* (coconut chicken) are superb. 3-course menus are good value at €16. **$$$**

Chez Alice 1 Rue des Sangliers, Hell-Bourg; ☎ 0262 478624; ⏲ for lunch & dinner Tue–Sun. Cuisine: Creole, French, Chinese. Unpretentious restaurant set back on a side street. **$$**

Crêperie Le Gall 55 Rue du Général de Gaulle, Hell-Bourg; ☎ 0262 478748; ⏲ 11.00–19.00 Sat–Thu. Cuisine: French, crêpes, snacks. A cosy, informal place on the main street. Serves a large range of crêpes, including the house speciality – 'La Créole', which comes with banana flambéed in local rum. Savoury snacks, salads & ice cream are also available. **$$**

Ti-Chouchou 42 Rue du Général de Gaulle, Hell-Bourg; ☎ 0262 478093; ⏲ for lunch & dinner Sat–Thu. Cuisine: Creole, French. Eat-in or take-away. As the name suggests, specialises in *chouchou*. Popular, so try to book in advance. **$$**

Other practicalities

Money and banking Neither Salazie nor Hell-Bourg has a bank but there is an **ATM** outside the post office in Salazie.

Communications There are **post offices** in Salazie, Hell-Bourg and Grand Ilet. **Internet access** is available at **Cyber C@se Creole** (*L'Orchidée Rose, 26 Rue Olivier Manès, Hell-Bourg; ☎ 0262 478722*). For details, see page 261.

Medical There is a **pharmacy** at Mare à Vielle Place in Hell-Bourg, and one in Salazie.

What to do in Cirque de Salazie

Hiking Most of Salazie's visitors come here, at least in part, for the hiking. The tourist office can provide information on hiking trails in the area, as well as provide advice on adventure sports such as **canyoning**. For details, see *Chapter 16, Activities*, page 341.

Mountain biking Numerous trails snake around Salazie, Hell-Bourg and Grand Ilet. For more information on mountain biking, see *Chapter 16, Activities*, pages 272–3.

SAINT EXPEDIT

As well as the roadside shrines to Christ and the Virgin Mary, there are many dedicated to Saint Expédit, which are typically red. Regarded as the national saint of Réunion, he is revered by Réunionnais of all religions.

Saint Expédit has taken on something of a sinister nature in the island's folklore. He is considered particularly effective and prompt (expeditious) at carrying out requests for revenge by placing curses on people. However, in return he demands payment, otherwise he will punish the person who requested his assistance. For this reason the red shrines are typically smothered by offerings, such as candles, flowers and red material, as well as messages of thanks.

Don't be surprised if you see decapitated statues of Saint Expédit in roadside shrines. The damage is either punishment for an unfulfilled request or has been done in order to break a curse that someone feels has been put on them by the saint.

The story of Saint Expédit is very confused. He is believed by many to have been a Roman legionnaire, named Expeditus, who was beheaded on 19 April AD303 in Malatya (Turkey) for not renouncing Christ.

However, some maintain that this story is a fabrication and that the saint's popularity in Réunion is the result of a misunderstanding. The story goes that at the time of the early colonists, the religious community was having difficulty impressing the importance of its values on the population, so wrote to the Vatican to request some religious relics to help them drive their message home.

Finally, at the end of the 19th century a small wooden box arrived bearing the word *expédit* (despatched). Inside were a few scattered bones. The religious community rejoiced – the relics that they had requested had at last arrived. After some discussion, they concluded that the remains must belong to Saint Expédit, as that was the inscription on the box.

Whichever version you believe, the Church's position is clear. In 1905, Pope Pius X demanded that Saint Expédit's name be struck off the list of martyrs and all images of him removed from churches. By this stage Saint Expédit was already adored throughout Réunion and his popularity has never wavered.

What to see in Cirque de Salazie

Maison Folio *(20 Rue Amiral Lacaze, Hell-Bourg;* **t/f** *0262 478098;* **e** *m.folio@wanadoo.fr; ⌚ 09.00–11.30 & 14.00–17.00 daily; admission adult/child under 10 €5/free)* A much-photographed Creole home which has preserved the elegant style of the 19th century. Built in 1870 and renovated in the late 1970s, the house, garden and furniture all accurately reproduce the era. Note that the kitchen and dining room are in a separate building at the back, which was the norm in Creole homes. In the garden, ornamental, medicinal and edible plants are typically bunched together in each flower bed. The stories told by the present owners provide an interesting insight.

Creole houses (Cases Créoles) *(Guided tours are arranged via the tourist office;* **t** *0262 478989 & operate 11.00, 15.30 Tue & on reservation; tour €8)* A leaflet on Hell-Bourg's Creole houses and the route you can follow to see them is available at the tourist office and costs €5. Alternatively, you can join a guided walking tour of Hell-Bourg, with a local guide providing information on the architecture, history and residents of the village's Creole homes. At this stage, the leaflet and the guided tour are available only in French.

CIRQUE DE MAFATE Spanning 72km², Mafate is the smallest and most tropical of the cirques. On its northern rim is the **Plaine d'Affouches**, which overlooks St-Denis and the north coast. On its western rim is **Piton Maïdo** (2,190m), which overlooks the dry west coast. To its south lies the Cirque de Cilaos.

Mafate is a wild, sparsely inhabited, mystifying place. Its name has suitably intriguing origins: it is said that a Malagasy sorcerer and runaway slave, named Mafaty (meaning 'dangerous one'), lived at the foot of **Le Bronchard** (1,261m). He was eventually caught in 1751 by François Mussard, a bounty hunter.

The cirque's first inhabitants were indeed runaway slaves after the agricultural colonisation of the island in the 1730s, then the *Créoles Blancs* (White Creoles) arrived following the abolition of slavery in 1848. Today, approximately 650 people reside in remote mountain hamlets, such as **Marla, La Nouvelle** and **Aurère**. They live off the land, in virtual isolation from the outside world. There are no roads, just 100km of walking trails. Supplies such as medication are brought in by helicopter, yet many of the Mafatais have never seen a car.

Visitors need to spend at least two days in Mafate to get a feel for the cirque. Access is on foot from Cilaos, via the **Col du Taïbit**, from Hell-Bourg via the **Col des Bœufs**, and from **Maïdo**, **Sans-Souci**, or **Dos d'Ane**. The easiest option is from Hell-Bourg; even easier is flying in by helicopter. If your time is limited, **Piton Maïdo**, which is accessible by car from St-Paul, provides superb views of the cirque.

There have been some terrible stories of hikers disappearing and even being found murdered in Mafate. Don't panic; this hasn't happened for a while! However, it is always safer to hike with other people, preferably a qualified guide, and a wise precaution is to tell someone where you're going and for how long.

Where to stay Many independent hikers choose to camp in this remote area. It can be a wonderful experience with fabulous starry skies. However, it does get very cold so bring along suitable clothing. If you do camp, be sure to clear up completely when you leave.

The alternatives to camping are *gîtes de montagne* and *gîtes d'étapes*. For details of these, see *Chapter 15, Accommodation*, pages 269-77.

Where to eat If you're staying in a *gîte*, you can order breakfast and dinner in advance. You'll need to bring any other food with you, to fuel all that walking. If you run out of snacks, don't despair – there are small food shops in most of Mafate's villages, including La Nouvelle, Marla, Roche Plate, Grande Place les Hauts, Ilet à Malheur, Aurère and Ilet aux Orangers. They are usually closed on Sunday afternoon and Monday morning.

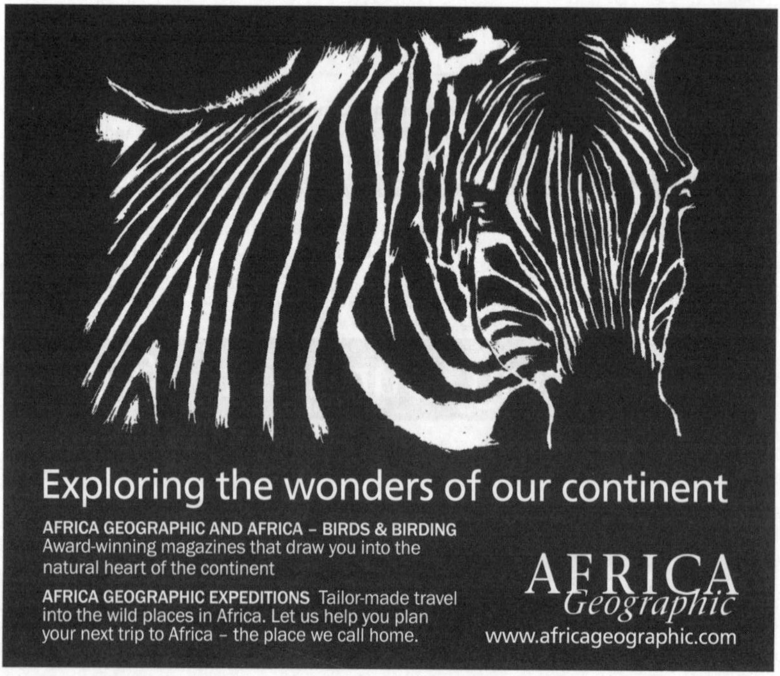

Appendix 1

LANGUAGE

To speak Creole, the slightest knowledge of French will be useful for the formalities: for instance, 'Good morning' is '*Bon-zoor*'. Here are some useful phrases that differ from the French. They have been written phonetically (as they should be pronounced).

USEFUL PHRASES

	Mauritian Creole	Réunionnais Creole
How are you?	*Ki man yeah?*	*Komon ee lay?*
Very well, and you?	*Mwa bee-an, eh oo?*	*Lay la eh oo?*
I'm not well	*Mwa pa bee-an*	*Mi lay pa bee-an*
What is your name?	*Ki oo non?*	*Komon oo apel?*
How old are you?	*Ki arj too on?*	*Kay laz oo nayna?*
What are you doing?	*Ki toe pay fare?*	*Ko sa oo fay?*
I don't understand	*Mwa pa kompran*	*Mi kompran pa*
Speak slowly	*Pa koz tro veet*	*Koz doosmon*
I don't speak Creole	*Mwa pa koz Kreol*	*Mi koz pa Kreol*
I don't know	*Mwa pa konnay*	*Mi konnay pa*
How much is it?	*Koomian sa?*	*Koomian i koot?*
It's too expensive	*Li tro ser*	*Lay tro ser*
Good/That's fine	*Li bon*	*Lay bon*
Where are you going?	*Kot oo pay allay?*	*Oo sa oo sa va?*
I want to go to …	*Mwa oo-lay al …*	*Mi vay allay a …*
Take me to the hotel	*Amen mwa lotel*	*Amen a mwa a lotel*
I want to stay	*Mwa pay restay*	*Mi vay restay*
Would you like a drink?	*Oo poo bwah keek soz?*	*Oo vay bwah keek soz?*
I'd like wine	*Mwa oo-lay do van*	*Mi voodray do van*
What's this?	*Ki etay sa?*	*Ko sa ee lay?*
I love you	*Mwa kontan twa*	*Mi em a-oo*
Goodbye	*Sallaam*	*Na wa/nooa troov*

PRONOUNCING PLACE NAMES

Stressed syllables are shown in bold.

Baie du Tombeau	Beige-tom-**bo**
Beau Bassin	Bo Bass**a**
Belle Mare	Bel-mar
Case Noyale	Kaz noy-**al**
Curepipe	Kewr-**peep**
Grand Bassin	Gron Bass**a**

Gris Gris	Gree-gree
Ile aux Aigrettes	Eel-oh-say**gret**
Ile aux Cerfs	Eel-oh-**sair**
Mahébourg	Mayberg *or* Mah-ay-bour
Morne Brabant	Morn Bra**bon**
Port Louis	Por(t) Loo-**ee**
Port Mathurin	Por(t) Ma-to-**ra**
Quatre Bornes	Katr born
Réduit	**Ray**dwee
Rodrigues	Rod**reegs**
Rose Hill	Roh**zill**
Souillac	**Soo**-ee-yak
Triolet	**Tree**-oh-lay
Trou aux Biches	Troo-oh-**beesh**
Trou d'Eau Douce	Troodoh-**doo**
Vacoas	**Va**-kwa

In Réunion (Ray-oo-nee-on), standard French pronunciation applies.

Appendix 2

FURTHER INFORMATION

GENERAL

Books

Adams, Douglas and Carwardine, Mark *Last Chance to See* William Heinemann, London, 1990. Beautifully written and illustrated, including a section on the endangered Mascarene wildlife (especially Mauritian birds).

Ellis, Dr Matthew and Wilson-Howarth, Dr Jane *Your Child Abroad: A Travel Health Guide* Bradt, 2005 (2nd edition). An invaluable guide for those travelling or resident overseas with babies and children of all ages.

Georges, Eliane and Vaisse, Christian *The Indian Ocean* Evergreen, 1998. Many beautiful photos but the information is inaccurate in parts.

Ventor, A J *Where to Dive in Southern Africa and off the Islands* Ashanti Publishing, 1991. Excellent for divers and non-divers alike. Well-written general reviews of all the Mascarenes, plus all the necessary information for divers and snorkelling enthusiasts.

Websites

www.fco.gov.uk/travel Foreign and Commonwealth Office website with up-to-date country-specific advice. Should be consulted prior to travel.

www.nhs.uk/healthcareabroad National Health Service website giving general travel health advice and country-specific inoculation recommendations. Also, everything you need to know about obtaining, completing and using an EHIC form.

www.weddings.co.uk Website providing information on getting married abroad, including lists of necessary documentation and other administrative procedures.

MAURITIUS AND RODRIGUES

Books

History

Editions Pacifique *Historical Postcards of Mauritius.*

Riviere, Lindsay *Historical Dictionary of Mauritius* Scarecrow Press, London, 1982.

Vaughn, Megan *Creating the Creole Island, Slavery in 18th-century Mauritius* Duke University Press, 2005. Excellent insight into Mauritius as a land of slaves and their masters.

Natural history

Atachia, Michael *Sea Fishes of Mauritius* Mauritius, 1984.

Durrell, Gerald *Golden Bats and Pink Pigeons* Fountain, 1979.

Michel, Claude *Birds of Mauritius* Mauritius, 1986.

Michel, Claude *Marine Molluscs of Mauritius* Mauritius, 1985.

Michel, Claude and Owadally, A W *Our Environment, Mauritius* Mauritius, 1975.

Owadally, A W *A Guide to the Royal Botanical Gardens, Pamplemousses* Mauritius, 1978.

Sinclair, Ian, and Langrand, Olivier *Birds of the Indian Ocean Islands* Struik/New Holland, 2004. The definitive field guide for birdwatchers visiting the western Indian Ocean. Includes many interesting discoveries made during the 1990s.
Ventor, A J *Underwater Mauritius* Media House Publications, South Africa, 1988.

Language

Lee, Jacques K *Mauritius: Its Creole Language* Green Print, 2008.

Activities

Mountain, A and Halbwachs, Y *The Dive Sites of Mauritius* Struik, 1996.

Travel guides/tourist booklets

MTPA *Mauritius Info Guide* Mauritius Tourism Promotion Authority. General information plus lists of restaurants, hotels and activity operators. Maps of Mauritius and Port Louis. Brief section on Rodrigues. Free.
MTPA *What's On in Mauritius* B&T directories, annually. General information, including activities, shopping and places of interest. Maps of the island, Port Louis, Curepipe and Grand Baie. Free.
MTPA *Rodrigues: Your Guide* Mauritius Tourism Promotion Authority. Background and practical information, including hotels and restaurants. Map of the island. Free.

General

Andrews et al *Best of Mauritian Cooking* Times Editions, 1994.
Baptiste, Françoise *Les Délices de Rodrigues* Payenké, 2008. Excellent Rodriguan recipe book.
Macmillan, Allister *Mauritius Illustrated (1914)* Editions du Pacifique, 1991.
Mauritius from the Air Nouvelles Editions du Pacifique, 1994.
Ramdoyal, Ramesh *Festivals of Mauritius* Edition Indian Ocean.
Sookhee, Lalita *Mauritian Delights* Mauritius, 1985.
Vaisse, Christian *Living in Mauritius* Editions du Pacifique, 1989.

Newspapers

Mauritius News, 'The first Mauritian Newspaper Overseas' published monthly; 583 Wandsworth Road, London SW8 3JD; ☎ 020 7498 3066; e editor@mauritiusnews.co.uk; www.mauritius-news.co.uk

Websites

www.gov.mu Mauritian Government website with extensive information, including the latest economic news and links to all departments and government bodies.

http://statsmauritius.gov.mu Up-to-date statistics on Mauritius.

www.tourism-mauritius.mu Mauritius Tourist Promotion Authority website. Contains background and practical information, including visa requirements. Provides details of hotels, restaurants and things to see in Mauritius.

www.orange.mu General website with news, sport, chat rooms and search engine.

www.maurinet.com Designed for tourists and business visitors. Hotel and restaurant contact details can be easily found, as well as the usual background information. The business guide contains listings of company contact details for a multitude of sectors.

www.tourism-rodrigues.mu MTPA website on Rodrigues. General tourist information. Very comprehensive.

www.themauritiusyellowpage.com Directory of businesses. Good in theory but searches do not work as well as they might.

http://metservice.intnet.mu Weather and cyclone information.

www.airmauritius.com Website of the airline. Includes schedule and route details, as well as online booking.

REUNION
Books
Natural history

Moyne-Picard, Marylène and Dutrieux, Eric *Fonds sous-marins de L'Ile de la Réunion* Ouest France, 1997. Guide to the marine environment around Réunion, plus information on the best dive sites. In French only.

Activities

Colas, Pascal *Le Paradis du Canyoning* Edition Maison de la Montagne, 1995. Information on canyoning in Réunion. In French only.

Fédération Française de la Randonnée Pédestre *Topoguide: L'Ile de la Réunion.* Comprehensive guide to the GR R1 and GR R2 trails, including maps. In French only.

Office Nationale des Forêts *Itinéraires Réunionnais* Bat' Karé. Information on hiking and suggested trails. In French only.

Office Nationale des Forêts *Sentiers Marmailles* Bat' Karé. 42 easy walks of less than three hours, designed with children in mind. In French only.

Reynaud, Luc *52 Balades et Randonnées Faciless à La Réunion* Orphie, 2003. 52 easy and moderate hikes. In French only.

Travel guides/tourist booklets

Comité du Tourisme de la Réunion *Guide des 24 Communes.* Focuses on the places of interest in each of the island's 24 communes. In French only.

Comité du Tourisme de la Réunion *Le Guide Run.* Published annually. Invaluable information on what to see in each region, plus hotel and restaurant contact details. In French and English.

Heissat, Robert and Puget, Anny *Bonjour La Réunion* Les Créations du Pelican, 1993. Colourful photos and text with good sections on culture, natural history and each region. In French only.

General

Gélabert, Serge *La Réunion Fruit d'une Passion* Serge Gélabert, 1998. Largely photos with some text on the island. In French only.

Gélabert, Serge and Javel, Mamy *La Réunion des Mille et Une Saveurs* Serge Gélabert, 1998. Excellent Creole recipe book. In French only.

Grenson, Jan. *La Cuisine de la Réunion* Editions Orphie, 2004. Réunionnais recipes, from *punch* to *cari.* In French only.

Websites

www.la-reunion-tourisme.com/www.reunion.fr Website of the Comité du Tourisme de la Réunion. A must for anyone planning a trip. Packed with information available in English, German and French about every aspect of the country. Includes calendar of events, tourism statistics and photographs.

www.ilereunion.com General website in French only, with hotel, restaurant and activities information. Useful descriptions of each region and major towns with things to see. Also, weather and traffic information and useful phone numbers.

www.creole.org Aims to give a feel of what Réunion is actually like, with an emphasis on culture. Contains photographs, Creole recipes, accommodation and restaurant information. Mostly in French, although parts are in English.

www.reunion-nature.com Excellent website with information on hiking accommodation and all outdoor activities. Online booking service.

www.reunion-directory.com General tourist information plus a directory of companies in tourism, industry, agriculture and service sectors. Good descriptions and links for hotels. Mostly in French, although some parts are in English.

www.runweb.com Plenty of practical tourist information. Available in French, English, Spanish and Chinese.

www.meteo-reunion.com Weather information for the island, including satellite pictures and cyclone news.

Index

Page numbers in **bold** refer to major entries; those in *italics* indicate maps.
Pages 1–194 refer to Mauritius, pages 195–231 to Rodrigues, pages 233–345 to Réunion